"The Handbook shows the realization of Ward Edwards's original dream of a field made exciting by the continual interplay between normative analyses, descriptive research, and prescriptive interventions, bridging critical gaps between the normative ideal and descriptive reality."

Baruch Fischhoff, *Carnegie Mellon University and President of Society for Risk Analysis*

"Fifty years of research have created an impressive body of knowledge and theory about human judgment and decision making. This comprehensive and authoritative handbook will serve as a valuable text and reference for students, scholars, and decision makers."

Paul Slovic, *University of Oregon and President of Decision Research Institute*

Blackwell Handbooks of Experimental Psychology

This outstanding series of handbooks provides a cutting-edge overview of classic research, current research and future trends in experimental psychology.

- Each handbook draws together 25–30 newly commissioned chapters to provide a comprehensive overview of a subdiscipline of experimental psychology.
- The international team of contributors to each handbook has been specially chosen for its expertise and knowledge of each field.
- Each handbook is introduced and contextualized by leading figures in the field, lending coherence and authority to each volume.

The Blackwell Handbooks of Experimental Psychology will provide an invaluable overview for advanced students of experimental psychology and for researchers as an authoritative definition of their chosen field.

Blackwell Handbook of Perception
Edited by Bruce Goldstein

Blackwell Handbook of Judgment and Decision Making
Edited by Derek J. Koehler and Nigel Harvey

Blackwell Handbook of Judgment and Decision Making

Blackwell Handbook of Judgment and Decision Making

Edited by

Derek J. Koehler and Nigel Harvey

Blackwell
Publishing

© 2004 by Blackwell Publishing Ltd
except for editorial material and organization © 2004 by Derek J. Koehler and Nigel Harvey

BLACKWELL PUBLISHING
350 Main Street, Malden, MA 02148-5020, USA
108 Cowley Road, Oxford OX4 1JF, UK
550 Swanston Street, Carlton, Victoria 3053, Australia

The right of Derek J. Koehler and Nigel Harvey to be identified as the Authors of the Editorial Material in this Work has been asserted in accordance with the UK Copyright, Designs, and Patents Act 1988.

First published 2004 by Blackwell Publishing Ltd

Library of Congress Cataloging-in-Publication Data

Blackwell handbook of judgment and decision making / edited by Derek J. Koehler and Nigel Harvey.— 1st ed.
    p. cm.
  Includes bibliographical references and index.
  ISBN 1–4051–0746–4 (hardcover : alk. paper)
  1. Decision making. 2. Judgment. I. Koehler, Derek J. II. Harvey, Nigel. III. Title.

BF448.B57 2004
153.4′6—dc22

2004010356

A catalogue record for this title is available from the British Library.

Set in 10.5/12.5pt Adobe Garamond
by Graphicraft Limited, Hong Kong

For further information on
Blackwell Publishing, visit our website:
http://www.blackwellpublishing.com

Contents

Contributors

Jonathan Baron
Department of Psychology
University of Pennsylvania

James R. Bettman
Fuqua School of Business
Duke University

Lyle A. Brenner
Warrington College of Business
University of Florida

Jerome R. Busemeyer
Department of Psychology
Indiana University

Gretchen B. Chapman
Department of Psychology
Rutgers University

Junsong Chen
China Europe International Business
School

Incheol Choi
Department of Psychology
Seoul National University

Jong An Choi
Department of Psychology
Seoul National University

Nicholas Epley
Department of Psychology
Harvard University

Simon Gächter
Department of Economics (FEW-HSG)
University of St. Gallen

Markus Glaser
School of Business Administration
University of Mannheim

Gerd Gigerenzer
Max Planck Institute for Human
Development

William M. Goldstein
Department of Psychology and
Committee on Human Development
University of Chicago

Richard Gonzalez
Department of Psychology
University of Michigan

Robin Gregory
Decision Research, Vancouver

Dale Griffin
Sauder School of Business
University of British Columbia

Christopher K. Hsee
Graduate School of Business
University of Chicago

Jesse Itzkowitz
Department of Psychology
University of Florida

Joseph G. Johnson
Department of Psychology
Indiana University

Gideon Keren
Department of Technology Management
Eindhoven University of Technology

Gary Klein
Klein Associates

Natalia Kotchetova
School of Accountancy
University of Waterloo

David A. Lagnado
Department of Psychology
University College London

Richard P. Larrick
Fuqua School of Business
Duke University

Robyn A. LeBoeuf
Warrington College of Business
University of Florida

Shenghua Luan
Department of Psychology
University of Florida

Craig R. M. McKenzie
Department of Psychology
University of California, San Diego

Ara Norenzayan
Department of Psychology
University of British Columbia

Markus Nöth
School of Business Administration
University of Mannheim

David Over
Department of Psychology
University of Sunderland

John W. Payne
Fuqua School of Business
Duke University

Jennifer K. Phillips
Klein Associates

Nick Pidgeon
School of Environmental Sciences
University of East Anglia

Jeffrey J. Rachlinski
Cornell Law School

Daniel Read
Department of Operational Research
London School of Economics and
Political Science

Neal J. Roese
Department of Psychology
University of Illinois

Yuval Rottenstreich
Graduate School of Business
University of Chicago

Steven Salterio
Queen's School of Business
Queen's University

Paul J. H. Schoemaker
The Wharton School
University of Pennsylvania

Eldar Shafir
Department of Psychology
Princeton University

David R. Shanks
Department of Psychology
University College London

Suzanne Shu
Graduate School of Business
University of Chicago

Winston R. Sieck
Klein Associates

Steven A. Sloman
Department of Cognitive and Linguistic
Sciences
Brown University

Dilip Soman
Rotman School of Management
University of Toronto

Robert D. Sorkin
Department of Psychology
University of Florida

Karl H. Teigen
Department of Psychology
University of Oslo

Martin Weber
School of Business Administration
University of Mannheim

George Wu
Graduate School of Business
University of Chicago

Jiao Zhang
Graduate School of Business
University of Chicago

Figures and Tables

Figures

Tables

Preface

Over the past several decades, researchers investigating the psychology of judgment and decision making have offered counterintuitive findings, profound insights, and practical prescriptions regarding the means by which people make judgments and choices. In the process, the field has grappled with fundamental questions about human rationality and has influenced the thinking of scholars in areas ranging from law to medicine to business.

There are two features that distinguish the field of judgment and decision making from other topics studied by psychologists. First, research in this area has been unusually attuned to the distinction between normative characterizations of how a rational agent ought to behave, and descriptive characterizations of how people actually behave. As a consequence, researchers in this field have long been concerned with questions of human rationality. Second, judgment and decision making research is often conducted with practical questions and applied settings in mind, and with an implicit or explicit concern with the ways in which judgments and decisions might be improved.

Understanding how people make judgments and decisions is an enterprise of such importance that its study is spread across many disciplines. The recent Nobel Prize in Economics awarded to Daniel Kahneman, for work conducted with the late Amos Tversky, is a particularly vivid indication of the increasing recognition and impact of the field. Conferences on judgment and decision making attract a diverse set of researchers who otherwise would probably not see much of each other, given their distinct backgrounds in cognitive and social psychology, management, marketing, accounting, public policy, and medicine, to name just a few of the areas in which the research is thriving. Likewise, this handbook brings together an international group of authors whose work is otherwise found in books and journals in a wide variety of areas of scholarly inquiry.

The field of judgment and decision making research is no longer in its infancy. Its origins can be found most directly in research conducted in the 1950s and 1960s, though the impact of even earlier innovators continues to be felt. Work by Kahneman and Tversky and their colleagues in the early 1970s brought increasing attention (and new researchers) to the field. By the 1980s, the field was sufficiently distinct and accomplished to support dedicated journals and edited collections. The 1980s and 1990s also saw the field spread from its origins in psychology to other disciplines, a trend that had already begun in the 1970s. At present, it is probably the case that most judgment and decision making research is conducted outside psychology departments, reflecting in part the heavy recruiting of researchers in this area by business schools. The membership of the field's professional societies now numbers many hundreds, and attendance at their conferences continues to grow.

The *Blackwell Handbook of Judgment and Decision Making* is intended both as a state-of-the-art report on current topics of interest to researchers in the field, and as an overview of the important findings and themes in this area for interested outsiders, including scholars in other disciplines and non-academic professionals. Although there are a number of fine edited collections, this is – to the best of our knowledge – the first handbook of judgment and decision making research. The field, it seems to us, is overdue for such a treatment.

Part I provides a glimpse at the many approaches that have been taken in the study of judgment and decision making, which in turn reflect the diverse backgrounds and disciplines from which the research has been approached. Chapters in this part sketch some of the central themes and controversies that have emerged in the field, often arising when the different approaches clashed with one another. Such clashes are not a thing of the past, as the various perspectives offered in this and subsequent parts of the *Handbook* will make readily apparent.

Parts II and III portray the major findings in the field, divided in the conventional manner into parts on judgments and on decisions. Judgment, in this context, is defined as the set of evaluative and inferential processes that people have at their disposal and can draw on in the process of making decisions. Decision making is treated quite broadly, covering not only the traditional topics of riskless and risky choice, but also examining the roles of social, emotional, and cultural influences.

Part IV describes some of the major areas of application of judgment and decision making research. The chapters in this part demonstrate the wide impact that judgment and decision making research has exerted on other fields, and also provide some examples of how such research has been expanded and enriched by application to important problems in a variety of professional contexts.

Our goal in putting together the handbook was to provide the reader with a sense of some of the key insights that have been achieved by the exciting work that has been conducted in the increasingly influential field of judgment and decision making research. The success of a handbook, of course, depends entirely on the authors. In our case, we were fortunate to receive contributions from some of the best in the field. We are grateful to the authors for their hard work in producing excellent chapters in (for the most part) a timely fashion, and for putting up with what must have seemed like a never-ending stream of email from the editors.

Additional thanks go to Christine Cardone, Sarah Coleman, and Phyllis Wentworth at Blackwell for their help with the editorial work, to Scott McAllister for checking and correcting references, and to Jonathan Baron and Dale Griffin for their helpful suggestions regarding the *Handbook*'s content and contributors during its early stages. Our work in preparing this book was supported by the Natural Sciences and Engineering Research Council of Canada and the Social Sciences and Humanities Research Council of Canada (Koehler) and the Economic and Social Research Council's Centre for Economic Learning and Social Evolution (Harvey).

Derek J. Koehler
Department of Psychology
University of Waterloo

Nigel Harvey
Department of Psychology
University College London

PART I

Approaches

1

Rationality and the Normative/ Descriptive Distinction

David Over

Introduction

Normative theories for cognition aim to tell us how we ideally should or ought to reason, make judgments, and take decisions. These theories, particularly formal logic, probability theory, and decision theory, give us rules to follow or conform to that supposedly make our thought rational. Descriptive theories in psychology try to describe how people actually think. Descriptive results showing that people are out of line with a suggested normative rule may be grounds for concluding that their thinking is fallacious or biased. However, there are sometimes serious disputes about whether a proposed normative theory or rule is really relevant to people's rationality. Whether a theory, or one of its rules, is truly "normative" or relevant in some context depends, at the deepest level, on our definition of "rationality."

This chapter will begin with a definition of rationality that is most often appealed to, explicitly or implicitly, in the study of judgment and decision making. According to this definition, our mental states or processes are rational when they help us to achieve our goals. We shall see how this "instrumental" notion of rationality can be used to try to determine whether a proposed normative theory or rule is relevant in some instance. This notion can also be used to try to say when it is too difficult for people to apply an ideal normative theory, and when a "rule of thumb" or heuristic should be relied on instead.

We shall then consider how evolutionary psychology supports the instrumental view of rationality. Our capacity to reason did not evolve by natural selection because reasoning has an intrinsic value as an "elevated" state of mind, but rather because it increased the reproductive success of our ancestors. Evolutionary psychology has also drawn attention to innate modules or instincts that embody helpful heuristics for goal satisfaction. However, instrumental rationality cannot be reduced, as we shall see, to evolutionary "rationality." Finally, we shall illustrate how problems can sometimes be reformulated to make them easier to solve by means of normative rules, to the benefit of our goal satisfaction and so instrumental rationality.

Instrumental Rationality

People and their mental states or processes and actions are rational when they meet the right cognitive standards. Normative theories and rules are supposed to lay down these standards, but there are disputes about what the right theories and rules are for this (Cohen, 1983; Stein, 1996; Stanovich, 1999; Stanovich & West, 2000). How are these disputes to be settled? Or at least, what points are relevant to settling them? To get clearer about these questions, we must make some points about the concept of rationality itself.

There is a distinction between what is often called epistemic rationality, on the one hand, and rationality of action, on the other. This distinction is between rational belief and rational inference, on the one hand, and rational action, on the other. A rational belief is based on a generally reliable mental process. A rational inference has a conclusion that is true, or at least probably true, given its premises. A rational action is a good one for us to perform, in a sense of "good" that has to be clarified. For example, suppose a friend tells us that an acquaintance of ours is 55 years old and has had a heart attack. Our friend always tells us the truth, and we believe her. Our belief is rational because we have reliable mental processes that enable us to recognize her, as our friend, and to remember her honesty. We infer that our acquaintance has had a heart attack. This inference is rational, as it is the trivially valid inference in formal logic of inferring q from "p & q". Our next step may be to decide to take more exercise than did our acquaintance. The presupposition here is that staying healthy is one of our goals. If this is so, then taking more exercise will be a "good" and "rational" action for us to take, in the sense that it will help us to achieve that goal.

There is also a distinction between theoretical and practical reasoning. What we ordinarily call "reason" is usually theoretical reason: it is aimed at acquiring rational beliefs about the world using rational inferences. Practical reason is often a matter of what we ordinarily call "judgment" and is aimed at selecting rational actions. Consider a lazy man, a couch potato, for example. His theoretical reasoning enables him to infer that lack of exercise is increasing his weight. This reasoning could be scientific, or based on the commonplace observation that weight gain can result from lack of exercise. Once he has established this conclusion, by means of theoretical reasoning, he may then use practical reasoning to make a judgment about the best corrective action to take. He might, say, decide to go jogging every day. This practical conclusion does not necessarily follow from the theoretical one. Even if the couch potato knows, by theoretical reasoning, that lack of exercise is causing him to put on weight, he might decide, as a result of practical reasoning, that it is not worth it to him to make a change in his lifestyle. He may not highly value the goal of weighing less. Even if he does want, a little, to be thinner, he may want other goals more, such as lying comfortably on his couch. Theoretical reasoning is rational when its use reliably leads us to beliefs that are true or at least probably true. But in our practical reasoning, we aim to decide which actions are the best for us to take, in light of our individual goals.

The field of judgment and decision making is mainly concerned with action and with judgments that are useful in decision making about action. Thus the field should tell us a great deal about practical reasoning. In fact, work on judgment and decision making usually presupposes a definition of rationality that makes rational action basic or primary in a deeper sense. This is the instrumental view of rationality. According to this view, rational action to achieve goals is the primary notion, and rational belief and rational inference are secondary and derived. The fundamental standard for instrumental rationality is having reliable means to achieve goals. The goals are very often objective in the sense of being external ends, such as making a great deal of money. But the goals are not objective in the sense that all rational people will agree on them. In the instrumental sense, one can aim to make a great deal of money and be rational, and equally one can find a less materialistic purpose in life and be rational. People have goals as a result of their subjective desires, which are expressed in preferences that vary from person to person. Theoretical reason is an instrument for achieving the goals, and it has no intrinsic value independent of the goals. The great empiricist philosopher Hume (1978, Book II, Section III, originally published 1739–40) was first to articulate this instrumentalist position clearly and to argue for it forcibly: "Reason is, and ought only to be the slave of the passions, and can never pretend to any other office than to serve and obey them."

Almost all discussions of rationality in cognitive psychology and cognitive science presuppose this instrumentalist understanding of rationality, the history of which can be traced back to Hume through later empiricist and pragmatist thinkers. An example of its explicit statement in recent cognitive work, in another vivid and striking metaphor, is in Simon (1983, pp. 7–8): "Reason is wholly instrumental. It cannot tell us where to go; at best it can tell us how to get there. It is a gun for hire that can be employed in the service of any goals we have, good or bad." It should be noted that Hume and Simon are talking about our underlying or primary "passions" or goals. Reason cannot tell us to prefer good health to bad health, but given that we prefer the former, reason can help us to the derived goal of getting more exercise, for the sake of our health.

Instrumental rationality is presupposed in almost all discussions in cognitive psychology about normative rules and their proper application, but its consequences are not always spelt out so clearly. In yet another clear statement of it, Baron (2000, p. 53) defines rational thinking as:

> whatever kind of thinking best helps people to achieve their goals. If it should turn out that following the rules of logic leads to eternal happiness, then it is "rational thinking" to follow the rules of logic (assuming that we all want eternal happiness). If it should turn out, on the other hand, that carefully violating the laws of logic at every turn leads to eternal happiness, then it is these violations that should be called rational.

Normative theories and their rules, like formal logic and its rules, are supposed to provide standards of rationality. From the instrumental point of view, however, a proposed normative theory, or one of its rules, is relevant to us in some context if and only if keeping in line with it will help us to attain our goals in that context, giving us goal satisfaction. Formal decision theory is an attempt to lay down normative rules for maximizing our goal satisfaction (Baron, 2000, Chapter 10, and this volume, Chapter 2). In the theory, goal satisfaction is measured by subjective utility. If our preferences among the possible outcomes of actions, or possible goals, are consistent with the axioms of the theory, then decision theorists can represent our subjective utilities with numbers. If our subjective probability judgments are consistent, or "coherent," with the axioms of probability theory, then decision theorists can represent these judgments with numbers as well. The two numbers can be multiplied together to give the subjective expected utility of a possible outcome or goal for us. The final objective of the rules of decision theory is to help us maximize subjective expected utility.

Formal decision theory is too strong in some respects, particularly in requiring an unbounded ability to make coherent probability judgments. It is also weak in other respects. In particular, the formal theory does not require our subjective probability judgments to correspond to objective probabilities, which are usually defined by reference to the frequencies of objective events (Baron, 2000, pp. 97–8). But most supporters of instrumental rationality do require this. They are "externalist" in that they define rationality in terms of having objectively reliable perceptual, cognitive, and motor "instruments" for goal satisfaction. Assuming this definition of rationality, we can criticize formal decision theory for being too strong in some respects and too weak in others (Evans & Over, 1996).

Simon (1957, 1983) has argued, in influential work, that we adopt a notion of bounded rationality and "satisficing," which is satisfying ourselves while falling short of the ideal of maximizing subjective expected utility. Simon's instrumental definition of rationality justifies the value he places on bounded rationality and a satisficing strategy in decision making. Reasoning consistently with supposed normative rules is worthwhile for rational action as long as it is an effective instrument for achieving goals. A debate about whether a proposed normative rule is relevant in some context should turn on whether the rule would be of help in getting to the desired goals. Our beliefs and judgments may sometimes be too vague or sloppy to be fully consistent with logic, probability theory, or decision theory. That does not necessarily mean that we should spend time and energy making our beliefs and judgments precise or consistent. We will sometimes have the best chance of getting to reasonably satisfying goals if we do not worry too much about exactly what is consistent with some possibly relevant normative theory. Moreover, it is not necessarily a good idea for us to appeal to logic, probability, and decision theory, even if our beliefs and judgments are consistent, and these theories would, ideally, tell us how to maximize our goal satisfaction. It can be too difficult for us, with our limited abilities, to apply these theories and their rules to particular cases. For these reasons, we can sometimes do better by relying on heuristics, which are bounded and satisficing procedures for performing inferences or making decisions. Heuristics can be efficient because they are often applied relatively automatically and quickly and with reasonable reliability. They can be justified instrumentally because they can help us to reach two goals: an end state that we desire and getting there without expending too much time and energy.

For example, suppose we are trying to make a judgment about whether to trust a man who is smiling at us. We might recall many people who smiled at us and were trustworthy, and only a few who smiled at us and were not. We are using the availability heuristic (Tversky & Kahneman, 1973) for probability judgment if we conclude, from these memories, that it is highly probable that the man is trustworthy. The use of the availability heuristic can go wrong and produce badly biased results. Tversky and Kahneman (1973) stressed the existence of these biases, but also pointed out that the availability heuristic has some "ecological validity," as objectively "frequent events are easier to recall or imagine than infrequent events." This heuristic is far from meeting the highest scientific standards for gathering data on the objective frequency of events, but then ordinary people cannot possibly meet those ideal standards. It is thus fine for them to use the availability heuristic for quick decisions when it has reasonable ecological validity.

By relying on heuristics in general, we can more or less implicitly conform to the normative rules of logic, probability theory, or decision theory. But this does not mean that we are explicitly following those rules. There is a distinction between implicitly conforming to, or complying with, rules and explicitly following them (Smith, Langston, & Nisbett, 1992). The most informal and intuitive way to make the distinction is in terms of consciousness. When people are following rules, they are consciously trying to apply and keep themselves in line with the rules. We could test whether people are following rules by asking them to report the contents of their working memory in explicit think-aloud protocols. These protocols can provide evidence of rule following. For example, if people speak aloud what they are thinking while trying to pass a driving test, they may allude to the rules of good driving that they have been taught by their instructor. Intending to overtake or pass another car, they might mention looking in their rearview mirror before pulling out. This would be good evidence of rule following. But of course, to perform this activity safely, they must process a great deal of visual data, which they will do automatically, implicitly, and unconsciously. They will be unable to report from their working memories how they are determining the distance another car is in front of them. There are rules for working out this distance correctly, but people do not explicitly follow them. It is rather that they have dedicated cognitive processes, below the level of consciousness, that implicitly comply with or conform to these rules.

It may not seem that there is anything that would ordinarily be called "reasoning" or "rationality" in judging the distance between one car and another. Nevertheless, making this judgment efficiently and reliably is a cognitive part of achieving the goal of passing another car safely. The dedicated processes, in the eyes and the brain, are effective "instruments" for reaching that goal and are, in that respect, in no way inferior to the "instrument" of reason. What we ordinarily tend to call "reasoning" has to do with explicitly following rules, which we can mention, to some extent, when we give our reasons for our judgments and decisions. But in terms of instrumental rationality, all efficient and reliable "instruments" for achieving goals are equal, whether conscious or unconscious, explicit or implicit, controlled or automatic.

Truth itself is only relevant to us given our preferences. Our preferences determine our goals and how much we want them, including even the epistemic goal of acquiring true beliefs. In short, epistemic utility is just a kind of subjective utility (Evans & Over,

1996). There is no one who wants only to have true beliefs and nothing else. There are dedicated scientists who have a strong preference for following the normative rules of scientific research and for the truth about the topics they are studying. Even they want other things in their academic lives, such as promotions and Nobel Prizes, and they have many other goals in other parts of their lives. Not even they want to devote all their time and energy to trying to ensure that all their beliefs are consistent and true. This is a logically impossible goal in any case. There is no logically bounded way to prove that our beliefs are consistent. Above the most elementary level, formal logic is an unbounded system, and since all other normative theories rest on it, these are unbounded as well. Sometimes finite bounds do exist for establishing consistency in relatively simple beliefs, but the bound may be one that we could not reach in our lifetime nor in many millions or billions of years. (See Oaksford & Chater, 1998, Chapter 4, on the significance of these points for cognitive psychology.)

Rationality of action should have priority, in the instrumental view, over rational belief and inference. For what is the use of a true belief or a valid inference if it does not help us to achieve a goal we have? Suppose that a hospital patient is so highly confident that she will recover from an illness that her confidence is far above the objective probability of her recovery. Even so, her overconfidence may make her objective chance of recovery as high as possible. If she followed the highest normative standards for rational belief, to get a well-calibrated belief, she would become less optimistic and more passive in taking steps to aid her recovery. That might lower her objective chance of recovery: she would be well calibrated but at a lower level. Convincing herself that she will definitely recover gives her, in this case, rationality of action. She performs the action that gives her the best objective chance of getting what she most wants. And it is hard to deny that she is rational full stop: her rationality of action has "trumped" her lack of "rational" belief.

More deeply still, instrumental rationality lies at the foundation, it can be argued, of what it means to have beliefs and desires and to perform actions. We will accept that a creature has beliefs and desires, and has performed actions, only if we can discern some successful goal achievement in its behavior. Beliefs and desires are just those mental states that work together to produce action. And action has to be more than random or undirected physical movement. It has to have goals, and it can only be seen to have goals if it has some success in reaching certain end states. In fact, if we could not identify some successful goal activity in a "creature," we could not call it a living thing at all, but would put it down as an inanimate object. For this reason, some philosophers have argued that even primitive tropic responses, like that of plant in growing towards the light, should be called a goal directed activity and a type of extremely primitive instrumental rationality (Bermúdez, 2002).

Evolution and Rationality

The instrumental understanding of rationality receives considerable support from evolutionary psychology. Why was the increasing ability to reason selected for in our evolutionary ancestors? That did not happen because reason has some intrinsic value. Many philosophers and religious thinkers, who were not empiricists or pragmatists, have held that theoretical reason not only has some necessary intrinsic value, but that this value is much greater than the value of desire, especially "base" desire. But evolution by natural selection has promoting reproductive success as its only "value," and "base" desires are essential for that. Reason has no more intrinsic value than a giraffe's long neck. Increasing neck length in the giraffe's evolutionary ancestors, and increasing ability to reason in ours, increased reproductive success. Both qualities were selected for because they were good instruments for achieving this goal. Increasing neck length made more food available to the giraffe's ancestors. Increasing ability to reason helped our ancestors to communicate, cooperate, innovate, and plan more effectively, allowing them to get more food and facilitating successful reproduction in other ways. Reason is instrumental because it serves this goal of evolution, directly and indirectly, for example by enabling us to invent useful instruments in the most literal sense of tools.

It will sometimes be better to trust completely to a primitive instinct than to spend time using reasoning to try to infer what we should do. Instincts can embody heuristics that are generally effective means of achieving reproductive success, yielding goals that almost everyone places a high value on. Suppose that we are sick after eating some exotic new food and our instinctive reaction is to avoid it in future. Is this rational? It does not conform to the canons of scientific research, but given the instrumental analysis of rationality, we can argue that it is rational. Relying on this reaction may well help us to avoid sickness from eating the wrong kind of food. True, we will sometimes be mistaken about which foods have truly made us sick. But unless we have a scientific interest in food poisoning, we may well prefer not getting sickness again to knowing exactly which foods cause the sickness. The public health authorities could well take a different view if we got sick after a restaurant meal. But we would anyway usually lack the authority and scientific expertise to discover the truth in such a case, and we could trust to our instinct as the grounds of our future action. Hume would have approved. He famously argued that instinct is often better than reason for ordinary judgments about causation (Hume, 1975, Section 45, originally published 1748–51).

The instinct, for reacting against novel foods when sickness follows eating them, is a dedicated or domain-specific module. It may help prevent food poisoning but does nothing to prevent other causes of illness. Modules like this embody content-specific heuristics for making inferences or decisions about particular problems. Another example of this type of module is for face recognition (Nakayama, 2001). Both of these modules appear to be innate in a strong sense, but other modular instincts can be more flexible and open to modification by learning. We may have some instinctive tendency to trust smiling faces, but obviously we can learn to be more skeptical of smiles and even to become quite subtle at detecting ones that are less trustworthy. Domain-specific modules can be innate instincts in a weak sense, by arising from "biased" learning that has been "preprogrammed" by natural selection (Cummins & Cummins, 1999).

One can sometimes show that a content-specific heuristic has ecological validity by assuming that the heuristic is applied in a domain or an environment with a fixed and relatively homogeneous structure. We can sometimes even "let the environment do the work" in giving us instrumental rationality (Gigerenzer, Todd, & the ABC Research

Group, 1999). However, not all domains are homogeneous, and there can be unpredictable changes in almost all domains. Almost any heuristic is bound to fail under some conditions (Kahneman, 2000). Even if this is a very rare occurrence for some heuristic, we cannot say that its potential failure is always insignificant. It is possible that a failure in some context will deny us a vital goal, such as preserving our lives. Just as we cannot argue, from an instrumental point of view, that formal rules are necessarily superior to heuristics, so we cannot argue that heuristics are necessarily superior to formal rules.

There is evidence that the mind operates content-specific heuristics, in domain-specific modules, but sometimes overrides these by following content-independent, formal rules. Those who are persuaded by this evidence propose dual process theories of the mind (Fodor, 1983; Evans & Over, 1996; Sloman, 1996; Stanovich, 1999; Stanovich & West, 2000; Kahneman & Frederick, 2002). In these theories, the two types of mental process are classified as being in System 1 or System 2. System 1 is that of domain-specific modules running content-specific heuristics. It operates automatically and rapidly by means of parallel processing. Its workings are almost totally hidden from consciousness and are "encapsulated," meaning that its output is unaffected by higher level cognition. For example, we do not know the details of the operation of our face recognition module, and we cannot help seeing a face-like appearance, even if we believe at a higher level that this appearance is just a trick of the light or our angle of view. System 1 can at best only more or less implicitly conform to content-independent normative rules, though it can do that very quickly and efficiently. Conscious, explicit rule following takes place in System 2. Normative rules sometimes help describe the very operation of System 2. It operates relatively slowly and sequentially, and is severely restricted by working memory capacity. But System 2 can sometimes override the results of System 1 when this is to our benefit. For example, we may be unable to help seeing a non-smiling, sinister face-like appearance in the bushes, but we will not run away if we have good reason to believe, due to System 2, that there cannot be a real face there. System 2 can compensate for System 1 when System 1 fails because its ecological validity is low in some context. System 2 can also work out new ways of responding effectively to unusual or novel events.

It is easy to say in theory, given the instrumental analysis of rationality, when System 2 should override System 1. That is when doing so will help us to achieve our goals in some context. However, it can be difficult, and sometimes impossible, in practice to decide when to override. That is partly the question of when it is best to take our time and expend energy to try to infer an exactly correct answer by means of formal rules. Or alternatively, when it is best to reply on fast and efficient, but rough and ready, heuristics that may, or may not, give us a good enough answer, depending on our luck. We could make general recommendations. If the problem is important given our utility judgments – for example our lives are at stake – and we have plenty of time and energy, then we should use System 2 as best we can. If the problem is less important, or we are pressed for time, then we should probably rely on System 1.

Both System 1 and System 2 are the result of evolution by natural selection, but System 2 gives us the ability to pursue goals that are detached from reproductive success, for example by practicing birth control. System 1 is much more tied to relatively inflexible instincts than System 2, which has been put on a "long leash" by our genes precisely to help us be flexible (Stanovich & West, 2003). Some people do not have reproductive success as one of their personal goals at the level of System 2, although that goal is, in effect, built into System 1. The immediate consequence is that we cannot define rationality simply in evolutionary terms, or replace the rules of logic, probability theory, and decision theory by evolutionary "rules" for reproductive success.

Rode, Cosmides, Hell, and Tooby (1999, p. 302) claim that:

> One should not expect the cognitive architectures of evolved organisms to be "rational" when rationality is defined as adherence to a normative theory drawn from mathematics or logic. One should expect their cognitive architecture to be ecologically rational: well designed for solving the adaptive problems their ancestors faced during their evolutionary history.

As this quote indicates, some evolutionary psychologists have a negative attitude to logic, probability theory, and decision theory as standards of rationality. They wish to define rationality by reference to "specialized cognitive mechanisms that evolution has built into the mind for specific domains of inference and reasoning . . ." (Gigerenzer, Todd, & the ABC Research Group, 1999, p. 30). In part, this attitude is a result of the fact that evolutionary psychologists presuppose a specific type of instrumental rationality, for which the sole underlying goal is reproductive success. This evolutionary approach sometimes goes to the extreme of implying that there is never value in formal rule following for ordinary judgment and decision making. However, following formal rules can have instrumental value in achieving some goals. The evidence is strong that people generally have some formal logical ability, some deductive competence (Evans & Over, 1996). And across a wide range of problems, people of higher cognitive ability tend to have greater ability to follow formal rules to get the solution (Stanovich, 1999; Stanovich & West, 2000).

Instrumental rationality cannot be reduced to evolutionary or ecological rationality, as suggested by the above evolutionary psychologists (Over, 2002; Stanovich & West, 2003). Suppose we are hungry and considering a choice between eating a chocolate bar or a carrot. An instinct makes us like foods full of fat or sugar. As the chocolate bar has more fat and sugar in it than the carrot, we will have some tendency to prefer the chocolate to the carrot. This instinct was beneficial under primitive conditions, when maximum calorie intake was necessary for reproductive success, but it may damage health in technologically advanced societies (Strassmann & Dunbar, 1999). We cannot say that making this choice now has instrumental rationality merely because the cognitive structure that brings it about facilitated the goal of reproductive success for our ancestors early in human (and pre-human) evolutionary history. We may not have the goal of reproductive success, and might wish to avoid having children or more children. Thanks to System 2, we may have a better idea, than our instinct implicitly does, of a healthy diet in contemporary society. With good health as a goal, we cannot call a cognitive structure "rational" if naively relying on it gives us a heart attack. More generally, heuristics that evolved by natural selection under primitive conditions can go badly wrong in technological society. There is no justification for complacency about the true instrumental rationality of instincts in the contemporary world, given that our instincts were designed to work well under conditions that may no longer exist.

Prescriptive Rules

An example of a prescriptive rule for a healthy diet would be to try to lower our intake of foods high in fat and sugar. This is vague but is more efficient for it. A prescriptive rule can be defined as a guide for helping us to get closer to a normative ideal (Baron, 2000, p. 32, and this volume, Chapter 2). There may well be an ideally healthy diet for each of us given our individual genetic make-ups, but it would be almost impossible for us to find out what this ideal is and to follow its rules. We may, however, be able to follow prescriptive "rules of thumb," like trying to cut down on foods high in fat and sugar.

Formal logic, probability theory, and decision theory are unbounded theories. It is impossible to be sure, in general, that one is being consistent with them. Some of the individual rules of these theories can be trivially easy to follow, but the theories themselves can only be thought of as ideal standards. This is where prescriptive rules can be of help, enabling us to approach the ideal to some extent by advising us when to use a satisficing heuristic. But sometimes it is easier to follow a normative rule to solve a problem if the problem is reformulated in a specific way. Another kind of prescriptive rule can advise us how to do this to our benefit. Recently psychologists have paid much attention to the fact that some probability word problems become relatively easy when they are expressed in terms of "frequencies," or more accurately, in terms of proportions in finite sets. Tversky and Kahneman (1983) were the first to get results of this kind.

When one proposition logically implies another, it is a rule of probability theory that the first proposition cannot be more probable than the second proposition. This is an excellent example of how a logical rule can help us to make probability judgments by constraining them in a certain respect. For example, as we have noted above, it is trivial that "p & q" logically implies q, and by the definition of logical implication, that means that "p & q" cannot possibly be true and q false. It immediately follows that the probability of "p & q" cannot be greater than the probability of q, since if this were the case, there would be some possibility that "p & q" was true and q false. However, Tversky and Kahneman (1983) found that people do sometimes violate this conjunction rule, committing the "conjunction fallacy." One example Tversky and Kahneman used was about a survey of adult males in British Columbia. The participants were asked a question about a proposition of the logical form "p & q": "What percentage of the men surveyed both are over 55 years old and have had one or more heart attacks?" and a question about the proposition q: "What percentage of the men surveyed have had one or more heart attacks?" People tended to commit the conjunction fallacy by giving a higher percentage answer to the question about "p & q" than to the question about q.

There have been many further experiments on, and interpretations of, the conjunction fallacy. It may be that people have a pragmatic presupposition that a question about men is about men of an average age, or somehow excludes older men. However, this objection and others to the original experiment can be overcome with the right materials (Sides, Osherson, Bonini, & Viale, 2002). An important fact is that people of higher cognitive ability are less prone to the conjunction fallacy (Stanovich & West, 1998). They are apparently more capable of thinking in abstract and formal terms. This is an ability that is bound to stand them in good stead in contemporary society, helping them to attain many goals that they desire (Stanovich & West, 2003).

There is a way of reformulating conjunction problems that helps more people to get the right answer. Tversky and Kahneman (1983) discovered how to do this by using proportions in finite, easy to imagine sets or classes to represent frequencies (see also this volume, Chapter 8). They reformulated their question in a set or class version by asking about a survey of 100 adult males in British Columbia. The "p & q" question became: "How many of the 100 participants both are over 55 years old and have had one or more heart attacks?" The "q" question became: "How many of the 100 participants have had one or more heart attacks?" The participants in Tversky and Kahneman's experiment did much better with this version in avoiding the conjunction fallacy.

Tversky and Kahneman explained that the reformulated version made the subset, or class inclusion, relation "transparent." There is a direct correspondence between elementary logic and finite set theory. By that correspondence, the set corresponding to a conjunction "p & q" is necessarily included in the set corresponding to q. This inclusion relation can be made as clear as possible with a geometric or graphic representation, e.g. in terms of Euler circles (Sloman & Over, 2003; Sloman, Over, & Slovak, 2003). Begin by thinking of the 100 men surveyed as gathered in a circle. Inside that first circle we can form a second circle round all of those surveyed men who have had at least one heart attack. Suppose that we judge that there will be 10 of those, so this second circle will go round those 10 men. Within that second circle, we can form a third circle of those men who are over 55 years old and have had at least one heart attack. The number of those in this third circle obviously cannot be greater than 10: perhaps there are 6 men in it. Grasping that the third circle has fewer, or at least no more, men than the second circle is an especially transparent way of avoiding the conjunction fallacy.

A prescriptive rule would be to transform probability questions about percentages into questions about proportions in finite sets. If that lacks full clarity, another prescriptive rule would be to draw Euler circles to represent the finite sets. Following these prescriptions, we could make formal normative rules transparent in their application and be able to follow them. The prescriptive rules, recommending these transformations, could be rational, helping us to achieve goals, as long as following them did not cost too much time or trouble or otherwise diminish goal satisfaction. There is a long tradition in logic and probability theory of using geometric or graphic representations, especially of sets, to make formal relations, and normative rules derived from them, as clear as possible. (This tradition goes back through Venn and Euler to Leibniz. See Kneale & Kneale, 1962, on the history, and Stenning, 2002, for recent work.)

Another example of how graphic representations can help people be rational has been extensively investigated recently by psychologists. Suppose that we have been given the following information about men who have taken too little exercise and eaten far too much fat and sugar. The "base rate" probability that one of these men has had a heart attack is 0.4. The conditional probability is 0.6 that that one of these men is over 55 years old given that he has had a heart attack. And the conditional probability is 0.2 that one of these men is over 55 years old given he has not had a heart attack. Then we are asked for the probability that one of these men had a heart attack given that he is over 55 years old. We can get the answer to this word problem by using Bayes' rule, which is a formal theorem of probability theory. The answer is approximately 0.67. Research has shown that most people would have trouble with this problem in this kind of formulation (Casscells, Schoenberger, & Graboys, 1978; Cosmides & Tooby, 1996).

The word problem can, however, be given in a set form and represented geometrically or graphically. Using logical trees is a nice way to bring out the underlying logical points (see Jeffrey, 1967, for the logical theory of these trees). Suppose we represent the probabilities as proportions in a set of 100 members. This set is a kind of ideal finite set with subsets in exact proportions to the relevant probabilities. Applying elementary logic, we know that this set can be divided into two separate branches, representing the subset of men who have had a heart attack and the disjoint subset of men who have not had a heart attack. There will be 40 men who have had a heart attack in the left-hand branch and 60 who have not had a heart attack in the right-hand branch. Applying logic again to the left-hand branch of 40 men who have had a heart attack, we have two disjoint sub-branches of these men: 24 with a heart attack and over 55; and 16 with a heart attack and not over 55. Now we turn to the right-hand branch of 60 men who have not had a heart attack. Applying logic yet again, we have two disjoint sub-branches of these men: 12 without a heart attack and over 55; and 48 without a heart attack and not over 55.

Finally, we ask for the proportion of men who have had a heart attack and are over 55 out of all the men over 55. We get the total number of men over 55 from the two left-hand sub-branches above. That is 24 + 12 = 36. The number of men who have had a heart attack and are over 55 is 24, and thus transparently our answer is 24 out of 36. People would find it easier to get the right answer when the problem is in this form (Gigerenzer & Hoffrage, 1995; Cosmides & Tooby, 1996; Brase, Cosmides, & Tooby, 1998).

Tversky and Kahneman would say that the second representation of the problem is easy to solve because the set or class structures in it make the relevant formal rules transparent and easy to follow. An alternative, evolutionary claim is that the second version is easy because it is about the results of natural sampling (Kleiter, 1994), and that people have a special adaptation for understanding this (Gigerenzer & Hoffrage, 1995, 1999; Cosmides & Tooby, 1996; Brase, Cosmides, & Tooby, 1998). Sometimes this evolutionary claim is combined with the statement that the second version is easier because it requires fewer computational steps than the first version (Gigerenzer & Hoffrage, 1995, 1999). But however many steps it takes, each step in a transparent derivation must represent elementary logical and set operations. The derivation must also end in a clearly displayed subset relation between a "p & q" set of objects (men who have had a heart attack and are over 55) and a "q" set of objects (men over 55). In the end, it must come down to avoiding the conjunction fallacy in the way Tversky and Kahneman (1983) specified (Over, 2003).

We do have to be careful when thinking of the problem in natural sampling terms. As noted above, the representation of the probabilities as proportions in finite sets is an ideal procedure. Sometimes the results of natural sampling are called "natural frequencies" (Gigerenzer & Hoffrage, 1999), but we must remember that these are sample frequencies that may not equal objective frequencies. We have so far discussed using elementary logical rules and set operations to solve word problems. The normative rules for trying to get unbiased sample frequencies are another topic altogether. Even if we followed the most exacting scientific rules to try to ensure that we got an unbiased sample, we might well not find that, out of 100 men actually sampled, exactly 40 would have had a heart attack. If we did not use scientific sampling procedures, but relied on our memories, then we could get badly biased results, for the reasons Tversky and Kahneman (1973) gave when discussing the availability heuristic.

The evidence is that people can be biased in actual sampling (Lagnado & Shanks, 2002). We probably could not even state very accurately the total number of men we know over 55 years old. People can also find it hard to use the results of natural sampling as these are not normalized (Harries & Harvey, 2000). For some inferences, it obviously helps to recognize, for instance, that both 30 out of 40 and 69 out of 92 are, to normalize, the same as 75 percent. Graphic or geometric representations can be an aid in overcoming this limitation of natural sampling.

It can be difficult, or even impossible, to use actual natural sampling because of vagueness in the language. Suppose we are asked for the actual proportion of men who are depressed out of all the men we know over 55 years old. The difficulty here is that "depressed" is a vague term, and we cannot separate men we know exactly into the depressed and the not depressed. Of course, we could just ignore this difficulty when presented with a word problem, by assuming that, somehow or other, the separation had been made.

Then too the results of natural sampling are sometimes used to damaging effect in decision making. Suppose our couch potato recalls that something is wrong with him almost every time he goes to see his doctor. His weight, blood pressure, or cholesterol is too high. He wishes very much to avoid having a health problem, and he decides that the way to do that is not to go to the doctor. It seems to him, from his natural sampling, that the chance is very high that something is wrong with him given that he goes to the doctor. Sadly, "magical" thinking like this is not uncommon. The trouble is that natural sampling does not necessarily inform us about causation (Over & Green, 2001).

There is an interesting debate about the significance of natural sampling. (See Girotto & Gonzalez, 2001, 2002, and Hoffrage, Gigerenzer, Krauss, & Martignon, 2002.) But no matter what the value of natural sampling as actual sampling, logical trees are a transparent way of representing the results. Logical trees are also widely used as "decision trees" to make decisions transparent (see Baron, 2000, p. 318, for an example). These uses of logical trees illustrate how the right kind of representation can bring the normative and the descriptive together. Research in cognitive psychology, and in judgment and decision making, should not only tell us how close, or far apart, the normative and descriptive can be in human thought and decision making. It should also find prescriptions for transparent representations that enable people to be consistent with normative theories.

Concluding Comments

Most cognitive psychologists presuppose the instrumental definition of rationality when they discuss the value of a formal rule or a heuristic for some purpose. There are, however, philosophers who criticize instrumental rationality (Nozick, 1993). Most of the criticisms focus on the fact that instrumental rationality allows only a very limited assessment of the rationality of goals, particularly of underlying or primary goals. True, many supporters of instrumental rationality have followed Hume (1975, Book II, Section III) in holding that desires and goals can sometimes be called irrational when they depend on false beliefs. Taking this line, we would say that it was irrational to fear what should be an obvious optical illusion of a sinister face and to have goal of running away from it as quickly as possible.

We could also call someone irrational who had the cognitive illusion that there is a difference between two clearly equivalent ways of describing, or "framing," a decision problem. Psychologists have discovered that such failures of extensionality in people's thought can affect their preferences and goals. Kahneman (1994) points out that these cases and others of false belief, e.g. about what will give us pleasure or pain in the future, pose problems for the formal theory of decision making. These are not necessarily problems for instrumental rationality, but we cannot go far in using this sense of rationality to criticize goals as "irrational," though we may still condemn them on moral or legal grounds. As the quote from Simon (1983) above implies, people can be rational in the pursuit of bad goals, which might, say, be cruel or unjust. Most cognitive psychologists would follow Simon in seeing an important distinction between cognitive normative standards and moral or legal normative standards.

Acknowledgment

Research for this chapter was supported by a research leave grant from the Arts and Humanities Research board of the UK.

References

Baron, J. (2000) *Thinking and Deciding* (3rd edn.). Cambridge: Cambridge University Press.

Bermúdez, J. L. (2002) Rationality and psychological explanation without language. In J. L. Bermúdez and A. Millar (eds.), *Reason and Nature: Essays in the Theory of Rationality*. Oxford: Oxford University Press.

Brase, G. L., Cosmides, L., & Tooby, J. (1998) Individuation, counting, and statistical inference: The role of frequency and whole-object representations in judgment under uncertainty, *Journal of Experimental Psychology*, 127, 3–21.

Casscells, W., Schoenberger, A., & Graboys, T. (1978) Interpretation by physicians of clinical laboratory results, *New England Journal of Medicine*, 299, 999–1001.

Cohen, L. J. (1983) Can human rationality be experimentally demonstrated? *Behavioral and Brain Sciences*, 4, 317–70.

Cosmides, L. & Tooby, J. (1996) Are humans good intuitive statisticians after all? Rethinking some conclusions from the literature on judgment under uncertainty, *Cognition*, 58, 1–73.

Cummins, D. D. & Cummins, R. (1999) Biological preparedness and evolutionary explanation, *Cognition*, 73, 37–53.

Evans, J. St. B. T. & Over, D. E. (1996) *Rationality and Reasoning*. Hove: Psychology Press.

Fodor, J. (1983) *The Modularity of Mind.* Cambridge, MA: The MIT Press.

Gigerenzer, G. & Hoffrage, U. (1995) How to improve Bayesian reasoning without instruction: Frequency formats, *Psychological Review*, 102, 684–704.

Gigerenzer, G. & Hoffrage, U. (1999) Overcoming difficulties in Bayesian reasoning: Reply to Lewis and Keren (1999) and Mellers and McGraw (1999), *Psychological Review*, 106, 425–30.

Gigerenzer, G., Todd, P., & the ABC Research Group (1999) *Simple Heuristics that Make Us Smart.* New York: Oxford University Press.

Girotto, V. & Gonzalez, M. (2001) Solving probabilistic and statistical problems: A matter of information structure and question form, *Cognition*, 78, 247–76.

Girotto, V. & Gonzalez, M. (2002) Chances and frequencies in probabilistic reasoning: Rejoinder to Hoffrage, Gigerenzer, Krauss, and Martignon, *Cognition*, 84, 353–9.

Harries, C. & Harvey, N. (2000) Are absolute frequencies, relative frequencies, or both effective in reducing cognitive biases? *Journal of Behavioral Decision Making*, 13, 431–44.

Hoffrage, U., Gigerenzer, G., Krauss, S., & Martignon, L. (2002) Representation facilitates reasoning: What natural frequencies are and what they are not, *Cognition*, 84, 343–52.

Hume, D. (1975) *Enquiries Concerning the Human Understanding and Concerning the Principles of Morals*, (ed. P. H. Nidditch) (3rd edn.). Oxford: Clarendon Press.

Hume, D. (1978) *A Treatise of Human Nature*, (ed. P. H. Nidditch) (2nd edn.). Oxford: Clarendon Press.

Jeffrey, R. C. (1967) *Formal Logic: Its Scope and Limits.* New York: McGraw-Hill.

Kahneman, D. (1994) New challenges to the rationality assumption, *Journal of Institutional and Theoretical Economics*, 150/1, 18–36.

Kahneman, D. (2000) A psychological point of view: Violations of rational rules as a diagnostic of mental processes, *Behavioral and Brain Sciences*, 23, 681–3.

Kahneman, D. & Frederick, S. (2002) Representativeness revisited: Attribute substitution in intuitive judgment. In T. Gilovich, D. Griffin, and D. Kahneman (eds.), *Heuristics and Biases: The Psychology of Intuitive Judgment.* Cambridge: Cambridge University Press.

Kleiter, G. (1994) Natural sampling: Rationality without base rates. In G. H. Fisher and D. Laming (eds.), *Contributions to Mathematical Psychology, Psychometrics, and Methodology.* New York: Springer-Verlag.

Kneale, W. & Kneale, M. (1962) *The Development of Logic.* Oxford: Oxford University Press.

Lagnado, D. & Shanks, D. R. (2002) Probability judgment in hierarchical learning: A conflict between predictiveness and coherence, *Cognition*, 83, 81–112.

Nakayama, K. (2001) Modularity in perception, and its relation to cognition and knowledge. In E. B. Goldstein (ed.), *Blackwell Handbook of Perception.* Oxford: Blackwell.

Nozick, R. (1993) *The Nature of Rationality.* Princeton, NJ: Princeton University Press.

Oaksford, M. & Chater, N. (1998) *Rationality in an Uncertain World: Essays on the Cognitive Science of Human Reasoning.* Hove, UK: Psychology Press.

Over, D. E. (2002) The rationality of evolutionary psychology. In J. L. Bermúdez and A. Millar (eds.), *Reason and Nature: Essays in the Theory of Rationality.* Oxford: Oxford University Press.

Over, D. E. (2003) From massive modularity to metarepresentation: The evolution of higher cognition. In D. E. Over (ed.), *Evolution and the Psychology of Thinking: The Debate.* Hove, UK: Psychology Press.

Over, D. E. & Green, D. W. (2001) Contingency, causation, and adaptive inference, *Psychological Review*, 108, 682–4.

Rode, C., Cosmides, L., Hell, W., & Tooby, J. (1999) When and why do people avoid unknown probabilities in decisions under uncertainty? Testing some predictions from optimal foraging theory, *Cognition*, 72, 269–304.

Sides, A., Osherson, D., Bonini, N., & Viale, R. (2002) On the reality of the conjunction fallacy, *Memory & Cognition*, 30(2), 191–8.

Simon, H. A. (1957) *Models of Man: Social and Rational.* New York: Wiley.

Simon, H. A. (1983) *Reason in Human Affairs.* Stanford, CA: Stanford University Press.

Sloman, S. A. (1996) The empirical case for two systems of reasoning, *Psychological Bulletin*, 119, 3–22.

Sloman, S. A. & Over, D. E. (2003) Probability judgment from the inside and out. In D. E. Over (ed.), *Evolution and the Psychology of Thinking: The Debate.* Hove, UK: Psychology Press.

Sloman, S. A., Over, D. E., & Slovak, L. (2003) Frequency illusions and other fallacies, *Organizational Behavior and Human Decision Processes*, 91, 296–309.

Smith, E. E., Langston, C., & Nisbett, R. (1992) The case for rules in reasoning. *Cognitive Science*, 16, 1–40.

Stanovich, K. E. (1999) *Who is Rational? Studies in Individual Differences in Reasoning.* Mahwah, NJ: Lawrence Erlbaum Associates.

Stanovich, K. E. & West, R. F. (1998) Individual differences in framing and conjunction effects. *Thinking and Reasoning*, 4, 289–317.

Stanovich, K. E. & West, R. F. (2000) Individual differences in reasoning: Implications for the rationality debate? *Behavioral and Brain Sciences*, 23, 645–726.

Stanovich, K. E. & West, R. F. (2003) Evolutionary versus instrumental goals: How evolutionary psychology misconceives human rationality. In D. E. Over (ed.), *Evolution and the Psychology of Thinking: The Debate.* Hove, UK: Psychology Press.

Stein, E. (1996) *Without Good Reason: The Rationality Debate in Philosophy and Cognitive Science.* Oxford: Oxford University Press.

Stenning, K. (2002) *Seeing Reason: Image and Language in Learning to Think.* Oxford: Oxford University Press.

Strassmann, B. I. & Dunbar, R. I. M. (1999) Human evolution and disease: Putting the stone age in perspective. In S. C. Stearns (ed.), *Evolution in Health and Disease.* Oxford: Oxford University Press.

Tversky, A. & Kahneman, D. (1973) Availability: A heuristic for judging frequency and probability, *Cognitive Psychology*, 5(2), 207–32.

Tversky, A. & Kahneman, D. (1983) Extensional versus Intuitive reasoning: The conjunction fallacy in probability judgment, *Psychological Review*, 90, 293–315.

2

Normative Models of Judgment and Decision Making

Jonathan Baron

Introduction: Normative, Descriptive, and Prescriptive

The study of judgment and decision making (JDM) is traditionally concerned with the comparison of judgments to standards, standards that allow evaluation of the judgments as better or worse. I use the term "judgments" to include decisions, which are judgments about what to do. The major standards come from probability theory, utility theory, and statistics. These are mathematical theories or "models" that allow us to evaluate a judgment. They are called normative because they are norms.[1]

This chapter is an introduction to the main normative models, not including statistics. I shall try to develop them informally, taking a more philosophical and less mathematical approach than other writers. Anyone who wants a full understanding should work through the math, for which I provide citations.

One task of our field is to compare judgments to normative models. We look for systematic deviations from the models. These are called biases. If no biases are found, we may try to explain why not. If biases are found, we try to understand and explain them by making descriptive models or theories. With normative and descriptive models in hand, we can try to find ways to correct the biases, that is, to improve judgments according to the normative standards. The prescriptions for such correction are called prescriptive models. Whether we say that the biases are "irrational" is of no consequence. If we can help people make better judgments, that is a good thing, whatever we call the judgments they make without our help.

Of course, "better" implies that the normative models truly define what better means. The more certain we are of this, the more confidence we can have that our help is really help. The history of psychology is full of misguided attempts to help people, and they continue to this day. Perhaps our field will largely avoid such errors by being very careful about what "better" means. If we can help people, then the failure to do so is a harm. Attention to normative models can help us avoid the errors of omission as well as those of commission. In sum, normative models must be understood in terms of their role in looking for biases, understanding these biases in terms of descriptive models, and developing prescriptive models (Baron, 1985).

As an example, consider the sunk-cost effect (Arkes & Blumer, 1985). People throw good money after bad. If they have made a down payment of $100 on some object that costs an additional $100, and they find something they like better for $90 total, they will end up spending more for the object they like less, in order to avoid "wasting" the sunk cost of $100. This is a bias away from a very simple normative rule, which is, "Do whatever yields the best consequences in the future." A prescriptive model may consist of nothing more than some instruction about such a rule. (Larrick, Morgan, & Nisbett (1990) found such instruction effective.)

In general, good descriptive models help create good prescriptive models. We need to know the nature of the problem before we try to correct it. Thus, for example, it helps us to know that the sunk-cost effect is largely the result of an over-application of a rule about avoiding waste (Arkes, 1996). That helps because we can explain to people that this is a good rule, but is not relevant because the waste has already happened.

The application of the normative model to the case at hand may be challenged. A critic may look for some advantage of honoring sunk costs, which might outweigh the obvious disadvantage, within the context of the normative model. In other cases, the normative model is challenged. The fact that theories and claims are challenged does not imply that they are impossible to make. In the long run, just as scientific theories become more believable after they are corrected and improved in response to challenges, so, too, may normative models be strengthened. Although the normative models discussed in this chapter are hotly debated, others, such as Aristotle's logic, are apparently stable (if not all that useful), having been refined over centuries.

The role of academic disciplines

Different academic disciplines are involved in the three types of models. Descriptive models are clearly the task of psychology. The normative model must be kept in mind, because the phenomenon of interest is the deviation from it. This is similar to the way psychology proceeds in several other areas, such as abnormal psychology or sensation and perception (where, especially recently, advances have been made by comparing humans to ideal observers according to some model).

Descriptive models account not only for actual behavior but also for reflective judgments. It is possible that our reflective intuitions are also biased. Some people, for example, may think that it is correct to honor sunk costs. We must allow the possibility that they are, in some sense, incorrect.

The prescriptive part is an applied field, like clinical psychology, which tries to design and test ways of curing psychological disorders. (The study of perception, although it makes use of normative models, has little prescriptive work.) In JDM, there is no single discipline for prescriptive models. Perhaps the closest is the study of decision analysis, which is the use of decision aids, often in the form of formulas or computer programs, to help people make decisions. But education also has a role to play, including simply the education that results from "giving away" our findings to students of all ages.

Normative models are properly the task of philosophy. They are the result of reflection and analysis. They cannot depend on data about what people do in particular cases, or on intuitions about what people ought to do, which must also be subject to criticism. The project of the branch of JDM that is concerned with normative models and biases is ultimately to improve human judgment by finding what is wrong with it and then finding ways to improve it. If the normative models were derived from descriptions of what most people do or think we would be unable to find widespread biases and repair them.

Although the relevant philosophical analysis cannot involve data about the judgment tasks themselves, it must include a deeper sort of data, often used in philosophy, about what sort of creatures we are. For example, we are clearly beings who have something like beliefs and desires, and who make decisions on the basis of these (Irwin, 1971). A normative model for people is thus unlikely to serve as well for mosquitoes or bacteria.

Justification of normative models

How then can normative models be justified? I have argued that they arise through the imposition of an analytic scheme (Baron, 1994, 1996, 2000). The scheme is designed to fit the basic facts about who we are, but not necessarily to fit our intuitions.

Arithmetic provides an example (as discussed by Popper, 1962, who makes a slightly different point). The claim that $1 + 1 = 2$ is a result of imposing an analytic frame on the world. It doesn't seem to work when we add two drops of water by putting one on top of the other. We get one big drop, not two. Yet, we do not say that arithmetic has been dis-confirmed. Rather, we say that this example does not fit our framework. This isn't what we mean by adding. We maintain the simple structure of arithmetic by carefully defining when it applies, and how.

Once we accept the framework, we reason from it through logic (itself the result of imposition of a framework). So no claim to absolute truth is involved in this approach to normative models. It is a truth relative to assumptions. But the assumptions, I shall argue, are very close to those that we are almost compelled to make because of who we are. In particular, we are creatures who make decisions based on beliefs and (roughly) desires.

Acts, states, and consequences

One normative model of interest here is expected-utility theory (EUT), which derives from an analysis of decisions into acts, uncertain states of the world, and consequences (outcomes). We have beliefs about the states, and desires (or values, or utilities) concerning the consequences. We can diagram the situation in the following sort of table.

	State X	*State Y*	*State Z*
Option A	Outcome 1	Outcome 2	Outcome 3
Option B	Outcome 4	Outcome 5	Outcome 6

The decision could be which of two trips to take, and the states could be the various possibilities for what the weather will be, for example. The outcomes could describe the entire experiences of each trip in each weather state. We would have values or utilities for these outcomes. EUT, as a normative model, tells us that we should have probabilities for the states, and that the expected utility of each option is determined from the probabilities of the states and the utilities of the outcomes in each row.

Before I get into the details, let me point out that the distinction between options and states is the result of a certain world view. This view makes a sharp distinction between events that we control (options) and events that we do not control (states). This view has not always been accepted. Indeed, traditional Buddhist thought tries to break down the distinction between controllable and uncontrollable events, as does philosophical determinism. But it seems that these views have had an uphill battle because the distinction in question is such a natural one. It is consistent with our nature.

Another important point is that the description of the outcomes must include just what we value. It should not include aspects of the context that do not reflect our true values, such as whether we think about an outcome as a gain or a loss (unless this *is* something we value). The point of the model is to provide a true standard, not to find a way to justify any particular set of decisions.

Reflective equilibrium

An alternative way of justifying normative models is based on the idea of "reflective equilibrium" (Rawls, 1971). The idea comes most directly from Chomsky (1957; see Rawls, 1971, p. 47), who developed his theory of syntax on the basis of intuitions about what was and what was not a sentence of the language. Rawls argues that, like the linguists who follow Chomsky, we should develop normative theories of morality (a type of decision making) by starting with our moral intuitions, trying to develop a theory to account for them, modifying the theory when it conflicts with strong intuitions, and ultimately rejecting intuitions that conflict with a well-supported theory. Such an approach makes sense in the study of language. In Chomsky's view, the rules of language are shaped by human psychology. They evolved in order to fit our psychology abilities and dispositions, which, in turn, evolved to deal with language.

Does this approach make sense in JDM? Perhaps as an approach to descriptive theory, yes. This is, in fact, its role in linguistics as proposed by Chomsky. It could come up with a systematic theory of our intuitions about what we ought to do, and our intuitions about the judgments we ought to make. But our intuitions, however systematic, may be incorrect in some other sense. Hence, such an approach could leave us with a normative model that does not allow us to criticize and improve our intuitions.

What criterion could we use to decide on normative models? What could make a model incorrect? I will take the approach here (as does Over in Chapter 1, this volume) that decisions are designed to achieve goals, to bring about outcomes that are good according to values that we have. And other judgments, such as those of probability, are subservient to decisions. This is, of course, an analytic approach. Whatever we call what it yields, it seems to me to lead to worthwhile questions.

Utility (Good)

The normative models of decision making that I shall discuss all share a simple idea: the best option is the one that does the most good. The idea is that good, or goodness, is "stuff" that can be measured and compared. Scholars have various concepts of what this stuff includes, and we do not need to settle the issue here. I find it useful to take the view that good is *the extent to which we achieve our goals* (Baron, 1996). Goal achievement, in this sense, is usually a matter of degree: goals can be achieved to different extents. Goals are *criteria* by which we evaluate states of affairs, more analogous to the scoring criteria used by judges of figure-skating competitions than to the hoop in a basketball game. The question of "what does the most good" then becomes the question of "what achieves our goals best, on the whole."

If this question is to have meaningful answers, we must assume that utility, or goodness, is *transitive* and *connected*. Transitivity means that if A is better than B (achieves our goals better than B, has more utility than B) and B is better than C, then A is better than C. This is what we mean by "better" and is, arguably, a consequence of analyzing decisions in this way. Connectedness means that, for any A and B, it is always true that either A is better than B, B is better than A, or A and B are equally good. There is no such thing as "no answer." In sum, connectedness and transitivity are consequences of the idea that expected utility measures the extent to which an option achieves our goals. Any two options either achieve our goals to the same extent, or else one option achieves our goals better than the other; and if A achieves our goals better than B, and B achieves them better than C, then it must be true that A achieves them better than C.[2]

Sometimes we can judge directly the relation between A and B. In most cases, though, we must deal with trade-offs. Option A does more good than B in one respect, and less good in some other respect. To decide on the best option, we must be able to compare *differences* in good, i.e., the "more good" with the "less good." Mathematically, this means that we must be able to measure good on an interval scale, a scale on which intervals can be ordered.

Connectedness thus applies even if each outcome (A and B) can be analyzed into parts that differ in utility. The parts could be events that happen in different states of the world, happen to different people, or happen at different times. The parts could also be attributes of a single outcome, such as the price and quality of a consumer good.

Some critics have argued that this is impossible, that some parts cannot be traded off with other parts to arrive at a utility for the whole. For example, how do we compare two safety policies that differ in cost and number of deaths prevented? Surely it is true descriptively that people have difficulty with such evaluations. The question is whether it is reasonable to assume, normatively, that outcomes, or "goods" can be evaluated as wholes, even when their parts provide conflicting information.

One argument where we can assume this is that sometimes the trade-offs are easy. It is surely worthwhile to spend $1 to save a life. It is surely not worthwhile to spend the gross domestic product of the United States to reduce one person's risk of death by one in a million this year. In between, judgments are difficult, but this is a property of all judgments. It is a matter of degree. Normative models are an idealization. The science of psychophysical scaling is built on such judgments as, "Which is larger, the difference between the loudness of tones A and B or the difference between B and C?" When subjects in experiments make a large number of such judgments, their average responses are orderly, even though any given judgment feels like a wild guess. This is, arguably, the sort of creatures we are. We have some underlying order, wrapped in layers of random error. (See Broome, 1997, and Baron, 2002, for related arguments.)

Another sort of challenge to the idea of a single utility for whole outcomes is that utility judgments are easily influenced by extraneous manipulations. I have argued that all of these manipulations do not challenge utility as a normative ideal (Baron, 2002). The general argument is that it is possible to understand the effects of manipulations as distortions of a true judgment. On the other hand, utilities change as a result of reflection. They are not hard wired, and the theory does not require them to be. They are best seen as something more like concepts, formed on the basis of reflection, and constantly being modified (Baron, 2002).

Expected-utility Theory (EUT)

Expected-utility theory (EUT) deals with decisions under uncertainty, cases in which we analyze outcomes into parts that correspond to outcomes in different states of the world. The theory says that the overall utility of an option is the expected utility. That is, the utility averaged across the various possible states, with the outcomes weighted according to the probability of the states. It is analogous to calculating the average, or expected, winning from a gamble. If you get $12 when a die comes up with a 1 and $0 otherwise, the average winning is $2, because the probability of a 1 is 1/6. But EUT deals with utility, not money. The mathematical and philosophical basis of this theory developed in the twentieth century (Ramsey, 1931; de Finetti, 1937; von Neumann & Morgenstern, 1947; Savage, 1954; Krantz, Luce, Suppes, & Tversky, 1971; Wakker, 1989).

Table 2.1 shows an example of several bets, with A and B being the uncertain states. These could be whether a coin is heads or tails, or whether it rains tomorrow or not. The outcomes in each cell are gains in dollars. The expected utility (EU) of an option is computed, according to EUT, by multiplying the utility (U) of each outcome by its probability (p), and then summing across the possible outcomes. We would thus have to assign a probability to states A and B. The EU of option S is thus $p(A)U(300) + p(B)U(100)$. To decide between options S and T we would ask which has greater EU, so we would look at the difference. This amounts to:

Table 2.1 Four choices illustrating tradeoff consistency

Choice 1 Option	State A	B	Choice 2 Option	State A	B
S	$300	$100	U	$500	$100
T	$420	$0	V	$630	$0

Choice 3 Option	State A	B	Choice 4 Option	State A	B
W	$300	$210	Y	$500	$210
X	$420	$100	Z	$630	$100

$$[p(A)U(\$300) + p(B)U(\$100)] - [p(A)U(\$420) + p(B)U(\$0)]$$

or

$$p(A)[U(\$300) - U(\$420)] + p(B)[U(\$100) - U(\$0)]$$

or (more intuitively)

$$p(A)[U(\$100) - U(\$0)] - p(B)[U(\$420) - U(\$300)].$$

Note that we need only know the differences of the utilities in each column, not their values. We ask which difference matters more to us, which has a greater effect on the achievement of our goals. Note also that the probabilities matter. Since the first term is multiplied by $p(A)$, the higher $p(A)$, the more we favor option T over option S. This is a basic principle of decision making: options should be favored more when the probability of good outcomes (our degree of belief in them) is higher and the probability of bad outcomes is lower. This principle follows from the most basic assumptions about what decisions involve (e.g., Irwin, 1971).

Table 2.1 can be used to illustrate an argument for EUT (Köbberling & Wakker, 2001). As usual, the rows are acts, the columns are states, and the cells are outcomes. In Choice 1, Option S yields $300 if event A happens (e.g., a coin comes up heads) and $100 if B happens. Köbberling & Wakker (2001) consider patterns like those for Choices 1–4. Suppose you are indifferent between S and T in Choice 1, between U and V in choice 2, and between W and X in Choice 3. Then you ought to be indifferent between Y and Z in Choice 4. Why? Because rational indifference means that the reason for preferring T if A happens, the $120 difference, is just balanced by the reason for preferring S if B happens. Thus, we can say that the difference between 300 and 420 in State B just offsets the difference between 0 and 100 in State A. If you decide in terms of overall good, then the 300–420 difference in A is just as good (on the whole, taking into account the probability of A) as the 0–100 difference in B. Similarly, if you are indifferent in Choice 2, then the 500–630 difference just offsets the same 0–100 difference. So the 500–630 difference is also just as good. And if you are indifferent in Choice 3, then the 500–630 difference in A just offsets the 100–210 difference in B. So all these differences are equal in terms of good. In this case, you ought to be indifferent in Choice 4, too.

This kind of "tradeoff consistency," in which Choices 1–3 imply the result of Choice 4, plus a couple of other much simpler principles, *implies expected-utility theory.* In particular, you can use one of the differences, like the 100–210 difference in B, as a measuring rod, to measure off equal intervals under A. Each of these differences represents the same utility difference. Note that this is all we need. We do not need to know what "zero utility" is, because decisions always involve comparison of options. (Even doing nothing is an option.) And the unit, like many units, is arbitrary. Once we define it, we must stick with it, but we can define it as we like. In this example, the 100–210 difference under B is a unit. If tradeoff consistency failed, we would not be able to do this. The utility measure of some difference in State A would change depending on what we used as the unit of measurement.

Later I shall explain why this analysis also implies that we need to multiply by probability. It should be clear for now, though, that the conditions for EU are met if we multiply the utility difference in column A by the same number in all the tables, and likewise for column B.

Why should tradeoff consistency apply? The critical idea here is that good (or bad) results from what happens, not from what does not happen. Thus, *the effect on goal achievement of changing from one outcome to another in State A (e.g., $300 to $420 in Table 2.1 cannot change as a function of the difference between the two outcomes in State B (e.g., $100 vs. $0 or $210 vs. $100), because the states are mutually exclusive.* This conclusion is the result of imposing an analytic scheme in which everything we value about an outcome is assigned to the cell in which that outcome occurs. If, for example, we experience emotions that result from comparing what happened to what did not happen, then the experience of those emotions must be considered part of the outcome in the cell representing what happened. (In cases like those in Table 2.1, this could mean that the outcome is not fully described by its monetary value, so that the same monetary value could be associated with different outcomes in different sub-tables.)

Note that we are also assuming that the idea of differences in utility is meaningful. But it must be meaningful if we are to make such choices at all. For example, if States A and B are equally likely, then any choice between S and T must depend on which difference is larger, the difference between the outcomes in A (which favor option T) or the difference between the outcomes in B (which favor S). It makes sense to say that the difference between 200 to 310 has as much of an effect on goodness as the difference between 0 and 100.

In sum, the justification of EUT is based on the idea that columns of the table have independent effects on goodness, because we analyze decisions so that all the relevant consequences of a given option in a given state fall into a single cell. Consequences do not affect goodness when they do not occur. Once we assume this framework, then we can use the difference between consequences under one state as a measuring stick, to mark off units of utility in another state, and vice versa. We can assign utilities to outcomes in such a way that the option that does the most good on the whole is always a weighted sum, where each column has its own weight (see Baron, 2000, for related argument). The next step is to show what this weight has to do with probability.

Probability

The idea of probability has a long history, although the idea that probability is relevant to decision making is only a few hundred years old (Hacking, 1975). Scholars have distinguished several different ways of thinking about what probability means. A standard classification distinguishes three general approaches: necessary (logical), objectivistic, and personal (Savage, 1954).

The logical view sees probability as an extension of logic, often by analysis of situations into possible worlds and their enumeration. It is the view that is often implicit in the early chapters of textbooks of probability and statistics, where probability is introduced in terms of gambling. There is a sense in which the probability of drawing a king from a deck of cards is necessarily 1/13. That is part of what we mean by a "fair deck." Similarly, the probability of drawing a red card is 1/2, and the probability of drawing a red king is 1/26.

The logical view is not very useful for calculation of insurance premiums or analysis of experiments. Thus, the later chapters of statistics books generally switch to the view of probabilities as objective, as relative frequencies. By this view, the probability of drawing a king from a deck is ultimately defined as the relative frequency of kings to draws with an infinite number of draws. Likewise, the probability that you will live to be 100 years old is to be determined by counting the number of people like you who did and who did not live that long.

Two problems arise with this view. One is that "like you" is definable in many ways, and the frequencies are different for different definitions. Another is that sometimes we like to talk about the probability of unique events, such as the probability that the Democratic Party will win the next US presidential election – not just elections in general, but that one in particular. Now it may be that such talk is nonsense, but the personal view assumes that it is not. And this is not a fringe view. It is often called Bayesian because it was advanced in a famous essay of Thomas Bayes (1764/1958), although had earlier antecedents (Hacking, 1975). The idea of the personal view is that probability is a measure of a person's degree of belief in the truth of propositions (statements that can have a truth value). Thus, two people can have different probabilities for the same proposition.

You might think that the personal view is so loose that anything goes. It is true that it does not assume a right answer about the probability of some proposition. But it does have some requirements, so it can serve as a normative model of probability judgments. Two sorts of requirements have been proposed: calibration and coherence.

Calibration is, in a way, a method for incorporating the objective view into the personalist view. But it solves the problem of multiple classification by classifying the judgments themselves. Thus, all of a given judge's judgments of the form, "The probability of X is 0.8" are put together. If we then discover the truth behind each judgment, we should expect that 80 percent of the propositions are true.

Coherence is the requirement that sets of judgments must obey certain rules. The following are the basic rules that define the concept of coherence:

- The probability of a proposition's being true, plus the probability of its being false (called the probability of the *complement* of the proposition), must equal 1. A probability of 1 represents certainty.
- Two propositions, *A* and *B*, are *mutually exclusive* if they cannot both be true at the same time. If you believe that *A* and *B* are mutually exclusive, then $p(A) + p(B) = p(A \text{ or } B)$: That is, the probability of the proposition "either *A* or *B*" is the sum of the two individual probabilities. If we assume that "It will rain" and "It will snow" are mutually exclusive propositions (that is, it cannot both rain and snow), then the probability of the proposition "It will rain or it will snow" is the sum of the probability of rain and the probability of snow. This rule is called *additivity*.
- A definition: The *conditional probability of proposition A given proposition B* is the probability that we would assign to *A* if we knew that *B* were true, that is, the probability of *A* conditional on *B* being true. We write this as $p(A/B)$. For example, $p(\text{king/face card}) = 1/3$ for an ordinary deck of cards (in which the face cards are king, queen, and jack).
- The *multiplication rule* says that $p(A \& B) = p(A/B) \cdot p(B)$. Here *A & B* means "both *A* and *B* are true." For example, if we think that there is a 0.5 probability of a given person being female and that the probability of a female's being over 6 feet tall is 0.02, then our probability for the person being a female over 6 feet tall is $p(\text{tall \& female}) = p(\text{tall/female}) \cdot p(\text{female}) = (0.02) \cdot (0.5) = 0.01$.
- In a special case, *A* and *B* are *independent*. Two propositions are independent for you if you judge that learning about the truth or falsity of one of them will not change your degree of belief in the other one. For example, learning that a card is red will not change my belief that it is a king. In this case, we can say that $p(A/B) = p(A)$, since learning about *B* does not change our probability for *A*. The multiplication rule for independent propositions is thus $p(A \& B) = p(A) \cdot p(B)$, simply the product of the two probabilities. For example, $p(\text{king \& red}) = p(\text{king}) \cdot p(\text{red}) = (1/13) \cdot (1/2) = 1/26$.

Such rules put limits on the probability judgments that are justifiable. For example, it is unjustifiable to believe that the probability of rain is 0.2, the probability of snow is 0.3, and the probability of rain *or* snow is 0.8. If we make many different judgments at one time, or if our past judgments constrain our present judgments, these constraints can be very strong. These constraints do not determine a *unique* probability for any proposition, however. Reasonable people can still disagree.

The two main rules here are additivity and multiplication. The rule concerning complements is a special case of additivity, simply defining the probability of a true proposition as 1. And the independence rule is a special case of the multiplication rule for the case in which the conditional probability and the unconditional probability are the same. Notice that all the rules are here defined in terms of relations among beliefs (following von Winterfeldt & Edwards, 1986).

Coherence rules and expected utility

Why are these rules normative? You might imagine a less demanding definition of coherence, in which the only requirement is that stronger beliefs (those more likely to be true) should be given higher numbers. This would meet the most general goal of quantifying the strength of belief. Or, looking at it another way, you might imagine that some transformation of p would do just as well as p itself. Why not p^2, or $p + 0.5$. Such transformations would violate either the addition rule or the multiplication rule, or both.[3] A major argument for the two rules comes from the use of probability in decisions.

In the section on EUT, I argued that the states – represented by columns – had corresponding weighting factors, which multiplied the utilities of each outcome in each column. EUT says that these are probabilities, and it does make sense to give more weight to outcomes in states that are more likely to happen. This requirement as stated, however, implies only an ordinal concept of probability, one that allows us to rank beliefs for their strength. As stated so far, it does not imply that probabilities must follow the coherence rules.

To see how it actually does imply coherence, consider the possibility of re-describing decisions in ways that do not affect good (goal achievement). Such a re-description should not affect the conclusions of a normative model about what we should do. This principle, called "extensionality" (Arrow, 1982) or "invariance" (Tversky & Kahneman, 1986), is important in the justification of several forms of utility theory.

First consider the addition rule. We can subdivide any state into two states. For example, if a state is about the weather tomorrow, for a decision about what sort of outing to take, we could subdivide the state "sunny" into "sunny and this coin comes up heads" and "sunny and this coin comes up tails." Any normative theory should tell us that this subdivision should not affect our decision. It is clearly irrelevant to good, to the achievement of our goals. Yet, if probability is not additive, it could change our decision.

For example, suppose that $p(S)$ is 0.4, where S is "sunny." If we subdivide into sunny-heads and sunny-tails, the probability of each would be 0.2. Additivity applies, and our decision would not change. In particular, if P is "picnic," H is "heads," and T is "tails," $p(S)U(PS) = p(SH)U(PSH) + p(ST)U(PST)$. The utilities here are all the same, of course. Now suppose we transform p so that additivity no longer applies. For example, we add .1 to each p. In this case, we would add .1 to the left side of the last equation (because there is one probability) and 0.2 to the right side (because there are two), and the equality would no longer hold. Of course this would not necessarily change our decision. The same option (e.g., movie, vs. picnic) might win. But it might not, because the calculated EU of picnic might increase. The only way to avoid such effects of arbitrary subdivision is to require that the addition rule apply to the weights used to multiply the states.

Now consider the multiplication rule. This relates to a different kind of invariance. Our choices should not be affected if we narrow down the space of possibilities to what matters. Nor should it matter what series of steps got us to the consequences, so long as

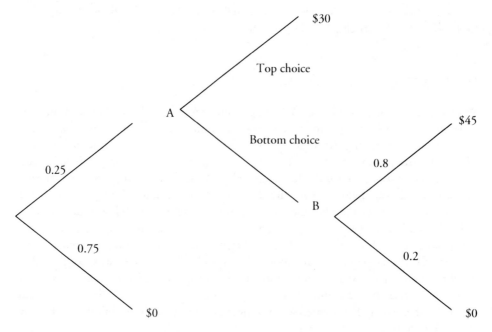

Figure 2.1 Illustration of consequentialism: A is a choice; B is a chance event

the consequences represent fully everything that affects our good. (Again, this is a requirement of the analytic scheme that we impose.) The irrelevance of the series of steps is called "consequentialism" (Hammond, 1988), although that term has other meanings.

Consider the sequence of events in Figure 2.1, a classic case originally discussed by Allais (1953; and discussed further by Kahneman & Tversky, 1979; McClennan, 1990; and Haslam & Baron, 1993). You have a 0.25 probability of getting to point A. If you don't get there, you get $0. If you get there, you have a choice between Top and Bottom, the two branches. Top gets you $30 for sure. Bottom gets you a 0.8 probability of $45, but if you don't get $45 you get $0.

You can think about the choice you must make from your point of view now, before you know whether you get to A. That situation is represented as follows:

Probability	*0.75*	*0.20*	*0.05*
Top	$0	$30	$30
Bottom	$0	$45	$0

Alternatively, you can think about your choice from your point of view if you get to A.

Probability	*0.8*	*0.2*
Top	$30	$30
Bottom	$45	$0

If the money is all you care about – and we are assuming that it is, since this is just an example where the money stands for any consequences that are the same when they have the same labels – then the choice that is better for you (the one that achieves your goals better) should not depend on when you make it. It depends only on the outcomes. This is because the time of making the choice does not affect which option is better (achieves your goals more).

Notice how the probabilities of 0.20 and 0.05 come about. They are the result of the multiplication rule for probabilities. The 0.20 is the product $p(A)p(\$45/A)$, that is, the probability of A times the conditional probability of $45 given A. If the multiplication rule did not hold, then the numbers in the top table would be different. The relative EU of the two options could change as well. In particular, the relative utility of the two options depends on the ratio of the probability of $45 and the probability of $0 in case Bottom is chosen. In sum, if the multiplication rule were violated, consequentialism could be violated.[4]

In sum, EUT requires that the basic coherence constraints on probability judgments be met. If they are not met, then different ways of looking at the same situation could lead to different conclusions about what to do. The situation is the "same" because everything that affects goodness (goal achievement) is the same, and this is a result of how we have analyzed the situation.

Bayes's theorem

The multiplication and additivity rules together imply a famous result, developed by Bayes, called Bayes' theorem. The result is a formula, which can be used for reversing a conditional probability. For example, if H is a hypothesis (the patient has a bacterial infection) and D is a datum (the throat culture is positive), we can infer $p(H/D)$ from $p(D/H)$ and other relevant probabilities. If we make judgments of both of these probabilities, we can use the formula to determine whether these judgments are coherent. The formula is a normative model for some judgments.

Specifically, we can calculate $p(H/D)$ from the multiplication rule, $p(H \ \& \ D) = p(H/D) \cdot p(D)$, which implies

$$p(H/D) = \frac{p(H \ \& \ D)}{p(D)} \tag{2.1}$$

Equation 2.1 does not help us much, because we don't know $p(H \ \& \ D)$. But we do know $p(D/H)$ and $p(H)$, and we know from the multiplication rule that $p(D \ \& \ H) = p(D/H) \cdot p(H)$. Of course $p(D \ \& \ H)$ is the same as $p(H \ \& \ D)$, so we can replace $p(H \ \& \ D)$ in Equation 2.1 to get:

$$p(H/D) = \frac{p(D/H) \cdot p(H)}{p(D)} \tag{2.2}$$

Equation 2.2 is useful because it refers directly to the information we have, except for $p(D)$. But we can calculate that too. There are two ways for D to occur; it can occur with H or without H (that is, with ^-H). These are mutually exclusive, so we can apply the additivity rule to get:

$$p(D) = p(D \ \& \ H) + p(D \ \& \ ^-H)$$
$$= p(D/H) \cdot p(H) + p(D/^-H) \cdot p(^-H)$$

This leads (by substitution into equation 2.2) to Equation 2.3:

$$p(H/D) = \frac{p(D/H) \cdot p(H)}{p(D/H) \cdot p(H) + p(D/^-H) \cdot p(^-H)} \qquad (2.3)$$

Equations 2.2 and 2.3 are called *Bayes' theorem*. In Equation 2.3, $p(H/D)$ is usually called the *posterior probability* of H, meaning the probability after D is known, and $p(H)$ is called the *prior probability*, meaning the probability before D is known. $p(D/H)$ is sometimes called the *likelihood* of D.

Utilitarianism

Utilitarianism extends the basic normative model of EUT to people as well as states. So far I have been talking about "our goals" as if it didn't matter whether decisions were made for individuals or groups. But the best option for one person is not necessarily the best for another. Such conflict between people is analogous to the conflict that arises from different options being better in different states of the world. We can extend our basic table to three dimensions.

Utilitarianism, of course, is a traditional approach to the philosophy of morality and law, with antecedents in ancient philosophy, and developed by Bentham (1948[1843]), Mill (1863), Sidgwick (1962[1907]), Hare (1981), Broome (1991), Baron (1993), and Kaplow and Shavell (2002), among others. It holds that the best choice is the one that does the most good. This is just what utility theory says, in general, but utilitarianism requires the somewhat controversial claim that utility can be added up across people just as it can across uncertain states. In utilitarianism, "each person counts as one, no person as more than one," so the idea of weighting is absent.

Utilitarianism is, in fact, very closely related to EU theory. It is difficult to accept one and not the other. When a group of people all face the same decision, then the two models clearly dictate the same choice. For example, suppose that we have a choice of two policies for distribution of annual income among some group of people. Plan A says that half of them, chosen at random, will get $80,000 per year and half will get $40,000. Plan B gives everyone $55,000. Suppose that, given each person's utility for money, plan A has a higher EU for each person (before it is known which group he is in). Utilitarianism would require the choice of plan A in this case: the total utility of A would necessarily be higher than B. The difference between EU and utilitarianism is that utilitarianism multiplies the average utility of $80,000 by the number of people who get it, etc., while EU multiplies the same average utility by each person's probability of getting it. It is easy to see that these calculations must yield the same result.

Suppose, on the other hand, we take a non-utilitarian approach to distribution. We might think that fairness requires a more equal distribution, at the cost of some loss in total utility, so we might choose B. In this case, viewed from the perspective of each person *ex ante* (before it is determined who is in which group), *everyone* is worse off than under plan A.

Kaplow and Shavell (2002) show how *any* non-utilitarian principle of distribution can yield results like this, in which nobody is better off and at least some people are worse off. The fact that these situations are highly hypothetical is not relevant, for a *normative* theory should apply everywhere, even to hypothetical situations. Of course, this argument, by taking an *ex-ante* perspective, assumes that people's good can be represented by EUT. But that is the point; EUT and utilitarianism are intimately connected.

Broome (1991) argues more formally that, if the utility of each person is defined by EU, then, with some very simple assumptions, the overall good of everyone is a sum of individual utilities. In particular, we need to assume the "Principle of Personal Good" (Broome, 1991, p. 165): "(a) Two alternatives are equally good if they are equally good for each person. And (b) if one alternative is at least as good as another for everyone and definitely better for someone, it is better." This is a variant of the basic idea of "Pareto optimality." This variant assumes that the probabilities of the states do not depend on the person. It is as though the theory was designed for decision makers with their own probabilities.

To make this argument, Broome (1991) considers an array like the following. Each column represents a state of nature (like those in the expected-utility table above). Each row represents a person. There are s states and h people. The entries in each cell represent the utilities for the outcome for each person in each state. For example u_{12} is the utility for person 1 in state 2.

$$
\begin{array}{cccc}
u_{11} & u_{12} & \cdots & u_{1s} \\
u_{21} & u_{22} & \cdots & u_{2s} \\
\cdot & \cdot & \cdots & \cdot \\
\cdot & \cdot & \cdots & \cdot \\
u_{h1} & u_{h2} & \cdots & u_{hs}
\end{array}
$$

The basic argument, in very broad outline, shows that total utility is an increasing function of both the row and column utilities, and that the function is additive for both rows and columns. Expected-utility theory implies additivity for each row. For a given column, the Principle of Personal Good implies that the utility for each column is an increasing function of the utilities for the individuals in that column. An increase in one entry in the cell has to have the same effect on both the rows and the columns, so the columns must be additive too.[5]

Conclusion

I have sketched some of the arguments for some of the major normative models used in JDM. I have emphasized one approach, based on the idea that models are justified by the imposition of an analytic framework, based on very fundamental assumptions about the nature of humans.

The importance of the analytic framework may be illustrated in terms of the way it handles apparent counter-examples. Consider the following three choices offered (on different days) to a well-mannered person (based on Petit, 1991):

1 Here is a (large) apple and an orange. Take your pick; I will have the other.
2 Here is an orange and a (small) apple. Take your pick; I will have the other.
3 Here is a large apple and a small apple. Take your pick; I will have the other.

It would make sense to choose the large apple in Choice 1 and the orange in Choice 2. But a polite person would choose the small apple in Choice 3, thus (apparently) violating transitivity. It is impolite to choose the large apple when the only difference is size, but it is acceptable to choose the larger fruit when size is not the only difference. But Choice 3 is not just between a large apple and a small apple. It is between "a large apple plus being impolite" and a small apple. The impoliteness associated with the large apple reduces its utility and makes it less attractive. Transitivity is not actually violated. When we use utility theory to analyze decisions, we must make sure to include all the relevant consequences, not just those that correspond to material objects.

For the sake of brevity, I have omitted some extensions of utility theory that are important in JDM. One important extension is multiattribute utility theory (see Chapters 16 & 17, this volume), which applies when the "parts" of utility are attributes such as the price, speed, and memory size of a computer. The attributes must have independent effects on utility for the simplest version of this model to be relevant, so it requires proper analysis, which is not always possible. This model is discussed by Keeney and Raiffa's classic work (1993[1976]) and by Keeney (1992), among other works.

A second model concerns choice over time, when outcomes occur at different times (see Chapter 21, this volume). A different form of the idea of dynamic consistency is often applied to this situation: the decision should not change as a function of when it is made, so long as the outcomes are not affected (Baron, 2000, Chapter 19).

Finally, I have omitted some of the more intricate arguments that have occupied scholars over the last few decades (e.g., Bachrach & Hurley, 1991). It is my hope that, in the long view of history, most of these arguments will be seen as necessary for the purpose of arriving at a good theory, but ultimately irrelevant once the theory is refined and widely understood. The idea of utility theory is simple – do the most good – and its simplicity, like that of arithmetic, may be what lasts.

Notes

1 The term "normative" is used similarly in philosophy, but differently in sociology and anthropology, where it means something more like "according to cultural standards."
2 Another way to understand the value of transitivity is to think about what happens if you have *in*transitive preferences. Suppose X, Y, and Z are three objects, and you prefer owning X to owning Y, Y to Z, and Z to X. Each preference is strong enough so that you would pay a

little money, at least 1 cent, to indulge it. If you start with Z (that is, you own Z), I could sell you Y for 1 cent plus Z. (That is, you pay me 1 cent, then I give you Y, and you give me Z.) Then I could sell you X for 1 cent plus Y; but then, because you prefer Z to X, I could sell you Z for 1 cent plus X. If your preferences stay the same, we could do this forever, and you will have become a *money pump*.

3   The square does not violate the multiplication rule: $p^2 q^2 = (pq)^2$. But it does violate the addition rule: in general $p^2 + q^2 \neq (p + q)^2$. Addition of a constant violates both rules.

4   Another way to look at this situation is to adopt the perspective of some scholars of probability, who say "all probabilities are conditional." Probabilities that seem not to be conditional are simply conditional on your current beliefs. The change from the perspective of the original decision maker to that of the person at point A simply involves a narrowing of the frame of reference. Again, this should not affect the relative goodness of the two options.

5   For details, see Broome (1991), particularly, pp. 68, 69, and 202.

References

Allais, M. (1953) Le comportement de l'homme rationnel devant le risque: Critique des postulats et axioms de l'école américaine, *Econometrica*, 21, 503–46.

Arkes, H. R. (1996) The psychology of waste, *Journal of Behavioral Decision Making*, 9, 213–24.

Arkes, H. R. & Blumer, C. (1985) The psychology of sunk cost, *Organizational Behavior and Human Decision Processes*, 35, 124–40.

Arrow, K. J. (1982) Risk perception in psychology and economics, *Economic Inquiry*, 20, 1–9.

Bachrach, M. O. L. & Hurley, S. L. (eds.) (1991) *Foundations of Decision Theory: Issues and Advances*. Oxford: Blackwell.

Baron, J. (1985) *Rationality and Intelligence*. New York: Cambridge University Press.

Baron, J. (1993) *Morality and Rational Choice*. Dordrecht: Kluwer.

Baron, J. (1994) Nonconsequentialist decisions (with commentary and reply), *Behavioral and Brain Sciences*, 17, 1–42.

Baron, J. (1996) Norm-endorsement utilitarianism and the nature of utility, *Economics and Philosophy*, 12, 165–82.

Baron, J. (2000) *Thinking and Deciding* (3rd edn.). New York: Cambridge University Press.

Baron, J. (2002) Value trade-offs and the nature of utility: Bias, inconsistency, protected values, and other problems. Paper for conference on behavioral economics. American Institute for Economic Research, Great Barrington, MA, July.

Bayes, T. (1958) An essay towards solving a problem in the doctrine of chances, *Biometrika*, 45, 293–315. (Original work published 1764.)

Bentham, J. (1948) *An Introduction to the Principles of Morals and Legislation*. Oxford: Blackwell. (Original work published 1843.)

Broome, J. (1991) *Weighing Goods: Equality, Uncertainty and Time*. Oxford: Basil Blackwell.

Broome, J. (1997) Is incommensurability vagueness? In R. Chang (ed.), *Incommensurability, Incomparability, and Practical Reason* (pp. 67–89). Cambridge, MA: Harvard University Press.

Chomsky, N. (1957) *Syntactic Structures*. The Hague: Mouton.

de Finetti, B. (1937) Foresight: Its logical laws, its subjective sources (trans. H. E. Kyburg, Jr. and H. E. Smokler). In H. E. Kyburg, Jr. and H. E. Smokler (eds.), *Studies in Subjective Probability*. New York: Wiley, 1964.

Hacking, I. (1975) *The Emergence of Probability*. New York: Cambridge University Press.

Hammond, P. H. (1988) Consequentialist foundations for expected utility, *Theory and Decision*, 25, 25–78.

Hare, R. M. (1981) *Moral Thinking: Its Levels, Method and Point.* New York: Oxford University Press.

Haslam, N. & Baron, J. (1993) Rationality and resoluteness: Review of "Rationality and dynamic choice: Foundational explorations," by E. F. McClennan, *Journal of Mathematical Psychology*, 37, 143–53.

Irwin, F. W. (1971) *Intentional Behavior and Motivation: A Cognitive Theory.* Philadelphia: Lippincott.

Kahneman, D. & Tversky, A. (1979) Prospect theory: An analysis of decision under risk, *Econometrica*, 47, 263–91.

Kaplow, L. & Shavell, S. (2002) *Fairness Versus Welfare.* Cambridge, MA: Harvard University Press.

Keeney, R. L. (1992) *Value-focused Thinking: A Path to Creative Decisionmaking.* Cambridge, MA: Harvard University Press.

Keeney, R. L. & Raiffa, H. (1993) *Decisions with Multiple Objectives: Preference and Value Tradeoffs.* New York: Cambridge University Press. (Originally published 1976.)

Köbberling, V. & Wakker, P. P. (2001) *A Tool for Qualitatively Testing, Quantitatively Measuring, and Normatively Justifying Expected Utility.* Department of Quantitative Economics, University of Maastricht, Maastricht, The Netherlands, online at: http://www.fee.uva.nl/creed/wakker/newps.htm

Krantz, D. H., Luce, R. D., Suppes, P., & Tversky, A. (1971) *Foundations of Measurement* (vol. 1). New York: Academic Press.

Larrick, R. P., Morgan, J. N., & Nisbett, R. E. (1990) Teaching the use of cost–benefit reasoning in everyday life, *Psychological Science*, 1, 362–70.

McClennan, E. F. (1990) *Rationality and dynamic choice: Foundational Explorations.* New York: Cambridge University Press.

Mill, J. S. (1863) *Utilitarianism.* London: Collins.

Petit, P. (1991) Decision theory and folk psychology. In M. O. L. Bachrach and S. L. Hurley (eds.), *Foundations of Decision Theory: Issues and Advances* (pp. 147–67). Oxford: Blackwell.

Popper, K. R. (1962) Why are the calculi of logic and arithmetic applicable to reality? Chapter 9 in *Conjectures and Refutations: The Growth of Scientific Knowledge*, pp. 201–14. New York: Basic Books.

Ramsey, F. P. (1931) Truth and probability. In R. B. Braithwaite (ed.), *The Foundations of Mathematics and Other Logical Essays by F. P. Ramsey* (pp. 158–98). New York: Harcourt, Brace.

Rawls, J. (1971) *A Theory of Justice.* Cambridge, MA: Harvard University Press.

Savage, L. J. (1954) *The Foundations of Statistics.* New York: Wiley.

Sidgwick, H. (1962) *The Methods of Ethics* (7th edn., 1907). Chicago: University of Chicago Press. (First edition published 1874.)

Tversky, A. & Kahneman, D. (1986) Rational choice and the framing of decisions, *Journal of Business*, 59, S251–S78.

von Neumann, J. & Morgenstern, O. (1947) *Theory of Games and Economic Behavior* (2nd edn.). Princeton: Princeton University Press.

von Winterfeldt, D. & Edwards, W. (1986) Decision analysis and behavioral research. New York: Cambridge University Press.

Wakker, P. (1989) *Additive Representation of Preferences: A New Foundation of Decision Analysis.* Dordrecht: Kluwer.

3

Social Judgment Theory: Applying and Extending Brunswik's Probabilistic Functionalism

William M. Goldstein

Introduction

Brunswikian research on judgment began in the mid-1950s (Hammond, 1955), at about the same time that research on preferential choice was beginning to attract attention in psychology (e.g., Edwards, 1954). Although the processes of judgment and choice are intricately interwoven, they have been pursued as separate fields of research by largely different groups of psychologists with different intellectual roots, metatheories, goals, and methods (Goldstein & Hogarth, 1997).

Students of preferential choice were initially inspired by von Neumann and Morgenstern's (1947) work. Their axiomatization of expected-utility theory produced advances in psychological measurement, and in addition it could be used to argue that it was *rational* to maximize expected utility. Psychologists with interests in psychophysics, measurement, and mathematical modeling took notice of the work and began conducting experiments in which people's deviations from expected-utility theory (i.e., from a presumed standard of *rationality*) were considered the interesting phenomena. By the mid-1960s, similar research on probability assessment was also undertaken – people's deviations from Bayes' theorem were considered suboptimal and in need of explanation (e.g., Edwards, 1968) – and this line of research evolved into the heuristics and biases approach (e.g., Tversky & Kahneman, 1974).

The point of departure for Brunswikian judgment research, in contrast, was an analogy with perception. Brunswik (1952, 1956) portrayed perception as a kind of Helmholtzian inferential process. Objects in the environment can be perceived only via the stimulation of people's sensory organs and, Brunswik argued, this immediately available sensory information is virtually always ambiguous. (For example, a retinal projection of a given size can indicate either a distant large object or a close small object.) Therefore, people must infer or construct a percept from a collection of sensory cues that provide only incomplete and fallible information. Hammond (1955) drew an analogy to clinical judgment. Specifically, a patient's behaviors, expressions, and test scores provide ambiguous cues to the patient's personality and diagnosis, just as sensory cues provide ambiguous information about environmental objects. In both cases the clinician/perceiver must use multiple cues and indicators to infer something that goes beyond the cues themselves. In addition to drawing this analogy, Hammond also applied Brunswik's larger metatheory, Probabilistic Functionalism, to the study of judgment. Brunswik's functionalism (see below) directs attention to the adaptiveness of a psychological process, and for judgment as well as perception it is apparent that accuracy is crucial. Thus, Brunswikian research on judgment has taken *accuracy*, not rationality, as its central concern.

Research on the accuracy of judgment achieved high visibility in the 1950s because of the surprising finding that people's intuitive predictions tend to be less accurate than those of simple statistical models (Meehl, 1954). Buoyed by interest in this phenomenon, research of a Brunswikian nature was able to attract attention and adherents. Substantive findings, methodological advances, and conceptual developments followed Hammond's (1955) demonstration of the applicability of Brunswikian principles to research on judgment, so that 20 years later Hammond and his colleagues could offer a distinctively Brunswikian metatheory of judgment, called Social Judgment Theory (SJT; Hammond, Stewart, Brehmer, & Steinmann, 1975). Since then, SJT has been applied to numerous substantive areas, expanded conceptually, and supplemented by a theory of the variety of modes of thinking called Cognitive Continuum Theory (Hammond, Hamm, Grassia, & Pearson, 1987). (For a sequence of books covering various aspects and applications of the Brunswikian approach to judgment, see Rappoport & Summers, 1973; Hammond & Joyce, 1975; Hammond & Wascoe, 1980; Brehmer & Joyce, 1988; Doherty, 1996; Hammond, 1996, 2000; Juslin & Montgomery, 1999; Hammond & Stewart, 2001).

This chapter begins with a review of Brunswikian principles of psychology. The full scope of Brunswik's thinking cannot be covered in a few pages, but I hope to demonstrate both the cogency and the generality of his viewpoint. I then sketch the application of Brunswikian principles to judgment, the development of SJT, and some selected lines of Brunswikian research on judgment. Finally I consider some explicit comparisons with other approaches.

Elements of Brunswik's Probabilistic Functionalism

Much of the appeal of Brunswikian judgment research is that it is grounded in a larger perspective on the nature of psychology, its definitive problems, and proper methodology. Therefore, I first review some principles that inform Brunswikian research in general (Brunswik, 1952, 1956; Doherty & Tweney, in press; Hammond, 1966; Hammond & Stewart, 2001). I will try to convey the core of Brunswik's Probabilistic Functionalism by elaborating on four interrelated concepts: (1) functionalism; (2) vicarious functioning; (3) probabilism; and (4) representative design.

Functionalism

Psychology in a Darwinian spirit

To begin, Brunswik was a thoroughgoing functionalist. He felt that the goal of psychology was to explicate how organisms become attuned to and manage to get things done (i.e., to "function") in their environments. Unlike many earlier functionalists, however, Brunswik placed equal importance on both the organism and the environment. He conceived of psychology as addressing "the interrelationships between organism and environment," and he thought that psychology should view organism and environment as "equal partners" in an interrelationship that "has the essential characteristic of a 'coming-to-terms'" (Brunswik, 1957, p. 5). "Coming to terms," for Brunswik, had a particular significance, but elaboration must be deferred a bit.

Regional reference

To develop a precise vocabulary for organism–environment interactions, Brunswik described the organismic and environmental systems as each having its own "surface and depth, or overt and covert regions" (Brunswik, 1957, p. 5). Brunswik labeled variables as distal, proximal, peripheral, or central, according to their positions on causal chains connecting ("deep" parts of) the environment with ("deep" parts of) the organism. In perception, the causal chain extends from the environment to the organism. The distal variable is a remote property of the environment (e.g., the size of an object). Proximal variables (also called "cues") refer to the patterns that meet the sensory surfaces of the organism (e.g., retinal images). Peripheral variables refer to sensory excitation and neural transmission, and central variables are intraorganismic perceptions (e.g., the apparent size of the object). Regarding overt action, the causal direction is reversed, extending from the organism to the environment. Central variables refer to such intraorganismic matters as motivation. Peripheral variables indicate neural transmission and motor excitation. Proximal variables (also called "means") refer to body movements or events, and distal variables indicate remote "effects" or "ends." In many investigations, the correspondence of events across the environment–organism interface (i.e., between the proximal and peripheral layers) is deemphasized, and the causal chains are therefore somewhat simplified: (1) distal variables to proximal cues to central perceptions; and (2) central motivations to proximal means to distal ends.

Central–distal versus peripheral focusing of achievement

Regarding the "coming to terms" mentioned above, Brunswik emphasized that this concerns "the rapport between the central, covert layers of the two systems" (Brunswik, 1957, p. 5). That is, Brunswik stressed the correspondence between distal and central events, and his reasons for doing so follow from his functionalist orientation. Brunswik's functionalism portrayed organisms as confronting complex environments that they must perceive accurately enough and in which they must act effectively enough to perform important tasks (e.g., survival and procreation). Accurate perception and effective action, moreover, are matters of central–distal correspondence, or as Brunwik would say, "achievement" (or "attainment" or "functional validity"). After all, it does the organism little good to "see" the surface of its retina, so to speak. It needs to see the objects in its ecology. Similarly, one's own body movements per se are seldom important (e.g., which hand dials the phone). Rather, it is the consequences of these body movements that are important (e.g., reaching the desired party). Thus, the organism's survival and well-being depend on the abilities: (1) to bring its (central) perceptions into line with (distal) objects; and (2) to bring about (distal) states of affairs that coincide with its (central) desires. Unfortunately for the organism, the only information directly available to it is the stimulation of its sensory surfaces (i.e., peripheral/proximal cues), and the only performances that are directly controllable by the organism involve its own motor processes (i.e., peripheral/proximal means). Whatever degree of central–distal correspondence the organism achieves, it brings it about by the *mediation* of peripheral/proximal events and processes. Moreover, as discussed below, this mediation is virtually always imperfect. In sum, Brunswik's functionalism is one in which organisms interact with the environment "through a glass" (and perhaps darkly).

The important problems of psychology

These observations permit us to be more precise about "the interrelationships between organism and environment" that Brunswik saw as the crucial problems of psychology. Because organisms will not be able to achieve close central–distal correspondence with all distal variables of potential interest, psychologists need to know where organisms can and do focus. An inventory of the kinds of objects "attained" by an organism would provide a description of its abilities and performance, and Brunswik favored the pursuit of such inventories. In fact, because a central–distal correspondence can be mediated by proximal/peripheral variables in many different ways, Brunswik's early writings emphasized the classification of achieved objects over the study of the processes by which organisms attain distal variables. Brunswik's later writings, by contrast, did include the study of mediational processes as an important problem in psychology. However, he distinguished between studies of "macromediation" and "micromediation." The former examine "the gross characteristics or macrostructure of the pattern of proximal and peripheral mediation between the distal and central foci," and thereby address "the problem of the grand strategy of mediation" (Brunswik, 1957, p. 8). The latter "attempt to break down the cognitive process further into its component parts," and thus concern "mediational tactics" (p. 9). As Brunswik (p. 9) put it, "Achievement and its strategy are molar problems; tactics is a molecular problem," and it is clear that he felt the former problems should precede and inform the latter.

Vicarious functioning

Stabilization of the end stage and diversity of preceding stages

Explicating "the grand strategy of mediation," for Brunswik, requires a pivotal concept: vicarious functioning. To introduce this concept, Brunswik (1952) discussed the problem of defining the "behavior" that is the subject matter of psychology. As Brunswik (1952, p. 17) asked rhetorically: "Was the incidental stumbling of a person over an obstacle to be considered behavior or nonbehavior?" He answered that psychologists are interested in *purposive* behavior, but that purposive behavior must be recognized by an objectively observable pattern. The pattern proposed by most theorists emphasized the multiplicity and flexibility of means to a given goal state, or as Brunswik preferred to put it, the "'stabilization' of the end stage" and the "diversity of preceding stages" (p. 17). Brunswik borrowed the term "vicarious functioning" from Hunter (1932). Hunter indicated that whereas the physiological functions of one organ are rarely taken over by another, the behavior studied by psychologists typically has a contrasting property. Specifically, if the parts of the body normally used in a performance are impaired, other parts of the body can function "vicariously" to perform the behavior. Brunswik generalized the spirit of Hunter's examples, and used the term "vicarious functioning" to refer more generally to exchangeability of means to an end.

Brunswik continued, though, because he saw that perception as well as overt behavior involved "'stabilization' of the end stage" and "diversity of preceding stages." In perception the end stage is the formation of the percept and the preceding stages refer to the organism's collection and integration of sensory information. That is, Brunswik, like Helmholtz, saw that percepts are inferred from proximal cues, but in addition he saw that varying sets of proximal cues will be available under different environmental conditions. Therefore, organisms must be sensitive to a *multiplicity* of cues, and they need to display the same *flexibility* in their use of cues as in their deployment of means to achieve ends. Brunswik referred to multiplicity and flexibility in using both cues and means as "vicarious functioning," and he took vicarious functioning (broadly construed to include multiplicity, flexibility, intersubstitutability, and combination of both cues and means) to be the core feature that makes "behavior" interesting to psychologists.

The lens model

Brunswik's lens model results from a pictorial representation of vicarious functioning. Figure 3.1 shows the lens model as it appeared in Brunswik's (1952, p. 20) book. For perception, the image portrays a distal stimulus at one focus (the "initial focal variable") emitting a scatter of rays, representing proximal cues, among which the organism selects a subset to be recombined into the central perception at the other focus (the "terminal focal variable"). For action, a central motivational state is pictured as the initial focal variable, and the rays represent proximal means among which the organism selects, all of which lead to the same distal end shown as the terminal focal variable. On different trials, organisms select different subsets of cues or means, and the composite picture shows the collection of cues or means that are used over a large number of trials. Figure 3.2 shows the lens model as it was adapted (Hammond, 1955; Hammond et al., 1975) for the study of judgment. Modeled on the case of perception, the to-be-judged criterion variable Y_e plays the role of the distal stimulus at the initial focus, while the person's judgments Y_s play the role of central perceptions at the terminal focus. The proximal cues $X_1, X_2, \ldots, X_n$ constitute the information available to the judge, and are related to the criterion by ecological validities (i.e., cue–criterion correlations) and to the judgments by cue utilization coefficients (i.e., cue–judgment correlations). Judgmental

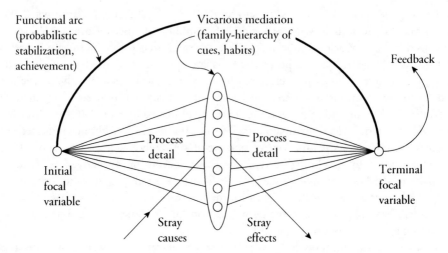

Figure 3.1 The lens model: Composite picture of the functional unit of behavior

Source: Reproduced with permission from E. Brunswik (1952) *International Encyclopedia of Unified Science* (vol. I, no. 10): *The Conceptual Framework of Psychology* (p. 20). Chicago: University of Chicago Press.

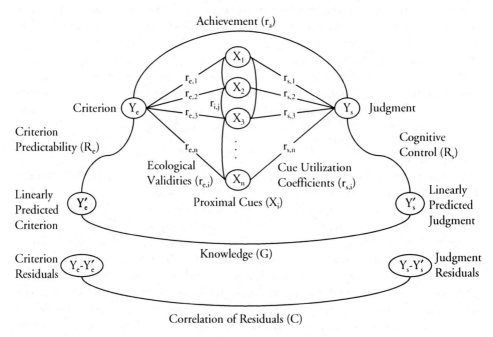

Figure 3.2 Brunswik's lens model as modified for Social Judgment Theory (SJT), shown together with components of the lens model equation

accuracy or achievement is assessed by the correlation between judgment and criterion values.

The lens model illuminates what Brunswik meant by calling variables "focal." He meant that they could be brought into stable relationships with each other via vicarious functioning, by contrast with "the relative chaos in the regions intervening between focal variables" (Brunswik, 1952, p. 20). Moreover, because it is central and distal variables that are focal, the lens model reinforces Brunswik's emphasis on central–distal relationships (i.e., achievement) as the key subject matter of psychology. Not only, as argued earlier, does Brunswik's functionalism identify these relationships as having primary importance to the organism, but the lens model specifies these relationships as the likeliest to be stable enough to support scientific investigation. This, in turn, supports the functional approach and the emphasis on the molar problems of "achievement and its strategy."

The lens model also helps to reveal what is involved in explicating the "grand strategy" by which an organism achieves a stable central–distal relationship: the organismic and environmental systems must be analyzed separately and compared. Expressed in terms of perception, the environment must be studied to determine the ecological "texture": (1) the identity of the features that correlate with the distal object (and are therefore potential proximal/peripheral cues); (2) the strengths of the relationships between the distal object and the (potential) cues (i.e., the ecological validities of the cues); and (3) the interrelationships among the cues (for this is partly what permits vicarious functioning). Regarding the organismic system, it must be determined which of the (potential) cues are actually used, and in what strengths. Finally, the systems must be compared to see if the organism's utilization of cues is commensurate with the ecological validities.

It may seem counterintuitive that a key part of the project – investigation of ecological texture – involves studying the environment apart from any organism's response to it. However, Brunswik cautioned against omitting it. Ultimately, assessing the appropriateness of cue utilization depends on knowledge of the ecological texture. Brunswik expressed his position more generally when he wrote, "psychology has forgotten that it is a science of organism–environment relationships, and has become a science of the organism" (Brunswik, 1957, p. 6). Brunswik strongly implied that approaches that remained "encapsulated" within the organism were abandoning functionalism and courting a kind of solipsism.

Probabilism

Although, in principle, the relationship between proximal/peripheral and distal variables must be determined in studies of ecological texture, Brunswik was convinced that these relationships would virtually always prove to be somewhat unreliable, ambiguous, or "equivocal." At least, this was the argument for individual cues and means. The extent to which an organism could combine cues and select means to overcome their limitations when taken singly is, of course, the problem of achievement – the main subject of research.

The equivocality of means may be more readily apparent than that of cues. A proverb reminds us that the best laid plans of mice and men oft go astray, and it is easy to see that failure is possible even in simple cases. Regarding perception, Brunswik gave numerous examples of proximal cues that were ambiguous, and he suggested that this would be typical. A trapezoidally shaped retinal image may be due to a rectangular object seen at an angle, or the object may actually be trapezoidal. Of two objects, the one with the larger retinal projection may be the closer, or its larger image may be due to its great physical size. These two examples are telling, because they indicate a pattern: in both cases the cue is ambiguous not because of an inherently probabilistic environment, but because of incompleteness of the information. Without challenging determinism, Brunswik argued that organisms usually have access to sets of proximal cues that are incomplete or otherwise inadequate for applying the laws that govern distal objects and distal–proximal relationships. He wrote, "The universal lawfulness of the world is of limited comfort to the perceiver or behaver not in a position to apply these laws . . .," and that "ordinarily organisms must behave as if in a semierratic ecology" (Brunswik, 1955, p. 209). That is, the environment must appear to organisms to be probabilistic, even if in a philosophical sense it is deterministic. To emphasize the organism's predicament, Brunswik coined the metaphor that the perceptual system must act as an "intuitive statistician" (e.g., Brunswik, 1956, p. 80).

From these observations, Brunswik drew an important implication for psychological theory. Specifically, certain parts of the project to explicate achievement and its strategy must be expressed in probabilistic terms. First, as just argued, the environment, or that part of it accessible to an organism, must appear to it to be probabilistic. Therefore, studies of ecological texture, which aim to describe the relationships between distal variables and the *accessible* proximal/peripheral cues and means, must describe a set of probabilistic relationships. For example, although the relationship between size of retinal projection and size of distal object is deterministic for objects at a fixed distance from the organism, the relationship is probabilistic when it must be taken over objects at the various distances the organism encounters in its environment. Second, in addition to ecological texture, achievement itself must be described in probabilistic terms. The reason is that, faced with ambiguous, apparently probabilistic cues, "[a]ll a finite, sub-divine individual can do when acting [or perceiving] is . . . to make a posit, or wager" (Brunswik, 1943, p. 259), and wagers are occasionally lost. Brunswik (1943, p. 270) concluded that "there can be no truly molar psychology dealing with the physical relationships of the organism with its environment unless it gives up the nomothetic ideal in favor of a thoroughly statistical conception."

Representative design

The last aspect of Brunswikian theory to be discussed was and remains one of the most controversial. By the 1950s it was commonly appreciated that participants in psychological investigations must be sampled at random from a specified population for the findings to generalize beyond the participants themselves. Brunswik argued similarly that for findings to generalize beyond the particular stimuli and conditions employed in the study, they also must be sampled to be representative of the ecology. Such experiments had what Brunswik called a "representative design," in contrast to the more typical "systematic design" where experimenters manipulate the stimuli and conditions to produce orthogonal independent variables.

Recall that Brunswik's project to study achievement and its strategy decomposed into four parts: (1) the study of achievement itself, (2) the study of ecological texture, (3) the study of the organism's utilization of cues, and (4) a comparison of the ecological and organismic systems. It is relatively easy to see the importance of representative design for the first two of these four parts. Clearly, achievement can be made excellent or poor by the use of stimuli that, in the appropriate sense, are easy or hard. Little is revealed about achievement in the natural environment unless the stimuli and conditions are representative of those that occur naturally. Even more clearly, the ecological texture of relationships among distal and proximal/peripheral variables cannot be studied adequately in a set of stimuli that distorts the relationships to be studied. The real controversy surrounding the use of representative design centers on its application to studies of cue utilization, and only a sketch of the issues can be given here, stated in terms of the sampling of stimuli.

One argument for representative design, even in studies of cue utilization, holds that the logic of statistical inference requires the probability sampling of units from populations. Generalizing beyond the specific stimuli employed in the study requires this no less than generalizing beyond the specific participants. Some might find this argument unconvincing, either because there are other, nonstatistical, bases for generalization (e.g., theory-guided inference), or because they are not convinced that organisms are sufficiently sensitive to their task environments for the orthogonalization of stimulus properties to affect their cue utilization. A Brunswikian might reply that sensitivity to the task environment is itself a matter for empirical investigation.

A second argument for representative design meets a similar objection, and one might give a similar reply. Specifically, the heart of cue utilization, and from a Brunswikian perspective the main interest in a study of cue utilization, is vicarious functioning. Therefore, organisms should be given full scope to display the vicarious functioning they normally employ in their environment. Moreover, vicarious functioning includes the flexible selection of cues, i.e., allowing some cues on occasion to substitute for other cues, on the basis of prior learning of cue intercorrelations in the environment. Deliberately destroying these cue intercorrelations in an orthogonal design could easily produce "intercombinations of variates [that] may be incompatible in nature or otherwise grossly unrealistic" (Brunswik, 1955, p. 205). Encountering such strange stimuli might confuse the participants, or prevent them from taking the experiment seriously, or at least make them wary of relying on the intersubstitutability of cues that would normally characterize their vicarious functioning. As before, a critic might suggest that participants are not so sensitive to their task environments, and a Brunswikian might reply that sensitivity to task environment is an empirical question.

As a final comment on representative design, it should be noted that Brunswikian research is not hostile to experimental research (as opposed to correlational research) per se. Rather, it is opposed to certain kinds of manipulations of stimulus properties when coupled with the untested assumption that organisms are insensitive to these changes. However, it is fully compatible with Brunswikian research to study the way that organisms adapt to new task environments by manipulating the environments and observing the learning that takes place as organisms adjust to the new ecology. In fact, a great deal of Brunswikian judgment research takes this general form. This research has amply demonstrated people's sensitivity to their task environments, while indicating a corresponding need for experimenters to be cautious about assumptions of insensitivity.

Application of Brunswikian Principles to Research on Judgment

Hammond and his colleagues have applied Brunswikian theory specifically to judgment, and extended it in various ways, to create Social Judgment Theory (SJT; Brehmer, 1988; Brehmer & Joyce, 1988; Hammond, Rohrbaugh, Mumpower, & Adelman, 1977; Hammond et al., 1975). In this section, I outline some of the developments that led to SJT and related lines of research. Unfortunately, space limitations necessitate a highly selective and condensed review, with references restricted mainly to landmark papers and to other literature reviews.

A demonstration of the applicability of Brunswikian principles

As mentioned earlier, Hammond (1955) urged that a Brunswikian approach be taken to the study of clinical judgment, drawing an analogy between clinical judgment and perception. (Others have used a perception/judgment analogy differently, emphasizing the speed and/or automaticity of the processes; see Chapter 5.) In his main example, Hammond reanalyzed data in which clinical psychologists judged patients' IQ scores on the basis of their Rorschach responses. Beyond demonstrating the applicability of Brunswikian principles, Hammond's examples provided a blueprint for the kinds of analyses that would be appropriate to assess achievement, model the environment, model the organism, and compare the environmental and organismic models. One of these analyses, specifically the modeling of organisms with multiple regression techniques, was given greater visibility in a well-known paper by Hoffman (1960). These techniques and associated lines of empirical research evolved to form what is known as "policy capturing" research. (For reviews of the methods, see Cooksey, 1996a, 1996b; Stewart, 1988. Brehmer and Brehmer, 1988, review such issues as: (1) whether the judgment process is adequately described by a linear model; (2) the number of cues that judges do or can use; (3) judgmental consistency; (4) judges' insight into their own judgment processes; and (5) individual differences in judgment. See also Holzworth, 2001a.)

A weakness in Hammond's (1955) paper was that only a qualitative comparison of the environmental and organismic models could be offered. That shortcoming was remedied by the development of the lens model equation.

The lens model equation

The lens model equation (LME) is a formula for decomposing the achievement coefficient, i.e., the correlation between criterion (environmental distal variable) and judgment (organismic central response), for a given set of proximal cues. A decomposition was first offered by Hursch, Hammond, and Hursch (1964), but it is Tucker's (1964) modification that is generally known as the LME:

$$r_a = GR_eR_s + C\sqrt{1 - R_e^2}\ \sqrt{1 - R_s^2},$$

where (see Figure 3.2):

r_a is the achievement coefficient, i.e., the correlation between the criterion variable Y_e and the judgment variable Y_s;

R_e is the multiple correlation of the criterion variable with the proximal cues;

R_s is the multiple correlation of the judgments with the proximal cues;

G is the correlation between the linear components of the criterion and judgment variables, i.e., the correlation between the values Y_e' that are predicted by linear regression of the criterion variable on the proximal cues and the values Y_s' that are predicted by linear regression of the judgments on the proximal cues; and

C is the correlation between the nonlinear components of the criterion and judgment variables, i.e., the correlation between the residuals $Y_e - Y_e'$ and the residuals $Y_s - Y_s'$.

The indices R_e and R_s indicate the linear predictability of the two systems, environmental (criterion) and organismic (judgment), respectively. If neither system has any consistent nonlinear or configural dependence on the proximal cues (a commonly satisfied assumption that implies $C \approx 0$), then R_s indicates the consistency with which the judge executes the systematic component of his or her judgment, and therefore the index is called "cognitive control" (Hammond & Summers, 1972). Under the same assumption, G indicates the extent to which the systematic component of the judge's performance is related to the systematic component of the task environment, and therefore is called "knowledge." The LME reveals the fact that even when knowledge is perfect ($G = 1$), achievement is limited by the consistency with which this knowledge is executed (R_s) and the consistency of the task environment (R_e).

The LME has become a standard tool of Brunswikian research. It was first applied to clinical judgment by Hammond, Hursch, and Todd (1964), and was first applied to multiple-cue probability learning tasks (see below) by Hammond and Summers (1965). Various extensions of the LME have been offered, and some authors have embedded the LME in other decompositions of performance (see Stewart, 2001).

Individual learning

Brunswik portrayed organisms as having to adapt to environments whose distal properties were indicated only probabilistically by proximal cues. This raises the question of how organisms learn probabilistic relationships, and Brunswikian researchers have produced a large literature on the subject using a paradigm called multiple-cue probability learning (MCPL). On each trial of an MCPL study, the respondent examines a profile of cue values, and predicts the value of a criterion variable. In a study using outcome feedback, the respondent is then told the correct criterion value and must learn the cue–criterion relationships over many trials. The MCPL task was first studied by Smedslund (1955), and its popularity rose after Hammond and Summers (1965) showed how to analyze its data with the LME. Among the factors that researchers have examined are: (1) the slope and shape of the functions relating cue and criterion variables; (2) inter-correlations among cues; (3) the optimal rule for combining cues; (4) dynamic task environments; and (5) world knowledge as prompted by labels of cues and criterion variables. For a review, see Klayman (1988a); also see comments by Holzworth (2001b).

In general, learning from outcome feedback tends to be surprisingly slow and limited. Todd and Hammond (1965) introduced the notion of "cognitive feedback," where respondents are shown statistical properties over blocks of trials rather than the outcomes of single trials. For example, comparing the ecological validities of the cues with one's own cue utilization coefficients enables one to see if one is misallocating importance to the cues. The result is that learning is generally faster and better than with outcome feedback. Doherty and Balzer (1988; Balzer, Doherty, & O'Connor, 1989) proposed that cognitive feedback be decomposed into: (1) task information (e.g., information about cue-criterion relations); (2) cognitive information (e.g., information about cue-judgment relations); and (3) functional validity information (e.g., r_a, G, C). Their literature reviews suggested that task information is the component of cognitive feedback that is responsible for improved performance, and subsequent experiments have supported this conclusion.

Rather than a bottom-up process of associating cue and criterion values in MCPL tasks, Brehmer and his colleagues have suggested that people use outcome feedback to test a priori hypotheses about: (1) rules for combining cues; (2) weights to be placed on the cues; and (3) shapes of the cue-criterion functions (Brehmer, 1974). Moreover, Brehmer suggested that people test their hypotheses in a relatively fixed order. This description of the process helps to explain the disappointing rate and degree of learning from outcome feedback. Learning will be slow when the correct hypothesis is low in the respondent's hierarchy of hypotheses. In fact, the respondent may fail entirely to find the correct combination rule and cue-criterion functions if conditions promote the premature acceptance of an incorrect hypothesis that is high in the hierarchy (e.g., probabilistic feedback that cannot definitively reject a hypothesis, see Brehmer, 1980, for a review). In addition to its explanatory value, Brehmer's approach helped to relate MCPL studies to research on the processes of concept formation, hypothesis testing, information gathering, and rule discovery, and it encouraged Brunswikian judgment researchers to address these issues (Doherty, Mynatt, Tweney, & Schiavo, 1979; Klayman, 1988b; Klayman & Ha, 1987, 1989; Mynatt, Doherty, & Tweney, 1978).

Interpersonal conflict and interpersonal learning

Most psychological studies of conflict assume its roots to be motivational, with the parties wanting different things or receiving different payoffs. Hammond (1965, 1973) argued that conflicts can also have cognitive sources, in that people can have shared goals but still differ in their assessments of the situation and the appropriate action. To study cognitive conflict, Hammond proposed the Interpersonal Conflict Paradigm. This involves a training phase, when two participants are separated and taught with an MCPL task to use cues differently in making judgments, and a conflict phase, when the participants are brought together and instructed to make further judgments by consensus. The participants are both motivated by the same desire to make accurate judgments, but the training phase has taught them to see things differently. The conflict between participants is indicated by the discrepancy between their initial judgments in each trial in the conflict phase as they start trying to reach consensus on that trial. In addition to enabling the study of cognitive conflict, this paradigm can also be used to study the kind of interpersonal learning whereby one participant learns from the other about the skillful performance of the task (Earle, 1973). A different kind of interpersonal learning can be studied in a procedure called the Interpersonal Learning Paradigm (Hammond, Wilkins, & Todd, 1966), which adds a third phase to the Interpersonal Conflict Paradigm. In this third phase the participants are again separated and each is asked to judge new cases as well as to predict the other participant's judgments of these cases. Thus, one can study what participants learn *about* each other (i.e., what they learn about the judgmental systems of their partners) as well as what participants learn *from* each other (i.e., how their own judgmental systems are changed due to exposure to their partners). (It is the social nature of these lines of research that injected the social element into SJT.)

The LME was described above as applying to the correlation between judgments and criterion values. However, the LME applies to the correlation between any two variables that are each, in turn, related to the same set of cues. Therefore, one can use it to decompose the correlation between two people's judgments. Changes in the LME components of this correlation, over blocks of trials, indicate the results of interpersonal learning and conflict. Examining the LME as applied to the agreement between two people reveals an important point. Specifically, even if G equals 1 and C equals 0, so that the two participants "agree in principle" (i.e., their systematic use of the cues is identical), it is still impossible for the two people to reach perfect agreement unless both execute their judgment strategies with perfect consistency. Thus, cognitive conflict between people need not result only from different judgment strategies, but can also result from the imperfect control with which people implement their strategies. In fact, one typically finds in interpersonal conflict experiments that participants quickly reduce the systematic discrepancy between themselves and their partners (i.e., G increases), but they also suffer losses in the consistency of their judgment strategies, with the result that overall disagreement remains relatively constant despite the participants' "agreement in principle" (Hammond & Brehmer, 1973).

Many of the same factors that have been manipulated in MCPL studies have also been examined in investigations of interpersonal learning and conflict, producing a large literature. Hammond et al. (1975) review the effects of task consistency, ecological validity of cues, cue-criterion function forms, and cue intercorrelations. For other reviews and discussions, including extensions to negotiations and small-group processes, see Adelman, Henderson, & Miller, 2001; Brehmer, 1976; Cooksey, 1996b, Mumpower, 1988, 2001; Rohrbaugh, 1988, 2001.

Other areas of research

The areas of research reviewed above contributed directly to the development of SJT. Some related research was mentioned along the way. However, this brief review cannot begin to convey the range of Brunswikian-inspired research on judgment. Among the many topics that investigators have addressed are people's insight into their judgment policies, expert judgment and disagreement among experts, and the effects of aging, drugs, and stress on judgment. Researchers have examined judgments of risk, aesthetics, fairness, sexism, personality, and the rapport between people. A Brunswikian approach to studying judgment has been taken in the domains of medicine, education, law, accounting, child welfare, and meteorological forecasting. Two lines of research deserve special attention because of the way they have either modified or built on SJT.

Cognitive Continuum Theory

Cognitive Continuum Theory (CCT; Hammond, 1996; Hammond et al., 1987) goes beyond SJT by presenting substantive hypotheses about the interactions between cognitive processes and task environments. By hypothesizing that specific task features affect processes in particular ways, CCT seeks to transcend the simple observation that different task environments evoke different cognitive processes. Space constraints prevent a complete treatment of CCT (see Hammond, 1996, pp. 147–202.) I will emphasize two core premises of CCT: (1) that different modes of cognition can be arranged on a continuum between intuition and analysis; and (2) that tasks can be similarly ordered on a continuum according to the kind of cognition they are likely to induce.

CCT is rooted in Brunswik's (1952, p. 24; 1956, pp. 89–99; 1966) distinction between "perception" and "thinking" (see Goldstein & Wright, 2001). More precisely, Brunswik distinguished between different strategies for using proximal cues: (1) an inflexible "certainty-geared" strategy that attempts to "duplicate the environmental laws . . . [using] a machine-like interaction" (Brunswik, 1966, p. 488); and (2) an "uncertainty-geared" strategy that "utilizes a whole family of cues of more or less limited trustworthiness" (p. 488) in a "check-and-balance system" (p. 489). An experiment (Brunswik, 1956, pp. 89–93) supported the hypothesis that "thinking" tasks would evoke the certainty-geared strategy and "perceptual" tasks would evoke the uncertainty-geared strategy. However, Brunswik argued that "thinking" is not a homogeneous class of processes, writing that "[t]here obviously are many cases of so-called thinking, which also [i.e., like the uncertainty-geared strategy of perception] use the weighing of vicarious or competitive multiple evidence" (Brunswik, 1966, p. 490). Finally, Brunswik suggested that "thinking" and "perception" should both be considered as special cases of a larger category of "reasoning-type inferences" that he termed "ratiomorphic," for "[i]n this light perception and the different varieties of thinking begin to reveal themselves as but different forms of imperfect reasoning, each with its own particular brands of virtues and of 'stupidity,' if the term be permitted" (Brunswik, 1966, p. 491).

CCT adapts and extends these ideas in several ways. First, in the context of judgment and decision tasks, the uncertainty-geared strategy is identified with intuition and the certainty-geared strategy is identified with analysis. Departing from the common practice of defining analysis and then defining intuition as the absence or opposite of analysis, CCT describes features of both modes of cognition. (For example, intuition is said to involve relatively low cognitive control and conscious awareness, and relatively rapid information processing; see Hammond et al., 1987.)

Second, in keeping with Brunswik's remark about the heterogeneity of "thinking" processes, CCT rejects the notion that judgments and decisions must be based entirely on intuition or analysis in their pure forms. Rather, CCT portrays judgments and decisions as involving many cognitive elements, some intuitive and some analytic, with different strategies calling on various blends of the two. Therefore, CCT posits that intuition and analysis represent the extremes of a continuum of modes of cognition. Most judgments and decisions are expected to include both analytic and intuitive elements, and therefore to be located somewhere in the "quasi-rational" interior of the cognitive continuum (to borrow another term from Brunswik). (For a different view of how intuition and analysis might interact, see Kahneman & Frederick, 2002; Chapter 5.) Hammond et al. (1987) constructed a Cognitive Continuum Index (CCI) to assess the location of a judgment strategy in use.

Third, CCT posits that cognitive tasks, as well as judgment strategies, can be ordered on a continuum. Specifically, CCT asserts that certain task properties are likely to induce more intuitive processing and other task properties are likely to induce more analytic processing, so that a package of task properties could occupy a position anywhere along a continuum from extreme intuition-induction to extreme analysis-induction. To assess the location of a task, Hammond et al., (1987) constructed a Task Continuum Index (TCI).

An experiment conducted by Hammond et al. (1987) tested CCT and related hypotheses about the interactive effects of task characteristics and mode of cognition on the quality of performance. Respondents made judgments in nine different tasks. Examining the TCI for the nine tasks showed that it accorded with expectations about which conditions would be relatively intuition- versus analysis-inducing. Examining TCI and CCI values together supported CCT's hypothesis that the task conditions would induce modes of cognition with corresponding properties. The data also showed that analytic cognition was not uniformly superior to intuitive and quasi-rational cognition in terms of the accuracy achieved. Rather, results suggested that intuitive and quasi-rational cognition may enable people to draw on substantive knowledge, perhaps coded nonverbally, that is less available to them when thinking analytically. Finally, the effect of adjusting one's mode of cognition to the demands of the task was examined by correlating $|TCI - CCI|$ with r_a. Participants tended to have better achievement when their mode of cognition corresponded to the task properties. (See also Cooksey, 2000; Dunwoody, Haarbaur, Mahan, Marino, & Tang, 2000; Hamm, 1988; Hammond, 2000; and Mahan, 1994.)

Fast and frugal heuristics

Gigerenzer and his colleagues (Gigerenzer & Kurz, 2001; Gigerenzer, Todd, & the ABC Research Group, 1999; Chapter 4) returned to the Brunswikian origins of SJT and reconsidered certain aspects. First, they note that Brunswik emphasized the adaptiveness of an organism's behavior, but that accuracy of judgment is only one facet of its adaptiveness, along with speed and the ability to make use of limited information. Second, although Brunswik suggested (e.g., 1952, p. 24) that linear regression might represent vicarious functioning, Gigerenzer and his colleagues question its adequacy because linear regression ignores: (1) the search for cues; (2) the decision to stop searching for cues; and (3) the way some cues might substitute for (rather than integrate with) other cues. Third, these investigators embrace the goal of modeling psychological processes, a goal that Brunswik accepted only late in his career and then gave relatively low priority. On the grounds of psychological process, Gigerenzer and his colleagues again question the plausibility of linear regression as a process model of judgment.

Gigerenzer and his colleagues propose, instead of linear regression, that people have a repertoire of domain-specific heuristics that are computationally simple (i.e., fast) and sparing in their information requirements (i.e., frugal). Such heuristics would be adaptive in a world where decisions must often be made quickly and with limited information, provided that accuracy does not suffer unduly. Therefore, the investigators have studied the accuracy of some stunningly simple heuristics. For example, suppose that the task is to infer which of two objects (e.g., cities) has the higher value on some criterion (e.g., larger population). If only one of the objects is recognized, the "recognition heuristic" concludes that the recognized object has the higher value. It is clearly fast and frugal. Its accuracy can also be impressive, depending on the information environment. (Less obviously, in an environment where the recognition cue is highly valid, greater knowledge can impair performance because recognizing both objects makes the recognition heuristic inapplicable and forces the use of a less valid cue.) Czerlinski, Gigerenzer, & Goldstein (1999) examined two-alternative choice tasks and compared the accuracy of four decision rules: (1) the Take The Best heuristic, which answers according to the single most valid cue that discriminates between the objects; (2) the Minimalist heuristic, which takes the cues in a random order and answers according to the first one that discriminates between the objects; (3) linear regression; and (4) a unit-weighted linear model. Averaging across 20 environments, multiple regression was most accurate when the models were being fitted, with an accuracy of 77 percent, followed by Take The Best (75 percent), unit weighting (73 percent), and Minimalist (69 percent). However, when predicting new cases, Take The Best had the highest accuracy (71 percent), followed by unit weighting (69 percent), multiple regression (68 percent), and Minimalist (65 percent). Thus, in a variety of environments, simple heuristics can do as well as or better than decision rules that require much more information and computation.

The research agenda for this approach is: (1) to propose heuristics that are "fast and frugal;" (2) to investigate the properties of environments where these heuristics perform well; (3) to study the metaheuristics by which people choose the heuristic to apply; and (4) to see if people actually use the proposed heuristics and metaheuristics in particular task environments. This program bears some resemblance to the research program known as "heuristics and biases" (H&B; Gilovich, Griffin, & Kahneman, 2002; Kahneman, Slovic, & Tversky, 1982; Chapter 5). Both approaches propose that people use simple heuristics, and both seek to find the conditions under which they are employed. However, Gigerenzer and Todd (1999) emphasize three differences between these approaches. First, they point to a divergence in attitudes regarding heuristics. In their own view, "heuristics [are seen] as the way the human mind can take advantage of the structure of information in the environment to arrive at reasonable decisions" (Gigerenzer & Todd, 1999, p. 28). In contrast, they characterize the H&B approach as seeing "heuristics as unreliable aids that the limited human mind too commonly relies upon despite their inferior decision-making performance" (p. 28). Second, they argue that their own candidate heuristics are specified in precise computational terms, while H&B researchers are more vague in their description of heuristics. Third, Gigerenzer and Todd evaluate the performance of heuristics against correspondence-based criteria (i.e., accuracy), whereas H&B researchers usually focus on coherence criteria (e.g., conformity with the laws of probability). (See below for further discussion of correspondence and coherence.)

Other research that resembles the work on fast and frugal heuristics, as well as CCT, is the work of Payne, Bettman, and Johnson (1993) on the adaptive decision maker. In all three research programs, an attempt is made: (1) to characterize the variety of judgment and decision strategies that people have in their repertoires; (2) to specify the task conditions that elicit the use of different strategies; and (3) to assess the consequences of using one or another strategy in particular task environments. However, both Gigerenzer and Todd (1999, pp. 26–7) and Hammond (1996, pp. 213–17) differentiate their work from that of Payne et al. by drawing attention to their own emphasis on correspondence-based criteria of performance in contrast to Payne et al.'s use of coherence criteria (conformity to subjective expected utility or to a weighted additive combination rule). (See also Payne et al.'s comments (1993, pp. 104–7) on Hammond et al. (1987).)

Comparisons Between Social Judgment Theory and Other Approaches to Judgment and Decision Research

In this final section, I briefly compare SJT and other approaches, with special attention to H&B research. (For more extensive comparisons between SJT and other approaches, see Cooksey, 1996b; Hammond, McClelland, & Mumpower, 1980.) Comparing SJT and H&B reveals that investigators agree about certain basic issues, but disagree about the implications for substantive theory and methodological practice. I think these differences reflect more than simple disagreements about the cogency of Brunswik's arguments, and instead indicate divergence in interests, scientific goals, and metatheoretical assumptions.

Agreement about issues and disagreement about implications

Uncertainty and probabilism
Brunswik argued that organisms must function in environments that they cannot perceive with complete accuracy and where their actions may not be effective. A similar emphasis on uncertainty is commonplace among judgment and decision researchers. The metaphor that "life is a gamble" has largely dominated research on preferential choice since the 1940s (Goldstein & Weber, 1995). The H&B program took form and grew by addressing judgment under uncertainty (Kahneman et al., 1982). However, despite consensus about the importance of uncertainty, researchers have drawn different implications for scientific practice. Whereas Brunswikian researchers have followed Brunswik's advice to construct probabilistic models, other researchers are more varied in their use of probabilistic and deterministic models. It isn't that non-Brunswikians avoid probabilistic models on principle. Rather, they seem to consider it a matter of the investigator's taste.

Importance of the task environment and representative design
Researchers also agree about the importance of the task environment. A cornerstone of the Brunswikian approach is that the task environment will affect both judgmental accuracy (e.g., via R_e in the LME) and psychological processes (e.g., by enabling and

channeling vicarious functioning). Among non-Brunswikians, a growing appreciation for the influence of task conditions on psychological processes has been a theme of judgment and decision research for over 30 years. Tversky's (1969) remarks on sequential versus simultaneous display of choice alternatives provide an early example. Payne's (1982) important review paper represents a milestone. Again, however, there is disagreement about the implications. Brunswik argued that organisms' sensitivity to task conditions necessitated representative design for results to generalize beyond the laboratory. Non-Brunswikians' attitudes toward representative design are mixed, even though they routinely acknowledge the connection between sensitivity to task conditions and generalizability of results. For example, in a discussion of the representativeness heuristic, Kahneman and Frederick (2002) considered the relative merits of between-subjects and within-subjects factorial designs:

> Rapidly successive encounters with objects of rigidly controlled structure are unique to the laboratory, and the solutions they evoke are not likely to be typical. . . . The between-subjects design in contrast, mimics the haphazard encounters in which most judgments are made and is more likely to evoke the casually intuitive mode of judgment that governs much of mental life in routine situations . . .
>
> (Kahneman & Frederick, 2002, pp. 72–3)

Thus, non-Brunswikians do credit the arguments in favor of representative design. However, they have stopped short of advocating it as a general practice. (In fact, one substantive debate involves the effects of representative design on the calibration of people's probability judgments. For different positions on this matter, see Juslin, 2001; Koehler, Brenner, & Griffin, 2002.)

Behind the disagreements: Different interests, scientific goals, and metatheoretical positions

Accuracy/correspondence versus rationality/coherence

Return now to the issue concerning probabilistic models. Brunswik emphasized the probabilistic nature of *achievement*, and argued that models of achievement therefore should be probabilistic. Brunswik did not argue that an individual's response to a given profile of proximal cues would be probabilistic. In fact, he argued (1956, p. 92) that the "flash-like speed" of "intuitive perception . . . could hardly be achieved without . . . stereotypy and superficiality in the utilization of cues," suggesting that an individual's responses to specific profiles of cues might be deterministic. On this view, the appropriateness of probabilistic vs. deterministic models depends on a more fundamental issue: whether one's purposes are served better by examining responses to specific profiles or by relating those responses to the environment.

Both SJT and H&B researchers are concerned with the quality of judgment and decision making. However, their intellectual backgrounds and interests have led them to embrace different standards of performance. Brunswik's functionalism led SJT to emphasize the adaptiveness of judgment, interpreted as meaning primarily *accuracy* of judgment, until Gigerenzer's recent expansion to include speed and cognitive simplicity. Because of its emphasis on accuracy, SJT research has largely focused on judgments where a criterion could be found or defined, "policy capturing" research notwithstanding. By contrast, research inspired by von Neumann and Morgenstern concentrated on preferential choice, and subsequent work (out of which H&B developed) examined people's probability judgments (often of unique events). These variables – preferential choice and probability judgment (of single events) – don't lend themselves easily to comparisons with external criteria. In the absence of criteria, perhaps the natural standards are those of consistency or coherence, and expected utility theory and Bayes' theorem were taken as standards of *rationality* against which people's judgments and choices could be assessed. This, of course, involves examining people's responses to specific stimuli, for which deterministic models are plausible.

The coherence-based H&B program has generally emphasized people's irrationality, while correspondence-based SJT researchers sometimes have found good accuracy, depending on task characteristics. Hammond (1996) argued that these different conclusions may be reconcilable because coherence and correspondence criteria are often independent and one form of competence may not generalize to the other. That is, one can be accurate without being rational (e.g., "right for the wrong reasons") and one can be rational without being accurate (e.g., holding a coherent worldview that is out of touch with reality). (There are also instances of incoherence that entail limits on accuracy. This fact may permit H&B researchers to argue that they are interested in rationality for the same reason that SJT researchers are interested in accuracy, namely the implications for adaptation to the environment. An SJT researcher might reply, then, that adaptation to the environment, i.e., correspondence criteria, should be studied directly whenever possible.)

Environmental adaptation versus causal processes
Regarding representative design, I believe that H&B researchers are ambivalent because they agree only partly with Brunswik's position that the goal of psychology is to explicate how organisms adjust to and accomplish important tasks in their environments. Other potential goals may militate against representative design. For example, researchers may want to study *whether* and/or the *conditions under which* an effect can be produced, apart from the typicality of those conditions. More problematically, the desire to study the *causal processes* underlying an effect may create a dilemma: distinguishing between potentially causal factors may require disentangling variables that are confounded in the environment, yet that very restructuring of variables may change the psychological processes.

Both SJT and H&B are concerned with psychological processes. However, despite exceptions, it seems fair to say that in general the two approaches differ in both the level of process description that is deemed appropriate and the emphasis placed on discovering psychological processes as compared with other scientific goals. Specifically, H&B researchers seem to advocate a relatively detailed level of process description. By contrast, SJT researchers are generally content to employ mathematical models that describe the combination of information "paramorphically" (Doherty & Brehmer, 1997; Hoffman, 1960; for an exception, see Gigerenzer et al., 1999).

In addition, SJT researchers inherited some of Brunswik's predispositions against an exclusive emphasis on internal processes. Brunswik regarded studies of "encapsulated" organisms as uninformative about functional adaptation. This, in itself, implies only that studies of cognitive processes should not ignore the task environment. However, a deeper ambivalence was evident in some of Brunswik's comments that research should concentrate on distal–central relationships. The internal cognitive processes of vicarious functioning are stabilizing (i.e., they produce stable relationships between central and distal variables), but are themselves unstable (i.e., they exhibit flexibility and variability), and, therefore, are likely to be difficult to study. As noted earlier, Brunswik did eventually admit the study of vicarious functioning, but he placed it lower in his priorities than studying achievement.

By contrast, H&B researchers appear to put their primary emphasis on psychological processes, with a secondary emphasis on finding conditions that elicit irrationality. (An exception is the work of Payne et al., 1993, which focuses on the task conditions that induce people to use particular decision strategies.) This concentration on psychological process seems consistent with the field's origins. Whereas Brunswik had ties to neo-behaviorism, the H&B approach evolved at a time when American psychology was rejecting behaviorism's exclusive concentration on the external circumstances of behavior and embracing the study of internal processes. However, as remarked earlier, the goals of studying causal processes and the conditions that elicit effects may necessitate departures from representative design.

Judgmental error versus judgmental adequacy

Finally, H&B researchers' emphasis on cognitive processes over environmental adaptation, I believe, has generated another difference from SJT researchers. Specifically, the desire to study psychological processes has led to the methodological practice of trying to elicit irrationality, because irrational behavior can be diagnostic of psychological processes. The popularity of this methodological device has conveyed at least the appearance that H&B researchers are more concerned with finding and categorizing judgmental error than with assessing judgmental adequacy.

Summary

In this chapter I have attempted to characterize and review SJT, the application of Brunswikian principles to research on judgment and decision making. I began with an overview of Brunswik's approach to psychology in general, describing his positions regarding functionalism, vicarious functioning, probabilism, and representative design. Next, I related some of the main steps in the development of SJT, including Hammond's application of Brunswikian principles to judgment, and the devising of the LME. Thereafter, I reviewed some of the major lines of SJT research, including work on individual learning, interpersonal conflict, and interpersonal learning, and I described two extensions of SJT, namely Hammond et al.'s CCT and Gigerenzer et al.'s fast and frugal heuristics. Finally, I compared SJT to other approaches, with special attention to H&B

research. I find that SJT and H&B researchers agree on such issues as the importance of uncertainty and task environments in influencing judgments and decisions, but they disagree about the theoretical and methodological implications. My assessment is that these disagreements can be traced to differences in metatheoretical positions and scientific priorities that, in turn, can be understood in terms of the intellectual histories and interests of the two groups of scholars.

Acknowledgment

The author would like to thank the following people for helpful comments on previous drafts of this chapter: Will Bennis, Michael Doherty, Gerd Gigerenzer, Kenneth Hammond, and Nigel Harvey.

References

Adelman, L., Henderson, D., & Miller, S. (2001) Vicarious functioning in teams. In K. R. Hammond and T. R. Stewart (eds.), *The Essential Brunswik: Beginnings, Explications, Applications* (pp. 416–23). Oxford: Oxford University Press.
Balzer, W. K., Doherty, M. E., & O'Connor, R., Jr. (1989) Effects of cognitive feedback on performance, *Psychological Bulletin*, 106, 410–33.
Brehmer, A. & Brehmer, B. (1988) What have we learned about human judgment from thirty years of policy capturing? In B. Brehmer and C. R. B. Joyce (eds.), *Human Judgment: The SJT View* (pp. 75–114). Amsterdam: North-Holland Elsevier.
Brehmer, B. (1974) Hypotheses about relations between scaled variables in the learning of probabilistic inference tasks, *Organizational Behavior and Human Performance*, 11, 1–27.
Brehmer, B. (1976) Social judgment theory and the analysis of interpersonal conflict, *Psychological Bulletin*, 83, 985–1003.
Brehmer, B. (1980) In one word: Not from experience, *Acta Psychologica*, 45, 223–41.
Brehmer, B. (1988) The development of social judgment theory. In B. Brehmer and C. R. B. Joyce (eds.), *Human Judgment: The SJT View* (pp. 13–40). Amsterdam: North-Holland Elsevier.
Brehmer, B. & Joyce, C. R. B. (eds.) (1988) *Human Judgment: The SJT View*. Amsterdam: North-Holland Elsevier.
Brunswik, E. (1943) Organismic achievement and environmental probability, *Psychological Review*, 50, 255–72.
Brunswik, E. (1952) *International Encyclopedia of Unified Science* (vol. I, no. 10): *The Conceptual Framework of Psychology*. Chicago: University of Chicago Press.
Brunswik, E. (1955) Representative design and probabilistic theory in a functional psychology, *Psychological Review*, 62, 193–217.
Brunswik, E. (1956) *Perception and the Representative Design of Psychological Experiments* (2nd edn.). Berkeley: University of California Press.
Brunswik, E. (1957) Scope and aspects of the cognitive problem. In H. E. Gruber, K. R. Hammond, and R. Jessor (eds.), *Contemporary Approaches to Cognition: A Symposium Held at the University of Colorado* (pp. 5–31). Cambridge: Harvard University Press.
Brunswik, E. (1966) Reasoning as a universal behavior model and a functional differentiation between "perception" and "thinking." In K. R. Hammond (ed.), *The Psychology of Egon Brunswik* (pp. 487–94). New York: Holt, Rinehart and Winston.

Cooksey, R. W. (1996a) The methodology of social judgement theory. In M. E. Doherty (ed.), *Social Judgement Theory* (special issue of *Thinking and Reasoning*, 2(2/3), 141–73). East Sussex, UK: Psychology Press.

Cooksey, R. W. (1996b) *Judgment Analysis: Theory, Methods, and Applications.* San Diego: Academic Press.

Cooksey, R. W. (2000) Commentary on "Cognitive adaptation and its consequences: A test of cognitive continuum theory," *Journal of Behavioral Decision Making*, 13, 55–9.

Czerlinski, J., Gigerenzer, G., & Goldstein, D. G. (1999) How good are simple heuristics? In G. Gigerenzer, P. M. Todd, and the ABC Research Group (eds.), *Simple Heuristics that Make us Smart* (pp. 97–118). New York: Oxford University Press.

Doherty, M. E. (ed.) (1996) *Social Judgement Theory* (special issue of *Thinking and Reasoning*, 2(2/3), 105–248), East Sussex, UK: Psychology Press.

Doherty, M. E. & Balzer, W. K. (1988) Cognitive feedback. In B. Brehmer and C. R. B. Joyce (eds.), *Human Judgment: The SJT View* (pp. 163–97). Amsterdam: North-Holland Elsevier.

Doherty, M. E. & Brehmer, B. (1997) The paramorphic representation of clinical judgment: A thirty-year retrospective. In W. M. Goldstein and R. M. Hogarth (eds.), *Research on Judgment and Decision Making: Currents, Connections, and Controversies* (pp. 537–51). Cambridge: Cambridge University Press.

Doherty, M. E., Mynatt, C. R., Tweney, R. D., & Schiavo, M. D. (1979) Pseudodiagnosticity, *Acta Psychologica*, 43, 111–21.

Doherty, M. E. & Tweney, R. D. (in press) Reasoning and task environments: The Brunswikian approach. In K. I. Manktelow and M. C. Chung (eds.), *Psychology of Reasoning: Historical and Philosophical Perspectives.* Hove, GB: Psychology Press.

Dunwoody, P. T., Haarbaur, E., Mahan, R. P., Marino, C., & Tang, C.-C. (2000) Cognitive adaptation and its consequences: A test of cognitive continuum theory, *Journal of Behavioral Decision Making*, 13, 35–54.

Earle, T. C. (1973) Interpersonal learning. In L. Rappoport and D. A. Summers (eds.), *Human Judgment and Social Interaction* (pp. 240–66). New York: Holt, Rinehart and Winston.

Edwards, W. (1954) The theory of decision making, *Psychological Bulletin*, 51, 380–417.

Edwards, W. (1968) Conservatism in human information processing. In B. Kleinmuntz (ed.), *Formal Representation of Human Judgment* (pp. 17–52). New York: Wiley.

Gigerenzer, G. & Kurz, E. M. (2001) Vicarious functioning reconsidered: A fast and frugal lens model. In K. R. Hammond and T. R. Stewart (eds.), *The Essential Brunswik: Beginnings, Explications, Applications* (pp. 342–47). Oxford: Oxford University Press.

Gigerenzer, G. & Todd, P. M. (1999) Fast and frugal heuristics: The adaptive toolbox. In G. Gigerenzer, P. M. Todd, and the ABC Research Group (eds.), *Simple Heuristics that Make us Smart* (pp. 3–34). New York: Oxford University Press.

Gigerenzer, G., Todd, P. M., & the ABC Research Group (eds.) (1999) *Simple Heuristics that Make us Smart.* New York: Oxford University Press.

Gilovich, T., Griffin, D., & Kahneman, D. (eds.) (2002) *Heuristics and Biases: The Psychology of Intuitive Judgment.* Cambridge: Cambridge University Press.

Goldstein, W. M. & Hogarth, R. M. (1997) Judgment and decision research: Some historical context. In W. M. Goldstein and R. M. Hogarth (eds.), *Research on Judgment and Decision Making: Currents, Connections, and Controversies* (pp. 3–65). Cambridge: Cambridge University Press.

Goldstein, W. M. & Weber, E. U. (1995) Content and discontent: Indications and implications of domain specificity in preferential decision making. In J. R. Busemeyer, R. Hastie, and D. L. Medin (eds.), *The Psychology of Learning and Motivation* (vol. 32): *Decision Making From a Cognitive Perspective* (pp. 83–136). San Diego: Academic Press.

Goldstein, W. M. & Wright, J. H. (2001) "Perception" versus "thinking": Brunswikian thought on central responses and processes. In K. R. Hammond and T. R. Stewart (eds.), *The Essential Brunswik: Beginnings, Explications, Applications* (pp. 249–56). Oxford: Oxford University Press.

Hamm, R. M. (1988) Moment-by-moment variation in experts' analytic and intuitive cognitive activity, *IEEE Transactions on Systems, Man, and Cybernetics*, 18, 757–76.

Hammond, K. R. (1955) Probabilistic functionalism and the clinical method, *Psychological Review*, 62, 255–62.

Hammond, K. R. (1965) New directions in research on conflict resolution, *Journal of Social Issues*, 21, 44–66.

Hammond, K. R. (ed.) (1966) *The Psychology of Egon Brunswik*. New York: Holt, Rinehart and Winston.

Hammond, K. R. (1973) The cognitive conflict paradigm. In L. Rappoport and D. A. Summers (eds.), *Human Judgment and Social Interaction* (pp. 188–205). New York: Holt, Rinehart and Winston.

Hammond, K. R. (1996) *Human Judgment and Social Policy: Irreducible Uncertainty, Inevitable Error, Unavoidable Injustice*. New York: Oxford University Press.

Hammond, K. R. (2000) *Judgments Under Stress*. New York: Oxford University Press.

Hammond, K. R. & Brehmer, B. (1973) Quasi-rationality and distrust: Implications for international conflict. In L. Rappoport and D. A. Summers (eds.), *Human Judgment and Social Interaction* (pp. 338–91). New York: Holt, Rinehart and Winston.

Hammond, K. R., Hamm, R. M., Grassia, J., & Pearson, T. (1987) Direct comparison of the efficacy of intuitive and analytical cognition in expert judgment, *IEEE Transactions on Systems, Man, and Cybernetics*, SMC-17, 753–70.

Hammond, K. R., Hursch, C. J., & Todd, F. J. (1964) Analyzing the components of clinical inference, *Psychological Review*, 71, 438–56.

Hammond, K. R. & Joyce, C. R. B. (eds.) (1975) *Psychoactive Drugs and Social Judgment: Theory and Research*. New York: Wiley.

Hammond, K. R., McClelland, G., & Mumpower, J. (1980) *Human Judgment and Decision Making: Theories, Methods, and Procedures*. New York: Praeger Scientific.

Hammond, K. R., Rohrbaugh, J., Mumpower, J., & Adelman, L. (1977) Social judgment theory: Applications in policy formation. In M. Kaplan and S. Schwartz (eds.), *Human Judgment and Decision Processes in Applied Settings* (pp. 1–30). New York: Academic Press.

Hammond, K. R. & Stewart, T. R. (eds.) (2001) *The Essential Brunswik: Beginnings, Explications, Applications*. Oxford: Oxford University Press.

Hammond, K. R., Stewart, T. R., Brehmer, B., & Steinmann, D. (1975) Social judgment theory. In M. F. Kaplan and S. Schwartz (eds.), *Human Judgment and Decision Processes* (pp. 271–312). New York: Academic Press.

Hammond, K. R. & Summers, D. A. (1965) Cognitive dependence on linear and nonlinear cues, *Psychological Review*, 72, 215–24.

Hammond, K. R. & Summers, D. A. (1972) Cognitive control, *Psychological Review*, 79, 58–67.

Hammond, K. R. & Wascoe, N. E. (eds.) (1980) *Realizations of Brunswik's Representative Design*. San Francisco: Jossey-Bass.

Hammond, K. R., Wilkins, M. M., & Todd, F. J. (1966) A research paradigm for the study of interpersonal learning, *Psychological Bulletin*, 65, 221–32.

Hoffman, P. J. (1960) The paramorphic representation of clinical judgment, *Psychological Bulletin*, 57, 116–31.

Holzworth, R. J. (2001a) Judgment analysis. In K. R. Hammond and T. R. Stewart (eds.), *The Essential Brunswik: Beginnings, Explications, Applications* (pp. 324–7). Oxford: Oxford University Press.

Holzworth, R. J. (2001b) Multiple cue probability learning. In K. R. Hammond and T. R. Stewart (eds.), *The Essential Brunswik: Beginnings, Explications, Applications* (pp. 348–50). Oxford: Oxford University Press.

Hunter, W. S. (1932) The psychological study of behavior, *Psychological Review*, 39, 1–24.

Hursch, C. J., Hammond, K. R., & Hursch, J. L. (1964) Some methodological considerations in multiple-cue probability studies, *Psychological Review*, 71, 42–60.

Juslin, P. (2001) Representative design: Cognitive science from a Brunswikian perspective. In K. R. Hammond and T. R. Stewart (eds.), *The Essential Brunswik: Beginnings, Explications, Applications* (pp. 404–8). Oxford: Oxford University Press.

Juslin, P. & Montgomery, H. (eds.) (1999) *Judgment and Decision Making: Neo-Brunswikian and Process-Tracing Approaches*. Mahwah, NJ: Erlbaum.

Kahneman, D. & Frederick, S. (2002) Representativeness revisited: Attribute substitution in intuitive judgment. In T. Gilovich, D. Griffin, and D. Kahneman (eds.), *Heuristics and Biases: The Psychology of Intuitive Judgment* (pp. 49–81). Cambridge: Cambridge University Press.

Kahneman, D., Slovic, P., & Tversky, A. (eds.) (1982) *Judgment Under Uncertainty: Heuristics and Biases*. Cambridge: Cambridge University Press.

Klayman, J. (1988a) On the how and why (not) of learning from outcomes. In B. Brehmer and C. R. B. Joyce (eds.), *Human Judgment: The SJT View* (pp. 115–62). Amsterdam: North-Holland Elsevier.

Klayman, J. (1988b) Cue discovery in probabilistic environments: Uncertainty and experimentation, *Journal of Experimental Psychology: Learning, Memory, and Cognition*, 14, 317–30.

Klayman, J. & Ha, Y. (1987) Confirmation, disconfirmation, and information in hypothesis testing, *Psychological Review*, 94, 211–28.

Klayman, J. & Ha, Y. (1989) Hypothesis testing in rule discovery: Strategy, structure and content, *Journal of Experimental Psychology: Learning, Memory, and Cognition*, 15, 596–604.

Koehler, D. J., Brenner, L., & Griffin, D. (2002) The calibration of expert judgment: Heuristics and biases beyond the laboratory. In T. Gilovich, D. Griffin, and D. Kahneman (eds.), *Heuristics and Biases: The Psychology of Intuitive Judgment* (pp. 686–715). Cambridge: Cambridge University Press.

Mahan, R. P. (1994) Stress-induced strategy shifts toward intuitive cognition: A cognitive continuum framework approach, *Human Performance*, 7, 85–118.

Meehl, P. E. (1954) *Clinical Versus Statistical Prediction: A Theoretical Analysis and a Review of the Evidence*. Minneapolis: University of Minnesota Press.

Mumpower, J. L. (1988) An analysis of the judgmental components of negotiation and a proposed judgmentally-oriented approach to mediation. In B. Brehmer and C. R. B. Joyce (eds.), *Human Judgment: The SJT View* (pp. 465–502). Amsterdam: North-Holland Elsevier.

Mumpower, J. L. (2001) Brunswikian research on social perception, interpersonal learning and conflict, and negotiation. In K. R. Hammond and T. R. Stewart (eds.), *The Essential Brunswik: Beginnings, Explications, Applications* (pp. 388–93). Oxford: Oxford University Press.

Mynatt, C. R., Doherty, M. E., & Tweney, R. D. (1978) Consequences of confirmation and disconfirmation in a simulated research environment, *Quarterly Journal of Experimental Psychology*, 30, 395–406.

Payne, J. W. (1982) Contingent decision behavior, *Psychological Bulletin*, 92, 382–402.

Payne, J. W., Bettman, J. R., & Johnson, E. J. (1993) *The Adaptive Decision Maker*. New York: Cambridge University Press.

Rappoport, L. & Summers, D. A. (eds.) (1973) *Human Judgment and Social Interaction*. New York: Holt, Rinehart and Winston.

Rohrbaugh, J. (1988) Cognitive conflict tasks and small group processes. In B. Brehmer and C. R. B. Joyce (eds.), *Human Judgment: The SJT View* (pp. 199–226). Amsterdam: North-Holland Elsevier.

Rohrbaugh, J. (2001) The relationship between strategy and achievement as the basic unit of group functioning. In K. R. Hammond and T. R. Stewart (eds.), *The Essential Brunswik: Beginnings, Explications, Applications* (pp. 384–7). Oxford: Oxford University Press.

Smedslund, J. (1955) *Multiple Probability Learning*. Oslo: Akademisk Forlag.

Stewart, T. R. (1988) Judgment analysis: Procedures. In B. Brehmer and C. R. B. Joyce (eds.), *Human Judgment: The SJT View* (pp. 41–74). Amsterdam: North-Holland Elsevier.

Stewart, T. R. (2001) The lens model equation. In K. R. Hammond and T. R. Stewart (eds.), *The Essential Brunswik: Beginnings, Explications, Applications* (pp. 357–62). Oxford: Oxford University Press.

Todd, F. J. & Hammond, K. R. (1965) Differential feedback in two multiple-cue probability learning tasks, *Behavioral Science*, 10, 429–35.

Tucker, L. (1964) A suggested alternative formulation in the developments by Hursch, Hammond, and Hursch, and by Hammond, Hursch, and Todd, *Psychological Review*, 71, 528–30.

Tversky, A. (1969) Intransitivity of preferences, *Psychological Review*, 76, 31–48.

Tversky, A. & Kahneman, D. (1974) Judgment under uncertainty: Heuristics and biases, *Science*, 185, 1124–31.

von Neumann, J. & Morgenstern, O. (1947) *Theory of Games and Economic Behavior* (2nd edn.). Princeton: Princeton University Press.

4

Fast and Frugal Heuristics: The Tools of Bounded Rationality

Gerd Gigerenzer

Introduction

If you open a book on judgment and decision making, chances are that you will stumble over the following moral: Good reasoning must adhere to the laws of logic, the calculus of probability, or the maximization of expected utility; if not, there must be a cognitive or motivational flaw. Don't be taken in by this fable. Logic and probability are mathematically beautiful and elegant systems. But they do not describe how actual people – including the authors of books on decision making – reason, as the subsequent story highlights. A decision theorist from Columbia University was struggling whether to accept an offer from a rival university or to stay. His colleague took him aside and said, "Just maximize your expected utility – you always write about doing this." Exasperated, the decision theorist responded, "Come on, this is serious."

I will introduce you to the study of cognitive heuristics: how people actually make judgments and decisions in everyday life, generally without calculating probabilities and utilities. The term *heuristic* is of Greek origin and means "serving to find out or discover." In the title of his Nobel Prize-winning paper of 1905, Albert Einstein used the term *heuristic* to indicate an idea that he considered incomplete, due to the limits of our knowledge, but useful (Holton, 1988). For the Stanford mathematician G. Polya (1954), heuristic thinking was as indispensable as analytical thinking for problems that cannot be solved by the calculus or probability theory – for instance, how to find a mathematical proof. The advent of computer programming gave heuristics a new prominence. It became clear that most problems of any importance are computationally intractable, that is, we do not know the optimal solution, nor a method for how to find it. This holds even for well-defined problems such as chess, the classic computer game Tetris, and the traveling salesman problem (Michalewicz & Fogel, 2000). The same uncertainty holds for less well-structured problems, such as which job offer to accept, what stocks to invest in, and whom to marry. When optimal solutions are out of reach, we are not paralyzed to inaction or doomed to failure. We can use heuristics to discover good solutions.

What is a Heuristic?

Imagine you want to build a robot that can catch balls – fly balls, as in baseball and cricket. (It's a thought experiment – no such robots exist yet.) For the sake of simplicity, consider situations where a ball is already high up in the air and will land in front of or behind the player. How would you build such a robot? One vision is *omniscience*: you aim at giving your robot a complete representation of its environment and the most sophisticated computational machinery. First, you might feed your robot the family of parabolas, because, in theory, balls have parabolic trajectories. In order to select the right parabola, the robot needs to be equipped with instruments that can measure the ball's initial distance, initial velocity, and projection angle. Yet in the real world, balls do not fly in parabolas, due to air resistance, wind, and spin. Thus, the robot would need further instruments that can measure the speed and direction of the wind at each point of the ball's flight, in order to compute the resulting path and the point where the ball will land, and to then run there. All this would have to be completed within a few seconds – the time a ball is in the air.

An alternative vision exists, which does not aim at complete representation and information. It poses the question: Is there a smart heuristic that can solve the problem? One way to discover heuristics is to study experienced players. Experimental studies have shown that players actually use several heuristics. One of these is the *gaze heuristic*. When a fly ball approaches, the player fixates the ball and starts running. The heuristic is to adjust the running speed so that the angle of gaze remains constant (or within a certain range; see McLeod & Dienes, 1996). The angle of gaze is the angle between the eye and the ball, relative to the ground. In our thought experiment, a robot that uses this heuristic does not need to measure wind, air resistance, spin, or the other causal variables. It can get away with ignoring every piece of causal information. All the relevant information is contained in one variable: the angle of gaze. Note that a player or robot using the gaze heuristic is not able to compute the point at which the ball will land. But the player will be there where the ball lands.

The gaze heuristic is a fast and frugal heuristic. It is fast because it can solve the problem within a few seconds, and it is frugal because it requires little information, just the angle of gaze. In general, a heuristic is a rule, such as "fixate the ball, start running, and adjust your running speed so that the angle of gaze remains constant." But a rule is not necessarily a heuristic, unless it embodies three qualities:

1   *Heuristics exploit evolved capacities.* A heuristic is *simple* relative to the evolved or learned capacities of an organism. For example, it is easy for humans to track a moving object against a noisy background; two-month-old babies can already hold

their gaze on moving targets (Rosander & Hofsten, 2002). Tracking objects, however, is difficult for a robot; a computer program that can solve this problem as well as a human mind can does not yet exist. (Similarly, in contrast to robots, humans are able to run.) Thus, the gaze heuristic is simple for humans but not for robots. Simplicity is not only a characteristic of beauty; it also allows making *fast, frugal, transparent*, and *robust* judgments. The gaze heuristic, like all heuristics, is transparent in the sense that it can be easily understood and taught to a novice, and the term *robust* refers to the ability of heuristics to generalize to new situations (see below). To summarize, a heuristic exploits hard-wired or learned cognitive and motor processes, and these features make it simple.

2   *Heuristics exploit structures of environments.* The rationality of heuristics is not logical, but ecological. Ecological rationality implies that a heuristic is not good or bad, rational or irrational per se, only relative to an environment. It can exploit certain structures of environments, or change an environment. For instance, the gaze heuristic transforms the complex trajectory of the ball in the environment into a straight line. All heuristics are to some degree domain-specific; they are designed to solve specific classes of problems. The gaze heuristic can solve problems that involve the interception of moving objects. If you learn to fly an airplane, you will be taught a version of it: When another plane is approaching, and you fear a collision, then look at a scratch in your windshield and observe whether the other plane moves relative to that scratch. If it does not, dive away quickly. For the pilot, the goal is to avoid a collision, whereas for the outfielder, the goal is to produce a collision. The nature of the heuristic is the same. To summarize, evolved capacities can make a heuristic simple, while the structure of the environment can make it smart.

3   *Heuristics are distinct from "as-if" optimization models.* The idea of calculating the ball's trajectory by solving differential equations is a form of optimization. When optimization is proposed to explain human behavior (as opposed to building artificial systems), this is called *as-if* optimization. In Richard Dawkins' (1976, p. 96) words: "When a man throws a ball high in the air and catches it again, he behaves as if he had solved a set of differential equations in predicting the trajectory of the ball." As-if optimization models are silent about the actual process, although it is sometimes suggested that the measurements and calculations might happen unconsciously. The gaze heuristic, however, illustrates that the logic of a heuristic, conscious or unconscious, can be strikingly distinct from as-if optimization. This yields an advantage. With a good model of a heuristic, one can deduce predictions that cannot be obtained from an as-if optimization model. The gaze heuristic, for instance predicts that players catch the ball while running, which follows from the fact that the player must move to keep the angle of gaze constant. Similarly, when the ball is thrown to the side of the player, one can predict that the player will run a slight arc, as can be observed in baseball outfielders and in dogs who catch Frisbees (e.g., Shaffer & McBeath, 2002).

In summary, a model of a heuristic is a rule whose purpose is to describe the actual process – not merely the outcome – of problem solving.

What is Bounded Rationality?

In models of unbounded rationality, all relevant information is assumed to be freely available to everyone. In this framework the question is, if humans had perfect information and all eternity at their disposal, how would they behave? Models of bounded rationality put us back into our human skin and try to answer the question, how do humans who have little time and knowledge behave? However, Simon's (1955, 1956) term *bounded rationality* itself has become associated with three disparate programs: the study of optimization under constraints, the study of cognitive illusions, and the study of fast and frugal heuristics.

The term *bounded* can refer to constraints in the environment, such as information costs, and to constraints in the mind, such as limited memory (Todd, 2001). Adding one or more constraints to the program of as-if optimization results in optimization under constraints (Conlisk, 1996). For instance, the idea of measuring all causal variables that determine the trajectory of a ball's flight, subject to some constraint such as time, illustrates this program of as-if optimization. In personal conversation, Herb Simon once remarked with a mixture of humor and anger that he had considered suing authors who misused his concept of bounded rationality to construct even more unrealistic models of the human mind.

The study of cognitive illusions evolved in opposition to optimization, but also linked itself to the study of bounded rationality (e.g., Camerer, 1998; Kahneman, Slovic, & Tversky, 1982, p. xii). Its primary aim is to show that optimization is descriptively invalid, that is, to demonstrate that people's judgments do not actually follow the laws of probability or the maximization of expected utility. The result is a list of deviations from norms, which are interpreted as cognitive fallacies, emphasizing irrationality rather than rationality. The assumption is that these deviations can reveal the underlying cognitive processes (see Chapter 5, this volume).

How would this program approach the problem of how players catch a ball? Let us continue the thought experiment. One might try to demonstrate that players actually make systematic errors when computing the point where the ball will land. A player might be positioned on a fixed point in the field, a fly ball is thrown, and the player is asked to predict where the ball will hit the ground. If players cannot predict very well, such as underestimating their distance to the point where the ball will land, this error would be attributed to people's limited cognitive abilities. It might be labeled the *optimistic bias* in baseball, because underestimation suggests that players think they might catch the ball even when they can't. A debiasing training might be offered to players. In this thought experiment, the cognitive illusions program would correctly conclude that the optimizing model is descriptively disproved, but the optimistic bias would not lead to the discovery of the gaze heuristic or other heuristics that players use. Just like the optimization model, the cognitive illusions program would overlook that the actual goal of the player is not to predict where the ball will land, but to be there where the ball lands. The rationality of heuristics is not simply a means to a given end; the heuristic itself can define what the end is.

Table 4.1 Twelve examples of phenomena that were first interpreted as "cognitive illusions" (left) but later revalued as reasonable judgments given the environmental structure

Is a phenomenon due to a "cognitive illusion"...	*... or to an environmental structure plus an unbiased mind?*
Overconfidence bias (defined as miscalibration)	"Miscalibration" can be deduced from an unbiased mind in an environment with unsystematic error, causing regression toward the mean (Dawes & Mulford, 1996; Erev et al., 1994)
Overconfidence bias (defined as mean confidence minus proportion correct)	"Overconfidence bias" can be deduced from an unbiased mind in an environment with unrepresentative sampling of questions; disappears largely with random sampling (Juslin, Winman, & Olsson, 2000)
Hard-easy effect	"Hard-easy effect" can be deduced from an unbiased mind in an environment with unsystematic error, causing regression toward the mean (Juslin et al., 2000)
Overestimation of low risks and underestimation of high risks	This classical phenomenon can be deduced from an unbiased mind in an environment with unsystematic error, causing regression toward the mean (Gigerenzer & Fiedler, 2004)
Contingency illusion	"Contingency illusion" can be deduced from an unbiased mind performing significance tests on samples with unequal sizes, such as minorities and majorities (Fiedler, Walther, & Nickel, 1999)
Most drivers say they drive safer than average	The distribution of the actual numbers of accidents is highly skewed, which results in the fact that most drivers (80% in one US study) have less accidents than the average number of accidents (Lopes, 1992; Gigerenzer, 2002)
Availability bias (letter "R" study)	"Availability bias" largely disappears when the stimuli (letters) are representatively sampled rather than selected (Sedlmeier, Hertwig, & Gigerenzer, 1998)
Preference reversals	Consistent social values (e.g., don't take the largest slice; don't be the first to cross a picket line) can create what look like preference reversals (Sen, 2002)
Probability matching	Probability matching is suboptimal for an individual studied in isolation, but not necessarily for individuals in an environment of social competition (Gallistel, 1990)
Conjunction fallacy	"Conjunction fallacy" can be deduced from the human capacity for semantic inference in social situations (Hertwig & Gigerenzer, 1999)
False consensus effect	This "egocentric bias" can be deduced from Bayes' rule for situations where a person has no knowledge about prior probabilities (Dawes & Mulford, 1996)
Violations of logical reasoning	A number of apparent "logical fallacies" can be deduced from Bayesian statistics for environments where the empirical distribution of the events (e.g., P, Q, and their negations) is highly skewed (McKenzie & Amin, 2002; Oaksford & Chater, 1994) and from the logic of social contracts (Cosmides & Tooby, 1992)

The general argument is that an unbiased mind plus environmental structure (such as unsystematic error, unequal sample sizes, skewed distributions) is *sufficient* to produce the phenomenon. Note that other factors can also contribute to some of the phenomena. The moral is not that people would never err, but that in order to understand good and bad judgments, one needs to analyze the structure of the problem or of the natural environment.

Simon's vision of bounded rationality was neither optimization under constraints nor cognitive illusions (Gigerenzer, 2004). His notion of rationality was an ecological one: the match between mind and environment. This is best illustrated in an analogy he offered: "Human rational behavior is shaped by a scissors whose blades are the structure of task environments and the computational capabilities of the actor" (Simon, 1990, p. 7). If looking only at one blade, one cannot fully understand how the human mind works, just as one cannot understand how scissors cut.

For instance, as Table 4.1 illustrates, as soon as researchers began to study the structure of information in the environment, what looked like a dull cognitive illusion often turned out to be a sharp pair of scissors. In a series of experiments, for example, participants answered general-knowledge questions. The typical finding was that when participants were 100 percent confident of giving a correct answer, the average number correct was lower, such as 80 percent. This phenomenon was labeled *overconfidence bias* or *miscalibration* and interpreted as a cognitive illusion. A glance at the environmental structure, however, reveals a large unsystematic error, which *in the absence of any cognitive bias* leads to regression towards the mean, that is, the average number correct is always lower than a high confidence level. When one plots the data the other way round, the unsystematic error produces a pattern that looks like *underconfidence*: When participants answered 100 percent correctly, their mean confidence was lower, such as 80 percent. Rather than being a cognitive illusion, the phenomenon seems largely a consequence of environments with substantial unsystematic error (Erev, Wallsten, & Budescu, 1994; but see Chapter 9, this volume, for a different view).

Models of Heuristics

A model of a heuristic specifies: (1) a process rule; (2) the capacities that the rule exploits to be simple; and (3) the kinds of problems the heuristic can solve, that is, the structures of environments in which it is successful. The latter two are Simon's blades. Models of heuristics need to be distinguished from mere labels. For instance, terms such as *representativeness* and *availability* are common-sense labels without specification of a process and the conditions under which a heuristic succeeds and fails. These need to be developed into testable models; otherwise they can post hoc account for almost everything (see Gigerenzer, 1996, 2000; Gigerenzer & Murray, 1987, Chapter 5; Gigerenzer & Regier, 1996; Kahneman & Tversky, 1996).

There do already exist a number of testable models for heuristics, such as satisficing (Selten, 2001; Simon, 1982), elimination by aspect (Tversky, 1972), and various heuristics for multiattribute choice discussed in Payne, Bettman, & Johnson (1993), and Chapter 6, this volume. Much of this earlier work addressed heuristics for preferences, not for inferences, that is, for problems where no external criterion of success exists. Criteria for the accuracy of heuristics were typically internal, such as whether they used all of the information or how closely they mimicked the gold standard of a weighted additive model. Because there were no external criteria for accuracy, the true power of heuristics could not be demonstrated. Some concluded that heuristics generally lead to irrational judgments, at best to second-best choices. For instance, when Keeney and Raiffa (1993) discussed lexicographic heuristics, they repeatedly inserted warnings that such a strategy "is more widely adopted in practice than it deserves to be" because "it is naively simple" and "will rarely pass a test of 'reasonableness'" (pp. 77–8). But the authors failed to report such a test – preferences alone cannot reveal how accurate heuristics really are. In this chapter I will report such tests.

I will focus on heuristics for inferences – such as comparative judgments, classification, and estimation. From the seminal work on heuristics with simple unit weights (such as +1 and −1; see Dawes, 1979), we know that the predictive accuracy of simple heuristics can be as high as or higher than that of the gold standard of weighing and adding. For instance, unit weights predicted the academic performance of students as well as or better than multiple regression (Dawes & Corrigan, 1974), and the Take The Best heuristic predicted the outcomes of the basketball games in the 1996 NBA season as well as Bayes's rule, but did so faster and with less information (Todorov, 2002). Models of heuristics for classification, estimation, comparative judgments, and choice are discussed in Gigerenzer, Todd, and the ABC Research Group (1999), Gigerenzer and Selten (2001), and Todd and Gigerenzer (2000). In what follows, I will select a few heuristics and discuss the ecological rationality and the empirical evidence.

Recognition Heuristic

Imagine you are a contestant in a TV game show and face the $1 million question: "Which city has more inhabitants: San Diego or San Antonio?" What is your answer? If you are American, then your chances of finding the right answer, San Diego, are not bad. Some two thirds of undergraduates at the University of Chicago did (Goldstein & Gigerenzer, 2002). If, however, you are German, your prospects look dismal because most Germans know little about San Diego, and many have not even heard of San Antonio. How many correct inferences did the less knowledgeable German group that we tested achieve? Despite a considerable lack of knowledge, 100 percent of the Germans answered the question correctly. How can people who know less about a subject nevertheless make more correct inferences? The answer is that the Germans used a fast and frugal heuristic, the recognition heuristic: If you recognize the name of one city but not the other, then infer that the recognized city has the larger population. The Americans could not use the heuristic, because they had heard of both cities. They knew too much.

The recognition heuristic is useful when there is a strong correlation – in either direction – between recognition and criterion. For simplicity, we assume that the correlation is positive. For two-alternative choice tasks, the heuristic can be stated as follows:

> *Recognition heuristic*: If one of two objects is recognized and the other is not, then infer that the recognized object has the higher value with respect to the criterion.

The recognition heuristic builds on an evolved capacity for recognition – such as face, voice, and name recognition. No computer program yet exists that can perform face recognition as well as a human child does. Note that the capacity for recognition is different from that for recall. For instance, one may recognize a face but not recall anything about who that person is (Craik & McDowd, 1987).

> *Ecological rationality*: The recognition heuristic is successful when ignorance is systematic rather than random, that is, when recognition is strongly correlated with the criterion.

The direction of the correlation between recognition and the criterion can be learned from experience, or it can be genetically coded. Substantial correlations exist in competitive situations, such as between name recognition and the excellence of colleges, the value of the products of companies, and the quality of sports teams. Consider forecasting the outcomes of the 32 English FA Cup third-round soccer matches, such as Manchester United versus Shrewsbury Town. Ayton and Önkal (1997) tested 50 Turkish students and 54 British students. The Turkish participants had very little knowledge about (or interest in) English soccer teams, while the British participants knew quite a bit. Nevertheless, the Turkish forecasters were nearly as accurate as the English ones (63 percent versus 66 percent correct). Their predictions were consistent with the recognition heuristic in 627 out of 662 cases (95 percent). Experimental studies by Goldstein and Gigerenzer (2002) indicate that in situations where the recognition heuristic is ecologically rational, people rely on it in about 90 percent of all cases.

One way to measure the degree of ecological rationality of the recognition heuristic (the correlation between recognition and criterion) is the *recognition validity* α, which is the proportion of times a recognized object has a higher criterion value than an unrecognized object in a reference class, such as cities, companies, or sports teams:

$$\alpha = R/(R + W) \tag{4.1}$$

where R is the number of correct (right) inferences the recognition heuristic would achieve, computed across all pairs in which one object is recognized and the other is not, and W is the number of incorrect (wrong) inferences under the same circumstances.

The recognition heuristic should not be confused with labels such as *availability* (Tversky & Kahneman, 1974) or *familiarity* (Griggs & Cox, 1982). Availability refers to ease of recall, not recognition. The recognition heuristic implies several counterintuitive phenomena that cannot be deduced from any other theory I am aware of. For instance, recognition information tends to dominate further knowledge, in rats as well as in people, even if there is conflicting evidence (Goldstein & Gigerenzer, 2002). Next, I will deduce a counterintuitive phenomenon, the *less-is-more effect*, and the conditions under which it will occur.

The less-is-more effect

Equation 4.2 specifies the proportion of correct answers c on an exhaustive test of all pairs of N objects (such as cities, soccer teams) for a person that recognizes n of these objects:

$$c = \frac{2n(N - n)}{N(N - 1)}\alpha + \frac{(N - n)(N - n - 1)}{N(N - 1)}\frac{1}{2} + \frac{n(n - 1)}{N(N - 1)}\beta \tag{4.2}$$

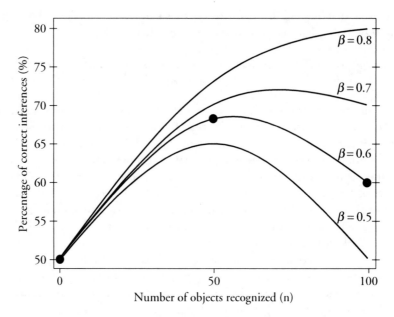

Figure 4.1 The less-is-more effect is a consequence of the recognition heuristic

The effect occurs when the recognition validity α is larger than the knowledge validity β. The curves shown are for $\alpha = 0.8$. A less-is-more effect can occur between people with the same β, as shown by the middle and right-hand points. It can also occur between people with different knowledge validities. For instance, a person who recognizes only half of the objects ($n = 50$) and has no useful knowledge ($\beta = 0.5$) will make more correct inferences than a person who recognizes all objects ($n = 100$) and has useful knowledge ($\beta = 0.6$)

The three terms on the right side of the equation correspond to the three possibilities: a person recognizes one of the two objects, none, or both. The first term accounts for the correct inferences made by the recognition heuristic, the second term for guessing, and the third term equals the proportion of correct inferences made when knowledge beyond recognition is used. The *knowledge validity* β is the relative frequency of getting a correct answer when both objects are recognized, which is computed like the recognition validity. All parameters in Equation 4.2 can be independently measured.

When one plots Equation 4.2, a counterintuitive implication can be seen (Figure 4.1). Consider first the curve for $\beta = 0.5$, that is, for people who have no predictive knowledge beyond recognition. A person that has heard of none of the objects will perform at chance level (50 percent, left side). A person that has heard of all objects will also perform at chance level (50 percent, right side). Only a person who has heard of some but not all objects can use the recognition heuristic, and her accuracy will first increase with n but then decrease again. The reason is that the recognition heuristic can be used most often when about half of the objects are recognized, in comparison to when all or none are recognized. When half of the objects are recognized, a person can use the recognition heuristic about half of the time, which results in some 65 percent (40 percent for $\alpha = 0.8$ plus 25 percent for guessing) correct inferences, as can be calculated from Equation 4.2. The next curve with three dots shows a less-is-more effect in the presence of knowledge beyond mere recognition, for $\beta = 0.6$. The left dot represents a person who has not heard of any objects, while the dot on the right represents someone who has heard of all objects and has recall knowledge that does better than chance. The middle dot represents a person who recognizes less objects but gets more correct inferences. In general, assuming that α and β are constant, the following result can be proven (Goldstein & Gigerenzer, 2002):

Less-is-more effect: The recognition heuristic will yield a less-is-more effect if $\alpha > \beta$.

A less-is-more effect can emerge in at least three different situations. First, it can occur between two groups of people, when a more knowledgeable group makes worse inferences than a less knowledgeable group in a given domain. An example is the performance of the American and German students on the question of whether San Diego or San Antonio is larger. Second, a less-is-more effect can occur between domains, that is, when the same group of people achieve higher accuracy in a domain in which they know little than in a domain in which they know a lot. For instance, when American students were tested on the 22 largest American cities (such as New York versus Chicago) and on the 22 largest German cities (such as Cologne versus Frankfurt), they scored a median 71.0 percent (mean 71.1 percent) correct on their own cities but slightly higher on the less familiar German cities, with a median of 73.0 percent correct (mean 71.4 percent). This effect was obtained despite a handicap: Many Americans already knew the three largest US cities in order, and did not have to make any inferences (Goldstein & Gigerenzer, 2002). A similar less-is-more effect was demonstrated with Austrian students, whose scores for correct answers were slightly higher for the 75 largest American cities than for the 75 largest German cities (Hoffrage, 1995; see also Gigerenzer, 1993). Third, a less-is-more effect can occur during knowledge acquisition, that is, when an individual's performance curve first increases but then decreases again.

Less-is-more in groups

Consider now group decision making. Three people sit in front of a computer screen on which questions such as "Which city has more inhabitants: San Diego or San Antonio?" are displayed. The task of the group is to find the correct answer through discussion, and they are free to use whatever means. In this task, the correct solution is difficult to "prove" by an individual group member; thus, one might expect that the majority determines the group decision (the *majority rule*; see Gigone & Hastie, 1997). Consider now the following conflict. Two group members have heard of both cities and each concluded independently that city A is larger. But the third group member has not heard of A, only of B, and concludes that B is larger (relying on the recognition heuristic). After the three members finished their negotiation, what will their consensus be? Given that two members have at least some knowledge about both cities, one might expect that the consensus is always A, which is also what the majority rule predicts. In fact, in more than half of all cases (59 percent), the group voted for B (Reimer & Katsikopoulos, 2003). This number rose to 76 percent when two members relied on mere recognition.

That group members let their knowledge be dominated by others' lack of recognition may seem odd. But in fact this apparently irrational decision increased the overall accuracy of the group. This result can be analytically deduced (Reimer & Katsikopoulos, 2003) and intuitively seen from Figure 4.1. When the recognition heuristic is used in group decisions, then a less-is-more effect results if $\alpha > \beta$, just as in Figure 4.1, but more strongly. Consistent with the theory, Reimer and Katsikopoulos (2003) observed when two groups had the same average α and β, the group who recognized *fewer* cities (smaller *n*) typically had *more* correct answers. For instance, the members of one group recognized on average only 60 percent of the cities, and those in a second group 80 percent; but the first group got 83 percent answers correct in a series of over 100 questions, whereas the second only 75 percent. Thus, group members seem to intuitively trust the recognition heuristic, which can improve accuracy and lead to the counterintuitive less-is-more effect between groups.

Heuristics Based on Reasons

When recognition is not valid, or people know too much, heuristics can involve search for reasons or cues. A few years after his voyage on the *Beagle*, the 29-year-old Charles Darwin divided a scrap of paper (titled, "This is the Question") into two columns with the headings "Marry" and "Not Marry" and listed supporting reasons for each of the two possible courses of action, such as "nice soft wife on a sofa with good fire" opposed to "conversation of clever men at clubs." Darwin concluded that he should marry, writing "Marry – Marry – Marry Q.E.D" decisively beneath the first column (Darwin, 1969[1887], pp. 232–3). The following year, Darwin married his cousin, Emma Wedgwood, with whom he eventually had 10 children. How did Darwin decide to marry, based on the possible consequences he envisioned – children, loss of time, a constant companion? He did not tell us. But we can use his "Question" as a thought experiment to illustrate various visions of decision making.

Darwin searched in his memory for reasons. There are two visions of search: optimizing search and heuristic search. Following Wald's (1950) optimizing models of sequential analysis, several psychological theories postulated versions of sequential search and stopping rules (e.g., Busemeyer & Townsend, 1993; see Chapter 7, this volume). In the case of a binary hypothesis (such as to marry or not marry), the basic idea of most sequential models is the following: A threshold is calculated for accepting one of the two hypotheses, based on the costs of the two possible errors, such as wrongly deciding that to marry is the better option. Each reason or observation is then weighted and the evidence is accumulated until the threshold for one hypothesis is met, at which point search is stopped, and the hypothesis is accepted. If Darwin had followed this procedure, he would have had to estimate, consciously or unconsciously, how many conversations with clever friends are equivalent to having one child, and how many hours in a smoky abode can be traded against a lifetime of soft moments on the sofa. Weighting and adding is a mathematically convenient assumption, but it assumes that there is a common currency for all beliefs and desires in terms of quantitative probabilities and utilities. These models are often presented as *as-if* models, whose task is to predict the outcome rather than the process of decision making, although it has been suggested that the calculations might be performed unconsciously using the common currency of neural activation.

The second vision of search is that people use heuristics – either social heuristics or reason-based heuristics – that exploit some evolved capacities. Social heuristics exploit the capacity of humans for social learning and imitation (imitation need not result in learning), which is unmatched among the animal species. For instance, the following heuristic generates social facilitation (Laland, 2001):

> *Do-what-the-majority-do heuristic*: If you see the majority of your peers display a behavior, engage in the same behavior.

For the marriage problem, this heuristic makes a man start thinking of marriage at a time when most other men in one's social group do, say, around age 30. It is a most frugal heuristic, for one does not even have to think of pros and cons. Do-what-the-majority-do tends to be ecologically rational when (1) the observer and the demonstrators of the behavior are exposed to similar environments that (2) are stable rather than changing, and (3) noisy, that is, where it is hard to see what the immediate consequence of one's action is (Boyd & Richerson, 1985; Goldstein, Gigerenzer, Hogarth, et al., 2001).

Darwin, however, seems to have based his decision on reasons. I will describe two classes of heuristics that search for reasons. Unlike optimizing models, they do not both weight and add cues. One class of heuristics dispenses with adding, and searches cues in order (a simple form of weighing). I will refer to this class as *one-reason decision making*. The second class dispenses with weighing, and adds up cues until a threshold is met. I will refer to the second class as *tallying* heuristics. Each of the heuristics consists of three building blocks: a rule for search, stopping, and decision making. I will specify some of the conditions under which each class of heuristics will be successful, and in order to do this, I will turn to inference rather than preference.

Take The Best and tallying

Consider the task of predicting which alternative, *a* or *b*, has the higher value on a criterion, where *a* and *b* are elements of a set of *N* alternatives (which can be actions, objects, events). The prediction can be based on *M* binary cues $(1, 2, \ldots, i, \ldots, M)$, where the cue values 1 and 0 indicate higher and lower criterion values, respectively. To illustrate, consider an experiment by Newell, Weston, & Shanks (2003). The participants were presented with a series of choices between the shares of two fictional companies. In each trial, two companies were presented on a computer screen, and the participants were asked to infer which share would prove to be more profitable. To help find the more profitable share, participants could acquire information concerning six cues, such as: "Does the company invest in new projects?" and "Does the company have financial reserves?" The cost of information about each cue was 1p (penny). After participants had bought as many cues as they desired, they made their choice, and feedback was given whether the answer was correct. When the answer was correct, the participants received

7p minus the amount they had spent searching for information. How do people make an inference when they have to search for information?

One hypothesis about how people make inferences is the *Take The Best* heuristic (Gigerenzer & Goldstein, 1999), which is a form of one-reason decision making. It consists of three building blocks: a search rule, a stopping rule, and a decision rule:

Take The Best:
1   Search by validity: Search through cues in order of their validity. Look up the cue values of the cue with the highest validity first.
2   One-reason stopping rule: If one object has a positive cue value (1) and the other does not (0 or unknown), then stop search and proceed to Step 3. Otherwise exclude this cue and return to Step 1. If no more cues are found, guess.
3   One-reason decision making: Predict that the object with the positive cue value (1) has the higher value on the criterion.

The validity of a cue i is defined as $v_i = R_i/P_i$, where R_i = number of correct predictions by cue i, and P_i = number of pairs where the values of cue i differ between objects. In the Newell, Weston and Shanks (2003) task, for example, the participant would start by looking up the most valid cue for predicting profitability, and see if the two companies differed with respect to that cue. If they did, the participant would stop search and choose accordingly; if not, the participant would look up the next most valid cue, and repeat the process until a choice is made. By using this stopping rule, participants can draw inferences without having to look up all of the available cue values.

Now consider an example for a tallying heuristic, which relies on adding but not on weighing (or order):

Tallying:
1   Random search: Search through cues in random order. Look up the cue values.
2   Stopping rule: After m $(1 < m \leq M)$ cues, stop search and determine which object has more positive cue values (1), and proceed to Step 3. If the number is equal, return to Step 1 and search for another cue. If no more cues are found, guess.
3   Tallying rule: Predict that the object with the higher number of positive cue values (1) has the higher value on the criterion.

Versions of tallying have been discussed in the literature, such as unit-weight models in which all cues $(m = M)$, or the m significant cues are looked up (Dawes, 1979). Unlike as-if models, which predict outcomes only, these models of heuristics predict process and outcome, and can be subjected to a stronger test. In Newell, Weston, and Shanks's study (2003), each of the three building blocks was tested independently.

Search rule. In theory, participants can search through cues in many different ways. If they looked up all six cues (which is unlikely, given the pay-off function), there would be 6! = 720 different orders. The search rule of the tallying heuristic does not predict a specific order, but the search rule from the Take The Best heuristic makes a strong prediction. People will search by one of these orders, the one defined by v_i. In order to learn the validities, Newell, Weston, and Shanks (2003) exposed each participant to 120 learning trials, with feedback (correct/incorrect) given after each response. The six cues varied in their validity. The learning phase was followed by a test phase with 60 trials.

During the test phase, 75 percent of the participants followed the search rule of Take The Best. When there were only two cues, this number increased to 92 percent. Thus, the great majority of participants did not search randomly, but in order of validity.

Stopping rule. The logical possibilities for stopping search are fewer than those for search. There are six possibilities, after the first, second, . . ., sixth cue (not counting the possibility that people would not search but simply guess). Tallying postulates that participants add up more than one cue, but leaves open how many (i.e., the number m must be independently estimated). In contrast, Take The Best postulates that search is stopped immediately after the first discriminating cue is found, not beforehand and not later. Note that each stopping rule can be valid independent of the results for the search rule. For instance, people can search in one of the 719 orders not consistent with v_i but stop after the first discriminating cue is found, or search can follow validity but is only stopped after all cues have been looked up. Thus, the empirical result for the search rule does not constrain the stopping behavior. Newell, Weston, and Shanks (2003) reported that in 80 percent of all cases (where participants bought any information at all), participants did not continue beyond a single discriminating cue, and this number increased to 89 percent when there were only two cues. This means that the great majority stopped search immediately after they found the first cue that made a difference.

Decision rule. In theory, participants can use infinite ways to combine the information concerning six cues. This includes linear models, weighted or unweighted. If a person follows the one-reason stopping rule, this constrains the ways to arrive at a decision (whereas, as mentioned before, the search rules impose no constraints on the stopping and decision rules). If only one piece of discriminating information is obtained, it seems that the only reasonable decision rules left are forms of one-reason decision making. The multiple-reason stopping rule, in contrast, would not constrain possible decision rules. Newell, Weston, and Shanks (2003) report that the decision rule of Take The Best was followed by their participants in 89 percent of trials, both for six and two cues.

There are now a substantial number of experiments that have analyzed under what conditions people use Take The Best (e.g., Bröder, 2000, 2003; Newell & Shanks, 2003; Newell, Weston, and Shanks, 2003) and where Take The Best was compared with other heuristics or optimizing models in the same task (Bröder, 2000, 2002; Bröder & Schiffer, 2003a, 2003b; Lee & Cummins, in press; Newell, Rakow, Weston, & Shanks, in press; Rieskamp & Hoffrage, 1999; Rieskamp & Otto, 2004; Todorov, 2002). Comparatively little experimental work has examined tallying (Bröder, 2000; Rieskamp & Hoffrage, 1999). One-reason decision making has been observed in high-stake decisions. British magistrates tend to make bail decisions on the basis of one good reason only (Dhami, 2003; Dhami & Ayton, 2001), and so do British general practitioners when they prescribe lipid-lowering drugs (Dhami & Harries, 2001). Many parents rely on one reason to decide which doctor to drive to in the night when their child becomes seriously ill (Scott, 2002).

Take The Best and tallying have been proposed and tested as components of a number of judgmental processes, such as in probabilistic mental models theory (Gigerenzer, Hoffrage, & Kleinbölting, 1991; Slegers, Brake, & Doherty, 2000) and RAFT, the first process model for the hindsight bias (Hoffrage, Hertwig, & Gigerenzer, 2000). We know from many studies that hindsight bias sometimes occurs and sometimes does not. The process model can predict for each participant and question whether hindsight bias

Hindsight Bias: Confidence

Question: Which has more cholesterol, cake or pie?

Cues	Original	Feedback	Recall
Saturated fat (80%)	cake ? pie	"cake"	cake > pie
Calories (70%)	cake > pie		stop search
Protein (60%)	stop search		
Choice	cake		cake
Confidence	70%		80%

Figure 4.2 A process model of hindsight bias

Participants learn cues (saturated fat, calories, protein) and their validities (in parentheses) in order to judge which of two supermarket food items has more cholesterol. There are three points in time: original judgment, feedback, and recall of the original judgment. The original judgment is generated by Take The Best, which implies that cues are looked up in memory in the order of validity. In the example given, the first cue, saturated fat, does not stop search, because the participant is ignorant of whether cake or pie has a higher value (indicated by "?"). The second cue stops search because the participant learned that cake has more calories than pie (indicated by ">"). The answer is *cake* and the confidence is 70 percent, that is, the validity of the cue. At the second point in time, feedback is given that *cake* was correct. Feedback is automatically used to update missing information in memory about cues (question marks). Thus, at the time of the recall, the "?" for saturated fat is likely to have changed into ">", following the direction of feedback. Recall of the original judgment again follows Take The Best, but now the first cue stops search and the recalled answer is *cake* as before, whereas the recalled confidence is 80 percent, which is incorrect and known as hindsight bias. By manipulating what participants know and don't know, one can predict for each question whether hindsight bias will occur or not. *Source*: Hoffrage et al. (2000)

will or will not occur (Figure 4.2). The bias itself seems to be a byproduct of an adaptive memory updating process.

Ecological Rationality

What structures of environments can each of the two heuristics exploit? Consider a situation with five binary cues, as in Figure 4.3 (left), where the weights correspond to the order of cues in Take The Best. In an environment where the weights of the cues (e.g., beta weights) decrease exponentially, such as $1/2$, $1/4$, $1/8$, and so on, no linear model, including multiple regression, can outperform the faster and more frugal Take The Best. The proof is in Martignon & Hoffrage (1999, 2002). One can see this result intuitively because the sum of all cue weights to the right of a cue can never be larger than this cue's weight – they cannot compensate for the cues with higher weights. This type of environment is structured by *noncompensatory information*. Here, relying on one reason and ignoring the rest is as accurate as integrating all reasons by any linear method. Given the superior robustness of frugal heuristics (see below), Take The Best is actually likely to be more accurate.

Tallying will not do well with noncompensatory information. It can exploit environments where the cue weights do not differ much. In the extreme case shown in

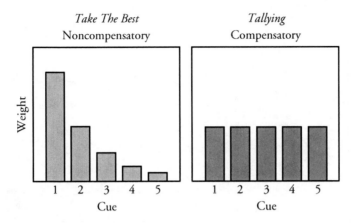

Figure 4.3 Ecological rationality of Take The Best and tallying

The environment on the left side has perfectly noncompensatory information (the weights of five binary cues decrease exponentially); the one on the right side has perfectly compensatory information (all weights are equal). Take The Best (but not tallying) can exploit noncompensatory information, and tallying (but not Take The Best) can exploit compensatory information.

Source: Martignon & Hoffrage (1999)

Figure 4.3 (right), where all cues have the same weights, one can see that a tallying heuristic that tallies all cues ($m = M$) will lead to the same accuracy as any linear model.

There are further structures that these two heuristics can exploit (Forster, Martignon, Vitouch, & Gigerenzer, 2003; Martignon & Hoffrage, 1999, 2002). For instance, when information is scarce, that is, the data points are few compared to the number of cues, then Take The Best and other simple heuristics will generally be of advantage compared to multiple regression and other statistical models that need large learning samples (Gigerenzer et al., 1999; Chater, Oaksford, Nakisa, & Redington, 2003).

How Do People Know Which Heuristic to Use?

Research suggests that people hardly ever make conscious decisions about which heuristic to use, but that they quickly and unconsciously tend to adapt heuristics to changing environments, provided there is feedback (Payne et al., 1993). This adaptive process is illustrated by an experiment by Rieskamp and Otto (2004). Participants took on the role of bank consultants with the task of evaluating which of two companies applying for a loan was more creditworthy on the basis of six cues, such as qualification of employees and profitability (similar to the experiment by Newell et al., 2003, except that there were no costs for looking up cue values). For the first 24 pairs of companies, no feedback was provided as to the correctness of the participant's inference. Participants followed Take The Best in only about 30 percent of the cases, which is not unusual for situations where information is free. In the following trials, feedback was given. For one group of participants, the environment was noncompensatory (see Figure 4.3), that is, the company that was more creditworthy was determined by the cue with the highest validity (on which

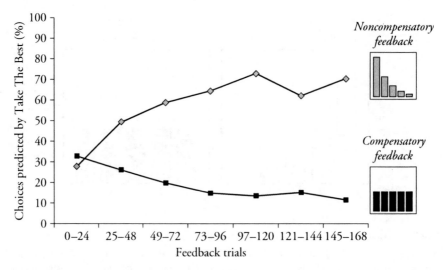

Figure 4.4 How people adapt their heuristics to the structure of environment

Source: Based on Rieskamp & Otto (2004)

the two companies differed) in about 90 percent of the cases. For the second group, the environment was compensatory, that is, feedback was determined by the weighted additive rule in about 90 percent of the cases. Did people intuitively adapt their heuristics to the structure of the environment? As can be seen in Figure 4.4, feedback about the structure of the environment changed the frequency of using Take The Best. People learned without instruction that different heuristics are successful in different environments. Bröder (2003) reported that people with higher IQs are better at detecting the structure of the environment, and consequently in knowing which heuristic to use. While individual correlates of strategy use are difficult to find, individual correlates of strategy adaptation seem to be easier to demonstrate.

   This experiment illustrates individual learning by feedback. Which heuristic to use for which problem can also be learned by evolutionary and cultural learning. For instance, a female guppy comes already equipped with a heuristic for mate choice, which resembles Take The Best (Dugatkin, 1996). When she has to decide between two potential mates, the most important cue seems to be the extent of orange color. If one male is noticeably more orange than the other, this cue is sufficient to stop search and decide in favor of him. Evolutionary learning is slowest, while social learning is the fastest way to learn what heuristic to use when. A novice baseball outfielder, pilot, or sailor can be taught the gaze heuristic in a few minutes.

Robustness

A good heuristic needs to be robust. *Robustness* is the ability to make predictions about the future or new events, whereas *fitting* refers to the ability to fit the past or already known

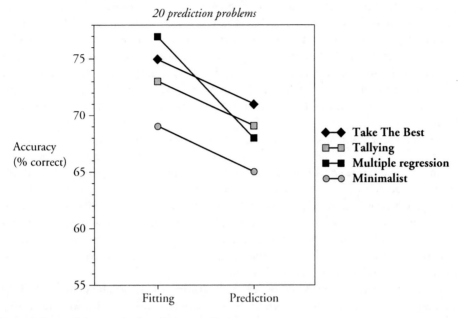

Figure 4.5 Simplicity can lead to higher predictive accuracy

The predictive power of three heuristics is compared to that of multiple regression in 20 problems. Two of the heuristics (Take The Best and minimalist) are from the one-reason decision-making family; the third is from the tallying family (unit weight linear model). The 20 prediction problems include psychological, economic, environmental, biological, and health problems. Most were taken from statistical textbooks, where they served as good examples for the application of multiple regression. The number of cues varied between 3 and 19, and these were binary or dichotomized at the median. For each of the 20 problems and each of the four strategies, the 95 percent confidence intervals were ≤ 0.42 percentage points. Although multiple regression has the best fit, two of the heuristics have higher predictive accuracy.
Source: Czerlinski et al. (1999)

data. An excellent fit can mean little more than *overfitting* (Mitchell, 1997; Roberts & Pashler, 2000). To define overfitting, we need to distinguish between a learning sample from which a model estimated its parameters and the test sample on which it is tested. Both samples are randomly drawn from the same population.

> *Definition*: A model O *overfits* the learning sample if there exists an alternative model O' such that O has a smaller error than O' in the learning sample but a larger error in the test sample. In this case, O' is called the more *robust* model.

Consider Figure 4.5, which shows the accuracy of three heuristics compared to multiple regression, averaged across 20 real-world problems (Czerlinski, Gigerenzer, & Goldstein, 1999). In each problem, the task was to predict which of two objects scores higher on a criterion. For instance, one problem was to predict which Chicago public high school has the higher dropout rate. The cues included the attendance rates of the students, the socioeconomic and ethnic compositions of the student bodies, the sizes of the classes, and the scores of the students on various standardized tests. Other problems involved the prediction of people's attractiveness judgments, of homelessness rates, of professors' salaries, and of adolescents' obesity at age 18. The three heuristics were Take The Best, minimalist (which is like take the best but searches cues in random order), and a tallying heuristic that looks up all cues ($m = M$), that is, a unit-weight linear rule. Take The Best and minimalist were most frugal; they looked up, on average, only 2.4 and 2.2 cues before they stopped search. Tallying and multiple regression looked up all cue information (exhaustive search), which amounted to an average of 7.7 cues. How accurate were the heuristics?

The important point is to distinguish between data fitting and prediction. In data fitting, the test set is the same as the training set, and here it is a mathematical truism that models with more adjustable parameters generally do better. Consequently, multiple regression had the best fit. However, the true test of a model concerns its predictive accuracy, which was tested by cross-validation, that is, the four models learned their parameters on half of the data, and were tested on the other half. The predictive accuracy of Take The Best and tallying was, on average, higher than that of multiple regression. This result may sound paradoxical because multiple regression processed all the information and more than each of the heuristics did.

Figure 4.5 shows that multiple regression overfitted the data relative to both Take The Best and tallying (see also Dawes, 1979). An intuitive way to understand overfitting is the following: a set of observations consists of information that generalizes to the other samples, and of information that does not (e.g., noise). If one extracts too much information from the data, one will get a better fit (a higher *explained variance*), but one will mistake more noise for predictive information. The result can be a substantial decrease in one's predictive power. Note that both forms of simplifying – dispensing either with adding or with weighting – resulted in greater robustness. Minimalist, however, which dispensed with both weighting and adding, extracted too little information from the data.

In general, the predictive accuracy of a model increases with its fit, decreases with its number of adjustable parameters, and the difference between fit and predictive accuracy gets smaller with larger number of data points (Akaike, 1973; Forster & Sober, 1994). The general lesson is that in judgments under uncertainty, one has to ignore information in order to make good predictions. The art is to ignore the right kind. Heuristics that promote simplicity, such as using the best reason that allows one to make a decision and ignore the rest, have a good chance of focusing on the information that generalizes.

These results may appear counterintuitive. More information is always better; more choice is always better – so the story goes. This cultural bias makes contrary findings look like weird oddities (Hertwig & Todd, 2003). Yet experts base their judgments on surprisingly few pieces of information (Shanteau, 1992), and professional handball players make better decisions when they have less time (Johnson & Raab, 2003). People can form reliable impressions of strangers from video clips lasting half a minute (Ambady & Rosenthal, 1993), shoppers buy more when there are fewer varieties (Iyengar & Lepper, 2000), and zero-intelligence traders make as much profit as intelligent people do in experimental markets (Gode & Sunder, 1993). Last but not least, satisficers are reported to be more optimistic and have higher self-esteem and life satisfaction, whereas maximizers excel in depression, perfectionism, regret, and self-blame (Schwartz, Ward, Monterosso, Lyubomirsky, White, & Lehman, 2002). Less can be more.

The Building Blocks of Heuristics

One way to think of the relation between heuristics and their building blocks is the periodic table in chemistry, where there are many elements but only few particles. Just as the same particles combine to new chemical elements, the same building blocks can construct new heuristics to deal with new tasks. Consider the following problem.

A man is rushed to the hospital with serious chest pains. The doctors suspect acute ischemic heart disease (myocardial infarction) and need to make a decision, and they need to make it quickly: Should the patient be assigned to the coronary care unit or to a regular nursing bed with ECG telemetry? In a Michigan hospital, doctors sent 90 percent of their patients to the coronary care unit. This defensive decision making led to overcrowding, decreased the quality of care provided, and became a health risk for patients who should not have been in the unit. An expert system with some 50 probabilities and a logistic regression did better than the physicians, but physicians do not like to use these systems because they are not transparent, that is, they don't understand them. To find a solution, researchers at the University of Michigan Hospital (Green & Mehr, 1997) used the building blocks of Take The Best to design a classification heuristic in the form of a fast and frugal tree (Figure 4.6). If a patient has a certain anomaly in his electrocardiogram (the so-called ST segment), he is immediately admitted to the coronary

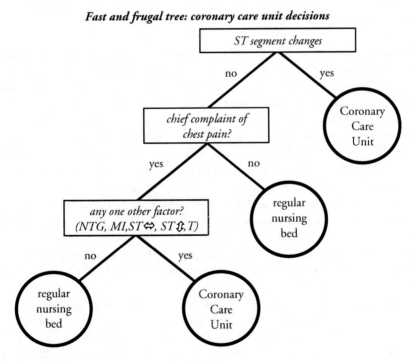

Fast and frugal tree: coronary care unit decisions

Figure 4.6 A heuristic for coronary care unit allocation

Source: Based on Green & Mehr (1997)

care unit. No other information is required. If that is not the case, a second variable is considered: whether the patient's primary complaint is chest pain. If this is not the case, he is immediately classified as low risk and assigned to a regular nursing bed. No further information is considered. If the answer is yes, then a third, composite question is asked to finally classify the patient.

Green and Mehr (1997) report that the fast and frugal tree was more accurate (as measured by the occurrence of myocardial infarction) than physician's decisions. It had a higher sensitivity and a smaller false positive rate. The heuristic was also more accurate than the expert system that had all the information that the fast and frugal tree had, and more.

A fast and frugal tree is defined as a classification tree that allows for a classification at each level of the tree. It has $M + 1$ exits or end nodes (M is the number of variables or cues). In contrast, the number 2^M of end nodes of a complete tree increases exponentially, which makes complete trees computationally intractable for large numbers of variables. A fast and frugal tree has the same building blocks as Take The Best: ordered search, one-reason stopping rule, and one-reason decision making. When the clinical cues follow the structure of Figure 4.3 (left), one can show that no logistic regression can be more accurate than the heuristic. When the clinical cues follow a more compensatory structure (Figure 4.3, right), then a tallying heuristic will be more accurate. A tallying heuristic for the care unit allocation problem is as follows (Forster et al. 2003):

> *Tally Three*: If three positive cue values are present, stop search and send patient to the coronary care unit.

Both heuristics for classification are transparent, that is, physicians can understand their logic easily and therefore are more willing to accept and actually use them than a logistic regression. The predictive accuracy of these heuristics is high: (1) if they can exploit the structure of the environment (see Figure 4.3), and (2) because simplicity tends to promote robustness. Note that the logistic regression may have had an excellent fit in the clinical population where it was originally validated, but it is now applied in a Michigan hospital with a patient population that differs to an unknown extent. That is, unlike the situation in Figure 4.5, where the training and test samples were drawn from the same population, robustness here refers to an unknown population.

Systematic teaching of fast and frugal decision making is currently being introduced into medicine as an alternative to classical decision theory (Elwyn, Edwards, Eccles, & Rovner, 2001), and also as an explication of the superb intuitions of master clinicians (Naylor, 2001; see also Chapter 15, this volume). Fast and frugal trees have been proposed as normative guidelines, such as when to prescribe antibiotics to young children (Fischer et al., 2002).

For classification problems with a larger number of categories, heuristics can rely on *elimination* rather than one-reason decision making or tallying. This building block is part of *categorization by elimination* (Berretty, Todd, & Martignon, 1999) and of a heuristic that can solve problems that involve quantitative estimation, *QuickEst* (Hertwig, Hoffrage, & Martignon, 1999). It was used earlier for preferential choice in *elimination by aspects* (Tversky, 1972). Building blocks for heuristics not covered in this chapter include aspiration levels (as in mate choice; see Todd & Miller, 1999), social notions of equity (as in parental investment; see Hertwig, Davis, & Sulloway, 2002), social norms (as in conformism; see Boyd & Richerson, 2001), and emotional processes, whose function can be analog to that of cognitive building blocks, yet stronger and longer lasting (see the chapters in Gigerenzer & Selten, 2001). For instance, falling in love can be seen as a powerful stopping rule that ends search for a partner and fosters commitment. Disgust can limit the choice set, and social norms can free us from having to think about how to make decisions all the time.

The Adaptive Toolbox

The study of smart heuristics is concerned with identifying (1) the building blocks of heuristics, and (2) the structures of environments that a given heuristic can exploit, that is, the kind of problems it can solve. In other words, its first objective is the study of the adaptive toolbox, and the second that of ecological rationality, with aims that are both descriptive and prescriptive. The study of the adaptive toolbox aims at description, including individual differences in the use of heuristics, and the change in the adaptive toolbox over the life course (Gigerenzer, 2003). Models of heuristics allow for qualitative predictions, such as whether players will catch a ball while running or the conditions in which hindsight bias will and will not occur. They also allow for quantitative predictions, such as the proportion of correct answers when using the recognition heuristic. Consistent with Bayesian model testing (MacKay, 1992), the strongest tests can be obtained from: (1) counterintuitive predictions, such as the less-is-more effect in individual and group decision making, and (2) models with zero adjustable parameters, such as the search, stopping, and decision rules of Take The Best.

The study of ecological rationality, in contrast, is descriptive and prescriptive. Its results concerning the match between heuristics and structures of environments can be used to derive hypotheses about people's adaptive use of heuristics. These results also carry prescriptive force. For instance, when the available information is noncompensatory, we can recommend a fast and frugal tree for classification, or Take The Best for paired comparison, because these heuristics will predict as well as any linear model, yet faster, more frugally, and more transparently. If in addition the available information is scarce, we expect that the heuristics will be more accurate, because they tend to be robust. Most problems that worry our minds and hearts are computationally intractable – no machine or mind can find the optimal solution. The systematic study of fast and frugal heuristics can provide normative recommendations on an empirical basis, even when we can never know the best solution.

In this chapter, I invited you to a journey into a land of rationality that is different from the familiar one we know where the sun of enlightenment shines down in beams of logic and probability. The new land of rationality we set out to explore is shrouded in a dim mist of uncertainty, populated with people who have limited time and knowledge, but with smart heuristics at their disposal. Welcome, and I hope you feel at home in this world.

Acknowledgment

I am grateful for comments by Jerome R. Busemeyer, Anja Dieckmann, Barbara Fasolo, William Goldstein, Nigel Harvey, Ralph Hertwig, Ulrich Hoffrage, Oswald Huber, Derek Koehler, Craig McKenzie, Ben R. Newell, Torsten Reimer, Jörg Rieskamp, Lael Schooler, and Peter Todd.

References

Akaike, H. (1973) Information theory and an extension of the maximum likelihood principle. In B. N. Petrov and F. Csaki (eds.), *2nd International Symposium on Information Theory* (pp. 267–81). Budapest: Akademiai Kiado.

Ambady, N. & Rosenthal, R. (1993) Half a minute: Predicting teacher evaluations from thin slices of nonverbal behavior and physical attractiveness, *Journal of Personality and Social Psychology*, 64, 431–41.

Ayton, P. & Önkal, D. (1997) Forecasting football fixtures: Confidence and judged proportion correct. Unpublished manuscript.

Berretty, P. M., Todd, P. M., & Martignon, L. (1999) Categorization by elimination: Using few cues to choose. In G. Gigerenzer, P. M. Todd, and the ABC Research Group, *Simple Heuristics that Make Us Smart* (pp. 235–57). New York: Oxford University Press.

Boyd, R. & Richerson, P. J. (1985) *Culture and the Evolutionary Process*. Chicago: University of Chicago Press.

Boyd, R. & Richerson, P. J. (2001) Norms and bounded rationality. In G. Gigerenzer and R. Selten (eds.), *Bounded Rationality: The Adaptive Toolbox* (pp. 281–96). Cambridge, MA: MIT Press.

Bröder, A. (2000) Assessing the empirical validity of the "Take The Best"-heuristic as a model of human probabilistic inference, *Journal of Experimental Psychology: Learning, Memory, and Cognition*, 26, 1332–46.

Bröder, A. (2002) Take The Best, Dawes' Rule, and compensatory decision strategies: A regression-based classification method, *Quality & Quantity*, 36, 219–38.

Bröder, A. (2003) Decision making with the "adaptive toolbox": Influence of environmental structure, intelligence, and working memory load, *Journal of Experimental Psychology: Learning, Memory, and Cognition*, 29, 611–25.

Bröder, A. & Schiffer, S. (2003a) Bayesian strategy assessment in multi-attribute decision making, *Journal of Behavioral Decision Making*, 16, 193–213.

Bröder, A. & Schiffer, S. (2003b) Take The Best versus simultaneous feature matching: Probabilistic inferences from memory and effects of representation format, *Journal of Experimental Psychology: General*, 132, 277–93.

Busemeyer, J. R. & Townsend, J. T. (1993) Decision field theory: A dynamic-cognitive approach to decision making in an uncertain environment, *Psychological Review*, 100, 432–59.

Camerer, C. F. (1998) Bounded rationality in individual decision making, *Experimental Economics*, 1, 163–83.

Chater, N., Oaksford, M., Nakisa, R., & Redington, M. (2003) Fast, frugal, and rational: How rational norms explain behavior, *Organizational Behavior and Human Decision Processes*, 90, 63–86.

Conlisk, J. (1996) Why bounded rationality? *Journal of Economic Literature*, 34, 669–700.

Cosmides, L. & Tooby, J. (1992) Cognitive adaptations for social exchange. In J. H. Barkow, L. Cosmides, and J. Tooby (eds.), *The Adapted Mind: Evolutionary Psychology and the Generation of Culture* (pp. 163–228). Oxford: Oxford University Press.

Craik, F. I. M. & McDowd, M. (1987) Age differences in recall and recognition, *Journal of Experimental Psychology: Learning, Memory and Cognition*, 14, 474–79.

Czerlinski, J., Gigerenzer, G., & Goldstein, D. G. (1999) How good are simple heuristics? In G. Gigerenzer, P. M. Todd, and the ABC Research Group, *Simple Heuristics that Make Us Smart* (pp. 97–118). New York: Oxford University Press.

Darwin, C. (1969) *The Autobiography of Charles Darwin, 1809–1882*. New York: Norton. (Original work published 1887.)

Dawes, R. M. (1979) The robust beauty of improper linear models in decision making, *American Psychologist*, 34, 571–82.

Dawes, R. M. & Corrigan, B. (1974) Linear models in decision making, *Psychological Bulletin*, 81, 95–106.

Dawes, R. M. & Mulford, M. (1996) The false consensus effect and overconfidence: Flaws in judgment, or flaws in how we study judgment? *Organizational Behavior and Human Decision Processes*, 65, 201–11.

Dawkins, R. (1976) *The Selfish Gene*. Oxford: Oxford University Press.

Dhami, M. K. (2003) Psychological models of professional decision-making, *Psychological Science*, 14, 175–80.

Dhami, M. K. & Ayton, P. (2001) Bailing and jailing the fast and frugal way, *Journal of Behavioral Decision Making*, 14, 141–68.

Dhami, M. K. & Harries, C. (2001) Fast and frugal versus regression models in human judgement, *Thinking & Reasoning*, 7, 5–27.

Dugatkin, L. A. (1996) Interface between culturally based preferences and genetic preferences: Female mate choice in Poecilia reticulata, *Proceedings of the National Academy of Sciences, USA*, 93, 2770–3.

Elwyn, G., Edwards, A., Eccles, M., & Rovner, D. (2001) Decision analysis in patient care, *The Lancet*, 358, 571–4.

Erev, I., Wallsten, T. S., & Budescu, D. V. (1994) Simultaneous over- and underconfidence: The role of error in judgment processes, *Psychological Review*, 101, 519–27.

Fiedler, K., Walther, E., & Nickel, S. (1999) Covariation-based attribution: On the ability to assess multiple covariates of an effect, *Personality & Social Psychology Bulletin*, 25, 607–22.

Fischer, J. E., Steiner, F., Zucol, F., Berger, C., Martignon, L., Bossart, W., et al. (2002) Use of simple heuristics to target macrolide prescription in children with community-acquired pneumonia, *Archives of Pediatrics and Adolescent Medicine*, 156, 1005–8.

Forster, M., Martignon, L., Vitouch, O., & Gigerenzer, G. (2003, forthcoming) Simple heuristics versus complex predictive instruments: Which is better and why? Manuscript submitted for publication.

Forster, M. & Sober, E. (1994). How to tell when simpler, more unified, and less *ad hoc* theories will provide more accurate predictions, *British Journal of the Philosophy of Science*, 45, 1–35.

Gallistel, C. R. (1990) *The Organization of Learning*. Cambridge, MA: MIT Press.

Gigerenzer, G. (1993) The bounded rationality of probabilistic mental models. In K. I. Manktelow and D. E. Over (eds.), *Rationality: Psychological and Philosophical Perspectives* (pp. 284–313). London: Routledge.

Gigerenzer, G. (1996) On narrow norms and vague heuristics: A rebuttal to Kahneman and Tversky (1996), *Psychological Review*, 103, 592–6.

Gigerenzer, G. (2000) *Adaptive Thinking: Rationality in the Real World*. New York Oxford University Press.

Gigerenzer, G. (2002) *Calculated Risks: How to Know When Numbers Deceive You*. New York: Simon & Schuster. (UK edition: *Reckoning with Risk. Learning to Live with Uncertainty*. London: Penguin.)

Gigerenzer, G. (2003) The adaptive toolbox and lifespan development: Common questions? In U. M. Staudinger and U. E. R. Lindenberger (eds.), *Interactive Minds: Life-span Perspectives on the Social Foundation of Cognition* (pp. 319–46). Cambridge: Cambridge University Press.

Gigerenzer, G. (2004) Striking a blow for sanity in theories of rationality. In M. Augier and J. G. March (eds.), *Models of a Man: Essays in Memory of Herbert A. Simon* (pp. 389–409). Cambridge, MA: MIT Press.

Gigerenzer, G. & Fiedler, K. (2004) Minds in environments: The potential of an ecological approach to cognition. Manuscript submitted for publication.

Gigerenzer, G. & Goldstein, D. G. (1999) Betting on one good reason: The Take The Best heuristic. In G. Gigerenzer, P. M. Todd, and the ABC Research Group, *Simple Heuristics that Make Us Smart* (pp. 75–95). New York: Oxford University Press.

Gigerenzer, G., Hoffrage, U., & Kleinbölting, H. (1991) Probabilistic mental models: A Brunswikian theory of confidence, *Psychological Review*, 98, 506–28.

Gigerenzer, G. & Murray, D. J. (1987) *Cognition as Intuitive Statistics*. Hillsdale, NJ: Erlbaum.

Gigerenzer, G. & Regier, T. (1996) How do we tell an association from a rule? Comment on Sloman (1996), *Psychological Bulletin*, 119, 23–6.

Gigerenzer, G. & Selten, R. (eds.) (2001) *Bounded Rationality: The Adaptive Toolbox*. Cambridge, MA: MIT Press.

Gigerenzer, G., Todd, P. M., & the ABC Research Group (1999) *Simple Heuristics that Make Us Smart*. New York: Oxford University Press.

Gigone, D. & Hastie, R. (1997) The impact of information on small group choice, *Journal of Personality and Social Pscyhology*, 72, 132–40.

Gode, D. K. & Sunder, S. (1993) Allocative efficiency of markets with zero-intelligence traders: Market as a partial substitute for individual rationality, *Journal of Political Economy*, 101, 119–37.

Goldstein, D. G. & Gigerenzer, G. (2002) Models of ecological rationality: The recognition heuristic, *Psychological Review*, 109, 75–90.

Goldstein, D. G., Gigerenzer, G., Hogarth, R. M., Kacelnik, A., Kareev, Y., Klein, G., et al. (2001) Group report: Why and when do simple heuristics work? In G. Gigerenzer and R. Selten (eds.), *Bounded Rationality: The Adaptive Toolbox* (pp. 173–90). Cambridge, MA: MIT Press.

Green, L. & Mehr, D. R. (1997) What alters physicians' decisions to admit to the coronary care unit? *The Journal of Family Practice*, 45, 219–26.

Griggs, R. A. & Cox, J. R. (1982) The elusive thematic-materials effect in Wason's selection task, *British Journal of Psychology*, 73, 407–20.

Hertwig, R., Davis, J. N., & Sulloway, F. J. (2002) Parental investment: How an equity motive can produce inequality, *Psychological Bulletin*, 128, 728–45.

Hertwig, R. & Gigerenzer, G. (1999) The "conjunction fallacy" revisited: How intelligent inferences look like reasoning errors, *Journal of Behavioral Decision Making*, 12, 275–305.

Hertwig, R., Hoffrage, U., & Martignon, L. (1999) Quick estimation: Letting the environment do the work. In G. Gigerenzer, P. M. Todd, & the ABC Research Group, *Simple Heuristics that Make Us Smart* (pp. 209–34). New York: Oxford University Press.

Hertwig, R. & Todd, P. M. (2003). More is not always better: The benefits of cognitive limits. In D. Hardman and L. Macchi (eds.), *Reasoning and Decision Making: A Handbook* (pp. 213–31). Chichester: Wiley.

Hoffrage, U. (1995) Zur Angemessenheit subjektiver Sicherheits-Urteile: Eine Exploration der Theorie der probabilistischen mentalen Modelle [The adequacy of subjective confidence judgments: Studies concerning the theory of probabilistic mental models]. Unpublished doctoral dissertation, University of Salzburg, Austria.

Hoffrage, U., Hertwig, R., & Gigerenzer, G. (2000) Hindsight bias: A by-product of knowledge updating? *Journal of Experimental Psychology: Learning, Memory, and Cognition*, 26, 566–81.

Holton, G. (1988) *Thematic Origins of Scientific Thought* (2nd edn.). Cambridge, MA: Harvard University Press.

Iyengar, S. S. & Lepper, M. R. (2000) When choice is demotivating: Can one desire too much of a good thing? *Journal of Personality and Social Psychology*, 79, 995–1006.

Johnson, J. G. & Raab, M. (2003) Take the first: Option generation and resulting choices, *Organizational Behavior and Human Decision Processes*, 91, 215–29.

Juslin, P., Winman, A., & Olsson, H. (2000) Naive empiricism and dogmatism in confidence research: A critical examination of the hard-easy effect, *Psychological Review*, 107, 384–96.

Kahneman, D., Slovic, P., & Tversky, A. (eds.) (1982) *Judgment Under Uncertainty: Heuristics and Biases*. Cambridge, UK: Cambridge University Press.

Kahneman, D. & Tversky, A. (1996) On the reality of cognitive illusions. A reply to Gigerenzer's critique, *Psychological Review*, 103, 582–91.

Keeney, R. L. & Raiffa, H. (1993) *Decisions with Multiple Objectives*. Cambridge, UK: Cambridge University Press.

Laland, K. N. (2001) Imitation, social learning, and preparedness as mechanisms of bounded rationality. In G. Gigerenzer and R. Selten (eds.), *Bounded Rationality: The Adaptive Toolbox* (pp. 233–47). Cambridge, MA: MIT Press.

Lee, M. D. & Cummins, T. D. R. (in press) Evidence accumulation in decision making. Unifying "Take the best" and "rational" models, *Psychonomic Bulletin & Review*.

Lopes, L. L. (1992) Risk perception and the perceived public. In D. W. Bromley and K. Segerson (eds.), *The Social Response to Environmental Risk* (pp. 57–73). Boston: Kluwer Academic Publishers.

Lynch, P. (1994) *Beating the Street*. New York: Schuster & Schuster.

MacKay, D. J. C. (1992) Bayesian interpolation, *Neural Computation*, 4, 415–47.

McKenzie, C. R. M. & Amin, M. B. (2002) When wrong predictions provide more support than right ones, *Psychonomic Bulletin & Review*, 9, 821–8.

McLeod, P. & Dienes, Z. (1996) Do fielders know where to go to catch the ball or only how to get there? *Journal of Experimental Psychology: Human Perception and Performance*, 22, 531–43.

Martignon, L. & Hoffrage, U. (1999) Why does one-reason decision making work? A case study in ecological rationality. In G. Gigerenzer, P. M. Todd, and the ABC Research Group, *Simple Heuristics that Make Us Smart* (pp. 119–40). New York: Oxford University Press.

Martignon, L. & Hoffrage, U. (2002) Fast, frugal and fit: Lexicographic heuristics for paired comparison, *Theory and Decision*, 52, 29–71.

Michalewicz, Z. & Fogel, D. B. (2000) *How to Solve It: Modern Heuristics*. New York: Springer.

Mitchell, T. M. (1997) *Machine Learning*. New York: McGraw-Hill International.

Naylor, C. D. (2001) Clinical decisions: From art to science and back again, *The Lancet*, 358, 523–4.

Newell, B. R., Rakow, T., Weston, N. J., & Shanks, D. R. (in press) Search strategies in decision-making: The success of "success," *Journal of Behavioral Decision Making*.

Newell, B. R. & Shanks, D. R. (2003) Take the best or look at the rest? Factors influencing "one-reason" decision-making, *Journal of Experimental Psychology: Learning, Memory, and Cognition*, 29, 53–65.

Newell, B. R., Weston, N., & Shanks, D. R. (2003) Empirical tests of a fast and frugal heuristic: Not everyone "takes-the-best," *Organizational Behavior and Human Decision Processes*, 91, 82–96.

Oaksford, M. & Chater, N. (1994) A rational analysis of the selection task as optimal data selection, *Psychological Review*, 101, 608–31.

Payne, J. W., Bettman, J. R., & Johnson, E. J. (1993) *The Adaptive Decision Maker*. Cambridge, UK: Cambridge University Press.

Polya, G. (1954) *Mathematics and Plausible Reasoning, Vol. 1: Induction and Analogy in Mathematics*. Princeton, NJ: Princeton University Press.

Reimer, T. & Katsikopoulos, K. (2003) Group decision-making, recognition heuristic, and less-is-more effect. Manuscript submitted for publication.

Rieskamp, J. & Hoffrage, U. (1999) When do people use simple heuristics, and how can we tell? In G. Gigerenzer, P. M. Todd, and the ABC Research Group, *Simple Heuristics that Make Us Smart* (pp. 141–67). New York: Oxford University Press.

Rieskamp, J. & Otto, P. E. (2004) Adaptive strategy selection in decision making: The learning rule theory. Manuscript submitted for publication.

Roberts, S. & Pashler, H. (2000) How persuasive is a good fit? A comment on theory testing, *Psychological Review*, 107, 358–67.

Rosander, K. & Hofsten, C. von (2002) Development of gaze tracking of small and large objects, *Experimental Brain Research*, 146, 257–64.

Schwartz, B., Ward, A., Monterosso, J., Lyubomirsky, S., White, K., & Lehman, D. R. (2002) Maximizing versus satisficing: Happiness is a matter of choice, *Journal of Personality and Social Psychology*, 83, 1178–97.

Scott, A. (2002). Identifying and analysing dominant preferences in discrete choice experiments: An application in health care, *Journal of Economic Psychology*, 23, 383–98.

Sedlmeier, P., Hertwig, R., & Gigerenzer, G. (1998) Are judgments of the positional frequencies of letters systematical biased due to availability? *Journal of Experimental Psychology: Learning, Memory, and Cognition*, 24, 754–70.

Selten, R. (2001) What is bounded rationality? In G. Gigerenzer and R. Selten (eds.), *Bounded Rationality: the Adaptive Toolbox* (pp. 13–36). Cambridge, MA: MIT Press.

Sen, A. (2002) *Rationality and Freedom*. Cambridge, MA: Harvard University Press.

Shaffer, D. M. & McBeath, M. K. (2002) Baseball outfielders maintain a linear optical trajectory when tracking uncatchable fly balls, *Journal of Experimental Psychology: Human Perception and Performance*, 28, 335–48.

Shanteau, J. (1992) How much information does an expert use? Is it relevant? *Acta Psychologica*, 81, 75–86.

Simon, H. A. (1955) A behavioral model of rational choice, *Quarterly Journal of Economics*, 69, 99–118.

Simon, H. A. (1956) Rational choice and the structure of environments, *Psychological Review*, 63, 129–38.

Simon, H. A. (1982) *Models of Bounded Rationality*. Cambridge, MA: MIT Press.

Simon, H. A. (1990) Invariants of human behavior, *Annual Review of Psychology*, 41, 1–19.

Slegers, D. W., Brake, G. L., & Doherty, M. E. (2000) Probabilistic mental models with continuous predictors, *Organizational Behavior and Human Decision Processes*, 81, 98–114.

Todd, P. (2001) Fast and frugal heuristics for environmentally bounded minds. In G. Gigerenzer and R. Selten (eds.), *Bounded Rationality. The Adaptive Toolbox* (pp. 51–70). Cambridge, MA: MIT Press.

Todd, P. M. & Gigerenzer, G. (2000) Precis of *Simple Heuristics that Make Us Smart*, *Behavioral and Brain Sciences*, 23, 727–80.

Todd, P. M. & Miller, G. F. (1999) From pride to prejudice to persuasion: Satisficing in mate search. In G. Gigerenzer, P. M. Todd, and the ABC Research Group, *Simple Heuristics that Make Us Smart* (pp. 287–308). New York: Oxford University Press.

Todorov, A. (2002) Predicting real outcomes: When heuristics are as smart as statistical models. Unpublished manuscript.

Tversky, A. (1972) Elimination by aspects: A theory of choice, *Psychological Review*, 79, 281–99.

Tversky, A. & Kahneman, D. (1974) Judgment under uncertainty: Heuristics and biases, *Science*, 185, 1124–31.

Wald, A. (1950) *Statistical Decision Functions*. New York: Wiley.

5

Yet Another Look at the Heuristics and Biases Approach

Gideon Keren and Karl H. Teigen

Introduction

The research approach that has become to be known as the *heuristics and biases* research program, initially launched in the beginning of the 1970s by Amos Tversky and Daniel Kahneman (1974), has been highly influential in shaping the field of judgment and decision making. Its main aim was to study people's intuitions about uncertainty and the extent to which they were compatible with the normative probability calculus. It stimulated hundreds of articles designed to test the robustness as well as the limitations of this approach. Like any successful research program it did not escape critical evaluation. Indeed, several authors raised their doubts regarding the ecological validity and logical soundness of this approach (e.g., Cohen, 1981; Gigerenzer 1991, 1996). Even the originators of this highly successful program have, during the course of time as research results accumulated, changed their perspective and suggested new interpretations (e.g., Tversky and Kahneman, 1974 vs. Kahneman and Frederick, 2002). Indeed, given abundant new studies and an increasing list of heuristics and biases, the understanding of the term has gradually changed, and acquired some new interpretations.

The success of the heuristic and biases research program to attract so much attention and stimulate an ever increasing stream of studies can be explained on several grounds. First, having been launched shortly after the so called "cognitive revolution," it raised interest for two opposing reasons. On the one hand, this research program and its method of investigation matched well the principles underlying the cognitive paradigm and the belief that human behavior could (and should) be explained mainly in cognitive terms. It offered a new experimental methodology to the study of cognitive processes. At the same time it implicitly challenged some tacit assumptions about the abilities and the limits of the cognitive system. It was probably this latter aspect that associated the heuristics and biases research program with the broad problem of rationality. The dispute concerning rationality, implied by the empirically exhibited biases, had implications not just for psychology. It challenged the fundamental assumptions underlying economic theory. Thus, the initial results reported by Kahneman and Tversky (1972, 1973; Tversky & Kahneman, 1972, 1974) carried an important message not just for psychology but for the social sciences in general.

Second, this research program evolved from previous investigations that laid the ground for the systematic study of how people cope with uncertainty and, in particular, the extent to which they obey the probability calculus. Precursors included the study of probability matching (Hake & Hyman, 1953), Meehl's (1954) essay on clinical versus statistical prediction, John Cohen's (1960, 1964) pioneering research on chance, skill, and luck, and the work of Ward Edwards and his colleagues who tried to asses the extent to which people behave as Bayesian statisticians (for a review, see Peterson & Beach, 1967). Kahneman and Tversky's heuristics and biases consolidated and in some respects challenged this previous work, and contained the outline of a novel, coherent, and meaningful framework.

Third, many of the demonstrations of biases were simple, easy to comprehend and thus very compelling. Indeed, for participants in these experiments the potential errors and inconsistencies were rather opaque (and some of the critics of these experiments argued that change of presentation may be sufficient to eliminate the observed biases). However, when presented in a transparent frame, to readers who were supposedly familiar with the basics of probability theory and who examined the experimental results analytically, the discrepancy between the intuitive and the analytical mode of reasoning became immediately evident.

Notwithstanding, simple introspection suggested to the honest reader that he or she might also be vulnerable to several of the observed biases. Consider for instance the letter frequency problem (Tversky & Kahneman, 1972) intended to demonstrate the availability heuristics. Participants were asked to estimate the likelihood that a given letter will appear in the first or third position of a word. For example, is the letter R more likely to appear in the first or the third position? Evidently, the majority of the participants judged the likelihood to be larger in the first position despite the fact that the letter R is more likely to be in the third position. Tversky and Kahneman suggested that people estimate the likelihoods of the two categories (first or third position) by roughly assessing the ease with which instances of the two categories come to mind. Taking a quick sample, it is mentally much easier to retrieve words with the letter R in the first rather than in the third place. Obviously, researchers reading the article were not more knowledgeable (than the average participant) about the frequency of different letters in different positions of a word. However, by placing oneself in the participants' role and attempting to simulate what participants in this task have done (in a way, using the simulation heuristic), it is easy to imagine that one would use exactly the same strategy supposedly used by the participants. Many of the problems used by Kahneman and Tversky were persuasive because they lent themselves easily to be imagined by the reader. So in a way, and perhaps paradoxically, the success of the heuristics and biases program could be partly attributed to a clever use of the simulation heuristic, whereby a conclusion appears convincing by being easily constructed as a part of a good scenario (Kahneman & Tversky, 1982b). It is of course impossible to provide a complete and detailed treatment of this innovative and stimulating research program in a single chapter. An extensive coverage is provided in Kahneman, Slovic and Tversky (1982), and Gilovich, Griffin, and Kahneman (2002), both of which carry, not incidentally, the same title. In this chapter we cover a small selection of the existing literature and highlight what seems to us to be some of the more important facets of the area. We first examine more closely the meaning of the two key concepts of "bias" and "heuristics." Subsequently, we offer a brief discussion in which the heuristic and bias program is related to perceptual processes on the one hand, and to the psychology of reasoning on the other hand. The following two sections contain a brief description of the three heuristics (representativeness, availability, and anchoring) and some more recent developments. Finally, a two-stage framework is proposed in which, borrowing from prospect theory, it is suggested that the processes underlying probability judgments consist of an *editing* and an *evaluation* phase.

What is a Bias?

The heuristics and biases approach rests on the marriage between two key concepts, neither of which are unproblematic and unambiguous by themselves. We will discuss them in turn.

According to the *Oxford English Dictionary* (2002), the term "bias" was originally used to describe a slanting line (e.g., the diagonal in a square), and the oblique motion of a loaded bowling ball; it also referred to the asymmetric construction of the bowling ball achieved by loading it on one side with lead, as exemplified in a Shakespearean passage: "Well, forward, forward thus the bowle should run. And not unluckily against the bias" (Shakespeare, 1596, *The Taming of the Shrew* IV, v. 25).

These usages illustrate two distinctions still implied in various contexts of the modern term. First, biases are often used to describe deviations from a norm (as with Shakespeare's bowl) but, in another more neutral sense, they can simply indicate a tendency to slant in one way rather than another (like the diagonal). For instance, the term "positivity bias" has been used to describe a preponderance of positive over negative evaluations in person perception and, more generally, in everyday language (Kanouse & Hanson, 1971; Peeters, 1971). This does not in itself indicate any errors of judgment, unless we believe that, in reality, positive and negative events should balance each other out. On the other hand, the concept of a "desirability bias" (Budescu & Bruderman, 1995) implies a tendency to assign exaggerated probability estimates to desired outcomes, not because of the amount of supporting evidence, but simply because we want them to come true. Such biases can be regarded as systematic, suboptimal judgments, sometimes labeled "errors," or even "fallacies."

Another distinction concerns bias as a cause versus bias as an effect. The bias of the bowl can be its shape or loading, causing it to deviate from a straight run. It also designates its trajectory, resulting from the lopsided construction. In the psychology of judgment, biases were originally conceived as effects (to be explained, for instance, by heuristics), rather than causes. But in many contexts, they have been used as explanations rather than phenomena to be explained. For example, in studies of logical tasks, Evans (1989) suggested that many errors of deductive reasoning can be explained on the basis of a more general "matching bias," namely the tendency to endorse conclusions that are linguistically compatible with the premises (this may in turn be regarded as a manifestation of a more general principle of relevance). Similarly, "confirmation bias" in hypothesis testing can be conceived as a general strategy for testing hypotheses through verification rather than falsification procedures (Wason, 1960; Klayman & Ha, 1987), either by searching for positive instances rather than negative ones, or by finding observed confirmations more compelling than disconfirmations. It has alternatively been described as a general outcome of these and similar mechanisms (e.g., matching), reflecting the fact that hypotheses, for whatever reason, appear to be more easily retained than rejected.

The concept of a bias in the latter sense, namely as a systematic deviation from a norm (or as an inclination towards one judgment rather than another), does not in itself imply one specific kind of explanation. Biases can be the result of cognitive limitations, processing strategies, perceptual organizing principles, an egocentric perspective, specific motivations (e.g. "self-serving biases" in social psychology), affects, and cognitive styles. In the heuristics and biases tradition, the general approach has been to regard biases as a more or less regular by-product of some more general principles of judgment, labeled heuristics, to which we now turn.

What is a Heuristic?

Paraphrasing William James, "everyone knows what heuristics are" or, at least, that is the impression given by the literature on heuristics and biases, where a definition of heuristics is rarely, if ever, attempted. The reason could also be that the term heuristics was, in this program, used in a deliberately imprecise way, more as a hint about the role of the psychological processes involved than as a description of their precise nature.

Following the Webster dictionary, the term heuristics implies inventing or discovering, and more specifically designates a method of education or a computer program that, searching for a solution or answer to a given question, proceeds along empirical lines using rules of thumb. It has been originally dubbed by Polya (1945) as a sort of reasoning "not regarded as final and strict but as provisional and plausible only, whose purpose is to discover the solution of the present problem" (p. 115). Being "provisional" rather than final, a heuristic approach will necessarily be incomplete and error prone. Einstein called his first Nobel Prize-winning paper on quantum physics (1905): "On a heuristic point of view concerning the generation and transformation of light," using the term "heuristic" rather than "theory" to indicate that he regarded it at this stage only as a useful approximation to truth.

The term has been adopted and applied both in computer science and in the (psychological) domain of problem solving as a prescriptive method in which a problem solver (or a machine in the case of artificial intelligence) proceeds along empirical guidelines to discover solutions or answers. Such procedures entail both advantages and risks, as they may lead us by a short cut to the goal we seek or they may lead us down a blind alley. Heuristics are, in this literature, often contrasted with algorithms, which are explicit and detailed rules that guarantee a correct result, but could be effortful and time-consuming, and hence impractical in situations characterized by limited cognitive resources.

The meaning of the term heuristics, as first used by Kahneman and Tversky, was highly similar to its use in the problem-solving literature, by being considered to be simplified methods intended to cope with humans' limited processing capacity. They were also error prone, leading generally to acceptable (although imprecise) estimates, but under certain circumstances, to systematic biases. Finally, they could be contrasted with normative, "algorithmic," procedures for estimating probabilities, which may require full statistical information of all outcomes involved, knowledge of the basic principles of probability theory (like combinatorial rules and Bayes' theorem), as well as cognitive capacity to carry out calculations based on these principles. However, one question remained: While heuristics in computer science and problem solving usually are explicit strategies, that can be applied (mostly with success) or not applied, it was not at all clear whether (or when) the judgmental heuristics described by Kahneman and Tversky were deliberate and under the control of the individual. Current views (Kahneman & Frederick, 2002) seem to suggest that the mechanisms underlying heuristics are essentially automatic, and supposedly do not operate under the individual's awareness. We elaborate on this point later.

Two Metaphors

The psychology of judgment can be conceived as occupying a middle ground between the psychology of thinking and the psychology of perception. It may be slow and deliberate, like problem solving, and quick and immediate, like for instance distance perception, where we seemingly jump to the conclusion (e.g. "a car is approaching") without conscious knowledge of the premises, or "cues," on which this conclusion is based (for a discussion of these two metaphors within the framework of Brunswikian social judgment theory, see Chapter 3, this volume).

It has been known for a long time that the subjective conclusions drawn in both areas are sometimes nonveridical, or incorrect. In the literature on deductive reasoning, such errors have traditionally been called *fallacies*, whereas perceptual mistakes have typically been called *illusions*. Classic texts on logic have often included a chapter on fallacies (e.g., Mill, 1856), in many ways reminiscent of the "biases" apparently rediscovered in the heuristics and biases tradition. Similarly, treatises on sensation and perception have contained lists of visual (and other) illusions as an integral part. The traditional distinction between fallacies and illusions is nicely illustrated by two volumes appearing in the same "International Scientific Series" more than one hundred years ago, one by psychologist James Sully (1882), entitled *Illusions*, the second on *Fallacies*, by the logician Alfred Sidgwick (1883). However, both authors admitted that the distinction between illusions, defined as errors of "immediate, self-evident, or intuitive knowledge," and fallacies, denoting false inferences or errors of reasoning, is hard to draw. If one wants to draw attention to the *process* involved in drawing a conclusion (even a perceptual one), the reasoning or inferential metaphor seems particularly apt; if, on the other hand, emphasis is put on the immediate or inevitable *gut feeling* of what is the case, the perceptual metaphor will be more appropriate.

Indeed, Kahneman and Tversky often drew a parallel between heuristics and biases, and comparable perceptual processes. It is in this respect that the term "cognitive illusions" was introduced as an analog to visual illusions. Though rarely described in these terms, many of the Gestalt laws, such as grouping or closure, constitute non-deliberate automatic processing. In a similar vein, and congruent with current interpretations (e.g., Griffin, Gonzalez, & Varey, 2001; Kahneman & Frederick, 2002), we assume that many "heuristic" judgments are performed automatically and cannot be entirely controlled. In other contexts, the term "fallacies" has been employed (e.g., the conjunction fallacy, the gambler's fallacy, and the "planning fallacy"), pointing more directly to the logical inconsistencies involved.

The perceptual metaphor, applied to subjective probability judgments, did not originate with Kahneman and Tversky, but can be traced back at least to Pierre Simon Laplace, one of the founders of probability theory. In his *Essai philosophique sur les probabilités* (1816) he included a chapter called "Illusions in probability estimation." Here, the reader is told that "the mind has its illusions, like the sense of vision" (p. 182), which need to be corrected by "reflection and calculation." Still, the subjective probabilities that are based on everyday experience, and exaggerated by hope and fear, are more striking than those that are merely a result of calculation. Subjective probabilities are, according to Laplace, governed by the principles of association, the main being contiguity (strengthened by repetition), and resemblance. These are, like heuristics, basically sound and helpful principles, but can occasionally be misleading. Indeed, the parallel between the laws of association and the heuristics suggested by Kahneman and Tversky is more than superficial, repetition frequency corresponding to availability, and resemblance corresponding to the representativeness heuristic. In a remarkable chapter on "Unphilosophical probabilities," David Hume (1976[1739]) made the same point, by showing how people judge probability by how "fresh" an event is in memory; unfortunately memorability is not only affected by frequency, but also by recency and vividness. This is of course an early, but quite accurate, description of the currently popular "availability heuristic."

The Domain of Heuristics and Biases

What kinds of phenomena lend themselves to "heuristic" approaches, and in which areas do we find "biased" outcomes of such an approach? The original focus of the heuristics and biases program was clearly within the field of prediction under uncertainty and estimation of probabilities and frequencies. In these areas many responses that are incompatible with normative considerations have been documented (as testified by Hume and Laplace), and the suspicion arose that people are not just inaccurate or lack the skills for calculating probabilities, but that they use an entirely different approach from that of the mathematician.

Soon, the search for biases was generalized to the whole area of judgment and decision making (JDM), giving rise to decision biases like the status quo bias (e.g., Kahneman, Knetsch, & Thaler, 1991), omission bias (Spranca, Minsk, & Baron, 1991), and outcome bias (Baron & Hershey, 1988). We may also speak of choice heuristics (Frederick, 2002), and specific heuristics tailored to concrete judgment tasks (Gigerenzer, Todd, and the ABC Research Group, 1999).

In an even wider sense, the concepts of heuristics and biases have – separately or in combination – been applied to areas outside the JDM field, both within cognitive psychology (hypothesis testing, inductive and deductive reasoning) and by social psychologists studying issues of social cognition (Nisbett & Ross, 1980). In particular, biases are frequently discussed within the framework of attribution theory, as for instance "the correspondence bias" (Gilbert & Malone, 1995), referring to the tendency to draw inferences about a person's dispositions from his or her behaviors (also called "overattribution," and "the fundamental attribution error"), the "actor–observer bias", and various "self-serving" biases, referring to patterns of attribution that tend to protect or boost the person's self-esteem. Biases have also been found in the area of self–other comparisons, where people commonly judge themselves as better, more lucky, or more special than other people (above-average bias, illusory optimism, and false uniqueness effect). Pronin, Lin and Ross (2002) recently demonstrated that people are even biased to think that they are less biased than others!

The remaining part of this chapter will be devoted mainly to a discussion of predictions and probability judgments, being the original core area of the heuristics and biases approach, but also with an eye to related developments in judgment and decision making, more broadly conceived. Biases in other areas of cognitive and social psychology are beyond the scope of the present chapter.

Three Canonical Heuristics

In their early work, Tversky and Kahneman (1974) described three judgmental heuristics for estimating probabilities, frequencies, and other uncertain quantities. These three, labeled representativeness, availability, and anchoring and adjustment, respectively, were not introduced as the *only* three, not even as the three most important heuristics, yet they have since the time of their introduction occupied a unique position as "prototypical" or canonical heuristics within the heuristics and biases approach.

Representativeness

Probability judgments are rarely completely unconditional. Some go from hypothesis to data, or from population to sample or, more generally, from a Model M to some instance or event X, associated with the model (Tversky & Kahneman, 1982). Such judgments could be: what is the probability of getting five heads in a row from an unbiased coin; or what is more likely: that the best student in the class this year will perform equally well, less well, or even better next year? Another set of probability questions goes the opposite way, from data to hypothesis, sample to population, or more generally from X to M. We observe the five heads, and wonder whether the coin is unbiased or not; or, we observe that the student is performing less well the following year, and wonder about the most likely explanation. The first set of problems can be regarded as problems of prediction, the second as problems of diagnosis, or explanation.

In three early important papers, Kahneman and Tversky (1972, 1973; Tversky & Kahneman, 1971) demonstrated that both types of probability judgments are often performed as a simple comparison between X and M. If X looks like a typical instance of M, it will be regarded as a probable outcome. In such cases, predictions are said to be performed by a "representativeness heuristic." Accordingly, we may think that five heads in a row is not a very likely outcome, because it does not fit our model of a random series; whereas we think it is likely that a good student will remain at the top of his class, because this looks like a typical thing for a good student to do.

M can also be diagnosed from X by the same mechanism. When five heads actually appear, we may suspect the coin of being loaded; if the student's achievement is more mediocre next year, we look for causal rather than statistical explanations (perhaps he was overworked, or spoiled by his initial success). Such probability judgments by similarity, which are the essence of the "representativeness heuristic," seemed well suited to explain several well-known biases of probability judgments, like the gamblers' fallacy and the problem of non-regressive predictions. It could also make observers (including scientists) place undue weight on characteristics of small samples (facetiously termed "belief in the law of small numbers" by Tversky & Kahneman, 1971), and to neglect base rates in diagnostic judgments.

One of the more striking manifestations of representativeness reasoning is to be found in the so-called conjunction fallacy. Here the predicted outcome, X, is typically a combination of a high-probability and a low-probability event, where the first is a good and the second a poor match for the model (Linda as a feminist, and Linda as a bank teller). The conjunction (a feminist bank teller) is, by the logic of probability theory, less likely than both its components (the number of feminist bank tellers cannot exceed the number of bank tellers), but from a similarity point of view, the picture looks different. One typical and one atypical characteristic can give the conjunction an appearance of being neither likely, nor completely unlikely, but something in between (Tversky & Kahneman, 1983).

Representativeness captures an aspect of probability that, in many languages, is embedded in the probability vocabulary itself, namely its verisimilitude, or likeness to truth (cf. French: "vraisemblable," German: "Wahrscheinlich," Swedish: "sannolik," Polish: "prawdopodobny"). It has been conceived as a very general mechanism, applicable both to singular and repeated events. It has also a high degree of ecological validity, since in most distributions, the central, or most typical value is at the same time the modal (most frequent) one. It is, at the same time, a quick and effortless type of judgment, requiring a minimum of cognitive resources. As a theoretical concept, critics have pointed out that it is underspecified and lends itself poorly to specific, falsifiable predictions (Olson, 1976; Gigerenzer, 1996).

Availability and simulation

The second main heuristic, introduced by Kahneman and Tversky (1973), was termed *availability*. In this case, events are not compared to a model in terms of similarity, they are instead evaluated according to the ease by which they can be imagined or retrieved from memory. Again, this refers to a class of phenomena, rather than one specific process. In the most concrete case, instances of the target event are simply recalled; if a number of instances are readily recalled, the event is judged to be frequent, and predicted with a high probability to happen again in the future. Events that are harder to recall, are regarded to be less frequent and less probable. Unfortunately, recall can be influenced by factors other than frequency, such as public exposure, vividness, primacy and recency, leading people for instance to overestimate highly publicized and dramatic risks (like terrorism and airplane accidents) and underestimate less spectacular ones (like diabetes and tobacco smoking). Recall can also be affected by retrieval principles and memory organization, as illustrated by the case of words with R in the first, vs. third position, described earlier in this chapter. Recent research indicates, however, that people are more accurate in estimating letter frequencies than implied by this classic demonstration (Sedlmeier, Hertwig, & Gigerenzer, 1998). Research by Schwarz, Bless, Strack, Klumpp, Rittenauer-Schatka, & Simons (1991) suggests that "ease of recall" is a more important determinant than "number of instances" recalled. The availability principle is thus more than a simple generalization from the size of the sample of recalled instances to the whole population of events. It also, and perhaps primarily, refers to the feelings of effort and effortlessness of mental productions.

This is even more transparent in the *simulation heuristic*, sometimes described as a subspecies of availability, namely "availability for construction" in contrast to "availability for recall" (Kahneman & Tversky, 1982b). In prediction, we often compare causal scenarios of the future, and tend to be most convinced by the story that is most easily imaginable, most causally coherent, appears to be most "natural" or normal, and is most easy to follow. Mental simulation is also observed in instances of counterfactual reasoning, when we discuss the probability of events that did not actually occur, but "could" have happened (see Chapter 7, this volume). In some respects, the simulation heuristic can be regarded as an implication of an *a priori fallacy* described by John Stuart Mill, namely to believe that what is natural for us to think must also exist, and what we cannot conceive, must be non-existent. More specifically, "even of things not altogether inconceivable, that we can conceive with the greatest ease is likeliest to be true" (Mill, 1856, p. 312). As with representativeness, the concepts of "availability" and "simulation" do not in themselves specify the processes that bring instances of type X easy to mind, or make models of type M easy to run. Rather, they invite investigators to look for factors that make X and M more retrievable and plausible and hence, more likely.

It may be constructive to point out that both representativeness and availability could be viewed as instances of categorization. Smith, Patalano, and Jonides (1998) proposed that categorization of an instance can be carried out either by applying a category defining rule to an instance in question, or by determining the instance's similarity to remembered exemplars of a category. Both representativeness and availability are supposedly based on processes of the latter type. For example, the lawyers/engineers study (Kahneman & Tversky, 1973) that was intended to demonstrate base-rate-neglect can be viewed as a categorization task in which participants have to judge whether a person (briefly described in a personality sketch) should be classified as a lawyer or an engineer depending on the judged similarity between the person's description and the respective prototypes of the two categories. Similarly, regarding availability, when participants attempt to estimate the frequency of the letter R in the first and third place of a word, they supposedly retrieve a few exemplars from the relevant categories and base their estimates on these exemplars (Smith & Medin, 1981).

The interpretation of studies on representativeness may differ depending on whether they are viewed as experiments on probability judgments or whether the focus is on categorization. Probability theory, which serves as the benchmark for assessing representativeness experiments, is a formal theory based on computational principles and as such lends itself exclusively to what Sloman (1996) has termed the rule-based system of reasoning. Categorization, in contrast, in which similarity plays a major role, is more likely to be performed by what Sloman calls the associative system. Examining representativeness (and availability) from these two different perspectives, may provide some useful insights.

Anchoring and adjustment

Judgments are also influenced by initial values, usually suggested by an external source. If asked whether I am willing to sell my old car for $2,000, I will think of it as less valuable than if I am offered $4,000, even if I find both offers "outrageously" low. In the first case, I may ask for $5,000 rather than $2,000, in the second I may ask for $7,000, with little awareness about the extent to which my own "independent" estimates are, in fact, influenced by the original suggestions. The estimates can in such cases be regarded as upwards or downwards "adjustments" of the suggested values, whereas the initial suggested values serve as "anchors," towards which the estimates are pulled. This process of *anchoring and adjustment* (Tversky & Kahneman, 1974) thus creates estimates that tend to be biased, or assimilated, in the direction of the anchor.

Despite the inbuilt bias, anchoring and adjustment is clearly an adaptive heuristic whenever the anchor is informative and relevant. In the car sale example, the offer from a prospective buyer provides helpful information about the market value of my car, and should legitimately be taken into account. Without any external hint, my own price expectations might be less biased, but more variable and inaccurate. Sensible people anchor their predictions about the future based on the situation today, resulting in a conservative bias (by judging the future to be more similar to the past than warranted), but a conservative bias may be better than an estimate anchored on a sanguine wish, or simply coming out of the blue. There is, however, no such thing as a foolproof heuristic; when people are uncertain, they can be influenced by an irrelevant anchor value (Wilson, Houston, Etling, & Brekke, 1996) or a completely implausible one (Strack & Mussweiler, 1997).

The anchoring and adjustment heuristic is more general than representativeness and availability, describing a process that applies equally well to frequency judgments, value judgments, magnitude judgments, and even causal attributions (Gilbert & Malone, 1995; Quattrone, 1982). In the area of probability judgment, anchoring phenomena have been used to explain the hindsight bias (where judgments about the past are biased by one's outcome knowledge), and various phenomena of overconfidence, for instance the tendency to produce too narrow confidence ranges in estimates of uncertain quantities (Alpert & Raiffa, 1982). In this case, the individual performs a guess about his or her most likely estimate, and makes (insufficient) adjustments upwards and downwards to incorporate the uncertainty involved. Alternatively, the lower estimate may function as an anchor for the higher estimate, or vice versa.

Despite the robustness of anchoring phenomena, there is no consensus about the mechanism behind them, not even whether actual adjustments are involved. Chapman and Johnson (2002) distinguish two main categories of explanations: insufficient adjustments (overweighing the anchor compared to other evidence), and selective activation and accessibility of evidence. In the first case, we could perhaps describe anchoring as a *primacy* effect; in the second case it functions as a special case of *priming* (Mussweiler & Strack, 2000). Epley (see Chapter 12, this volume) suggests that anchoring phenomena might be due to several, independent mechanisms.

Heuristics and Biases: A Current Evaluation

The introduction of the heuristics and biases program was enthusiastically adopted by researchers and has been followed by 30 years of intensive research and corresponding disputes. This accumulating research was often guided by the question concerning the extent to which the heuristics and the associated biases should be considered as evidence for failures of rationality (e.g., Cohen, 1981, 1983; Evans & Over, 1996; Gigerenzer, 1996; Stanovich & West, 2002).

Much of the research consolidated previous findings and at the same time delineated the circumstances and conditions under which specific biases would appear, and sometimes disappear. For instance, a review paper by Koehler (1996) on the base-rate fallacy (one of the more prominent biases linked to the representativeness heuristic) provides overall evidence for the robustness of the phenomenon. Yet, at the same time, Koehler points out possible methodological shortcomings indicating that researchers have been too quick to conclude that people simply "neglect" the base rates.

The continuous build up of the heuristics and bias research program extended in two ways. First, the number of newly identified biases has been constantly growing. For instance, in one of the more popular textbooks on judgment and decision making, Baron (2002) counts no less than 25 biases (see the term bias in his subject index). Second, new heuristics have appeared, but not at the same pace, and not as widely adopted as the three original ones. Among the newcomers are "the numerosity heuristic" (Pelham, Sumarta, & Myaskovsky, 1994), according to which the number of instances of a target is used to indicate its probability (regardless of the number of non-target instances); "the recognition heuristic" (Goldstein & Gigerenzer, 1999), which says that alternatives with known (recognized) labels are automatically believed to be a bigger, better, and safer than alternatives with unknown labels; and "the affect heuristic" (Slovic, Finucane, Peters, & MacGregor, 2002), referring to people's tendency to regard objects and activities with positive connotations as yielding positive outcomes with higher probability, and negative outcomes with lower probability, than objects with negative connotations. It has also been suggested that people often assess probabilities by heuristically comparing the target outcome only to its strongest competitor, rather than to the whole set of alternatives, creating the "alternative outcomes effect" (Windschitl & Wells, 1998), and that people, especially in hindsight, evaluate probabilities of a counterfactual outcome by their impression of how close it was to occurring, thus apparently adopting a "closeness" or "proximity" heuristic (Kahneman & Varey, 1990; Teigen, 1998).

In hindsight, it may have been unfortunate that heuristics and biases were introduced in unison, as a slogan or brand name, giving rise to the impression that the main task of heuristics was to produce biases, and that any bias was to be explained by a corresponding heuristic. Critics (e.g., Fiedler, 1983; Gigerenzer et al., 1999; Lopes, 1991) have pointed out that the proposed heuristics are vague and hence not readily testable, that they do not constitute a comprehensive model of probability judgments, and that they differ from problem-solving heuristics by being more often automatic than conscious and deliberate. Perhaps it is fair to say that they were introduced – like Einstein's model alluded to previously – not as a theory, but as a heuristic [sic] device suggesting rather than dictating ways of thinking about subjective probabilities. From the amount of research inspired by this approach, the idea of heuristics appears to have been a fruitful heuristic.

Two Stages of Probability Judgments

If probability judgments, and the possible biases associated with such judgments, are not to be explained by a finite set of concrete "heuristics," how could the judgment process (alternatively) be conceived?

Recent developments in research on heuristics (e.g. Kahneman & Frederick, 2002) suggest that probability judgments may result from an interaction between two modes of thinking: one intuitive, automatic, and immediate (labeled System 1), and another more analytic, controlled, and rule-governed form of reasoning (System 2). In this scheme, spontaneous System 1 judgments may or may not be biased, and these biases may or may not be endorsed, corrected, or adjusted by System 2. Typical heuristic judgments (e.g. impressions of representativeness and priming effects caused by anchoring) can be explained by operations that are dominated by the first rather than the second of these systems. Responses induced by the first system are spontaneous and often irresistible, bearing some similarity to output from the perceptual system. Like the perceptual apparatus, System 1 may occasionally wind up with (cognitive) illusions. System 2 processes are, on the other hand, more slow and deliberate. This does not necessarily mean that they are always compatible with normative prescriptions. Extensive empirical evidence suggests that we are capable of being mistaken in different ways, leading to violations of the laws of logic or probability calculus. We may lack the proper rule (e.g., regression towards the mean) leading to what has been termed errors of competence. We may strongly believe in rules that are irreconcilable with normative considerations (e.g., the gambler's fallacy). And, even if we are familiar with the proper rule, we are occasionally prone to make mistakes resulting in what has been termed errors of application.

Without necessarily endorsing the view that there are two distinct ways of thinking, as proposed by some models (Epstein, 1994; Sloman, 1996; Stanovich & West, 2002), we may profit from the two-phase analysis and posit that most instances of prediction and probability judgments include a phase in which candidate judgments are suggested or formulated, and a phase in which these proposals (or hypotheses) are evaluated. This is especially apparent in the case of anchoring and adjustment, where the anchor represents an externally suggested candidate value, to be modified and evaluated during the subsequent adjustment stage. In the case of representativeness, an initial prediction is made on the basis of how well a sample or a target outcome matches, or resembles, salient characteristics of the parent population, or outcome source. This prediction may subsequently be corrected and moderated by factors like base rates, beliefs about cue validity, or a record of previous prediction accuracy. Sometimes people use simple rules of thumb to ensure that some corrections are made. When asked about her confidence of testimony, an eyewitness (in a Norwegian murder case) recently claimed that she was "90 percent sure; when I do not say 100 percent, it is because I *never* say 100 percent." This witness evidently used a simple, deliberate principle to modify her immediate, perceptually based impression that the observed person was identical with the suspect. We could even call her use of a correction factor a "judgmental heuristic," with "heuristic" in this case indicating a consciously chosen strategy (to minimize errors of overconfidence) rather than an immediate, intuitive process. As proposed earlier, probability judgments are based on psychological principles of perception on one hand, and thinking and reasoning on the other. Supposedly, initial impressions and assessments (of a situation or an event) are mainly construed according to perceptual laws, whereas the subsequent evaluation phase is mainly based on deliberate conscious reasoning. Analogous to the two stages underlying choice behavior as postulated by prospect theory (Kahneman & Tversky, 1979), we suggest that probability judgments are governed by an initial *editing and encoding* phase followed by *evaluation*.

Phase 1: Editing (encoding)

The initial editing phase is composed of structuring and arranging the available incoming information in a meaningful way, preparing it for the subsequent evaluative–computational phase. Given a limited processing and memory capacity, editing is designed to encode the information in the simplest and most meaningful way. The manner by which the perceptual system is tuned to encode the available information is based on what Bruner (1957) has referred to as perceptual readiness and is founded on some underlying (Gestalt) principles. In a broader context, editing is guided by what Pomerantz and Kubovy (1986) have termed the simplicity principle, according to which the perceptual system is geared up to find the simplest perceptual organization (what the Gestalt psychologists referred to as prägnanz).

Editing is responsible for selection of information and transforming it into an internal representation which, among other things, would depend on stimulus characteristics like concreteness and vividness. For instance, as originally proposed by Meehl (1954), and demonstrated in countless studies, people are evidently more tuned to the singular (clinical) than to statistical evidence. It has been proposed that the clinical singular case is more vivid, and therefore is given priority in the editing phase. The strength of this vividness effect would depend on how the available information (verbal or non-verbal) presents itself. For instance, in the well-known lawyer/engineer problem (Kahneman & Tversky, 1973), participants were presented with both a personality sketch (of either a lawyer or an engineer) and with base-rates regarding the number of lawyers and engineers respectively. Evidently, participants made their judgment mainly on the basis of the specific description ignoring the normatively important base-rate information. Kahneman and Tversky assert that participants evaluate the likelihood of a particular description to be that of an engineer or a lawyer by the degree to which the particular description resembles (or is representative) of the typical stereotype associated with these two occupations. In the framework proposed here, the editing phase is particularly sensitive to singular narrative information, which frequently grabs the major attention at this initial stage. In particular, the vivid character of the stereotypical sketch descriptions of the lawyer and the engineer draws immediate attention and is encoded as highly salient. This encoding, like the editing phase in general, is recognition based and to a large extent automatic. It is insensitive to the accuracy, validity, or diagnosticity of such descriptions which, if at all, are assessed only at the subsequent evaluation stage.

The operations of the editing and the corresponding initial impressions are highly dependent on the order of the incoming information and the manner by which it is structured and arranged. Studies of anchoring show the importance of order (primacy effects). Studies of framing effects reveal how the same, objective, facts can have different impact dependent upon how they are presented (Tversky & Kahneman, 1981; Levin, Schneider, & Gaeth, 1998). For instance an 80 percent chance of success (positive frame) appears more encouraging than a 20 percent chance of failure (negative frame), by directing our attention towards a positive versus a negative target outcome. Framing can also be achieved by the choice of probability terms, the 80 percent probability of success can be described as a "highly probable" success or a "not completely certain" success, the first description being more optimistic than the second (Teigen & Brun, 2003).

Similar to framing, editing is also vulnerable to all sorts of format effects. For instance, much of the controversy concerning base-rate neglect (the tendency to overweight singular narrative information and undermine corresponding statistical information) is directly linked to how the information is presented. The difference between studies that demonstrate base-rate neglect compared with those that fail to find the effect (Koehler, 1996), is largely dependent on how the two types of information are presented. Different presentation formats enhance some aspects more than other, resulting in a different structure of the internal representation. Note that framing is not necessarily restricted to verbal descriptions. Perceptual stimuli (and situations) can be equally presented and perceived in more than one way.

Descriptions of target outcomes can also differ by specificity, or amount of detail. This is a central point in support theory (Tversky & Koehler, 1994; Rottenstreich &

Tversky, 1997), where it is claimed that people do not allocate probabilities to events, but to descriptions of events. Events that are described in such a way that they will generate a large amount of support (positive evidence and favorable arguments) will be estimated as more probable than those that are described in such a way that they will be more sparsely supported. The most important corollary of this view is that an "unpacked" outcome (for instance deaths by traffic accidents, natural disasters, terrorism, homicide, or suicide) is believed to be more probable than the corresponding "packed" outcome ("death from unnatural causes"), even if the latter include the former. Such "subadditivity" has been documented in many domains.

Phase 2: Evaluation

The editing phase determines which aspects of the incoming information will receive more or less attention, and arranges (structures) the information preparing it for the subsequent evaluation phase. This latter phase consists of assessing the different aspects of the available information obtained from the editing phase, eventually combining them into a probabilistic estimate (in a numerical or verbal form). The evaluation phase supposedly consists of deliberate cognitive processes that are, at least to some extent, based on what Bruner (1984) has termed the paradigmatic or logico-scientific mode of reasoning. This mode is regulated by requirements of consistency and non-contradiction, and in its most developed form fulfills the ideal of a formal mathematical system of description and explanation. However, there is overwhelming empirical evidence (much of which has been stimulated by the heuristics and biases approach) suggesting that the evaluation phase can also be prone to systematic errors and reasoning faults. Failures at the evaluation phase may be due to different reasons.

First, in many cases people are familiar with the appropriate (paradigmatic) way of thinking yet fail to apply it to the particular case thus resulting in what has been termed errors of application (Kahneman & Tversky, 1982a). For example, they presented (p. 127) participants with the following question: "As you know, a game of squash can be played either to 9 or to 15 points. Holding all other rules of the game constant, if A is a better player than B, which scoring system will give A a better chance of winning."

Most participants believed that the scoring rule should not make a difference, yet (with few exceptions) they were convinced after being told that A (the better player) would be better off with a scoring rule of 15 because an atypical outcome is less likely to occur in a large sample. The likelihood of "correct" applications at the evaluation phase depends on the extent to which the problem structure is transparent, and in turn on the manner by which it is encoded at the initial editing phase.

Second, the principles underlying statistical theory are neither easy to grasp nor always compatible with natural intuitions (Lewis & Keren, 1999). Indeed, themes like regression toward the mean or inverse probabilities are not just difficult to comprehend, but (or because) they are not part of our natural reasoning tools. Hence, the evaluation phase fails in those instances in which the proper rule, procedure, or more generally way of thinking, is unknown or not recognized resulting in what is referred to as errors of comprehension.

Third, there are several statistical and probabilistic phenomena on which we possess deeply rooted misconceptions, that may dominate the evaluative phase. By misconceptions is meant beliefs that are neither compatible with the physical world nor with normative considerations based on the paradigmatic mode of reasoning. Two of the most pervasive ones are a deficient understanding of randomness (e.g., Bar-Hillel & Wagenaar, 1993) as exemplified, for instance, by the belief in the "hot hand" (Gilovich, Vallone, & Tversky, 1985), and the failure to understand statistical independence as exhibited in the gambler's fallacy (Keren & Lewis, 1994).

When probability evaluations, even analytical and deliberate ones, sometimes differ from the normative rules, it could be due to the kind of probability concept people endorse. Even among probability theorists, there is no consensus about what is the true reference for a probability statement. Should probability statements be reserved for repeatable events, as claimed by proponents of the frequentistic approach, or are probability statements fundamentally statements about a person's ideal degree of confidence, as claimed by the personalistic school (de Finetti)? Can probability statements legitimately refer to unique situations by being descriptive of the causal propensities involved (Popper)? Lay people may, in different contexts, endorse versions of all these views, albeit in a less stringent and explicit form. For instance we may distinguish between "external" (sometimes called aleatory) and "internal" (epistemic) probabilities (Kahneman & Tversky, 1982c). In daily life, probability is for most of us a "polysemous" concept (Hertwig & Gigerenzer, 1999), referring on some occasions to relative frequencies, and in other situations simply to "plausibility." In many cases, people seem to think of probabilities as a kind of causal forces, or dispositions, manifesting themselves not only in outcome frequencies but also in the strength and latency of target outcomes. For instance, when people are told about the risk of an earthquake in a particular region during the next three years, they will believe that it will come sooner and be stronger if $p = .8$ than if $p = .6$ (Keren & Teigen, 2001). With such interpretations, probabilities tend to become viewed as characteristics of causal systems, with no urgent need to obey formal axioms of distributive probabilities.

Closing Comments

It is naturally impossible to cover, in a single chapter, all the aspects of the heuristic and bias research program and its implications for decision-making research. In this final section we briefly assess the achievements and the limitations of this research and the possible directions in which it may evolve in the future.

The heuristic and bias research program made several important contributions. First, it successfully combined perceptual principles with the psychology of thinking and reasoning, offering a new perspective on judgment under uncertainty. Second, it provided irrefutable evidence that humans' reasoning and decision-making capabilities, though certainly remarkable, are prone to systematic errors. Third, and as a consequence, it challenged the rigid assumptions of economic theory regarding "Homo economicus" and human rationality associated with it. Evidently, people are not always able to follow the prescriptions of normative theories (despite the fact, that these were originally constructed by the human mind) as is assumed by standard economic theory. Finally, it offered simple and clever methods for the study of probability judgments. Not undermining its inspiring achievements, a comprehensive theory that can encompass the different heuristics under one framework is still lacking. Different heuristics are explicated by different processes which are only partially linked. Given that the different heuristics are based on a wide range of perceptual and cognitive mechanisms, it is questionable whether an all-inclusive theory of heuristics and biases is feasible. One promising step has been the development of support theory (Rottenstreich & Tversky, 1997; Tversky & Koehler, 1994) according to which probability judgments correspond to an assessment of the relative balance of evidence for and against competing hypotheses. Though the theory can serve as a global framework for the heuristic approach, it does not explain how, and under what conditions, the different heuristics would be operating.

Most of the empirical demonstrations regarding the different heuristics are based on explicitly eliciting people's probability judgments. An open question is how different elicitation procedures induce different heuristics, leading to different biases. Are different heuristics deeply rooted facets of the cognitive system, or are they mainly brought to mind (online) by the specific elicitation method employed? This question has both theoretical and practical implications. Attempting to answer this question may provide a useful guideline for future theoretical research. From a more practical viewpoint, it may have an important contribution to the development of enhanced corrective (often referred to as debiasing) methods.

References

Alpert, M. & Raiffa, H. (1982) A progress report on the training of probability assessors. In D. Kahneman, P. Slovic, and A. Tversky (eds.), *Judgment Under Uncertainty: Heuristics and biases* (pp. 294–305). Cambridge: Cambridge University Press.

Bar-Hillel, M. & Wagenaar, W. A. (1993) The perception of randomness. In G. Keren and C. Lewis (eds.), *A Handbook for Data Analysis in the Behavioral Sciences: Methodological Issues*. Hillsdale, NJ: Lawrence Erlbaum.

Baron, J. (2002) *Thinking and Deciding* (3rd edn.). Cambridge: Cambridge University Press.

Baron, J. & Hershey, J. C. (1988) Outcome bias in decision evaluation, *Journal of Personality and Social Psychology*, 54, 569–79.

Bruner, J. S. (1957) On perceptual readiness, *Psychological Review*, 54, 123–49.

Bruner, J. S. (1984) Narrative and paradigmatic modes of thought. Paper presented at the annual APA meeting, Toronto (August 25, 1984).

Budescu, D. V. & Bruderman, M. (1995) The relationship between the illusion of control and the desirability bias, *Journal of Behavioral Decision Making*, 8, 109–25.

Chapman, G. B. & Johnson, E. (2002) Incorporating the irrelevant: Anchors in judgments of belief and value. In T. Gilovich, D. Griffin, and D. Kahneman (eds.), *Heuristics and Biases: The Psychology of Intuitive Judgment* (pp. 120–38). Cambridge: Cambridge University Press.

Cohen, J. (1960) *Chance, Skill, and Luck*. Baltimore: Penguin.

Cohen, J. (1964) *Behavior in Uncertainty*. New York: Basic Books.

Cohen, L. J. (1981) Can human irrationality be experimentally demonstrated? *Behavioral and Brain Sciences*, 4, 317–70.

Cohen, L. J. (1983) The controversy about irrationality, *Behavioral and Brain Sciences*, 6, 510–17.

Epstein, S. (1994) Integration of the cognitive and the psychodynamic unconscious, *American Psychologist*, 49, 709–24.

Evans, J. St. B. T. (1989) *Bias in Human Reasoning: Causes and Consequences.* Hove, UK: Erlbaum.

Evans, J. St. B. T. & Over, D. E. (1996) *Rationality and Reasoning.* Hove, UK: Psychology Press.

Fiedler, K. (1983) On the testability of the availability heuristic. In R. W. Scholz (ed.), *Decision Making Under Uncertainty* (pp. 109–19). Amsterdam: North-Holland.

Frederick, S. (2002) Automated choice heuristics. In T. Gilovich, D. Griffin, and D. Kahneman (eds.), *Heuristics and Biases: The Psychology of Intuitive Judgment* (pp. 548–58). Cambridge: Cambridge University Press.

Gigerenzer, G. (1991) How to make cognitive illusions disappear: Beyond "heuristics and biases," *European Review of Social Psychology*, 2, 83–115.

Gigerenzer, G. (1996) On narrow norms and vague heuristics: A reply to Kahneman and Tversky, *Psychological Review*, 103, 592–6.

Gigerenzer, G., Todd, P. M., & the ABC Research Group (1999) *Simple Heuristics that Make Us Smart.* Oxford: Oxford University Press.

Gilbert, D. T. & Malone, P. S. (1995) The correspondence bias, *Psychological Bulletin*, 117, 21–38.

Gilovich, T., Griffin, D., & Kahneman, D. (2002) *Heuristics and Biases.* Cambridge: Cambridge University Press.

Gilovich, T., Vallone, R., & Tversky, A. (1985) The hot hand in basketball: On the misperception of random sequences, *Cognitive Psychology*, 17, 295–314.

Goldstein, D. G. & Gigerenzer, G. (1999) The recognition heuristic: How ignorance makes us smart. In G. Gigerenzer, P. Todd, & the ABC Research Group, *Simple Heuristics that Make Us Smart* (pp. 37–58). Oxford: Oxford University Press.

Griffin, D., Gonzalez, R., & Varey, C. (2001) The heuristics and biases approach to judgment under uncertainty. In A. Tesser and N. Schwarz (eds.), *Blackwell Handbook of Social Psychology: Intra-individual Processes* (pp. 207–35). Oxford: Blackwell.

Hake, H. W. & Hyman, R. (1953) Perception of the statistical structure of a random series of binary symbols, *Journal of Experimental Psychology*, 45, 64–74.

Hertwig, R. & Gigerenzer, G. (1999) The "conjunction fallacy" revisited: How intelligent inferences look like reasoning errors, *Journal of Behavioral Decision Making*, 12, 275–305.

Hume, D. (1976) *A Treatise on Human Nature.* Oxford: Clarendon Press (Original published in 1739).

Kahneman, D. & Fredrick, S. (2002) Representativeness revisited: Attribute substitution in intuitive judgments. In T. Gilovich, T. D. Griffin, and D. Kahneman (eds.), *Heuristics and Biases: The Psychology of Intuitive Judgment* (pp. 49–81). Cambridge: Cambridge University Press.

Kahneman, D., Knetsch, J. L., & Thaler, R. H. (1991) The endowment effect, loss aversion, and status quo bias, *Journal of Economic Perspectives*, 5, 193–206.

Kahneman, D., Slovic, P., & Tversky, A. (1982) *Judgment Under Uncertainty: Heuristics and Biases.* Cambridge: Cambridge University Press.

Kahneman, D. & Tversky, A. (1972) Subjective probability: A judgment of representativeness, *Cognitive Psychology*, 3, 430–54.

Kahneman, D. & Tversky, A. (1973) On the psychology of prediction, *Psychological Review*, 80, 237–51.

Kahneman, D. & Tversky, A. (1979) Prospect theory: An analysis of decision under risk, *Econometrica*, 47, 263–91.

Kahneman, D. & Tversky, A. (1982a) On the study of statistical intuitions, *Cognition*, 11, 123–41.

Kahneman, D. & Tversky, A. (1982b) The simulation heuristic. In D. Kahneman, P. Slovic, and A. Tversky (eds.), *Judgment Under Uncertainty: Heuristics and Biases* (pp. 201–8). Cambridge: Cambridge University Press.

Kahneman, D. & Tversky, A. (1982c) Variants of uncertainty, *Cognition*, 11, 143–57.

Kahneman, D. & Varey, C. A. (1990) Propensities and counterfactuals: The loser that almost won, *Journal of Personality and Social Psychology*, 59, 1101–10.

Kanouse, D. E. & Hanson, L. R. (1971) Negativity in evaluations. In E. E. Jones, D. E. Kanouse, H. H. Kelley, R. E. Nisbett, S. Valins, and B. Weiner (eds.), *Attribution: Perceiving the Causes of Behavior* (pp. 47–62). Morristown NJ: General Learning Press.

Keren, G. & Lewis, C. (1994) The two fallacies of gamblers: Type I and Type II, *Organizational Behavior and Human Decision Processes*, 60, 75–89.

Keren, G. & Teigen, K. H. (2001) The probability-outcome correspondence principle: A dispositional view of the interpretation of probability statements, *Memory & Cognition*, 29, 1010–21.

Klayman, J. & Ha, Y.-W. (1987) Confirmation, disconfirmation, and information in hypothesis testing, *Psychological Review*, 94, 211–28.

Koehler, J. (1996) The base-rate fallacy reconsidered: Descriptive, normative, and methodological challenges, *Behavioral and Brain Sciences*, 19, 1–53.

Laplace, P. S. (1816) *Essai philosophique sur les probabilités*. Paris: Courcier.

Levin, P., Schneider, S. L., & Gaeth, G. J. (1998) All frames are not created equal: A typology and critical analysis of framing effects, *Organizational Behavior and Human Decision Processes*, 76, 149–88.

Lewis, C. & Keren, G. (1999) On the difficulties underlying Bayesian reasoning: A comment on Gigerenzer and Hoffrage, *Psychological Review*, 106, 411–16.

Lopes, L. L. (1991) The rhetoric of irrationality, *Theory and Psychology*, 1, 65–82.

Meehl, P. E. (1954) *Clinical Versus Statistical Prediction: A Theoretical Analysis and a Review of the Evidence*. Minneapolis: University of Minnesota Press.

Mill, J. S. (1856) *A System of Logic*. London: Parker.

Mussweiler, T. & Strack, F. (2000) Comparing is believing: A selective accessibility model of judgmental anchoring. In W. Stroebe and M. Hewstone (eds.), *European Review of Social Psychology*, 10 (pp. 135–67). Chichester, UK: Wiley.

Nisbett, R. E. & Ross, L. (1980) *Human Inference: Strategies and Shortcomings of Social Judgment*. Englewood Cliffs, NJ: Prentice-Hall.

Olson, C. L. (1976) Some apparent violations of the representativeness heuristic in human judgment, *Journal of Experimental Psychology: Human Perception and Performance*, 2, 599–608.

Oxford English Dictionary (2002). Oxford: Oxford University Press, online at: http://dictionary.oed.com

Peeters, G. (1971) The positive-negative asymmetry: On cognitive consistency and positivity bias, *European Journal of Social Psychology*, 1, 455–74.

Pelham, W. B., Sumarta, T. T., & Myaskovsky, L. (1994) The easy path from many to much: The numerosity heuristic, *Cognitive Psychology*, 26, 103–33.

Peterson, C. & Beach, L. R. (1967) Man as an intuitive statistician, *Psychological Bulletin*, 68, 29–46.

Polya, G. (1945) *How to Solve it: A New Aspect of Mathematical Method*. Princeton: Princeton University Press.

Pomerantz, J. R. & Kubovy, M. (1986) Theoretical approaches to perceptual organization: Simplicity and likelihood principles. In K. R. Boff, L. Kaufman, and J. P. Thomas (eds.), *Handbook of Perception and Human Performance: Volume II. Cognitive Processes and Human Performance* (pp. 1–45). New York: Wiley.

Pronin, E., Lin, D. Y. & Ross, L. (2002) The bias blind spot: Perception of bias in self versus others, *Personality and Social Psychology Bulletin*, 28, 369–81.

Quattrone, G. A. (1982) Overattribution and unit formation: When behavior engulfs the person, *Journal of Personality and Social Psychology*, 42, 593–607.

Rottenstreich, Y. & Tversky, A. (1997) Unpacking, repacking, and anchoring: Advances in support theory, *Psychological Review*, 104, 406–15.

Schwarz, N., Bless, H., Strack, F., Klumpp, G., Rittenauer-Schatka, H., & Simons, A. (1991) Ease of retrieval as information: Another look at the availability heuristic, *Journal of Personality and Social Psychology*, 61, 195–202.

Sedlmeier, P., Hertwig, R., & Gigerenzer, G. (1998) Are judgments of the positional frequencies of letters systematically biased due to availability? *Journal of Experimental Psychology: Learning, Memory, and Cognition*, 24, 754–70.

Sidgwick, A. (1883) *Fallacies: A View of Logic from the Practical Side*. London: Kegan Paul, Trench & Co.

Sloman, S. A. (1996) The empirical case for two systems of reasoning, *Psychological Bulletin*, 119, 3–22.

Slovic, P., Finucane, M., Peters, E., & MacGregor, D. (2002) The affect heuristic. In T. Gilovich, T. D. Griffin, and D. Kahneman (eds.), *Heuristics and Biases: The Psychology of Intuitive Judgment* (pp. 397–420). Cambridge: Cambridge University Press.

Smith, E. E. & Medin, D. L. (1981) *Categories and Concepts*. Cambridge, MA : Harvard University Press.

Smith, E. E., Patalano, A. L., & Jonides, J. (1998) Alternative strategies of categorization, *Cognition*, 65, 167–96.

Spranca, M., Minsk, E., & Baron, J. (1991) Omission and commission in judgment and choice, *Journal of Experimental Social Psychology*, 27, 76–105.

Stanovich, K. E. & West, R. F. (2002) Individual differences in reasoning: Implications for the Rationality debate? In T. Gilovich, T. D. Griffin, and D. Kahneman (eds.), *Heuristics and Biases: The Psychology of Intuitive Judgment* (pp. 421–40). Cambridge: Cambridge University Press.

Strack, F. and Mussweiler, T. (1997) Explaining the enigmatic anchoring effect: Mechanisms of selective accessibility, *Journal of Personality and Social Psychology*, 73, 437–46.

Sully, J. (1882) *Illusions: A Psychological Study*. London: Kegan Paul, Trench & Co.

Teigen, K. H. (1998) When the unreal is more likely than the real: Post hoc probability judgments and counterfactual closeness, *Thinking and Reasoning*, 4, 147–77.

Teigen, K. H. & Brun, W. (2003) Verbal probabilities: A question of frame? *Journal of Behavioral Decision Making*, 16, 53–72.

Tversky, A. & Kahneman, D. (1971) Belief in the law of small numbers, *Psychological Bulletin*, 76, 105–10.

Tversky, A. & Kahneman, D. (1972) Availability: A heuristic for judging frequency and probability, *Cognitive Psychology*, 5, 207–32.

Tversky, A. & Kahneman, D. (1974) Judgment under uncertainty: Heuristics and biases, *Science*, 185, 1124–31.

Tversky, A. & Kahneman, D. (1981) The framing of decisions and the psychology of choice. *Science*, 211, 453–8.

Tversky, A. & Kahneman, D. (1982) Judgments of and by representativeness. In D. Kahneman, P. Slovic, and A. Tversky (eds.), *Judgment Under Uncertainty: Heuristics and Biases* (pp. 84–98). Cambridge: Cambridge University Press.

Tversky, A. & Kahneman, D. (1983) Extensional versus intuitive reasoning: The conjunction fallacy in probability judgment, *Psychological Review*, 90: 293–315.

Tversky, A. & Koehler, D. J. (1994) Support theory: A nonextensional representation of subjective probability, *Psychological Review*, 101, 547–67.

Wason, P. (1960) On the failure to eliminate hypotheses in a conceptual task, *Quarterly Journal of Experimental Psychology*, 12, 129–40.

Wilson, T. D., Houston, C. E., Etling, K. M., & Brekke, N. (1996) A new look at anchoring effects: Basic anchoring and its antecedents, *Journal of Experimental Psychology: General*, 125, 387–402.

Windschitl, P. D. & Wells, G. L. (1998) The alternative-outcomes effect, *Journal of Personality and Social Psychology*, 75, 1411–23.

6

Walking with the Scarecrow: The Information-processing Approach to Decision Research

John W. Payne and James R. Bettman

Introduction

From the mid-twentieth century on, the "information-processing" approach has been a theoretical and methodological framework (paradigm) driving much research on human judgment and choice. Part of the so-called "cognitive revolution" in psychology, this approach builds upon the pioneering work of Herbert A. Simon. By the time this volume is published, it will be almost exactly 50 years since Simon's path-breaking 1955 article on the concept of bounded rationality. Our chapter takes its title from the classic tale of the Wizard of Oz (Baum, 1903), in which the Tin Man seeks a heart, the Lion courage, and the Scarecrow a brain. The information-processing approach to decision research has traditionally focused on understanding the cognitive (mind/brain) aspects of decision making; however, as noted later in this chapter, recent work has attempted to integrate the cognitive with more emotional and motivational aspects of decision making (Luce, Bettman, & Payne, 2001; Shiv & Fedorikhin, 1999).

Simon captures three key aspects of the information-processing approach to decision research in the following quotes:

1   A theory of human rationality "must be as concerned with procedural rationality – the ways in which decisions are made – as with substantive rationality – the content of those decisions" (Simon, 1981, p. 57).

2   In terms of models of procedural rationality, "the task is to replace the global rationality of economic man with a kind of rational behavior that is compatible with the access to information and the computational capacities that are actually possessed" by humans (Simon, 1955, p. 99).

3   "Human rational behavior is shaped by a scissors whose two blades are the structure of task environments and the computational capabilities of the actor" (Simon, 1990, p. 7).

As the first quote states, focusing on the processes of judgment and choice and using various methods to trace decision processing are hallmarks of the information-processing approach, in contrast to the traditional focus in economics on *what* decisions are made rather than *how* they are made. The second quote stresses the need to replace the assumptions of classical economic theory about the rational decision maker (a person with complete knowledge, a stable system of preferences, and unlimited computational skill) with a view of the decision maker more compatible with humans' memory systems and computational capacities. Simon (1955) argued that limits on computational capacity are particularly important constraints upon the definition of rational choice, i.e., people exhibit only "bounded" rationality.

The last quote implies that understanding decision processing must reflect the intersection of cognitive limitations with the demands of different decision tasks. One consistent and striking conclusion from many studies of decision behavior is that judgments and choices are highly contingent upon a variety of task and context factors, due to the interaction between properties of both the human information-processing system and decision environments (Payne, 1982).

A related point is that decision researchers increasingly believe that preferences for and beliefs about objects or events of any complexity are often constructed – not merely revealed – in the generation of a response to a judgment or choice task, at least in part due to limitations in information-processing capacity (Bettman, 1979; Payne, Bettman, & Johnson, 1992; Slovic, 1995). That is, people are seen as constructing preferences and beliefs on the spot when needed, instead of having known, well-defined, and stable preferences. Further, preferences are not generated by some invariant algorithm such as Bayesian updating or expected utility calculations, but instead are generated by the contingent use of a variety of different decision heuristics or simplification mechanisms. Such use of *multiple* simplifying mechanisms (heuristics) for judgment and choice under various task and context contingencies yields the incompletely evoked and labile preferences and beliefs that typify a constructed response.

Next we present some of the key conceptual and methodological aspects of this information-processing approach to decision research. Later we illustrate the approach by focusing on a program of research (the Adaptive Decision Maker framework) dealing with choice among alternative courses of action. We end the chapter by considering how the information-processing framework can be extended to include noncognitive factors such as emotion and how the information-processing approach relates to current dual-process theories of thinking.

Information-processing Concepts and Methods

Attention as the scarce resource

A core idea of the information-processing approach is that conscious attention is *the* scarce resource for decision makers (Simon, 1978). Thus, people are generally highly selective about what information is attended to and how it is used. Understanding what drives selective attention in decision making is a critical task for decision research.

There are two major types of attention, voluntary and involuntary (Kahneman, 1973). Voluntary attention describes devoting attention to information that individuals perceive is relevant to current goals, e.g., prevention of harm (Higgins, 2002). Attention also can be captured involuntarily by aspects of the environment that are novel, unexpected, potentially threatening or otherwise affect-related, or simply perceptually salient, e.g., changes and losses relative to some aspiration, target, or reference level. Simon (1983) has argued that emotions focus attention and help overcome the limits of our one-at-a-time information-processing system. Importantly, people may be *unaware* that their attention has been focused on certain aspects of the task environment, and that their decisions consequently have been influenced.

Many common context and task effects in decision making, indicative of constructed values and beliefs, result from selective attention due to making different aspects of the judgment and choice environment salient. For instance, one of the most striking task effects in decision research is that the preference order between two gambles (prospects) often reverses, contingent upon whether the response requested is a direct choice between the gambles or a bidding price for each gamble. Although several factors likely contribute to such preference reversals, one of the explanations offered is the compatibility between a feature of the response mode and an aspect of the gambles, e.g., the need to express a bidding response in terms of dollars may direct increased attention towards the payoffs of the gamble being evaluated. At a more general level, selective attention may involve not only differential attention paid to the various aspects of a single alternative, such as gamble payoffs versus probabilities, but also a greater focus on the best and worst outcomes of a gamble as compared to intermediate outcomes, as in recent work on rank-dependent utility models of risky choice (see Chapter 20, this volume), or differential attention paid to features across multiple alternatives, e.g., the common versus unique dimensions of the alternatives.

A critical point is that decision processing in which attention is highly selective does not necessarily produce poor decisions. To the extent that a decision maker's selective attention maps onto the relevant aspects of the environment and ignores the irrelevant aspects, even highly simplified choice mechanisms are likely to yield good (satisfactory) decisions (Johnson & Payne, 1985). However, to the extent an individual selectively attends to irrelevant information or ignores relevant information, poor decisions can result. If attention is the scarce resource of a decision maker, then helping individuals manage attention is critical for improving decisions. Many decision aids have substantial value in simply helping to ensure that attention is spread more evenly across the features of an option and across multiple options (see Chapter 16, this volume).

The distinction between the *cost of processing* an item of information and the cost of acquiring information is related to the idea of attention as the scarce resource. Deliberation (processing information) about a decision is a costly activity (Conlisk, 1996), and we should consider processing costs as well as the costs of acquiring information in modeling decision making. An increase in the cognitive (or emotional) cost of processing an item of information, like the cost of acquiring an item of information, will lead to greater use of simplification mechanisms that minimize information processing. The cost of acquiring and processing an item of information may also affect the order in which information is processed, as well as whether or not an item is processed at all. Finally, because processing is costly, people tend to accept information in the form in which it is given rather than expending cognitive effort to transform it (Slovic, 1972).

Serial processing

Generally, the information-processing approach assumes that decision making involves the serial manipulation of symbols that reflect the internal representation of a problem. That is, one step in thought follows, *and is influenced by*, another. However, as Simon (1979) has noted, the specification that "the human information processing system is serial is a highly controversial claim" (p. 4). As we discuss in more detail below, several researchers have argued for dual-process views of thinking (e.g., Kahneman & Frederick, 2002; Sloman, 1996), with one type of processing that is parallel, relatively automatic, associative, and fast ("System 1") and another that is serial, effortful, and rule-based ("System 2"). Most decision researchers in the information-processing tradition accept the possibility of parallel processing in some judgments; however, we focus most on those aspects of decision processing that are serial and attention-demanding, i.e., System 2 thinking.

Heuristic judgment and choice strategies

The central idea of bounded rationality (Simon, 1955) is that limited cognitive capacity requires the use of mechanisms (heuristics) involving the selective and simple use of information to solve decision problems. Further, information-processing researchers argue that heuristics generally produce *satisfactory* outcomes. There are several reasons for the use of simplifying heuristics. First, individuals must sometimes use simplification mechanisms because there is no other choice; i.e., limited cognitive capacity or limited time for processing may act as constraints on feasible processing in a specific environment. Second, individuals may simplify because of the cost in time or effort of using the scarce resource of computational capacity. Finally, a person may use simplification mechanisms because they have worked satisfactorily in the past and are readily available in memory.

Simon (1955) proposed that one important simplification of decision processing was to stop search after the first satisfactory solution to the decision problem is obtained rather than exhaustively search for the best (optimal) solution to a problem. A related idea is that decision consequences are valued using simple payoff schemes, where the outcomes of a decision are seen as either being satisfactory or unsatisfactory relative to some aspiration level or reference value. Dynamic aspects of decision behavior can be captured by changes in the aspiration level or reference point. Although heuristics involving satisficing and simple payoff schemes can often lead to reasonable choices, they also can result in choice biases. Using satisficing to guide search and alternative selection, for instance, means that the order in which alternatives are considered can greatly impact the alternative selected. Using simple payoff schemes means that decisions will not consider reasoned trade-offs among conflicting objectives.

Other heuristic mechanisms may involve problem redefinition. Kahneman and Frederick (2002), for instance, argue that people may solve a difficult judgment problem by attribute substitution, i.e., substituting an easier to solve definition of the problem. For example, the more difficult question of how likely it is that a person with characteristics X is currently doing a job with characteristics Y may be answered by substitution of the easier to answer question of how similar the characteristics of X are to the characteristics of Y. The more similar the two sets of characteristics (the more representative), the higher the judged probability. Like selective attention effects, the redefinition of the problem may or may not be something of which the decision maker is aware. Note that use of attribute substitution means that potentially relevant information for probability forecasts, e.g., the base-rates of different jobs, may be neglected.

A critical assumption of the information-processing approach to judgment and choice is that an individual possesses a variety of heuristic strategies for solving decision problems, i.e., a "repertoire," "toolkit," or "toolbox" of strategies (Payne, Bettman, & Johnson, 1993; see Chapter 4, this volume), acquired through experience and more formal training. We have long argued that the use of multiple heuristics contingent upon task demands is a way for humans with limited cognitive capabilities to intelligently adapt to complex decision environments (Payne, Bettman, & Johnson, 1988).

In sum, heuristics provide methods for solving complex problems with limited information processing; heuristics also generally produce satisfactory outcomes. However, the use of heuristic (selective) processes for information processing also means that decision errors can occur; importantly, such errors in judgment and choice will tend to be systematic (predictable). Consequently, systematic human error in decision making does not *require* motivated irrationality but can be the result of a limited information processor trying to do the best that he or she can. Further, the potential biases or errors in reasoning that result should not be viewed as fragile effects that can easily be made to disappear; they are important regularities in decision behavior. These cognitive, as opposed to motivational, aspects of decision errors have important implications for evaluating and aiding decisions.

Methodological Considerations

The information-processing approach to decision research also shares some methodological features. As stressed earlier (quote 1), the information-processing approach emphasizes the study of *how* decisions are made, not just what decisions are made (Simon, 1978). As a result, decision researchers within the information-processing framework often *complement* an analysis of final judgments or choices with the results of "process-tracing" techniques such as verbal reports of processing during the task, i.e., verbal protocols; the monitoring of information search; and response times (Svenson, 1996). The use of process-tracing methods is consistent with the idea that an understanding of decision processes "must be sought through microscopic analysis rather than through indirect and remote interpretations of gross aggregative data" (Simon, 1982, p. 204).

Verbal protocols

Protocol analysis is one approach to gathering detailed data on decision-making processes (e.g., Hastie, Schkade, & Payne, 1998). The essence of a verbal protocol analysis is to ask a subject to give continuous verbal reports, i.e., "to think aloud," while performing some task of interest to the researcher. The researcher treats the verbal protocol as a record of the subject's ongoing problem-solving or decision behavior and interprets what is said as an indication of the subject's state of knowledge at a particular point in time or the use of a particular operation to transform one state of knowledge into another (Newell & Simon, 1972).

Monitoring information search

Monitoring information acquisition behavior is one of the most popular process-tracing methods used by decision researchers. To implement this method, the choice or judgment task is structured so that the subject must seek information so that what and how much information is sought, in what order it is acquired, and how long each piece of information is examined can be monitored easily.

Several methods for monitoring information acquisition behavior have been utilized in the past, ranging from simple "information boards" (e.g., Payne, 1976) to sophisticated eye-movement tracking (Russo & Dosher, 1983). However, today the most common approach is to use computerized information retrieval systems for presenting and recording information acquisition (e.g., Jacoby, Mazursky, Troutman, & Kuss 1984; Payne & Braunstein, 1978), including systems designed for use over the Internet (Edwards & Fasolo, 2001). For recent examples of monitoring information acquisition in studies of predictions and preferential choice, see Newell and Shanks (2003) and Costa-Gomes, Crawford, and Broseta (2001).

Response time

One advantage of information-processing models in decision research is that they provide a natural way of accounting for differences in the time it takes to make particular judgments or choices, due to the ideas of stages of processing, different operations within each stage, and the more general serial processing viewpoint. Thus, information-processing researchers often include response time measures as part of the information that is collected when people make a judgment or choice. For an example of the use of response times to study choice behavior, see Bettman, Johnson & Payne (1990).

An Example of the Information-processing Approach: The Adaptive Decision Maker

We illustrate the use of information-processing methods and concepts by reviewing a program of research on choice among alternative courses of action, often seen as the heart of the decision-making process. A key assumption of this program of research is that how individuals decide how to decide reflects considerations of cognitive effort as well as the accuracy of various information-processing strategies (Payne et al., 1993). The goal of minimizing cognitive effort fits well within the concept of "bounded rationality" advocated by Simon (1955). It is further assumed that how people make decisions is generally adaptive and intelligent, if not always optimal, given multiple goals for a decision.

Task analysis

Given the importance of the structure of task environments in understanding human behavior (Simon, 1990), an important first step is a task analysis. A typical multiattribute choice problem, for instance, consists of a set of m options where each option i (alternative) is described by a vector of n attribute values $(x_{i1}, x_{i2}, \ldots, x_{in})$, with each attribute value reflecting the extent to which each option meets the objectives (goals) of the decision maker for that attribute. A key feature of almost all choice problems is the presence of value conflicts, since usually no single alternative is best (most preferred) on all attributes. Attributes generally vary with respect to their desirability to the decision maker, the uncertainty of actually receiving the attribute value, and the willingness of the decision maker to accept a loss on one attribute for a gain on another attribute. The presence of value conflict, and the fact that a rule for resolving the conflict often cannot be drawn from memory, is why preferential choice problems are generally solved using processes of information acquisition and evaluation rather than simply pattern recognition and response.

Strategies for multiattribute choice problems

How do people solve multiattribute choice problems? Research has shown that an individual uses a variety of different information-processing strategies contingent upon task demands, e.g., the number of alternatives to be considered. Different individuals also tend to use different strategies. Some of those strategies involve the processing of all relevant information about the available alternatives and explicit consideration of the tradeoffs among values (i.e., they are compensatory), whereas other heuristic strategies use information in a more limited and often very selective fashion and avoid tradeoffs (i.e., they are non-compensatory). Some decision strategies process information primarily by alternative, with multiple attributes of a single option processed before another option is considered. Other strategies are more attribute-focused, and the values of several alternatives on a single attribute are examined before information on another attribute is considered.

A classic decision-making strategy is the weighted additive strategy (WADD), which captures trade-off processing and is often considered to be a normative rule for decisions. To implement WADD, a measure of the relative importance (weight) of an attribute is multiplied by the attribute's value for a particular alternative, the products are summed over all attributes to obtain an overall value for that alternative, and the alternative with the highest overall summed evaluation is selected (i.e., WADD is a maximizing strategy). Thus, the WADD strategy uses all the relevant decision information. The weighting and summing of the resulting values potentially allows for a poor value on one attribute to be compensated for by a good value on another attribute. The WADD strategy is also an alternative-based strategy for processing information in that a summary evaluation of one alternative is reached before processing moves on to the next alternative in the choice set. Expected Value, Expected Utility, and various non-linear expectation models for risky decisions are strategies related to WADD (see Chapter 20, this volume).

People sometimes make decisions in ways consistent with WADD and related expectation models; however, these strategies can be very effortful to implement using scarce cognitive resources. Hence, years of decision research have made clear that people often make decisions using simpler decision processes (heuristics). For example, people frequently use a lexicographic strategy (LEX), where the alternative with the best value on the most important attribute is selected (assuming that there are no ties on this attribute). The LEX strategy is a clear example of a choice heuristic, in that people using the strategy are assumed to be highly selective regarding what information is used. The LEX strategy also uses attribute-based information processing. A very similar model for inferential judgments is the take the best heuristic (see Chapter 4, this volume).

In spite of its highly selective use of information, in some task conditions the very simple LEX choice heuristic can produce similar decisions as more information-intensive strategies like WADD (Johnson & Payne, 1985). In some decision environments (e.g., tasks where there is high variance in decision weights across attributes), there is relatively little cost in terms of decision quality associated with using a LEX strategy to make a choice. This is a critical point, because it implies that the use of a heuristic like the LEX strategy may be an adaptive response to some decision tasks for a decision maker who has a goal of saving cognitive effort as well as making the best possible choice. That is, although heuristics may not be optimal strategies in the narrow sense of decision accuracy alone, they may be reasonable ways to solve many decision problems.

Although the LEX heuristic performs well in some environments, it can lead to errors such as intransitive patterns of choice when combined with the idea that people have a just-noticeable-difference structure on attribute values (a lexicographic semi-order) (Tversky, 1969). As would be expected, the more the task environment is characterized by multiple important attributes, the less well the LEX strategy does in making a high quality decision (Johnson and Payne, 1985). For a similar point in terms of the take the best heuristic, see Martignon and Krauss (2003).

Simon (1955) proposed a satisficing (SAT) strategy for decisions. In SAT, each attribute's value for the option currently under consideration is compared to a predetermined cutoff level for that attribute. If any attribute fails to meet the cutoff level, the option is rejected and the next option is considered. SAT is alternative-based because multiple attributes can be considered for an alternative, although there will generally be variance in how much information is processed for each alternative. Importantly, the first option in a choice set passing the cutoffs for all attributes is selected, so people are not assumed to maximize; stopping after a satisfactory alternative has been identified can save a lot of information processing. If no option passes all the cutoffs, the levels can be relaxed and the process repeated. Busemeyer and Johnson offer a model for preference that combines elements of the LEX, SAT, and WADD strategies (see Chapter 7, this volume).

Elimination by aspects (EBA) is a commonly used decision strategy that contains elements of both the LEX and SAT strategies. EBA eliminates options that do not meet a minimum cutoff value or do not have a desired aspect for the most important attribute. This elimination process is repeated for the second most important attribute and continues with the next most important attributes, with processing continuing until a single option remains (Tversky, 1972). EBA focuses on attributes as the basis for processing information, is noncompensatory, and does not use all potentially relevant information. To the extent that the order in which the attributes are used reflects the decision maker's basic values, this heuristic may work well. However, to the extent that the attributes used reflect "irrelevant" factors of selective attention such as the salience of particular attributes in a display, the EBA strategy may not perform well in terms of decision accuracy.

Decision makers may also use combined choice strategies. A typical combined strategy has an initial phase in which some alternatives are eliminated and a second phase in which the remaining options are analyzed in more detail. One frequently observed combination is initial use of EBA to reduce the choice set to two or three options followed by a compensatory strategy such as WADD to select among those. An implication of using combined strategies is that the "properties" of the choice task may change as the result of using a particular strategy first. For example, the initial use of a process for eliminating dominated alternatives from a choice set, an often advocated procedure, will make the conflict among attribute values more extreme, perhaps then triggering the application of a new strategy on the reduced set of options.

Strategy selection

A critical question for the information-processing approach to decision research is how, and why, does a decision maker select one decision strategy instead of another for a particular task? A hypothesis that has led to a great deal of research is that strategy selection is guided by goals of both minimizing cognitive effort and achieving a satisfactory level of decision accuracy (Beach & Mitchell, 1978; Payne, 1976).

The different decision strategies described above seemingly require different amounts of computational effort; however, we need a more precise level of analysis to compare decision strategies in terms of cognitive effort. We have taken the approach of decomposing choice strategies like WADD and EBA into more basic components called elementary information processes (EIPs), with a specific decision strategy defined in terms of a specific collection and sequence of EIPs. Newell and Simon (1972) suggest that the number of EIPs needed for a strategy to complete a task provides a measure of the cognitive processing effort for that strategy for that task. The set of EIPs we have used includes such operations as reading information, comparing values, adding values, and eliminating options or attributes from consideration. We can then characterize each strategy by a sequence of such operations. A lexicographic choice strategy, for example, would involve a number of reading and comparison EIPs, but no compensatory EIPs such as adding or multiplying.

A particular set of EIPs represents a theoretical judgment regarding the appropriate level of decomposition for choice processes. For instance, one could further decompose a multiplication EIP into more detailed elementary information processes. One could also use more general processing components, e.g., a rule for selective search and a rule for stopping search. We believe that the level of decomposition represented by EIPs such as reading information or comparing values, however, is sufficiently detailed to provide useful measures of the relative cognitive effort of various decision strategies in differing task environments. Such EIPs are similar to those postulated for other cognitive tasks and have been successfully used to predict decision times and self-reports of decision effort (Bettman et al., 1990).

To measure the cognitive effort of specific decision strategies in various task environments more precisely, strategies can be modeled as production systems (Newell & Simon, 1972). A production system consists of a set of productions expressed as (condition)–(action) pairs, a task environment, and a (typically limited) working memory. The actions in a production are performed (fired) only when the condition matches the contents of working memory, which can contain both information read from the environment and information deposited by the actions of other production rules. Actions can include both changes to the task environment (e.g., eliminate option A from further consideration) and the creation of new states of knowledge (e.g., gamble one has the best chance of winning). Once decision strategies have been represented in the form of production systems, the performance of those strategies can be assessed using computer simulation, another method widely used in the information-processing approach.

Simulation of effort and accuracy in decision environments

We have used production system representations of decision strategies and computer simulation to explore the cognitive effort and accuracy of various strategies in a wide variety of decision environments (Johnson & Payne, 1985; Bettman, Johnson, Luce, & Payne, 1993; Payne, Bettman, & Luce, 1996; see also, Chapter 4, this volume). Typically, we have used the performance of normative models for the task, e.g., WADD or expected value, as the standards for accuracy. In preference tasks, as opposed to inference tasks, individual differences in values must be acknowledged to define what constitutes an accurate or high quality decision. It is also likely that individuals adjust their standard for accuracy as a function of task demands (see Chapter 7, this volume).

Several conclusions about decision heuristics are suggested by these simulation results. First, heuristic choice strategies can be highly accurate with substantial savings in cognitive effort. Thus, the use of choice heuristics can be a reasonable (adaptive) response for a decision maker concerned with both minimizing the use of scarce cognitive resources and making good decisions. Second, no single heuristic does well across all environments in terms of accuracy. The lack of generalized good performance for any given heuristic across all task environments is one of the costs of heuristic processing. This result suggests that *if a decision maker wants to achieve both a reasonably high level of accuracy and low effort (by using heuristics), he or she must use a repertoire (toolbox) of heuristic strategies, with selection contingent upon situational demands.*

Third, the cognitive effort required with heuristics increases more slowly than the effort required to use WADD as the choice task is made more complex. Fourth, the accuracy advantage of strategies like WADD is greatest in contexts with greater levels of conflict among the attribute values (i.e., more negative intercorrelation among the attributes) or lower dispersion (more nearly equal values) in the probabilities of the outcomes or the weights of the attributes of the alternatives in a choice set. More generally, one advantage of more "normative" strategies like WADD is that accuracy tends to be less sensitive to changes in task and context factors than is the case for heuristics. One exception to this general conclusion is the case of time pressure; although increased time pressure hurts the accuracy of all choice strategies, the biggest impact in terms of lowering accuracy is for WADD, because time often expires before computations can be completed. In cases of substantial time pressure, the simple LEX rule is often "best" in terms of maintaining decision accuracy (Payne et al., 1988; Payne et al., 1996). That is, it is best to examine some, albeit limited, information about each option under severe time pressure rather than to examine some options in more depth and not examine others at all.

Experiments examining adaptive strategy selection

Simulation results highlight how an idealized adaptive decision maker might shift choice strategies as task and context demands change. Do actual decision makers behave adaptively? In our experimental work, described next, participants make choices among options under various choice environment properties such as time pressure, and we observe the details of their information processing. Hypotheses regarding how observable aspects of processing may change are derived from the simulations. In the various experiments summarized below, we use process-tracing methods to measure the extent to which such aspects of processing vary with changes in the decision task. These aspects include the amount of information processed, the selectivity of information processing, the degree of alternative-based versus attribute-based processing, and the extent to which attribute-based processing involves multiple alternatives. Each of these aspects of processing can be related to prototypical decision strategies. For example, the EBA strategy uses less than complete information, is selective across alternatives, and uses relatively more attribute-based processing that can extend over multiple alternatives (n > 2); on the other hand, WADD uses complete information, is not selective, and is alternative based. The experiments also include the use of within subject designs to provide a strong test of adaptivity, the use of performance contingent payoffs, and the assessment of final choices and judgments as well as process measures of behavior.

What has been learned from such experiments? One clear result is that people increase their use of choice heuristics such as EBA and satisficing as the decision task becomes more complex. For instance, people process information quite differently if faced with many alternatives (four or more) than if faced with just two or three alternatives in a choice set. Importantly, these strategy shifts as a function of task complexity occur within subjects. That is, the same individual will use a more compensatory strategy in some situations and a more heuristic strategy in other situations. This result directly supports the critical idea that a person has a repertoire of decision strategies. In addition, there is evidence that people sometimes adapt their processing in top-down fashion. The following excerpts from verbal protocols of two decision makers illustrate this point: (1) "Well, with these many apartments (six) to choose from, I'm not going to work through all the characteristics. Start eliminating them as soon as possible" (Payne, 1976); (2) "With just two [gambles] to choose from, I'm going to go after all the information. It won't be that much trouble" (Payne and Braunstein, 1978). Thus, people sometimes plan a priori how to solve various types of problems. However, we also believe that strategy selection proceeds at other times in a much more bottom-up, constructive fashion, with little or no conscious awareness of a strategy being selected. Instead, people adjust their processing during the course of solving a decision problem in an "opportunistic" fashion as they learn more about the structure of the decision.

Another result is that processes like WADD are more likely to be used when decision accuracy is emphasized more than saving decision effort (Creyer, Bettman, & Payne, 1990), consistent with the general idea of a cost–benefit tradeoff underlying strategy selection. A less obvious prediction from the simulations, verified in the experimental results, is that the use of processes such as WADD is greater in task environments characterized by greater levels of conflict among the attribute values (i.e., more negative intercorrelation among the attributes) (Bettman et al., 1993). Simulation results show that in domains characterized by negative correlations among attributes, the relative penalty in decision quality for using a heuristic is greater. Interestingly, subjects who shifted strategies more in response to different levels of attribute correlation were better performers in terms of average payoffs.

One of the most important decision task variables is time pressure. Time pressure can result because a decision must be made by a certain point in time or because errors in judgment or choice can result from either deciding too soon (rush-to-judgment) or from delaying decisions too long (opportunity-cost). One of the major advantages of heuristic decision rules is that they can lead to quicker decisions, and, as noted above, our simulation results suggest that simple heuristics such as LEX perform better than WADD in terms of maintaining decision accuracy in the face of substantial time pressure, both for time pressure that is the result of a fixed time constraint for making a decision and for opportunity-cost time pressure. Shifting to strategies more like the LEX rule is associated with higher payoffs under such time pressure. Thus, adaptive decision behavior is characterized by more selective and more attribute-based processing under time pressure. There is also evidence of a hierarchy of responses to time pressure. People shift towards strategies like LEX as time pressure is increased, but this shift in processing tends to occur only after the decision maker first tries to respond by simply increasing the speed with which he or she tries to carry out the current decision strategy. Finally, we predict that those subjects who adapt more to time pressure by shifting strategies, and not just by working faster, will perform better, i.e., achieve greater decision accuracy. These predictions have been verified in several experiments (Payne et al., 1988; Payne et al., 1996).

Such results support the claim that decision makers often use choice heuristics in adaptive ways. However, we have also shown that contingent strategy use is not always appropriate. In one of the Payne et al. (1996) studies, for example, we found that people were not adaptive in terms of decision accuracy under competing time pressure and correlation structure demands. In particular, greater responsiveness to correlation structure under no time pressure resulted in higher payoffs, whereas greater responsiveness to correlation structure under time pressure led to lower payoffs; shifting to more alternative-based, non-selective processing strategies in response to negative correlation is not adaptive under conditions of time pressure.

To summarize, our program of research shows that an individual uses a variety of strategies to solve multiattribute choice problems, including heuristic strategies involving highly selective information processing. We can predict the conditions under which certain types of decision strategies are more or less likely to be used, based upon such factors as the number of options, time pressure, information format, response mode, attribute correlational structure, and so on. Next, we briefly review an extension of the Adaptive Decision Maker framework that includes emotion and other goals for a decision.

Emotion and Other Goals: Bringing Together the Scarecrow and the Tin Man

Cognitive effort and decision accuracy are two primary determinants of decision behavior. However, it is increasingly clear that strategy selection and other forms of decision behavior also are influenced by other goals, often developed constructively on the spot. Note that these goals can apply both to the processes of the decision and the products of the decision.

A choice goals framework for decision making

Bettman, Luce, and Payne (1998) suggest that four important meta-goals for choice are maximizing the accuracy of a decision, minimizing the cognitive effort required for the decision, minimizing the experience of negative emotion while making the decision and afterwards, and maximizing the ease of justification of a decision. This set of goals adds two goals relating to negative emotion and justification to the standard accuracy/effort approach.

Different subsets of these goals are likely to be relevant in different situations depending upon such factors as the importance and irreversibility of the decision and the timeliness and ambiguity of the feedback available on performance relative to each goal. For instance, effort feedback is generally much easier to obtain than accuracy feedback (Einhorn, 1980). This is one reason why cognitive effort considerations may play such a big role in explaining decision behavior. Obviously, however, the usefulness of a choice goals framework is compromised if too many goals are postulated, such as a different goal for each decision. Accordingly, we have focused on the limited subset of goals listed above, because we believe these four meta-goals capture many of the most important motivational aspects relevant to decision making.

Minimizing negative emotion

Although not all decisions are likely to evoke emotional responses, it is clear that people sometimes face emotion-laden choices. For instance, consumers find certain tradeoffs more emotionally difficult than others, e.g., trading off the increased safety of a larger vehicle against environmental damage due to poorer gas mileage. At the extreme, people often resist even thinking about such issues as the value in monetary terms of saving a human life or accepting a decrease in environmental quality. Tetlock (2002) has referred to such tradeoffs of sacred versus profane considerations as taboo tradeoffs. Note that the nature of emotion-laden choices is such that the ensuing negative emotion is associated with the decision itself and not with some unrelated ambient negative mood.

How might the negative emotions experienced while making a choice involving difficult tradeoffs impact strategy selection and decision making? One approach is to argue that emotion will interfere with decision processes, degrading cognitive performance (e.g., Hancock & Warm, 1989). Thus, one could modify the models of decision strategies illustrated above by assuming that any cognitive operation will both take more time and contain more error as negative emotion is increased. This suggests that decision makers adapting to negative emotion will simply shift to easier-to-implement decision strategies, analogous to the effects of increasing task complexity.

Another approach to broadening information-processing theories to account for the influence of emotions is to argue that decision makers may directly adapt to the negative emotion itself. People can respond to emotion-laden tasks in two related, but separate ways. One way is to use what Folkman and Lazarus (1988) have called problem-focused coping. That is, negative emotions associated with a task are dealt with by trying to solve the problem as well as possible, in effect treating negative emotions as a signal of decision importance. Trying to solve the decision problem effectively will increase the weight given to the goal of maximizing accuracy. As noted above, the motivation to perform accurately is often associated with more extensive processing of information. Extensive processing of information is the most readily available (to oneself) and observable (to others) indicator of one's motivation to be accurate. This suggests that instead of leading to the use of easier heuristic strategies, increased negative emotion associated with a decision should lead to more extensive processing.

A second way of coping with emotion-laden decisions is to take actions to directly minimize emotion by changing the amount or content of thought about the decision (emotion-focused coping). At one extreme, this can involve avoidant behaviors such as refusing to make any decision (Anderson, 2003), letting another make the decision for you, or showing an increased preference for the status quo option or any other option that is more easy to justify to oneself or others (Luce, 1998). A related strategy is not to avoid the decision altogether but instead to avoid whatever specific aspects of the decision problem one finds most distressing, even under high levels of trade-off-induced negative emotion. For example, an individual undertaking an automobile purchase may refuse to consider the possibility that he or she may be involved in a life-threatening accident, yet may be quite willing to carefully assess other aspects of the purchase decision (e.g., the cost, reliability, and styling of various cars). We believe that explicitly making tradeoffs generates negative emotions, so one hypothesis is that individuals may cope with emotion-laden decisions by avoiding tradeoffs and adopting non-compensatory strategies such as LEX. Any attribute-based processing strategy is likely to minimize confronting the possibility that one attribute must be sacrificed to gain another (Hogarth, 1987).

Thus, if individuals try to directly adapt to negative emotion, the arguments above imply that people will simultaneously process more extensively (reflecting an accuracy goal) and in a more attribute-based fashion (reflecting a goal of minimizing negative emotion by avoiding difficult tradeoffs) in emotion-laden choices. In a series of studies involving either the selection of a child to support through a charity or a job choice, Luce, Bettman, & Payne (1997) found these predicted shifts in processing (i.e., a simultaneous increase in the amount of processing and more attribute-based processing). In other studies, we have also found less willingness to trade off higher values on a quality attribute for a lower price as the quality attribute under consideration increases in emotional tradeoff difficulty, regardless of which attribute is seen as more important (Luce, Payne, & Bettman, 1999, 2000).

To further demonstrate the necessity of considering an emotion-minimization goal, we examine reactions to increased decision conflict (more negative intercorrelation among the attributes). In the Bettman et al. (1993) studies of choice among gambles summarized above, increased conflict among attributes resulted in more processing, less selectivity in processing, and more alternative-based processing, consistent with increased use of strategies like WADD. In the Luce et al. (1997) studies, on the other hand, increased conflict was associated with more extensive and more attribute-based processing. In combination, these two sets of studies suggest that decision makers tend to confront between-attribute tradeoffs required by decision conflict explicitly when attributes are relatively low in emotional tradeoff difficulty, but they avoid these explicit tradeoffs when attributes are higher in emotional tradeoff difficulty. Somewhat ironically, decision makers may be more willing to use the types of conflict-confronting processes associated with normative decision rules for less emotion-laden choices than they are for more emotion-laden and sometimes more crucial decisions. See Luce et al., (2001) for more details on the work summarized above.

Maximizing ease of justification

The choice goals framework advocated by Bettman et al. (1998) also includes the goal of easily justifying a decision to others or to oneself (Tetlock, 2002). Due to space limitations, we do not review research indicating that ease of justification cannot be fully accounted for by accuracy and effort considerations. We stress, however, that maximizing ease of justification may involve the use of a different type of decision heuristic based on easily seen and communicable relationships among options, such as simply choosing the compromise option in a set. We have called such heuristics relational heuristics (Bettman et al., 1998); changes in the set of options under consideration change the relationships among the options and therefore some of the potential reasons for choosing among the options. To illustrate, consider research on the "asymmetric dominance" effect (Huber, Payne, & Puto, 1982; Simonson & Tversky, 1992). One classic assumption of rational choice theories is *regularity*, i.e., adding a new alternative to a choice set cannot increase the probability of choosing a member of the original choice set. However, people's choices do not always obey regularity. In particular, adding an option to a choice set that is dominated by one option in the original set but not by the other (an asymmetric dominance relationship) has the remarkable effect of actually increasing the choice share of the dominating alternative, violating the principle of regularity. In an important study dealing with the need to justify a decision, Simonson (1989) showed that an increased need for justification led to a greater asymmetric dominance effect.

Boxes 6.1 and 6.2 provide summaries of the major elements of the "Adaptive Decision Maker" framework and the major results from that program of research. Chapter 4, this volume, summarizes a very related program of research dealing with "fast and frugal" heuristics for predictive and probability judgments.

Dual Process Theories

Another extension of the information-processing perspective is dual process views of thinking. Recent theorizing in psychology (e.g., Hogarth, 2001; Kahneman & Frederick, 2002; Sloman, 1996) has argued for two modes of thinking characterized by different properties. One type of thinking, called System 1 thinking, is relatively unconscious, automatic, highly associative, rapid, contextualized, parallel, evolved early, is relatively independent of language, and generates feelings of certitude. System 1 thinking is related to what is commonly called intuition and also to the "affect heuristic," which reaches good–bad assessments in a rapid, automatic, and relatively effortless manner (Slovic, Finucane, Peters, & MacGregor, 2002). System 2 thinking is controllable, conscious, constrained by working memory, rule-based, serial, develops with age and is vulnerable to aging, is related to language, and is less characterized by feelings of certitude. System 2 thinking is commonly called analytic. These two systems probably represent the ends of a continuum rather than two distinct categories (Hammond, 1996).

As noted earlier, Simon (1979) argues strongly for the serial nature of the higher-level cognitive, attention-demanding, information-processing activities that characterize much

---

Box 6.1 Assumptions of the Adaptive Decision Maker Framework

People have a constrained repertoire (toolbox) of strategies for solving decision problems, including choice heuristics like the lexicographic choice rule and elimination-by-aspects; relational heuristics that focus on the ordinal relationships among options, such as choosing an asymmetrically dominating option or a compromise option; and more compensatory strategies like weighted additive value.

Strategies for solving decision problems are acquired through experience and training as well as potentially being "hardwired."

Constraints on the repertoire of strategies available to solve a specific problem include knowledge of strategies and cognitive limits on the implementation of a strategy in particular task environments.

Different strategies have differing advantages and disadvantages for any particular decision task, and these relative advantages and disadvantages are contingent upon task, context, social, and individual difference factors.

The advantages and disadvantages of strategies relate to the meta-goals of decision makers. Four important meta-goals for decision making are maximizing the accuracy of the decision, minimizing the cognitive effort required for the decision, minimizing the experience of negative emotion while making the decision and afterwards, and maximizing the ease of justification for the decision.

Strategies are sequences of mental operations used to transform an initial state of knowledge into an achieved goal state where the decision problem is viewed as solved. The relative cognitive effort needed to execute a particular strategy in a specific task environment reflects both the number *and* types of mental operations used. Certain mental operations, e.g., making tradeoffs, will also tend to be more emotionally difficult and less easy to justify to others as the basis for choice.

Individuals select among strategies in an adaptive fashion that can lead to reasonable performance on the meta-goals of accuracy, effort, the experience of negative emotion, and justification.

Strategy selection is sometimes a conscious top-down process reflecting learned contingencies, but it also can be a bottom-up process responding in an opportunistic fashion to information encountered during the decision process.

---

decision making. In terms of dual-process models of cognition, therefore, the focus of Simon's work and much of the decision research reviewed in this chapter is System 2 thinking, although relational heuristics may be more akin to System 1. However, there is growing awareness that information processing below the level of consciousness (i.e., System 1) may have a far greater impact on judgments and choices than previously realized (Bargh & Chartrand, 1999; Hogarth, 2001). To be fair, Simon (1983) also argued that any kind of serious, complex thinking employs both analytical and intuitive thought in varying proportions and in various ways.

Box 6.2 Results from the Adaptive Decision Maker Research Program

Heuristic strategies such as the lexicographic rule that involve highly selective processing of information and that use only relatively simple mental operations can provide relatively high levels of decision accuracy with substantial savings of both effort and the experience of negative emotion.

No single choice heuristic performs well in terms of accuracy, effort, negative emotion, and justification across changes in the task environment. As a result, people shift strategies as a function of task and context demands consistent with the relative emphasis placed on accuracy, effort, negative emotion, and justification.

Although not perfectly adaptive, people often change strategies appropriately given changes in features of the decision problem. Furthermore, the more adaptive the decision maker, the better the relative performance.

Effort considerations may be more salient than accuracy considerations in the selection of a strategy due to ease of assessment.

Strategies like weighted additive value that impose greater information processing demands are generally less sensitive to changes in the task environment than simplifying heuristics in terms of accuracy but are more sensitive in terms of effort. However, under some conditions (e.g., time constraints), a heuristic strategy can be more accurate than a strategy like weighted additive value.

People use a hierarchy of responses to time pressure: acceleration of processing, then increased selectivity of processing, and finally changes in strategies.

Emotion-laden choices are characterized by more extensive, more selective, and more attribute-based processing. In general, emotion-laden choices encourage avoidant behaviors.

Many context effects can be accounted for by general heuristics that focus on the ordinal relationships among options; these relationships often are viewed as reasons or justifications for choice.

People have greater difficulties in properly assessing and adapting to context factors than to task factors, which is one source of failure in adaptivity.

We believe that an important direction for broadening the information-processing framework is to examine how processes of judgment that evoke little or no attention demands (System 1 thinking) interact with "higher" level, attention-demanding, cognitive processes (System 2 thinking). One hypothesis is that an initial judgment involving little or no effort and no conscious awareness is arrived at quickly via System 1 thinking and that such an initial judgment may then either be expressed immediately or be confirmed or corrected by more effortful, conscious, System 2 processing (e.g., Cobos, Almaraz, & García-Madruga, 2003).

Correction of System 1 thinking by System 2 thinking is one way in which the two modes of thinking may interact. Another possible way the two types of thinking may interrelate is expressed in "selection" models (Gilbert & Gill, 2000). Selection models argue that the mode of processing is selected based on such factors as cognitive load or time pressure. For instance, one would expect System 1 thinking to be selected when cognitive load was high or time was short, a variant of the adaptive strategy selection ideas expressed earlier in this chapter. Correction models, on the other hand, suggest that people generally start with System 1 processes and then may or may not engage in System 2 processing. That is, System 1 is the default processing mode, always exerting an influence on judgments and choices, and the results of System 1 are sometimes corrected and sometimes not corrected by System 2 processing. Note that the results of System 1 judgments may also influence any later System 2 thinking through such effects as predecisional information distortion (Russo, Meloy, & Medvec, 1998).

An evolutionary, adaptive argument for the value of a corrective approach to judgment is that our environment has been structured so that most of the time quick, low-effort judgmental systems yield good answers, with the corrective system only needed to deal with more unusual cases. Hogarth (2001) argues that a mark of intelligence among humans is learning when intuition (System 1 thinking) may be erroneous and how to use deliberate (System 2) thought appropriately to correct such judgments. However, Wilson and Brekke (1994) suggest that correction processes may be relatively rare. Correction of an initial judgment requires awareness of the potential for bias or error *and* the ability *and* the motivation to correct the flawed judgment process. If either awareness or ability or motivation is lacking, correction will not take place. Thus, many judgments we observe may be the result of System 1 thinking rather than more analytical System 2 thought. However, modern technological society, with frequent and often large changes in the decision environment, may require more and more System 2 thinking. That is, more experientially based System 1 thinking may perform more poorly the more it is asked to deal with events to be experienced in a future that might be different from the past.

Although System 2 thinking has been the focus of much of the research within the information-processing approach to decisions, particularly preferential choice, there is still much to learn about the nature of System 1 decision making and how Systems 1 and 2 may interact. Such learning may be facilitated by adapting some of the concepts and methods of the information-processing approach. For example, it may be possible to engage in "process-tracing" for System 1 thinking by using new techniques in neuroscience to provide time-ordered data localized to particular brain areas (Breiter, Aharon, Kahneman, Dale, & Shizgal, 2001). Developing computational models of specific System 1 judgment strategies (e.g., relational heuristics), as has been done for System 2 choice strategies, may also help in understanding how the various systems of thinking interact.

Conclusion

In the 50 years since Simon's (1955) classic article on bounded rationality, much has been learned about the processes of decision making. There is now a strong research foundation for Simon's conjectures about the nature of decision processes. People often make judgments and choices using simplifying mechanisms (heuristics) that are attuned to and constrained by people's limited computational capabilities. Many heuristics for judgment and choice have been, and continue to be, identified. Some of those heuristics reflect simple rules for System 2 thinking and some represent more perceptually based (System 1) thinking.

Importantly, the same individual has been shown to use many different heuristics contingent upon task demands. Simon's point that "human rational behavior is shaped by a scissors whose two blades are the structure of task environments and the computational capabilities of the actor" (Simon, 1990, p. 7) has been verified over and over again.

Use of multiple heuristics contingent upon task demands often leads to reasonable (satisfactory) decision outcomes. It is clear, however, that using heuristics can lead to predictable and significant decision errors. The task-contingent nature of human decision processing also means that people systematically violate the principles of descriptive, procedural, and context invariance traditionally assumed by economic models. As a result, the view that preferences and beliefs are frequently constructed as needed on the spot, rather than simply retrieved from memory, is becoming increasingly accepted and has important implications for the understanding, assessment, and improvement of decisions (Payne, Bettman, & Schkade, 1999).

Taken together, the past 50 years of decision research using concepts and process-tracing methods from the information-processing approach have resulted in a more complex, yet more realistic, view of the processes of actual human decision making. Although a theory should be no more complex than necessary, a good theory of the psychology of judgment and choice behavior should be complex enough to capture the key cognitive and emotional mechanisms leading to a decision. Increasingly, there is less need to "satisfice" in our models of decision behavior. Many of the once "revolutionary" ideas of Simon have now been empirically verified and have become part of the mainstream in decision research.

References

Anderson, C. J. (2003) The psychology of doing nothing: Forms of decision avoidance result from reason and emotion, *Psychological Bulletin*, 129, 139–67.

Bargh, J. A. & Chartrand, T. L. (1999) The unbearable automaticity of being, *American Psychologist*, 54, 462–79.

Baum, L. F. (1903 [1984]) *The Wizard of Oz*. New York: Grosset and Dunlop.

Beach, L. R. & Mitchell, T. R. (1978) A contingency model for the selection of decision strategies, *Academy of Management Review*, 3, 439–49.

Bettman, J. R. (1979) *An Information Processing Theory of Consumer Choice*. Reading, MA: Addison-Wesley.

Bettman, J. R., Johnson, E. J., Luce, M. F., & Payne, J. W. (1993) Correlation, conflict, and choice, *Journal of Experimental Psychology: Learning, Memory, and Cognition*, 19, 931–51.

Bettman, J. R., Johnson, E. J., & Payne, J. W. (1990) A componential analysis of cognitive effort in choice, *Organizational Behavior and Human Decision Processes*, 45, 111–39.

Bettman, J. R., Luce, M. F., and Payne, J. W. (1998) Constructive consumer choice processes, *Journal of Consumer Research*, 25, 187–217.

Breiter, H. C., Aharon, I., Kahneman, D., Dale, A., & Shizgal, P. (2001) Functional imaging of neural responses to expectancy and experience of monetary gains and losses, *Neuron*, 30, 619–39.

Cobos, P. L., Almaraz, J., & García-Madruga, J. A. (2003) An associative framework for probability judgment: An application to biases, *Journal of Experimental Psychology: Learning, Memory, and Cognition*, 29, 80–96.

Conlisk, J. (1996) Why bounded rationality? *Journal of Economic Literature*, 34, 669–700.

Costa-Gomes, M., Crawford, V. P., & Broseta, B. (2001) Cognition and behavior in normal-form games: An experimental study, *Econometrica*, 69, 1193–235.

Creyer, E. H., Bettman, J. R., & Payne, J. W. (1990) The impact of accuracy and effort feedback and goals on adaptive decision behavior, *Journal of Behavioral Decision Making*, 3, 1–16.

Edwards, W. & Fasolo, B. (2001) Decision technology, *Annual Review of Psychology*, 52, 581–606.

Einhorn, H. J. (1980) Learning from experience and suboptimal rules in decision making. In T. S. Wallsten (ed.), *Cognitive Processes in Choice and Decision Behavior* (pp. 1–20). Hillsdale, NJ: Erlbaum.

Folkman, S. & Lazarus, R. S. (1988) Coping as a mediator of emotion, *Journal of Personality and Social Psychology*, 54, 466–75.

Gilbert, D. T. & Gill, M. J. (2000) The momentary realist, *Psychological Science*, 11, 394–8.

Hammond, K. R. (1996) *Human Judgment and Social Policy: Irreducible Uncertainty, Inevitable Error, Unavoidable Injustice*. New York: Oxford University Press.

Hancock, P. A. & Warm, J. S. (1989) A dynamic model of stress and sustained attention, *Human Factors*, 31, 519–37.

Hastie, R., Schkade, D. A., & Payne, J. W. (1998) A study of juror and jury judgments in civil cases: Deciding liability for punitive damages, *Law & Human Behavior*, 22, 287–314.

Higgins, E. T. (2002) How self-regulation creates distinct values: The case of promotion and prevention decision making, *Journal of Consumer Psychology*, 12, 177–91.

Hogarth, R. M. (1987) *Judgement and Choice* (2nd edn.). New York: Wiley.

Hogarth, R. M. (2001) *Educating Intuition*. Chicago: University of Chicago Press.

Huber, J., Payne, J. W., & Puto, C. P. (1982) Adding asymmetrically dominated alternatives: Violations of regularity and the similarity hypothesis, *Journal of Consumer Research*, 10, 31–44.

Jacoby, J., Mazursky, D., Troutman, T., & Kuss, A. (1984) When feedback is ignored: Disutility of outcome feedback, *Journal of Applied Psychology*, 69, 531–45.

Johnson, E. J. & Payne, J. W. (1985) Effort and accuracy in choice, *Management Science*, 31, 394–414.

Kahneman, D. (1973) *Attention and Effort*. Englewood Cliffs, NJ: Prentice-Hall.

Kahneman, D. & Frederick, S. (2002) Representativeness revisited: Attribute substitution in intuitive judgment. In T. Gilovich, D. Griffin, and D. Kahneman (eds.), *Heuristics and Biases: The Psychology of Intuitive Judgment* (pp. 49–81). Cambridge: Cambridge University Press.

Luce, M. F. (1998) Choosing to avoid: Coping with negatively emotion-laden consumer decisions, *Journal of Consumer Research*, 24, 409–33.

Luce, M. F., Bettman, J. R., & Payne, J. W. (1997) Choice processing in emotionally difficult decisions, *Journal of Experimental Psychology: Learning, Memory, and Cognition*, 23, 384–405.

Luce, M. F., Bettman, J. R., & Payne, J. W. (2001) *Emotional Decisions: Tradeoff Difficulty and Coping in Consumer Choice*, Monographs of the *Journal of Consumer Research*, 1. Chicago: University of Chicago Press.

Luce, M. F., Payne, J. W., & Bettman, J. R. (1999) Emotional trade-off difficulty and choice, *Journal of Marketing Research*, 36, 143–59.

Luce, M. F., Payne, J. W., & Bettman, J. R. (2000) Coping with unfavorable attribute values in choice, *Organizational Behavior and Human Decision Processes*, 81, 274–99.

Martignon, L. & Krauss, S. (2003) Can L'Homme Eclaire be fast and frugal? Reconciling Bayesianism and bounded rationality. In S. L. Schneider and J. Shanteau (eds.), *Emerging Perspectives on Judgment and Decision Research* (pp. 108–22). Cambridge: Cambridge University Press.

Newell, A. & Simon, H. A. (1972) *Human Problem Solving*. Englewood Cliffs, NJ: Prentice-Hall.

Newell, B. R. & Shanks, D. R. (2003) Take the best or look at the rest? Factors influencing "one reason" decision making, *Journal of Experimental Psychology: Learning, Memory, and Cognition*, 29, 53–65.

Payne, J. W. (1976) Task complexity and contingent processing in decision making: An information search and protocol analysis, *Organizational Behavior and Human Performance*, 16, 366–87.

Payne, J. W. (1982) Contingent decision behavior, *Psychological Bulletin*, 92, 382–402.

Payne, J. W., Bettman, J. R., & Johnson, E. J. (1988) Adaptive strategy selection in decision making, *Journal of Experimental Psychology: Learning, Memory, and Cognition*, 14, 534–552.

Payne, J. W., Bettman, J. R., & Johnson, E. J. (1992) Behavioral decision research: A constructive processing perspective, *Annual Review of Psychology*, 43, 87–131.

Payne, J. W., Bettman, J. R., & Johnson, E. J. (1993) *The Adaptive Decision Maker*. Cambridge: Cambridge University Press.

Payne, J. W., Bettman, J. R., & Luce, M. F. (1996) When time is money: Decision behavior under opportunity-cost time pressure, *Organizational Behavior and Human Decision Processes*, 66, 131–52.

Payne, J. W., Bettman, J. R., and Schkade, D. A. (1999) Measuring constructed preferences: Towards a building code, *Journal of Risk and Uncertainty*, 19, 243–70.

Payne, J. W. and Braunstein, M. L. (1978) Risky choice: An examination of information acquisition behavior, *Memory & Cognition*, 6, 554–61.

Russo, J. E. & Dosher, B. A. (1983) Strategies for multiattribute binary choice, *Journal of Experimental Psychology: Learning, Memory, and Cognition*, 9, 676–96.

Russo, J. E., Meloy, M. G., & Medvec, V. H. (1998) Predecisional distortion of product information, *Journal of Marketing Research*, 35, 438–52.

Shiv, B. & Fedorikhin, A. (1999) Heart and mind in conflict: The interplay of affect and cognition in consumer decision making, *Journal of Consumer Research*, 26, 278–92.

Simon, H. A. (1955) A behavioral model of rational choice, *Quarterly Journal of Economics*, 69, 99–118.

Simon, H. A. (1978) Rationality as process and as product of thought, *American Economic Review*, 68, 1–16.

Simon, H. A. (1979) *Models of Thought*. New Haven, CT: Yale University Press.

Simon, H. A. (1981) *The Sciences of the Artificial* (2nd edn.). Cambridge, MA: MIT Press.

Simon, H. A. (1982) *Models of Bounded Rationality*. Cambridge, MA: MIT Press.

Simon, H. A. (1983) *Reason in Human Affairs*. Stanford, CA: Stanford University Press.

Simon, H. A. (1990) Invariants of human behavior, *Annual Review of Psychology*, 41, 1–19.

Simonson, I. (1989) Choice based on reasons: The case of attraction and compromise effects, *Journal of Consumer Research*, 16, 158–74.

Simonson, I. & Tversky, A. (1992) Choice in context: Tradeoff contrast and extremeness aversion, *Journal of Marketing Research*, 29, 281–95.

Sloman, S. A. (1996) The empirical case for two systems of reasoning, *Psychological Bulletin*, 119, 3–22.

Slovic, P. (1972) From Shakespeare to Simon: Speculation – and some evidence – about man's ability to process information, *Oregon Research Institute Bulletin*, 12(3), 1–29.

Slovic, P. (1995) The construction of preference, *American Psychologist*, 50, 364–71.

Slovic, P., Finucane, M., Peters, E., & MacGregor, D. G. (2002) The affect heuristic. In T. Gilovich, D. Griffin, and D. Kahneman (eds.), *Heuristics and Biases: The Psychology of Intuitive Judgment* (pp. 397–420). Cambridge: Cambridge University Press.

Svenson, O. (1996) Decision making and the search for fundamental psychological regularities: What can be learned from a process perspective? *Organizational Behavior and Human Decision Processes*, 65, 252–67.

Tetlock, P. E. (2002) Social functionalist frameworks for judgment and choice: Intuitive politicians, theologians, and prosecutors, *Psychological Review*, 109, 451–71.

Tversky, A. (1969) Intransitivity of preferences, *Psychological Review*, 76, 31–48.

Tversky, A. (1972) Elimination by aspects: A theory of choice, *Psychological Review*, 79, 281–99.

Wilson, T. D. & Brekke, N. (1994) Mental contamination and mental correction: Unwanted influences on judgments and evaluations, *Psychological Bulletin*, 116, 117–42.

7

Computational Models of Decision Making

Jerome R. Busemeyer and Joseph G. Johnson

What Are Computational Models of Cognition?

In his classic book on computational vision, Marr (1982) proposed three levels of theories about cognitive systems. At the highest level, theories aim to understand the abstract goals a system is trying to achieve; at an intermediate level, theories are designed to explain the dynamic processes used to achieve the top level goals; and at the bottom level, theories attempt to describe the neurophysiologic substrate of the second level. Judgment and decision-making researchers have generally been concerned with theorizing at the higher and more abstract levels. From this higher point of view, explanations based on principles such as context dependent weights, loss aversion, and anchoring-adjustment are considered satisfactory. This chapter presents arguments for viewing decision making from the perspective of a lower level microanalysis. By doing so, we can try to answer deeper questions such as: why decision weights change across contexts, why people are loss averse, and why adjustments sometimes are inadequate to overcome the influence of anchors.

Computational models are constructed from simple units that conform to a small number of elementary principles of cognition, but a large number of these simple units are connected together to form a dynamic system. Although the properties of the individual units are simple, the emergent behavior of the ensemble becomes fairly complex. Computational models appear in a variety of forms, but this chapter focuses on a class known as artificial neural networks, connectionist networks, or parallel distributed processing systems (see Grossberg, 1988; and Rumelhart & McClelland, 1986, for general overviews of these models). This class of computational models is designed to form a bridge that mediates between the neural and behavioral sciences.

Generally speaking there are two major types of connectionist or artificial neural network models: feedforward models mainly concerned with learning from experience, and recursive models mainly concerned with performance. This chapter focuses on the latter type because, traditionally, decision researchers have studied problems with full information that do not require learning. There are also two major categories of problems that decision researchers have examined: one emphasizing preferential choice among valued options; another emphasizing probabilistic inference about a set of hypotheses. This chapter is restricted to the topic of preferential choice behavior.

How Does the Brain Make Decisions?

Several decades ago, the brain was an impenetrable black box, but with recent advances in neuroscience, we can start to look inside. It is informative to point out a conclusion arising from converging evidence obtained through neuroscience research on decision making. Neuroscientists have examined decision-making processes in the brains of macaque monkeys using single cell recording techniques (for reviews, see Gold & Shadlen, 2001, 2002; Platt, 2002; Schall, 2001), as well as from the brains of humans using evoked response potentials (Gratton, Coles, Sirevaag, Erickson, & Donchin, 1988). A simple but important conclusion from this work is that decisions in the brain are based on the dynamic accumulation of noisy activation for each action, and the action whose activation first exceeds a threshold is chosen. This process is illustrated in Figure 7.1, for three actions, with each trajectory representing the cumulative activation (i.e., preference state) for an action. The horizontal axis represents deliberation time and the vertical axis indicates the activation for each action at each moment in time. In this figure, action A reaches the threshold first, and is chosen at time $T = 425$.

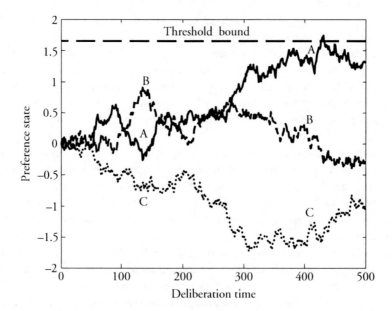

Figure 7.1 The decision process for a choice among three actions

This dynamic decision process is known as a sequential sampling process (DeGroot, 1970). It forms the basis of decision models used in a wide variety of cognitive applications including sensory detection (Smith, 1995), perceptual discrimination (Laming, 1968; Link & Heath, 1975; Usher & McClelland, 2001; Vickers, 1979), memory recognition (Ratcliff, 1978); categorization (Nosofsky & Palmeri, 1997; Ashby, 2000), probabilistic inference (Wallsten & Barton, 1982) and preferential choice (Aschenbrenner, Albert, & Schmalhofer, 1984; Busemeyer, 1985).

Computational Models for Decision Making

Several artificial neural network or connectionist models have been recently developed for judgment and decision tasks: some placing more emphasis on the neural processing aspects (Grossberg & Gutowski, 1987; Levin & Levine, 1996; Usher & McClelland, 2002), and others placing more emphasis on applications to judgment and decision making (Dougherty, Gettys, & Ogden, 1999; Holyoak & Simon, 1999; Guo & Holyoak, 2002; Read, Vanman, & Miller, 1997). Due to limitations of space, here we will focus on our own work, known as decision field theory (DFT; Busemeyer & Townsend, 1993; Roe, Busemeyer, & Townsend, 2001).

DFT uses a sequential sampling process to make decisions, consistent with the other areas of cognition. The theory has been applied to a variety of traditional decision-making problems including decision making under uncertainty (Busemeyer & Townsend, 1993), selling prices and certainty equivalents (Busemeyer & Goldstein, 1992; Townsend & Busemeyer, 1995), multiattribute decision making (Diederich, 1997), multialternative decision making (Roe et al., 2001), and decision rule learning (Johnson & Busemeyer, in press).

To introduce DFT, it will be helpful to consider an example problem. Suppose you have to choose a penalty program for a young offender, convicted of a serious crime, from one of three options: (A) a mild 5 year imprisonment, with a population of inmates that only have minor convictions, and a possibility for parole in 2 years; (B) a moderate 15 year imprisonment, with a population of inmates with moderately serious convictions, and a possibility for parole in 7 years; or (C) a severe 30 year imprisonment with a population of hardcore criminals with no possibility for parole. If we assume that the offender may be either corrigible (labeled event *g* for good) or incorrigible (labeled event *b* for bad), then Table 7.1 displays the six types of possible consequences for this decision. For

Table 7.1 Hypothetical decisions about penalty for a crime

Action	Event g: Corrigible	Event b: Incorrigible
A: Mild penalty	m_{A1}: Reform to normal life	m_{A2}: Release dangerous man
B: Moderate penalty	m_{B1}: Damage the man	m_{B2}: Delay danger
C: Severe penalty	m_{C1}: Destroy a life	m_{C2}: Safely incarcerate

example, if a mild penalty is chosen (option A) but the criminal is incorrigible (state b), then the outcome is the release of a dangerous man who will very likely repeat the crime (outcome m_{A2}).

According to DFT, the decision maker deliberates over these courses of action by thinking about the various possible consequences of each action. This is driven by attention shifting between the possible events from moment to moment over a period of time. For example, at one moment the decision maker may remember something (e.g., the kind face of the offender) that makes her think the offender can be reformed – focusing attention to the event "corrigible" momentarily – and then she is appalled by the thought of wasting his life, locked behind bars for 30 years. But at another moment, she may recall a recent story in which a parolee committed a horrible crime – shifting attentional focus to the possibility of the "incorrigible" event – and she may feel a cold fear arise from the idea of releasing another on the streets in a few years. These affective reactions to the consequences of each action give rise to an overall sense of desirability for each action under each event (the values associated with each m in Table 7.1). At each moment, the values of the focal event are evaluated and compared, and the resulting comparisons are accumulated over time to form a preference state. The preference state for an action represents the integration of all the preceding affective reactions produced by thinking about that action during deliberation. This deliberation process continues until the accumulated preference for one action reaches a threshold, which determines the choice and the deliberation time of the decision (refer back to Figure 7.1).

The *threshold bound* for the decision process, symbolized θ, is a key parameter for controlling speed and accuracy tradeoffs. If θ is set to a low threshold, then only a weak preference is required to make a choice. In this case, decisions are made very quickly, which may be reasonable for trivial decisions of small consequence. However, a low threshold would cause the decision to be based on little thought about the consequences, which is likely to lead to a choice with bad unforeseen outcomes. For more serious decisions, θ is set to a very high threshold, so that a very strong preference is required to make a decision. In this case, deliberation takes longer, but the decision is based on a more thoughtful evaluation of all the consequences, producing a choice that is more likely to result in a positive outcome. Impulsive individuals may tend to use lower thresholds, while perspicacious individuals may tend to use higher thresholds.

The dynamic system used to generate this deliberation process is presented next, and the connectionist network is represented in Figure 7.2. The three actions corresponding to the mild, moderate, and severe penalty option are labeled A, B, and C, and the corrigible and incorrigible events are labeled 1 and 2, respectively, in this figure. The network has three layers of simple units that perform the following computations.

The inputs into this network, shown on the far left, represent the affective evaluations of the possible consequences of a decision. These *values* are assumed to be generated by a motivational system (hence the symbol m_{ij}), which is not explicitly represented here (but see Busemeyer, Townsend, & Stout, 2002). For example, m_{A1} represents the positive evaluation of the consequence produced by reforming the offender and allowing him to return to society as a productive citizen, and m_{A2} represents the negative evaluation of the consequence produced by releasing a dangerous man back into society.

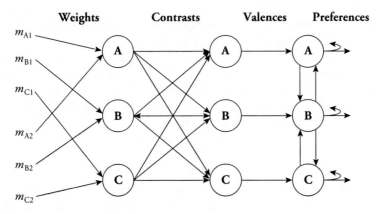

Figure 7.2 Connectionist network representation of DFT

The connections, linking the inputs to the first layer of nodes, are designed to represent an attention process. At any moment in time, the decision maker is assumed to attend to one of the possible events leading to consequences for each action. For example, if the decision maker thinks the criminal is incorrigible, then at that moment, option A is evaluated at m_{A2}, option B is evaluated at m_{B2}, and option C is evaluated at m_{C2}. However, if something comes to mind which makes the decision maker switch her attention and think that the offender can be reformed, then at that later moment, option A is evaluated at m_{A1}, option B is evaluated at m_{B1}, and option C is evaluated at m_{C1}. Thus, the inputs to the first layer fluctuate from one moment (time t) to another moment (time $t+h$) as the decision maker's attention switches from one possible event to another. The probability of attending to a particular event at each moment reflects the decision maker's underlying subjective probability or belief that the offender is corrigible. To formalize these ideas, we define $W_1(t)$ and $W_2(t) = 1 - W_1(t)$ as stochastic variables, called the *attention weights*, which fluctuate across time. For example, attention may be focused at time t on the corrigible event so that $W_1(t) > W_2(t)$, but a moment later at time $t+h$, attention may switch to the incorrigible event so that $W_2(t+h) > W_1(t+h)$. The first layer of the network computes a weighted value for each option i within a set of n options as follows:

$$U_i(t) = W_1(t) \cdot m_{i1} + W_2(t) \cdot m_{i2} + \varepsilon_i(t). \tag{7.1}$$

The last "error" term, $\varepsilon_i(t)$, represents the influence of irrelevant features (e.g., in an experiment, these are features outside of an experimenter's control). The above equation looks like the classic weighted additive utility model, but unlike the classic model, the attention weights are stochastic rather than deterministic (see Fischer, Jia, & Luce, 2000, for a related model). Although, the mean values of the attention weights over time correspond to the deterministic weights used in classic weighted additive models (e.g., attribute weights in multiattribute utility theory).

The connections linking the first and second layers are designed to perform comparisons among weighted values of the options, to produce what are called valences.

A positive valence for one option indicates that the option has an advantage under the current focus of attention, and a negative valence for another option indicates that the option has a disadvantage under the current focus of attention. For example, if attention is currently focused on event *1* (corrigible), then action A has an advantage over other options, and option C has a disadvantage under this state. But these valences reverse when attention is switched to event *2* (incorrigible). The second layer computes the *valence* for each option *i* within a set of *n* options by comparing the weighted value for option *i* with the average of the other $(n - 1)$ options:

$$v_i(t) = U_i(t) - U_j(t), \tag{7.2}$$

where $U_j(t) = \sum_{k \neq i} U_k(t)/(n - 1)$. Valence is closely related to the concept of advantages and disadvantages used in Tversky's (1969) additive difference model. Note, however, that the additive difference model assumed complete processing of all features, whereas the present theory assumes a sequential sampling process that stops when a threshold is crossed.

The connections, between the second and third layers, and the interconnections among the nodes in the third layer, form a network that integrates the valences over time into a *preference state* for each action. This is a recursive network, with positive self-recurrence within each unit (denoted s_{ii}), and negative lateral inhibitory connections between units (denoted s_{ik}). Positive self-feedback is used to integrate the valences produced by an action over time, and lateral inhibition produces negative feedback from other actions. The third layer computes the preference state for option *i* from a set of *n* options according to the linear dynamic system:

$$P_i(t+h) = s_{ii} \cdot P_i(t) + v_i(t+h) - \sum_{k \neq i} s_{ik} \cdot P_k(t). \tag{7.3}$$

Conceptually, the new state of preference is a weighted combination of the previous state of preference and the new input valence. The initial preference state for an option, $P_i(0)$, at the start of a decision problem represents a preference recalled from past experience. This is used to explain carry over effects from previous decisions or past experience, such as the status quo effect (Samuelson & Zeckhauser, 1988).

Inhibition is also introduced from the competing alternatives. We assume that the strength of the lateral inhibition connection is a decreasing function of the dissimilarity between a pair of alternatives. For example, in Table 7.1, options A and C are more dissimilar than options A and B, and so the lateral inhibition between A and C (s_{AC}) would be smaller than that between options A and B (s_{AB}). Lateral inhibition is commonly used in artificial neural networks and connectionist models of decision making to form a competitive system in which one option gradually emerges as a winner dominating over the other options (cf. Grossberg, 1988; Rumelhart & McClelland, 1986). As shown later in this chapter, this concept serves a crucial function for explaining several paradoxical phenomena of preferential choice.

In summary, a decision is reached by the following deliberation process: as attention switches from one event to another over time, different affective values are probabilistically selected, these values are compared across actions to produce valences, and finally these valences are integrated into preference states for each action. This process continues until the preference for one action exceeds a threshold criterion, at which point in time the winner is chosen. Formally, this is a Markov process, and matrix formulas have been mathematically derived for computing the choice probabilities and distribution of choice response times (for details, see Busemeyer & Townsend, 1992; Busemeyer & Diederich, 2002; Diederich & Busemeyer, 2003). Alternatively, Monte Carlo computer simulation can be used to generate predictions from the model. (However, all of the predictions presented below were computed from the matrix formulas.)

What Do Computational Models Contribute to Decision Theory?

Computational models are a lot more complex than the algebraic models commonly used by decision theorists. One could argue that computational models are too microscopic in their view, and they have little to show for their increased cost in complexity. Can computational models provide a gain in explanatory power that has not been achieved by the algebraic models? To answer this question, we will review a set of empirical phenomena that have resisted a coherent explanation by their algebraic counterparts (see Chapter 17, this volume, for a discussion of multiattribute utility theory).

To review these empirical phenomena within a common framework, it will be helpful to place the example decision problem, shown in Table 7.1, into a two dimensional representation, shown in Figure 7.3a. The first dimension represents the evaluation of the options from the perspective that the offender is corrigible, and the second dimension represents the evaluation of the options from the perspective that the offender is incorrigible. Consider option A from Table 7.1. From the perspective that the offender is corrigible, then option A has a very high value; but from the perspective that the offender is incorrigible, then option A has a very low value. Thus option A is high on the first dimension and low on the second. Alternatively, option C has a low value from the corrigible perspective, but option C has a high value from the incorrigible perspective. Similarly, option B is midway between options A and C. We can also imagine other

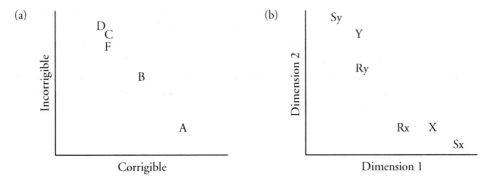

Figure 7.3 Two-dimensional representations of actions: (a) for example problem; and (b) used to examine loss aversion

possible options in this space, which are variations of those shown in Table 7.1. Option D is another penalty program that is even more severe than option C; and option F is severe like option C, but it is deficient, perhaps because there is less security at that institution. These examples will be used to illustrate the essential properties of the empirical phenomena reviewed below.

Similarity effect

This refers to the effect, on choice probabilities, produced by adding a competitive option D to an earlier choice set containing only A and C, where option D is very similar to option C. Suppose that in a binary choice between A and C, options A and C are chosen equally frequently so that $Pr[C \mid \{A,C\}] = Pr[A \mid \{A,C\}]$. Adding a new option D to this choice set, mainly takes away probability from the nearby option C, and leaves the probability of choosing option A unaffected. The empirical result is that the probability ordering for A and C changes from equality with the binary choice set, to $Pr[A \mid \{A,C,D\}] > Pr[C \mid \{A,C,D\}]$ for the triadic choice set, producing a violation of a choice principle called independence of irrelevant alternatives (see Tversky, 1972, for a review). This robust empirical finding eliminates a large class of probabilistic choice models called simple scalability models, which includes for example, Luce's (1959) ratio of strength model. Tversky (1972) elegantly explained these results with a theory he called the elimination by aspects model of choice. Tversky (1972) also proved that the elimination by aspects model satisfies another important choice principle called regularity, which is considered next.

Attraction effect

This refers to the effect, on choice probabilities, of adding a decoy option F to an earlier choice set containing only options A and C, where the decoy F is similar to, but also dominated by, option C. Suppose, once again, that in a binary choice between A and C, options A and C are chosen equally frequently so that $Pr[C \mid \{A,C\}] = 0.50$. A second robust finding is that adding the decoy option F to this choice set enhances the probability of the nearby dominant option C, so that $Pr[C \mid \{A,C,F\}] > Pr[C \mid \{A,C\}]$, which produces a violation of the regularity principle (Huber, Payne, & Puto, 1982; see Heath & Chatterjee, 1995, for a review). Consequently, this result cannot be explained by Tversky's (1972) elimination by aspects model. This violation of regularity also rules out a large class of random utility models of choice (Luce & Suppes, 1965), including Thurstone's (1959) preferential choice theory.

Compromise effect

This refers to the effect, on choice probabilities, of adding an intermediate option B to an earlier choice set containing only two extreme options A and C, where the compromise

B is midway between the two extremes. Suppose, that all the binary choices are equal so that $Pr[A \mid \{A,B\}] = Pr[A \mid \{A,C\}] = Pr[B \mid \{B,C\}] = 0.50$. A third robust finding is that adding the compromise option B to a set containing A and C enhances the probability of the compromise option so that $Pr[B \mid \{A,B,C\}] > Pr[A \mid \{A,B,C\}] = Pr[C \mid \{A,B,C\}]$, which is another violation of the independence between irrelevant alternatives principle (Simonson, 1989; see Tversky & Simonson, 1993 for a review). Tversky and Simonson (1993) proposed a context-dependent preference model based on the principle of loss aversion to explain the attraction and compromise effects. However, the context-dependent preference model cannot account for the similarity effect (see Roe et al., 2001, for a proof). Thus no model was proposed to account for all three simultaneously.

A common explanation

DFT provides an explanation for all three phenomena using a common set of principles (see Roe et al., 2001, for details). In other words, we do not need to change any of the assumptions of the model across phenomena, and neither do we need to change any of the model parameters. The same assumptions always apply, and the same parameters can be used to predict all three effects. The mathematical basis for these predictions is derived elsewhere (see Roe et al., 2001; Busemeyer & Diederich, 2002), and here we only present an intuitive discussion.

First consider the similarity effect – that is, the effect of adding option D to an earlier set containing A and C. The attention-switching property is essential for explaining this effect. On the one hand, whenever attention is focused on the corrigible event (corresponding to the first dimension in Figure 7.3a), then option A alone gets a large positive advantage, while options C and D both have negative valences; on the other hand, whenever attention is focused on the incorrigible event (corresponding to the second dimension in Figure 7.3a), then both options C and D have positive valences, while option A gets a large negative valence. If an individual happens to pay more attention to the corrigible event, then option A will tend to be chosen; but if an individual happens to pay more attention to the incorrigible event, then either option C or option D tend to be chosen. Therefore, option D only takes away probability from its neighboring option, C, and it does not affect the probability of choosing the more distant option, A.

Next consider the attraction effect. In this case the lateral inhibition mechanism serves a crucial purpose. Neuroscientists long ago established the fact that the strength of lateral inhibitory connections decreases as a function of distance, and this property is responsible for generating contour and edge enhancement effects in vision (cf. Anderson, 1997, Chapter 4). According to DFT, lateral inhibition produces an attraction effect for preference in the same way that it produces an edge enhancement effect for vision. During deliberation, the preference state for the dominated alternative F is driven toward a negative state because it competes with the nearby dominant alternative C. The negative preference state associated with option F feeds back through a negative inhibitory connection to option C, producing a bolstering (disinhibitory) effect on option C. This

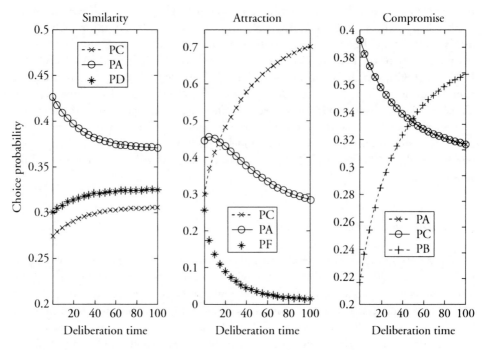

Figure 7.4 DFT predictions for similarity, attraction, and compromise effects

bolstering effect is not applied to option A because it is too distant from F, and the lateral inhibitory link is too weak. Thus option C shines out by being close to an unattractive alternative, F.

Note that the attention switching and lateral inhibition processes are assumed to be operating all the time for both the similarity and attraction effects. These two components operate in synchrony to generate both effects. As a matter of fact, it is the interaction between these two processes that is essential for producing the compromise effect. In this case, if attention happens to focus on some irrelevant features favoring the compromise option, B, then this sends lateral inhibition to the neighboring extreme options A and C, decreasing their strength, which then builds up an advantage for the compromise option.

The predictions for all three effects were computed from DFT as follows. We simply set the values (m_{ij} in Equation 7.1) proportional to the coordinates shown in Figure 7.3a, and the probabilities of attending to each dimension were equal ($\Pr[W_1(t) = 1] = \Pr[W_2(t) = 1] = 0.50$). The self-feedback loop coefficient was set to $s = 0.94$, the lateral inhibitory coefficient for nearby options (e.g., s_{CD}) was set to 0.04, and the lateral inhibitory coefficient for distant options (e.g., s_{AC}) was set to 0.001. The standard deviation of the error, ε, due to irrelevant dimensions was set equal to 1.25. Figure 7.4 shows the predictions for the triadic choice probabilities plotted as a function of deliberation time, separately for each effect. As can be seen in this figure, a common set of assumptions, and exactly the same parameters, reproduces all three effects.

An interesting prediction that follows from the above explanations for the attraction and compromise effects is that they should become stronger as deliberation time increases. In other words, if decision makers are encouraged to deliberate longer, then the attraction and compromise effects will increase. This is because lateral inhibitory effects grow in strength during deliberation. Two experiments have now been reported that confirm these dynamic predictions of the model (Simonson, 1989; Dhar, Nowlis, & Sherman, 2000).

Loss aversion

An influential article by Tversky and Kahneman (1991) provides the most compelling evidence for loss aversion. The basic ideas are illustrated in Figure 7.3b, where each letter shown in the figure represents a choice option described by two attributes; such as for example, consumer products that vary in size and quality, or jobs that vary in salary and interest. In this case, option X is high on dimension 1 but low on dimension 2, whereas option Y is low on dimension 1 but high on dimension 2.

The first study manipulated a reference point, using either option R_x or R_y. Under one condition, participants were asked to imagine that they currently owned the commodity R_x, and they were then given a choice of keeping R_x or trading it for either commodity X or commodity Y. From the reference point of R_x, option X has a small advantage on dimension 1 and no disadvantage on dimension 2, whereas Y has both large advantages (dimension 2) and disadvantages (dimension 1). Under these conditions, R_x was rarely chosen, and X was strongly favored over Y. Under another condition, participants were asked to imagine that they owned option R_y, and they were then given a choice of keeping R_y or trading it for either X or Y. From the reference point of R_y, Y has a small advantage and no disadvantages, whereas X now has both large advantages and disadvantages. Under this condition, R_y was rarely chosen again, but now Y was slightly favored over X. (The smaller effect using R_y may indicate that dimension 2 was less important than dimension 1.) Tversky and Kahneman (1991) interpreted this pair of results as a loss aversion effect, because X was favored when Y entailed large losses relative to the reference point R_x, but the opposite occurred when X entailed large losses relative to the reference point R_y.

DFT provides an explanation for this loss aversion effect through the lateral inhibition mechanism. To derive predictions from DFT, we simply set the values (m_{ij} in Equation 7.1) proportional to coordinates of the options in Figure 7.3b. We set the probability of attending to the first dimension equal to 0.55, and the probability of attending to the second dimension equal to 0.45. The remaining parameters were the same as used to generate Figure 7.4. These predictions are shown in Figure 7.5, which shows the probability of the triadic choices as a function of deliberation time, separately for the two reference point conditions. As can be seen in this figure, DFT reproduces the loss aversion effect – that is, the change in preference for option X relative to Y depending on the reference point. It is important to note that exactly the same parameters are used for both reference point conditions. This reversal of preference does not depend on the probability of attending to each dimension – if we set the probabilities equal to 0.50

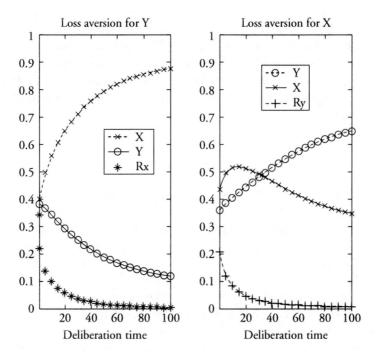

Figure 7.5 DFT predictions for loss aversion effect

then the reversal becomes even stronger, although symmetric in size. In fact, the result depends primarily on the lateral inhibition parameter – if it is set to zero, then the effect is predicted to disappear.

The second study also manipulated a reference point, but in this case, using either option S_x or S_y. In one condition, participants were asked to imagine that they trained on job S_x, but that job would end, and they had to choose between two new jobs X or Y. From this reference point, job X has small advantages and disadvantages over S_x, whereas Y has large advantages and disadvantages. Under these conditions, option X was strongly favored over option Y. In a second condition, participants were asked to imagine that they trained on job S_y, and in this case, preferences reversed, and option Y was strongly favored over option X. Tversky and Kahneman (1991) also interpreted these results as a loss aversion effect.

To apply DFT to this study, we assume that each option is described by three dimensions: the values of the first two dimensions (e.g., salary and interest) are taken from the positions of the options shown in Figure 7.3b, and the third dimension represents job availability. Jobs X and Y both have a positive value on dimension 3 (they are available), whereas jobs S_x and S_y both have negative values on dimension 3 (they are no longer available). For example, option S_x is assigned a slightly higher value on dimension 1 than option X, a slightly lower value on dimension 2 than option X, and it has a large negative value on dimension 3. We assumed an equal probability of attending to each of the three dimensions, and the remaining parameters were the same as used to generate

Figure 7.4. The asymptotic choice probability results predicted by the theory are $\Pr[X \mid \{X,Y,S_x\}] = 0.87$, and conversely $\Pr[Y \mid \{X,Y,S_y\}] = 0.87$; that is, DFT again reproduces the reversal in preference as a function of the reference point. In sum, we find that both loss aversion effects, as well as attraction and compromise effects, all can be derived from the lateral inhibitory mechanism of DFT.

Discrepancies between WTA and WTP

Another phenomenon interpreted in terms of loss aversion (Tverksy & Kahneman, 1991) concerns disparities between the price individuals are willing to accept to sell something they own (WTA or selling prices), versus the price they are willing to pay to acquire something they do not own (WTP or buying prices). For example, Kahneman, Knetsch, and Thaler (1990) gave one group of subjects a mug and asked them how much they would be willing to accept to give up the mug, whereas another group was simply given some money and asked how much they would be willing to pay to buy the mug. They found that participants were willing to buy the mug for only about $3, but they were asking a much higher price of $7 to sell the mug. This price difference is interpreted as the loss aversion effect produced by an owner giving up his or her mug.

At first glance, one might argue that differences between buying and selling prices are simply a strategic effect: a person may deliberately underestimate the WTP and over-estimate the WTA to gain an advantage. But this simple explanation implies that buying and selling prices would still produce the same rank orders. In fact, this is not the case. Birnbaum, Yeary, Luce, & Zhou (2002) review several studies that report preference reversals between WTP and WTA. For example, Birnbaum and Sutton (1992) presented subjects with the following two gambles: gamble G gives a 0.5 probability of winning $96, otherwise $0; gamble F gives a 0.5 probability of winning $48, otherwise $36 dollars. On the average, subjects gave a higher WTP to gamble F than gamble G, but at the same time they gave a higher WTA to gamble G than gamble F. Birnbaum and Sutton (1992) explained these effects as a change in decision weight that depends on the buyer or seller point of view.

Must these discrepancies between WTA and WTP be explained by changes in decision weights or values? Or can these discrepancies simply be a product of the computational processes used to generate prices? Below we show how a computational model can explain discrepancies between different measures of preference using a common set of weights and values.

The basic idea is that prices are selected by a series of covert comparisons (refer to Figure 7.6). To find a price equivalent to a gamble, the decision maker must search for a candidate price that produces an indifference response. During each step of this search process, the decision maker compares a candidate price to the gamble, and this comparison may result in one of three judgments: if the candidate price is preferred, then the price is decremented by a small amount and the search continues (a left transition in Figure 7.6); if the gamble is preferred, then the price is incremented by a small amount and the search continues (a right transition in Figure 7.6); if the comparison produces an indifference judgment, then the search stops and the candidate price is reported as the price

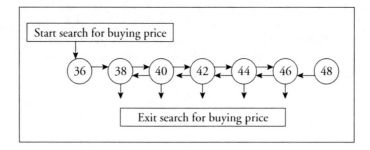

Figure 7.6 Illustration of the search process for finding the buying price of a gamble

(a downward transition in Figure 7.6). We simply use DFT to perform this comparison process, which provides the probabilities for the three judgments at each stage of the search process (see Busemeyer & Goldstein, 1992, for details). Then Markov chain theory is used to determine the distribution of prices generated by the search process (see Busemeyer & Townsend, 1992, for the mathematical derivations).

We assume that the feasible set of prices that one may attach to a gamble is bounded by the minimum and maximum possible outcomes of the gamble. Then, when asked to find a maximum WTP for a gamble, we assume that the search process starts near the minimum of the feasible set of prices, biased away from paying excess money. However, when asked to find a minimum WTA, we assume that the search process starts near the maximum of the feasible set of prices, biased toward earning extra money. This simple scheme was used to find buying and selling prices for gambles F and G used by Birnbaum and Sutton (1992). In this case, we simply set the values (m_{ij} in Equation 7.1) equal to the stated dollar values of the gambles, and we simply set the probability of attending to each event equal to the stated probabilities. Figure 7.7 shows the distribution of prices produced by this model for WTP (top panel) and WTA (bottom panel).

As can be seen in Figure 7.7, the predicted buying prices (or WTP) are lower than the predicted selling prices (or WTA), accounting for the well-known disparity between these measures. More importantly, preference reversals occur for buying and selling prices: referring to the top panels, the mean WTP for gamble F is larger than for gamble G; referring to the bottom panels, the mean WTA is larger for gamble G than for gamble F.

There is an intuitive explanation for these computational results. The price for gamble F is restricted to a small range, which makes the price insensitive to changes in the starting position produced by the selling or buying price task. However, the price for gamble G has a wide range of possible values, and it is more strongly affected by the starting position produced by buying and selling tasks. This idea is similar to earlier anchoring and adjustment models of preference reversal (e.g., Goldstein & Einhorn, 1987). However, unlike these earlier anchoring and adjustment theories, the amount of adjustment is not a free parameter in DFT, because it is derived from the dynamics of the search process.

Preference reversals also occur between prices and choices (Lichtenstein & Slovic, 1971; see Slovic & Lichtenstein, 1983, for a review) and between certainty and probability

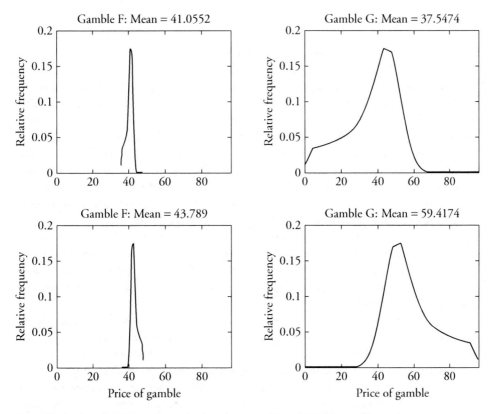

Figure 7.7 Predicted WTP or buying prices (top panels) and WTA or selling prices (bottom panels)

equivalents (Hershey & Schoemaker, 1985). The matching model of DFT can also reproduce these types of preference reversals using a common set of weights and values as inputs into the choice and price processes (Busemeyer & Goldstein, 1992; Townsend & Busemeyer, 1995).

In summary, previous explanations for discrepancies between various measures of preference have relied on the assumption that the utility function is changed by the preference task. In some cases, the values of the payoffs entering the utility function are assumed to change as a result of changes in loss aversion (Tversky & Kahneman, 1991). In other cases, the decision weights for the probabilities entering the utility function are assumed to change as a result of changes in attention (Birnbaum & Sutton, 1992; Tversky, Sattath, & Slovic, 1988). Computational models can provide an alternative explanation for these discrepancies: a common set of weights and values are used for all of these tasks, and instead, the discrepancies are explained by the dynamic processes used to generate responses for each of these tasks. This chapter has only reviewed a small subset of the findings in this area, and further research is needed to determine whether or not the DFT is adequate to account for all of the known findings concerning preference reversals.

Preference reversals under time pressure

Up to this point we have argued that computational models, such as DFT, provide a deeper level analysis of several traditional effects from the decision-making literature. Now we turn to new predictions that arise from the dynamic nature of the model.

There is a growing body of evidence showing that it is possible to reverse an individual's preference by changing the amount of time given to make the decision. For example, Svenson and Edland (1987) asked people to choose among apartments under short vs. long time deadlines. Under the short time deadlines, the lower rent apartment was chosen more frequently; but under longer time deadlines, they preferred apartments with higher rents that provided other attractive features. Diederich (2003b) extended these findings by asking individuals to choose between two gambles, and each gamble could yield either a monetary reward or a blast of noise punishment. Choice probabilities changed under time pressure for all participants, and in many cases, the change was large enough to reverse their preferences. For example, if avoiding noise was more important than winning money, then the low noise gamble was chosen more frequently under short deadlines, but the high monetary payoff gamble was chosen more frequently under the longer deadlines.

A common explanation for these effects is that decision makers switch strategies (Payne, Bettman, & Johnson, 1993; see also Chapter 6, this volume). Under short deadlines, it is hypothesized that decision makers use a non-compensatory heuristic strategy such as a lexicographic rule or an elimination by aspects rule. These strategies are quick and easy to execute but are not very accurate in the sense of maximizing weighted additive utility. Under longer deadlines, decision makers can use the more time-consuming compensatory strategy such as a weighted additive rule, which increases accuracy.

Sequential sampling models provide an alternative view, which simply assumes that individuals reduce their threshold criterion under time pressure. Diederich (1997) developed a multiattribute version of DFT, which assumes individuals sequentially sample information over time, but they begin processing the most important dimension, and later switch to process the other less important dimensions. Under short deadlines, a low threshold is used, only the most important dimension tends to get processed, and so this dimension alone determines the choice. Under long deadlines, a high threshold is used, and now there is sufficient time to process additional attributes. If these additional attributes disagree with the most important attribute, then this additional processing can reverse the direction of the evolving preference state. Diederich (2003b) showed that this model provided a very accurate quantitative account of the preference reversals under time pressure that she observed.

Are Computational Models Testable?

One might argue that computational models are so complex that they cannot be empirically tested. On the contrary, it is possible to rigorously test these models both quantitatively as well as qualitatively. For example, to quantitatively test DFT, one can estimate all of the model parameters from a set of binary choice probabilities, and then use these same parameters to predict other measures of preference including choice response times, triadic choice probabilities, and buying/selling prices (see, for examples, Dror, Busemeyer, & Basola, 1999; Diederich & Busemeyer, 1999; Diederich, 2003a, 2003b). Qualitative tests of the theory are also possible: on the one hand, DFT predicts violations of strong stochastic transitivity, but on the other hand it predicts that weak stochastic transitivity will be satisfied (Busemeyer & Townsend, 1993). In agreement with the first qualitative prediction, violations of strong stochastic transitivity frequently occur (see Mellers & Biagini, 1994, for a review); but contrary to the second qualitative prediction, violations of weak stochastic transitivity also have been reported under special conditions (see Gonzàlez-Vallejo, 2002, for a recent review and explanation for this result).

What Are Some Alternative Computational Models?

Up to this point we have highlighted one computational model, decision field theory, but there are a growing number of new computational models for decision making. Two that have addressed topics reviewed in this chapter are briefly described below.

Competing accumulator model

Usher and McClelland (2001, 2002) have recently proposed a competing accumulator model that shares many assumptions with decision field theory, but departs from this theory on a few crucial points. The connectionist network of the competing accumulator model is virtually the same as shown in Figure 7.2. However, this model makes different assumptions about: (a) the evaluations of advantages and disadvantages (what we call valences in Equation 7.2); and (b) the dynamics of response activations (what we call preference states in Equation 7.3). First, they adopt Tversky and Kahneman's (1991) loss aversion hypothesis so that disadvantages have a larger impact than advantages. Using our own notation, the valence for alternative $i \in \{A,B,C\}$, and $i \neq j \neq k$, is computed as follows:

$$v_i(t) = F[U_i(t) - U_j(t)] + F[U_i(t) - U_k(t)] + c, \tag{7.4}$$

where $F(x)$ is a nonlinear function that satisfies the loss aversion properties presented in Tversky and Kahneman (1991). Thus, rather than deriving loss aversion effects indirectly from the dynamics as we have done, they build this effect directly into the model. Second, they use a nonlinear dynamic system that restricts the response activation to remain positive at all times, whereas we use a linear dynamical system that permits positive and negative preference states. The non-negativity restriction was imposed to be consistent with their interpretation of response activations as neural firing rates.

Usher and McClelland (2002) have shown that the competing accumulator model can account for the main findings concerning the similarity effect, the attraction effect, and the compromise effect, using a common set of parameters. Like decision field theory, this model uses an attention switching mechanism to produce similarity effects, but unlike decision field theory, this model uses loss aversion to produce the attraction and compromise effects. Further research is needed to discriminate between these two models.

ECHO model

Guo and Holyoak (2002; see also Glockner, 2002) proposed a different kind of connectionist network, called ECHO, adapted from Thagard and Millgram (1995). In this model, there is a special node, called the external driver, representing the goal to make a decision, which is turned on when a decision is presented. The driver node is directly connected to the attribute nodes, with a constant connection weight. Each attribute node is connected to an alternative node with a bidirectional link, which allows activation to pass back and forth from the attribute node to the alternative node. The connection weight between an attribute node and an alternative node is determined by the value of the alternative on that attribute (our m_{ij}). There are also constant lateral inhibitory connections between the alternative nodes.

The decision process works as follows. Upon presentation of a decision problem, the driver is turned on and applies constant input activation into the attribute nodes, and each attribute node then activates each alternative node (differentially depending on value). Each alternative node then provides positive feedback to each attribute node, and negative feedback to the other alternative nodes. Activation in the network evolves over time according to a nonlinear dynamic system, which keeps the activations bounded between zero and one. The decision process stops as soon as the changes in activations fall below some threshold. At that point, the probability of choosing an option is determined by a ratio of activation strengths.

Guo and Holyoak (2002) used this model to explain the similarity and attraction effects. To account for these effects, they assumed that the system first processes the two similar alternatives, and during this time, the lateral inhibition produces a competition between these two options. After this initial comparison process is completed, the system processes all three options, including the dissimilar option. In the case of the similarity effect, the initial processing lowers the activation levels of the two similar options; in the case of the attraction effect, the initial processing enhances the activation level of the dominating option. Thus lateral inhibition between alternatives plays a crucial role for explaining both effects. Although the model has been shown to account for the similarity and attraction effects, at this point, it has not been shown to account for the compromise effect or loss aversion effects.

The ECHO model makes an important prediction that differs from both DFT and the competing accumulator model. The ECHO model predicts that as one option becomes dominant during deliberation, this will enhance the activation of the attribute nodes favored by the dominant alternative. The enhancement is caused by the feedback from the alternative node to the attribute node, which tends to bias the evaluation of the attributes over time. This property of the model is related to the dominance-seeking principle included in other decision-making theories (Montgomery, 1989; Svenson, 1992). Holyoak and Simon (1999) tested this hypothesis by asking individuals to rate attribute importance at various points during deliberation, and they report evidence for increases in the importance of attributes that are favored by the dominant alternative during deliberation.

Concluding Comments

During the past 40 years, decision theorists have let the utility function do most of the work of explaining choice results. By positing the simplest possible hypotheses about the choice processes, all the explanatory power falls upon the utility function itself. Consequently, during this 40 year span of time, the forms of utility functions have become increasingly complex (see Luce, 2000, for a review). However, it is possible that if theorists work harder in understanding the complexities inherent in the choice processes, then the underlying utility representations may become simpler and more coherent. As others have argued (cf. Plott, 1996), it may be too early for decision theorists to accept the conclusion that utilities are constructed on the fly for every variation of task and context, and instead it may be possible to retain a stable underlying value system that is expressed through a very complex choice process.

References

Anderson, J. A. (1997) *An Introduction to Neural Networks*. Cambridge, MA: MIT Press.

Aschenbrenner, K. M., Albert, D., & Schmalhofer, F. (1984) Stochastic choice heuristics, *Acta Psychologica*, 56(1–3), 153–66.

Ashby, F. G. (2000) A stochastic version of general recognition theory, *Journal of Mathematical Psychology*, 44, 310–29.

Birnbaum, M. H. & Sutton, S. E. (1992) Scale convergence and utility measurement, *Organizational Behavior and Human Decision Processes*, 52, 183–215.

Birnbaum, M. H., Yeary, S., Luce, R. D., & Zhou, L. (2002, submitted) Contingent valuation, endowment, or viewpoint effects: Testing properties in judgments of buying and selling prices of lotteries.

Busemeyer, J. R. (1985) Decision making under uncertainty: Simple scalability, fixed sample, and sequential sampling models, *Journal of Experimental Psychology: Learning, Memory, and Cognition*, 11, 538–64.

Busemeyer, J. R. & Diederich, A. (2002) Survey of decision field theory, *Mathematical Social Sciences*, 43, 345–70.

Busemeyer, J. R. & Goldstein, W. M. (1992) Linking together different measures of preference: A dynamic model of matching derived from decision field theory, *Organizational Behavior and Human Decision Processes*, 52, 370–96.

Busemeyer, J. R. & Townsend, J. T. (1992) Fundamental derivations from decision field theory, *Mathematical Social Sciences*, 23, 255–82.

Busemeyer, J. R. & Townsend, J. T. (1993) Decision field theory: A dynamic cognition approach to decision making, *Psychological Review*, 100, 432–59.

Busemeyer, J. R., Townsend, J. T., & Stout, J. C. (2002) Motivational underpinnings of utility in decision making: Decision field theory analysis of deprivation and satiation. In S. Moore (ed.), *Emotional Cognition*. Amsterdam: John Benjamins.

DeGroot, M. H. (1970) *Optimal Statistical Decisions*. New York: McGraw-Hill.

Dhar, R., Nowlis, S. M., & Sherman, S. J. (2000) Trying hard or hardly trying: An analysis of context effects in choice, *Journal of Consumer Psychology*, 9, 189–200.

Diederich, A. (1997) Dynamic stochastic models for decision making under time constraints, *Journal of Mathematical Psychology*, 41(3), 260–74.

Diederich, A. (2003a) Decision making under conflict: Decision time as a measure of conflict strength, *Psychonomic Bulletin and Review*, 10(1), 167–75.

Diederich, A. (2003b) MDFT account of decision making under time pressure, *Psychonomic Bulletin and Review*, 10(1), 157–66.

Diederich, A. & Busemeyer, J. R. (1999) Conflict and the stochastic dominance principle of decision making, *Psychological Science*, 10, 353–9.

Diederich, A. & Busemeyer, J. R. (2003) Simple matrix methods for analyzing diffusion models of choice probability, choice response time, and simple response time, *Journal of Mathematical Psychology*, 47(3), 304–22.

Dougherty, M. R. P., Gettys, C. F., & Ogden, E. E. (1999) MINERVA-DM: A memory process model for judgements of likelihood, *Psychological Review*, 106, 108–209.

Dror, I. E., Busemeyer, J. R., & Basola, B. (1999) Decision making under time pressure: An independent test of sequential sampling models, *Memory and Cognition*, 27, 713–25.

Fischer, G. W., Jia, J., & Luce, M. F. (2000) Attribute conflict and preference uncertainty: The RandMAU model, *Management Science*, 46, 669–84.

Glockner, A. (2002) The maximizing consistency heuristic: Parallel processing in human decision making, thesis, Heidelberg University.

Gold, J. I. & Shadlen, M. N. (2001) Neural computations that underlie decisions about sensory stimuli, *Trends in Cognitive Neuroscience*, 5, 10–16.

Gold, J. I. & Shadlen, M. N. (2002) Banburismas and the brain: Decoding the relationship between sensory stimuli, decisions, and reward, *Neuron*, 36, 299–308.

Goldstein, W. & Einhorn, H. J. (1987) Expression theory and the preference reversal phenomena, *Psychological Review*, 94, 236–54.

Gonzàlez-Vallejo, C. (2002) Making trade-offs: A probabilistic and context-sensitive model of choice behavior, *Psychological Review*, 109(1), 137–55.

Gratton, G., Coles, M. G., Sirevaag, E. J., Erickson, C. J., & Donchin, E. (1988) Pre- and poststimulus activation of response channels: A psychophysiological analysis, *Journal of Experimental Psychology: Human Perception and Performance*, 14, 331–44.

Grossberg, S. (1988) *Neural Networks and Natural Intelligence*. Cambridge, MA: MIT Press.

Grossberg, S. & Gutowski, W. E. (1987) Neural dynamics of decision making under risk: Affective balance and cognitive-emotional interactions, *Psychological Review*, 94(3), 300–18.

Guo, F. Y. & Holyoak, K. J. (2002) Understanding similarity in choice behavior: A connectionist model. In W. D. Gray and C. D. Schunn (eds.), *Proceedings of the Twenty-fourth Annual Conference of the Cognitive Science Society* (pp. 393–8). Mahwah, NJ: Erlbaum.

Heath, T. B. & Chatterjee, S. (1995) Asymmetric decoy effects on lower-quality versus higher-quality brands: Meta analytic and experimental evidence, *Journal of Consumer Research*, 22, 268–84.

Hershey, J. C. & Schoemaker, P. J. H. (1985) Probability versus certainty equivalence methods in utility measurement: Are they equivalent? *Mangement Science*, 31, 1213–31.

Holyoak, K. J. & Simon, D. (1999) Bidirectional reasoning in decision making by constraint satisfaction, *Journal of Experimental Psychology: General*, 128(1), 3–31.

Huber, J., Payne, J. W., & Puto, C. (1982) Adding asymmetrically dominated alternatives: Violations of regularity and the similarity hypothesis, *Journal of Consumer Research*, 9(1), 90–8.

Johnson, J. G. & Busemeyer, J. R. (in press) Rule-based decision field theory: A dynamic computational model of transitions among decision-making strategies. To appear in T. Betsch (ed.), *The Routines of Decision Making*. Mahwah, NJ: Erlbaum.

Kahneman, D., Knetsch, J., & Thaler, R. (1990) Experimental tests of the endowment effect and the Coase theorem, *Journal of Political Economy*, 98(6), 1325–48.

Laming, D. R. (1968) *Information Theory of Choice-reaction Times*. New York: Academic Press.

Levin, S. J. & Levine, D. S. (1996) Multiattribute decision making in context: A dynamic neural network methodology, *Cognitive Science*, 20, 271–99.

Lichtenstein, S. & Slovic, P. (1971) Reversals of preference between bids and choices in gambling decisions, *Journal of Experimental Psychology*, 89, 46–55.

Link, S. W. & Heath, R. (1975) A sequential theory of psychological discrimination, *Psychometrika*, 40, 77–111.

Luce, R. D. (1959) *Individual Choice Behavior: A Theoretical Analysis*. New York: Wiley.

Luce, R. D. (2000) *Utility of Gains and Losses*. Mahwah, NJ: Erlbaum.

Luce, R. D. & Suppes, P. (1965) Preference, utility, and subjective probability. In R. D. Luce, R. R. Bush, and E. Galanter (eds.), *Handbook of Mathematical Psychology* (vol. 3, pp. 249–410). New York: Wiley.

Marr, D. (1982) *Vision*. Cambridge, MA: MIT Press.

Mellers, B. A. & Biagini, K. (1994) Similarity and choice, *Psychological Review*, 101, 505–18.

Montgomery, H. (1989) From cognition to action: The search for dominance in decision making. In H. Montgomery and O. Svenson (eds.), *Process and Structure in Human Decision Making* (pp. 23–49). New York: Wiley.

Nosofsky, R. M. & Palmeri, T. J. (1997) An exemplar based random walk model of speeded classification, *Psychological Review*, 104, 266–300.

Payne, J. W., Bettman, J. R., & Johnson, E. J. (1993) *The Adaptive Decision Maker*. New York: Cambridge University Press.

Platt, M. L. (2002) Neural correlates of decisions, *Current Opinion in Neurobiology*, 12(2), 141–8.

Plott, C. R. (1996) Rational individual behavior in markets and social processes: The discovered preference hypothesis. In K. Arrow, E. Collombatto, M. Perlaman, and C. Schmidt (eds.), *The Rational Foundations of Economic Behavior*. London: Macmillan.

Ratcliff, R. (1978) A theory of memory retrieval, *Psychological Review*, 85, 59–108.

Read, S. J., Vanman, E. J., & Miller, L. C. (1997) Connectionism, parallel constraint satisfaction and gestalt principles: (Re)introducing cognitive dynamics to social psychology, *Personality and Social Psychology Review*, 1, 26–53.

Roe, R., Busemeyer, J. R., & Townsend, J. T. (2001) Multi-alternative decision field theory: A dynamic connectionist model of decision-making, *Psychological Review*, 108, 370–92.

Rumelhart, D., & McClelland, J. L. (1986) *Parallel Distributed Processing: Explorations in the Microstructure of Cognition* (vol. 1). Cambridge, MA: MIT Press.

Samuelson, W. & Zeckhauser, R. (1988) Status quo bias in decision making, *Journal of Risk and Uncertainty*, 1, 7–59.

Schall, J. D. (2001) Neural basis of deciding, choosing, and acting, *Nature Reviews: Neuroscience*, 2, 33–42.

Simonson, I. (1989) Choice based on reasons: The case of attraction and compromise effects, *Journal of Consumer Research*, 16, 158–74.

Slovic, P. & S. Lichtenstein. (1983) Preference reversals: A broader perspective, *American Economic Review*, 73, 596–605.

Smith, P. L. (1995) Psychophysically principled models of visual simple reaction time, *Psychological Review*, 102(3), 567–93.

Svenson, O. (1992) Differentiation and consolidation theory of human decision making: A frame of reference for the study of pre- and post-decision processes, *Acta Psychologica*, 80, 143–68.

Svenson, O. & Edland, A. (1987) Change of preferences under time pressure: Choices and judgments, *Scandinavian Journal of Psychology*, 28, 322–30.

Thagard, P. & Millgram, E. (1995) Inference to the best plan: A coherence theory of decision. In A. Ram and D. B. Leake (eds.), *Goal-driven Learning* (pp. 439–54). Cambridge, MA: MIT Press.

Thurstone, L. L. (1959) *The Measurement of Values*. Chicago: University of Chicago Press.

Townsend, J. T. & Busemeyer, J. R. (1995) Dynamic representation of decision-making. In R. F. Port and T. van Gelder (eds.), *Mind as Motion* (pp. 101–20). Cambridge, MA: MIT Press.

Tversky, A. (1969) Intransitivity of preferences, *Psychological Review*, 76, 31–48.

Tversky, A. (1972) Elimination by aspects: A theory of choice, *Psychological Review*, 79(4), 281–99.

Tversky, A. & Kahneman, D. (1991) Loss aversion in riskless choice: A reference dependent model, *Quarterly Journal of Economics*, 106, 1039–61.

Tversky, A., Sattath, S., & Slovic, P. (1988) Contingent weighting in judgment and choice, *Psychological Review*, 95, 371–384.

Tversky, A. & Simonson, I. (1993) Context dependent preferences, *Management Science*, 39, 1179–89.

Usher, M. & McClelland, J. L. (2001) On the time course of perceptual choice: A model based on principles of neural computation, *Psychological Review*, 108, 550–92.

Usher, M. & McClelland, J. L. (2002) Decisions, decisions: Loss aversion, information leakage, and inhibition in multi-attribute choice situations. Unpublished note.

Vickers, D. (1979) *Decision Processes in Visual Perception*. New York: Academic Press.

Wallsten, T. S. & Barton, C. (1982) Processing probabilistic multidimensional information for decisions, *Journal of Experimental Psychology: Learning, Memory, and Cognition*, 8, 361–84.

PART II

Judgments

8

Inside and Outside Probability Judgment

David A. Lagnado and Steven A. Sloman

The Inside/Outside Distinction

Four brothers have gone for a day at the races. They are preparing to bet on the big race. Harpo is a complete novice. He knows that there are eight horses running, but nothing much else. He figures that the chance of each horse winning is 1/8. Chico is also a novice, but he notices that one of the horses is called "Sure Thing." He figures that this horse has got to win and puts all his money on it. Zeppo is a race track expert (he organized the trip). He has pored over the *Racing Post* all morning, looking at the previous form of each horse. He manages to identify ten past races very similar to the big race today, all with the same eight horses. "Best Shot" has won eight out of these ten races, so he figures its chances are 8/10. Finally, Groucho is also an expert. Indeed he had dinner with the stable boy last night (he paid). He happens to know that "Some Dope" has been given a new wonder drug that pretty much guarantees it will win. He places his bets accordingly.

Ignoring the relative merits of each strategy for the moment, we can classify these four probability judgments into two broad classes. Harpo and Zeppo, despite their difference in expertise, are both reasoning from the *outside*. They are thinking of the outcome as a member of a set of events or possibilities, and basing their judgments on an appropriate proportion of these. Chico and Groucho, despite their differences, are reasoning from the *inside*. They are basing their judgments on knowledge (or belief) about the properties of a specific horse. These two strategies have roots that can be traced back to conceptions of probability judgment in both philosophy and psychology.

The epistemic/aleatory distinction in the philosophy of probability

Ever since its inception, the formal notion of probability has been interpreted in two main senses: either in terms of reasonable degrees of belief or in terms of statistical distributions within classes of events. Hacking (1975) terms the former sense *epistemic*, because it concerns states of knowledge or belief, and the latter *aleatory*, because it concerns frequencies or proportions generated by stochastic processes in the world. Philosophical analyses of probability have reinforced this distinction (Carnap, 1950; Ramsey, 1931). Although some theorists have argued for the exclusivity of one approach over the other, the general consensus is that both are important (Gillies, 2001). Certainly from a normative point of view, both provide valid interpretations of the probability calculus. On the epistemic view, the laws of probability furnish laws of *coherence* for our degrees of belief; to violate these laws lays a person open to a Dutch book. That is, if you bet in accordance with an incoherent set of beliefs an opponent can win money from you regardless of the actual outcomes of the events bet upon (Ramsey, 1931). On the statistical view, the laws consist in combination rules for relative frequencies.

The epistemic/aleatory distinction outlined here concerns valid interpretations of the probability calculus, and in that sense speaks to issues of normativity. It is the *ideal* reasoner that has perfectly coherent beliefs or attunes their judgments to the appropriate relative frequencies. However, the philosophical debate has also focused on how people actually employ probability judgments. Do we understand talk of probability in terms of expressions of confidence in what will happen or in terms of relative frequencies? Once again the received opinion is that both interpretations have a certain domain of applicability. Sometimes we use probability statements to express the degree of support our evidence lends to it, on other occasions we use them to refer to a proportion in a class of events. Neither reading alone is sufficient to capture all important aspects of usage.

A parallel distinction appears in people's judgments of probability. This idea is apparent in early work by Meehl (1954) on clinical prediction, and also underpins the general framework endorsed by Kahneman and Tversky (1982a).

Clinical vs. statistical prediction

Meehl (1954) was concerned with a basic methodological issue in clinical psychology, to predict how an individual will behave (e.g., Will they re-offend once released from prison? Will they commit suicide due to their depression?). Meehl contrasts "clinical" prediction, which involves an assessment of the individual case at hand, and attempts to isolate the causally relevant factors that determine subsequent behaviour, with statistical or actuarial prediction, in which a person is assigned to a class of like individuals, and a statistical table of relevant frequencies is used to infer future behaviour. Dawes (1996) summarizes a wealth of research showing the superiority of the statistical approach, despite strongly held beliefs to the contrary within the clinical community: "People's behaviour and feelings are best predicted by viewing them as members of an aggregate and by determining what variables generally predict for that aggregate and how. That conclusion contradicts experts' claims to be able to analyze an individual's life in great detail and determine what caused what."

Although concerned with prediction rather than probability judgment per se, and with experts rather than lay people, the contrast between clinical and statistical methods suggests that a similar distinction may operate in our everyday predictive activities. It also cautions us that despite our apparent "expertise" in everyday judgment situations, we too may suffer from the neglect of a more statistical approach. Indeed this is exactly the perspective adopted by Kahneman and Tversky (1982a) when they introduced the inside/outside distinction.

The inside vs. outside view

In their essay "Variants of uncertainty" (1982a), Kahneman and Tversky maintain that people reach judgments of probability in a variety of ways. In particular, they distinguish a *distributional* mode, where "the case in question is seen as an instance of a class of similar cases, for which the relative frequencies of outcomes are known or can be estimated," with a *singular* mode, "in which probabilities are assessed by the propensities of the particular case at hand." This is illustrated by consideration of the "planning fallacy" whereby people estimate the time of completion of a project on the basis of factors specific to that particular project, and neglect available information about how long similar projects have taken to complete. In the light of various experimental studies they conjecture that people tend to use the singular mode, even though it is more likely to lead to erroneous judgments. Thus "people generally prefer the singular mode, in which they take an 'inside view' of the causal system that most immediately produces the outcome, over an 'outside view', which relates the case at hand to a sampling schema."

Adopting the basic insight and terminology introduced by Tversky and Kahneman we will characterize an inside perspective on probability judgment as one that focuses on the individual case, and its attendant properties. A judgment of probability is reached by assessing the relation between this case and the to-be-judged category or outcome. In contrast, an outside perspective considers some set or reference class of instances to which the individual case belongs. The distributional properties of this set form the basis for a judgment of probability. To illustrate, consider the case of Hilary, who is applying for a prestigious job vacancy. What are her chances? An inside view will focus just on Hilary's qualities (intelligence, loyalty) and suitability for the post. A judgment of probability will be reached on the basis of how well these features fit the job specification and selection process. In contrast, an outside view would consider one or more sets that Hilary is a member of – the set of other candidates, the set of occasions on which Hilary has applied for previous jobs, etc. Knowledge about distributions over these sets would inform an outside probability judgment.

A survey of the modern literature on probability judgment reveals two types of models that, for the most part, can be classified as taking an inside or an outside view. However, the relation between inside and outside views is complicated. First, sometimes people try to view a category from the outside – by examining instances – but the sheer number of category instances makes counting ineffective. In such a case, the instances retrieved may be treated as a representative sample and may be subject to property-based comparison (a typical inside view operation) in order to arrive at a probability judgment. Second, outside views of categories reveal inclusion relations among categories that are hidden from the inside view. Therefore, a variety of phenomena of probability judgment reflect the effect of variables that cause people to change from an inside to an outside perspective.

Our discussion will divide into two parts. In the first we will concentrate on models and phenomena that reveal the operation of the inside perspective. In the second we will consider models that take a broadly outside perspective, in so far as they involve the explicit consideration of sets of instances. However, while some of the models in this section adopt a purely outside view, others admit of varying degrees of contamination through inside factors.

Inside Models

Similarity: Probability judgment from property overlap

The representativeness heuristic of probability judgment has been defined in a variety of ways, starting with the earliest discussions by Tversky and Kahneman (1973). Its dominant sense concerns similarity (Kahneman & Frederick, 2002). An event is judged representative, and therefore probable, to the degree that it is similar to a model of the event being judged. Your judged probability that George plays saxophone reflects your judged similarity between George and your model of the typical saxophone player.

Evidence for the representativeness heuristic as defined in terms of similarity is vast and broad. Many studies have shown how representative judgment can lead to the neglect of base-rate information, violations of basic laws of probability, and a near perfect correlation between people's judgments of similarity and probability (for a recent review see Kahneman & Frederick, 2002). For example, Bar-Hillel and Neter (1993) presented students with the following kind of question: "Danielle is sensitive and introspective. In high school she wrote poetry secretly . . . Though beautiful, she has little social life, since she prefers to spend her time reading quietly at home rather than partying. What does she study?" Participants then ranked a list of subject categories according to one of several criteria such as probability, suitability or willingness to bet. The lists included nested subordinate–superordinate pairs (e.g., in the case of Danielle both "Literature" and "Humanities") specifically designed so that the character profile fitted the subordinate category better than the superordinate. There were two main findings. First, people consistently ranked the subordinate category as more probable than the superordinate, in violation of the extension law of probability (whereby a subordinate cannot be more probable than a superordinate category that contains it). Bar-Hillel and Neter termed this a disjunction error. Second, probability rankings were almost perfectly correlated with both suitability and willingness-to-bet rankings (and in a subsequent experiment with actual betting behavior). This suggests that participants in the different judgment conditions used the same underlying process, and one that was not based on an extensional understanding of probability.

Such findings illustrate people's propensity to take an inside view and neglect the distributional properties of the problem situation. The character profile of Danielle conjures up a stereotype of a sensitive Literature student, and people base their judgments on this picture rather than the structural fact that Literature is a subset of the Humanities. The plausibility of this kind of process, however, depends on a viable model of the similarity judgment itself. Many such models exist. Most models of similarity have been defined in terms of distance or lack of overlap of dimensional values or properties (Shepard, 1980). The contrast model of similarity (Tversky, 1977) considers not only the degree to which the properties and values of objects are distinct, but also the degree of commonality among objects. Smith and Osherson (1989) applied a version of the contrast model to probability judgments for both conjunction and base-rate problems.

One consequence of a feature weighting model like Tversky's (1977) is that a complex feature profile can be highly similar to a target category in some respects, but highly dissimilar in other respects. In accordance with this possibility, Yamagishi (2002) showed that people sometimes make non-complementary binary probability judgments i.e., for two mutually exclusive and exhaustive events A and ~A, their ratings for p(A) and p(~A) sum to over 1, in violation of the laws of probability.

Using enriched descriptions of "Linda" and "Bill" from Tversky and Kahneman's (1983) conjunction problems, Yamagishi replicated the finding that judgments of similarity were highly correlated with judged probability, and also showed that judgments of dissimilarity were highly correlated with judged negation probability (the probability that an individual was *not* a member of the target category). For example, an enriched description of Linda (now called "Rhonda") added features such as "is pro-life" and "is very active in her church" that contrasted with the typical feminist features such as "deeply concerned with issues of discrimination and social justice." Subsequent judgments of the probability that Rhonda belonged to various categories (e.g., bank teller, feminist bank teller, league of women's voters) were highly correlated with judgments of similarity between Rhonda and these categories. A similar correlation obtained between judgments of the probability that Rhonda was not a member of these categories and judgments of how dissimilar she was from them.

The representativeness heuristic is, in essence, the proposal that judgments of probability are governed by the same mental processes that determine categorization via similarity to a prototype. X is judged likely to be an instantiation of event category Y to the degree that X is a good example of Y. Goodness-of-example is also a key determinant of judgments of the typicality of a category within a superordinate (Hampton, 1998) and has been viewed as a measure of the similarity of an instance to a category prototype (Rosch, 1973).

However, other categorization models also exist that appear to take an outside view: They attribute typicality and category name judgments, not to similarity to a prototype, but to similarity to a set of exemplars (e.g., Nosofsky, 1984). Correspondingly, one can now find a model of probability judgment that also appeals to exemplar processing (MINERVA-DM: Dougherty, Gettys, & Ogden, 1999). This model accounts for some of the phenomena attributed to the representativeness heuristic, and fits a variety of other probability judgment data. However, much of the work of this model is not done by the analysis of exemplars per se, but rather by the similarity relations that determine how exemplars are selected for processing. To this extent, the key to understanding certain judgment phenomena remains the acknowledgment that people tend to view events from the inside, in terms of their properties, and to make judgments by comparing the properties of an event to those of a model of the event being judged.

Associative theories of probability judgment

Associative models of probability judgment (e.g., Gluck & Bower, 1988; Shanks, 1991) are also prototype theories. What distinguishes them is their reliance on an incremental error-driven learning mechanism. This restricts their applicability to judgment situations where people are exposed to sequentially learned information. The central idea is that during this exposure people learn to associate cues (properties or features) with outcomes (typically another property or a category prediction), and that these learned associations form the basis for subsequent probability judgments.

Within this associative framework several studies have demonstrated biases in probability judgments that are analogs of biases typically found in the heuristics and biases program. For example, Gluck and Bower (1988) demonstrated an analog of base-rate neglect. In an online paradigm people learn to diagnose two fictitious diseases on the basis of sets of symptoms, and then rate the probability of these diseases given a particular target symptom. The learning environment is arranged so that the conditional probability of each disease is equal, but the overall probability (base rate) of one is high and the other low. Given this structure, the target symptom is a better predictor of the rare disease than the common one, and in line with the associative model people give higher ratings for the conditional probability of the rare disease. The associative account of this probability bias relies on cue competition effects, and cannot be explained by exemplar models such as MINERVA-DM (Cobos, Almaraz, & Garcia-Madruga, 2003).

Lagnado and Shanks (2002) extended this approach to disjunction errors. People learned to diagnose diseases at two levels of a hierarchy, and were then asked to rate the conditional probabilities of subordinate (e.g., Asian flu) and superordinate categories (e.g., flu). The learning environment was arranged so that a target symptom was a better predictor of a subordinate disease than it was of that disease's superordinate category. In line with the associative account, people rated the conditional probability of the subordinate higher, even though this violated the extension rule of probability whereby the conditional probability of a subordinate cannot be higher than its superordinate. This suggests that people ignored the subset relation between the diseases, and based their conditional probability judgments on the degree of association between symptom and disease categories.

As well as replicating the base-rate effect, Cobos et al. (2003) demonstrated a conjunction effect, where people rated the probability of a conjunction of symptoms higher than one of its conjuncts, and a conversion effect, where they confused the conditional probability of symptom given disease with that of disease given symptom. Both of these biases can be accommodated by an associative model but not by an exemplar-based one.

These learning studies, in common with many one-shot judgment problems, suggest that people base their probability judgments on the degree to which a cue or property is associated with an outcome category, and neglect extensional information provided by the base rates or the set structure of the problem space.

Causality: Probability judgment from relational explanation

That people often judge probability by considering the properties of a prototypical event, as opposed to the distributional properties of a category, seems indisputable in light of the evidence. That those properties are treated as independent is far from evident however. Certain examples of the conjunction fallacy already suggest that probability judgment cannot, in general, be reduced to overlap among independent properties. Consider the following problem from Tversky and Kahneman (1983):

> Mr. F. was randomly selected from a representative sample of adult males. Which is more probable?
>
> a)   Mr. F. has had one or more heart attacks.
> b)   Mr. F. has had one or more heart attacks and he is over 55 years old.

Of their participants, 58 percent chose b) even though the conjunction rule of probability prescribes a). One account of this is that a Mr. F. who is over 55 and has had one or more heart attacks is more similar to people's expectations of adult males than a Mr. F. who has simply had one or more heart attacks. But an account that is at least as compelling is that the aged Mr. F. is more representative because being over 55 is causally relevant to having had a heart attack. Representativeness may draw on the relation between the properties, a relation that is in essence explanatory (age is part of the explanation for heart problems).

Explanatory relations serve as the foundation for various kinds of judgment. To illustrate, Pennington and Hastie (1993) have shown that mock jurors are more likely to attribute guilt to a hypothetical accused if the evidence is presented in chronological rather than random order. They interpret the effect in terms of explanatory coherence – evidence shown in chronological order facilitates the construction of a story that provides motivation and, more generally, allows the construction of a causal model of events. The key is that jurors are only willing to consider the probability of guilt sufficiently high if the judgment is supported by a causal model. Strong evidence per se does not automatically lead people to conclude guilt; the evidence must sustain a causal model.

Causal explanation in inductive inference

One domain of probability judgment concerns conditional probability: How do people update their beliefs about categories given information about other, related categories? Psychologists have approached this question using arguments with a particular form, such as: "*Moose use norepinephrine as a neurotransmitter.* Therefore, deer use norepinephrine as a neurotransmitter," in which a predicate ("uses norepinephrine as a neurotransmitter") is attributed to one or more premise categories and participants are asked to make a judgment about their belief that the predicate is also true of the conclusion category.

A number of phenomena have been demonstrated with such arguments (for a review, see Sloman & Lagnado, in press). One clear fact concerns arguments like the above that use predicates that participants know very little about and cannot use to reason with. Such arguments are judged strong to the extent that the premise and conclusion categories are similar (Rips, 1975). In fact, consider:

> *Every individual bird has sesamoid bones.* Therefore, every individual robin has sesamoid bones.
> and
> *Every individual bird has sesamoid bones.* Therefore, every individual ostrich has sesamoid bones.

Not only are both arguments often assigned a probability of less than 1, even by those people who agree that all robins and ostriches are birds, but people on average assign higher conditional probability to the first, more typical, conclusion than the second (Sloman, 1998). Here the adoption of an inside, similarity-based perspective leads people to neglect a relevant structural constraint (that a property possessed by every member of the superordinate set must be possessed by every member of any of its subsets).

Similarity relations are flexible however, and they change when predicates can be used to reason with (Heit & Rubinstein, 1994). The conditional probability that hawks have an anatomical property (like "has a liver with two chambers") is greater when told that chickens have the property than when told that tigers do. But given a behavioral predicate that concerns hunting (like "prefers to feed at night"), the probability that hawks have it is higher when conditioned on tigers rather than chickens. The interpretation of a predicate picks out a set of relevant properties of the categories under consideration.

The process by which causal knowledge selects relevant features is essentially a process of explanation. Induction is mediated by people's efforts to explain why a predicate would obtain of a category on the basis of relations among category features (Sloman, 1994) or by constructing a causal model to explain how a conclusion could be the causal effect of the premise (Medin, Coley, Storms, & Hayes, 2003).

For example, Medin et al. demonstrate that people find the argument: "Bananas contain retinum, therefore monkeys do," more convincing than the argument: "Mice contain retinum, therefore monkeys do," even though mice and monkeys are more similar than bananas and monkeys. Because monkeys are known to eat bananas but not mice, the causal path of ingestion mediates the first argument but not the second.

Here people are basing their probability judgments on the plausibility of causal explanations connecting premise and conclusion, an essentially inside operation, rather than invoking appropriate sets or reference classes.

Mental simulation

Judgments of conditional probability are closely related to probability judgments of conditional if–then statements (Over & Evans, 2003). The outline of a method to determine such probabilities was mentioned by Ramsey (1931) and theories of the meaning of conditional statements based on Ramsey's test have been developed by Stalnaker (1968) and Lewis (1976). A natural interpretation of Ramsey's proposal as a psychological hypothesis – as a strategy for judgment – is that to judge the probability of q given p, one first imagines a world in which p is true and then examines that world to see what the probability is that q holds in it.

This is basically the idea of the mental simulation heuristic, suggested by Kahneman and Tversky (1982b) as a common means by which people can make probability assessments. Thus people construct an appropriate causal model of the situation and then "run" it using certain parameter settings (e.g., those specified in the antecedent of the conditional). The ease of achieving a target outcome is then taken as a measure of the probability of that outcome, given the initial conditions. Estimates for the probability of an event reached by such a procedure require an inside view; they involve focus on individual scenarios or stories, not the distributional properties of a set of cases.

The simulation heuristic is particularly applicable to situations where people make plans or predictions about the future. A robust empirical finding, termed the *planning fallacy*, is that people tend to underestimate the amount of time that it will take to complete a task or project. An example is the tendency of students to underestimate how long it will take them to finish an academic assignment. Buehler, Griffin and Ross (1994) found that students nearing the end of a one-year honors thesis underestimated their completion time by an average of 22 days.

The planning fallacy probably arises because people estimate time using mental simulations of the project or task, generating a plausible set of steps from initiation to completion. This focus on plausible scenarios can override the consideration of outside factors, such as the past frequencies of delayed completion. The effect obtained even when people made frequency rather than probability judgments, and estimated how many out of 10 tasks would be completed by a relevant date (Griffin & Buehler, 1999). In spite of a prompt to take an outside perspective, and judge completion in terms of the distribution across a set of similar cases, people persisted in taking an inside view.

Single-path or restricted path reasoning

More generally, there is a wealth of evidence suggesting that people's probability judgments are modulated by the number of alternative scenarios they construct. The judged probability of a target outcome increases when people imagine multiple causes of that outcome, but decreases when they imagine multiple causes of an alternative outcome (Koehler, 1994). Further, in reaching their judgments people tend to restrict themselves to considering a minimal number of possible scenarios, often just one.

To illustrate, Dougherty, Gettys, and Thomas (1997) gave people text-based vignettes about a real-life situation (e.g., the circumstances leading up to the death of a firefighter) and then asked them for both a probability judgment and a list of the thoughts they had had in reaching this judgment. They found that participants used a mixture of single-path and several-path strategies, and that the former led to higher probability estimates than the latter. Moreover, although people initially generated several causal scenarios, they tended to eliminate the less plausible of these prior to making their probability judgment. The single-path strategy clearly requires an inside view, and it appears that even when a few alternative paths are entertained, people still adopt an inside strategy to reach their final judgment, but modulate this with knowledge of alternative paths.

Similar simplifying strategies are also apparent when people make probability judgments or predictions based on uncertain premises. Early research on cascaded inference (Steiger & Gettys, 1972) looked at multistage inferences, where the first step involves a probabilistic inference based on a known premise, and the second involves a further probabilistic inference conditional on this uncertain judgment. For example, suppose you want to bet on a horse in the Grand National, and you know that rain will favor "Water Boy." You see dark clouds gathering by the race track (this is your known premise). From this you estimate the probability of rain (this is your first step inference). Finally you estimate the probability that "Water Boy" wins given this inference (this is the second step). In such cascaded inference problems people adopt a "best guess" or "as if" strategy: they make their second inference *as if* the most probable outcome at the first step is true rather than probable. In our example this involves assuming that it will rain, and basing your probability estimate that "Water Boy" wins on this assumption. A normatively more justifiable procedure is to compute a weighted sum over all the alternative pathways using a modified version of Bayes' theorem (Jeffrey, 1965). Even with just a few alternatives this would lead to a complex computation; it is not surprising that people use a simplifying heuristic. In effect this heuristic amounts to abandoning an outside perspective across multiple possible chains of events, and focusing on the single most probable, and therefore presumably the most representative, path.

An independent but very similar line of research has been developed in category inference (Murphy & Ross, 1994). The starting point was Anderson's rational model of categorization (1991) and in particular his claim that when making a prediction on the basis of an uncertain categorization people follow a Bayesian rule that computes a weighted average over all potential categories. In contrast to this *multiple category* view, Murphy and Ross provided evidence for a *single category* view where just the most probable category is used to make a prediction. For example, consider the task of predicting whether the insect flying towards you on a dark night is likely to sting you. Let the potential categories in this situation be *Fly*, *Wasp*, or *Bee*. According to the multiple category view you compute a weighted average across all three categories in order to determine the probability of being stung. In contrast, on the single category view you base your prediction only on the most probable category and ignore alternative categories.

Ross and Murphy (1996) gave a heuristic explanation of these findings in terms of the availability of categories in memory, and showed that people can incorporate multiple categories when these are made more accessible. However, representativeness also appears to be involved; that is, people focus on the most representative category to guide subsequent inference. Lagnado and Shanks (2003) extended this line of research to online learning situations involving hierarchical categories. They too found strong evidence that people focused on the most probable category in order to make a subsequent probability estimate, and showed that these estimates were readily manipulated by priming people to different hierarchical levels (e.g., subordinate or superordinate). These results were explained in terms of the associative links that people build up during learning, and their subsequent activation in the judgment phase. For example, if you think of an individual as a likely Broadsheet reader then you activate the associated property of voting Conservative, whereas if you think of the same individual as a *Guardian* reader (a subset of Broadsheet readers) you activate the associated property of voting Labour.

These three sets of studies converge on the same conclusion despite quite different paradigms. Also, they all show a strong influence of the inside perspective; one that avoids consideration of multiple alternative paths, and focuses on a single most probable case.

Finally, studies have shown that even when people are presented with a full set of alternative outcomes, so that the correct probability for a target outcome is transparent, their intuitive assessments of uncertainty (measured by non-numeric verbal means) are modulated by irrelevant features of the distribution of alternatives (Windschitl, Young, & Jenson, 2002). For example, people express greater optimism about winning a 59 ticket raffle in which they hold 17 tickets and the other competitors hold 9, 9, 8, 8, and 8 respectively than when they hold 17 tickets and the other competitors hold 16, 7, 7, 6, and 6. This *alternative outcomes* effect can be explained by a heuristic comparison process that focuses on the target outcome and its strongest competitor. Furthermore, in a learning paradigm where people must base their judgments on memory for the frequencies of past outcomes, the effect is also reflected in their numerical probability estimates.

These studies imply a dissociation between an outside view probability judgment (given by computing the proportion of favorable outcomes) and a more intuitive probability judgment reflected in verbal reports. They suggest that the latter is based on a comparison process characteristic of the inside perspective. Moreover, the findings further support the idea that people severely restrict the set of possibilities they consider in order to reach a probability judgment.

Outside Models

Mental model theory of extensional reasoning

An explicitly outside perspective on probabilistic reasoning is taken by Johnson-Laird, Legrenzi, Girotto, Legrenzi and Caverni (1999) in their mental model theory of extensional reasoning. They argue that naïve reasoners – those who are unfamiliar with the probability calculus – can nevertheless infer the probabilities of events in an extensional fashion. Here extensional reasoning consists in "inferring the probability of an event from the different possible ways in which it could occur." The central claim is that people reach probability judgments through the construction of mental models of the problem situation, and subsequent computations over these models.

One key claim of the model theory is that because people construct mental models that focus on what is presumed true, their mental partition of the problem space sometimes fails to correspond to the full set of mutually exclusive and exhaustive possibilities. This can explain a variety of erroneous probabilistic inferences. Another key claim is that in the absence of information to the contrary people assume that each mental model is equiprobable. For example, suppose that you have lost sight of your companions on a country walk. You come to a junction where the road splits into three separate paths. With no extra information, you assign each path a probability of $^1/_3$. In addition, once an equiprobable partition is made, people can compute the probabilities of compound events by proportionality. If two of the paths lead up the hill, and one leads down the hill, the probability that your companions went up the hill is $^2/_3$.

Various studies (e.g., Girotto & Gonzalez, 2003) show that naïve reasoners, including children, can compute probabilities based on these principles. Moreover, the typical errors made by participants can be attributed to inappropriate partitions of the problem space (see also Fox & Rottenstreich, 2003). This is also held to underlie common mistakes in probability puzzles such as the Monty Hall problem and Bertrand's three-card problem (Johnson-Laird et al., 1999).

The principle of equiprobability does a lot of work for the model theory, but is inadequate as a means for establishing probabilities a priori (Gillies, 2001). Problem spaces often admit of different partitions, and in such cases the equiprobability principle can lead to the same event being assigned inconsistent probabilities. To illustrate, if you divide the earlier problem space into equiprobable paths, the probability that your friends went up the hill is $^2/_3$. However, if you divide the space of possibilities into either "going up the hill" or "going down the hill," then the probability of this same event is $^1/_2$.

Although this is fine if the principle is intended as a psychological heuristic (indeed it helps to explain people's reasoning errors once a particular partitioning is assumed), such examples undermine its status as a logical principle. This severely restricts the model theorists' claims that extensional probabilistic reasoning is deductive. If people are presented with a unique equiprobable partition, then they can deduce other probabilities. But creating an appropriate partition is the main problem in many situations, and this does not reduce to deduction.

A related problem for the model theory, and indeed any extensional theory, concerns the differential weighting of mental models. In many situations we do have some prior weighting of the possibilities. Thus we may see that a coin has an irregular shape, and infer that one side is favoured over the other. The model theory proposes that we encode these weightings by means of numerical tags attached to each model. But the theory does not tell us how to infer such weights when the principle of equiprobability does not apply. Here it appears that we must rely on inside judgments – e.g., about the causal properties of the coin, about its similarity to a normal coin, etc.

In sum, people can sometimes reason from the outside, and possibly do so by constructing mental models, but the weighting of these models is not a logical matter, and will often depend on inside judgments.

Availability: The construction of a set of instances

Tversky and Kahneman (1973) introduced availability as a heuristic method for estimating frequencies or probabilities. People use the availability heuristic whenever they base their estimates on the ease with which instances or occurrences come to mind. Despite the simplicity of its formulation, the heuristic covers a range of cases. For one, it applies both to the recall of previous occurrences (e.g., how often you remember team X beating team Y) and to the generation of possible occurrences (e.g., how many ways you can imagine a novel plan going wrong). Second, it need not involve *actual* recall or generation, but only an assessment of the ease with which these operations *could* be performed. Our discussion will focus on cases of actual recall or generation because these are most relevant to current models of probability judgment. Issues concerning the subjective feeling of ease of recall rather than the content of recall lie beyond the scope of this chapter (see Schwarz & Vaughn, 2002).

As Tversky and Kahneman point out, availability is an ecologically valid cue to frequency because in general frequent events are easier to recall than infrequent ones. However, the clearest evidence that people use this heuristic comes from studies where it leads to biased estimates. For example, under timed conditions people generate far more words of the form _ _ _ _*ing* than of the form _ _ _ _ _*n*_ , even though the first class is a subset of the second. This shows that the first form is more available in memory than the second. Further, when one group estimates how many words in four pages of a novel have the form _ _ _ _*ing*, and another answers the same question for the form _ _ _ _ _*n*_ , estimates are much higher for the first. This suggests that in making their frequency estimates people relied on the ease with which they could retrieve instances (Tversky & Kahneman, 1983).

The availability heuristic furnishes one method for constructing a sample of events or instances. A more general account of sampling is advanced by Fiedler (2000). This extends the analysis from memory-based search to environmental search. Both kinds of search require an outside perspective, and both can lead to biases in the resulting set of instances. For one, the environment might be sampled in a biased way. Fiedler cites an example concerning the assessment of lie detectors. Many validity studies of such devices incorporate a pernicious sampling bias: of all the people who fail the test, validity assessments only include those who subsequently confess. Those who fail the test but are telling the truth are not counted (cf. positive test strategies, Klayman & Ha, 1987). Another common route to error is when people sample from a biased environment such as the media that over-represent sensational and newsworthy events.

Systematic biases can also arise when one generates a sample from one's own memory. This can occur due to the intrusion of associative memory processes (Kelley & Jacoby, 2000). Alternatively, it can result from the biased generation of possibilities or scenarios. For example, people tend to recruit reasons to support their own views, and neglect counterarguments or reasons that support opposing conclusions (Kunda, 1990). In all these cases people take a step towards an outside perspective by gathering a set of instances. Subsequent judgments may be flawed because the sample is atypical of the wider population. Fiedler (2000) argues that many judgmental biases arise because – rather than in spite – of our ability to process sample information accurately. Samples are often biased, and we lack the metacognitive abilities to correct for such biases.

The availability heuristic involves the generation of a set of instances, but it does not specify how people go from this set to a probability judgment. In certain cases this will be relatively transparent, such as when more instances of horse A winning a race rather than horse B are recalled and thus A is predicted to beat B. However, many situations will be more complicated. Suppose A and B have never raced against each other, and A has only raced in easy races, B in hard ones. In this case you may need to weight their number of wins differentially, and for this availability offers little guide.

The main role of availability in probability judgment, therefore, is to facilitate the selection or construction of a set of instances. Where this process leads to just one instance, the reasoner is likely to rely on an inside judgment (of similarity or association) to reach a probability estimate. Where it leads to a set of instances, the reasoner has a choice. They can resort to an inside strategy by simply averaging across properties of these instances, as they appear to do in frequency versions of the planning fallacy (Griffin & Buehler, 1999). Or they can use the distributional properties of the set to reach a probability judgment from the outside.

Nested sets

One of the virtues of the inside view is that it can take advantage of the rich knowledge normally associated with properties of the category being judged. However, this focus on the internal structure of a category causes the neglect of the distributional structure of category instances. In particular, an inside view fails to represent class inclusion relations. An outside view, in contrast, makes these relations transparent. By representing a distribution of instances, simple relations among sets of instances are represented automatically (Tversky & Kahneman, 1983). Sloman and Over (2003) describe the nested-sets hypothesis as the view that: (1) All else being equal, people prefer an inside view; but (2) representing instances requires an outside view that can make set inclusion relations transparent.

Evidence in favor of the nested-sets hypothesis includes demonstrations that presenting problems in the context of diagrams that reveal nested-set relations reduces the incidence of conjunction errors and base-rate neglect (Agnoli & Krantz, 1989; Cosmides & Tooby, 1996; Sloman, Over, & Slovak, 2003). Also, when asked to depict their thought processes on paper, people who get problems correct are more likely to draw pictures that represent nested-set relations (Sloman et al., 2003).

The nested-sets hypothesis is also supported by evidence that presenting problems in terms of the frequency of instances facilitates performance over presentation in terms of single-event probabilities (Cosmides & Tooby, 1996; Fiedler, 1988; Tversky & Kahneman, 1983). The frequency frame induces an outside perspective by asking participants to think about multiple instances of the category instead of assuming their more usual inside property-based perspective.

The frequency effect has sparked a lively debate over the status of the fallacies of probability judgment. Theorists like Gigerenzer (2000) and Cosmides and Tooby (1996) have argued that probability judgment must be understood in its ecological context. Errors arise on this view when participants are asked to make judgments of single-event probabilities because people did not evolve to make such judgments. Rather, they evolved to make judgments using natural frequencies. In response, Kahneman and Tversky (1996) pointed out that errors have been demonstrated using judgments of frequency since the onset of their heuristics and biases program, and that detractors have failed to provide an account of the systematic biases that the program has uncovered. Moreover, frequency formulations (even via natural sampling) are neither necessary nor sufficient for facilitation. Facilitation has been observed with judgments of probability (Girotto & Gonzalez, 2001; Johnson-Laird et al., 1999; Sloman et al., 2003), and errors have been observed with judgments of frequency (Bar-Hillel & Neter, 1993; Gluck & Bower, 1988; Lagnado & Shanks, 2002, 2003). The evolutionary rationale is itself suspect as people may well have evolved to use devices like causal models to make single-event probability judgments (Sloman & Over, 2003).

The bulk of the data do indeed show that presenting a problem in terms of frequency can reduce the incidence of error in probabilistic judgment. The current evidence suggests, however, that this is not the effect of natural frequency via natural sampling per se, but is mediated by the elicitation of an outside perspective that makes nested-set relations transparent. In short, people can reason extensionally whether or not they have to process "natural frequencies" (cf. Girotto & Gonzalez, 2001).

Statistical heuristics

The untutored approach to probabilistic reasoning often involves an inside view. What are the factors that promote a shift from an inside to an outside perspective? An influential developmental claim is that people's statistical intuitions stem from their learning about the nature of randomizing devices (e.g., coin tosses, card draws, spinners). Piaget and Inhelder (1951) argued that the child's concept of uncertainty derives from an understanding of physical causality, from causal mechanisms and the predictability of the outcomes they generate. Initially children struggle to comprehend randomizing devices, and invoke ad hoc causal explanations to account for the lack of predictability. Gradually they develop a better understanding; they appreciate the unpredictability of individual outcomes and the relevance of repeated trials.

Drawing on these ideas, Nisbett, Krantz, Jepson and Kunda (1983) argued that people possess *statistical heuristics* – "intuitive, rule-of-thumb inferential procedures that resemble formal statistical procedures." Examples of such heuristics include the preference for more rather than less evidence, intuitions about variability, and an appreciation of base rates in certain contexts. People are supposed to apply these heuristics to randomizing devices at a relatively early age, and later on to probabilistic causal systems (e.g., sports events, weather forecasts). Given that we do possess such heuristics, why do we often persist in reasoning from the inside? Nisbett et al. identified three relevant factors.

First, the use of statistical heuristics depends on the clarity of the sample space and the sampling process. Thus typical chance set-ups promote the use of these heuristics because both the space of alternative outcomes (e.g., the faces of a coin or die) and the repeatability of trials are clear and well defined. Indeed most games of chance are specifically designed to make these features transparent. For example, the symmetry of the different faces of a die, and the similarity of each separate die throw, make it much easier to take a distributional or outside perspective. This is supported by Girotto and Gonzalez's (2003) findings that in a variety of problems with well-defined sample spaces adults and children reason extensionally. It is also supported by Nisbett et al.'s demonstration that under appropriate conditions people obey the law of large numbers (see also Sedlmeier & Gigerenzer, 2000;

Fiedler, 2000) and appreciate that homogeneous properties require less confirmatory evidence than heterogeneous ones.

A related factor is the transparency of the randomizing element itself. With throws of the dice or spins of the roulette wheel the haphazard nature of the process is readily apparent. Likewise in ball games the movement of the ball reveals elements of randomness. This contrasts with many social domains where the randomizing factor is less tangible. For example, because of the lack of cues to the random elements in job interviews, people are prone to regard the interview as a "portrait in miniature" rather than a sample from a population.

In support of this claim, Nisbett et al. showed that participants shift from inside to outside reasoning according to the salience of the random process, and Gigerenzer, Hell, and Blank (1988) have shown that base-rate neglect in the lawyers/engineers problem is reduced if people perform the random sampling themselves. Base-rate neglect in the medical diagnosis problem is also reduced when the random sampling in the problem is made explicit (Cosmides & Tooby, 1996).

A third factor cited by Nisbett et al. involves cultural prescriptions to think statistically. They report various studies showing how statistical training promotes the adoption of an outside perspective, and this has been echoed in recent work on training people to reason statistically (Sedlmeier, 1999). Nisbett et al. draw the moral that the driving force in the shift from inside to outside reasoning is cultural evolution. This contrasts with theorists who argue that certain statistical reasoning abilities are hard-wired (Cosmides & Tooby, 1996; Gigerenzer, 2000), and require appropriate representations. A third view is that the ability to reason extensionally develops from other more basic cognitive operations (cf. Heyes, 2003).

Finally, the argument that our conception of random mechanisms develops from our prior understanding of causal systems cuts two ways. As well as suggesting conditions that facilitate an outside view, it suggests reasons that can undermine or distort it; vestiges of our primitive notion of a causal system remain in our ordinary notions of a random process. Both the gambler's fallacy and the hot hand fallacy are testament to this. In the case of the gambler's fallacy people often justify their fallacious inferences (e.g., that after a run of coin tosses resulting in heads, the next toss is more likely to fall tails) by claiming that things must eventually balance out. This is to conceive of chance as a self-correcting process rather than a genuinely random one (cf. Tversky & Kahneman, 1982). Similarly, when basketball fans believe that after a run of successful baskets a player is more likely to succeed with their next shot (Gilovich, Vallone & Tversky, 1985), they defend these erroneous beliefs by appeal to causal explanations (e.g., a "hot" player is more motivated or confident). In both cases people impose causal structure upon random sequences of events.

Conclusions

So what are the guidelines that demarcate an outside from an inside probability judgment? To start with, an outside view requires the enumeration of a relevant set of instances or possibilities. But this alone is insufficient. Probability judgments must be based on some distributional property of this set, such as a proportion or relative frequency. Moreover, reasoning from an outside perspective often requires attending to structural relations among instances (such as nested-set relations) rather than just causal or similarity relations. Finally, although both inside and outside perspectives can lead to fallacious reasoning, the nature of these errors typically differs. Inside judgments tend to violate the laws of probability because they are driven by natural assessments (such as similarity or association) unconstrained by probabilistic coherence. By contrast, outside-view errors tend to arise from an incomplete or inappropriate specification of the problem space.

Our survey suggests an essential tension between the two perspectives. To reach an unbiased probability judgment from the outside requires both an appropriate representation of the problem and a distributional perspective across the relevant units. But the task of achieving a good representation often relies on inside judgments – grouping units by similarity, determining relevance by causality, weighting alternatives by associative strength. And each of these factors can inhibit our ability to see the wider field. The outside view requires that we transcend the specific case, and yet it is the specific case, and all its properties, that make our representations of the world so compelling.

References

Agnoli, F. & Krantz, D. H. (1989) Suppressing natural heuristics by formal instruction: The case of the conjunction fallacy, *Cognitive Psychology*, 21, 515–50.

Anderson, J. R. (1991) The adaptive nature of human categorization, *Psychological Review*, 98, 409–29.

Bar-Hillel, M. & Neter, E. (1993) How alike is it versus how likely is it: A disjunction fallacy in probability judgments, *Journal of Personality and Social Psychology*, 65, 1119–31.

Buehler, R., Griffin, D., & Ross, M. (1994) Exploring the "planning fallacy": Why people underestimate their task completion times, *Journal of Personality and Social Psychology*, 67, 366–81.

Carnap, R. (1950) *Logical Foundations of Probability*. Chicago: University of Chicago Press.

Cobos, P. L., Almaraz, J., & Garcia-Madruga, J. A. (2003) An associative framework for probability judgment: An application to biases, *Journal of Experimental Psychology: Learning, Memory, and Cognition*, 29, 80–94.

Cosmides, L. & Tooby, J. (1996) Are humans good intuitive statisticians after all? Rethinking some conclusions from the literature on judgment under uncertainty, *Cognition*, 58, 1–73.

Dawes, R. M. (1996) *House of Cards: Psychology and Psychotherapy Built on Myth*. New York: The Free Press.

Dougherty, M. R. P., Gettys, C. F., & Ogden, E. E. (1999) MINERVA-DM: A memory processes model for judgments of likelihood, *Psychological Review*, 106, 180–209.

Dougherty, M. R. P., Gettys, C. F., & Thomas, R. P. (1997) The role of mental simulation in judgments of likelihood, *Organizational Behavior and Human Decision Processes*, 70, 135–48.

Fiedler, K. (1988) The dependence of the conjunction fallacy on subtle linguistic factors, *Psychological Research*, 50, 123–9.

Fiedler, K. (2000) Beware of samples! A cognitive-ecological sampling approach to judgment biases, *Psychological Review*, 107, 659–76.

Fox, C. R. & Rottenstreich, Y. (2003) Partition priming in judgment under uncertainty, *Psychological Science*, 14, 195–200.

Gigerenzer, G. (2000). *Adaptive Thinking: Rationality in the Real World.* New York: Oxford University Press.

Gigerenzer, G., Hell, W., & Blank, H. (1988) Presentation and content: The use of base rates as a continuous variable, *Journal of Experimental Psychology: Human Perception and Performance,* 14, 513–25.

Gillies, D. (2001) *Philosophical Theories of Probability.* London: Routledge.

Gilovich, T., Vallone, R., and Tversky, A. (1985) The hot hand in basketball: On the misperception of random sequences, *Cognitive Psychology,* 17, 295–314.

Girotto, V. & Gonzalez, M. (2001) Solving probabilistic and statistical problems: A matter of information structure and question form, *Cognition,* 78, 247–76.

Girotto, V. & Gonzalez, M. (2003) Probabilistic reasoning and combinatorial analysis. To appear in V. Girotto and P. Johnson-Laird (eds.), *The Shape of Reason: Essays in Honour of Paolo Legrenzi.* Hove, Psychology Press.

Gluck, M. A. & Bower, G. H. (1988) From conditioning to category learning: An adaptive network model, *Journal of Experimental Psychology: General,* 117, 227–47.

Griffin, D. & Buehler, R. (1999) Frequency, probability, and prediction: Easy solutions to cognitive illusions, *Cognitive Psychology,* 38(1), 48–78.

Hacking, I. (1975) *The Emergence of Probability.* Cambridge: Cambridge University Press.

Hampton, J. A. (1998) Similarity-based categorization and fuzziness of natural categories, *Cognition,* 65, 137–65.

Heit, E. & Rubinstein, J. (1994) Similarity and property effects in inductive reasoning, *Journal of Experimental Psychology: Learning, Memory, and Cognition,* 20, 411–22.

Heyes, C. M. (2003) Four routes of cognitive evolution, *Psychological Review,* 110(4), 713–27.

Jeffrey, R. (1965) *The Logic of Decision.* New York: McGraw-Hill.

Johnson-Laird, P. N., Legrenzi, P., Girotto, V., Legrenzi, M., and Caverni, J.-P. (1999) Naïve probability: A mental model theory of extensional reasoning, *Psychological Review,* 106, 62–88.

Kahneman, D. & Frederick, S. (2002) Representativeness revisited: Attribute substitution in intuitive judgment. In T. D. Gilovich, D. W. Griffin, and D. Kahneman (eds.), *Heuristics and Biases: The Psychology of Intuitive Judgment* (pp. 49–81). New York: Cambridge University Press.

Kahneman, D. & Tversky, A. (1982a) Variants of uncertainty. In D. Kahneman, P. Slovic, and A. Tversky (eds.), *Judgment under Uncertainty: Heuristics and Biases.* Cambridge: Cambridge University Press.

Kahneman, D. & Tversky, A. (1982b) The simulation heuristic. In D. Kahneman, P. Slovic, and A. Tversky (eds.), *Judgment under Uncertainty: Heuristics and Biases.* Cambridge: Cambridge University Press.

Kahneman, D. & Tversky, A. (1996) On the reality of cognitive illusions, *Psychological Review,* 103, 3, 582–91.

Kelley, C. M. & Jacoby, L. L. (2000) Recollection and familiarity: Process-dissociation. In E. Tulving and F. I. M. Craik (eds.), *The Oxford Handbook of Memory.* New York: Oxford University Press.

Klayman, J. & Ha, Y-W. (1987) Confirmation, disconfirmation, and information in hypothesis testing, *Psychological Review,* 94, 211–28.

Koehler, D. J. (1994) Hypothesis generation and confidence in judgment, *Journal of Experimental Psychology: Learning, Memory, and Cognition,* 20, 461–9.

Kunda, Z. (1990) The case for motivated reasoning, *Psychological Bulletin,* 108, 480–98.

Lagnado, D. A. & Shanks, D. R. (2002) Probability judgment in hierarchical learning: A conflict between predictiveness and coherence, *Cognition,* 83, 81–112.

Lagnado, D. A. & Shanks, D. R. (2003) The influence of hierarchy on probability judgment, *Cognition,* 89, 157–78.

Lewis, D. (1976) Probabilities of conditionals and conditional probabilities, *Philosophical Review*, 85, 297–315.

Medin, D. L., Coley, J. D., Storms, G., & Hayes, B. (2003) A relevance theory of induction, *Psychonomic Bulletin and Review*, 10(3), 517–32.

Meehl, P. E. (1954) *Clinical vs. Statistical Prediction: A Theoretical Analysis and a Review of the Evidence*. Minneapolis, MN: University of Minnesota Press.

Murphy, G. L. (1996) Category-based predictions: Influence of uncertainty and feature associations, *Journal of Experimental Psychology: Learning, Memory, and Cognition*, 22, 736–53.

Murphy, G. L. & Ross, B. H. (1994) Predictions from uncertain categorizations, *Cognitive Psychology*, 27, 148–93.

Nisbett, R. E., Krantz, D. H., Jepson, D. H., & Kunda, Z. (1983) The use of statistical heuristics in everyday inductive reasoning, *Psychological Review*, 90, 339–63.

Nosofsky, R. M. (1984) Choice, similarity, and the context theory of classification, *Journal of Experimental Psychology: Learning, Memory, and Cognition*, 10, 104–14.

Over, D. E. & Evans, J. St. B. T. (2003) The probability of conditionals: The psychological evidence, *Mind and Language*, 18(4), 340–58.

Pennington, N. & Hastie, R. (1993) Reasoning in explanation-based decision making, *Cognition*, 49, 123–63.

Piaget, J. & Inhelder, B. (1951) *The Genesis of the Idea of Chance in the Child*. Paris: Presses Universitaires de France.

Ramsey, F. P. (1931) *The Foundations of Mathematics and Other Logical Essays*. London: Routledge and Kegan Paul.

Rips, L. (1975) Inductive judgments about natural categories, *Journal of Verbal Learning and Verbal Behavior*, 14, 665–81.

Rosch, E. H. (1973) Natural categories, *Cognitive Psychology*, 4, 328–50.

Schwarz, N. & Vaughn, L. (2002) The availability heuristic revisited: Ease of recall and content of recall as distinct sources of information. In T. D. Gilovich, D. W. Griffin, & D. Kahneman (eds.), *Heuristics and Biases: The Psychology of Intuitive Judgment* (pp. 103–19). New York: Cambridge University Press.

Sedlmeier, P. (1999) *Improving Statistical Reasoning: Theoretical Models and Practical Implications*. Mahwah, NJ: Lawrence Erlbaum Associates.

Sedlmeier, P. & Gigerenzer, G. (2000) Was Bernoulli wrong? On intuitions about sample size, *Journal of Behavioral Decision Making*, 13, 133–9.

Shanks, D. R. (1991) A connectionist account of base-rate biases in categorization, *Connection Science*, 3, 143–62.

Shepard, R. N. (1980) Multidimensional scaling, tree-fitting, and clustering, *Science*, 210, 390–8.

Sloman, S. A. (1994) When explanations compete: The role of explanatory coherence on judgments of likelihood, *Cognition*, 52, 1–21.

Sloman, S. A. (1998) Categorical inference is not a tree: The myth of inheritance hierarchies, *Cognitive Psychology*, 35, 1–33.

Sloman, S. A. & Lagnado, D. A. (in press) The problem of induction. To appear in R. Morrison and K. Holyoak (eds.), *Handbook of Thinking and Reasoning*.

Sloman, S. A. & Over, D. E. (2003) Probability judgment: From the inside and out. In D. E. Over (ed.), *Evolution and the Psychology of Thinking: The Debate*. Hove: Psychology Press.

Sloman, S. A., Over, D. E., & Slovak, L. (2003) Frequency illusions and other fallacies, *Organizational Behavior and Human Decision Processes*, 91, 296–309.

Stalnaker, R. (1968) A theory of conditionals, *American Philosophical Quarterly Monograph Series*, 2, 98–112.

Steiger, J. H. & Gettys, C. F., (1972) Best-guess errors in multistage inference, *Journal of Experimental Psychology*, 92, 1–7.

Smith, E. E. & Osherson, D. N. (1989) Similarity and decision making. In S. Vosniadou & A. Ortony (eds.), *Similarity and Analogical Reasoning* (pp. 60–75). New York: Cambridge University Press.

Tversky, A. (1977) Features of similarity, *Psychological Review*, 84, 327–52.

Tversky, A. & Kahneman, D. (1973) Availability: A heuristic for judging frequency and probability, *Cognitive Psychology*, 5, 207–32.

Tversky, A. & Kahneman, D. (1982) Evidential impact of base rates. In Kahneman, D., Slovic, P., and Tversky, A. (eds.), *Judgment under Uncertainty: Heuristics and Biases*. Cambridge: Cambridge University Press.

Tversky, A. & Kahneman, D. (1983) Extensional versus intuitive reasoning: The conjunction fallacy in probability judgment, *Psychological Review*, 90, 293–315.

Windschitl, P. D., Young, M. E., & Jenson, M. E. (2002) Likelihood judgment based on previously observed outcomes: The alternative-outcomes effect in a learning paradigm, *Memory and Cognition*, 30, 469–77.

Yamagishi, K. (2002) Proximity, compatibility, and noncomplementarity in subjective probability, *Organizational Behavior and Human Decision Processes*, 87, 136–55.

9

Perspectives on Probability Judgment Calibration

Dale Griffin and Lyle Brenner

Introduction

"The Games could no more have a deficit than a man could have a baby!" So quoth Jean Drapeau, mayor of Montreal, shortly before the 1967 Montreal Summer Olympics ran a $2 billion deficit. Are such unrealistic pronouncements typical of human intuitive judgment? Such questions do not hold merely academic interest. For example, each reader of this chapter will probably be faced with choosing a course of action based on a physician's judgment about the outcome of a medical intervention.

Despite the importance of understanding the intuitive judgments of physicians, judges, and politicians, the study of probability calibration is primarily a laboratory-based enterprise, with theoretical controversies resolved (or not resolved) with reference to laboratory findings. There are two primary reasons for this apparently myopic focus. Jean Drapeau's quote illustrates one: expert pronouncements usually serve multiple functions beyond communicating the judge's own beliefs. Such judgments also serve to persuade, to inspire, and even to undermine opposing viewpoints. Second, the methods and paradigms for studying probability judgment were shaped by investigators who were interested not in the quality of likelihood judgments but in people's ability to monitor their own knowledge. Thus there are thousands of studies on confidence in trivia knowledge, compared to a handful of studies on the calibration of experts in the field (Koehler, Brenner, & Griffin, 2002).

Our review proceeds as follows. First, we review some general background necessary for understanding the theoretical controversies in the field. We then outline some classic findings as defined by the paradigm-setting review of Lichtenstein, Fischhoff, & Phillips (1982). We then describe five major classes of theories of judgmental calibration, and we examine how, and how well, these theories account for the dominant stylized facts in the literature. We conclude with a specific applied example and describe how the different theories account for the observed phenomena.

Calibration Curves: Graphical Displays of Calibration and Miscalibration

The quality of calibration can be assessed through *calibration curves* that represent a qualitative pattern of calibration, or through indices that summarize the degree of calibration quantitatively. We focus on graphical representations as they have had considerably more impact on conclusions in this field than summary indices (see, e.g., Yates, 1990).

Forced choice, half-range tasks

Laboratory studies of calibration have relied on a standard paradigm inherited from the cognitive psychologists studying metacognition, or one's knowledge about one's knowledge. A typical experiment consists of a subject answering many general knowledge or "almanac" questions (e.g., "Which is further north: Paris or New York?"), and then rating his/her confidence, in the form of a probability, that the chosen answer is correct. The questions are typically presented with 2 choices so that the possible probability ratings in the chosen alternative range from 50 per cent to 100 per cent.

Accuracy rates (Y) are plotted against confidence ratings (X) in a calibration curve. Overconfidence occurs when confidence exceeds accuracy; underconfidence occurs when accuracy exceeds confidence (see Figure 9.1). Mixed cases occur when a curve starts out on one side of the identity line (often above the line representing underconfidence for relatively low probabilities such as 0.5 or 0.6) and then crosses the identity line (typically below the line representing overconfidence for higher probabilities). In these cases, it is essential to examine the calibration curve in tandem with the response proportions at each level of expressed probability (Wallsten, 1996). The same mixed pattern may indicate aggregate overconfidence if most of the judgments are made with high confidence or aggregate underconfidence if most of the judgments are made with low confidence.

Full-range tasks

One common source of confusion (resulting from the predominance of half-range tasks) is that there are distinct patterns of judgment referred to by the label "overconfidence." When probabilities are assigned to a focal hypothesis on the full 0 to 1 probability scale, we can distinguish between two forms of overconfidence: *overprediction*, depicted by curve A in Figure 9.2, the tendency to assign probabilities that are consistently too *high*; and *overextremity*, depicted by curve C, the tendency to assign probabilities that are consistently too *extreme* (i.e., too close to either 0 or 1). In the case of binary hypotheses,

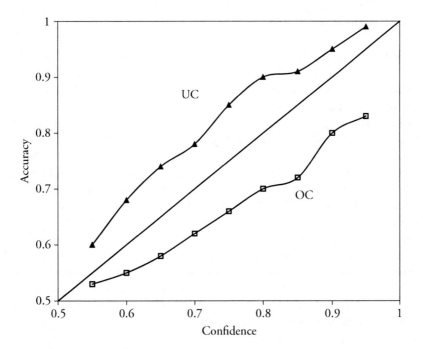

Figure 9.1 Sample half-range calibration curves

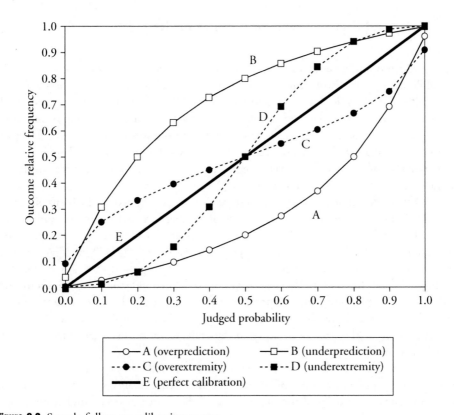

Figure 9.2 Sample full-range calibration curves

overextremity indicates an overestimation of whatever hypothesis the judge considers most likely. Thus, overconfidence, the poster child of judgmental biases, as a simple summary term does not uniquely identify one of these patterns (Wallsten & Budescu, 1983). Underestimation and underextremity can be defined similarly; underestimation (curve B) refers to assigning consistently too low probabilities to the focal hypothesis, and underextremity (curve D) refers to assigning probabilities that are not sufficiently extreme (i.e., probabilities too close to the middle of the scale.) Combinations of under- or over-prediction and either of the extremity biases are also possible, and result in lines that cross the diagonal at points other than 50 percent. (See Harvey (1997) for a similar analysis.)

Liberman & Tversky (1993) called patterns of overextremity "generic overconfidence," and patterns of overprediction "specific overconfidence." Because overprediction refers to overconfidence in a specific designated hypothesis, it may be thought of as a bias towards that particular hypothesis. In contrast, in the case of binary hypotheses, overextremity indicates an overestimation of whatever hypothesis the judge considers most likely, and in that sense is independent of the focal hypothesis. Both overprediction and overextremity can be distinguished from optimistic overconfidence, which may be thought of as a specific form of overprediction – overestimation of the probability of events thought to be beneficial to the judge.

The Roots and Stylized Facts of Calibration Research

Early research on judgmental calibration was not aimed at discovering how people used probabilities, but in discovering how well people could assess or monitor their own knowledge. For example, Fullerton and Cattell (1892), Henmon (1911), and others all studied how well observers could introspect about whether their perceptions or college test answers were correct, and in particular whether observers could successfully report "partial knowledge." Henmon summarized his results as follows: "While there is a posit-ive correlation on the whole between degree of confidence and accuracy the degree of confidence is not a reliable index of accuracy" (pp. 200–1).

Two other parallel streams of early research were summarized by Lichtenstein et al. Research within meteorology on the accuracy of weather forecasts began very early in the twentieth century and unlike the psychological research, dealt exclusively with expert forecasters in the field. Research in the signal detection theory (SDT) paradigm studied the accuracy of confidence ratings in perceptual tasks during the 1950s and 1960s. The findings in these disparate fields were very similar: a preponderance of overconfidence, both in the overextremity and overprediction forms, with the degree of overconfidence depending on the difficulty of the task, and some scattered examples of underprediction. Lichtenstein et al. then reviewed scores of laboratory studies using almanac questions that showed the same pattern.

The Lichtenstein et al. review has been cited over 600 times, and usually for the following three points (in order of popularity): the predominance of overconfidence in the 2AFC almanac paradigm; the dependence of the degree of overconfidence on item difficulty; and the superb calibration of professional weather forecasters predicting rain in a Midwestern American city. In the manner of most secondary citations, the points are usually oversimplified compared to the comprehensive treatment in the review. The predominance of overconfidence was found across tasks, expertise, format, and method, across physicians and CIA operatives, weather forecasters and clinical psychologists. It is clearly not merely an artifact of the trivia or general knowledge paradigm. Furthermore, given that the amount of overconfidence is usually dramatic even with judgments of complete certainty, and with other forms of elicitation (e.g., odds, bets), the effect is not solely due to unfamiliarity with the probability scale or measurement artifacts due to the scale endpoints.

Similarly, the difficulty or "hard–easy" effect is not a hothouse phenomenon created by the clever concoction of a misleading set of general knowledge items. It has been found when participants differing in ability are compared, when participants with differing amounts of training are compared, and when item difficulty is defined by intrinsic qualities of the items rather than percent correct, as well as on post hoc comparisons of high-accuracy versus low-accuracy items. In each case, the most difficult items or domains showed strong overconfidence, which declined and turned into underconfidence for the easiest items or domains. The same qualitative pattern was found in a signal detection study (Pollack and Decker, 1958), which examined the discriminability of words presented on earphones under conditions of high or low noise. An analog to the difficulty effect was found when the proportions of "true" statements were manipulated in a one-alternative true–false task: overprediction when true statements were rare and underprediction when true statements were common.

The difficulty effect implies that there is a negative correlation between overall over/underprediction (Bias) and accuracy (Acc). It might appear that the difficulty effect is a statistical artifact, simply because the measure of overconfidence used contains the measure of difficulty: Bias = Conf − Acc. Let us examine this claim by calculating the covariance between Bias and Acc:

$$\mathrm{Cov(Bias,Acc) = Cov(Conf,Acc) - Var(Acc)}$$

Note that this quantity certainly can be positive (contrary to the difficulty effect) if the correlation between Conf and Acc is large enough:

$$\mathrm{Corr(Conf,Acc) > SD(Acc) \ / \ SD(Conf).}$$

Thus, the difficulty effect is not a necessary feature of the method of data analysis, but is equivalent to a sufficiently low correlation between average confidence and accuracy across items.

From these "classic" and robust findings, we can summarize several "stylized facts" that theories of calibration need to explain.

1 Overconfidence is the predominant finding.
2 The degree of overconfidence depends on item difficulty (in the 2AFC case) and item base rate (in the full-range case). The calibration curve is relatively flat rather than rising with increasing probability.

3   Underconfidence is regularly found in very easy tasks and with very high base rates.
4   Excellent calibration is possible.

Theoretical Perspectives on Calibration

We now turn to five competing psychological accounts of probability calibration, and provide a conceptual framework for organizing the maze of empirical results. The five broad perspectives and their most important characteristics are summarized in Table 9.1. This set of theories is by no means exhaustive and we make no attempt to determine the "winner" of the theory competition, for our view is that these theories are like lenses that serve to organize the calibration data in different ways.

Optimistic overconfidence

The most influential perspective on miscalibration – at least for those outside the field itself – is the *optimistic overconfidence* perspective: people are notoriously subject to wishful thinking and self-enhancement, and thus provide probability estimates that are distorted by these self-serving motivations. This fits the dictionary definition of overconfidence: "The state or quality of being impudently or arrogantly self-confident" (*Roget's Thesaurus*, 1985). Biases thus reflect unwarranted arrogance or hubris, and overconfidence in the form of overprediction (curve A in Figure 9.2) should predominate and should vary according to the desirability of the outcome.

Conceptual background
The optimistic overconfidence perspective builds on several findings in the psychological literature: the *better than average effect* (e.g., Larwood & Whittaker, 1977, for managers; Svenson, 1981, for drivers; Alicke, 1985, for personal traits), the tendency to rate oneself as above the mean in positive skills and traits; *unrealistic optimism* (e.g., Weinstein, 1980), the tendency to rate oneself as more likely to experience positive events and less susceptible to negative events than others; *self-serving attributions* (e.g., Miller & Ross, 1975), the tendency to take credit for success and avoid blame for failure; and the *illusion of control* (e.g., Langer, 1975), the tendency to rate oneself as having some degree of control over random events. The account is further bolstered by the ubiquity of the *planning fallacy* (e.g., Buehler, Griffin, & Ross, 1994; Kahneman & Tversky, 1979), the tendency to believe that tasks will be completed more quickly and successfully in the future than they have been in the past, and *partisan belief polarization* (Hastorf & Cantril, 1954; Lord, Ross, & Lepper, 1979), the tendency for opposing partisans to interpret the same evidence as supporting their own divergent beliefs.

Conceptual critique
Both the generality of and the bases for self-enhancing forms of optimism have been questioned. Ironically, one of the papers most commonly cited to support the notion of

Table 9.1 Characteristics of theoretical models of calibration

	Optimistic overconfidence	Confirmatory bias	Case-based judgment	Ecological models	Error models
Primary assumption and emphasis	People are motivated to think well of themselves	People have information-processing bias to confirm hypotheses	Subjective probability is nonextensional and primarily focused on features of the case at hand (neglects relevant class-based evidence)	People adapt to and internalize statistical cues in natural environments; judged probabilities are unbiased estimates of ecological validity	Random error contaminates probability judgments; calibration of underlying beliefs is different than calibration of stated probabilities
Predicted biases	Overprediction	Overextremity	All patterns possible: Depends on information environment	Most patterns with nonrepresentative item selection; good calibration with representative item selection	Some amount of overextremity is attributable to random error in responses; overextremity and underextremity depending on method of data analysis
Expressed judgment represents	Hopes, wishes, self-enhancement	Proportion of evidence favoring most likely hypothesis	Evaluation of strength of evidence in case at hand	Reflection of ecological cue validity in natural environment	Internal "true-belief" probability plus random response error
Explanation for underprediction and/or underextremity	Underprediction: Depressive personality	None	Underprediction: High base rate Underextremity: High discriminability	Underprediction: Oversampling of high-probability items Underextremity: Sampling too many extreme-probability items	Underextremity: Items grouped by objective probability and inverse regression operating

Table 9.1 (cont'd)

	Optimistic overconfidence	Confirmatory bias	Case-based judgment	Ecological models	Error models
Explanation for predominance of overconfidence	Most people are optimistic	Confirmation is typical mode of reasoning	Forecasts are typically made for rare or difficult-to-predict outcomes	Studies of unrepresentative domains/items	Most predictions contain substantial random error
Explanation for overprediction and/or over-extremity	Overprediction: Focal hypothesis is positive/self-enhancing	Overprediction: Bias towards evidence for *focal* hypothesis Overextremity: Bias towards evidence for *more likely* hypothesis	Overprediction: Low base rate Overextremity: Low discriminability	Overprediction: Sampling too many low-probability items Overextremity: Sampling too many moderate-probability items	Overextremity: Large amount of random error in judgment
Explanation for the difficulty effect	None	More overlooked reasons for difficult items/domains	Changing discriminability and/or changing base rate of set neglected	Oversampling of difficult items varies from set to set	Regression effect between mean judgment and mean accuracy
Explanation for good calibration	No personal interest or motive	Even-handed consideration of alternative hypothesis	Moderate base rate and discriminability	Representative sample of items from natural environment	Little or no response error is necessary but not sufficient
Implications for debiasing	Reduce hubris; recruit arm's-length judges	Explicit consideration of reasons for the alternative and against the focal	Training to increase attention to base rate and discriminability	Avoid nonrepresentative sampling; use frequency estimates when nonrepresentative	Reduce response error; Adjust for random error in analysis

self-serving attributions (Miller & Ross, 1975) advanced the claim that it is virtually impossible to separate motivational causes of self-serving attributions from informational causes. In particular, they note that people have much greater experience with success than with failure, and may thus explain them differently, even without any motivation to feel superior. In the same vein, recent commentators have noted that comparative optimism ("how do you compare to the average person?"), one form of unrealistic optimism, may be due in part to an attentional bias and therefore less general than previously believed (Kruger, 1999). The common tendency to rate oneself as in the ninety-fifth percentile of drivers seems to be caused partly by an excessive focus on the self, with a corresponding lack of attention to the others serving as the basis of comparison. Thus, for domains where people have a high absolute level of skill (e.g., driving) comparative optimism is found, but for domains where people have a low absolute level of skill (e.g., juggling), comparative pessimism is found, consistent with the argument that people anchor on their own level of skill and then adjust insufficiently for the comparative nature of the judgment (Kruger, 1999). (This interpretation does not hold for the many demonstrations of unrealistic optimism using "indirect" measures where individuals separately rate their own standing and the average person's standing.)

The planning fallacy, too, may be interpreted in informational terms: because the base rate of meeting predicted deadlines is relatively low, neglecting past experiences will give rise to apparently optimistic predictions. This interpretation is bolstered by the finding that the planning fallacy is equally pronounced in Japan and in Canada, despite the fact that the Japanese showed self-blaming attributions (Buehler, Otsubo, Lehman, Heine, & Griffin, 2003). Furthermore, the degree of optimism about future events is controlled by the temporal distance to the event, with events in the near future being regarded in a more evenhanded fashion (Gilovich, Kerr, & Medvec, 1993; Liberman & Trope, 1998; Shepperd, Ouellette, & Fernandez, 1996). All in all, these ambiguities and limitations in the optimistic bias account should lead to greater caution in its use as a *general* explanation of miscalibration.

Fitting stylized facts

The optimistic overconfidence account is only able to directly address the first stylized fact, the prevalence of overconfidence. For example, financial forecasts over the past century have been consistently over-optimistic (Hogarth & Makridakis, 1981). A survey of almost 3,000 new business owners revealed unrealistic optimism about their own business succeeding (81 percent probability of success for their own business vs. 59 percent probability of businesses like theirs, whereas a realistic estimate is somewhere in the range of 30 to 70 percent, Cooper, Woo, & Dunkelberg, 1988). However, as noted above, these findings are open to interpretation in terms of information-based biases.

Confirmatory bias

A second broad perspective, largely eschewing motivational underpinnings, is the *confirmatory bias* perspective: People naturally search for evidence that supports their chosen hypothesis. Biases in calibration should thus reflect hypothesis-confirmation biases in attention, information gathering, and interpretation; consequently, overconfidence in the form of overextremity (curve C in Figure 9.2) should predominate.

Conceptual background

This account, too, is well supported by basic psychological evidence. When people test simple hypotheses about the relations between numbers and letters (e.g., Wason, 1968) or attempt to determine the personality type of an individual (e.g., Snyder & Swann, 1978) or even when teachers decide on a grade for a schoolchild (Rosenthal & Jacobson, 1966) they selectively search for confirmatory instances to "test" their theories.

Koriat, Lichtenstein, and Fischhoff (1980) argued that overconfidence arises in part from people's tendency to recruit evidence from memory that confirms the focal hypothesis. They offered a two-stage model in which the judge first selects her preferred option on the basis of a knowledge search, and then assesses her confidence by recruiting reasons supporting the preferred answer. The stronger and more numerous the reasons that are recruited, the greater is the confidence expressed in the selected answer. Because this process inclines the judge to overlook reasons *against* the selected answer, she is likely to be overconfident that the selected answer is correct.

Koriat et al. reported two results consistent with their model. First, asking subjects to generate reasons favoring and opposing both options reduced overconfidence relative to a control condition in which no such reasons were generated. Second, asking subjects to generate reasons contradicting their preferred alternative reduced overconfidence while generation of supporting reasons had no effect. Hoch (1985) also reported results consistent with the confirmatory search model in a study of predictions of graduating business school students regarding the outcome of their job searches. Asking students to generate reasons why the target event would *not* occur substantially reduced the observed overconfidence, whereas asking them to generate reasons supporting the target event's occurrence had no influence (see also Brenner, Koehler, & Tversky, 1996).

Conceptual critique

Considerable experimental evidence suggests that a confirmatory bias – like a tendency towards optimism – is responsible for creating *some* amount of overconfidence, particularly overextremity. However, direct evidence for its role and prevalence in probability judgments is scarce. The fact that providing reasons against a hypothesis can reduce overconfidence in general knowledge does not provide privileged support to the confirmatory bias account. Overconfidence may be created by any one of the mechanisms we discuss and still be reduced through strictures to "consider the opposite" (Lord, Lepper, & Preston, 1984). More studies are needed to distinguish the relative effects of hypotheses that are believed to be true and hypotheses that are wished to be true, as well as to distinguish confirmatory overconfidence from that caused by informational biases, such as neglecting the outcome base rate.

Fitting stylized facts

McKenzie (1997) offers a model that includes a parameter reflecting the extent to which evidence regarding alternative hypotheses is weighted in the confidence assessment, which ranges from 0 (complete neglect) to 1 (full weighting, equal to that placed on evidence regarding focal hypothesis). Anything less than a weight of 1 will produce overly extreme judgments. His model departs from the earlier confirmatory bias approaches in that he assumes that people have an unbiased sample of confirmatory evidence but simply neglect other evidence. A confirmatory bias model is used by Yates, Lee, Sieck, Choi, & Price (2002) to explain cultural differences in overconfidence. Such models can help to explain the prevalence of overconfidence reported in the literature using general knowledge questions. They are also, arguably, consistent with the observation of the difficulty effect. For easy tasks, there are likely to be proportionally few neglected reasons, since the majority of the evidence will point to the preferred (and correct) answer. On this account, we would expect substantial overconfidence for difficult tasks but not for easy tasks.

Confirmatory bias models cannot naturally accommodate the base-rate effects found in full-range tasks or underextremity or underprediction, though underconfidence is commonly observed with easy tasks. Confirmatory bias may be one piece of the miscalibration puzzle, but it is not the whole story.

Case-based judgment

A third approach is the *case-based judgment* perspective, associated with the heuristics and biases and related literatures. From this perspective, judgment biases reflect the way that people intuitively perceive and assess relevant evidence. People focus on case-specific factors and neglect the information structure of the environment, leading to a pattern of miscalibration that includes all the curves drawn in Figure 9.2 (including the diagonal line of perfect calibration). The case-based perspective rests on the assumption that intuitive judgments of probability or likelihood are non-extensional; that is, that they are based on an evaluation of the individual case with little consideration of the set or class from which the case is drawn. Well-known findings in the heuristics and biases literature such as base-rate neglect, non-regressive prediction, neglect of sample size, and the conjunction fallacy are demonstrations of the non-extensional nature of intuitive probability judgment (Kahneman, Slovic, & Tversky, 1982). This view is also consistent with much recent research indicating that judgments are often constructed based on internal sensations and cues (e.g., Koriat & Levy-Sadot, 1999).

Lichtenstein et al. (1982, pp. 316–17) provided an early description of the neglect perspective when they noted that "the hard–easy effect seems to arise from assessors' inability to appreciate how difficult or easy a task is." The neglect perspective was formalized in Ferrell & McGoey's (1980) Decision Variable Partition (DVP) model with cutoff parameters that were insensitive to changing evidence diagnosticity or outcome base rates. This model was successful in reproducing the difficulty effect in both the 2AFC case (where difficulty was neglected) and in the full-range case (where base rate was neglected). Griffin & Tversky (1992) noted the applicability of the heuristics and biases principles to the calibration context and proposed a *strength-weight* model of judged probability. According to this model, people intuitively focus on the strength of the evidence (how extreme is the evidence *in this case*) and then slightly adjust for the weight of the evidence (class-based factors such as sample size, base rate, and diagnosticity of the evidence). Such underadjustment leads to overconfidence when strength is high and weight is low and underconfidence when strength is low and weight is high; good calibration will generally occur when both are moderate. Furthermore, this model also unifies conservatism biases in belief updating (e.g., Phillips & Edwards, 1966) with the representativeness heuristic, as the underextremity typical of conservatism is found with evidence of high diagnosticity (weight) but the overextremity typical of the representativeness heuristic is found with evidence of low diagnosticity (weight).

Random Support Theory (RST; Brenner, 2003) supplements qualitative accounts such as the strength-weight model by characterizing the degree of case-based neglect in a given set of calibration data. RST, like Ferrell's DVP, uses a signal detection framework to link different outcomes to different confidence states in the judge; however, RST embeds the signal detection model within the broad non-extensional model of probability judgment provided by Support Theory (Tversky & Koehler, 1994; Rottenstreich & Tversky, 1997). An advantage of support-based models is that, in many cases, people can assess directly the extent to which the available evidence supports a given hypothesis. Koehler, Brenner, and Tversky (1997) report the results of a number of studies in which direct ratings of support are used successfully to fit probability judgments.

Conceptual critique

The empirical demonstrations used to underpin the heuristics and biases program have been the subject of many criticisms, ranging from claims that participants misunderstood the instructions to claims that the results might be restricted to paper and pencil tests of probabilistic reasoning. Each individual criticism may have some force with regard to a particular demonstration of a particular phenomenon. However, the large body of work is highly consistent and cannot be written off as a byproduct of experimental ingenuity or leading questions (Gilovich, Griffin & Kahneman, 2002). Furthermore, the calibration of experts in the field is consistent with the case-based model (Koehler et al., 2002, see Figure 9.3).

The chief difficulty with this class of models is that although people underweight class factors, they do use them to a degree that varies across situations. How does this happen? Does information about the weight of the evidence contaminate the assessment of its strength, without any attempt at Bayesian integration? Or is there something like an anchoring-and-adjustment mechanism that gives priority to the case-based evaluation but nonetheless consists of a separate evaluation for weight? These questions are critical issues for this account to address.

Fitting stylized facts

At the time of the Lichtenstein et al. (1982) review, the only existing model precise enough to be fit to empirical data was the decision variable partition model (DVP) of Ferrell and McGoey (1980). In the tradition of signal detection theory, this model describes confidence judgment as a process of partitioning an internal decision variable (which might be thought of as a feeling of confidence) into confidence categories that are used in making the overt judgment or response. Specifically, the model starts with the usual signal detection assumption that the decision variable can be represented using two unit-normal distributions, one for true or correct hypotheses and the other for false

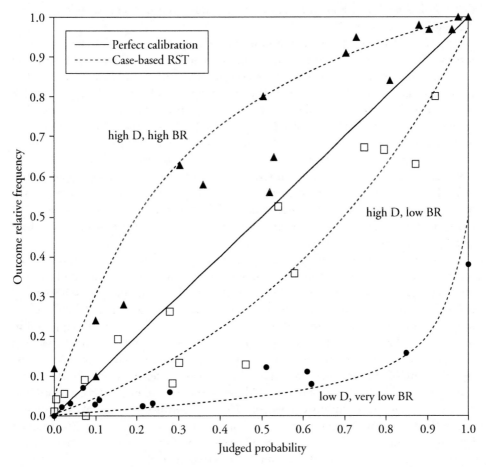

Figure 9.3 Calibration of physicians' probability judgments

or incorrect hypotheses. The former is assumed to have a higher mean than the latter, with the distance between them representing the discriminability of true and false hypotheses. The decision variable itself is not scaled in terms of probability; instead, the judgment is assumed to arise from a partition of the decision variable which assumes only that confidence is a monotonically increasing function of the decision variable.

The set of cutoff values established by the judge to create this partition is a crucial aspect of the partition model. Perhaps most impressive is the model's performance when supplemented by the assumption that the judge's set of cutoffs is insensitive to changes in task difficulty or base rate in the absence of performance feedback (Ferrell & McGoey, 1980; Smith & Ferrell, 1983; Suantak, Bolger, & Ferrell, 1996). Although there exists, for any given level of proportion correct, a set of cutoffs that would ensure perfect calibration (Gu & Wallsten, 2001), Ferrell and colleagues have found that the miscalibration observed in experimental contexts is often well accounted for by a single set of cutoffs that is not changed over large variations in the task environment. This insensitivity can produce any of the calibration patterns pictured in Figure 9.2, however, the model is agnostic about the nature of the underlying decision variable or where the cutoffs come from.

Brenner's RST model can fit the same range of data as the DVP model, but it incorporates a psychological theory of the determinants of confidence (support theory) and thus provides a more parsimonious and intuitive set of output parameters. The underlying dimension is now made up of two distributions of perceived *support*, for true and for false hypotheses. The distance between these two distributions is the discriminability parameter α. The set of cutoffs used in DVP is replaced by the focal bias parameter β (indicating sensitivity to base rate) and the extremity parameter σ (indicating sensitivity to discriminability). These parameters can be used to characterize almost any observed pattern of calibration in terms of the underlying process of support evaluation. However, highly specific predictions are made by constraining β and σ (usually fixing β to represent base-rate neglect, and setting σ to near 1, indicating a moderate degree of variability in judged probabilities), while allowing discriminability and base rate to be free parameters of the environment.

Accounting for all the stylized facts then requires some additional assumptions. The prevalence of overconfidence implies that most judgment tasks that are studied (and probably most that are of interest in the real world) are difficult (leading to overextremity) and the outcomes of interest are rare (leading to overprediction). The difficulty effect implies that people tend not to alter the extremity by which they translate support into probability when the diagnosticity of evidence or the discriminability of the hypotheses change. Underprediction reflects those settings where the outcomes of interest are extremely common. Finally, there are some settings where the diagnosticity of the evidence is moderate and base rates are moderate – these settings should give rise to good calibration, even for untutored intuitive judgment. However, settings where good calibration is achieved in spite of extreme diagnosticity or extreme base rates require explanation beyond the basic theory (e.g., the calibrated prediction of rain in Chicago requires some explanation because the base rate of rain was moderately low).

Ecological probability

A fourth perspective is the *ecological probability* perspective; the key premise here is that people have highly accurate, adaptive knowledge of the probability of events in their natural environment. Because experiments rarely use stimuli that are representative of natural environments, studies find (or create) artificial biases in probabilistic judgment. Biases thus represent distortions induced by misleading empirical settings, and miscalibration should disappear when items are representative of the natural environment.

The above summary characterizes the second of two Brunswikian models that are relevant to calibration research. There is a long tradition of *lens model* approaches initiated by Brunswik himself (see Chapter 3, this volume). As Hammond noted (1998) "In short, ecological validity refers to the potential utility of various cues for organisms in their ecology (or natural habitat). Of course, the difference between the ecological validity of a cue and its actual use by an organism provides important information about the effective use of information by that organism." This is the central goal of the Brunswikian lens model social judgment theory approach: to determine what cues are used in judgment and how cue utilization compares to the ideal ecological validity of those cues (Hammond & Stewart, 2001). Most of these studies have focused on expert judgments, including many studies of meteorologists making probability judgments about weather events (e.g., Lusk, Stewart, Hammond, & Potts, 1990).

In a second wave of Brunswikian models of calibration, the focus on the use or misuse of ecologically valid cues by experts in the field has been replaced by the assumption of known ecological validities and by studies of students answering general knowledge questions. These models were motivated by May's (1986) observation that almanac studies finding overconfidence often used items hand-chosen to be challenging or even tricky, and her finding that judgments of overall accuracy ("how many did you get right?") rarely showed the same degree of overconfidence. The first and probably best-known model of this type was the Probabilistic Mental Model (PMM) account developed by Gigerenzer, Hoffrage, and Kleinbölting (1991). A probabilistic model recruits a *reference class* from the natural environment (e.g., "all large cities in Germany"), and the reference class in turn recruits a series of cues. Confidence is determined by the cue validity, and "good calibration is to be expected if cue validities correspond to ecological validities" (Gigerenzer et al., 1991, p. 509). In general, items sampled from a well-defined reference class should meet this standard and show good calibration. If items are selected in a non-representative fashion, miscalibration will be observed.

In the first study testing these predictions, the calibration of a "representative set" of questions was compared with that of a "selected set" of general knowledge questions. The representative set was generated by randomly selecting 25 cities out of the 65 German cities with populations over 100,000. Participants judged pairs of these cities, decided which was larger, and indicated their confidence. After each block of 50 questions, participants estimated the number correct. The city-judgment task was substantially easier (72 percent) than the general knowledge task (52 percent), and in fact was much better calibrated overall, although judges showed substantial overextremity in the half-range task. Note that this finding is in accord with the difficulty effect as well as the selection effect. The authors attempt to address this ambiguity by selecting a portion of the city pairs that matched the difficulty of the general knowledge questions. As predicted by both the difficulty effect and the PMM, overconfidence in this selected set of difficult city questions showed substantial overconfidence. The same design in a second study led to a similar accuracy/difficulty confound (75 percent vs. 56 percent) and similar differences in calibration. Importantly, estimates of aggregate accuracy (frequency estimation over a set of problems) matched the observed accuracy rate of the difficult general knowledge questions and were substantially lower than the observed accuracy rate of the easier city questions. From these results, the authors concluded that overconfidence "disappeared" with representative sampling or with aggregate frequency judgments.

An extensive review of over 95 data sets (Juslin, Winman, & Olsson, 2000) found that the natural confounding of difficulty and representative versus selected data sets is almost complete. From the few studies that allowed the comparison at equal levels of difficulty, the overconfidence effect was much stronger for selected rather than representative sets (note, however, that regression artifacts make this comparison difficult to interpret). Although both overconfidence and underconfidence have been found with representative items, they rarely if ever show the extreme level of overconfidence found with difficult general item sets (possibly because the relatively easy representative sets allow less scope for overconfidence).

Conceptual critique

A central weakness of the second wave of ecological models is their continued focus on general knowledge and almanac questions, even ones randomly selected from world cities, countries, or death rates. Although it is important to question the role of difficult or tricky item sets (Keren, 1991), the research paradigm has lost the most important aspect of Brunswik's representative design: the actual environment and actual experts who have experience in selecting and using cues in that environment. Preliminary evidence from the limited number of calibration studies on experts in their natural environments reveals a dramatic pattern of miscalibration (Koehler et al., 2002) and should spur studies that examine cue use as well as ecological validity for representative judgments by lawyers, physicians, economic forecasters, and meteorologists. Furthermore, although it is both conceptually and practically difficult to define the appropriate reference class from which to sample items, representative design is satisfied by definition for the day-to-day judgments of experts.

   The superior calibration of frequency judgments compared to probability judgments has found little support in subsequent studies. Instead, when frequency judgments are based on the same evidence as probability judgments, they show similar patterns of overconfidence (Brenner, Koehler, Liberman, & Tversky, 1996); otherwise, aggregate frequency judgments are simply lower than average confidence, leading to better overall calibration on difficult sets and poorer calibration on easy sets (Griffin & Buehler, 1999). Griffin and Tversky (1992) argued that the comparison of selected and representative sets should take into account not only the difficulty of the questions but also the strength of the impressions generated by the questions. Using random sampling from the same reference class (American states), they showed that holding accuracy constant at a low level, question sets that recruited strong impressions led to overconfidence while those that recruited weak impressions led to good overall calibration. Thus, neither representative samples nor specific levels of accuracy are sufficient to determine good calibration.

Fitting stylized facts

As described, the ecological models can account for overconfidence, the difficulty effect, and even underconfidence by invoking appropriately biased selection criteria. Good calibration should be associated with a representative sample. Although the key forms of miscalibration have been found even with representative sampling, the ecological models' assumption of an unbiased underlying representation of a true, ecological probability also has been incorporated in some of the error models that are reviewed below.

Error model

A fifth perspective is the *error model* or psychometric perspective. Error models attempt to separate the core underlying beliefs of the judge from the observed expressed probability judgments. In general, such approaches imply that uncorrected judgments will show overextremity biases, and that observed overextremity will be improved by correcting for or reducing the random response error.

Conceptual background

The psychometric justification for this approach is simple: when random error is added, the correlation between variables is attenuated. Erev, Wallsten, & Budescu (1994) proposed using the psychometric approach in the calibration domain by assuming that observed probability judgments reflect a systematic component (covert confidence) plus some amount of random error. Following this logic, even if the underlying true scores are unbiased, a significant amount of random error added at the response stage would lead to a lower correlation between judged probability and outcome than between true probability and outcome, and this, due to the effects of regression to the mean, would lead to observed overextremity.

The psychometric analogy also implies that the conclusions drawn by regressing or plotting Y (outcome frequency) as a function of X (judged probability) can be different from those drawn by regressing or plotting X on Y. If items can be classified by some objective probability, for example, general knowledge items can be classified by percent correct, then confidence can be plotted as a function of, or conditioned on, objective probability. If true underlying confidence is perfectly calibrated but random error is added, a regressive pattern is produced where high subjective probabilities are matched with lower outcomes (overconfidence in the high end of the scale) when the data are conditioned on judgment – but items with high objective probabilities are matched with lower subjective probabilities (underconfidence in the high end of the scale) when the data were conditioned on outcome. This pattern was labeled "simultaneous overconfidence and underconfidence" by Erev et al.

Conceptual critique

The results of Erev et al. can be interpreted in two ways, as a methodological prescription and as a descriptive model of probability judgment. The methodological prescription highlights the perils of diagnosing overconfidence on the basis of the calibration curve, since "error alone" can produce the appearance of overconfidence in such a curve even when underlying beliefs are unbiased. Brenner, Koehler, Liberman, and Tversky (1996) noted that the standard measure of overconfidence in 2AFC tasks, namely the difference between mean confidence and mean accuracy, provides an unbiased estimate of overconfidence which is not subject to the same kind of regression effect apparent in the calibration curve. Brenner (2000) questioned the logic of a model where observed overconfidence is relabeled based on assumptions about an unmeasured "latent" construct (see also Wallsten, Erev & Budescu, 2000).

Budescu, Wallsten, and Au (1997) assessed the relative contributions of random error and systematic bias (i.e., over- or underconfidence) to overall miscalibration. The reliability of probability judgments was assessed from replicate judgments and used to estimate the degree of miscalibration expected on the basis of error alone (i.e., in the absence of systematic bias), which was then used to construct a less strict standard of "ideal" performance than that which is usually employed, the identity line of perfect calibration.

(Klayman, Soll, González-Vallejo, & Barlas, 1999, offer another method for separating effects of systematic error and unreliability of judgments.) Using this method, Budescu et al. (1997) found substantial overextremity, even after correcting for the unreliability of the assessments, in a full-range task involving the relative populations of pairs of cities. As a descriptive model, then, the assumption of an unbiased "true score" subject to error is not a sufficient account of the miscalibration found in this and other laboratory tasks.

Error models are generally agnostic on whether the well-calibrated judge *should* take response error into account. Given that feedback from the environment should operate on observed judgments, one would expect learning to occur that would mitigate the effects of error by encouraging regressive adjustments to observed judgments. Clearly, patients would not be reassured upon learning that their miscalibrated physicians were suffering only from response error and their underlying probability assessments were perfectly calibrated (Brenner, 2000).

Fitting stylized facts

The error model approach as instantiated by Budescu et al. (1997) follows from Wallsten and González-Vallejo's (1994) stochastic judgment model, and is similar to Ferrell and McGoey's (1980) pioneering DVP signal detection model, invoking two normal distributions of covert confidence, one for true and the other for false statements. The underlying confidence measure is translated into stated probability by means of a set of cutoffs. The key innovation is in the modeling of within-state (i.e. within the true or false distributions) variance: Total within-state variance (σ^2) is composed of the variance between items within states (σ_b^2) and variance within items (σ_e^2). σ_e^2 is interpreted as random error and is estimated by measuring multiple judgments of the same item (or "reversed" items, assuming binary complementarity). The probability assigned by the cutoff is perturbed by random error (on a log-odds scale).

Like Ferrell's DVP model, error models are sufficiently flexible in setting the cutoff levels so as to model any of the patterns presented in Figure 9.2. However, the psychometric approach is naturally designed to model overextremity. Error models are thus easily able to account for the prevalence of overconfidence, the tendency towards low confidence–accuracy correlations, and consequently the difficulty effect. However, it is not clear how error alone can produce any form of underconfidence.

Several researchers (Björkman, 1994; Juslin & Olsson, 1997; Juslin, Wennerholm, & Olsson, 1999; Soll, 1996) have recently offered modified ecological models in which stochastic error components have been introduced. In such models, the "internal" probability is only an estimate of the corresponding ecological probability, unbiased but subject to sampling error. Soll (1996), Juslin and Olsson (1997), and Budescu, Erev, and Wallsten (1997) have shown, using simulations, that a modified ecological model incorporating sampling error can produce overconfidence that increases with task difficulty.

One version of these models is able to account for underextremity in half-range judgments (summarized in Juslin et al., 1999). A key difference between this and other error models is that the perturbation takes place on the bounded probability scale rather than on the unbounded log-odds scale. Thus very easy tasks (the example used in the simulation was 0.95) are modeled by an underlying distribution producing many very extreme ecological probabilities, and in general added error will asymmetrically affect these probabilities so as to make the resulting judgments *underextreme* (as values such as 0.95 are limited in how much positive error can be added). Note, however, that all error models are designed to account for extremity biases; patterns of general bias such as overprediction and underprediction are not accommodated in such models.

Application and Example

Figure 9.3 presents calibration data from nine studies of practicing physicians' judgments about actual patients (adapted from Koehler et al., 2002). Each study was categorized in terms of the base rate of outcome (divided into high, moderate, and very low) and the physicians' ability to discriminate between cases when the event occurred and when it did not (moderately high or low). Each point on the graph represents a set of judgments and outcomes aggregated within a study by judged probability; a given study provided several data points. The data summarized in Figure 9.3 reveal that, across the different sets of medical events, physicians' probability judgments were sometimes too low (underprediction when base rate was high and discriminability was high), sometimes slightly too high (when base rate was low and discriminability was high), and sometimes much too high (overprediction when base rate was very low and discriminability was low).

It is instructive to consider how each of the five perspectives we have outlined might explain this pattern of data and would approach the problem of debiasing the physicians' judgments (see Chapter 16, this volume). The optimistic overconfidence perspective naturally leads to an expectation that overprediction would arise when outcomes were desirable and underprediction when outcomes were undesirable. However, this categorization does not account for the observed patterns in the data. The confirmatory bias perspective naturally leads to an expectation that more likely outcomes would be overpredicted and less likely outcomes would be underpredicted. In fact, the reverse is true. The case-based perspective naturally leads to an expectation that rare events will be overpredicted and common events will be underestimated (the dotted line refers to the predictions of RST assuming base rate and diagnosticity are completely neglected). This fits the obtained pattern, and leads to the suggestion that physicians' should be debiased with training on using set-based characteristics to overcome their case-based focus. The ecological perspective might suggest that, even though all judgments were made about real patients by expert physicians in their specific area of expertise, the categorization by base rate and discriminability still involves a selection effect. Averaged across all three groupings, the degree of bias is small and hence the ecological cues used by physicians may be unbiased. However, this approach offers little solace to the misclassified patients and no clear guidance as to how the categorized judgments may be debiased. Finally, the psychometric approach can explain the imperfect slopes of the lower two lines, but not the substantial vertical displacement, in terms of random error added at the response stage.

To the extent that there can be a "winner" in this competition among models, we believe the decision should be driven primarily by the philosophical and practical "fit" of the models to the problems we are trying to solve, rather than simply by the statistical goodness of fit of a model to experimental data.

References

Alicke, M. D. (1985) Global self-evaluation as determined by the desirability and controllability of trait adjectives, *Journal of Personality & Social Psychology*, 49, 1621–30.

Björkman, M. (1994) Internal cue theory: Calibration and resolution of confidence in general knowledge, *Organizational Behavior & Human Decision Processes*, 58, 386–405.

Brenner, L. (2000) Should observed overconfidence be dismissed as a statistical artifact? Critique of Erev, Wallsten, and Budescu (1994), *Psychological Review*, 107, 943–6.

Brenner, L. A. (2003) A random support model of the calibration of subjective probabilities, *Organizational Behavior & Human Decision Processes*, 90, 87–110.

Brenner, L. A., Koehler, D. J., Liberman, V., & Tversky, A. (1996) Overconfidence in probability and frequency judgments: A critical examination, *Organizational Behavior & Human Decision Processes*, 65, 212–19.

Brenner, L. A., Koehler, D. J., & Tversky, A. (1996) On the evaluation of one-sided evidence, *Journal of Behavioral Decision Making*, 9, 59–70.

Budescu, D. V., Erev, I., & Wallsten, T. S. (1997) On the importance of random error in the study of probability judgment. Part I: New theoretical developments, *Journal of Behavioral Decision Making*, 10, 157–71.

Budescu, D. V., Wallsten, T. S., & Au, W. T. (1997) On the importance of random error in the study of probability judgment: Part II. Applying the stochastic judgment model to detect systematic trends, *Journal of Behavioral Decision Making*, 10, 173–88.

Buehler, R., Griffin, D., & Ross, M. (1994) Exploring the "planning fallacy": Why people underestimate their task completion times, *Journal of Personality & Social Psychology*, 67, 366–81.

Buehler, R., Otsubo, Y., Lehman, D. R., Heine, S. J., & Griffin, D. (2003) *Culture and Optimism: The Planning Fallacy in Japan and North America*. Manuscript submitted for publication.

Cooper, A. C., Woo, C. Y., & Dunkelberg, W. (1988) Entrepreneurs' perceived chances for success, *Journal of Business Venturing*, 3, 97–108.

Erev, I., Wallsten, T. S., & Budescu, D. V. (1994) Simultaneous over- and underconfidence: The role of error in judgment processes, *Psychological Review*, 101, 519–27.

Ferrell, W. R. & McGoey, P. J. (1980) A model of calibration for subjective probabilities, *Organizational Behavior & Human Decision Processes*, 26, 32–53.

Fullerton, G. S. & Cattell, J. McK. (1892) On the perception of small differences: With special reference to the extent, force and time of movement, *Publications of the University of Pennsylvania: Philosophical Series*, no. 2.

Gigerenzer, G., Hoffrage, U., & Kleinbölting, H. (1991) Probabilistic mental models: A Brunswikian theory of confidence, *Psychological Review*, 98, 506–28.

Gilovich, T., Griffin, D. W., & Kahneman, D. (2002) *Heuristics and Biases: The Psychology of Intuitive Judgment*. New York: Cambridge University Press.

Gilovich, T., Kerr, M., & Medvec, V. H. (1993) Effect of temporal perspective on subjective confidence, *Journal of Personality & Social Psychology*, 64, 552–60.

Griffin, D. & Buehler, R. (1999) Frequency, probability, and prediction: Easy solutions to cognitive illusions? *Cognitive Psychology*, 38, 48–78.

Griffin, D. & Tversky, A. (1992) The weighing of evidence and the determinants of confidence, *Cognitive Psychology*, 24, 411–35.

Gu, H. & Wallsten, T. S. (2001) On setting response criteria for calibrated subjective probability estimates, *Journal of Mathematical Psychology*, 45, 551–63.

Hammond, K. (1998) Ecological Validity: Then and Now, online at: http://brunswik.org/notes/essay2.html.

Hammond, K. R. and Stewart, T. R. (eds.) (2001) *The Essential Brunswik: Beginnings, Explications, Applications*. New York: Oxford University Press.

Harvey, N. (1997) Confidence in judgment, *Trends in Cognitive Sciences*, 1, 78–82.

Hastorf, A. H. & Cantril, H. (1954) They saw a game; a case study, *Journal of Abnormal & Social Psychology*, 129–34.

Henmon, V. A. C. (1911) The relation of the time of a judgement to its accuracy, *Psychological Review*, 18, 186–201.

Hoch, S. J. (1985) Counterfactual reasoning and accuracy in predicting personal events, *Journal of Experimental Psychology: Learning, Memory, & Cognition*, 11, 719–31.

Hogarth, R. & Makridakis, S. (1981) Forecasting and planning: An evaluation, *Management Science*, 27, 115–38.

Juslin, P. & Olsson, H. (1997) Thurstonian and Brunswikian origins of uncertainty in judgment: A sampling model of confidence in sensory discrimination, *Psychological Review*, 104, 344–66.

Juslin, P., Wennerholm, P., & Olsson, H. (1999) Format dependence in subjective probability calibration, *Journal of Experimental Psychology: Learning, Memory, & Cognition*, 25, 1038–52.

Juslin, P., Winman, A., & Olsson, H. (2000) Naive empiricism and dogmatism in confidence research: A critical examination of the hard-easy effect, *Psychological Review*, 107, 384–96.

Kahneman, D. & Tversky, A. (1979) Intuitive prediction: Biases and corrective procedures, *TIMS Studies in Management Science*, 12, 313–27.

Kahneman, D., Slovic, P., & Tversky, A. (1982) *Judgment Under Uncertainty: Heuristics and Biases*. Cambridge: Cambridge University Press.

Keren, G. (1991) Calibration and probability judgments: Conceptual and methodological issues, *Acta Psychologica*, 77, 217–73.

Klayman, J., Soll, J. B., González-Vallejo, C., & Barlas, S. (1999) Overconfidence: It depends on how, what, and whom you ask, *Organizational Behavior & Human Decision Processes*, 79, 216–47.

Koehler, D. J., Brenner, L., & Griffin, D. (2002) The calibration of expert judgment: Heuristics and biases beyond the laboratory. In T. Gilovich, D. Griffin, & D. Kahneman (eds.), *Heuristics and Biases: The Psychology of Intuitive Judgment* (pp. 686–715). Cambridge: Cambridge University Press.

Koehler, D. J., Brenner, L. A., & Tversky, A. (1997) The enhancement effect in probability judgment, *Journal of Behavioral Decision Making*, 10, 293–313.

Koriat, A. & Levy-Sadot, R. (1999) Processes underlying metacognitive judgments: Information-based and experience-based monitoring of one's own knowledge. In S. Chaiken and Y. Trope (eds.), *Dual-Process Theories in Social Psychology*. (pp. 483–502). New York, NY: Guilford.

Koriat, A., Lichtenstein, S., & Fischhoff, B. (1980) Reasons for confidence, *Journal of Experimental Psychology: Human Learning & Memory*, 6, 107–18.

Kruger, J. (1999) Lake Wobegon be gone! The "below-average effect" and the egocentric nature of comparative ability judgments, *Journal of Personality & Social Psychology*, 77, 221–32.

Langer, E. J. (1975) The illusion of control, *Journal of Personality & Social Psychology*, 32, 311–28.

Larwood, L. & Whittaker, W. (1977) Managerial myopia: Self-serving biases in organizational planning, *Journal of Applied Psychology*, 62, 194–8.

Liberman, N. & Trope, Y. (1998) The role of feasibility and desirability considerations in near and distant future decisions: A test of temporal construal theory, *Journal of Personality & Social Psychology*, 75, 5–18.

Liberman, V. & Tversky, A. (1993) On the evaluation of probability judgments: Calibration, resolution, and monotonicity, *Psychological Bulletin*, 114, 162–73.

Lichtenstein, S., Fischhoff, B., & Phillips, L. D. (1982) Calibration of probabilities: The state of the art to 1980. In D. Kahneman, P. Slovic, & A. Tversky (eds.), *Judgment under Uncertainty: Heuristics and Biases* (pp. 306–34). Cambridge: Cambridge University Press.

Lord, C. G., Lepper, M. R., & Preston, E. (1984) Considering the opposite: A corrective strategy for social judgment, *Journal of Personality & Social Psychology*, 47, 1231–43.

Lord, C. G., Ross, L., & Lepper, M. R. (1979) Biased assimilation and attitude polarization: The effects of prior theories on subsequently considered evidence, *Journal of Personality & Social Psychology*, 37, 2098–109.

Lusk, C. M., Stewart, T. R., Hammond, K. R. and Potts, R. J. (1990) Judgment and decision making in dynamic tasks: The case of forecasting the microburst, *Weather and Forecasting*, 5, 627–39.

May, R. S. (1986) Inferences, subjective probability and frequency of correct answers: A cognitive approach to the overconfidence phenomenon. In B. Brehmer, H. Jungermann, P. Lourens, and A. Sevoaan (eds.), *New Directions in Research on Decision Making* (pp. 175–89). Amsterdam: North Holland.

McKenzie, C. R. M. (1997) Underweighting alternatives and overconfidence, *Organizational Behavior & Human Decision Processes*, 71, 141–60.

Miller, D. T. & Ross, M. (1975) Self-serving biases in the attribution of causality: Fact or fiction? *Psychological Bulletin*, 82, 213–25.

Phillips, L. D. & Edwards, W. (1966) Conservatism in a simple probability inference task, *Journal of Experimental Psychology*, 346–54.

Pollack, I. & Decker, L. R. (1958) Confidence ratings, message reception, and the receiver operating characteristic, *Journal of the Acoustical Society of America*, 286–92.

Rosenthal, R. & Jacobson, L. (1966) Teachers' expectancies: Determinants of pupils' IQ gains, *Psychological Reports*, 115–18.

Rottenstreich, Y. & Tversky, A. (1997) Unpacking, repacking, and anchoring: Advances in support theory, *Psychological Review*, 104, 406–15.

Shepperd, J. A., Ouellette, J. A., & Fernandez, J. K. (1996) Abandoning unrealistic optimism: Performance estimates and the temporal proximity of self-relevant feedback, *Journal of Personality & Social Psychology*, 70, 844–55.

Smith, M. & Ferrell, W. R. (1983) The effect of base rate on calibration of subjective probability for true–false questions: Model and experiment. In P. Humphreys, O. Svenson, & A. Vari (eds.), *Analyzing and Aiding Decisions*. Amsterdam: North-Holland.

Snyder, M. & Swann, W. B. (1978) Behavioral confirmation in social interaction: From social perception to social reality, *Journal of Experimental Social Psychology*, 14, 148–62.

Soll, J. B. (1996) Determinants of overconfidence and miscalibration: The roles of random error and ecological structure, *Organizational Behavior & Human Decision Processes*, 65, 117–37.

Suantak, L., Bolger, F., & Ferrell, W. R. (1996) The hard-easy effect in subjective probability calibration, *Organizational Behavior & Human Decision Processes*, 67, 201–21.

Svenson, O. (1981) Are we all less risky and more skillful than our fellow drivers? *Acta Psychologica*, 47, 143–8.

Tversky, A. & Koehler, D. J. (1994) Support theory: A nonextensional representation of subjective probability, *Psychological Review*, 101, 547–67.

Wallsten, T. S. (1996) An analysis of judgment research analyses, *Organizational Behavior & Human Decision Processes*, 65, 220–26.

Wallsten, T. S. & Budescu, D. V. (1983) Encoding subjective probabilities: A psychological and psychometric review, *Management Science*, 29, 151–73.

Wallsten, T. S., Erev, I., & Budescu, D. V. (2000) The importance of theory: Response to Brenner (2000), *Psychological Review*, 107, 947–9.

Wallsten, T. S. & González-Vallejo, C. (1994) Statement verification: A stochastic model of judgment and response, *Psychological Review*, 101, 490–504.

Wason, P. C. (1968) Reasoning about a rule, *Quarterly Journal of Experimental Psychology*, 273–81.

Weinstein, N. D. (1980) Unrealistic optimism about future life events, *Journal of Personality & Social Psychology*, 39, 806–20.

Yates, J. F. (1990) *Judgment and Decision Making*. Englewood Cliffs, NJ: Prentice Hall.

Yates, J. F., Lee, J.-W., Sieck, W. R., Choi, I., & Price, P. C. (2002) Probability judgment across cultures. In T. Gilovich, D. Griffin, & D. Kahneman (eds.), *Heuristics and Biases: The Psychology of Intuitive Judgment* (pp. 271–91). Cambridge: Cambridge University Press.

10

Hypothesis Testing and Evaluation

Craig R. M. McKenzie

Introduction

Imagine a physician examining a patient who exhibits certain symptoms. The physician would undoubtedly generate possible explanations, or hypotheses, regarding the cause of the symptoms. If additional evidence were needed to confidently diagnose the patient, the physician might need to decide which questions to ask the patient or which tests to order. Then, based on the answers to the questions or the results of the tests, the physician would update confidence in one or more hypotheses and perhaps feel confident enough to recommend a course of action. If still more evidence were needed – perhaps the test results were unexpected, leaving no obvious explanation of the patient's symptoms – decisions would have to be made again about how to gather more information.

The above scenario captures the essence of hypothesis development (Klayman, 1995), which is generally concerned with how we determine whether there is a match between what we think might be true about the world and what is in fact true about the world. The process is a complex set of behaviors, but for present purposes, it will be seen as consisting of three stages: Hypothesis generation, testing, and evaluation. In the above example, hypothesis *generation* occurs when the physician produces at least one hypothesis based on the patient's symptoms. What is (are) the most likely explanation(s) of the pattern of symptoms? Once the physician has a hypothesis, but is unsure whether it is correct, more information might be collected for *testing* the hypothesis: Which medical tests should be run, which questions should be asked? Once the hypothesis has been put to test, the results are used to *evaluate* the hypothesis. Do the results provide confirming or disconfirming evidence (or neither)? How strongly do the results (dis)confirm the hypothesis?

Hypothesis development is not limited to formal situations such as physicians diagnosing patients and scientists testing theories. More mundane examples include determining whether your new research assistant is reliable, or how to get a young child to eat more vegetables. As will be argued shortly, hypothesis development is probably even more mundane than you think: We constantly engage in it in order to make sense out of our infinitely complex environment.

Due to its ubiquity, complexity, and importance, hypothesis development has been, and continues to be, the focus of much psychological research. The purpose of this chapter is to provide an overview of some important issues in the psychology of hypothesis development. As the title suggests, the emphasis is on the second and third stages, namely, hypothesis testing and evaluation. The first section notes some key findings beginning in the 1950s regarding the importance of hypothesis development. The second section critically examines "confirmation bias," a term now used to describe people's purported tendency to be overly confident in their favored hypothesis. The third section reviews recent research indicating that consideration of the environment outside the laboratory is crucial for understanding hypothesis-testing behavior inside the laboratory. The chapter concludes with an overview of the main points and their implications for understanding how, and how well, people put their ideas to test.

Some Early Findings

Bruner, Goodnow, and Austin's (1956) book represents a milestone in research on hypothesis development, even though it was only indirectly concerned with the topic. Its primary focus was on "concept attainment," or how we learn to group objects into pre-existing categories. In a typical experiment, participants were presented with cards showing different shapes that varied in terms of size and color. There was a predetermined "concept" and participants were to learn, by choosing cards, which attributes distinguished exemplars from non-exemplars. The experiment usually began with the experimenter providing the participant with an exemplar of the concept to be learned. After each card was chosen by the participant, the experimenter revealed whether it was an instance of the concept. For example, the concept might be "triangle," in which case every chosen card with a triangle would receive a positive response from the experimenter and all others a negative response. In this way, the participant would learn to attend to shape and to ignore color and size.

For our purposes, what is most important about the research of Bruner et al. (1956) is how it paved the way for replacing the (behaviorists') passive view of the mind with one in which people actively organized their experience and brought their knowledge to bear on the task. In this case, participants often *actively engaged in hypothesis development* regarding the correct concept. For example, after being shown that a large red triangle was an instance of the concept, a participant might hypothesize that "large shapes" was the correct concept. This would then influence not only the next card selected, but also the interpretation of the subsequent feedback (depending on the specific strategy used). A different participant might hypothesize that "red triangles" was the correct concept and therefore behave differently. The insight that participants were actively testing hypotheses was crucial for understanding behavior – both success and failure – in these concept attainment tasks.

Other learning phenomena were later uncovered that both confirmed and extended Bruner et al.'s (1956) active hypothesis-development viewpoint. For example, non-learning sometimes occurred for presumably smart and motivated participants (e.g., Levine, 1971). Some participants simply failed to learn the concept or rule despite many trials with feedback. This is problematic for the passive view of the mind in which learning is gradual and automatic, but it makes sense from a hypothesis-development viewpoint: Non-learning occurred when participants failed to generate the correct hypothesis. Closely related was the finding that some learning tended to be all-or-none rather than gradual (e.g., Restle, 1965). Participants' performance was often at chance level until they generated the correct hypothesis and was virtually perfect thereafter.

Also related was the finding that organisms do not learn to make a connection between all events equally well. For example, in a classic study, Garcia and Koelling (1966) allowed thirsty rats to drink flavored water while simultaneously presented with a light and noise. Some rats were then mildly poisoned while others received a shock. Those who received the poison showed aversion to the flavor of the water, but not to the light and noise, while those who received the shock showed an aversion to the light and noise, but not to the flavor of the water. These findings indicate that certain hypotheses are more readily generated, or seen as more plausible a priori, in certain contexts. Again, a passive view of the mind cannot explain this.

All of the above research examined learning using discrete variables (e.g., shapes were either triangles or squares, red or blue). Interestingly, however, similar results have been found in tasks examining how participants learn to predict scaled criterion values based on scaled cue values. These cue-learning tasks are also solved through the process of hypothesis development. In this case, participants test a series of hypotheses about the possible functional form, and the hypotheses are tested in a systematic order (Brehmer, 1974; Sniezek & Naylor, 1978; for an overview, see Brehmer, 1980). Participants first check to see if the relationship is linear and positive. If this turns out to be incorrect, they test the hypothesis that the relationship is linear and negative, followed by an inverse U-shaped hypothesis, then a U-shaped hypothesis, and so on. The amount of time taken to discover the true relationship depends on how far down the participant's hypothesis hierarchy the true rule is.

The above findings indicate that it is simply not the case that hypothesis development is primarily the province of scientists testing theories and physicians diagnosing illnesses. We all engage in hypothesis development on a regular basis as we try to organize and impose structure on our complex world.

Given its prevalence and importance, how good are we at developing our hypotheses? Bruner et al. (1956) found that participants did not behave optimally. Because of the circumscribed (and usually deterministic) nature of the tasks, a participant could, in theory, rule out multiple hypotheses simultaneously with a single test. Instead, though, participants tended to use a win-stay, lose-shift strategy. If a test of the current hypothesis led to the expected positive response, participants would continue testing it. If a test led to an unexpected negative response, only then would they consider a different hypothesis. Thus, participants tended to test hypotheses in a serial fashion rather than in parallel, which led to inefficiencies; participants were not getting as much information out of each test as they could have. Nonetheless, it is worth noting that Bruner et al.

were impressed by participants' sensitivity to task demands. Participants tended to use more sophisticated strategies as task demands were reduced. Indeed, those who tried to use complex strategies when task demands were high sometimes performed worse than those using simpler strategies (for similar findings in the context of choice strategies, see Payne, Bettman, & Johnson, 1993).

In sum, hypothesis development is a ubiquitous means for coping with a complex world. Hypotheses enable us to interpret incoming data by telling us what to look for; they suggest what's relevant. Indeed, we must have some idea of what might be learned before we can learn it.

Confirmation Bias

Wason (1960) was not as sanguine as Bruner et al. (1956) with respect to people's hypothesis-development abilities. In particular, Wason viewed the common strategy of testing hypotheses serially, only revising hypotheses after receiving disconfirming evidence (Bruner et al.'s "successive scanning"), as being seriously deficient. He devised the "2-4-6" concept attainment task in order to demonstrate this.

In this task, participants were told that the experimenter had a rule in mind that produces triples of numbers, an example of which was 2-4-6. They were to produce triples of numbers in order to figure out the experimenter's rule. After announcing each triple, participants were told whether or not it conformed to the experimenter's rule. They could test as many triples as they wished and were to state what they thought was the correct rule only after they were highly confident they had found it. Few participants discovered the correct rule (with their first "highly confident" announcement), which was "numbers in increasing order of magnitude."

How could most participants be so confident in a wrong rule after being allowed to test it as much as they wished? The initial 2-4-6 example naturally suggests a hypothesis such as "increasing intervals of two" (which was the most commonly stated incorrect rule). They would then test their hypothesis by stating triples such as 8-10-12, 14-16-18, 20-22-24, and 1-3-5 – triples that were consistent with their hypothesized rule. Of course, each of these triples is consistent with the correct rule as well, and hence participants received a positive response from the experimenter ("Yes, it conforms to the rule"). This, in turn, led them to believe incorrectly that they had discovered the correct rule.

Wason (1960) claimed that participants appeared unwilling to test their hypotheses in a manner that would lead them to be disconfirmed (which is what Popper, 1959, claimed was how people ought to test hypotheses). The only way to disconfirm the "increasing intervals of two" hypothesis is to test triples that are *not* expected to conform to the hypothesis, such as 2-4-7 or 1-2-3 (Bruner et al. referred to these as "indirect tests"). Testing such triples would lead to unexpected "yes" responses from the experimenter, and participants would then (and only then) know that their hypothesis was wrong. Instead, Wason argued, participants tested their hypotheses in a way that led them to be confirmed. This came to be known as "confirmation bias" and created a stir because of the apparent dire implications: We test our hypotheses in a manner that leads

us to believe them, regardless of their correctness. This view of lay hypothesis development became dominant in psychology (Evans, 1989; Mynatt, Doherty, & Tweney,
1977, 1978; Nisbett & Ross, 1980; Snyder, 1981; Snyder & Campbell, 1980; Snyder &
Swann, 1978). As Nickerson (1998, p. 175) recently noted, "If one were to attempt to
identify a single problematic aspect of human reasoning that deserves attention above all
others, the confirmation bias would have to be among the candidates for consideration."

But what exactly is confirmation bias? The label has been applied to a variety of
phenomena (Fischhoff & Beyth-Marom, 1983; Klayman, 1995; Klayman & Ha, 1987;
Nickerson, 1998; Poletiek, 2001). For present purposes, I will refer to confirmation
bias as testing or evaluating a hypothesis such that inappropriately high confidence in
the hypothesis is the systematic result (Klayman, 1995; Nickerson, 1998). Accordingly,
I briefly review findings from hypothesis-testing and hypothesis-evaluation tasks separately
below.

Testing strategies and confirmation bias

Despite the enormous implications of confirmation bias, it has become clear that many
of the early claims were overstated. For example, it is now generally accepted that
hypothesis-testing strategies do not, by themselves, necessitate confirmation bias (Klayman,
1995; Poletiek, 2001). In order to discuss the testing stage of hypothesis development
and how it might relate to confirmation bias, I will move away from Wason's 2-4-6 task,
which involves hypothesis generation, testing, *and* evaluation. (I will return to the task
in the section on "Importance of the environment.") Using a simple probabilistic testing
task, I will first discuss how one *ought* to select among possible tests in order to determine, in the most efficient fashion, which of the competing hypotheses is most likely
true. Subsequently, I will discuss how people choose tests in such a task, and what
implications, if any, this has for confirmation bias.

Consider Table 10.1, which lists the proportion of whimsical creatures, Gloms and
Fizos, on the planet Vuma, possessing each of eight features (Skov & Sherman, 1986;
see also Slowiaczek, Klayman, Sherman, & Skov, 1992). For example, the first feature

Table 10.1 Percentage of Gloms and Fizos possessing each of eight features

Feature	Gloms (%)	Fizos (%)
1 – wear hula hoops	10	50
2 – eat iron ore	28	32
3 – have gills	68	72
4 – gurgle a lot	90	50
5 – play the harmonica	72	68
6 – drink gasoline	32	28
7 – smoke maple leaves	50	90
8 – exhale fire	50	10

regards whether the creatures wear hula hoops; 10 percent of Gloms do so and 50 percent of Fizos do so. Assume that there are equal numbers of Gloms and Fizos on the planet and there are only these two types of creature. If you had to ask a randomly sampled creature from Vuma about just one of the listed features in order to determine whether it was a Glom or a Fizo, which feature would you choose?

Deciding which question one ought to ask requires a fair amount of sophistication, even in this highly constrained and well-specified example. A complicating factor is that you don't know what answer the creature will give. We need to first think about the possible answers to a question (e.g., "Yes, I wear a hula hoop" or "No, I don't wear a hula hoop") in terms of their likelihood ratios, $p(D/H1)/p(D/H2)$, where D corresponds to data and $H1$ and $H2$ correspond to the competing hypotheses. In this context, the datum is the answer to the question ("yes" or "no") and the hypotheses are that the creature is a Glom ($H1$) or a Fizo ($H2$). To the extent that the likelihood ratio differs from 1, the datum is diagnostic, or helps discriminate between the hypotheses. For feature 1 in Table 10.1, the likelihood ratio for a "yes" answer is 0.1/0.5 and for a "no" answer is 0.9/0.5. Note that the first ratio is less than one and the second is greater than one. This is because the "yes" answer provides evidence against $H1$ and the "no" answer provides evidence for $H1$.

How confident should one be in $H1$ after receiving one of these answers? Bayes' theorem provides an answer. Generally:

$$p(H1/D) = p(H1)p(D/H1)/[p(H1)p(D/H1) + p(H2)p(D/H2)]. \qquad (10.1)$$

So, in the case of a "yes" response to a question about feature 1 ($F1$), confidence that the creature is a Glom should be:

$$p(\text{Glom}/F1) = 0.5(0.1)/[0.5(0.1) + 0.5(0.5)] = 0.17.$$

However, if the creature answers "no" ($\sim F1$), confidence in the Glom hypothesis should be:

$$p(\text{Glom}/\sim F1) = 0.5(0.9)/[0.5(0.9) + 0.5(0.5)] = 0.64.$$

Note that, relative to the prior confidence in the Glom hypothesis (0.5), the "yes" answer decreased confidence more than the "no" answer increased confidence because the former is more diagnostic than the latter. The former likelihood ratio is 1/5 and the latter is 9/5. One way to compare the diagnosticity of two data, when one likelihood ratio is greater than 1 and the other is less than 1, is to take the reciprocal of the ratio that is less than 1 and then make a direct comparison. In this case, 5/1 > 9/5. Another way is to take the absolute value of the log of each ratio (log likelihood ratio, or LLR):

$$\text{abs}[\log_2(1/5)] = 2.3 > \text{abs}[\log_2(9/5)] = 0.85.$$

Given that the different answers to the same question will be differentially diagnostic (except when the two likelihoods sum to 1), and the tester does not know which answer the creature will give, how should one choose a question? One way is to select the question with the highest *expected* LLR. In order to do so, one must calculate, for each question, the LLR of each possible answer ("yes" or "no") and how likely each answer is, which depends on both the frequency of the feature for each creature and how likely each hypothesis is. In the case of feature 1, you would expect to hear "yes" 30 percent of the time because 50 percent of the creatures are Gloms, 10 percent of whom will answer yes, and 50 percent of the creatures are Fizos, 50 percent of whom will answer "yes." Similarly, you expect to hear "no" 70 percent of the time. Thus, for feature 1, the expected (absolute) LLR is 0.3(2.3) + 0.7(0.85) = 1.285. Now just make such calculations for the remaining seven features so you can choose the feature with the highest expected LLR. Simple, right?

It's fair to say that choosing the most diagnostic question is not so simple, even in this simple example. How, then, do people choose which questions to ask? Given a set of questions as in Table 10.1, three factors seem to drive people's choices: Diagnosticity, positivity, and extremity. Diagnosticity essentially refers to expected LLR and has been found to be a major determinant of question selection (Bassok & Trope, 1984; Skov & Sherman, 1986; Slowiaczek et al., 1992; Trope & Bassok, 1982, 1983). In other words, one strong tendency is to select the questions that ought to be selected in order to test hypotheses most efficiently. In Table 10.1, features 1, 4, 7, and 8 have the highest expected LLR. Participants might tend to choose questions with the highest expected LLR because the measure is highly correlated with the algebraic difference between the two likelihoods (when the prior probabilities for the hypotheses are equal; Slowiaczek et al., 1992). That is, to the extent that the difference between the two percentages listed for a given feature in Table 10.1 is large, expected LLR is large. Participants might be sensitive to this difference, which correlates with expected LLR.

The second factor, positivity, is the tendency to ask questions that are expected to result in a "yes" response, given the truth of the working hypothesis (Klayman & Ha, 1987; Skov & Sherman, 1986; Bruner et al., 1956, referred to these as "direct tests"). This is analogous to the testing strategy that participants in Wason's (1960) 2-4-6 task appeared to use and is now commonly referred to as "positive hypothesis testing" (Klayman & Ha, 1987). For example, if testing the Glom hypothesis and forced to choose between asking about features 1 or 4 (which have the same expected LLR), participants tend to prefer feature 4.

Extremity, the final factor, refers to a preference for questions whose outcomes are very likely or unlikely under the working hypothesis relative to the alternate hypothesis. Thus, if testing the Glom hypothesis, participants prefer asking about feature 4 over feature 8, though asking about the features has the same expected LLR and both are positive tests.

These latter two tendencies look like they might lead to inappropriately high confidence in the hypothesis being tested, or confirmation bias. But they don't. At least not necessarily. Any testing strategy not solely concerned with diagnosticity will be inefficient (assuming equal costs of information and errors), but as long as the tester takes into account the test biases at the subsequent hypothesis-evaluation stage, no confirmation bias will result. As Klayman (1995) noted, participants in Wason's (1960) experiment erred not in their tendency to conduct positive tests (i.e., test triples that they expected to result in "yes" answers), but in failing to take this into account at the hypothesis-evaluation stage. In this case, they failed to notice that their strategy left open the possibility of false negative errors. Similarly, if one evaluates the hypothesis properly (Equation 10.1) following "extreme" questions, there will be no bias.

Even other forms of biased testing, such as a tendency to recruit facts or arguments to support, rather than refute, the working hypothesis do not necessitate confirmation bias if one takes the testing bias into account at the evaluation stage (Klayman, 1995). For example, one might be sensitive to how difficult it is to recruit positive evidence, or not be influenced much by the positive evidence, or be strongly influenced by even the slightest negative evidence (e.g., McKenzie, Lee, & Chen, 2002). In short, biased testing strategies lead to inefficiencies but do not necessitate confirmation bias.

Evaluation strategies and confirmation bias

While there is a huge literature on how people evaluate hypotheses after finding out the result of a test, I'll just mention a couple of phenomena that seem most relevant to confirmation bias (see Klayman, 1995, and Nickerson, 1998, for other examples). Perhaps the most obvious one is that people tend to be more skeptical of new information that is inconsistent with their favored hypothesis than consistent with it (Koehler, 1993; Lord, Ross, & Lepper, 1979). That is, participants sometimes downplay evidence against their favored hypothesis. Although this would appear to lead to confirmation bias, it can be normatively reasonable for prior beliefs to influence perceived evidence quality (Koehler, 1993; Lord et al., 1979). For instance, if someone were to tell you that Earth was cone-shaped, should you decrease confidence in your current belief about Earth's shape or dismiss the new "data"? The extent to which evidence inconsistent with a favored hypothesis ought to result in a change in confidence rather than be met with skepticism is a difficult normative issue. When both data and hypotheses are uncertain, the relationship between them is mutual; each can inform the other (Thagard, 1989). (Interestingly, the first significance tests were used to reject data [outliers], not hypotheses; Gigerenzer, Swijtink, Porter, Daston, Beatty, & Krüger, 1989, pp. 80–4.) It is of course possible that people are overly eager to dismiss evidence inconsistent with their beliefs, but without a clear normative benchmark, we cannot know for sure.

In addition, people sometimes interpret ambiguous evidence in ways that give the benefit of the doubt to their favored hypothesis. Whether you interpret someone's failure to return a smile from across the room as indicating the person didn't see you or the person is snubbing you will likely be influenced by whether the person is a good friend or is known for being socially distant. As Nisbett and Ross (1980) point out, however, this is not necessarily an error. Under these circumstances, it generally would be more likely true that the person didn't see you if he or she were a good friend, and it generally would be more likely true that the person was snubbing you if he or she were socially distant. It might very well be that people interpret ambiguous data in overly generous ways, but the complexity of the normative issue makes it difficult to know if or when people are making errors (Klayman, 1995).

Confirmation bias due to interactions between testing and evaluation

Although neither testing strategies nor evaluation strategies, by themselves, appear to lead to confirmation bias, some combinations of the two can (Klayman, 1995; Poletiek, 2001; Slowiaczek et al., 1992). Klayman (1995) notes three such combinations. First, confirmation bias can result from the combination of positive testing (in this case, asking questions that you expect a "yes" answer to, if your hypothesis is correct) and the fact that respondents are biased to answer "yes" to questions in social settings ("acquiescence bias"; Zuckerman, Knee, Hodgins, & Miyake, 1995). If interviewers do not take respondents' biases into account – and apparently they don't – this leads to higher confidence in the working hypothesis than is warranted. Though interesting, note that this example of confirmation bias is limited to asking yes/no questions in social settings.

Two other examples appear to have broader applicability. One is the combination of positive testing – in this case, asking about features expected to be present if the working hypothesis is true – and the fact that participants are more affected by the presence of features than by their absence (e.g., feature-positive effects; Jenkins & Sainsbury, 1969, 1970; Newman, Wolff, & Hearst, 1980). Because positive testing implies that the presence of features confirms the hypothesis and their absence disconfirms the hypothesis, and feature-positive effects imply that presence has more impact than absence, then evidence favoring the hypothesis will have the most impact.

The third and final combination noted by Klayman (1995) is that of preferring extremity and finding confirming and disconfirming outcomes more equal in terms of their informativeness than they really are (Slowiaczek et al., 1992). In terms of Table 10.1, the preference for extremity implies asking about features 1 and 4 if Glom were the working hypothesis (because for each feature the likelihood corresponding to Gloms is much closer to 0 or 1 than the corresponding likelihood for Fizos). Note that the confirming answer is "no" after asking about feature 1 and "yes" after asking about feature 4. Recall that confirming and disconfirming test outcomes are often differentially informative. For example, when testing the Glom hypothesis and asking about feature 1, it was shown earlier that the confirming "no" answer should increase confidence from 0.5 to 0.64, whereas the disconfirming "yes" answer should decrease confidence from 0.5 to 0.17. The latter change is larger because the disconfirming "yes" answer is more diagnostic than the confirming "no" answer. For both features 1 and 4, the confirming outcomes have likelihood ratios of 9/5 whereas the disconfirming outcomes have likelihood ratios of 5/1. Participants, however, tend to see the different test outcomes as more similar in terms of diagnosticity than they ought to. For example, Slowiaczek et al. (1992) found that participants reported confidence in the working Glom hypothesis of 0.62 and 0.27 to "no" and "yes" answers, respectively, for likelihoods analogous to feature 1 in Table 10.1. Note that the former confidence report is slightly too low, but that the latter is considerably too high, giving an overall edge to the working hypothesis. Generally, when selecting features that are more extreme under the working hypothesis, the confirming outcome is less diagnostic than the disconfirming outcome. (The reason, discussed in the next section, is that the disconfirming outcome under these conditions is rarer, or more surprising.) Because the weakly confirming and strongly disconfirming outcomes will be seen as being more similar in terms of their diagnosticity than they really are, confidence in the working hypothesis will tend to be higher than is warranted.

Confirmation bias summary

Early claims about confirmation bias appear to have been overstated. It is now generally accepted that neither hypothesis-testing strategies nor hypothesis-evaluation strategies, by themselves, appear to lead to confirmation bias, but working together they can (Klayman, 1995; Poletiek, 2001; Slowiaczek et al. 1992).

Importance of the Environment in General, and Rarity in Particular

The foregoing discussion was concerned with the typical formalizations associated with hypothesis testing and evaluation (e.g., likelihoods) that are often manipulated orthogonally in the laboratory. Sometimes overlooked in such analyses, however, is what the situation tends to be like outside the laboratory and how these "real world" conditions might influence behavior inside the laboratory. In this section, recent research on testing and evaluation behavior that has been influenced by considerations of the environment is discussed. In particular, the focus is on the *rarity of data*. How rare, or surprising, data are is a key notion in essentially all formal theories of hypothesis testing (Poletiek, 2001, Chapter 2) and it will be argued that people are highly sensitive to this variable. Indeed, even in tasks in which considerations of rarity might seem irrelevant, participants none-theless appear to make (reasonable) assumptions about rarity based on experience outside the laboratory, which can lead their behavior to be seen as less sensible than it really is.

Wason's "2-4-6" task

Klayman and Ha's (1987) analysis of Wason's "2-4-6" task illustrates the importance of taking into account environmental conditions in general, and rarity in particular, when trying to understand hypothesis-development behavior. Recall that Wason (1960) argued that people were prone to confirming their hypotheses because they tested triples they expected to lead to a "yes" response from the experimenter (positive hypothesis tests). Klayman and Ha pointed out that Popper (1959), whose view of hypothesis testing Wason considered normative, had prescribed testing hypotheses so that they are most likely to be disconfirmed; he did not say that one ought to test cases that the hypothesis predicts will fail to occur. In other words, Klayman and Ha distinguished between disconfirmation as a goal (as prescribed by Popper) and disconfirmation as a testing strategy. Wason (1960) confounded these two notions. Because the true rule ("increasing numbers") is more general than the tentative "increasing intervals of two" hypothesis, the only way to disconfirm the latter is by testing triples that are expected not to work (negative hypothesis tests). This, of course, is just what Bruner et al. (1956) found people tend not to do, which is why Wason designed his task as he did. But notice that the situation could easily be reversed: One could entertain a hypothesis that is more general than the true rule, in which case the only way to disconfirm the hypothesis is by testing cases hypothesized to work (and finding they do not) – exactly opposite from the situation in Wason's task. For example, an advertising executive might hypothesize that advertising a particular product on television is the key to success, whereas in fact only advertising on prime time television will work. In this situation, testing only cases hypothesized *not* to work (e.g., advertising on the radio) could lead to incorrectly believing the hypothesis (because all the cases that the hypothesis predicts will not work will, in fact, not work).

Whether positive testing is a good strategy, then, depends on the relationship between the hypothesized and true rule. Furthermore, positive testing is more likely than negative testing to lead to disconfirmation when (a) you are trying to predict a rare event, and (b) your hypothesized rule includes about as many cases as the true rule does (i.e., your hypothesis describes an equally rare event). Finally – and very important – the above two conditions (both involving rarity), Klayman and Ha (1987) argue, are commonly met in real-world hypothesis-testing situations, implying that positive hypothesis testing is generally more likely than negative hypothesis testing to lead to disconfirmation.

Thus, despite the results from Wason's (1960) 2-4-6 task, positive testing appears to be a highly adaptive strategy for testing hypotheses under typical real-world conditions. This virtual reversal of the perceived status of testing cases expected to work is primarily due to Klayman and Ha's *analysis of the task environment*. Seen independent of the environmental context in which it is usually used, positive testing can look foolish (as in Wason's task). Seen in its usual environmental context, it makes good normative sense. Klayman and Ha's work underscores the point that understanding hypothesis-development behavior requires understanding the context in which it usually occurs.

Wason's selection task

Wason is also well known for a second hypothesis-testing task: the selection task (Wason, 1966, 1968). In this task, which involves only testing (and not hypothesis generation or evaluation), participants have four cards in front of them. Imagine, for example, that each has a letter on one side and a number on the other. The visible side of one card has an "A" on it, a second has a "K", a third a "2", and the fourth a "7". You are to test whether the following rule is true or false: If a card has a vowel on one side, it has an even number on the other. Which cards must you turn over in order to test the rule?

According to one interpretation of the rule ("material implication"), propositional logic dictates that the A and 7 cards should be turned over. When testing "If P, then Q" (P → Q), only the combination of P and not-Q (a vowel on one side and an odd number on the other in the example) falsifies the rule; any other combination is consistent with the rule. Thus, turning over the "A" card is useful because an even number on the other side is consistent with the rule, but an odd number is not. Similarly, turning over the "7" card is useful because finding a consonant on the other side is consistent with the rule, but finding a vowel is not. By contrast, nothing can be learned by turning over the "K" and "2" cards because whatever is on the other side of either card is consistent with the rule. Therefore, there is no point in turning over these two cards according to propositional logic.

Which cards do participants select? The most common response is to select the "A" and "2" cards (P and Q). Typically, fewer than 10 percent of participants request the logically correct "A" and "7" (P and not-Q) combination (Wason, 1966, 1968). Participants tend to select the cards mentioned in the rule. This has traditionally been seen as a classic demonstration of irrationality.

However, Oaksford and Chater (1994; see also Nickerson, 1996) have shown that the P and Q cards are the most informative if one assumes (a) an inferential (Bayesian) approach to the task that treats the cards to be turned over as a sample from a larger population of interest, and (b) that P and Q are rare relative to not-P and not-Q (the "rarity assumption"). Their model enabled them to account for a wide variety of selection task findings and, equally important, led to predictions as to when participants would prefer to turn over the not-Q card. Indeed, as predicted, participants are more likely to turn over the not-Q card as P and Q become more common (Oaksford & Chater, 2003).

Thus, Oaksford and Chater (1994) make two assumptions that appear to reflect the real world. First, they assume an inferential approach that is appropriate in a probabilistic, rather than deterministic, environment. Second, they assume (and supporting empirical evidence is discussed below) that conditional rules or hypotheses tend to mention rare, not common, events, which plausibly describes everyday discourse. Normative principles, combined with considerations of the environment, can help explain behavior in the selection task.

Impact of confirming evidence

In most of the discussion thus far, there have been two kinds of confirming evidence: outcomes expected to occur that do occur and outcomes expected not to occur that don't. Judging by their preferred testing strategies, participants consider the former confirming outcomes more informative than the latter. For example, people are much more likely to perform positive hypothesis tests than negative hypothesis tests, suggesting that people are generally more concerned about whether what they expect to occur does occur than whether what they expect not to occur doesn't.

Generally, when evaluating hypotheses of the form P → Q, participants deem the combination of P and Q (P&Q outcomes) as more informative than not-P&not-Q outcomes, although both provide confirming evidence. Why? One possible reason comes from Oaksford and Chater's (1994) rarity assumption: When testing P → Q, maybe P and Q tend to be rare relative to not-P and not-Q. If so, then from a Bayesian perspective, the P&Q outcome *is* more informative than a not-P&not-Q outcome.

To see why a combination of rare events is most informative, consider testing a forecaster's claim of being able to predict the weather in San Diego, where rainy days are rare. Assume that the forecaster rarely predicts rain and usually predicts sunshine. On the first day, the forecaster predicts sunshine and is correct. On the second day, the forecaster predicts rain and is correct. Which of these two correct predictions would leave you more convinced that the forecaster can accurately predict the weather and is not merely guessing? The more informative of the two observations is the correct prediction of rain, the rare event, at least according to Bayesian statistics (Horwich, 1982; Howson & Urbach, 1989). Qualitatively, the reason is that it would not be surprising to correctly predict a sunny day by chance in San Diego because almost every day is sunny. That is, even if the forecaster knew only that San Diego is sunny, you would expect her to make lots of correct predictions of sunshine just by chance alone. Thus, such an observation does not help much in distinguishing between a knowledgeable forecaster and one who is merely guessing. In contrast, because rainy days are rare, a correct prediction of rain is unlikely to occur by chance alone and therefore provides relatively strong evidence that the forecaster is doing better than merely guessing. Generally, given two dichotomous variables, P and Q, when testing P → Q, a P&Q outcome will be more informative than a not-P&not-Q outcome whenever $p(P) < 1 - p(Q)$ (Horwich, 1982; Mackie, 1963). This condition is clearly met when both P and Q are rare ($p < 0.5$).

Thus, just as with the above account of Wason's selection task, it is possible to explain a preference for the confirming outcome mentioned in the hypothesis by adopting a Bayesian approach and by making the rarity assumption. Furthermore, the account leads to the prediction that this preference will be reversed when it is clear to participants that the hypothesis mentions common, not rare, events.

McKenzie and Mikkelsen (2000) tested this prediction. They found that participants evaluating abstract hypotheses tended to consider whichever combination of events was mentioned in the hypothesis to provide the strongest support. However, participants evaluating concrete hypotheses about variables they were familiar with tended to select the combination of rare events as most informative, regardless of whether the events were mentioned in the hypothesis. In other words, when the hypothesis mentioned common events, participants tended to consider the *un*mentioned confirming observation as providing the strongest support.

These results suggest that participants generally assume that mentioned observations are rare when evaluating abstract, unfamiliar hypotheses (the norm in the laboratory), but this default assumption is overridden when it is clear that it does not apply. Once again, participants' behavior is consistent with the qualitative use of Bayesian principles combined with reasonable assumptions about how the world usually works.

Direct evidence for the rarity assumption

The rarity assumption has been important for explaining, in qualitatively normative terms, purported errors in the hypothesis-development tasks discussed above. That is, if it is assumed that hypotheses tend to mention rare events, much explanatory power is gained. In fact, several authors have speculated that people do indeed tend to hypothesize about rare events (e.g., Einhorn & Hogarth, 1986; Klayman & Ha, 1987; Mackie,

1974; Oaksford & Chater, 1994). Rare or unexpected events "demand" explanation. We tend to hypothesize about the factors leading to success, not mediocrity; about the factors leading to being HIV+, not HIV−; about what caused a plane crash, not a normal flight; and so on. Consistent with these speculations, McKenzie, Ferreira, Mikkelsen, McDermott, & Skrable (2001) found that participants had a tendency – often a strong one – to phrase conditional hypotheses ("If _____, then _____") in terms of rare rather than common events. This provides an answer to the question of why, as a default strategy, people consider mentioned confirming observations to be more informative than unmentioned confirming observations: mentioned observations generally *are* more informative because they are rare.

Covariation assessment

Research on covariation assessment is concerned with evidence evaluation, and participants' assumptions about, and sensitivity to, the rarity of data can explain purported errors in this highly studied task as well. In a typical task, participants are asked to assess the relationship between two variables, each of which can be either present or absent, resulting in the familiar 2×2 matrix (see Table 11.1 in the next chapter). Cell A corresponds to the joint presence of the variables, Cell B to the presence of variable 1 and the absence of variable 2, Cell C to the absence of variable 1 and the presence of variable 2, and Cell D to the joint absence of the variables. Given the four cell frequencies, participants assess the direction or strength of the relationship (for reviews, see Allan, 1993; McKenzie, 1994; Chapter 11, this volume). Assessing how variables covary underlies such fundamental behaviors as learning, categorization, and judging causation. For our purposes, what is important about the normative model for this task is that all four cells are equally important (see Chapter 11 for details).

In contrast to the normative model, probably the most robust finding in studies of covariation assessment is that participants do not find the four cells equally important. In particular, Cell A has the largest impact on behavior and Cell D has the smallest impact (Jenkins & Ward, 1965; Kao & Wasserman, 1993; Levin, Wasserman, & Kao, 1993; Lipe, 1990; Smedslund, 1963; Ward & Jenkins, 1965; Wasserman, Dorner, & Kao, 1990). The typical order in terms of impact is A > B ≈ C > D. This differential impact of the four cells is routinely interpreted as nonnormative. For example, Kao and Wasserman (1993, p. 1365) state that, "It is important to recognize that unequal utilization of cell information implies that nonnormative processes are at work," and Mandel and Lehman (1998) attempted to explain differential cell utilization in terms of a combination of two reasoning biases.

If one views a covariation task as testing the hypothesis that there is a positive relationship between the two variables, then Cells A and D are evidence for the hypothesis and Cells B and C are evidence against it. Note that the larger impact of Cell A compared to Cell D – both of which provide confirming evidence for a positive relationship – is analogous to the larger impact of confirming observations that are mentioned in the hypothesis compared to those that are not mentioned. Also analogous is that one can adopt a Bayesian view of the covariation task in which participants (a) view the four cell observations as a sample from a larger population of interest and (b) assume that the presence of variables is rare ($p < 0.5$) and their absence common ($p > 0.5$) in the larger population. Note that this latter assumption is related to, but different from, the rarity assumption discussed earlier, which regarded how conditional rules or hypotheses are phrased.

Under these assumptions, Cell A (joint presence) is normatively more informative than Cell D (joint absence) for determining if there is a relationship between the variables rather than no relationship. Observing the rare observation, Cell A, distinguishes better between these two possibilities. Similar to the discussion about rarity earlier, if absence of the two variables is common, then it would not be surprising to see both variables absent, a Cell D observation, even if the variables were independent. In contrast, observing their joint presence would be surprising, *especially* if the variables were independent. Furthermore, under the current assumptions, Cells B and C (evidence against a positive relationship) fall in between Cells A and D in terms of informativeness, which is also consistent with the empirical findings. In short, assuming that presence is rare, a Bayesian account can naturally explain the perceived differences in cell informativeness (Anderson, 1990; Anderson & Sheu, 1995; McKenzie & Mikkelsen, 2000, in press).

Is the presence of an event or a feature usually rarer than its absence? That is, might it be adaptive to assume that presence is rare? The answer will depend on the specific circumstances, but in the majority of cases, the answer appears to be yes. Most things are not red, most things are not mammals, most people do not have a fever, and so on. Here's another way to think about the issue: Imagine two terms, "X" and "not-X" (e.g., red things and non-red things, accountants and non-accountants), where there is no simple, non-negated term for not-X. Which would be the larger category, X or not-X? Not-X appears to be the larger category in the vast majority of cases.

McKenzie and Mikkelsen's (in press) results support this idea. They discovered that a Cell A "bias" became a Cell D "bias" when they used variables that were familiar to the participants and it was clear that absence was rare, providing evidence that the robust Cell A bias demonstrated over the past four decades stems from (a) participants' Bayesian approach to the task, and (b) their default assumption (probably implicit) that presence is rare. A Bayesian approach, combined with an eye toward the structure of the natural environment, can help explain how people evaluate covariation evidence.

Environment summary

Several robust "errors" in hypothesis testing and evaluation can be explained by adopting a qualitatively Bayesian perspective that is influenced by the predictable structure of our natural environment. (For more on the influence of the "real world" on people's behavior, see Chapters 4 and 15.) In particular, participants appear to harbor strong assumptions about event rarity that reflect experiences outside the laboratory. Normative principles combined with considerations of the environment can provide compelling explanations of behavior.

Summary and Implications

Because hypothesis development is a ubiquitous behavior and plays a crucial role in understanding our complex world, early claims about confirmation bias were quite alarming. However, there is now a consensus that many of the early confirmation bias claims were overstated. Neither testing nor evaluation strategies alone appear to necessitate confirmation bias, though certain combinations of the two can (Klayman, 1995).

Laboratory studies can indicate people's general tendencies in testing and evaluating hypotheses. Often these tendencies do not coincide with what is considered optimal for the task of interest. What to conclude about real-world behavior based on these studies is not so straightforward, however. Participants' strategies might reflect what works in the real world, if not the particular laboratory task (e.g., Funder, 1987; Gigerenzer, Todd, & the ABC Research Group, 1999; Hogarth, 1981; McKenzie, 1994, 2003). I have argued that many "biases" can be explained by adopting a Bayesian perspective combined with assumptions about event rarity that appear to reflect our natural environment.

It is probably worth noting that I am *not* claiming that people never make errors. For example, if the selection task instructions make clear that only the four cards showing are of interest, then selecting the P and Q cards is an error (in Funder's, 1987, sense of "error"; see also McKenzie, 2003). Similarly, if the covariation task instructions make clear that participants are to summarize the relationship between the variables for only the observations presented, then giving more weight to joint presence observations is an error (McKenzie, 2003; McKenzie & Mikkelsen, in press). However, when discussing errors in their concept attainment tasks, Bruner et al. (1956, p. 240) wrote, "Little is added by calling them errors. They are dependent variables, these tendencies, whose determinants have yet to be discovered." Indeed. I would only add that, when adaptation to the environment is a crucial part of the explanation of such tendencies, even less is added by calling them errors.

In addition, I am not claiming that people are optimal Bayesians (see, e.g., McKenzie, 1994). Instead, I argue that participants are sensitive to the rarity of data, which is normatively defensible from a Bayesian perspective. People appear to behave in a *qualitatively* Bayesian manner in a variety of tasks that were not intended by the experimenters to be Bayesian tasks. The consistency in findings across these different tasks lends credence to the current viewpoint.

Finally, it will be obvious to most readers that I am hardly the first to argue that taking into account the environment is crucial for understanding behavior (see, e.g., Anderson, 1990; Brunswik, 1956; Gibson, 1979; Gigerenzer et al., 1999; Hammond, 1955; Marr, 1982; Simon, 1955, 1956; Toda, 1962; Tolman & Brunswik, 1935). Nonetheless, this approach is not exploited enough in research on judgment and decision making in general, and on hypothesis development in particular. I hope that I have convinced the reader that much can be gained by the approach. When robust "errors" occur in the laboratory, a fruitful strategy is to (a) ask about the conditions under which such behavior would make sense, (b) see if such conditions describe the natural environment, and (c) test resulting predictions. The importance of such an analysis lies not so much in its implications for how "good" performance is, but in its ability to provide a *deeper understanding* of behavior (see also Anderson, 1990). Almost 50 years ago, Bruner et al. (1956, p. 240) wrote: "These [strategies], though they may lead to inefficient behavior in particular problem-solving situations, may represent highly efficient strategies when viewed in the broader context of a person's normal life." The recent research described above appears to provide strong support for their hypothesis.

Acknowledgment

Preparation of this chapter was supported by NSF grants SES-0079615 and SES-0242049. For their helpful comments, the author thanks Nigel Harvey, Derek Koehler, Mike Liersch, John Payne, and Shlomi Sher.

References

Allan, L. G. (1993) Human contingency judgments: Rule based or associative? *Psychological Bulletin*, 114, 325–448.

Anderson, J. R. (1990) *The Adaptive Character of Thought*. Hillsdale NJ: Erlbaum.

Anderson, J. R. & Sheu, C-.F. (1995) Causal inferences as perceptual judgments, *Memory and Cognition*, 23, 510–24.

Bassok, M. & Trope, Y. (1984) People's strategies for testing hypotheses about another's personality: Confirmatory or diagnostic? *Social Cognition*, 2, 199–216.

Brehmer, B. (1974) Hypotheses about relations between scaled variables in the learning of probabilistic inference tasks, *Organizational Behavior and Human Performance*, 11, 1–27.

Brehmer, B. (1980) In one word: Not from experience, *Acta Psychologica*, 45, 223–41.

Bruner, J. S., Goodnow, J. J., & Austin, G. A. (1956) *A Study of Thinking*. New York: Wiley.

Brunswik, E. (1956) *Perception and the Representative Design of Psychological Experiments* (2nd edn.). Berkeley, CA: University of California Press.

Einhorn, H. J. & Hogarth, R. M. (1986) Judging probable cause, *Psychological Bulletin*, 99, 3–19.

Evans, J. St. B. T. (1989) *Bias in Human Reasoning: Causes and Consequences*. Hillsdale, NJ: Erlbaum.

Fischhoff, B. & Beyth-Marom, R. (1983) Hypothesis evaluation from a Bayesian perspective, *Psychological Review*, 90, 239–60.

Funder, D. C. (1987) Errors and mistakes: Evaluating the accuracy of social judgment, *Psychological Bulletin*, 101, 75–90.

Garcia, J. & Koelling, R. A. (1966) Relation of cue to consequence in avoidance learning, *Psychonomic Science*, 4, 123–4.

Gibson, J. J. (1979) *The Ecological Approach to Visual Perception*. Boston: Houghton Mifflin.

Gigerenzer, G., Swijtink, Z., Porter, T., Daston, L., Beatty, J., & Krüger, L. (1989) *The Empire of Chance: How Probability Changed Science and Everyday Life*. Cambridge: Cambridge University Press.

Gigerenzer, G, Todd, P. M., & the ABC Research Group (1999) *Simple Heuristics that Make Us Smart*. Oxford: Oxford University Press.

Hammond, K. R. (1955) Probabilistic functioning and the clinical method, *Psychological Review*, 62, 255–62.

Hogarth, R. M. (1981) Beyond discrete biases: Functional and dysfunctional aspects of judgmental heuristics, *Psychological Bulletin*, 47, 116–31.

Horwich, P. (1982) *Probability and Evidence*. Cambridge: Cambridge University Press.

Howson, C. & Urbach, P. (1989) *Scientific Reasoning: The Bayesian Approach*. La Salle, IL: Open Court.

Jenkins, H. M. & Sainsbury, R. S. (1969) The development of stimulus control through differential reinforcement. In N. J. Mackintosh and W. K. Honig (eds.), *Fundamental Issues in Associative Learning*. Halifax, Nova Scotia, Canada: Dalhousie University Press.

Jenkins, H. M. & Sainsbury, R. S. (1970) Discrimination learning with the distinctive feature on positive or negative trials. In D. Mostofsky (ed.), *Attention: Contemporary Theory and Analysis*. New York: Appleton-Century-Crofts.

Jenkins, H. M. & Ward, W. C. (1965) The judgment of contingency between responses and outcomes, *Psychological Monographs: General and Applied*, 79(1, whole no. 594).

Kao, S.-F. & Wasserman, E. A. (1993) Assessment of an information integration account of contingency judgment with examination of subjective cell importance and method of information presentation, *Journal of Experimental Psychology: Learning, Memory, and Cognition*, 19, 1363–86.

Klayman, J. (1995) Varieties of confirmation bias, *Psychology of Learning and Motivation*, 32, 385–418.

Klayman, J. & Ha, Y.-W. (1987) Confirmation, disconfirmation, and information in hypothesis testing, *Psychological Review*, 94, 211–28.

Koehler, J. J. (1993) The influence of prior beliefs on scientific judgments of evidence quality, *Organizational Behavior and Human Decision Processes*, 56, 28–55.

Levin, I. P., Wasserman, E. A., & Kao, S.-F. (1993) Multiple methods for examining biased information use in contingency judgments, *Organizational Behavior and Human Decision Processes*, 55, 228–50.

Levine, M. (1971) Hypothesis theory and nonlearning despite ideas S-R reinforcement contingencies, *Psychological Review*, 78, 130–40.

Lipe, M. G. (1990) A lens-model analysis of covariation research, *Journal of Behavioral Decision Making*, 3, 47–59.

Lord, C. G., Ross, L., & Lepper, M. R. (1979) Biased assimilation and attitude polarization: The effects of prior theories on subsequently considered evidence, *Journal of Personality and Social Psychology*, 11, 2098–109.

Mackie, J. L. (1963) The paradox of confirmation, *British Journal for the Philosophy of Science*, 13, 265–77.

Mackie, J. L. (1974) *The Cement of the Universe: A Study of Causation*. Oxford: Clarendon.

Mandel, D. R. & Lehman, D. R. (1998) Integration of contingency information in judgments of cause, covariation, and probability, *Journal of Experimental Psychology: General*, 127, 269–85.

Marr, D. (1982) *Vision*. San Francisco: W. H. Freeman.

McKenzie, C. R. M. (1994) The accuracy of intuitive judgment strategies: Covariation assessment and Bayesian inference, *Cognitive Psychology*, 26, 209–39.

McKenzie, C. R. M. (2003) Rational models as theories – not standards – of behavior, *Trends in Cognitive Sciences*, 7, 403–6.

McKenzie, C. R. M., Ferreira, V. S., Mikkelsen, L. A., McDermott, K. J., & Skrable, R. P. (2001) Do conditional hypotheses target rare events? *Organizational Behavior and Human Decision Processes*, 85, 291–309.

McKenzie, C. R. M., Lee, S. M., & Chen, K. K. (2002). When negative evidence increases confidence: Change in belief after hearing two sides of a dispute, *Journal of Behavioral Decision Making, 15*, 1–18.

McKenzie, C. R. M. & Mikkelsen, L. A. (2000) The psychological side of Hempel's paradox of confirmation, *Psychonomic Bulletin and Review, 7*, 360–66.

McKenzie, C. R. M. & Mikkelsen, L. A. (in press) A Bayesian view of covariation assessment, *Cognitive Psychology*.

Mynatt, C. R., Doherty, M. E., & Tweney, R. D. (1977) Confirmation bias in a simulated research environment: An experimental study of scientific inference, *Quarterly Journal of Experimental Psychology, 29*, 85–95.

Mynatt, C. R., Doherty, M. E., & Tweney, R. D. (1978) Consequences of confirmation and disconfirmation in a simulated research environment, *Quarterly Journal of Experimental Psychology, 30*, 395–406.

Newman, J., Wolff, W. T., & Hearst, E. (1980) The feature-positive effect in adult human subjects, *Journal of Experimental Psychology: Human Learning and Memory, 6*, 630–50.

Nickerson, R. S. (1996) Hempel's paradox and Wason's selection task: Logical and psychological puzzles of confirmation, *Thinking and Reasoning, 2*, 1–31.

Nickerson, R. S. (1998) Confirmation bias: A ubiquitous phenomenon in many guises, *Review of General Psychology, 2*, 175–220.

Nisbett, R. & Ross, L (1980) *Human Inference: Strategies and Shortcomings of Social Judgment.* Englewood Cliffs, NJ: Prentice-Hall.

Oaksford, M. & Chater, N. (1994) A rational analysis of the selection task as optimal data selection, *Psychological Review, 101*, 608–31.

Oaksford, M. & Chater, N. (2003) Optimal data selection: Revision, review, and re-evaluation, *Psychonomic Bulletin and Review, 10*, 289–318.

Payne, J. W., Bettman, J. R., & Johnson, E. J. (1993) *The Adaptive Decision Maker.* Cambridge: Cambridge University Press.

Poletiek, F. (2001) *Hypothesis-testing Behavior.* East Sussex: Psychology Press.

Popper, K. R. (1959) *The Logic of Scientific Discovery.* New York: Harper & Row.

Restle, F. (1965) Significance of all-or-none learning, *Psychological Bulletin, 64*, 313–25.

Simon, H. A., (1955) A behavioral model of rational choice, *Quarterly Journal of Economics, 69*, 99–118.

Simon, H. A. (1956) Rational choice and the structure of the environment, *Psychological Review, 63*, 129–38.

Skov, R. B. & Sherman, S. J. (1986) Information-gathering processes: Diagnosticity, hypothesis-confirmatory strategies, and perceived hypothesis confirmation, *Journal of Experimental Social Psychology, 22*, 93–121.

Slowiaczek, L. M., Klayman, J., Sherman, S. J., & Skov, R. B. (1992) Information selection and use in hypothesis testing: What is a good question and what is a good answer? *Memory and Cognition, 20*, 392–405.

Smedslund, J. (1963) The concept of correlation in adults, *Scandinavian Journal of Psychology, 4*, 165–73.

Sniezek, J. A. & Naylor, J. C. (1978) Cue measurement scale and functional hypothesis testing in cue probability learning, *Organizational Behavior and Human Performance, 22*, 366–74.

Snyder, M. (1981) Seek and ye shall find: Testing hypotheses about other people. In E. T. Higgins, C. P. Heiman, and M. P. Zanna (eds.), *Social Cognition: The Ontario Symposium on Personality and Social Psychology* (pp. 277–303). Hillsdale, NJ: Erlbaum.

Snyder, M. & Campbell, B. H. (1980) Testing hypotheses about other people: The role of the hypothesis, *Personality and Social Psychology Bulletin, 6*, 421–6.

Snyder, M. & Swann, W. B., Jr. (1978) Hypothesis-testing in social interaction, *Journal of Personality and Social Psychology*, 36, 1202–12.

Thagard, P. (1989) Explanatory coherence, *Behavioral and Brain Sciences*, 12, 435–502.

Toda, M. (1962) The design of a fungus-eater: A model of human behavior in an unsophisticated environment, *Behavioral Science*, 7, 164–83.

Tolman, E. C. & Brunswik, E. (1935) The organism and the causal structure of the environment, *Psychological Review*, 42, 43–77.

Trope, Y. & Bassok, M. (1982) Confirmatory and diagnosing strategies in social information gathering, *Journal of Personality and Social Psychology*, 43, 22–34.

Trope, Y. & Bassok, M. (1983) Information-gathering strategies in hypothesis testing, *Journal of Experimental Social Psychology*, 19, 560–76.

Ward, W. C. & Jenkins, H. M. (1965) The display of information and the judgment of contingency, *Canadian Journal of Psychology*, 19, 231–41.

Wason, P. C. (1960) On the failure to eliminate hypotheses in a conceptual task, *Quarterly Journal of Experimental Psychology*, 12, 129–40.

Wason, P. C. (1966) Reasoning. In B. M. Foss (ed.), *New Horizons in Psychology* (pp. 135–51). Harmondsworth, England: Penguin.

Wason, P. C. (1968) Reasoning about a rule, *Quarterly Journal of Experimental Psychology*, 20, 273–81.

Wasserman, E. A., Dorner, W. W., & Kao, S.-F. (1990) Contributions of specific cell information to judgments of interevent contingency, *Journal of Experimental Psychology: Learning, Memory, and Cognition*, 16, 509–21.

Zuckerman, M., Knee, C. R., Hodgins, H. S., & Miyake, K. (1995) Hypothesis confirmation: The joint effect of positive test strategy and acquiescence response set, *Journal of Personality and Social Psychology*, 68, 52–60.

11

Judging Covariation and Causation

David R. Shanks

Introduction

The ability to accurately perceive relationships in the environment is an essential component of adaptive behavior, as it allows powers of explanation, control, and prediction. It is easy to see the significance of our faculty for detecting such relations when one recognizes that almost all learning is fundamentally the learning of covariations. Because causal relations are constantly affecting peoples' behavior, it is perhaps fortunate that we are rather good at attending to, and acting on, these relations.

Much experimental research has been devoted to understanding how humans process covariance and causal information and to determining the cognitive processes underlying causal induction. Some of the key issues have been: (1) How accurate or biased are we in our judgments? (2) What is the role of generative mechanisms in the formation of causal beliefs? For instance, why does it seem implausible that there might be an inverse relationship between the number of unmarried people in a village and the population of fieldmice in the surrounding countryside (Glymour & Cheng, 1998)?[1] (3) How do prior expectations affect our judgments? (4) What is the relationship between covariation and causation? and (5) What can we say about the algorithms and mechanisms determining judgments of covariation and causation?

Although the paradigms used to study covariation and causal learning in the laboratory vary, they often involve presenting participants with information about a single cue or cause that can be present or absent, and about the presence or absence of an outcome or effect, e.g., firing shells and tank destruction, a baking ingredient and cake rising, or drug administration and side effects. The present chapter describes some of the findings from experiments of this sort and highlights some of the main factors that affect our judgments. It also devotes some time to the normative issue of specifying what our judgments should be – which is to say, what would an expert statistician judge a given relationship to be? I shall provide some reasons for thinking that the appropriate norm differs depending on whether one is judging covariation or causation. From this normative question follows fairly directly the interesting question of the extent to which people's covariation and causal judgments are well calibrated and if not, then in what ways they may be biased. Lastly, I briefly consider some of the theoretical explanations that have been offered to explain the mechanisms underlying our judgments.

A Normative Perspective on Covariation and Causation

Are people good judges of the extent to which variables are associated, be they continuous or discrete?[2] Whereas in the former case the standard correlation coefficient r is an appropriate statistical norm against which covariation judgments can be compared, in the latter case the χ^2 and φ coefficients $[\varphi = (\chi^2/N)^{1/2}]$ are often taken as appropriate measures (Allan, 1980; McKenzie, 1994). These coefficients are bi-directional in that they measure the dependence of event A on event B and the dependence of B on A. In many studies of covariation judgment (some exceptions are noted below), however, researchers are interested in a one-way dependence between cue A and outcome O (this is even more true in the case of causal judgments) and under these conditions an appropriate measure is:

$$\Delta P = P(O|A) - P(O|\sim A) \tag{11.1}$$

which bears a fairly simple relationship to χ^2 (Allan, 1980). Here, $P(O|A)$ and $P(O|\sim A)$ refer to the probability of the outcome O in the presence and absence, respectively, of the target cue A. When $P(O|A)$ exceeds $P(O|\sim A)$ the contingency is positive and we would say that A is indeed a predictor of the outcome, and when $P(O|\sim A)$ exceeds $P(O|A)$ the contingency is negative and we would say that C predicts the absence of the outcome. As the vast majority of research has focused on dichotomous (usually present/absent) events, Equation 11.1 will be the covariation benchmark we will consider in this chapter for unidirectional judgments. I will also briefly mention some studies that have used continuous variables.

The different combinations of the presence or absence of the cue and the outcome are often represented in a 2 × 2 matrix whose cells give the respective frequencies of the various combinations of events (Table 11.1). Using the common notation for this matrix, $P(O|A)$ is calculated as $a/(a + b)$ and $P(O|\sim A)$ as $c/(c + d)$.

Although it seems appropriate to view people's unidirectional judgments of *covariation* as well calibrated if they approximate ΔP, ΔP seems an inappropriate normative index of *causality*. One reason is that covariation is indeterminate with respect to the direction of causation. For instance, if $b = c$ then the value of ΔP would be identical and would fail to distinguish between C causing E and E causing C. Moreover, even when $b \neq c$, ΔP would often be nonzero if computed on the incorrect basis of E causing C. Another reason is that judgments of covariation and causation seem to differ in their reference classes: a covariation judgment generally concerns an observed sample of events whereas

Table 11.1 Combinations of the presence or absence of a target cue and an outcome

Target cue	Outcome	
	Present	Absent
Present	a	b
Absent	c	d

a–d represent the frequencies of the events.

a causal judgment refers to a larger population. Causal judgments require inferences that go beyond the observed data while covariation ratings seem to involve only a characterization of the observed data themselves.

Yet another reason to be very cautious about the relevance of measures of covariation such as ΔP to determining causation is that a cause need not be a covariate and a covariate need not be a cause. For example, consider the "ceiling problem." Suppose that the air force wishes to test some new bomb-targeting technology. In an operation, 16 bombers are dispatched, eight with the new technology, eight without. During the mission, all 16 aircraft successfully hit their targets and therefore ΔP in this circumstance is zero $[\Delta P = P(\text{Hit target} | \text{New technology}) - P(\text{Hit target} | {\sim}\text{New technology}) = 0]$. However, the air force would not conclude that the technology was ineffective; rather, there was not enough evidence to make a decision because the effect was always occurring at its maximal level. Hence a cause need not be a covariate. Similarly, consider the case of the relationship between thirst and intoxication. Although thirst covaries inversely with intoxication, it is plainly not causally related to intoxication: both are effects of a common cause, consuming alcohol. Hence a covariate need not be a cause.

Indeed, examples of Simpson's paradox illustrate how a cause can be negatively correlated with an effect and vice versa. Take the case of the relationship between the birth control pill and the occurrence of thrombosis. Hesslow (1976) pointed out that thrombosis tends to be less probable in women taking the pill, hence ΔP for this relationship is negative implying a preventative causal relationship. However the truth is that the pill is a cause, not a prevention, of thrombosis. How can this be? The answer is that pregnancy is another cause of thrombosis and is also a relatively more potent cause. The negative ΔP for the contraceptive pill comes about because taking the pill reduces the likelihood of a strong cause of thrombosis (i.e., pregnancy), leading to a reduction overall in the likelihood of thrombosis. Were one to study a group of women, some of whom had taken the pill and some of whom had not, and none of whom became pregnant, then the adverse effects of the pill on the likelihood of thrombosis would become apparent. Spellman (1996) has shown that people are capable of avoiding attributing causal influence to spurious causes in such cases of Simpson's paradox.

To account for the distinction between covariation, as measured by ΔP, and causality, Cheng (1997) proposed the power PC theory. This theory states that normative causal judgments are based on p, a combination of ΔP and the base-rate of the effect, with the latter being measured by $P(E|{\sim}C)$, where C is the target cause and E the effect. In the case of generative causes (i.e., $\Delta P > 0$), judgments should be determined by the computation:

$$p = \frac{\Delta P}{1 - P(E|{\sim}C)} \qquad (11.2)$$

where $\Delta P = P(E|C) - P(E|{\sim}C)$ as in Equation 11.1. It follows from Equation 11.2 that, for a normative judge, conditions of equivalent power should result in equal causal judgments regardless of the actual values of ΔP or $P(E|{\sim}C)$. Similarly, it should also be true that conditions with equal values of ΔP but different $P(E|{\sim}C)$ will result in judgments that vary directly with the value of the latter. Specifically, as $P(E|{\sim}C)$ approaches (but does not equal) 1, a candidate cause will be judged to have increasing generative power. However, if $P(E|{\sim}C) = 1$, the ratio is no longer defined and, as in the case of the air force, no conclusion about causality can be drawn.

One way to see the normative justification of Equation 11.2 is to think about an effect as either being caused by the target cause C or by some alternative cause or set of causes X. If C and X are independent, then what we would like to measure is the probability that if C occurs, it causes E. On this formulation,

$$P(E) = P(C) \cdot p_C + P(X) \cdot p_X(1 - P(C) \cdot p_C) \qquad (11.3)$$

which says that the probability of the effect occurring can be computed as the sum of two probabilities: (1) the probability of C occurring multiplied by the likelihood that, when C occurs, it causes E (p_C); and (2) if C does not cause E, the probability of X occurring multiplied by the likelihood that, when X occurs, it causes E (p_X). Cheng (1997) shows that this equation leads to Equation 11.2 if the unobservable term $P(X) \cdot p_X$ is estimated by $P(E|{\sim}C)$. She also gives a full description of the assumptions on which this formulation is based.

In sum, it appears that the appropriate normative benchmark is different for judgments of covariation (Equation 11.1) and causation (Equation 11.2). This difference arises because covariation does not imply causation and vice versa. In the case of the "ceiling problem" described above, it would be correct for the air force to judge that their new bomb-targeting technology did not covary ($\Delta P = 0$) with the target being hit in their trial, as $P(\text{Hit target}|\text{New technology}) = P(\text{Hit target}|{\sim}\text{New technology})$. However, it would be incorrect for them to conclude that there is no causal relationship between the new technology and hitting the target: perhaps in a sample of tests in which $P(\text{Hit target}|{\sim}\text{New technology})$ is less than 1.0, the new technology would increase the probability of the target being hit. Consistent with this, Equation 11.2 does not yield a value of $p = 0$ but instead says that p is undefined (the denominator of the equation is zero when the base-rate of the effect is 1.0). Thus the two normative formulae capture the intuition that covariation and causation are distinct entities. Note however that the difference between ΔP and p will be quite small when the base-rate of the effect is small. Indeed $\Delta P = p$ when the base-rate is zero.

Judgments of Covariation and Causation

With this normative framework in mind, we can begin to ask about the calibration of human judgments. Many studies have presented participants with summary information of the form represented in Table 11.1. In such circumstances people seem to be moderate judges of covariation as indexed by conformity to ΔP (these studies pre-dated the power theory and hence did not compare judgments to p). Quite a lot of evidence is consistent with the use of simpler judgment rules such as ones in which judgments are based on $(a + d) - (b + c)$ or on $(a - c)$. In another strand of research, participants are given information about correlated continuous variables in the form, for instance, of scatterplots of bivariate data or samples of pairs of digits drawn from a continuous bivariate distribution (Boynton, 2000; Broniarczyk & Alba, 1994; Well, Boyce, Morris, Shinjo, & Chumbley, 1988). Studies of this type have compared judgments to the correlation coefficient r and have attempted to derive a psychophysical function which captures the relationship between judgments of covariation and r. Once again, people are generally found to be moderate judges, with systematic deviations such as underestimation of low correlations. Boynton (2000) found that estimation of covariation from graphical scatterplots was well predicted by a model based on the relative elongation of the data points and the degree of dispersion from the best-fitting regression line. This model predicts that scatterplots with the same value of r can yield different judgments and that scatterplots differing in r can yield similar judgments.

Although many interesting findings have emerged from this body of research, studies such as these are not the principal focus here. The reason is that the ecological validity of such studies is probably rather limited, especially with respect to causal inference. Rarely are we confronted with scatterplots of correlated data or tabulated numerical case information as the basis for making a judgment. Far more common are situations in which we observe covariations as they unfold in time on a case-by-case basis, and in which we have the chance to entertain hypotheses which we can revise as more and more information is obtained. Of course one rarely draws inferences from pure observation alone; later I shall discuss some ways in which prior knowledge and expectancies affect causal judgment.

Accordingly, numerous experiments have presented participants with a series of learning trials defined by the events in Table 11.1 (see Chapter 10, this volume, for more on how people make use of the four cells of a 2 × 2 matrix). For instance, Collins and Shanks (2002) gave participants 80 learning trials in each of which they saw a different butterfly together with pictorial information about whether the butterfly had been treated with radiation, and participants were asked to indicate, using mouse-activated buttons, whether or not they expected a mutation to occur. They were then shown a color image of either a mutated or nonmutated butterfly. Thus each sample corresponded to one of the cell types *a–d*. At the end of the trial series participants made their causal judgments using a horizontal rating scale to estimate the "degree to which the radiation causes mutations." The scale had endpoints of −100 (radiation prevents mutation) to +100 (radiation causes mutation). Participants made a judgment by moving a slider with the mouse. When the participants were satisfied with their response, they could continue to the next set of records or next trial series. In other experiments of the same basic type, participants might be asked non-causal questions such as "to what extent does A predict O?" or "to what extent are A and O related?" Many studies have used a simulated medical diagnosis task in which participants judge the relationship between symptoms (the cues) and diseases (the outcome). Since symptoms do not cause diseases, judgments of the extent to which the symptoms predict or diagnose the disease are plainly not causal judgments.

In experiments such as these it is generally found that covariation and causal judgments are quite accurate. Specifically: (1) judgments tend to increase as $P(E|C)$ or $P(O|A)$ increases; (2) decrease as $P(E|{\sim}C)$ or $P(O|{\sim}A)$ increases; and (3) be fairly close to zero when $P(E|C) = P(E|{\sim}C)$ or $P(O|A) = P(O|{\sim}A)$. Numerous studies document this accuracy (e.g., Wasserman, Elek, Chatlosh, & Baker, 1993). To illustrate subjects' accuracy in causal judgment, consider an experiment by Wasserman et al. (1993). In that experiment, subjects were required to make judgments of the extent to which pressing a telegraph key (cause C) caused a white light to flash (effect E). Thus unlike the radiation/mutation example, this sort of judgment task asks participants to rate the efficacy of their own instrumental actions or interventions. They were presented with 25 different problems constructed by taking all possible pairings of $P(E|C)$ and $P(E|{\sim}C)$ with the values of 1.0, 0.75, 0.5, 0.25, and 0.0. In situations where $P(E|C)$ is greater than $P(E|{\sim}C)$, the action to some degree caused the outcome, whereas in situations where $P(E|C)$ is less than $P(E|{\sim}C)$, the action was a preventative cause which made the outcome *less* likely to occur. When $P(E|C)$ and $P(E|{\sim}C)$ were equal, there was no objective contingency between the action and outcome. These conclusions apply regardless of whether Equation 11.1 or 11.2 is taken as the norm.

Each condition lasted for one minute and was divided into 60 one-second intervals. If the participant responded during a given interval by pressing the telegraph key, then the white light flashed for 0.1 sec at the end of that interval with a probability $P(E|C)$, and if the subject did not respond during the 1 sec interval, the light flashed with probability $P(E|{\sim}C)$. Hence the maximum rate of the effect was 1/sec. At the end of each problem, the subjects rated the response–outcome relation on a scale from −100 ("prevents the light from occurring") to +100 ("causes the light to occur"), with 0 reflecting no causal effect.

In general the results, shown in Table 11.2, indicated an impressive degree of sensitivity to the conditional probabilities. As $P(E|C)$ is held constant at 1.0, judgments decrease as $P(E|{\sim}C)$ is raised from 0.0 to 1.0. Conversely, judgments increase (become

Table 11.2 Mean judgments of contingency, divided by 100, as a function of $P(E|C)$ and $P(E|{\sim}C)$ in Wasserman et al.'s (1993) Experiment 3

$P(E|C)$	$P(E|{\sim}C)$				
	0.00	*0.25*	*0.50*	*0.75*	*1.00*
1.00	0.85	0.52	0.37	0.13	−0.03
0.75	0.65	0.43	0.16	0.06	−0.12
0.50	0.37	0.19	0.01	−0.19	−0.34
0.25	0.12	−0.10	−0.14	−0.37	−0.58
0.00	−0.08	−0.45	−0.51	−0.66	−0.75

less negative) when $P(E|{\sim}C)$ is held constant at 1.0 as $P(E|C)$ is raised from 0.0 to 1.0. Judgments are close to zero when $P(E|C)$ and $P(E|{\sim}C)$ are equal. All of these effects are consistent with Equation 11.2. However, they are also consistent with Equation 11.1, so it is natural to ask whether judgments are closer to p than to ΔP. In fact, the converse is true, with ΔP and p accounting for about 97 percent and 88 percent of the variance in judgments, respectively.[3] Apparent violations of Equation 11.2 are clearly evident in the condition where $P(E|C)$ and $P(E|{\sim}C)$ are both 1.0. Participants judged that pressing the button had no causal influence whereas in truth the correct answer is that it is impossible to assess and that therefore no specific numerical rating should be preferred over any other: if the light would have flashed anyway, how can one judge whether the button-press might also be a cause?

How might we attempt to rationalize the ceiling effect described above? One reason why people might be willing to give judgments close to zero when $P(E|C)$ and $P(E|{\sim}C)$ are both 1.0 is because they believe that the presence of the cause C *could* have led (but did not) to a detectable change in some aspect of the effect such as its magnitude or rate. In Wasserman et al.'s experiment, the outcome certainly could in principle have occurred more than once per second. This speculation leads to the suggestion that participants' judgments should be very different if they are encouraged to believe that the effect is occurring at its maximal magnitude or rate and that a genuine ceiling effect is therefore present, and this idea has been tested and confirmed by De Houwer, Beckers, and Glautier (2002). These researchers asked participants to rate the causal relationship between a light appearing in a particular position and a tank blowing up in conditions in which $P(E|C) = P(E|{\sim}C) = 1.0$. When the effect was described as occurring at less than the maximum possible magnitude (10 on a scale from 0 to 20), causal judgments were very close to zero. This seems consistent with the data in Table 11.2 if we assume that Wasserman et al.'s participants believed that the effect could have occurred more frequently than it actually did. However when the effect (tank destruction) was described as occurring at its maximal possible magnitude (10 on a scale from 0 to 10), causal judgments were quite high. Thus participants seem to have recognized that determining the magnitude of causal influence depends on whether or not the effect is occurring at its maximal level. Perhaps if they had been instructed that the light could not flash more than once per second, and had been given the option to say that the extent of causal influence was indeterminate, Wasserman et al.'s participants would have chosen to do so in the case where the effect was at its maximal level.

Another aspect of Wasserman et al.'s data which violates the power calculation is evident in the fact that judgments were very different across conditions for which $P(E|C) = 1.0$ (the top row of the table), varying from 85 when $P(E|{\sim}C) = 0.0$ to 13 when $P(E|{\sim}C) = 0.75$ despite the fact that $p = 1$ in all these conditions. Similarly, judgments were different across conditions in which $P(E|C) = 0.0$ (the bottom row of the table), varying from −45 when $P(E|{\sim}C) = 0.25$ to −75 when $P(E|{\sim}C) = 1.0$ despite the fact that $p = -1$ in all these conditions. At face value, then, these results seem to provide evidence that people are not fully sensitive to the normative considerations captured in Equation 11.2.

There have been a number of further experimental tests of this bias in judgments whereby they vary from what is predicted by the power PC theory. In these studies the

Table 11.3 Cell frequencies, contingency (ΔP), and power (p) in Collins and Shanks' (2003) Experiment 1

Condition ($\Delta P/p$)	Cell frequencies				$P(E\,|\,C)$	$P(E\,|\,{\sim}C)$	ΔP	p
	a	b	c	d				
0.66/0.66	30	15	0	45	0.66	0.0	0.66	0.66
0.40/0.66	36	9	18	27	0.8	0.4	0.40	0.66
0.40/0.40	18	27	0	45	0.4	0.0	0.40	0.40

a, *b*, *c*, and *d* refer to the following combinations of cause and effect: cause/effect, cause/no-effect, no-cause/effect, no-cause/no-effect (see Table 11.1). $P(E\,|\,C)$ is the probability of the effect in the presence of the cause, $a/(a+b)$. $P(E\,|\,{\sim}C)$ is the probability of the effect in the absence of the cause, $c/(c+d)$.

logic has been to hold ΔP constant while varying p and vice versa. The results of these experiments have established two things: first, "standard" causal judgments do not conform particularly well to p; second, causal judgments elicited with counterfactual causal questions do conform well with p. The empirical basis for these conclusions is now reviewed.

The bulk of studies have obtained results that run counter to the theory's predictions. As an example, Collins and Shanks (2003) presented participants with the problem types illustrated in Table 11.3. Participants were required to judge the causal relationship between radiation and mutation in a sample of butterflies. The two critical conditions are labelled 0.66/0.66 and 0.40/0.66, with the first number in each designation referring to ΔP and the second to p. From the table it can be seen that in condition 0.40/0.66, for example, the values of $P(E\,|\,C)$ and $P(E\,|\,{\sim}C)$ were 0.8 and 0.4 which yield values of ΔP and p of 0.40 and 0.66, respectively, from Equations 11.1 and 11.2. The key point about these conditions is that they are identical in terms of p but differ in terms of ΔP, and hence allow us to determine which metric better characterizes judgments: if judgments are roughly equal in these conditions, then that would imply that they are normative with respect to power p, whereas if they differ, they would appear to be non-normative (there was also a control condition in which both p and ΔP were low, 0.4/0.4, for which both theories predict low judgments). Collins and Shanks found that when participants were asked after 30, 60, and 90 trials "To what extent does radiation cause mutations?" judgments differed significantly across the two conditions, as shown in the top panel of Figure 11.1. Judgments violated the norm specified by the power theory.

The effect of the probe question

However, before accepting this conclusion it is important to consider the precise judgment in a little more detail. Although it is true that causal learning research has not strongly supported the power PC theory, what has also emerged is the sense that participants are not fixed in employing a single causal induction strategy. Rather, qualitative differences in responding can be observed through subtle changes in the experimental

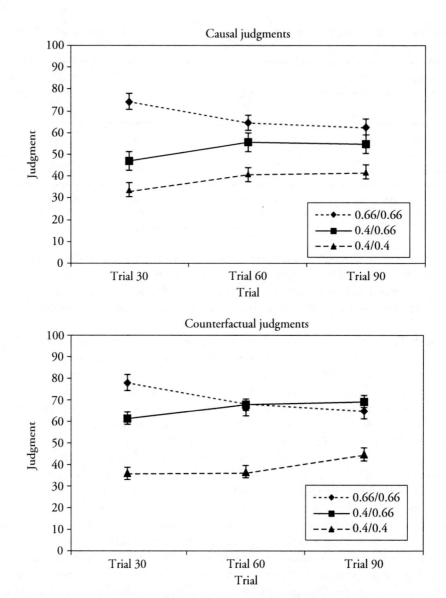

Figure 11.1 Causal (top panel) and counterfactual (lower panel) judgments (±SE) across judgment intervals for each condition in Collins and Shanks' (2003) Experiment 1

Each condition is denoted by two numbers, the first being the value of ΔP, the second the value of p. Under the causal question, final judgments differed in the conditions of equal power (0.66/0.66 and 0.40/0.66). Under a counterfactual probe, in contrast, judgments were consistent with p. See Table 11.3 for further details.

environment such as judgment interval (Collins & Shanks, 2002), magnitude of the effect (De Houwer et al., 2002), and the type of question that probes causal knowledge.

As an illustration of the latter variable, Matute, Arcediano, and Miller (1996) presented participants with information about administering medication to patients and possible side effects and reported competition between causes (i.e., discounted judgments if several cues were associated with the same outcome) when participants were probed with a causal question (e.g., "To what degree do you think that the cue is the cause of the outcome?"). However, when participants were probed with a probability question (e.g., "To what degree do you think the cue was followed by the outcome, even by chance?"), cue competition, one of the most fundamental and reliable phenomena in causal induction, was not evident.

Similar effects were reported by Gredebäck, Winman, and Juslin (2000) and Matute, Vegas, and De Marez (2002). Gredebäck et al. reported that blocking and conditioned inhibition, two specific instances of cue competition (see below), were dependent on the type of probe question, where the former was only evident with predictive and causal questions, but not with probability or frequency questions, and the latter only with a causal probe. Matute et al. found that responses to predictive test questions (e.g., "To what degree to you expect the outcome to occur on this trial?") were more susceptible to trial-order effects and extinction than were causal or contiguity question types.

Perhaps test-question effects could also be behind failures to validate the power PC theory. Buehner, Cheng, and Clifford (2003) argued that the causal probe questions used in most studies are suboptimal in two ways. First, they suggested that causal questions are often ambiguous with respect to the context in which the question applies. This could lead to participants using either ΔP or power to make their judgments depending on their interpretation (i.e., the question could refer to the current situation where alternative causes produce a proportion of the target effects *or* a situation where the participant should isolate the strength of a specific candidate). Second, Buehner et al. argue that a causal question could result in participants conflating causal power and reliability, i.e., a low causal rating could reflect either a weak belief that there is a strong causal relationship, or a strong belief in a weak relationship.

Rather than using a causal question, Buehner et al. (2003) proposed that a counterfactual probe is the appropriate manner to elicit judgments of causal power. They argued that a counterfactual question (i.e., asking participants how many cases out of 100, none of which showed an outcome, would show an outcome if the target cause was introduced) is still explicitly causal because it asks participants to consider the intervention of a candidate cause (such as administering radiation to DNA). Additionally, it instructs participants to assume that all other causes are held constant, or in terms of the power PC theory, prompts them to consider the base rate of the effect. Thus, Collins and Shanks went on to ask the following question: If judgments probed with a causal question tend not to be determined by *p*, would causal knowledge probed with a counterfactual question produce responding more consistent with the power PC theory?

The bottom panel of Figure 11.1 reveals the answer. Another group of participants answered the question "How many out of 100 butterflies, none of which would show an outcome if unradiated, do you estimate would show an outcome if radiated?" It is clear that these participants rated the radiation as equally effective in the critical 0.66/0.66 and 0.40/0.66 conditions. These results support Buehner et al.'s (2003) argument that a counterfactual probe question is the optimal way to elicit human judgments of causal strength.

It thus appears that what might at first sight appear to be superficial changes in the experimental environment such as question type and outcome magnitude can shape the responses given in causal judgment tasks. The results suggest that subtle changes in wording can have a major effect on the extent to which causal inferences conform to a normative prescription.

Judgment biases

A number of biases have been documented in causal and covariation judgment. One example is a primacy effect observed by Dennis and Ahn (2001) and Collins and Shanks (2002). As another example, it is commonly observed in conditions where $P(E|C) = P(E|\sim C)$ or $P(O|A) = P(O|\sim A)$ that judgments are greater than zero, and this bias is especially prevalent when only small samples of events have been witnessed (Shanks, 1993). For instance, Shanks, López, Darby, and Dickinson (1996) reported that judgments in a condition where $P(O|A) = P(O|\sim A) = 0.75$ were significantly higher than ones in a condition where $P(O|A) = P(O|\sim A) = 0.25$, but that they tended to converge with further exposure to the relevant events. Under the name "illusory correlation," a variant of this phenomenon was the subject of much study a few decades ago (Chapman & Chapman, 1969).

Yet another bias is that variations in $P(E|C)$ and $P(O|A)$ tend to have a greater impact on judgments than equivalent variations in $P(E|\sim C)$ and $P(O|\sim A)$. For example, the weight given to $P(O|A)$ in fitting participants' judgments was greater than that given to $P(O|\sim A)$ in studies reported by Lober and Shanks (2000) (this is also evident in the data pattern shown in Table 11.2). The basis of these effects is somewhat unclear, although several theoretical accounts have been offered. For instance, Cheng (1997) argued that a greater influence of $P(E|C)$ than $P(E|\sim C)$ is normative and consistent with the power theory.

Multiple cues

The scenario we have considered in all of the studies discussed thus far is remarkably stripped down compared to real-world judgment situations. For instance, we have paid no attention to the possibility that there might be a time lag between the events and that this lag might seriously affect the magnitude of the judged relationship (Buehner & May, 2003; Shanks, Pearson, & Dickinson, 1989) nor have we considered the role of prior expectations in covariation and causal judgment (Alloy & Tabachnik, 1984; Cobos, López, Caño, Almaraz, & Shanks, 2002). Yet another simplification is the focus on situations in which a single cue covaries with a single outcome. Here we consider the significant influences on judgments that emerge when the target cue is only one among several potential predictors of the outcome.

In brief, the presence of alternative predictors may either decrease or increase judgments of the target cue and such effects are now quite well understood (Dickinson, 2001). Consider a situation in which $P(E|C) = 1.0$ and $P(E|\sim C) = 0.0$ for some target putative cause C. We know that if all other events are held constant, participants will judge C to be strongly causally efficacious. However the presence of another potential

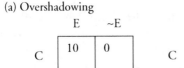

(a) Overshadowing

	E	~E
C	10	0
~C	0	0

	E	~E
C	10 **X**	0
~C	0	0

(b) Signaling

	E	~E
C	10	0
~C	10	0

	E	~E
C	10	0
~C	10 **X**	0

(c) Blocking and superlearning

	E	~E
C	10 **X**	0
~C	5 **X**	5 **Y**

	E	~E
C	10 **X**	0
~C	5 **Y**	5 **X**

	E	~E
C	10 **X**	0
~C	5 **Y**	5 **XY**

Figure 11.2 A variety of competition effects described in terms of contingency tables (see Table 11.1)

Numbers refer to frequencies of events involving permutations of the presence and absence of a cause C and an effect E. Bold letters (**X**, **Y**) refer to events where additional possible causes are also present.

cause can dramatically effect judgments for C. For example, if C always occurs together with another event, judgments will be discounted ("overshadowed" – see Figure 11.2a) (Cobos et al., 2002). It is as if the total amount of causal strength that an effect can support has to be shared out among potential causes. Figure 11.2 illustrates a number of other such cases. Figure 11.2b shows a pair of situations in both of which $P(E\,|\,C) = 1.0$ and $P(E\,|\,{\sim}C) = 1.0$. Here, we expect judgments to be close to zero. The interesting condition shown on the right is where all of the occurrences of the effect in the absence of the target cause are predicted by another event X. Experiments have shown that despite the fact that the conditional probabilities relating to C are identical in these two conditions, judgments will be much higher in the latter case in which a distinct "signal" for the occurrences of the effect in the absence of the target cause is present (Shanks, 1989). It is as if these effects are screened off or discounted in the assessment of the causal power of C. Figure 11.2c shows three sets of situations in all of which $P(E\,|\,C) = 1.0$ and $P(E\,|\,{\sim}C) = 0.5$. The target cue C is always accompanied by another cue X.

Note that in the left-hand panel, X also occurs on trials where C is absent, and on those trials the effect occurs (the complete set of trial types is therefore CX→E, X→E, Y→~E, where the notation refers to the potential causes present on different trial types and whether the target effect is present or absent), whereas in the centre panel, when X occurs on trials where C is absent, the effect does not occur (the set is CX→E, X→~E, Y→E). Numerous experiments have demonstrated that the causal connection between X and E which is learned in the former condition "blocks" learning a connection between C and E, relative to the latter control condition (e.g., Chapman & Robbins, 1990).

Lastly, the right-hand panel of Figure 11.2c again illustrates a condition in which $P(E|C) = 1.0$ and $P(E|{\sim}C) = 0.5$. The target cue C is always accompanied by another cue X, and X occurs on other occasions with Y and no effect, while Y predicts E by itself (the set is CX→E, XY→~E, Y→E). This scenario leads to "superlearning" (e.g., Aitken, Larkin, & Dickinson, 2000) with the relationship between C and E being judged especially strong (and in particular stronger than the control condition in the centre panel of Figure 11.2c). Thus judgments tend to increase moving from left to right across the three panels of the figure. Superlearning emerges in situations where one cue (X) is strongly preventative of an effect as a result of a negative contingency established on XY→~E and Y→E trials. When the effect is then seen to occur on trials in which X is combined with C, participants infer that C must have sufficient supernormal power to overcome the preventative effect of X. A drug which causes a headache when taken in conjunction with aspirin must have supernormal power to cause headache.

What all these cases illustrate is that judgments of a target relationship between C and E may vary as a function of the causal influence of other co-occurring events, even if the conditional probabilities $P(E|C)$ and $P(E|{\sim}C)$ are unaffected. How are we to explain such effects? This question has two answers, one normative and the other theoretical. From a normative perspective, the important point to realize is that ΔP and p can only accurately be measured across sets of events in which all other potential causal factors are held constant. Consider the relationship between coffee consumption and lung cancer. If coffee-drinkers happen to be more likely to smoke than non-coffee-drinkers, a positive value of ΔP might be obtained for this relationship despite the absence of a direct causal relationship. To determine whether coffee consumption and lung cancer are truly causally related, we need to know the probability of lung cancer in coffee-drinkers who smoke versus in non-coffee-drinkers who smoke, or the probability of lung cancer in coffee-drinkers who don't smoke versus in non-coffee-drinkers who don't smoke, that is, in situations in which relevant alternative potential causes (smoking) are held constant. A persuasive justification for this requirement can be found in Glymour and Cheng (1998). Just as in good experimental design, confounding factors have to be controlled or held constant. In the case of blocking, for example, ΔP has to be calculated across a subset of events instead of across all events. For the illustration given in Figure 11.2c, the relevant events are CX→E and X→E for the blocking condition and CX→E and X→~E for the control condition. Holding other things constant (i.e., the presence of X), ΔP is 0 in the first case and 1 in the second, justifying the blocking effect.

From a theoretical perspective, cue interaction effects tell us that a plausible causal induction mechanism will have to compute conditional, not unconditional contrasts. The ability of various candidate mechanisms to achieve this has been the subject of some exploration. For instance, associative learning models in which cause–effect relationships are incremented or decremented on a trial-by-trial basis according to an error-correcting learning algorithm (Dickinson, 2001) are known to compute conditional contrasts in a fairly broad range on situations (Cheng, 1997).

Chains of causal inferences

There is recent evidence from several studies that the causal power attributed to a cue can be affected by chains of retrospective inferences (De Houwer & Beckers, 2002; Denniston, Savastano, Blaisdell, & Miller, 2003; Melchers, Lachnit, & Shanks, 2004). In those experiments, cue A was presented in compound with another cue B and cue B was also presented on other occasions in compound with cue C. Both of these compounds were paired with an effect (AB→E, BC→E). Suppose that cue C is then subsequently presented by itself and either followed by the effect (C→E) or not (C→~E). "Retrospective revaluation" of cue B refers to the fact that the judged causal status of B is reduced in the condition where C was paired with E compared to the condition where C was not paired with E. It is as if participants reason that if C is alone sufficient to cause E, then it should be retrospectively attributed all of the available causal influence that can be allocated on BC trials, with B losing causal power. But in addition to this, (second-order) retrospective revaluation of cue A is also found with greater causal influence attributed to A in the C→E than in the C→~E group. This seems to provide evidence of a chain of backward inferences: if C is alone sufficient to cause E, then it should be retrospectively attributed all of the available causal influence that can be allocated on BC trials. This in turn means that the causal power attributed to B is reduced, but since B was also present on AB→E trials, A must therefore be attributed greater causal influence. The surprising fact about these chains is that they occur in online learning situations where the AB→E and BC→E events have to be retrieved from memory; they also, remarkably, appear to occur in animals (Denniston et al., 2003).

From a theoretical perspective, these effects may appear entirely in keeping with a rational view of causal judgment, but there is nevertheless an interesting feature of them which has considerable theoretical significance. Melchers et al. (2004) have found that forward and backward effects have a different basis as the nature of these inferences is very dependent on the order in which the relevant information is presented (Larkin, Aitken, & Dickinson, 1998). When the trials are presented in the backward order described above (i.e., AB→E and BC→E in the first stage, C→E or C→~E in the second stage), the magnitude of the retrospective revaluation of A correlates significantly with participants' memory for the stage 1 trial types: participants who can recall that A and B co-occurred and predicted the effect (there were many other trial types in the experiment so this is not a trivial thing to recollect), and that B and C together predicted the effect, tended to show large changes in their judgments of the causal power of A, while participants who failed to recall these event types showed much weaker revaluation effects. However when the events are presented in the reversed (forward) order (i.e., C→E or C→~E in the first stage, AB→E and BC→E in the second stage) the corresponding correlation is zero (Melchers et al., 2004). How can this be?

This result is one of the strongest pieces of evidence for believing that an incremental, associative process plays a role in causal judgment (Dickinson, 2001). Associative models are very sensitive to the order in which information is presented and provide rather different theoretical explanations for forward and backward effects. Fleshing out this assertion is beyond the scope of the present chapter, but demonstrations that covariation and causal judgments depend on trial order are not only of normative interest but have also been of considerable significance in attempts to characterize the mechanisms controlling such judgments. Although they certainly would find several of the results described in this chapter difficult to explain, associative models seem to capture some of the processes intrinsic to covariation and causal judgment.

Expectancies and Prior Knowledge

In this section I briefly review some evidence that, in addition to the "bottom-up" factors discussed so far, expectancies and prior knowledge may play an important role in causal judgments. Much fuller reviews of this issue were conducted by Alloy and Tabachnik (1984) and Jennings, Amabile, and Ross (1982).

To this point, all of the examples of causal reasoning I have considered have involved prediction from causes to effects. Information about the occurrence of some cause or set of causes is available and on the basis of that information we judge whether or not some effect is likely to occur. However it is also possible to infer causes from effects: that is to say, on the basis of information about the occurrence of an effect or set of effects, we can reason backwards to the occurrence of some cause or set of causes. Technically such inferences should be called "diagnostic" rather than "predictive." A doctor who observes some symptoms and judges that the patient has a certain disease is usually engaging in diagnostic reasoning: influenza (disease) causes high temperature (symptom), for instance.

The predictive/diagnostic distinction has been the subject of some investigation because different normative rules apply to them. Consider a situation in which a doctor is trying to judge the likelihood that a patient will develop high temperature on the basis of certain knowledge that the person has influenza, and let us assume for the sake of argument that the power of influenza to cause high temperature is close to 1 (Figure 11.3a). The doctor should rate this likelihood as high, and this judgment should, normatively, be unaffected by other symptoms (effects) such as fatigue which the doctor may or may not believe will also occur. To put it another way, the doctor should not care about other symptoms. Effects are independent of one another, conditional on their common cause, in the sense that the probability of an effect E1 given cause C is the same whether or not effect E2 is present (see Glymour & Cheng, 1998), that is $P(E1|C \& E2) = P(E1|C)$. The probability of lung cancer, given that one smokes, is the same regardless of whether or not one has yellow fingers. It is smoking that causes lung cancer, not yellow fingers.

Now imagine that the doctor is trying to judge the likelihood that the patient has influenza on the basis of certain knowledge that the person has a high temperature

(a)   (b)

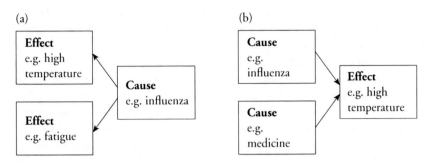

Figure 11.3 Effects of a common cause (panel a) and competing causes for an effect (panel b)

(Figure 11.3b). In this case the doctor's judgment should, normatively, be affected by other factors (causes) which may or may not also be present. For example, if the patient has just taken a medicine known to elevate body temperature, the inference from temperature to influenza is undermined even though the causal power of influenza to cause a high temperature is large. The two situations are not normatively the same. In the second (diagnostic) case, the doctor needs to know about alternative potential causes, whereas in the first (causal) case, he/she does not need to know about other co-occurring effects. The probability of cause C1 given effect E depends on whether or not cause C2 is present, that is $P(C1|E \& C2) \neq P(C1|E)$. The problems should yield different outcomes if participants' prior knowledge and expectancies about these constraints on causal influence are brought to bear.

A number of studies have presented participants with structurally identical inference problems requiring either predictive or diagnostic causal judgments. Although the outcomes of these studies have not been decisive, there does seem to be evidence that people are sometimes aware of the normative considerations and that they are sometimes unaware. In an experiment by Waldmann (2001) for instance, participants either saw repeated trials on which two causes predicted a single effect or trials on which two effects diagnosed a single cause. When asked to rate the strength of the causal link in the former case, judgments for one of the causes were discounted by the presence of the other cause. In contrast, when asked to rate causal strength in the latter (diagnostic) case, judgments for one of the effects were not discounted by the presence of the other effect. In contrast, in some rather similar causal judgment tasks, Cobos et al. (2002) found no difference between judgments in the predictive and diagnostic conditions, suggesting a normative violation. In all of these studies, considerable care was taken to check that participants fully understood the causal structure of the relevant events. Further research is needed to clarify the reasons why judgments do or do not respect this structural constraint.

Another example of the importance of people's interpretation of a causal scenario is provided by an elegant experiment by Buehner and May (2002). It is well known that causal judgments tend to be inversely related to the experienced time delay between cause and effect (Shanks et al., 1989). Buehner and May asked whether prior expectancies might alter this delay effect. In one condition they required their participants to judge the extent to which pressing a switch caused a light to illuminate, a condition designed to recruit prior expectations of an immediate causal influence. Under these circumstances participants rated the relationship as strong when the cause–effect delay was short but were very intolerant of longer cause–effect delays. In contrast, they were much more tolerant of longer cause–effect delays when the instructions led them to expect a delayed effect: in a second condition, participants judged the relationship between launching a grenade and a subsequent explosion. This scenario, of course, was designed to foster an expectation of a delay between cause and effect. Thus the very same experienced frequencies can lead to different causal judgments depending on people's expectations. In the extreme, one might imagine that judgments would be stronger at a long cause–effect delay than at a short one, though Buehner and May were not able to elicit this effect. Surely we would be more likely to attribute an upset stomach to something we have eaten when the delay is moderate (tens of minutes) than when it is instantaneous?

Concluding Comments

Contrary to a view commonly expressed in textbooks, people are quite good at detecting covariations and causal relations, especially when the events on which they are basing their judgments are distributed across time. Nevertheless, a number of normative violations have been repeatedly observed. This simple statement masks, however, a considerable amount of complexity in describing what exactly the norms are against which judgments of covariation and causation should be assessed. In the case of covariation, standard metrics such as r and ΔP are generally agreed to be appropriate, with the latter being particularly relevant when a directional covariation is being judged. In the case of causal relationships, in contrast, these measures do not seem to be appropriate: the "ceiling effect," for instance, suggests that $\Delta P = 0$ in cases where causation may be indeterminate. The power theory has been offered as a partial solution which makes a clear distinction between covariation and causation. Recent evidence is broadly consistent with the power theory provided that one acknowledges the potential for ambiguity in people's understanding of causal judgment questions.

Nevertheless, numerous findings have proven difficult to encompass within this normative framework. For example, causal judgments are very sensitive to the order in which information is presented and to the frequency with which judgments are elicited. These and other findings have led researchers to propose judgment models which bear little resemblance to normative judgment rules (e.g., Collins & Shanks, 2002; Maldonado, Catena, Cándido, & García, 1999).

One important area of research, which has only been touched on here, is the attempt to specify in algorithmic terms how judgments of covariation and causation are derived. A number of computational models have been proposed which tend to fall into two broad sets: those that assume some mental version of a judgment rule such as the ΔP rule (e.g., Cheng & Holyoak, 1995) and those that assume an incremental associative learning process (e.g., Dickinson, 2001). There is lively debate about the relative merits of these approaches (Shanks, Holyoak, & Medin, 1996).

A number of areas have been highlighted in the present chapter as important topics for further research. Among these are the significance of the wording of the probe question on conformity to normative standards, the basis of chains of causal inferences, and the basis of adaptation effects. These and other questions will continue to drive research in the rich field of covariation and causal judgment for some time to come.

Acknowledgments

The research described here was supported by a grant from the United Kingdom Biotechnology and Biological Sciences Research Council. The work is part of the program of the ESRC Centre for Economic Learning and Social Evolution, University College London. I thank Darrell Collins and Dave Lagnado for useful discussions on the content of this chapter.

Notes

1   When provided with a mechanism – unmarried people tend to have more cats than married ones – the relationship doesn't seem so bizarre.
2   The term "contingency" is often used to refer to unidirectional covariation between dichotomous or discrete variables. I shall use the term "covariation" to refer to relationships between both continuous and discrete variables.
3   One should be very cautious about drawing inferences from these correlations. Almost all judgment models are highly correlated with each other (McKenzie, 1994), so even if a model correlates well with judgments, another strategy might correlate even higher. More significant are cases where a given model makes a qualitative prediction which is either borne out or falsified by the data.

References

Aitken, M. R. F., Larkin, M. J. W., & Dickinson, A. (2000) Super-learning of causal judgements, *Quarterly Journal of Experimental Psychology*, 53B, 59–81.
Allan, L. G. (1980) A note on measurement of contingency between two binary variables in judgment tasks, *Bulletin of the Psychonomic Society*, 15, 147–9.
Alloy, L. B. & Tabachnik, N. (1984) Assessment of covariation by humans and animals: The joint influence of prior expectations and current situational information, *Psychological Review*, 91, 112–49.
Boynton, D. M. (2000) The psychophysics of informal covariation assessment: Perceiving relatedness against a background of dispersion, *Journal of Experimental Psychology: Human Perception and Performance*, 26, 867–76.
Broniarczyk, S. M. & Alba, J. W. (1994) Theory versus data in prediction and correlation tasks, *Organizational Behavior and Human Decision Processes*, 57, 117–39.
Buehner, M. J., Cheng, P. W., & Clifford, D. (2003) From covariation to causation: A test of the assumption of causal power, *Journal of Experimental Psychology: Learning, Memory, and Cognition*, 29, 1119–40.
Buehner, M. J. & May, J. (2002) Knowledge mediates the timeframe of covariation assessment in human causal induction, *Thinking and Reasoning*, 8, 269–95.

Buehner, M. J. & May, J. (2003) Rethinking temporal contiguity and the judgement of causality: Effects of prior knowledge, experience, and reinforcement procedure, *Quarterly Journal of Experimental Psychology*, 56A, 865–90.

Chapman, G. B. & Robbins, S. J. (1990) Cue interaction in human contingency judgment, *Memory & Cognition*, 18, 537–45.

Chapman, L. J. & Chapman, J. P. (1969) Illusory correlation as an obstacle to the use of valid psychodiagnostic signs, *Journal of Abnormal Psychology*, 74, 271–80.

Cheng, P. W. (1997) From covariation to causation: A causal power theory, *Psychological Review*, 104, 367–405.

Cheng, P. W. & Holyoak, K. J. (1995) Complex adaptive systems as intuitive statisticians: Causality, contingency, and prediction. In H. L. Roitblat and J.-A. Meyer (eds.), *Comparative Approaches to Cognitive Science* (pp. 271–302). Cambridge, MA: MIT Press.

Cobos, P. L., López, F. J., Caño, A., Almaraz, J., & Shanks, D. R. (2002) Mechanisms of predictive and diagnostic causal induction, *Journal of Experimental Psychology: Animal Behavior Processes*, 28, 331–46.

Collins, D. J. & Shanks, D. R. (2002) Momentary and integrative response strategies in causal judgment, *Memory & Cognition*, 30, 1138–47.

Collins, D. J. & Shanks, D. R. (2003) Conformity to the power PC theory of causal induction depends on type of probe question. Manuscript submitted for publication.

De Houwer, J. & Beckers, T. (2002) Higher-order retrospective revaluation in human causal learning, *Quarterly Journal of Experimental Psychology*, 55B, 137–51.

De Houwer, J., Beckers, T., & Glautier, S. (2002) Outcome and cue properties modulate blocking, *Quarterly Journal of Experimental Psychology*, 55A, 965–85.

Dennis, M. J. & Ahn, W.-K. (2001) Primacy in causal strength judgments: The effect of initial evidence for generative versus inhibitory relationships, *Memory & Cognition*, 29, 152–64.

Denniston, J. C., Savastano, H. I., Blaisdell, A. P., & Miller, R. R. (2003) Cue competition as a retrieval deficit, *Learning and Motivation*, 34, 1–31.

Dickinson, A. (2001) Causal learning: An associative analysis (The 28th Bartlett Memorial Lecture), *Quarterly Journal of Experimental Psychology*, 54B, 3–25.

Glymour, C. & Cheng, P. W. (1998) Causal mechanism and probability: A normative approach. In M. Oaksford and N. Chater (eds.), *Rational Models of Cognition* (pp. 295–313). Oxford: Oxford University Press.

Gredebäck, G., Winman, A., & Juslin, P. (2000) Rational assessments of covariation and causality. In L. R. Gleitman and A. K. Joshi (eds.), *Proceedings of the 22nd Annual Conference of the Cognitive Science Society*. Mahwah, NJ: Lawrence Erlbaum.

Hesslow, G. (1976) Two notes on the probabilistic approach to causality, *Philosophy of Science*, 43, 290–2.

Jennings, D. L., Amabile, T. M., & Ross, L. (1982) Informal covariation assessment: Data-based versus theory-based judgments. In D. Kahneman, P. Slovic, and A. Tversky (eds.), *Judgment Under Uncertainty: Heuristics and Biases* (pp. 211–30). Cambridge: Cambridge University Press.

Larkin, M. J. W., Aitken, M. R. F., & Dickinson, A. (1998) Retrospective revaluation of causal judgments under positive and negative contingencies, *Journal of Experimental Psychology: Learning, Memory, and Cognition*, 24, 1331–52.

Lober, K. & Shanks, D. R. (2000) Is causal induction based on causal power? Critique of Cheng (1997), *Psychological Review*, 107, 195–212.

Maldonado, A., Catena, A., Cándido, A., & García, I. (1999) The belief revision model: Asymmetrical effects of noncontingency on human covariation learning, *Animal Learning and Behavior*, 27, 168–80.

Matute, H., Arcediano, F., & Miller, R. R. (1996) Test question modulates cue competition between causes and between effects, *Journal of Experimental Psychology: Learning, Memory, and Cognition*, 22, 182–96.

Matute, H., Vegas, S., & De Marez, P. J. (2002) Flexible use of recent information in causal and predictive judgments, *Journal of Experimental Psychology: Learning, Memory, and Cognition*, 28, 714–25.

McKenzie, C. R. M. (1994) The accuracy of intuitive judgment strategies: Covariation assessment and Bayesian inference, *Cognitive Psychology*, 26, 209–39.

Melchers, K. G., Lachnit, H., & Shanks, D. R. (2004) Within-compound associations in retro-spective revaluation and in direct learning: A challenge for comparator theory, *Quarterly Journal of Experimental Psychology*, 56B, 25–53.

Shanks, D. R. (1989) Selectional processes in causality judgment, *Memory & Cognition*, 17, 27–34.

Shanks, D. R. (1993) Associative versus contingency accounts of category learning: Reply to Melz, Cheng, Holyoak, and Waldmann (1993), *Journal of Experimental Psychology: Learning, Memory, and Cognition*, 19, 1411–23.

Shanks, D. R., Holyoak, K. J., & Medin, D. L. (eds.) (1996) *The Psychology of Learning and Motivation vol. 34): Causal Learning.* San Diego, CA: Academic Press.

Shanks, D. R., López, F. J., Darby, R. J., & Dickinson, A. (1996) Distinguishing associative and probabilistic contrast theories of human contingency judgment. In D. R. Shanks, K. J. Holyoak, and D. L. Medin (eds.), *The Psychology of Learning and Motivation: Causal Learning* (vol. 34, pp. 265–311). San Diego, CA: Academic Press.

Shanks, D. R., Pearson, S. M., & Dickinson, A. (1989) Temporal contiguity and the judgment of causality, *Quarterly Journal of Experimental Psychology*, 41B, 139–59.

Spellman, B. A. (1996) Conditionalizing causality. In D. R. Shanks, K. J. Holyoak & D. L. Medin (eds.), *The Psychology of Learning and Motivation: Causal Learning* (vol. 34, pp. 167–206). San Diego, CA: Academic Press.

Waldmann, M. R. (2001) Predictive versus diagnostic causal learning: Evidence from an over-shadowing paradigm, *Psychonomic Bulletin & Review*, 8, 600–8.

Wasserman, E. A., Elek, S. M., Chatlosh, D. L., & Baker, A. G. (1993) Rating causal relations: The role of probability in judgments of response-outcome contingency, *Journal of Experimental Psychology: Learning, Memory, and Cognition*, 19, 174–88.

Well, A. D., Boyce, S. J., Morris, R. K., Shinjo, M., & Chumbley, J. I. (1988) Prediction and judgment as indicators of sensitivity to covariation of continuous variables, *Memory & Cognition*, 16, 271–80.

12

A Tale of Tuned Decks? Anchoring as Accessibility and Anchoring as Adjustment

Nicholas Epley

Introduction

Ralph Hull made a reasonable living as a magician milking a card trick he called "The Tuned Deck" (Hilliard, 1938). The trick itself was unremarkable – subjects removed a card (yes, any card), identified it, and returned it anonymously to the deck. Hull claimed he could hear the chosen card ring a tune when he struck the deck with his finger and, after the requisite deck-flicking, would (*voilà!*) remove the chosen card. This trick became famous not for its ability to stump the gullible public – nearly all can do that – but for its ability to stump fellow magicians. Hull enjoyed subjecting himself to the scrutiny of colleagues who attempted to eliminate, one by one, various explanations by depriving him of the ability to perform a particular slight of hand. But the real trick was over before it had even begun, for the magic was not in clever fingers but in a clever name. The blatantly singular referent cried out for a blatantly singular explanation, when in reality The Tuned Deck was not one trick but many. The search for a single explanation is what kept this multiply determined illusion so long a mystery.

The mind, of course, has its fair share of tuned decks – singular referents that actually describe multiple mental tricks. "Consciousness," for example, is exactly the kind of thing that *should* reside in a single seat, but appears to spread its real-estate around the brain and is actually the product of multiple regions operating in unity (Zeki, 2003). So too with attention (Nakayama & Joseph, 1998), intelligence (Duncan et al., 2000), language (Pinker, 1994), and memory (Schacter, 1996) – all singular referents describing multiply determined phenomena. Searching for a single explanation in these cases is likely to leave interested psychologists, like Hull's audiences, with little to say.

This chapter is intended to add one of the most widely studied biases in human judgment to this list of psychological tuned decks – judgmental anchoring. Across ever-expanding domains, people's estimates of uncertain qualities are biased in the direction of a salient comparison value or "anchor." Although easy to demonstrate, such anchoring biases have not been so easy to explain (Strack & Mussweiler, 1997). One reason for this difficulty, it appears, is that psychologists have been seeking a single solution. In fact, judgmental anchoring is not a single mental trick but a set of tricks. How many tricks? At least two.

Anchors Aweigh

People's judgments are often inordinately influenced by the first information that comes to mind. Assessments of others' perceptions are unduly tied to one's own (Kenny & DePaulo, 1993; Keysar & Barr, 2002), impressions of others' personalities overly influenced by automatic dispositional inferences (Gilbert, 2002), inferences about pairs of attributes based heavily on the first attribute evaluated (Rottenstreich & Tversky, 1997), and answers to general knowledge questions biased in the direction of irrelevant values considered early in the processing stream (Chapman & Johnson, 2002).

These effects, and many like them, have traditionally been called an "anchoring effect" – an umbrella description that includes almost any judgment that is assimilated to an anchor value. Anchors come in numerous varieties, are presented or activated in very different paradigms, and bias judgments in widely dispersed domains. For example, some anchors are generated by participants themselves whereas others are provided by an experimenter or external source. Most anchoring effects are observed in an experimental paradigm involving a two-step process involving an explicit consideration of the anchor value whereas others are produced in the absence of any explicit comparison. Anchoring effects have been observed in probability estimates (Plous, 1989), legal decisions (Englich & Mussweiler, 2001), general knowledge questions (Tversky & Kahneman, 1974), consumer purchases (Wansink, Kent, & Hoch, 1998), and population frequencies (Rottenstreich & Tversky, 1997), just to name a few. Although "anchoring" may provide a nice description of the behavioral effects observed in these varied contexts, it may not be especially helpful for understanding the psychological processes that produce them.

The proliferation of these anchoring effects began after Tversky and Kahneman (1974) included the anchoring and adjustment heuristic in their seminal paper describing three basic heuristics that guide intuitive judgment (the other two being availability and representativeness). Tversky and Kahneman argued that people sometimes simplify complicated assessments by "starting from an initial value that is adjusted to yield the final answer" (p. 1128). Presumably this adjustment process would involve some kind of iterative consideration of estimates ever further from the initial anchor until a plausible estimate is reached (Quattrone, 1982). Thus, a person might estimate the cost of a new Toyota Camry by inflating the cost of last year's model, or estimate the height of the second tallest mountain in the world (K-2) by adjusting down from the first (Mt. Everest). This heuristic simplifies judgment by substituting an easily accessible value that can be serially adjusted for a more complicated search that might involve a trip to the library. Although clearly helpful, Tversky & Kahneman (1974) suggested that "adjustments are typically insufficient" (p. 1128), leaving final estimates biased in the direction of the original anchor value.

To demonstrate the operation of this heuristic, Tversky & Kahneman (1974) developed a research paradigm that quickly acquired a research life of its own. This paradigm utilizes a two-stage process in which participants are initially asked to make a comparative assessment (e.g., Was Aristotle born before or after AD 1825?), followed by an absolute estimate (e.g., In what year was Aristotle actually born?). Countless experiments have demonstrated that people's absolute estimates are biased in the direction of the anchor value considered in the comparative assessment (for a review see Chapman & Johnson, 2002). People estimate, for example, that Aristotle was born in 140 BC if they first estimated whether he was born before or after AD 1825, but that he was born more than 1,000 years earlier if they first estimated whether he was born before or after 25,000 BC (Strack & Mussweiler, 1997).

The most obvious interpretation of these results is that participants take the anchor value as a hint to the answer, based on conversational logic that speakers mention only relevant information (Grice, 1975). However, the most interesting experiments utilizing this standard anchoring paradigm take great pains to inform participants that the anchor value was chosen randomly, or is completely uninformative. For example, anchoring effects are observed even when anchors are obtained by spinning a roulette wheel (Tversky & Kahneman, 1974), by using the participant's experiment number (Switzer & Sniezek, 1991), by adding a constant to the participant's phone number (Russo & Schoemaker, 1989), or by drawing a number from a hat (Cervone & Peake, 1986). Conversational logic may contribute to a great many anchoring effects in daily discourse, but it cannot explain the overwhelming number of demonstrations involving patently accidental anchors.

Instead, the results from this experimental paradigm have traditionally been interpreted as the product of insufficient adjustment from the anchor value considered in the comparative assessment. People start, the explanation goes, by rejecting the anchor value mentioned in the comparative assessment and then adjust in a serial, deliberate, and conscious fashion until they reach a plausible estimate. Because adjustments terminate at the outer range of plausible estimates, they tend to be insufficient (Quattrone, Lawrence, Finkel, & Andrus, 1981).

But while the race was on to demonstrate near and far that people incorporate irrelevant anchors into numeric estimates, nobody seemed to notice an experimental sleight of hand. In fact, recent research has demonstrated that the similarities between the anchoring and adjustment "heuristic" and the paradigm used to elucidate it are only skin deep. Ironically, the paradigm long used to reveal the anchoring and adjustment heuristic does not involve adjustment away from an anchor value at all. Instead, it appears that the anchoring and adjustment heuristic operates in an entirely different context, and the two-step procedure used to demonstrate it involves an entirely different process.

Heuristics versus Biases

Heuristics are short-cut rules used to simplify otherwise exceedingly difficult problems. One may not know, for example, whether another person is an athlete or not but can confidently guess by assessing the extent to which the person is similar to the proto-typical athlete. And a perfectly calibrated assessment of one's own assertiveness would require an elaborate memory search (or a review of one's diary), but an intuition can be generated by considering the ease with which instances of assertive behavior come to mind.

The anchoring and adjustment heuristic describes cases in which one automatically generates a value known to be close to the right answer but in need of adjustment. The automatic recruitment of an anchor value that is close but wrong is followed by a con-trolled process of serial adjustment away from that anchor to incorporate other relevant information. Quattrone (1982), for example, suggested that people explain others' behavior by initially anchoring on a dispositional attribution and subsequently adjusting to accom-modate situational constraints. Griffin & Tversky (1992) suggested that people deter-mine the weighting of information in judgment by initially anchoring on its strength or extremity and subsequently adjusting to accommodate its validity. And Keysar & Barr (2002) suggested people understand another's communication by anchoring on their own egocentric interpretation and only subsequently adjusting to accommodate the speaker's perspective. In all of these cases people begin with a readily accessible assess-ment – a dispositional inference, the extremity of information, one's own perspective – that is adjusted to arrive at an actual answer.

Notice, however, that the anchors provided in the standard anchoring paradigm are considerably different than these "self-generated" anchors. They are not values generated automatically by participants to simplify an otherwise difficult assessment, but rather ones provided by an experimenter or external source. These anchors are novel values that must be explicitly considered, no matter how irrelevant, to answer a comparative judg-ment. They are *not* instantly known without reflection to be wrong (even if they are completely implausible), nor are they automatically perceived to be close to the right answer and thus in need of only slight adjustment. Instead, they involve two deliberate attempts to answer two very different questions, one comparative and one absolute. This difference in the context in which anchors are generated, as well as the knowledge that comes attached to them, produces anchoring effects that look descriptively similar but that are psychologically distinct.

The remainder of this chapter will present evidence for multiple mechanisms in judgmental anchoring. It will focus on what is generally considered to be a single literature on anchoring effects in human judgment that actually comprises two distinct paths of research, one addressing the standard anchoring paradigm and another addressing the anchoring and adjustment heuristic.

Understanding the Paradigm: Anchoring as Accessibility

Many psychological findings depend upon a variety of situational factors, and it is therefore a refreshing truism that human judgment is guided by accessible information (Higgins, 1996). But *what* is accessible at any point in time, returning quickly to familiar territory, depends on a variety of situational factors. Patently irrelevant anchors can influence intuitive judgment when the situational factors are aligned in exactly the ways that heighten the accessibility of anchor-consistent information and diminish the accessibility of anchor-inconsistent information. As it happens, the standard anchoring paradigm – and the everyday contexts that mimic it – do just that.

Recall that the standard anchoring paradigm consists of two steps – an initial comparative assessment followed by an absolute judgment. In the comparative assessment, participants are asked to compare the (irrelevant) anchor value to a target, such as "Is the maximum speed of a house cat more or less than 35 mph?" (Jacowitz & Kahneman, 1995). Assuming that even the most ardent cat lover would not know their pet's maximum speed, participants must retrieve knowledge to generate an answer. Not all retrievable knowledge, however, is equally helpful. Knowledge related to the anchor value – e.g., knowledge about other fast-moving animals or objects – is more helpful than knowledge unrelated to it – e.g., knowledge about slow-moving animals – when assessing whether or not an anchor value is correct (Klayman & Ha, 1987). Consequently, participants' retrieval is guided by the hypothesis implied in the comparative assessment (Tversky, 1977). In particular, Mussweiler & Strack (1999) have suggested that people generate an answer to these comparative assessments by "testing the hypothesis that the target's value is equal to the anchor" (p. 138) – in other words, "Is the maximum speed of a house cat equal to 35 mph?" This is likely to increase the accessibility of anchor-consistent information and decrease the accessibility of anchor-inconsistent information. The subsequent absolute estimate – "What is the maximum speed of a house cat?" – is then biased in the direction of the anchor value because it is based upon the accessible information used to answer the comparative assessment. This "Selective Accessibility" account is also consistent with models that suggest anchors increase the consideration of common features between the target and anchor and decrease the consideration of unique features (Chapman & Johnson, 1994; Jacowitz & Kahneman, 1995).

At least four findings are consistent with this account and demonstrate that irrelevant anchors increase the accessibility of anchor-consistent information. First, people attend to shared features between the anchor and target more than to unique features. For example, participants in one experiment reported how much they would be willing to pay for an apartment after explicitly comparing it with the rent of an "anchor" apartment (Chapman & Johnson, 1999). Participants not only spent more time looking at attributes shared by the target and anchor value, but also spent more time looking at positive features when provided a high rent anchor than when provided a low rent anchor. Not surprisingly then, directing participants to attend to differences between the anchor and target substantially diminishes anchoring effects (Chapman & Johnson, 1999; Mussweiler, Strack, & Pfeiffer, 2000).

Second, participants who have just completed the standard anchoring paradigm are faster to identify words consistent with the implications of an anchor value than words inconsistent with it. Those who had just assessed, for instance, whether the annual mean temperature in Germany is more or less than 5°C subsequently recognized winter words (e.g., snow, ski) more quickly than summer words (e.g., beach, swim). The opposite occurred among participants who considered whether the annual mean temperature is more or less than 20°C (Mussweiler & Strack, 2000b).

Third, altering the hypothesis tested in the comparative assessment correspondingly influences the magnitude of anchoring effects. If the comparative assessment renders anchor-consistent evidence more accessible because people evaluate whether the anchor value is equal to the target, then asking them to first determine whether the anchor is *more* than the target value or not should increase absolute estimates and asking whether the anchor is *less* than the target value should decrease absolute estimates, exactly the effect reported by Mussweiler & Strack (1999). Participants in this experiment thought the Elbe River, for example, was longer after initially evaluating whether it was *longer* than 890 kilometers than after evaluating whether it was *shorter* than 890 kilometers.

Finally, participants who are knowledgeable in a particular domain and thus better able to generate evidence consistent with an extreme anchor value are less influenced by irrelevant anchor values than participants who are not knowledgeable (Mussweiler & Strack, 2000a; Wilson, Houston, Etling, & Brekke, 1996). In addition, people who are more confident in their estimates within the standard anchoring paradigm generally show weaker anchoring effects than people who are less confident, presumably because more confident participants found it easier to generate anchor-inconsistent information (Jacowitz & Kahneman, 1995; Wilson et al., 1996).

This evidence suggests that most of the action in producing anchoring effects within this paradigm comes in the first comparative assessment. Explicitly comparing a target with an anchor value – even an irrelevant one – facilitates the recruitment of information consistent with the anchor value, creating an accessible pool of systematically biased evidence. Altering the hypothesis considered in this comparative assessment alters the magnitude of anchoring effects considerably, and removing it altogether by simply priming participants with a numerical value before making an absolute estimate produces relatively weak and unreliable anchoring effects (Brewer & Chapman, 2002; Chapman & Bornstein, 1996; Wilson et al., 1996).

However, accessible information is not applied in *any* judgment, just when it is relevant to the judgment at hand (Higgins, 1996). The standard anchoring paradigm not only facilitates the recruitment of anchor-consistent information but also its applicability to an absolute estimate because the two steps in this procedure generally involve the same target. This close relation means that judges are likely to rely on the information generated during the comparative assessment to make an absolute estimate. Because that information is biased in the direction of the anchor value, so too are absolute estimates.

Two findings in particular highlight the importance of applicability in the standard anchoring paradigm. First, reducing the relevance of the information generated during the comparative assessment dramatically alters the magnitude of anchoring effects, sometimes eliminating them altogether. For example, participants in one experiment were asked whether the height of the Cathedral in Cologne was more or less than a high or low anchor value, and then estimated either the actual height or length of the Cathedral (Strack & Mussweiler, 1997). Anchoring effects appeared only when the comparative and absolute assessments were on the same dimensions, and disappeared when they were on different dimensions (see also Chapman & Johnson, 1994; Mussweiler & Strack, 2001b; Wong & Kwong, 2000). This is important not only for understanding the underlying mechanisms of these anchoring effects, but also for identifying boundary conditions. Making a numeric estimate will not automatically influence any subsequent judgment – as a quick perusal of the anchoring literature might suggest – only judgments that are clearly relevant.

The second finding demonstrating the importance of applicability is that the speed with which judges answer the comparative and absolute assessments tend to be negatively correlated (Mussweiler & Strack, 1999). This suggests that the more applicable the information generated during the comparative assessment is to the absolute estimate, the easier the absolute assessment is to make.

Collectively, the findings in this section strongly suggest that anchoring effects in the standard anchoring paradigm are produced by the biased accessibility of anchor consistent information, rather than by insufficient adjustment from an irrelevant anchor. Although many of the findings reviewed in this section are consistent with an insufficient adjustment account, it is not clear that any of them would have been predicted by it. More troublesome for an adjustment account within this paradigm is that manipulations that ought to influence a deliberate, effortful, and serial adjustment process do not influence responses. Distracting participants' attention with a simultaneous task, for example, ought to hinder people's ability to engage in effortful adjustment but it does nothing to responses in the standard anchoring paradigm (Epley & Gilovich, 2004b; Mussweiler & Strack, 1999). So too with financial incentives for accuracy and forewarning of bias that ought to lengthen adjustment by increasing the tendency to engage in effortful thought, but do not influence responses in the standard anchoring paradigm (for a review see Chapman & Johnson, 2002). An accessibility-based account of anchoring, however, has little trouble with these findings as accessibility effects are the paradigmatic example of automatic psychological processes that do not require attentional resources and are generally immune to deliberate corrective procedures.

Extending the Paradigm: Accessibility in Everyday Life

The preceding research can sound like just the kind of academic hair-splitting that irritates one's relatives, as the research can seem like a series of experiments about experiments. Although the standard anchoring paradigm is indeed an experimental task with its own unique attributes, it is important to remember that it is a proxy for some judgments that normal people care about a great deal.

For example, the outcome of an uncertain event seems more obvious or likely once the outcome is actually known. Although likely produced by multiple mechanisms (Hawkins & Hastie, 1991), this "hindsight bias" at least partly involves an implicit comparison of the target with a highly certain anchor value once the outcome is known (see Chapter 13, this volume). This outcome appears to bias the recruitment of evidence consistent with the occurrence of the outcome, increasing retrospective evaluations of likelihood (Koriat, Lichtenstein, & Fischhoff, 1980). Mimicking results in the standard anchoring paradigm, explicit warnings to avoid the hindsight bias do little to dampen its effect (Fischhoff, 1977), but explicitly considering the likelihood that the opposite outcome occurred diminishes the bias (Slovic & Fischhoff, 1977).

More generally, overconfidence seems partly produced by people's failure to consider the likelihood that one's response might be wrong, and biased by the recruitment of response-consistent evidence (Block & Harper, 1991). People are more confident, for example, in the accuracy of others' responses than in the accuracy of their own responses (Koehler, 1994). This presumably occurs because *evaluating* an answer, like evaluating an externally provided anchor, involves biased hypothesis testing and the recruitment of answer-consistent evidence whereas *generating* an answer requires an explicit consideration of alternative responses. As in the standard anchoring paradigm, explicitly asking participants to generate reasons inconsistent with their chosen answer substantially reduces overconfidence (Koriat et al., 1980).

Beyond confidence, social comparisons often involve an implicit or explicit evaluation of the extent to which one is similar or dissimilar to some selected target. Whether one is athletic, attentive, or attractive, for example, depends critically on the standard of comparison. People tend to assimilate their self-assessments toward targets quickly perceived to be similar to themselves (such as members of relevant in-groups) and contrast them away from targets perceived to be dissimilar (such as members of relevant out-groups). The recruitment of features shared with similar targets and unshared with dissimilar targets follows a pattern akin to those in the standard anchoring paradigm, and appears to influence self-assessments in relation to a standard through the same mechanisms (Mussweiler, 2003).

On a more applied level, some everyday contexts are structured in a fashion similar to the standard anchoring paradigm and therefore contain similar anchoring biases. Negotiations, for example, begin with an initial offer that must be explicitly considered. This offer acts as an anchor, as final estimates are consistently biased in the direction of the opening offer (Galinsky & Mussweiler, 2002). Similarly, sentencing decisions by court judges often begin with a suggested sentence by prosecution that acts as an anchor and biases subsequent decisions (Englich & Mussweiler, 2001), as do initial award requests in personal injury verdicts (Chapman & Bornstein, 1996), and listing prices in residential housing assessments (Northcraft & Neale, 1987). Finally, advertisers can make gluttons of us all by introducing anchors into consumer contexts to increase spending. Shoppers in one grocery store, for example, bought nearly twice the number of Snickers bars when the advertisement suggested buying "18 for your freezer" than when it suggested buying "some for your freezer" (Wansink et al., 1998). Each of these contexts naturally involves a salient comparison value whose relation to the target value is unknown and must be implicitly or explicitly assessed. Related contexts that share this feature are also likely to produce anchoring effects through accessibility-based mechanisms, and resulting biases likely reduced by strategies that increase the accessibility of anchor-inconsistent information.

Understanding the Heuristic: Anchoring as Adjustment

The preceding research makes it clear that serial adjustment cannot explain the influence of irrelevant anchor values on human judgment. It would be premature, however, to conclude that the anchoring and adjustment heuristic does not exist. Many anchor values encountered in daily life are quite different from those encountered in the standard anchoring paradigm. They are not values provided by an experimenter or some external source but rather values generated by people to simplify a complicated assessment – in other words, a heuristic. What, for example, is the boiling point of water on the top of Mt. Everest? Or when was George Washington elected President of the United States? Although virtually no one knows the answers to these questions, most can arrive at a reasonable estimate by adjusting from a value they do know. Most know that less heat is required to boil water at higher elevations and water must therefore boil on Everest at less than 212°F, or that the US declared its independence in 1776 and Washington must have been elected shortly thereafter. People make these judgments, it appears, by automatically generating a value that is clearly wrong but known to be close to the right answer and in need of some tinkering. These "self-generated" anchors differ from the "externally provided" anchors encountered in the standard anchoring paradigm because there is no need to consider whether the answer is equal to the anchor – one already knows it is not – and thus no spark to ignite mechanisms of selective accessibility. Instead, people must serially adjust from this anchor value until a plausible estimate is reached.

Several findings demonstrate not only that these self-generated anchors activate serial adjustment but also that this process differs considerably from accessibility-based mechanisms involved in the standard anchoring paradigm. For example, because the adjustment from a self-generated anchor value is conscious and deliberate, people can consciously report utilizing this heuristic when responding to self-generated anchor values as coded by independent raters, but not when responding to externally provided anchoring questions (Epley & Gilovich, 2001).

More compelling, however, are experiments that manipulate adjustment rather than simply measure it. If people adjust from self-generated anchor values that are known to be close to the right answer but in need of adjustment, then anything that influences people's willingness to accept or reject values that come to mind ought to influence the amount of adjustment as well. A person inclined to accept a value as a plausible estimate ought to adjust less than a person inclined to reject that value. Research on attitudes and persuasion suggests that such acceptance and rejection can be manipulated by altering participants' body movements while making judgments. In particular, people are more inclined to accept propositions as true when they listen to them while nodding their heads up and down than while shaking them from side to side (Wells & Petty, 1980). And indeed, participants provided estimates closer to a self-generated anchor when they were simultaneously nodding their heads up and down than when they were shaking them from side to side (Epley & Gilovich, 2001). In addition, participants provided their responses more quickly when nodding their heads than when shaking them, also consistent with a shortened process of serial adjustment. Participants' head movements, however, did not influence either estimates or response times within the standard anchoring paradigm, suggesting two very different mechanisms operating in these two contexts.

A similar asymmetry is found with psychologically similar proprioceptive movements such as pulling up versus pushing down on a table. People tend to respond more favorably to stimuli when adopting an approach posture through arm flexion than when adopting an avoidance posture through arm extension (Caccioppo, Priester, & Berntson, 1993). When responding to self-generated anchors, the favorable evaluation induced by arm flexion (like head nodding) leads participants to provide estimates closer to a self-generated anchor value than does the unfavorable evaluation produced by arm extension (Epley & Gilovich, 2004c). Again, arm position did not influence responses in the standard anchoring paradigm, demonstrating that "self-generated" anchors activate a process of adjustment that "experimenter-provided" anchors do not.

Arguably the most important feature of the anchoring and adjustment heuristic, and the reason it is used to explain a host of judgmental phenomena, is that adjustments tend to be insufficient. The problem with the existing (apparent) evidence for insufficient adjustment is that virtually all of it comes from the standard anchoring paradigm that clearly does not involve adjustment at all. However, two recent findings demonstrate that insufficient adjustment is a hallmark of self-generated anchor values as well. First, people's estimated answers to these questions tend to fall consistently short of the correct answers (Epley & Gilovich, 2004c). People estimate, for example, that George Washington was elected President of the United States somewhere around 1779 when he was actually elected in 1789, suggesting insufficient adjustment from the country's Declaration of Independence in 1776. And participants estimate that Vodka freezes around 1°F when it actually freezes closer to −20°, demonstrating insufficient adjustment from the freezing point of water at 32°F. Notice that a similar comparison to the actual answer within the standard anchoring paradigm is not meaningful because the relationship between the anchor value and answer is arbitrary. Not so, however, with the use of the anchoring and adjustment heuristic because these anchors are activated precisely because they are known to be close to the right answer but in need of adjustment. Second, participants who naturally generate, or who are led to generate, different self-generated anchors provide systematically different answers (Epley & Gilovich, 2004c). These results look similar to those seen in the standard anchoring paradigm, but are in contexts involving serial adjustment rather than selective accessibility.

Although Tversky & Kahneman (1974) offered no explanation for *why* adjustments tend to be insufficient, two subsequent accounts have focused on the attention-demanding nature of adjustment. Fans of one account note that anchors are activated automatically but adjustment requires attention (Gilbert, 2002). Because attention is a limited resource, anything that hinders a person's ability to expend it should shorten adjustment. In a world as complicated and attention demanding as ours, few judgments are given one's full attention, meaning that most adjustments will be insufficient. Several experiments have shown that responses to "self-generated" anchors are uniquely influenced by attentional demands (Epley & Gilovich, 2004b). In one, participants adjusted less when responding to a series of self-generated anchoring questions when they were simultaneously distracted by memorizing an eight-letter string than when they were not distracted. In another, participants who had consumed alcohol at a campus-wide party adjusted less from a series of self-generated anchors than participants who had not consumed alcohol. And finally, people who dislike effortful thinking – those low in Need for Cognition (Cacioppo & Petty, 1982) – adjust less from self-generated anchors than those who love effortful thinking. Neither busyness, drunkenness, nor cognitive laziness, however, influenced responses to externally provided anchors within the standard anchoring paradigm. Insufficient adjustment, it appears, is partly produced by insufficient thought.

A prescription for harder thinking, however, will cure insufficient adjustment only if people recognize the right answer when they reach it. This is obviously impossible, by definition, in any judgment under uncertainty. Fans of a second insufficient adjustment account have therefore suggested that anchoring and adjustment is likely to be characterized by a certain amount of "satisficing" as people adjust until they reach a value that appears plausible (Mussweiler & Strack, 2001a; Quattrone, 1982; Quattrone et al., 1981). Because this adjustment terminates at the outer range of plausible values, adjustments tend to be insufficient.

To test this account, participants received a series of 12 self-generated anchoring questions like those discussed earlier (Epley & Gilovich, 2004b). Participants in one condition simply answered each of these questions. Participants in the other condition provided a range of plausible answers to each question (e.g., What is the earliest Washington could plausibly have been elected President of the United States? What is the latest Washington could plausibly have been elected President of the United States?). Consistent with this satisficing account, the answers provided in the first condition were not centered within the ranges provided by the second. Instead, answers were strongly skewed towards the anchor value, on average falling at the fifteenth percentile of the plausible ranges provided by other participants. It appears that people adjust until they reach a plausible value, at which point adjustment stops.

Both of these mechanisms of insufficient adjustment suggest that a different strategy for debiasing must be adopted than the "consider the opposite" strategy effectively employed within the standard anchoring paradigm. In particular, both suggest that insufficient adjustments should be lengthened by inducing more careful and deliberate thought. Although experimental instantiations of these strategies – including forewarnings to avoid being biased by values that come quickly to mind and providing incentives for accuracy – do not influence responses to externally provided anchors in the standard anchoring paradigm (Chapman & Johnson, 2002; Wilson et al., 1996), *both* increase adjustment from self-generated anchors (Epley & Gilovich, 2004b). Accessibility effects are prime examples of automaticity and serial adjustment a prime example of controlled processing, meaning adjustment-based anchoring effects will be influenced by attention-dependent debiasing strategies but accessibility-based anchoring effects will not. Dissociations in the effectiveness of different debiasing strategies are therefore predictable. After all, not all anchors are alike.

Extending the Heuristic: Adjustment in Everyday Life

The anchoring and adjustment heuristic appears to be utilized when people automatically generate an anchor value known to be wrong but close to the right answer, and not when a novel anchor is provided by an external source. These circumscribed preconditions might seem to substantially reduce the scope of the anchoring and adjustment heuristic, except that so many everyday inferences appear to involve exactly these preconditions. Human inference often begins with an automatic process that provides a rough approximation and ends with a controlled process that subsequently refines or adjusts it. Whether such a dual-process judgment *actually* involves the anchoring and adjustment heuristic depends on whether the automatic approximation is known to be wrong, and if so, whether it is known to be close to the right answer and in need of slight adjustment. This more tightly tuned version of the anchoring and adjustment heuristic is likely to describe fewer phenomena than the unencumbered metaphor, but the decrease in population should be more than offset by the increase in accuracy. As it happens, this restricted pool of adjustment phenomena is still quite crowded.

For example, people appear to adopt others' perspectives by serially adjusting from their own. Because adjustments tend to be insufficient, adult perspective taking is often egocentrically biased. People tend to overestimate the extent to which others will share their thoughts and feelings (Keysar, 1994; Nickerson, 1999; Ross, Greene, & House, 1977; Van Boven, Dunning, & Loewenstein, 2000), overestimate the extent to which others notice both their internal states and emotions (Gilovich, Savitsky, & Medvec, 1998), and overestimate the extent to which others are noticing their very existence (Gilovich, Medvec, & Savitsky, 2000), just to name a few. Over time, of course, people learn that their own perspective may be quite different than another's, and parents commit far fewer egocentric errors than their children. Nevertheless, monitoring the time course of social thought via eye-tracking technology has shown that children and their parents are equally quick to look at objects suggested by an egocentric interpretation and differ only in the speed with which they shift that attention to accommodate another's differing perspective (Epley, Morewedge, & Keysar, 2004). A lifetime of learning doesn't reduce the tendency to form an egocentric response so much as increase the tendency to adjust from it.

Consistent with an anchoring and adjustment account of perspective taking, diminishing attentional resources (Kruger, 1999) or the time available to engage in serial adjustment (Epley, Keysar, Van Boven, & Gilovich, in press) increases the magnitude of egocentric biases. Increasing attentional resources, in contrast, by providing incentives for accuracy diminishes them (Epley, Keysar et al., in press). And asking participants to adopt another's perspective while nodding their heads up and down increases egocentric biases compared to when they are shaking their heads from side to side (Epley, Keysar et al., in press), consistent with the adjustment phenomena discussed earlier.

Similar effects seem to guide inferences about the future that are based on adjustments from best- or worst-case scenarios. What one hopes or fears will happen in some future event is often readily accessible but clearly more extreme than what is *likely* to happen, setting the stage for serial adjustment. Consistent with this account, participants in one experiment predicted how long it would take them to complete a variety of upcoming academic tasks. Although they generally underestimated how long it would take to complete these tasks, this "planning fallacy" was larger when participants were nodding their heads up and down than when they were shaking their heads from side to side (Epley & Gilovich, 2004a). This suggests that participants estimated their completion dates by anchoring on the date they hoped to complete the project and serially adjusted to a later date to accommodate inevitable delays.

Although the evidence for anchoring and adjustment is strongest in perspective taking and temporal prediction, these effects seem to be part of a larger family of inferences that involve adjustment from a self-generated anchor that is known to be close to the right answer but wrong. This includes people's attempts to adjust their inferences to reduce situational distortions (Gilbert & Gill, 2000), to adjust the predicted emotional impact of distressing events to accommodate the dampening effects of time (Gilbert, Gill, & Wilson, 2002), to adjust their relative ability estimates to accommodate others' ability levels as well as their own (Kruger, 1999), and to adjust the impact of a given piece of information in judgment to incorporate the reliability of the information into an assessment of its extremity (Griffin & Tversky, 1992). Each of these cases is marked by what appears to be insufficient adjustment, producing predictable biases in the direction of the initial anchor value. More important, biases that arise in at least some of these contexts are increased by attentional load (Gilbert & Gill, 2000; Gilbert, Gill, & Wilson, 2002; Kruger, 1999). Although the results of such load manipulations are ambiguous, influencing serial adjustment along with *any* effortful process, these findings are at least consistent with an anchoring and adjustment account. More work is clearly needed.

But by far the best-known application of the anchoring and adjustment heuristic is within the family of "correction" models that seek to explain how people identify the causes of their own and others' actions. Jones (1979) argued, for example, that it is easier to draw a connection between a person and their behavior than between a situation and the behavior, and Quattrone (1982) suggested that a dispositional inference may therefore serve as an anchor that is subsequently adjusted to incorporate situational constraints. Gilbert (1989, 2002) expanded this model and dropped the anchoring and adjustment terminology by proposing that people first "categorize" a person's behavior in terms of a general behavioral category (e.g., "George behaved arrogantly"), then "characterize" the person in terms of the category by forming a dispositional inference (e.g., "George is arrogant"), and finally "correct" that dispositional inference to accommodate situational constraints (e.g. "George is mildly arrogant"). Because characterization of the person is relatively automatic but situational correction is effortful, person perception will be dispositionally biased – which it is (Gilbert & Malone, 1995). Most of the data amassed to support this model demonstrates that cognitive load increases the dispositional bias.

However, Trope & Gaunt (2000) point out that these and other resource-depletion findings are also consistent with a slightly different kind of dual process account involving the integration of competing explanations rather than the adjustment of one to incorporate another. They demonstrate that manipulating the accessibility of situational constraints moderates dispositional inferences, much in the same way that the accessibility of anchor-inconsistent evidence moderates anchoring effects in the standard paradigm. Attentional load, their experiments suggest, may influence people's ability to consider situational information at all, and cognitive load does not increase dispositional biases when the situational constraints are highly accessible. This integration, or accessibility-based, account suggests that person perception may not involve any serial adjustment or effortful correction.

Like most debates within psychology, this one will likely be resolved by delineating domains of applicability. In fact, the research on "self-generated" anchors suggests a solution based on the apparent power of situational constraints. Recall that people are likely to utilize the anchoring and adjustment heuristic when an anchor value is perceived to be close to the right answer but wrong. This predicts that people are likely to serially adjust a dispositional inference when the situational constraints are relatively weak and the dispositional inference therefore appears close to the right answer but in need of slight adjustment. When the situational constraints are strong, however, the dispositional inference is unlikely to serve as a starting point in adjustment but rather as a data point in a process of integration. The moderating strength of situational constraints would provide a resolution similar to that between accessibility- and adjustment-based accounts of judgmental anchoring. This proposed truce, however, is currently awaiting empirical signatures.

Although additional experimentation is required to fully understand the impact of the anchoring and adjustment heuristic in daily life, this section should confirm that reports of its death were exaggerated. The anchoring and adjustment heuristic appears to be alive and well, as long as one looks in the right places.

The Future of an Illusion

Anchoring effects are ubiquitous in human judgment and from a distance can all look alike. This apparent unity is produced by the illusion that similar psychological outcomes are guided by a single psychological process. But scientific scrutiny reveals that this blurry forest is actually composed of different trees. Some anchoring effects, namely those that involve externally provided anchors whose relation to a target is unknown, influence judgments by increasing the accessibility of anchor-consistent information. Other anchoring effects, namely those involving "self-generated" anchors known to be close to the target but wrong, are produced by a process of insufficient adjustment. Both types are united by the general tendency for judgments to be assimilated to an anchor value, but differ dramatically in the mental tricks that produce them.

The microscopic dissection of these tricks would be a matter of intellectual triviality were it not that these details are critical for determining both the nature of inferential biases and also strategies for alleviating them. Accessibility-based anchoring effects will generally produce assimilation, but can occasionally produce contrast effects when the target and anchor are wildly different from one another and activate a search for features that differ between them (Strack & Mussweiler, 1997). Adjustment-based anchoring, in contrast, should only produce assimilation effects. Accessibility-based anchoring effects can be reduced by considering features of the anchor that differ from the target, whereas adjustment-based anchoring effects can be reduced by attentional effort and careful thought. The number of domains that involve one of these two kinds of anchoring effects is large and expanding, increasing the importance of attending to these underlying mechanisms even further.

As varied demonstrations of anchoring effects continue to increase, so may the family of mechanisms that produce them. Although accessibility and adjustment are two established mechanisms, others including conversational norms (Englich & Mussweiler, 2001), numeric priming (Wong & Kwong, 2000), and persuasion (Wegener, Petty, Detweiler-Bedell, & Jarvis, 2001) may make important contributions as well. Whether these additional mechanisms alone are sufficient to produce anchoring effects or merely serve to moderate accessibility and adjustment-based mechanisms is currently unclear, but there seems little doubt that an attempt to reduce this family to a single member will ultimately prove unfruitful.

It might therefore appear that the singular "anchoring effect" is an unhelpful and misleading term that ought to be diced up into its constituent elements and replaced by a new language that captures the variety of anchoring experiences. However, proliferation of psychological jargon is costly and should be restrained so long as the current language is not entirely misleading. The tricks underlying this psychological Tuned Deck are well on their way to being revealed, and the various mental tricks that a singular referent might have concealed is therefore of less concern. To the extent that an "anchoring effect" provides an accurate description of a psychological outcome, it is worth keeping, so long as one remembers that there are at least two psychological processes lurking beneath it.

Acknowledgments

Writing of this chapter was supported by NSF grant SES-0241544, facilitated by the editorial support of Erin Rapien, and improved by the helpful comments of Thomas Gilovich, Derek Koehler, and Neal Roese. I would like to thank Daniel Dennett for bringing the opening example to my attention.

References

Block, R. A. & Harper, D. R. (1991) Overconfidence in estimation: Testing the anchoring-and-adjustment hypothesis, *Organizational Behavior & Human Decision Processes*, 49, 188–207.

Brewer, N. T. & Chapman, G. B. (2002) The fragile basic anchoring effect, *Journal of Behavioral Decision Making*, 7, 223–42.

Cacioppo, J. T. & Petty, R. E. (1982) The need for cognition, *Journal of Personality and Social Psychology*, 42, 116–31.

Cacioppo, J. T., Priester, J. R., & Berntson, G. G. (1993) Rudimentary determinants of attitudes. II: Arm flexion and extension have differential effects on attitudes, *Journal of Personality and Social Psychology*, 65, 5–17.

Cervone, D. & Peake, P. K. (1986) Anchoring, efficacy, and action: The influence of judgmental heuristics on self-efficacy judgments and behavior, *Journal of Personality and Social Psychology*, 50, 492–501.

Chapman, G. B. & Bornstein, B. H. (1996) The more you ask for, the more you get: Anchoring in personal injury verdicts, *Applied Cognitive Psychology*, 10, 519–40.

Chapman, G. B. & Johnson, E. J. (1994) The limits of anchoring, *Journal of Behavioral Decision Making*, 7, 223–42.

Chapman, G. B. & Johnson, E. J. (1999) Anchoring, activation and the construction of value, *Organizational Behavior and Human Decision Processes*, 79, 115–53.

Chapman, G. B. & Johnson, E. J. (2002) Incorporating the irrelevant: Anchors in judgments of belief and value. In T. Gilovich, D. Griffin, and D. Kahneman (eds.), *Heuristics and Biases: The Psychology of Intuitive Judgment* (pp. 120–38). Cambridge: Cambridge University Press.

Duncan, J., Seitz, R. J., Kolodny, J., Bor, D., Herzog, H., Ahmed, A., et al. (2000) A neural basis for general intelligence, *Science*, 289, 399–401.

Englich, B. & Mussweiler, T. (2001) Sentencing under uncertainty: Anchoring effects in the courtroom, *Journal of Applied Social Psychology*, 31, 1535–51.

Epley, N. (2001) Mental correction as serial, effortful, confirmatory, and insufficient adjustment, *unpublished doctoral dissertation, Cornell University*.

Epley, N. & Gilovich, T. (2001) Putting adjustment back in the anchoring and adjustment heuristic: Differential processing of self-generated and experimenter-provided anchors, *Psychological Science*, 12, 391–6.

Epley, N. & Gilovich, T. (2004a) Adjusting to what will happen from what might happen: The anchoring and adjustment heuristic in intuitive prediction. Unpublished manuscript, Harvard University.

Epley, N., & Gilovich, T. (2004b) Anchoring and insufficient adjustment: When, why, and how to ameliorate. Unpublished manuscript, Harvard University.

Epley, N., & Gilovich, T. (2004c) Are adjustments insufficient? *Personality and Social Psychology Bulletin*, 30, 447–60.

Epley, N., Keysar, B., Van Boven, L., & Gilovich, T. (in press) Perspective taking as egocentric anchoring and adjustment, *Journal of Personality and Social Psychology*.

Epley, N., Morewedge, C., & Keysar, B. (in press) Perspective taking in children and adults: Equivalent egocentrism but differential correction, *Journal of Experimental Social Psychology*.

Fischhoff, B. (1977) Perceived informativeness of facts, *Journal of Experimental Psychology: Human Perception and Performance*, 3, 349–58.

Galinsky, A. & Mussweiler, T. (2002) First offers as anchors: The role of perspective-taking and negotiator focus, *Journal of Personality and Social Psychology*, 81, 657–69.

Gilbert, D. T. (1989) Thinking lightly about others: Automatic components of the social inference process. In J. S. Uleman and J. A. Bargh (eds.), *Unintended Thought* (pp. 189–211). New York: Guilford.

Gilbert, D. T. (2002) Inferential correction. In T. Gilovich, D. Griffin, and D. Kahneman (eds.), *Heuristics and Biases: The Psychology of Intuitive Judgment* (pp. 167–84). Cambridge: Cambridge University Press.

Gilbert, D. T. & Gill, M. J. (2000) The momentary realist, *Psychological Science*, 11, 394–8.

Gilbert, D. T., Gill, M. J., & Wilson, T. D. (2002) The future is now: Temporal correction in affective forecasting, *Organizational Behavior and Human Decision Processes*, 88, 430–44.

Gilbert, D. T. & Malone, P. S. (1995) The correspondence bias, *Psychological Bulletin*, 117, 21–38.

Gilovich, T., Medvec, V. H., & Savitsky, K. (2000) The spotlight effect in social judgment: An egocentric bias in estimates of the salience of one's own actions and appearance, *Journal of Personality and Social Psychology*, 78, 211–22.

Gilovich, T., Savitsky, K., & Medvec, V. H. (1998) The illusion of transparency: Biased assessments of others' ability to read our emotional states, *Journal of Personality and Social Psychology*, 75, 332–46.

Grice, H. P. (1975) Logic and conversation. In P. Cole and J. L. Morgan (eds.), *Syntax & Semantics* (vol. 3, pp. 41–58). New York: Academic Press.

Griffin, D. & Tversky, A. (1992) The weighing of evidence and the determinants of confidence, *Cognitive Psychology*, 24, 411–35.

Hawkins, S. A. & Hastie, R. (1991) Hindsight: Biased judgments of past events after the outcomes are known, *Psychological Bulletin*, 107, 311–27.

Higgins, E. T. (1996) Knowledge: Accessibility, applicability, and salience. In A. Kruglanski (ed.), *Social Psychology: Basic Principles* (pp. 133–68). New York: Guilford.

Hilliard, J. N. (1938) *Greater Magic: A Practical Treatise on Modern Magic*. Minneapolis: C. W. Jones.

Jacowitz, K. E. & Kahneman, D. (1995) Measures of anchoring in estimation tasks, *Personality and Social Psychology Bulletin*, 21, 1161–7.

Jones, E. E. (1979) The rocky road from acts to dispositions, *American Psychologist*, 34, 107–17.

Kenny, D. A. & DePaulo, B. M. (1993) Do people know how others view them? An empirical and theoretical account, *Psychological Bulletin*, 114, 145–61.

Keysar, B. (1994) The illusory transparency of intention: Linguistic perspective taking in text, *Cognitive Psychology*, 23, 165–208.

Keysar, B. & Barr, D. J. (2002) Self-anchoring in conversation: Why language users don't do what they "should." In T. Gilovich, D. Griffin, and D. Kahneman (eds.), *Heuristics and Biases: The Psychology of Intuitive Judgment* (pp. 150–66). Cambridge: Cambridge University Press.

Klayman, J. & Ha, Y. W. (1987) Confirmation, disconfirmation, and information in hypotheses testing, *Psychological Review*, 94, 211–28.

Koehler, D. J. (1994) Hypothesis generation and confidence in judgment, *Journal of Experimental Psychology: Learning, Memory, Cognition*, 20, 461–9.

Koriat, A., Lichtenstein, S., & Fischhoff, B. (1980) Reasons for confidence, *Journal of Experimental Psychology: Human Learning and Memory*, 6, 107–18.

Kruger, J. (1999) Lake Wobegon be gone! The "below-average effect" and the egocentric nature of comparative ability judgments, *Journal of Personality and Social Psychology*, 77, 221–32.

Mussweiler, T. (2003) Comparison processes in social judgment: Mechanisms and consequences, *Psychological Review*, 110, 472–89.

Mussweiler, T. & Strack, F. (1999) Hypothesis-consistent testing and semantic priming in the anchoring paradigm: A selective accessibility model, *Journal of Experimental Social Psychology*, 35, 136–64.

Mussweiler, T. & Strack, F. (2000a) Numeric judgment under uncertainty: The role of knowledge in anchoring, *Journal of Experimental Social Psychology*, 36, 495–518.

Mussweiler, T. & Strack, F. (2000b) The use of category and exemplar knowledge in the solution of anchoring tasks, *Journal of Personality and Social Psychology*, 78, 1038–52.

Mussweiler, T. & Strack, F. (2001a) "Considering the Impossible": Explaining the effects of implausible anchors, *Social Cognition*, 19, 145–60.

Mussweiler, T. & Strack, F. (2001b) The semantics of anchoring, *Organizational Behavior & Human Decision Processes*, 86, 234–55.

Mussweiler, T., Strack, F., & Pfeiffer, T. (2000) Overcoming the inevitable anchoring effect: Considering the opposite compensates for selective accessibility, *Personality and Social Psychology Bulletin*, 26, 1142–50.

Nakayama, K. & Joseph, J. S. (1998) Attention, pattern recognition and popout in visual search. In R. Parasuraman (ed.), *The Attentive Brain* (pp. 279–98). Cambridge, MA: MIT Press.

Nickerson, R. S. (1999) How we know – and sometimes misjudge – what others know: Imputing one's own knowledge to others, *Psychological Bulletin*, 125, 737–59.

Northcraft, G. B. & Neale, M. A. (1987) Experts, amateurs, and real estate: An anchoring-and-adjustment perspective on property pricing decisions, *Organizational Behavior and Human Decision Processes*, 39, 84–97.

Pinker, S. (1994) *The Language Instinct*. New York: William Morrow.

Plous, S. (1989) Thinking the unthinkable: The effect of anchoring on likelihood estimates of nuclear war, *Journal of Applied Social Psychology*, 19, 67–91.

Quattrone, G. A. (1982) Overattribution and unit formation: When behavior engulfs the person, *Journal of Personality and Social Psychology*, 42, 593–607.

Quattrone, G. A., Lawrence, C. P., Finkel, S. E., & Andrus, D. C. (1981) Explorations in anchoring: The effects of prior range, anchor extremity, and suggestive hints. Unpublished manuscript, Stanford University.

Ross, L., Greene, D., & House, P. (1977) The false consensus effect: An egocentric bias in social perception and attribution processes, *Journal of Experimental Social Psychology*, 13, 279–301.

Rottenstreich, Y. & Tversky, A. (1997) Unpacking, repacking, and anchoring: Advances in Support Theory, *Psychological Review*, 104, 406–15.

Russo, J. E. & Schoemaker, P. J. H. (1989) *Decision Traps*. New York: Simon and Schuster.

Schacter, D. L. (1996) *Searching for Memory: The Brain, the Mind, and the Past*. New York: Basic.

Slovic, P. & Fischhoff, B. (1977) On the psychology of experimental surprises, *Journal of Experimental Psychology: Human Perception and Performance*, 3, 544–51.

Strack, F. & Mussweiler, T. (1997) Explaining the enigmatic anchoring effect: Mechanisms of selective accessibility, *Journal of Personality and Social Psychology*, 73, 437–46.

Switzer, F. & Sniezek, J. A. (1991) Judgmental processes in motivation: Anchoring and adjustment effects on judgment and behavior, *Organizational Behavior and Human Decision Processes*, 49, 208–29.

Trope, Y. & Gaunt, R. (2000) Processing alternative explanations of behavior: Correction or integration? *Journal of Personality and Social Psychology*, 79, 344–54.

Tversky, A. (1977) Features of similarity, *Psychological Review*, 84, 327–52.

Tversky, A. & Kahneman, D. (1974) Judgment under uncertainty: Heuristics and biases, *Science*, 185, 1124–30.

Van Boven, L., Dunning, D., & Loewenstein, G. (2000) Egocentric empathy gaps between owners and buyers: Misperceptions of the endowment effect, *Journal of Personality and Social Psychology*, 79, 66–76.

Wansink, B., Kent, R. J., & Hoch, S. J. (1998) An anchoring and adjustment model of purchase quantity decisions, *Journal of Marketing Research*, 35, 71–81.

Wegener, D. T., Petty, R. E., Detweiler-Bedell, B. T., & Jarvis, W. B. G. (2001) Implications of attitude change theories for numerical anchoring: Anchor plausibility and the limits of anchor effectiveness, *Journal of Experimental Social Psychology*, 37, 62–9.

Wells, G. L. & Petty, R. E. (1980) The effects of overt head movements on persuasion: Compatibility and incompatibility of responses, *Basic and Applied Social Psychology*, 1, 219–30.

Wilson, T. D., Houston, C., Etling, K. M., & Brekke, N. (1996) A new look at anchoring effects: Basic anchoring and its antecedents, *Journal of Experimental Psychology: General*, 4, 387–402.

Wong, K. F. E. & Kwong, J. Y. Y. (2000) Is 7300 m equal to 7.3 km? Same semantics but different anchoring effects, *Organizational Behavior & Human Decision Processes*, 82, 314–33.

Zeki, S. (2003) The disunity of consciousness, *Trends in Cognitive Sciences*, 7, 214–18.

13

Twisted Pair: Counterfactual Thinking and the Hindsight Bias

Neal J. Roese

Introduction

Flip a fair coin. As it arcs through the air, it has two possible outcomes, heads or tails. At the moment it comes to rest, those two possibilities vanish, converted into two different species of outcome. Heads up. Heads is the factual outcome. Tails up is the outcome that did not occur. It could have occurred. The coin is fair, and so there was an even chance that tails might have been up. Tails is the counterfactual outcome.

Counterfactual means, literally, contrary to the facts. Counterfactual thoughts are thoughts of what might have been, of what could have happened had some detail or action been different. Hindsight bias refers to an exaggerated sense of certainty in the factual outcome's occurrence, defined relative to certainty of judgments made in fore-sight. In a sense, the hindsight bias reflects an inability to regain one's pre-outcome state of mind. Both counterfactual thinking and the hindsight bias are judgments of the past, both involve reconstructions based on blends of semantic and episodic memory, and both can be construed as forms of biased or heuristic reasoning (Connolly & Zeelenberg, 2002; Hawkins & Hastie, 1990; Roese, 1999).

When both classes of judgment are defined as probability estimates, differing only in their focus on factual versus counterfactual outcome likelihoods, the two judgments would be expected, on purely logical grounds, to be inversely related. Given a binary outcome structure, the greater the retrospective likelihood assigned to a factual event, the lower the likelihood that should be assigned to its alternative. The more certain you are that heads *had to* come up (you suspect a cheat . . .), the less likely you believe tails *would have* come up. As Kahneman and Varey (1990, p. 1103) pointed out, "X is neither necessary nor inevitable if it can properly be said that Y almost happened instead of [X]" (see also Arkes, Faust, Guilmette, & Hart, 1988; Davies, 1992; Fischhoff, 1976; Robbennolt & Sobus, 1997; Slovic & Fischhoff, 1977).

This is the traditional assumption of many theorists, yet new research casts considerable doubt on its generality. This chapter summarizes striking new discoveries on the link between counterfactual thinking and the hindsight bias. Some studies indicate that the two judgments can dissociate, as when a determinant variable influences one but not the other. Other studies reveal that the two judgments are often positively correlated. Yet other studies reveal that both judgments may be similarly distorted by affective motivational concerns. Taken together, these studies suggest that defining counterfactual thinking and the hindsight bias as inverse probability estimates misses an important part of how these judgments operate on a subjective level. Counterfactual thinking and the hindsight bias are sometimes inversely related, sometimes positively related, sometimes causally related. They are interwoven, twisted together like wires inside a coaxial cable. This twisted pair is united in its intimate role in the essential cognitive goal of making sense of the world and guiding effective action within it.

This chapter reviews four lines of recent research that offer new insights into the link between counterfactual thinking and the hindsight bias. These four lines of research emphasize:

1 dissociation based on a proximity heuristic;
2 accessibility experience;
3 causal inference; and
4 self-serving motivated inference.

Before turning to these four lines of research, brief reviews of the counterfactual and hindsight literatures are presented.

Counterfactual Thinking and Regret

Counterfactual thinking refers to thoughts of what might have been, of alternatives to past factual events, as in: "If not for voting irregularities in Florida, Gore might have become the new American president in 2000." The study of counterfactual thinking has mushroomed because such thoughts are common and influence a diverse range of judgments, such as biased hypothesis-testing, blame, expectancy, overconfidence, satisfaction, superstition, suspicion, and victim compensation (see Chapter 5, this volume; Mellers, 2000; Roese, 1997, for reviews). Regret is the more specific type of counterfactual that is self-focused, upward rather than downward in its direction of comparison (i.e., focuses on how the past might have been better rather than worse), and affectively unpleasant. For the sake of ease of presentation, counterfactual and regret are treated as synonymous in this review. Although the term counterfactual is hence used exclusively, the conclusions drawn below apply equally well to conceptions of regret.

According to a functional view of counterfactual thinking (Roese & Olson, 1997), counterfactual judgments constitute not so much a form of bias but rather an instrument of behavior regulation, performance enhancement, and goal pursuit. When people think about what might have been, they typically think of unmet personal desires, such as missed career opportunities or lost loves, and how these might have been achieved. Three lines of evidence support this functionalist approach. First, some types of counterfactuals facilitate performance (Roese, 1994). Second, those counterfactuals that facilitate performance are particularly likely to be generated in response to failure or salient achievement goals (Grieve, Houston, Dupuis, & Eddy, 1999; Roese & Hur, 1997; Sanna & Turley, 1996). Third, spontaneously generated counterfactuals tend to be upward (i.e., specifying how outcomes might have been better) rather than downward (i.e., specifying how outcomes might have been worse), again suggesting an overall emphasis on improvement (Nasco & Marsh, 1999; Roese & Olson, 1997). Roese (1997) argued that nearly all of the judgmental consequences of counterfactual thinking could be attributed to either of two mechanisms, contrast effects or causal inferences (Connolly & Zeelenberg, 2002, make a similar claim for regret in decision making).

Contrast effects occur when a judgment becomes more extreme via the juxtaposition of some anchor or standard. For example, a cup of coffee feels hotter, by contrast, if one has just been eating ice cream. In the same way, a factual outcome may appear worse if a more desirable alternative outcome is salient and better if a less desirable outcome is salient. In a variety of demonstrations, manipulation of counterfactual anchors influenced affective judgments such as satisfaction (e.g., Medvec & Savitsky, 1997; Mellers, Schwartz, Ho, & Ritov, 1997; Roese, 1994).

Counterfactuals also imply causal inferences (Wells & Gavanski, 1989), which produce psychological consequences that are independent of contrast effects. By virtue of their conditional structure and implicit reference to a parallel factual statement, counterfactual propositions exemplify the logic of Mill's method of difference. Consider the counterfactual, "If only Joan had bought house insurance, she would not have suffered financially after a fire ravaged her house." This counterfactual is implicitly connected to the parallel factual events that Joan did not buy insurance and Joan is suffering financially. If the perceiver believes that alteration of the decision to purchase insurance is enough to change Joan's financial situation, then the perceiver also believes that Joan's decision causally impacted her financial situation. Although there have been numerous demonstrations of the impact of counterfactual thinking on cause and blame judgments (e.g., Branscombe, Owen, Garstka, & Coleman, 1996; Creyer & Gürhan, 1997; Goldinger, Kleider, Azuma, & Beike, 2003; Harris, German, & Mills, 1996; Macrae, 1992; Markman & Tetlock, 2000; Roese & Olson, 1996), inconsistent findings have also appeared (Mandel, 2003; Mandel & Lehman, 1996; N'gbala & Branscombe, 1995). As we shall see, that counterfactual thinking influences causal inferences represents one mechanism by which counterfactuals can heighten, rather than reduce, the hindsight bias.

Hindsight Bias

Hindsight bias refers to an exaggerated belief in the likelihood of a given event's occurrence. More specifically, it is the tendency to believe that an event was predictable before it occurred, even though for the perceiver it was not. The hindsight bias represents more than simple learning from past experience; it describes an inability to retrieve a pre-outcome explanatory perspective. For this reason, it is sometimes labeled a "knew-it-all-along effect."

Importantly, the term hindsight bias has been applied to two rather different paradigms, and recent evidence suggests that they are probably independent phenomena. In the *hypothetical paradigm*, subjects make judgments about events, with information about the event (e.g., whether it in fact occurred or not) manipulated. In the *memory paradigm*, subjects answer obscure trivia questions, make confidence estimates, receive the correct answers, and then recall their original confidence estimates. Theory emphasizing judgmental repetition (Hertwig, Gigerenzer, & Hoffrage, 1997) and knowledge updating (Hoffrage, Hertwig, & Gigerenzer, 2000; see also Erdfelder & Buchner, 1998; Winman, Juslin, & Björkman, 1998) have been successfully applied to the memory paradigm. The present chapter focuses entirely on the hypothetical paradigm. Although these two paradigms may instantiate different psychological phenomena, there is converging agreement that both paradigms reflect the by-products of adaptive learning, as opposed to simple error (cf. Hoffrage et al., 2000; Roese & Olson, 1996).

Accordingly, a favored theoretical account of the hypothetical paradigm version of hindsight bias emphasizes memory integration (Fischhoff, 1975; Hawkins & Hastie, 1990). By way of rapid integration of new outcome information into existing memory structures, new and multiple semantic links are established. Essentially, new target outcome information is effortlessly embedded in knowledge structures, from which it is henceforth difficult to isolate. Selective accessibility of information congruent with the outcome, cued by the outcome itself, contributes to an overall feeling of understanding, and hence to a heightened feeling of having known it all along. This same process may underlie jurors' inability to disregard evidence presented inappropriately in court (Hawkins & Hastie, 1990).

Carli (1999) showed how memory reconstruction crucially contributes to hindsight bias. In her studies, subjects read detailed information regarding a romantic encounter, with outcome information manipulated (rape vs. no-outcome). One week later, subjects completed a 30-item memory test. Those receiving rape outcome information were more likely to misrecall details of the romantic encounter in a manner congruent with the rape. This outcome-congruent misrecall mediated hindsight judgments of outcome certainty (see also Agans & Shaffer, 1994; Joslyn, Loftus, McNoughton, & Powers, 2001, for similar although less direct evidence). Further, hindsight bias regarding an actual outcome increases with temporal distance from the outcome (Bryant & Brockway, 1997; Bryant & Guilbault, 2002; McGlynn, 2000), suggesting further that as accuracy of recall decreases with the passage of time, intuitive theory-guided memory reconstruction (e.g., Ross, 1989) contributes more to hindsight bias. These recent findings compellingly confirm the role of memory integration and reconstruction as a key basis of hindsight bias.

With the counterfactual and hindsight literatures briefly summarized, I turn now to the four lines of research revealing more complicated interconnections between the two kinds of judgment:

1   dissociation based on a proximity heuristic;
2   accessibility experiences;

3   causal inference; and
4   self-serving motivated inference.

It Nearly Happened: Evidence for Dissociation

To return to the coin toss example, counterfactuals and hindsight bias ought, on purely logical grounds and particularly in the context of binary outcomes, to be inversely related. If you believe that the coin that has just landed "tails" is rigged and that tails had a 0.65 probability of occurrence, then you must also believe that "heads" had a 0.35 probability. There are only two possibilities in this simplest of examples, and one directly specifies the other. You would think, then, that such likelihood estimates, even in more complicated situations, would always bear this simple inverse relation. They do not.

Teigen's (1998) research indicated that likelihood estimates for factual versus counterfactual outcomes are dissociated. That is, some determinant variables exert a relatively greater impact on one than the other. Teigen's research emphasized one such determinant variable – outcome closeness. To say that an alternative outcome nearly happened is to say that its probability of occurrence is retrospectively high and that the factual outcome was a fluke or oddity. If another rigged coin landed "heads" but you believe this likelihood was 0.15, then you also believe that "tails" nearly came up – tails was "close" to having occurred.

Teigen's insight was that if closeness is framed not in terms of probabilities but rather in terms of incidental spatial or numeric dimensions, a "feeling" of closeness, or *proximity heuristic*, may impinge upon judgment. Moreover, previous research has amply demonstrated how perceived closeness (either temporal or spatial) increases counterfactual thinking (Miller & McFarland, 1986; Kahneman & Tversky, 1982; Roese & Olson, 1996).

In one of Teigen's (1998) studies, subjects read a scenario in which two protagonists, Ivan and Boris, both escape death while playing Russian roulette. Both individuals had objectively identical chances of dying (with two bullets in a six-chamber revolver, the probability for both individuals was 0.33). However, when both open the chambers of their revolvers, Ivan discovers that the two bullets flank the chamber that was just fired (i.e., they are spatially close to the firing position) whereas Boris discovers that his two bullets are over on the other side of the chamber (i.e., they are spatially distant from the firing position). When the likelihood estimate was framed in terms of the factual outcome (likelihood of surviving), only 60 percent of subjects thought that both individuals had the same chance of surviving, demonstrating that a proximity heuristic was in play. But even more remarkably, when the same outcome was framed in terms of the counterfactual (likelihood of dying), a much lower 40 percent of subjects now claimed that both individuals had the same chance of dying. If factual and counterfactual likelihood estimates were mirror image judgments, these two rates would have been identical.

In another revealing study reported by Teigen (1998), sport outcomes were presented to students such that success and failure and home team versus opposing team were perfectly crossed in a factorial design, along with outcomes that were close versus a "blow-out" in terms of point spread. Also, likelihood judgments were made on either a factual or counterfactual basis. Collapsing across factors to examine only the 2 × 2 pattern involving close versus far and factual versus counterfactual, a striking pattern of dissociation appears. The manipulation of closeness produces a reliable effect on counterfactual estimates, with closer outcomes producing greater certainty than distant outcomes. By contrast, no such effect is apparent when the likelihood estimates target factual outcomes. Again, if factual and counterfactual likelihood estimates were mirror images, the closeness manipulation should have exerted equivalent (albeit opposite) effects on both. Teigen's research dramatically demonstrates how counterfactual thinking and the hindsight bias are dissociated, and points to the relatively greater sensitivity of counterfactual judgments to a proximity heuristic.

Hard to Do: Accessibility Experiences

Schwarz (1998) points out that frequency judgments (such as in the classic case of the availability heuristic) may be influenced by retrieved content from memory but also by the subjective experience of retrieval. Paradoxically, if it "feels" difficult to imagine ten examples of assertive behavior, then one may self-ascribe less assertiveness than when only two examples are retrieved. Sanna, Schwartz, and Stocker (2002) therefore reasoned that if generating many versus few counterfactual alternatives to a factual outcome "feels" more difficult, then judgments of certainty may be heightened rather than diminished. Using a variation of Fischhoff's (1975) British-Ghurka scenario (in which the presence or absence of outcome information regarding an obscure colonial war is manipulated), these authors found that generating ten rather than two thoughts about "how this scenario might have turned out differently" indeed increased hindsight certainty, defined using probability estimates for the factual outcome (0.68 vs. 0.54), relative to the no-outcome control (0.48). These findings demonstrate another mechanism by which counterfactual thinking and the hindsight bias might deviate from an inverse relation. To the extent that accessibility experiences directly impact feelings of certainty, then when the act of generating counterfactuals *feels difficult*, the likelihood of the factual outcome comes to be seen as even more inevitable.

Sanna, Schwartz, Small et al. (2002) provided further evidence by replicating the above effect with a different manipulation of accessibility experience. Rather than having participants generate either many or few alternative explanations, in this research participants generated the same number of alternative explanations but with a concurrent manipulation of frowning, which conveys proprioceptive signals indicative of mental effort. Greater subjective experience of effort in two experiments resulted in reduced hindsight bias. In further research, when subjective experiences of effortfulness were attributed to some other, arbitrary factor, the above effects were erased (Sanna & Schwarz, 2003). This new linkage between counterfactual thinking and the hindsight bias constitutes one example of the more general judgment phenomena involving accessibility experiences as heuristic cues.

Sense-Making: The Role of Causal Inference

A single counterfactual inference can heighten the hindsight bias, to the extent that it facilitates the explanatory coherence of an outcome, that is, if it makes sense of it. Earlier research showed that the more clearly an event can be explained in retrospect, the more inevitable it may come to be seen (Koriat, Lichtenstein, & Fischhoff, 1980; Wasserman, Lempert, & Hastie, 1991). Expectancy-discrepant outcomes stimulate attempts at causal explanation, and indeed such surprising outcomes produce paradoxically larger hindsight bias (Schkade & Kilbourne, 1991). If counterfactuals result in satisfying causal explanation, then they too will increase hindsight bias. For example, a sports fan might react to his or her team's loss with the counterfactual judgment that the team would have won were it not for an injury suffered in the third quarter. Without that injury, a victory would have been assured. In this way, the conditional counterfactual points to some causal feature that accounts for the outcome, yielding a satisfying feeling of explanation, comprehension, and post hoc certainty.

Roese and Olson (1996) presented three experiments supporting this reasoning. In Experiment 1, participants read a scenario describing a student preparing for but then performing poorly on an important exam. For half of the participants, the poor perform-ance was easily "undone" mentally through the imagined alteration of a salient anteced-ent action performed by the student. For the other participants, altering this antecedent action would not have changed the outcome. The hindsight bias was greater for those participants who could mentally undo the outcome. Parallel effects were obtained on a measure of causal inferences: the target antecedent action was seen as more causally important when altering this antecedent would have undone the outcome.

In the third experiment reported by Roese and Olson (1996), counterfactual think-ing was manipulated in two ways. First, actions within a scenario leading toward a focal outcome (missing a plane) were described as either exceptional or normal (previous research has shown that exceptional antecedents heighten counterfactual thinking, e.g., Kahneman & Tversky, 1982; Miller & Taylor, 1995). Second, outcome closeness, discussed already in the context of Teigen's research, was also manipulated, with the focal outcome described as either a near miss (missing the flight by 5 minutes) or a far miss (missing the flight by 1 hour). Both manipulations, according to previous research, reliably induce counterfactual thinking. The two manipulations differ, however, in the extent to which they alter causal ascriptions. Whereas the antecedent normality mani-pulation centers on the salience of an antecedent, and hence contributes to the mental linkage of antecedent to outcome that is the crux of causal inference, the closeness manipulation focuses only on an alternative outcome, with no specification of the means by which it might be achieved. Stated somewhat differently, the former is a manipula-tion of conditional counterfactuals, whereas the latter is a manipulation of close counter-factuals. Indeed, although both manipulations influenced counterfactual thinking (according to manipulation check thought-listings), only the former produced reliable shifts in causal judgments and the hindsight bias. Mediational analyses confirmed that changes in causal inferences underlay the facilitating effect of conditional counterfactual thinking on the hindsight bias. Thus, it is only when counterfactual thoughts engender satisfying causal explanations that they have the power to magnify the hindsight bias.

In a field study conducted at Northwestern University Wildcats football games (Roese & Maniar, 1997), fans approached after as opposed to before the game showed the typical hindsight bias regarding the chances of a victory (0.30 vs. 0.14). As a bit of background, it should be noted that the low expectations reflected the chronically poor performance of the Wildcats football team over previous decades. Happily, for fans as well researchers, testing occurred at three games during the Wildcats' 1995 winning season that resulted in a trip to the Rose Bowl. All three games were Wildcats victories – a surprise to fans in all three cases.

For subjects who were additionally prompted to describe either a key counterfactual or a key causal explanation, the hindsight bias was inflated to an even greater extent (0.55 and 0.49; relative to control, 0.14). The counterfactual and causal conditions resulted in equivalent magnification of the hindsight bias because both produced similar degrees of sense-making. Overall, this research indicated that counterfactuals inflate confidence in one's decision-making prowess only to the extent that the counterfactual proffers a causal explanation that satisfyingly accounts for the outcome at hand. In terms of underlying mechanism, these effects are identical to those in which individuals see future events as more likely after having explained why they *might* occur (Koehler, 1991; Sherman, Zehner, Johnson, & Hirt, 1983). Explanation increases likelihood estimates for events in both the past and future.

It is essential to recognize that not all counterfactuals, and hence not all causal explanations, similarly increase hindsight bias. When subjects are prompted to explain *why* an alternative outcome might have occurred, hindsight bias is reduced. Such an effect is an example of the more general "consider-the-alternatives" strategy for debiasing overconfident judgment (discussed in the next section). When the subject is asked to consider a *new* explanation for a different outcome, it *contradicts* an *initial* explanation that accounts for the factual outcome, reducing faith in that initial explanation, and hence reducing hindsight certainty that the factual outcome had to occur as it did. By contrast, the above research rests on effects in which a counterfactual conditional emphasizes that same initial explanation by showing how a different effect would have emerged in the absence of the factor named in that explanation. For example, explaining a sport victory by pointing to a star player may be emphasized by the counterfactual supposition that a loss would have resulted if the star player were sidelined, resulting in heightened certainty of a victory. But being asked to consider *other* factors that might *also* have led to a loss, such as superior coaching of the opponent team, weakens faith in the star player explanation, possibly reducing post hoc certainty of a victory (of course, if those other explanations are plausible, they might well increase post hoc certainty).

More generally, this research suggests a reconceptualization of hindsight bias that more broadly embraces the subjective experience of retrospective certainty. In the case of the armchair quarterback, watching the home team lose may result in the classic hindsight bias: the loss was predictable and inevitable, given, for example, certain foolish decisions made by the coach. But this same post hoc certainty applies equally well to counterfactuals, for example those decisions the coach *should have* made, that would have resulted in victory (and that the armchair quarterback *confidently believes* should have been made). An increase in confidence after outcome information becomes known can be directed at counterfactual as well as factual events (Roese & Olson, 1996, Experiment 2).

Hijacked by Motivation: Inconsistent Findings and Resolution

Both counterfactual thinking and the hindsight bias, like any judgment, may be hijacked by affective/motivational processes to take the form of self-serving comparisons. The prototypical self-serving bias centers on causal attributions that emphasize personal credit for success and blaming of others for failure (Miller & Ross, 1975). "My victory today rests on my talent alone; my failure yesterday was all my coach's fault . . ." an athlete might self-servingly say. Generating such self-serving biases is affectively rewarding (McFarland & Ross, 1982), and appears to be a common compensatory response to threat (Campbell & Sedikides, 1999).

Counterfactuals can be self-serving to the extent that they focus on mental alteration of own actions following success and on alteration of others' actions following failure (Roese & Olson, 1993). This pattern does occur, but relatively rarely. Most spontaneous counterfactual thoughts are evoked by problems and focus on how personal actions might have solved the problem, meaning that most counterfactuals tend to reflect self-blame. With regard to the widely used distinction between affective enhancement goals versus performance improvement goals, counterfactual thinking tends to instantiate the latter rather than the former (Roese & Olson, 1997; Roese, Sanna, & Galinsky, in press). Counterfactuals inform the individual of ways the past might have been improved, and thus reveal insights for future improvement (Roese, 1994).

For many years, reviews of the hindsight bias literature concluded that such judgments were rarely hijacked by motivational concerns, and instead reflected purely cognitive processes of knowledge updating and memory reconstruction (Christensen-Szalanski & Willham, 1991; Hawkins & Hastie, 1990). This conclusion derived from several demonstrations of little or no impact of incentive on hindsight bias (e.g., Leary, 1982). Challenging this traditional view are two lines of recent research. Curiously, however, these two lines make utterly contradictory predictions and provide utterly contradictory findings to support them. Although both note that it is affectively rewarding to exaggerate retrospectively the likelihood of success (one can take greater credit for skill, effort, and decision-making acumen that *over-determined* the positive outcome), they differ in their predictions for hindsight judgments regarding negative outcomes. In the first line of research, the hypothesis for negative outcomes is a reduction in hindsight bias; in the second, it is an increase in hindsight bias.

In the first line of research, individuals are thought to find consolation in the recognition that they had no knowledge of, and hence no responsibility for, an unpleasant outcome. For example, subjects playing a stock market decision-making game showed a reduced hindsight bias for their own negative stock outcomes, relative to the judgments of observers (Mark, Boburka, Eysell, Cohen, & Mellor, 2003). Further, laid-off workers gave lower estimates of the lay-off's likelihood than did workers who kept their jobs (Mark & Mellor, 1991), and supporters of the European Union's switch to the new Euro currency evidenced more hindsight bias in recalling economic advantage than disadvantage (Holzl, Kirchler, & Rodler, 2002). For team-based financial decision making, hindsight bias is greater for success than for failure (Louie, Curren, & Harich, 2000; see also Louie, 1999).

The idea behind the second line of research is that it is affectively consoling to exaggerate certainty for failure (increase in hindsight bias), because one can take refuge in the belief that despite one's best efforts, the failure would have happened anyway. For example, one study examined students' likelihood estimates of the outcome of the 1999 Israeli prime ministerial election (in which Ehud Barak defeated Benjamin Netanyahu), with estimates measured both before and after the election. Disappointed Netanyahu supporters were especially likely to exaggerate, after the fact, Barak's likelihood of victory (Tykocinski, 2001, Experiment 2). Using a scenario methodology, greater hindsight bias for negative than positive outcomes was enhanced by outcome importance (Experiment 1) and reduced when judgments were made for another person rather than oneself (Tykocinski, Pick, & Kedmi, 2002, Experiment 2; see also Bryant & Guilbault, 2002; Haslam & Jayasinghe, 1995; Sanna & Chang, 2003).

To reiterate, some research suggests a reduction whereas other work suggests an increase in the hindsight bias in response to personally negative outcomes. What accounts for this discrepancy in results? I suggest that the main reason for the discrepancy is theoretical misspecification centering on the conceptualization of external attribution.

The self-serving bias may be defined with regard to judgments along an internal versus external dimension of causal responsibility (i.e., causal locus) – in other words, one can be either more or less praiseworthy or more or less blameworthy for an outcome's occurrence. After failure, it is affectively rewarding to attribute causation externally: to blame others. Both research lines embrace this reasoning, but contort their conception of hindsight bias differently to achieve this same meaning of "blame others" (i.e., external attribution). In the Mark/Louie research, personal action is salient (i.e., stock decision making), and hindsight bias is defined in terms of one's own ability to have predicted *and therefore acted accordingly*. Given a bad outcome, the external attribution may be achieved by reducing hindsight certainty ("I could never have seen it coming"). By contrast, in the Tykocinski research, personal action is not salient: it is either irrelevant (as in predicting the outcomes of elections and sport matches) or overshadowed by salient external factors, such as traffic delays (as in all of the scenarios presented to subjects).

The apparent contradiction in findings disappears once we realize that regardless of paradigm, it is the external attribution that is heightened by a negative personal outcome. The two research programs simply construed hindsight bias differently to capture the notion of external attribution. In the Mark/Louie research, the external attribution takes the form of reduced hindsight for an outcome that implicates personal action ("I couldn't have prevented it *because* I couldn't have predicted it"), whereas in the Tykocinski research the external attribution takes the form of increased hindsight for an outcome that does not implicate personal action ("I couldn't have prevented it *because* other factors would have brought it about anyway"). A study of counterfactual thinking is compatible with this resolution. After making mock investment decisions and learning of their outcomes, subjects' counterfactual thoughts that targeted responsibility-mitigating excuses (e.g., "I couldn't have known Company A was in trouble," p. 319) were elevated under conditions of high accountability and surprising turns of event (Markman & Tetlock, 2000).

Despite the conceptual confusion, a clear pattern of self-serving bias, akin to the bias in causal inferences reviewed by Campbell and Sedikides (1999), is evident in hindsight judgments. The assertion that hindsight bias is immune to motivated influence, articulated in reviews of the previous generation of research (Christensen-Szalanski & Willham, 1991; Hawkins & Hastie, 1990), can now be laid to rest. Indeed, *any* form of judgment may be hijacked by higher-order motives or lower-level regulatory processes.

Consequences, Applications, and Debiasing

Both counterfactual thinking and the hindsight bias have received extensive attention in part because of their consequences for socially important phenomena, from responsibility ascription to "blaming-the-victim" effects. Demonstrations that both counterfactual (Goldinger et al., 2003) and hindsight (Carli & Leonard, 1989) judgments impact blame judgment emphasizes how causal inference is both determinant and consequence of both judgments.

An explosion of new research has applied concepts of hindsight bias, and also debiasing strategies, to legal settings, particularly regarding punitive judgments in liability cases. When making decisions about punitive damages in civil suits, for example, a key question is the extent to which the defendant should have known better and thus should have acted with foresight to have prevented whatever harm has prompted legal action (i.e., a counterfactual question). Hastie, Schkade, and Payne (1999) presented an experiment with mock jurors demonstrating a clear hindsight bias, in that identical judgments made in hindsight (relative to foresight, that is, without prior knowledge of the actual unfolding of events) showed substantially increased punitiveness. Similar findings were found in studies of mock juror decisions in cases involving a shipping accident causing flood damage (Kamin & Rachlinski, 1995), financial failure at a savings and loan institution (Stallard & Worthington, 1998), and allegedly illegal search and seizure (Casper, Benedict, & Perry, 1989).

Debiasing refers to techniques designed to mitigate bias in general (Arkes, 1991), and past research reflects a mix of successes and failures with regard to various debiasing strategies targeting a range of judgmental biases, of which hindsight bias is but one example. Hindsight bias has proven particularly resistant to debiasing. However, the "consider-alternatives" strategy appears to be effective. This strategy compels observers to consider, in detail, multiple causal pathways, rather than the single pathway that is the typical result of truncated, "miserly" judgment. Via consideration of alternative explanations, "new causal skids are greased": "if the occurring event cued its own causal chains, then considering the non-occurring event ought to accomplish the analogous result, thereby reducing the bias" (Arkes, 1991, p. 494). Evidence supporting this strategy appears in Arkes et al. (1988); Hirt and Markman (1995); Hoch (1985); Koriat et al. (1980); and Lord, Lepper, and Preston (1984). This strategy only works to the extent that full, deep, and vivid evidence corresponding to each alternative is presented. It is not sufficient merely to request that jurors, for example, ponder alternatives on their own; jurors must be immersed in relevant evidence and only then will they expend the effort necessary to bypass the hindsight bias (Kamin & Rachlinski, 1995). A more detailed review of debiasing procedures in general appears in Larrick (Chapter 16, this volume).

Conclusion

Counterfactual thinking and the hindsight bias are both forms of judgment aimed at past outcomes. One involves mental construction of alternative outcomes that might have occurred, and the other involves exaggerated certainty about the likelihood of the obtained outcome's occurrence. Much of their supporting literatures have assessed these two classes of judgment in isolation, but an underlying assumption over the years has been that the two judgments are inversely related in a simple, direct, and linear fashion. Four recent lines of research have shown this assumption to be overly simplistic, in that the relation between counterfactuals and hindsight bias is complex and varied. The judgments are differentially influenced by determinant variables such as perceived closeness, yet are joined at the hip by accessibility inferences and causal inferences. Moreover, the judgments are unified in their vulnerability to hijack by self-serving motives, compelling evidence for which was absent until very recently. Future research will no doubt elaborate further intriguing connections between these two classes of judgment.

Acknowledgments

This chapter was prepared while the author was supported by National Institute of Mental Health grant MH55578 and by the Canada Research Chair program. I appreciate the helpful comments of Nick Epley, Nigel Harvey, and Larry Sanna.

References

Agans, R. P. & Shaffer, L. S. (1994) The hindsight bias: The role of the availability heuristic and perceived risk, *Basic and Applied Social Psychology*, 15, 439–49.

Arkes, H. R. (1991) Costs and benefits of judgment errors: Implications for debiasing, *Psychological Bulletin*, 110, 486–98.

Arkes, H. R., Faust, D., Guilmette, T. J., & Hart, K. (1988) Eliminating the hindsight bias, *Journal of Applied Psychology*, 73, 305–7.

Branscombe, N. R., Owen, S., Garstka, T., & Coleman, J. (1996) Rape and accident counterfactual: Who might have done otherwise and would it have changed the outcome? *Journal of Applied Social Psychology*, 26, 1042–67.

Bryant, F. B. & Brockway, J. H. (1997) Hindsight bias in reaction to the verdict in the O. J. Simpson criminal trial, *Basic and Applied Social Psychology*, 19, 225–41.

Bryant, F. B. & Guilbault, R. L. (2002) "I knew it all along" eventually: The development of hindsight bias in reaction to the Clinton impeachment verdict, *Basic and Applied Social Psychology*, 24, 27–41.

Campbell, W. K. & Sedikides, C. (1999) Self-threat magnifies the self-serving bias: A meta-analytic integration, *Review of General Psychology*, 3, 23–43.

Carli, L. L. (1999) Cognitive reconstruction, hindsight, and reactions to victims and perpetrators, *Personality and Social Psychology Bulletin*, 25, 966–79.

Carli, L. L. & Leonard, J. B. (1989) The effect of hindsight on victim derogation, *Journal of Social and Clinical Psychology*, 8, 331–43.

Casper, J. D., Benedict, K., & Perry, J. L. (1989) Juror decision making, attitudes, and the hindsight bias, *Law and Human Behavior*, 13, 291–310.

Christensen-Szalanski, J. J. J. & Willham, C. F. (1991) The hindsight bias: A meta-analysis, *Organizational Behavior and Human Decision Processes*, 48, 147–68.

Connolly, T. & Zeelenberg, M. (2002) Regret in decision making, *Current Directions in Psychological Science*, 11, 212–16.

Creyer, E. H. & Gürhan, Z. (1997) Who's to blame? Counterfactual reasoning and the assignment of blame, *Psychology and Marketing*, 14, 209–22.

Davies, M. F. (1992) Field dependence and hindsight bias: Cognitive restructuring and the generation of reasons, *Journal of Research in Personality*, 26, 58–74.

Erdfelder, E. & Buchner, A. (1998) Decomposing the hindsight bias: A multinomial processing tree model for separating recollection and reconstruction in hindsight, *Journal of Experimental Psychology: Learning, Memory, and Cognition*, 24, 387–414.

Fischhoff, B. (1975) Hindsight ≠ foresight: The effect of outcome knowledge on judgment under uncertainty, *Journal of Experimental Psychology: Human Perception and Performance*, 1, 288–99.

Fischhoff, B. (1976) The effect of temporal setting on likelihood estimates, *Organizational Behavior and Human Performance*, 15, 180–94.

Goldinger, S. D., Kleider, H. M., Azuma, T., & Beike, D. R. (2003) "Blaming the victim" under memory load, *Psychological Science*, 14, 81–5.

Grieve, F. G., Houston, D. A., Dupuis, S. E., & Eddy, D. (1999) Counterfactual production and achievement orientation in competitive athletic settings, *Journal of Applied Social Psychology*, 29, 2177–202.

Harris, P. L., German, T., & Mills, P. (1996) Children's use of counterfactual thinking in causal reasoning, *Cognition*, 61, 233–59.

Haslam, N. & Jayasinghe, N. (1995) Negative affect and hindsight bias, *Journal of Behavioral Decision Making*, 8, 127–35.

Hastie, R., Schkade, D. A., & Payne, J. W. (1999) Juror judgments in civil cases: Hindsight effects on judgments of liability for punitive damages, *Law and Human Behavior*, 23, 597–614.

Hawkins, S. A. & Hastie, R. (1990) Hindsight: Biased judgment of past events after the outcomes are known, *Psychological Bulletin*, 107, 311–27.

Hertwig, R., Gigerenzer, G., & Hoffrage, U. (1997) The reiteration effect in hindsight bias, *Psychological Review*, 104, 194–202.

Hirt, E. R. & Markman, K. D. (1995) Multiple explanation: A consider-an-alternative strategy for debiasing judgments, *Journal of Personality and Social Psychology*, 69, 1069–86.

Hoch, S. J. (1985) Counterfactual reasoning and accuracy in predicting personal events, *Journal of Experimental Psychology: Learning, Memory, and Cognition*, 11, 719–31.

Hoffrage, U., Hertwig, R., & Gigerenzer, G. (2000) Hindsight bias: A by-product of knowledge updating? *Journal of Experimental Psychology: Learning, Memory, and Cognition*, 26, 566–81.

Holzl, E., Kirchler, E., & Rodler, C. (2002) Hindsight bias in economic expectations: I knew all along what I want to hear, *Journal of Applied Psychology*, 87, 437–43.

Kahneman, D. & Tversky, A. (1982) The simulation heuristic. In D. Kahneman, P. Slovic, and A. Tversky (eds.), *Judgment Under Uncertainty: Heuristics and Biases* (pp. 201–8). New York: Cambridge University Press.

Kahneman, D. & Varey, C. A. (1990) Propensities and counterfactuals: The loser that almost won, *Journal of Personality and Social Psychology*, 59, 1101–10.

Kamin, K. A. & Rachlinski, J. J. (1995) Ex post ≠ ex ante: Determining liability in hindsight, *Law and Human Behavior*, 19, 89–104.

Koehler, D. J. (1991) Explanation, imagination, and confidence in judgment, *Psychological Bulletin*, 110, 499–519.

Koriat, A., Lichtenstein, S., & Fischhoff, B. (1980) Reasons for confidence, *Journal of Experimental Psychology: Human Learning and Memory*, 6, 107–18.

Joslyn, S., Loftus, E., McNoughton, A., & Powers, J. (2001) Memory for memory, *Memory and Cognition*, 29, 789–97.

Leary, M. R. (1982) Hindsight distortion and the 1980 presidential election, *Personality and Social Psychology Bulletin*, 8, 257–63.

Lord, C. G., Lepper, M. R., & Preston, E. (1984) Considering the opposite: A corrective strategy for social judgment, *Journal of Personality and Social Psychology*, 47, 1231–43.

Louie, T. A. (1999) Decision makers' hindsight bias after receiving favorable and unfavorable feedback, *Journal of Applied Psychology*, 84, 29–41.

Louie, T. A., Curren, M. T., and Harich, K. R. (2000) "I knew we would win": Hindsight bias for favorable and unfavorable team decision outcomes, *Journal of Applied Psychology*, 85, 264–72.

Macrae, C. N. (1992) A tale of two curries: Counterfactual thinking and accident-related judgments, *Personality and Social Psychology Bulletin*, 18, 84–7.

Mandel, D. R. (in press) Judgment dissociation theory: An analysis of differences in causal, counterfactual, and covariational reasoning, *Journal of Experimental Psychology: General*.

Mandel, D. R. & Lehman, D. R. (1996) Counterfactual thinking and ascriptions of cause and preventability, *Journal of Personality and Social Psychology*, 71, 450–63.

Mark, M. M., Boburka, R. R., Eysell, K. M., Cohen, L. L., & Mellor, S. (2003) "I couldn't have seen it coming": The impact of negative self-relevant outcomes on retrospections about foreseeability, *Memory*, 11, 443–54.

Mark, M. M. & Mellor, S. (1991) Effect of self-relevance of an event on hindsight bias: The foreseeability of a layoff, *Journal of Applied Psychology*, 76, 569–77.

Markman, K. D. & Tetlock, P. E. (2000) Accountability and close counterfactuals: The loser that almost won and the winner that almost lost, *Personality and Social Psychology Bulletin*, 26, 1213–24.

McFarland, C. & Ross, M. (1982) Impact of causal attributions on affective reactions to success and failure, *Journal of Personality and Social Psychology*, 43, 937–46.

McGlynn, R. P. (2000) Hindsight bias and the O. J. Simpson verdict: A one-year follow-up, *Journal of Social Behavior and Personality*, 15, 293–301.

Medvec, V. H. & Savitsky, K. (1997) When doing better means feeling worse: A model of counterfactual cutoff points, *Journal of Personality and Social Psychology*, 72, 1284–96.

Mellers, B. A. (2000) Choice and the relative pleasure of consequences, *Psychological Bulletin*, 126, 910–24.

Mellers, B. A., Schwartz, A., Ho, K., & Ritov, I. (1997) Decision affect theory: Emotional reactions to the outcomes of risky options, *Psychological Science*, 8, 423–9.

Miller, D. T. & McFarland, C. (1986) Counterfactual thinking and victim compensation: A test of norm theory, *Personality and Social Psychology Bulletin*, 12, 513–19.

Miller, D. T. & Ross, M. (1975) Self-serving biases in the attribution of causality: Fact or fiction? *Psychological Bulletin*, 82, 213–25.

Miller, D. T. & Taylor, B. R. (1995) Counterfactual thought, regret, and superstition: How to avoid kicking yourself. In N. J. Roese and J. M. Olson (eds.), *What Might Have Been: The Social Psychology of Counterfactual Thinking* (pp. 305–31). Mahwah, NJ: Erlbaum.

Nasco, S. A. & Marsh, K. L. (1999) Gaining control through counterfactual thinking, *Personality and Social Psychology Bulletin*, 25, 556–68.

N'gbala, A. & Branscombe, N. R. (1995) Mental simulation and causal attribution: When simulating an event does not affect fault assignment, *Journal of Experimental Social Psychology*, 31, 139–162.

Robbennolt, J. K. & Sobus, M. S. (1997) An integration of hindsight bias and counterfactual thinking: Decision making and drug courier profiles *Law and Human Behavior*, 22, 671–83.

Roese, N. J. (1994) The functional basis of counterfactual thinking, *Journal of Personality and Social Psychology*, 66, 805–18.

Roese, N. J. (1997) Counterfactual thinking, *Psychological Bulletin*, 121, 133–48.

Roese, N. J. (1999) Counterfactual thinking and decision making, *Psychonomic Bulletin and Review*, 6, 570–8.

Roese, N. J. & Hur, T. (1997) Affective determinants of counterfactual thinking, *Social Cognition*, 15, 274–90.

Roese, N. J. & Maniar, S. D. (1997) Perceptions of purple: Counterfactual and hindsight judgments at Northwestern Wildcats football games, *Personality and Social Psychology Bulletin*, 23, 1245–53.

Roese, N. J. & Olson, J. M. (1993) Self-esteem and counterfactual thinking, *Journal of Personality and Social Psychology*, 65, 199–206.

Roese, N. J. & Olson, J. M. (1996) Counterfactuals, causal attributions, and the hindsight bias: A conceptual integration, *Journal of Experimental Social Psychology*, 32, 197–227.

Roese, N. J. & Olson, J. M. (1997) Counterfactual thinking: The intersection of affect and function. In M. P. Zanna (ed.), *Advances in Experimental Social Psychology* (vol. 29, pp. 1–59). San Diego, CA: Academic Press.

Roese, N. J., Sanna, L. J., & Galinsky, A. D. (in press) The mechanics of imagination: Automaticity and counterfactual thinking. To appear in J. A. Bargh, J. Uleman, and R. Hassin (eds.), *The New Unconscious*. New York: Cambridge University Press.

Ross, M. (1989) Relation of implicit theories to the construction of personal histories, *Psychological Review*, 96, 341–57.

Sanna, L. J. & Chang, E. C. (2003) The past is not what it used to be: Optimists' use of retroactive pessimism to diminish the sting of failure, *Journal of Research in Personality*, 37, 388–404.

Sanna, L. J. & Schwarz, N. (2003) Debiasing the hindsight bias: The role of accessibility experiences and (mis)attributions, *Journal of Experimental Social Psychology*, 39, 287–95.

Sanna, L. J., Schwarz, N., & Small, E. M. (2002) Accessibility experiences and the hindsight bias: I knew it along versus it could never have happened, *Memory and Cognition*, 30, 1288–96.

Sanna, L. J., Schwarz N., & Stocker S. L. (2002) When debiasing backfires: Accessible content and accessibility experiences in debiasing hindsight, *Journal of Experimental Psychology: Learning, Memory, and Cognition*, 28, 497–502.

Sanna, L. J. & Turley, K. J. (1996) Antecedents to spontaneous counterfactual thinking: Effects of expectancy violation and outcome valence, *Personality and Social Psychology Bulletin*, 22, 906–19.

Schkade, D. A. & Kilbourne, L. M. (1991) Expectation-outcome consistency and hindsight bias, *Organizational Behavior and Human Decision Processes*, 49, 105–23.

Schwarz, N. (1998) Accessible content and accessibility experiences: The interplay of declarative and experiential information in judgment, *Personality and Social Psychology Review*, 2, 87–99.

Sherman, S. J., Zehner, K. S., Johnson, J., & Hirt, E. R. (1983) Social explanation: The role of timing, set, and recall on subjective likelihood estimates, *Journal of Personality and Social Psychology*, 44, 1127–43.

Slovic, P. & Fischhoff, B. (1977) On the psychology of experimental surprises, *Journal of Experimental Psychology: Human Perception and Performance*, 3, 544–51.

Stallard, M. J. & Worthington, D. L. (1998) Reducing the hindsight bias utilizing attorney closing arguments, *Law and Human Behavior*, 22, 671–83.

Teigen, K. H. (1998) When the unreal is more likely than the real: Post hoc probability judgments and counterfactual closeness, *Thinking and Reasoning*, 4, 147–77.

Tykocinski, O. E. (2001) I never had a chance: Using hindsight tactics to mitigate disappointments, *Personality and Social Psychology Bulletin*, 27, 376–82.

Tykocinski, O. E., Pick, D., & Kedmi, D. (2002) Retroactive pessimism: A different kind of hindsight bias, *European Journal of Social Psychology*, 32, 577–88.

Wasserman, D., Lempert, R. O., & Hastie, R. (1991) Hindsight and causality, *Personality and Social Psychology Bulletin*, 17, 30–5.

Wells, G. L. & Gavanski, I. (1989) Mental simulation of causality, *Journal of Personality and Social Psychology*, 56, 161–9.

Winman, A., Juslin, P., & Björkman, M. (1998) The confidence-hindsight mirror effect in judgment: An accuracy-assessment model for the knew-it-all-along phenomenon, *Journal of Experimental Psychology: Learning, Memory, and Cognition*, 24, 415–31.

14

Forecasting and Scenario Planning: The Challenges of Uncertainty and Complexity

Paul J. H. Schoemaker

Introduction

Forecasting involves making predictions about an unknown question or issue. My focus here is on why uncertainty and complexity pose special challenges in forecasting and what to do about this. Figure 14.1 provides a typology of forecasts based on how uncertain the prediction is (x axis) and how complex the issue is (y axis). Complexity here refers to the number of variables and the extent to which they are interrelated. Uncertainty, in contrast, concerns the degree of available knowledge about the target

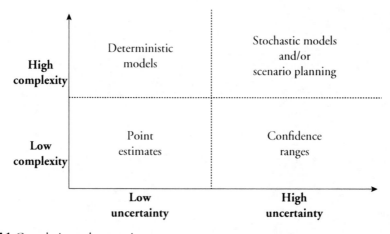

Figure 14.1 Complexity and uncertainty

variable, whether simple or complex (Schoemaker, 1993). Unrecognized complexity may appear as uncertainty, but they are conceptually distinct.

Low uncertainty–low complexity cases (LL for short) are often handled in the form of point estimates, for example when forecasting the demand for a known product in a stable environment. HL cases (high uncertainty–low complexity) typically entail a point forecast plus a confidence range or perhaps an entire probability distribution. The mean is of less interest here than the range over which the variable may vary. An example is trying to estimate the oil reserves in a new offshore field about to be prospected. Since complexity is low in both the LL and HL cases, it is justifiable to make numerical predictions about the variable of interest without extensively conditioning the forecast on key assumptions about other variables that may influence it. The uncertainty range (or an entire univariate probability distribution) may be able to capture and reflect the combined impact of these other secondary factors. However, when complexity is high, in the sense of there being strong interdependence among the multiple predictor variables, then such isolated forecasts become less valuable and perhaps dangerous.

The LH case (low uncertainty–high complexity) typically requires the formulation of a deterministic model in which the key variables of interest are explicitly related to each other. For instance, a short-term forecast about GNP growth may not be meaningful without specifying the key relationships among interest rates, consumer confidence, economic policy and the like. Econometric models seek to capture such relationships algebraically without explicit attention to uncertainty other than, perhaps, as exogenous shocks. The HH (high uncertainty–high complexity) case would require stochastic models that seek to include uncertainty explicitly, such as queuing models with random arrival times. There exist few stochastic models that capture global economic interactions well. It seems very hard to capture both the complexity and uncertainty components in HH cases. Scenario planning may offer a good compromise between a highly formal model and informal conjecture (Huss, 1988). It balances the need for discipline with the need to maintain an open mind and as such can provide a good starting point for HH cases. We shall later pay special attention to the HH case through scenario planning. First, however, we discuss the two dimensions of uncertainty and complexity in greater detail.

The Challenge of Uncertainty[1]

We define uncertainty as disagreement among forecasters, or doubts within a single forecaster, as to the correct value of an unknown quantity of interest. Years of behavioral research on judgment and decision making have unearthed a variety of cognitive limitations when people are confronted with uncertainty. We shall review just the major ones.

When forecasting, most humans suffer from *overconfidence*. We are too sure of our single view about the future and fail to consider alternative views sufficiently (Lichtenstein, Fischhoff, & Phillips, 1982; Ayton & McClelland, 1997; Klayman, Soll, Gonzàlez-Vallejo, & Barlas, 1999). Novices and experts alike appear to be overconfident in most of their predictions (Cerf & Navasky, 1984). We are overconfident, in part, because of our inability to envision all possible pathways into the future – a failure of imagination. But there are other reasons (Russo & Schoemaker, 1992).

Illusion of control

A motivational reason why people may be overconfident is that they harbor a deep-seated psychological need to feel in control. Langer (1975) showed that people harbor an insidious illusion of control, which gets stronger as they exert more effort in predicting the future. For example, lottery sales in Massachusetts increased markedly once people were allowed to pick their own lucky number rather than being assigned a number at random the old way (Perlmuter & Monty, 1977). This need for an illusion of control is widespread (Presson & Benassi, 1996) and may explain why gamblers blow on their dice or study the streaks in roulette. The illusion of control, however, may also contribute to our mental health (Taylor & Brown, 1988; Gillham, 2000) and thus is not all bad. Overconfidence just needs to be suppressed somewhat when making key forecasts or important decisions.

Information distortion

People's perceptions of risk and uncertainty are further distorted because the available information may not be representative of the real situation. We are overly aware of those parts of the world that produce the most noise or are most readily in our line of sight (Tversky & Kahneman, 1974). For example, when researchers asked subjects whether they thought lung cancer or automotive accidents caused more deaths annually in the USA, the majority guessed auto accidents. In fact, at the time of the study, there were about 140,000 deaths per year from lung cancer compared to about 40,000 from auto accidents. People learn about auto accidents from the media every day and their perceptions of risk are skewed accordingly (Huber, Wider, & Huber, 1997). Similarly, we overreact to shark attacks in the ocean or terrorist attacks in the sky and fail to put these risks in their proper statistical perspective. This bias towards overweighting the most readily available information operates in many subtle ways and can best be countered by asking where the hidden slants are in the data that are available to us.

Risk perception

When it comes to people's perceptions of risk, other factors play a role. We seem to dread most those risks we understand poorly (say radon gas in our basement) or those over which we have no control (such as flying a commercial airplane). And risks that occur in clusters, such as an airplane crash in which all people are killed, instill more fear than far greater risks that hit isolated individuals at random such as automobile accidents. Similarly, we react more strongly to uncertainties that are vividly portrayed or experienced, such as physical assault or a highly traumatic childbirth, than the less vivid statistical risks associated with various kinds of cancer (Fischhoff, 1983; Slovic, 1987).

Assessing or weighing probabilities

This is another area where people are not very good. Often they don't even look at this information. Several studies asked people to choose among uncertain alternatives and when given the opportunity to get additional information few inquired about data on probabilities (Kunreuther, Hogarth, & Meszaros, 2001; Magat, Viscusi, & Huber, 1987). This problem is especially acute when dealing with very low probabilities, such as the chance of catastrophic accidents or natural disasters. In such cases, people cannot readily distinguish between a 0.001 risk vs. a 0.0001 risk even though the latter is ten times less likely.

In sum, humans seem to have a hard time assessing and estimating risk and uncertainty appropriately. And the picture is not really better when it comes to complexity.

The Challenge of Complexity

Complexity, in our sense, refers to how many variables have to be considered and how deeply they interact for the prediction task at hand. Decision research has not focused as much on how humans cope with complexity (as opposed to uncertainty). The extensive literature on heuristics and biases mostly addresses how such mechanisms as anchoring, availability, or representativeness underlie and often bias subjects' estimates of uncertain quantities but do not address the issue of interrelatedness per se.

Combining variables

Early decision research within the lens model paradigm did address how well subjects could combine multiple predictor variables (Hammond, Hursch, & Todd, 1964; Dawes, Faust, & Meehl, 1989). The focus was mostly on subject's ability to aggregate cues additively rather than their skill in understanding cue interrelationships (which an additive model, by definition, cannot capture). The few studies that did focus on these so-called configural cues, which can be represented as cross product terms in a linear model, concluded that people seldom understand, learn or use interaction effects well in their predictions. These lens model studies further demonstrated subjects' difficulties in handling other forms of non-linearity, such as concave or convex cue relationships. Also, the lens model line of research highlighted the large amount of random error present in people's intuitive multivariate forecasts and the attendant need to use models as forecasting aids (Camerer, 1981). The phenomenon of bootstrapping – in which subjects are outperformed by their own subjective regression models in predicting new cases – has justly received much attention.[2] And linear models have been praised for their robust beauty (Dawes & Corrigan, 1974). Nonetheless, Feltovich, Ford, and Hoffman (1997) caution that when we abstract cues from a complex real-world situation, we inevitably create distortion (i.e., a reduction bias).

Understanding covariance

Other behavioral studies have examined why subjective estimates of correlation or covariation among variables suffer from some interesting distortions (Jennings, Amabile, & Ross, 1982). On the one hand, people tend to underestimate correlations among variables when their perceptions are purely atheoretical, e.g., data presented in spreadsheet form on golf scores between two players after several rounds of match play. On the other hand, humans tend to overestimate correlations when they are primarily based on a presumed causal theory. If we can easily envision a causal pathway that makes one variable dependent on another – such as being in a car accident while drinking or using a cell phone – people deem the correlation to be stronger than the data warrant. The basic conclusion is that humans don't process cue importance or cue interrelationships well when things get complex (i.e., multiple variables are involved). Furthermore, this limited ability to detect multivariate relationship deteriorates quickly when random noise is added to the equation, which introduces the uncertainty dimension (our HH case).

Cognitive simplification

The challenge of complexity relates directly to the notion of bounded rationality (Simon, 1997). Humans need to simplify the complex world that surrounds them and do so through such cognitive devices as associative networks, scripts, schemata, frames, and mental models (for their finer distinctions see Klayman & Schoemaker, 1993). In combination, these mental mechanisms provide much needed cognitive structure and simplification, which is essential for making sense of the complex patterns presented by the world (Gentner & Stevens, 1983; Johnson-Laird, 1983; Ranyard, 1997). Considering the avalanche of information bombarding us daily, these cognitive structures and processes help us filter out some things and focus on others. Instead of seeing a stream of disconnected pixels on our computer or television screens, we are able to see images and words. However, one drawback of such cognitive economy may be that our frames can greatly distort reality (Schoemaker & Russo, 2001). The essence of expertise seems to entail a judicious balancing of cognitive simplification while maintaining high functional competence (Klein, 2003).

Often people use such related processes as "pattern matching" and "story telling" to connect the new stimuli to the mental models in our heads. Hastie, Penrod, Pennington, & Willis (2002) studied jurors in mock murder trials and noticed how early on they develop stories or scripts about the initial data and then proceed to process additional information in line with these original stories. The problem is that we tend to become trapped by our frames or stories: we notice the confirming evidence more than that which does not fit (Klayman & Ha, 1987, 1989). We start to see patterns that are not really there or fail to see soon enough that new data may require a fundamental change in the storyline. When new information comes in, we try to force it into the existing frame rather than shifting our frames. Let's be mindful of Albert Einstein's admonition that "we should make things as simple as possible, but not simpler." The major dangers of frames are that they filter information, restrict our attention, become too engrained, and make our view seem more complete than it really is (Russo & Schoemaker, 2001). Frame awareness and adjustment can help overcome these dangers.

Dynamic complexity

The problem of complexity has at least two important dimensions: cross-sectional complexity, which concerns how variables interrelate at a given point in time versus dynamic complexity, which adds the time elements and the role of feedback loops. The lens model research cited above mostly addressed static complexity. The temporal dimension introduces additional challenges relating to observation, feedback and learning. Sterman (1989, 1999) specifically studied how people learn about complex relationships in simulated dynamic environments, such as a computer simulation of an airline company's strategic decisions or an electronics firm's new launch of a hit product that goes boom and bust. The subjects in these experiments were asked to assume the role of management and to make various strategic and operational decisions for a given period. After completing one round of decisions, they received abundant feedback (in the form of financial statements, market share data, operational statistics, etc.) and then were asked to repeat this process for 20 or more periods. In spite of extensive feedback after each period, subjects improved only slowly over time and had difficulty developing sound mental models about the deeper drivers of the simulation. They typically could not out-perform preprogrammed heuristics that used very simple adjustments from one period to the next, with a planning horizon and memory of no more than one period.

Senge (1990), Morecroft and Sterman (1994) and others used these dynamic simulations to reveal subjects' embedded mental models, which can be useful whenever executives face major changes in their industries. The science of surfacing and represent-ing mental models is still embryonic. The key is to understand better how complex interrelationships are mentally represented, which in turn may require a better science of networks (see Barabási, 2002). Much progress has been made in artificial intelligence (AI) using such approaches as neural nets, genetic algorithms, and expert systems. The tasks studied in AI are usually well structured and clearly bounded in domain, like chess or medical diagnoses. Nonetheless, these tasks are typically very complex and defy closed forum optimization. Also, a science of complexity is emerging, motivated by the desire of physicists, economists and others to better understand the behavior of complex sys-tems and our representations thereof (Varela, 1979). The fields of systems theory and cybernetics, dating back to Von Bertalanffy (1976), Wiener (1961), and Forrester (1961), pursued similar goals but have yet to achieve broad acceptance. But the effort is import-ant since complexity has been the stepchild of decision-making research when compared to its twin uncertainty.

Complexity research is related to such streams as catastrophe theory (Thom, 1984) and chaos models (Gleick, 1987; Ekeland, 1988; Baumol & Benhabib, 1989), which study the discontinuity and unpredictability of complex systems. These phenomena of insta-bility, as encountered in weather patterns, economic cycles as well as speculative bubbles, pose great challenges to forecasters but also major opportunities for those who do it well (Andreassen & Kraus, 1990). Typically, however, a deeper understanding is needed in order to recognize when turning or tipping points in markets may occur. And perhaps these bifurcations hinge on so many unobservable factors that forecasters can do little more than bound the range within which the system may oscillate. For example, relatively simple deterministic models with non-linear feedback loops can exhibit extreme sensitivity to minor deviations in the underlying variables, which may prompt observers to characterize it as a "chaotic, unpredictable system." However, in this case deterministic complexity is simply misdiagnosed as uncertainty since a deterministic model, by definition, does not contain any stochastic elements (Schuster, 1995).

It may seem ironic, in view of the above complexity discussion, that some of the best-calibrated forecasts are found among weather forecasters (Lichtenstein et al, 1982; Murphy & Winkler, 1984). These professionals realize that what they seek to predict is highly uncertain and complex (HH case). Consequently, they provide probabilistic forecasts and closely observe outcomes. Also, they are aided by good starting points based on computer-based weather forecasts. Over time, this man-machine approach – supplemented with accurate, repeated, and timely feedback as well as explicit rewards for good calibration – has developed into an effective forecasting system. The key to improvement is to understand the nature of the task, the limitations of humans, and the value of tools. The next section reviews further what kind of challenges humans are likely to encounter for different combinations of uncertainty and complexity.

Selected Research Findings

Having discussed uncertainty and complexity as separate dimensions, we now examine their combined effects. Based on an extensive behavioral literature (see Hastie, 2001; Gilovich, Griffin, & Kahneman, 2002) the following stylized biases or challenges appear to exist for the four quadrants of Figure 14.1.

Low uncertainty–low complexity (LL)

Single point forecasts are often plagued by tendencies to focus excessively on one value and reluctance to diverge from that initial estimate. Such point forecasts either start with a convenient reference point and then adjust to reflect other factors, or they seek to integrate numerous factors all at once. In the former approach, the process may suffer from anchoring with insufficient adjustment (Tversky & Kahneman, 1974). In the latter approach, various other biases may arise from availability effects to representativeness distortions (Kahneman, Slovic, & Tversky, 1982). When the time variable is added, researchers found that, for example, exponential growth is commonly underestimated and that other nonlinear effects are systematically misjudged (Wagenaar & Timmers, 1979). More recent information may be over weighted (recency bias) when integrating information over time (Lawrence & O'Connor, 1992; Bolger & Harvey, 1993). In general, the way information is retrieved in order to arrive at a synthesis judgment may suffer from recall and other availability biases (Tversky & Kahneman, 1973; Bolger & Harvey, 1998). Intuitive predictions usually also exhibit a high degree of inconsistency because information is processed in a haphazard fashion.[3] A caveat we should add is that most of the above biases were demonstrated in experimental settings rather than studying experts in real-world tasks. This may limit the generality of the overall findings.

High uncertainty–low complexity (HL)

Uncertainty ranges are typically too narrow: people are overly sure about the accuracy of their predictions (Lichtenstein et al., 1982; Klayman et al., 1999). Vivid information or easily recalled data may overly influence judgments (Tversky & Kahneman, 1974), both in terms of point estimates as well as ranges. New information may be too conservatively factored into people's revised forecasts (conservatism bias) whereas in other settings concrete new information may overshadow abstract prior probabilities (base-rate ignorance). In general, humans cannot systematically or comprehensively consider all factors and consequently they often misestimate the degree of uncertainty as well as consistency of their intuitive predictions (Kahneman & Tversky, 1982; Harvey, 1995; Dougherty, Gettys, & Thomas, 1997).

Low uncertainty–high complexity (LH)

When constructing models, in order to combine the multiple factors that matter, people often harbor simplistic notions about cause and effect (Tversky & Kahneman, 1980; Einhorn & Hogarth, 1986). They may ignore feedback loops or secondary interactions (Sterman, 1989, 1999). Surprisingly, intuitive predictions involving multiple variables are usually outperformed by linear regression models based on those very judgments (known as bootstrapping). Combining human and mechanical predictions typically beats either alone (Blattberg & Hoch, 1990; Hoch, 1994, 2001). The challenge is to discover the valid component of intuitive judgment amid the extensive noise that surrounds it (Whitecotton, Sanders, & Norris, 1998). Recent approaches in statistics have tried to address the LH case using vector autoregression (Tiao, 2001).

High uncertainty–high complexity (HH)

Limited behavioral research exists about human judgment under conditions of high complexity and high uncertainty. In this case, a focus on learning is more important than analysis per se. It is known that people dislike ambiguity and thus try to avoid such situations (Einhorn & Hogarth, 1985; Hogarth & Kunreuther, 1995; Fox & Tversky, 1995; Kunreuther et al., 1993). But if they have to function in such environments, humans do not easily learn about the deeper structures, especially if non-linear feedback loops exist or other complicating factors operate in the complex dynamic situation

(Sterman, 1989, 1999). Common mistakes when trying to learn in complex and uncertain environments include failing to entertain multiple hypotheses and placing too much weight on confirming rather than disconfirming evidence (Klayman & Ha, 1987, 1989).

Complexity and uncertainty clearly complicate our attempts at sound forecasting (O'Connor, Remus, & Griggs, 1993). In general, intuitive judgment should not be trusted in such cases unless the forecaster is highly expert and has much experience (Hogarth, 2001; Klein, 2003). Although both components (i.e., complexity as well as uncertainty) are very important in daily life, behavioral decision researchers have focused much more on judgment under uncertainty than on how humans deal with complexity. Most studies of complexity focus either on framing effects or heuristics and biases, but often in simplified laboratory settings where normative benchmarks can be easily established (for critiques of this line of research see Gigerenzer, 1991, 1996; Klein, 1998).

Tools to Improve Prediction

Fortunately, there are many tools to help overcome the numerous forecasting and decision-making traps alluded to above (Armstrong, 2001; Courtney, Kirkland, & Viguerie, 1997; Courtney, 2001). Our focus in this section will be limited to tools relevant to the four cases just discussed.

Low uncertainty–low complexity (LL case)

This is a situation where unbiased point estimates may be good enough. Although uncertainty and complexity do exist, they are probably of a variety that can be managed in the normal course of business. For instance, when McDonald's opens up yet another mainstream restaurant, it does so with the benefit of vast experience. The 20,000 or so previous restaurants McDonalds opened should give it high confidence about projected revenues, cost structures, competitive behaviors, etc. In this case, extrapolative forecasting, net present value analysis, and decision analytic methods such as sensitivity analysis are all that may be needed; doing much more will likely be overkill. The use of the systematic methods just mentioned, each of which demands welcome scrutiny about the input variables and some discipline about the information aggregation process, will largely eliminate the problems of human inconsistency, poor non-linear extrapolation and anchoring on convenient starting points. Of course, deeper biases may remain about hidden assumptions or misaligned mental models in which case further exercises need to be conducted to help surface and correct them (Fiol & Huff, 1992).

High uncertainty–low complexity (HL case)

In this situation, there is significant external uncertainty but of a kind that can be structured and analyzed quite easily. An example would be whether or not a small biotech company will receive a key patent or not. Whenever the possible outcomes can be clearly identified and probabilities assigned with some confidence, we are dealing with a HL case. The key assumption here is that the prediction task is sufficiently well understood to allow for a structured and complete analysis. The natural techniques here are event diagrams, fault trees, simulation and decision analysis, especially decision trees and value of information analyses such as Bayesian updates.[4] A sound application of these techniques should reduce the problem of overconfidence (narrow ranges) and biased estimates, but the earlier caveats about mental models and deeper assumptions (Bell, Raiffa, & Tversky, 1988; Kleindorfer, Kunreuther, & Schoemaker, 1993) still apply. It is especially important in HL cases to get unbiased estimates of the probabilities, many of which may be subjective in nature. This can be done through consensus forecasts or other statistical averaging techniques (Winkler, 1981).

Low uncertainty–high complexity (LH case)

In this case, the number of variables involved, and their interrelationships, will require a more systematic analysis. LH cases are typically amenable to some form of deterministic modeling. A simple approach would be to start with assumption analysis (Mason & Mitroff, 1981) since this may identify gaps or distortions in the fabric of presumed interrelationship. Next, an influence diagram could be constructed and/or an entire system dynamic model (see Sterman, 2000) to fully appreciate causal linkages over time (Einhorn & Hogarth, 1986). Another approach to consider is discovery-driven planning (McGrath & MacMillan, 1995), in which one works backward to see what assumptions and interim achievements would be required to achieve a particular end state. This technique will also help identify key drivers that should be monitored closely so that timely adjustments can be made in the forecasts if needed. In addition to these more holistic approaches, more focused techniques exist to improve the quality of judgments when matters get complex. Reason generation, role-playing, imagining unusual outcomes (outliers), comparisons against past cases, and panel techniques like Delphi polling can all improve judgments about input variables or causal relationships (see Armstrong, 2001).

High uncertainty–high complexity (HH case)

This greatest level of challenge is posed when both uncertainty and complexity are high. In the real world, this would correspond to cases of high ambiguity or chaos where too little knowledge exists to make reliable predictions. Assessing the future market size of genomics-based drugs is an example, as would be predicting the outcome of the war on terrorism. In such cases, the focus should be mostly on exploration and learning rather than on trying to synthesize whatever meager knowledge exists into a single point forecast or univariate range. Surfacing the deeper assumptions, challenging one's mental models and posing disconfirming questions would be good ways to start (Mason & Mitroff, 1981; de Geus, 1988). Exploring the issue from a system's perspective, with a focus on multiple causes and feedback loops, would also help. Whenever strong predictions are made in HH cases, it would be wise to work backwards and ask what one would have to believe for those predictions to be valid. For instance, what would it require for genomics-based drugs to exceed $10 billion in sales by 2010? Or what would it take for a particular war in the Middle East to be over within say 6 months? Scenario planning is especially good at deepening our understanding of the forces at work and in generating multiple viewpoints that capture the full range of uncertainty and complexity.

Scenario Planning[5]

This section focuses further on scenario planning since it is a proven, practical tool to handle HH cases. Unlike earlier tools discussed, scenario planning typically occurs within a rich organizational context, involving big picture issues and, perhaps, deep differences of view about the future. My treatment will reflect this organizational context, although the tool can be used as well by a single person working in isolation.

Scenarios focus on the *joint* effect of many factors. Scenario planning helps us understand how the various strands of a complex tapestry move if one or more threads are pulled. When you just *list* possible causes, as for instance in fault tree analysis (Dube-Rioux & Russo, 1988), you may tend to discount any one factor in isolation. But when you explore the factors together, you realize that certain combinations could magnify each others' impact or likelihood. For instance, an increased trade deficit may trigger an economic recession, which in turn creates unemployment and reduces domestic production. Although joint occurrences of events will always have a lower probability than each individual event alone, the conjunction fallacy may actually give greater psychological credence to causally coherent scenarios (Tversky & Kahneman, 1983). Ironically, scenario planning uses one bias (the conjunction fallacy) to help overcome other biases such as overconfidence and limited imagination.

Scenario planning starts by dividing our knowledge into two broad domains: things we believe we know something about and elements we consider uncertain or unknowable. The first component – trends – casts the past forward, recognizing that our world possesses considerable momentum and continuity. For example, we can safely make assumptions about demographic shifts and, perhaps, substitution effects for certain new technologies. The second component – true uncertainties – involve indeterminables such as future interest rates, outcomes of political elections, rates of innovation, fads and fashions in markets, and so on. The art of scenario planning lies in blending the known and the unknown into a limited number of internally consistent views of the future that span a very wide range of possibilities.

Numerous organizations have applied scenario planning to a broad range of issues, from relatively simple, tactical decisions to the complex process of strategic planning and vision building (Schwartz, 1991; van der Heijden, 1996; Ringland, 1998). I personally became persuaded by the power of scenario planning through my work with Royal Dutch/Shell, which has used scenarios since the early 1970s as part of a process for generating and evaluating its strategic options (Wack, 1985a, 1985b; Schoemaker & van der Heijden, 1992). Shell has been consistently better in its oil forecasts than other major oil companies, and saw the overcapacity in the tanker business and Europe's petrochemicals earlier than its competitors (Schwartz, 1991). Other firms have likewise benefited from scenario planning (Sunter, 1987).

How to Develop Scenarios

What follows is a brief description of how one might construct multiple scenarios, based on the approach developed by Royal Dutch/Shell and many other companies (Schoemaker, 1995). Again, in contrast to the earlier sections, which focused on the individual decision makers or forecasters, I adopt here more of an organizational perspective. Readers should also note that scenario planning can take many forms and that numerous variations exist (see Fahey & Randall, 1998) which makes it a very flexible and highly scaleable (from informal to formal) process.

1   *Define the scope*: Set the time frame and scope of analysis (e.g., products, markets, geographic areas, technologies).
2   *Identify the major stakeholders*: Who will have an interest in these issues? Who will be affected by them? Who could influence them? Think about each player's role, interests, and power position, and ask how and why they have changed over time. A stakeholder map could plot key stakeholders in terms of power and interest and examine this map over time.
3   *Identify basic trends*: What social, technological, economic, environmental, and political (STEEP) trends are sure to affect the issues you identified in step 1? Briefly define each trend (such as the aging population or greater broadband into homes) and explain how or why it is indeed relevant. You could list each trend on a chart to identify whether its impact on your *present strategy* is positive, negative, or neutral. For something to be labeled a trend, everyone must agree that the trend will continue directionally within the time frame considered; any issue on which there is disagreement within the team belongs in the next step.
4   *Identify key uncertainties*: What events, whose outcomes are uncertain, will significantly affect the issues concerning you? As above, consider factors that are political, economic, societal, etc. For each uncertainty, determine possible outcomes. It is not important to account for all the possible outcomes of each uncertainty; simplifying the range of outcomes is sufficient. For instance, you may want to think in terms of three possible interest rates (high, medium, and low) rather than hundreds of them. As before, you could score each outcome in terms of being positive, negative, or neutral relative to the current strategy. The purpose here is not to cover all possibilities, but to describe a wide range.
5   *Construct initial scenario themes*: Once you have identified trends and uncertainties, you have the main ingredients for scenario construction. The simplest approach is to identify two extreme worlds by putting all the positive outcomes in one and all the negatives in another and then sprinkle in the remaining "neutral" outcomes (Schoemaker, 1991). Note that positive, neutral, or negative are defined here relative

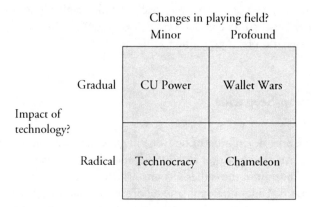

Figure 14.2 Basic scenario matrix

to the current strategy. So, a seemingly negative outcome (say greater environmental regulation) may later prove to be one of innovation and hidden opportunity provided a new strategy is adopted. A second, and probably better approach, is to select the two most significant uncertainties and then postulate two rather extreme outcomes for each uncertainty. These dichotomous uncertainties can then be crossed in a 2-by-2 matrix to generate four possible scenario themes as illustrated in Figure 14.2.[6]

6 *Build a scenario blueprint*: The next step is to add additional outcomes to each cell of the matrix, to reflect the role of the other uncertainties. This way a blueprint gets created that lists for every scenario what outcomes are presumed. In addition to playing out all uncertainties, we must add all the trends to each scenario. Assuming there are t trends and u uncertainties, each scenario is now an n-tuple (where $n = t + u$) consisting of all trends plus presumed outcomes for all uncertainties. Then we must ask if these initial scenario scripts are plausible, internally consistent, and sufficiently relevant. For example, an initial scenario may postulate both full employment and zero inflation. But that is an unlikely combination. To test internal consistency, ask: Are the trends compatible within the chosen time frame? (If not, remove the trends that don't fit.) Do the scenarios combine outcomes of uncertainties that go together? (If not, eliminate that possible pairing from the scenario.) Are major stakeholders placed in positions they do not like and can change? (If so, your scenario will evolve into something else; try to describe the new scenario, which is more stable.)

7 *Develop full-fledged scenarios*: By now, some general themes should begin to emerge. Once the building blocks have been arranged in various ways (steps 5 and 6 above), a more holistic view has to be adopted. The overall goal is to identify storylines and themes for the scenarios that cover a full range of possible outcomes for the uncertain issues at hand. It may be necessary to rearrange the scenario elements in order to create anywhere from two to five internally consistent and relevant scenarios. These scenarios should describe generically different futures, rather than variations

on one theme. They should cover a wide range of possibilities and clearly highlight competing perspectives. Although the trends, by definition, appear in all the scenarios, they can be given more or less weight in different scenarios. The key is to develop a compelling storyline for each scenario that captures a distinct viewpoint about how the future may play out. Thus, a good scenario is more than just an n-tuple of presumed outcomes and trends, but rather a coherent dynamic account of how a particular future may come about over time.

8   *Identify research needs*: At this point, you may need to do further research to flesh out your understanding of uncertainties and trends, as well as perhaps their inter-relationship over time. For example, do you really understand the causal chain of events, or how a key stakeholder might behave in a given scenario? Do you need to study new technologies not yet in the mainstream of your industry, but which may be someday? It can be helpful at this stage to draw analogies to earlier time periods or other industries to illustrate the essence of a scenario. For example, a scenario about the future of genomics might make reference to the early days of the computer industry to underscore the importance of standards, killer applications, or strategic alliances. It may also help to develop an influence diagram that captures the dynamic logic of each scenario (Morecroft & Sterman, 1994; Sterman, 2000). Such diagrams can help portray how various trends and key uncertainties are interrelated causally, including the role of feedback loops.

9   *Develop quantitative models*: Once you have influence diagrams, you can take any scenario to the next level of specificity by quantifying it. Using *i-think* or similar software, you can start specifying the key relationships in each scenario algebraic-ally resulting in a system dynamic representation. You can then use this model to simulate the consequences of various scenarios in terms of price behavior, growth rates, market share, and so on. Royal Dutch/Shell used such a model to make sure that oil prices, inflation, GNP growth, taxes, oil inventories, interest rates, and so forth were kept plausibly balanced within each of its scenarios. The benefit of such a simulation is that the scenarios are brought closer to the decision-making process. Managers may relate better to the specific numerical ranges implied by each scenario.

10   *Evolve toward decision scenarios*: Finally, through an iterative process, you must converge toward a limited number of distinctly different scenarios that you will eventually use to test your strategies and generate new ideas. Retrace steps 1 through 8 to see if the scenarios (and any quantitative models from step 9) address the real issues facing your company. Are they relevant? Internally consistent? Do they describe generically different futures rather than variations on one theme? Has each scenario been thought through towards its final conclusion (if any)? Have you discussed the scenarios with others, to get inputs and external validation or chal-lenge? If you answered "yes" to each of the questions above, you are done. If not, repeat the steps and refocus your scenarios the way an artist judges the balance and focal point in a painting. Half of this judgment is art, half is science. Once done, the scenarios can now be used as frameworks or inputs for more quantitative analyses of key decisions or projects using such techniques as payoff matrices, decision trees, options analysis, Monte Carlo simulation, or portfolio optimization.

Some Limitations of Scenario Planning

Although scenario planning has gained much adherence in industry, its subjective and heuristic nature leaves many academics uncomfortable. How do we know if we have the right scenarios? And how do we go from scenarios to decisions? These concerns are legitimate and scenario planning would gain in academic standing if more research were conducted on its comparative performance and underlying theoretical premises (Gregory & Duran, 2001; Harries, 2003). A recent collection of chapters by noted scenario planners (Fahey & Randall, 1998) failed to contain a single reference to an academic source! The technique was born from practice and its appeal is based more on anecdotal than scientific evidence. Furthermore, significant misconceptions remain about its intent and claims. Above all, scenario planning is a tool for collective learning, reframing perceptions and preserving uncertainty when the latter is pervasive. Too many decision makers want to bet on one future scenario, falling prey to the seductive temptation of trying to predict the future rather than to entertain multiple futures (Wright, 1999; van der Heijden, 2002). Another trap is to take the scenarios too literally, as though they were static beacons that map out a fixed future. In actuality, their aim is to bound the future but in a flexible way that permits learning and adjustment as the future unfolds.

One criticism of the 2-by-2 technique outlined above is that the matrix results in four somewhat arbitrary scenario themes.[7] If other key uncertainties had been selected, it might be argued, very different scenarios could emerge. How true this is depends on whether the matrix is viewed as just a starting point to be superseded by the ensuing blueprint or is considered as the grand architecture that nests everything else. In either case, however, the issue should not be which are the "right" scenarios but rather whether they delineate the range of possible futures appropriately. Any tool that tries to simplify a complex picture will introduce distortions, whether it is a geographic map or a set of scenarios. Seldom will complexity decompose naturally into simple states. But it might. Consider, for example, the behavior of water (the molecule H_2O) which, depending on temperature and pressure, naturally exists in just one of three states: gas, liquid or solid. The art of scenarios is to look for such natural states or points of bifurcation in the behavior of a complex system.

Apart from some inherent subjectivity in scenario design, the technique can suffer from various process and content traps that are enumerated in Schoemaker (1998). These traps mostly relate to how the process is conducted in organizations (such as team composition, role of facilitators, etc.) as well as the substantive focus of the scenarios (long vs. short term, global vs. regional, incremental vs. paradigm shifting, etc). One might think of these as merely challenges of implementation, but since the process component is integral to the scenario experience, they can also be viewed as weaknesses of the methodology itself. Limited safeguards exist against political derailing, agenda control, myopia and limited imagination when conducting scenario planning exercises within real organizations. But, to varying extents, all forecasting techniques will suffer from such organizational limitations. The benchmark to use is not perfection, especially when faced with high uncertainty and complexity, or even strict adherence to such normative precepts as procedural invariance and logical consistency, but whether the technique performs better than its rivals. And to answer this question fairly, performance must be carefully specified. It should clearly include some measures of accuracy as well as a cost–benefit analysis that considers the tradeoff between effort and accuracy. In addition, legitimation criteria may be important to consider as well as the ability to refine and improve the approach as more experience is gained.

A third limitation of scenario planning in organizational settings is its weak integration into other planning and forecasting techniques. Most companies have plenty of trouble dealing with just one future, let alone multiple ones. Typically, budgeting and planning systems are predicated on single views of the future, with adjustments made as necessary through variance analysis, contingency planning, rolling budgets, and periodic renegotiations. The weaknesses of these traditional approaches were very evident after the tragic attack of September 11, 2001 when many companies became paralyzed and quite a few just threw away the plan and budget. Their strategies were not future-proof and they lacked organized mechanisms to adjust to external turmoil. In cases of crisis, leadership becomes important but so does some degree of preparedness. Once the scenarios are finished, the real work starts of how to craft *flexible* strategies and appropriate monitoring systems (Schoemaker, 1992). Managers need a simple but comprehensive compass to navigate uncertainty from beginning to end. Scenario planning is just one component of a more complete management system, the details of which are beyond our scope but can be found in Schoemaker (2002). The point is that scenario thinking needs to be integrated with the existing planning and budgeting system, as awkward as this fit may be. The reality is that most organizations do not handle uncertainty well and that researchers have not provided adequate answers about how to plan under conditions of high uncertainty and complexity. In my view, this is an important new frontier in both research and practice.

Summary

Prediction and forecasting remain very human affairs that can only be partly relegated to models or machines. As such, we must appreciate the natural biases humans bring to this task as well as the tools that can help.[8] I discussed the biases using an uncertainty–complexity typology and reviewed various tools for different combinations of uncertainty and complexity. Each component remains a formidable challenge to forecasters and needs to be more fully acknowledged when prognostications are made. Uncertainty can be represented in various ways, such as indicating confidence levels, making underlying assumptions explicit, or through the explicit modeling of how uncertainties may play out. Likewise, complexity can be addressed in a variety of ways from graphic influence diagrams to full-fledged mathematical models and simulations.

Special attention was given to scenario planning as a powerful tool – for both individuals and groups – to come to terms with the uncertainties and complexities inherent in most predictions of any import. The focus in scenario planning is not so much on the computational complexity presented by the forecast, but rather its conceptual and epistemic complexities (see Chapter 5, this volume). The questions of what do we know and what we don't know, as well as the deeper epistemic issue of "do we know what we don't know?" is front and central in scenario planning. It brings uncertainty and complexity to the fore in ways that few other forecasting methods do. Unfortunately, scenario planning is not as well understood nor as widely practiced as it should be. Most managers have only a moderate level of familiarity with this important tool according to our surveys.[9] Other tools we have surveyed – from soft to hard – did not fare much better. This raises an interesting question about who is at fault: the managers or the tools? My guess is a bit of both: the tools are better than most managers realize but not quite as useful as their proponents would like to believe.

In closing, I recommend that we focus more on the uncertainties and complexities inherent in any forecast, instead of the point estimates: better decisions will likely result if we do so. Increasingly, our world is moving toward higher levels of uncertainty and complexity in which the seductive comfort of linear extrapolation and point forecasts will prove illusory and often dangerous. Pasteur's famous expression sums it up well: "Chance will only favor the prepared mind." How to prepare the individual and organizational mind to be favored by chance remains a daunting challenge, but I believe that scenario planning is pointing us in the right direction.

Notes

1   This section draws on Appendix A of my book *Profiting from Uncertainty* (2002), which further discusses the differences between risk, uncertainty and ambiguity. These distinctions hinge on the extent of expert agreement about the outcome space and the associated probability distributions.

2   Classic studies on bootstrapping include Wallace (1923); Meehl (1954); Hammond et al. (1964); Hoffman, Slovic, & Rorer (1968); Dawes & Corrigan (1974); Dawes, 1979; Camerer, (1981); and Dawes et al. (1989). Managerial applications of bootstrapping can be found in Hammond, Hamm, Grassia, & Pearson (1987); Ashton, Ashton, & Davis (1994); and Cooter & Erdmann (1995).

3   The subject of intuition is complex and controversial. Some sing its praises (Weston, 1989) while others plead caution (Simon & Prietula, 1989; Hayashi, 2001) or are highly skeptical (Dawes et al., 1989). For recent treatments of intuition, see Hogarth (2001), Myers (2002), and Klein (2003).

4   The formal or quantitative approach to decision making is well explained in Nau and Clemen (1996) or Raiffa (1968). A more advanced treatment can be found in Keeney and Raiffa (1976) and Kleindorfer et al. (1993).

5   This section draws upon Schoemaker (1995) as well as Chapter 4 in *Winning Decisions* by Russo and Schoemaker (2001).

6   The two dimensions of this particular scenario matrix specifically include the following. The technology dimension covers such issues as the role of internet banking and e-commerce (websites, portals, etc.), check imaging and processing (electronic vs. paper); new user verification methods such as Iris scans, smart cards with chips, the importance of data mining, new back-end systems to streamline operations, etc. The playing field question concerns the rules and regulations under which credit unions can operate (both state and Federal), the role of non-traditional new entrants, the scrutiny given by Congress (which had considered a bill to tax credit unions), as well as the game plans of the various players (from focusing on

profit to market share to competing on innovation). Each cell of this initial matrix was then developed in greater detail – by adding other trends and key uncertainties – resulting in four full-fledged scenarios. Readers can find complete descriptions of these four scenarios at www.cues.org.

7   The 2-by-2 technique is just one of several approaches to develop scenarios. An alternative method, involving multivariate techniques, is described in Schoemaker (1991).

8   The nature of these biases remains an active and important area of research in behavioral decision theory. Useful reviews can be found in Goldstein and Hogarth (1997), Connolly, Arkes, & Hammond (2000) or Gilovich et al. (2002). The organizational context is addressed in March (1998) and Klein (1998).

9   The respondents were general managers attending executive education programs at the Wharton School, University of Pennsylvania (N > 100). More detail can be found in Schoemaker and Randall (2002).

Acknowledgments

I received valuable comments on earlier drafts of this chapter from Richard Adler, Nigel Harvey, Gary Klein, V. Michael Mavaddat, Roch Parayre, and J. Edward Russo. I acknowledge each with much gratitude and absolve all of them from any blame.

References

Andreassen, P. B. & Kraus, S. J. (1990) Judgmental extrapolation and the salience of change, *Journal of Forecasting*, 9, 347–72.

Armstrong, J. S. (ed.) (2001) *Principles of Forecasting: A Handbook for Researchers and Practitioners.* Dordrecht, The Netherlands: Kluwer Academic Publishers.

Ashton, A. H., Ashton, R. H., & Davis, M. N. (1994) White-collar robotics: Levering managerial decision making, *California Management Review*, 37(1), 83–109.

Ayton, P. & McClelland, A. G. R. (1997) How real is overconfidence? *Journal of Behavioral Decision Making*, 10(3), 279–86.

Barabási, A.-L. (2002) *Linked: The New Science of Networks.* Boulder, CO: Perseus Publishing.

Baumol, W. J. & Benhabib, J. (1989) Chaos: Significance, mechanism, and economic applications, *Journal of Economic Perspective*, 3(1), 77–105.

Bell, D., Raiffa, H., & Tversky, A. (eds.) (1988) *Decision Making: Descriptive, Normative and Prescriptive Interactions.* New York: Cambridge University Press.

Blattberg, R. & Hoch, S. (1990) Database models and managerial intuition: 50% model + 50% manager, *Management Science*, 36(8), 887–99.

Bolger, F. & Harvey, N. (1993) Context-sensitive heuristics in statistical reasoning, *Quarterly Journal of Experimental Psychology*, 46A, 779–811.

Bolger, F. & Harvey, N. (1998) Heuristics and biases in judgmental forecasting. In G. Wright and P. Goodwin (eds.), *Forecasting with Judgment* (pp. 113–37). New York: Wiley.

Camerer, C. (1981) General conditions for the success of bootstrapping models, *Organizational Behavior and Human Performance*, 27, 411–22.

Cerf, C. & Navasky, N. (1984) *The Experts Speak.* New York: Pantheon Books.

Connolly, T., Arkes, H. R., & Hammond, K. R. (eds.) (2000) *Judgment and Decision Making: An Interdisciplinary Reader* (2nd edn.). New York: Cambridge University Press.

Cooter, R. & Erdmann, J. B. (1995) A model for predicting HEAL repayment patterns and its implications for medical student financing, *Academic Medicine*, 70(12), 1134–7.

Courtney, H. (2001) *20/20 Foresight*. Boston, MA: Harvard Business School Press.

Courtney, H., Kirkland, J., & Viguerie, P. (1997) Strategy under uncertainty, *Harvard Business Review*, November–December, 66–81.

Dawes, R. (1979) The robust beauty of improper linear models in decision making, *American Psychologist*, 34, 571–82.

Dawes, R. M. & Corrigan, B. (1974) Linear models in decision making, *Psychological Bulletin*, 81, 97–106.

Dawes, R., Faust, D., & Meehl, P. (1989) Clinical versus actuarial judgment, *Science*, 243, 1668–73.

De Geus, A. (1988) Planning as learning, *Harvard Business Review*, March–April, 70–4.

Dougherty, M. R. P., Gettys, C. F., & Thomas, R. P. (1997) The role of mental simulation in judgments of likelihood, *Organizational Behavior and Human Decision Processes*, 70(2), 135–48.

Dube-Rioux, L. & Russo, J. E. (1988) An availability bias in professional judgment, *Journal of Behavioral Decision Making*, 1, 223–37.

Einhorn, H. J. & Hogarth, R. M. (1985) Ambiguity and uncertainty in probabilistic inference, *Psychological Review*, 92, 433–61.

Einhorn, H. J. & Hogarth, R. M. (1986) Judging probable cause, *Psychological Bulletin*, 99, 3–19.

Ekeland, I. (1988) *Mathematics and the Unexpected*. Chicago, IL: University of Chicago Press.

Fahey, L. & Randall, R. (eds.) (1998) *Learning from the Future*. New York: Wiley.

Feltovich, P. J., Ford, K. M., & Hoffman, R. R. (1997) *Expertise in Context*. Menlo Park, CA: AAAI Press/The MIT Press.

Fiol, C. M. & Huff, A. S. (1992) Maps for managers: Where are we? Where do we go from here? *Journal of Management Studies*, 29(3), 267–85.

Fischhoff, B. (1983) Acceptable risk: The case of nuclear power, *Journal of Policy Analysis and Management*, 2, 559–75.

Forrester, J. W. (1961) *Industrial Dynamics*. Bala Cynwyd, PA: Pegasus Communications.

Fox, C. & Tversky, A. (1995) Ambiguity aversion and comparative ignorance, *Quarterly Journal of Economics*, 585–603.

Gentner, D. & Stevens, A. L. (eds.) (1983) *Mental Models*. Hillsdale, NJ: Laurence Erlbaum Associates.

Gigerenzer, G. (1991) How to make cognitive illusions disappear: Beyond "Heuristics and biases," *European Review of Social Psychology*, 2, 83–115.

Gigerenzer, G. (1996) On narrow norms and vague heuristics: A response to Kahneman and Tversky, *Psychological Review*, 103, pp. 592–6.

Gillham, J. E. (2000) *The Science of Optimism and Hope: Research Essays in Honor of Martin E. P. Seligman (Laws of Life Symposia Series, vol. 2.)*. Radner, PA: Templeton, Foundation Press.

Gilovich, T., Griffin, D., & Kahneman, D. (2002) *Heuristics and Biases: The Psychology of Intuitive Judgment*. New York: Cambridge University Press.

Gleick, J. (1987) *Chaos: Making a New Science*. New York: Viking Penguin, Inc.

Goldstein, W. M. & Hogarth, R. M. (eds.) (1997) *Research on Judgment and Decision Making: Currents, Connections, and Controversies*. New York: Cambridge University Press.

Gregory, W. L. & Duran, A. (2001) Scenarios and acceptance of forecasts. In J. S. Armstrong (ed.), *Principles of Forecasting: A Handbook for Researchers and Practitioners* (pp. 519–40). Dordrecht, The Netherlands: Kluwer Academic Publishers.

Hammond, K. R., Hamm, R. M., Grassia, J., & Pearson, T. (1987) Direct comparison of the efficacy of intuitive and analytical cognition in expert judgment, *IEEE Transactions on Systems, Man, and Cybernetics*, SMC-17, no. 5.

Hammond, K. R., Hursch, C. J., & Todd, F. J. (1964) Analyzing the components of clinical inference, *Psychological Review*, 71, 438–56.

Harries, C. (2003) Correspondence to what? Coherence to what? What is good scenario-based decision making? *Technological Forecasting & Social Change*, 5561, 1–21.

Harvey, N. (1995) Why are judgments less consistent in less predictable task situations? *Organizational Behavior and Human Decision Processes*, 63, 247–63.

Hastie, R. (2001) Problems for judgment and decision making, *Annual Review of Psychology*, 52, 653–83.

Hastie, R., Penrod, S. D., Pennington, N. & Willis, J. (2002) *Inside the Jury*. Clark, NJ: The Lawbook Exchange Ltd., November.

Hayashi, A. M. (2001) When to trust your gut, *Harvard Business Review*, 79, 59.

Hoch, S. J. (1994) Experts and models in combination. In R. Blattberg, R. Glazer, and J. D. C. Little (eds.), *The Marketing Information Revolution*. Harvard Business School Press.

Hoch, S. J. (2001) Combining models with intuition to improve decisions. In S. J. Hoch and H. C. Kunreuther, *Wharton on Making Decisions* (Chapter 5). New York: Wiley.

Hoffman, P. J., Slovic, P., & Rorer, L. G. (1968) An analysis-of-variance model for assessment of configural cue utilization in clinical judgment, *Psychological Bulletin*, 69, 338–49.

Hogarth, R. (2001) *Educating Intuition*. Chicago: University of Chicago Press.

Hogarth, R. & Kunreuther, H. (1995) Decision making under ignorance: Arguing with yourself, *Journal of Risk and Uncertainty*, 10, 15–36.

Huber, O., Wider, R., & Huber, O. (1997) Active information search and complete information presentation in naturalistic risky decision tasks, *Acta Psychologica*, 95, 15–29.

Huss, W. R. (1988) A move toward scenarios, *International Journal of Forecasting*, 4, 377–88.

Jennings, D. L., Amabile, T. M., & Ross, L. (1982) Informal covariation asessment: Data-based vs. theory-based judgments. In D. Kahneman, P. Slovic, & A. Tversky (eds.), *Judgment Under Uncertainty: Heuristics and Biases* (pp. 211–30). New York: Cambridge University Press.

Johnson-Laird, P. N. (1983) *Mental Models* (2nd edn.). Cambridge, MA: Harvard University Press.

Kahneman, D. & Tversky, A. (1982) The simulation heuristic. In D. Kahneman, P. Slovic, and A. Tversky (eds.), *Judgment Under Uncertainty: Heuristics and Biases* (pp. 201–10). New York: Cambridge University Press.

Kahneman, D., Slovic, P., & Tversky, A. (eds.) (1982) *Judgment Under Uncertainty: Heuristics and Biases*. New York: Cambridge University Press.

Keeney, R. & Raiffa, H. (1976) *Decisions with Multiple Objectives: Preferences and Value Tradeoffs*. New York: John Wiley & Sons.

Klayman, J. & Ha, Y. W. (1987) Confirmation, disconfirmation, and information in hypothesis testing, *Psychological Review*, 94(2), 211–28.

Klayman, J. & Ha, Y. W. (1989) Hypothesis testing in rule discovery: Strategy, structure and content, *Journal of Experimental Psychology: Learning, Memory, and Cognition*, 15(4), 496–604.

Klayman, J. & Schoemaker, P. J. H. (1993) Thinking about the future: A cognitive perspective, *Journal of Forecasting*, 12, 161–8.

Klayman, J., Soll, J.-B. Gonzalez-Vallejo, C., & Barlas, S. (1999) Overconfidence: It depends on how, what, and whom you ask, *Organizational Behavior and Human Decision Processes*, 79(3), 216–47.

Klein, G. (2003) *Intuition at Work*. New York: Doubleday.

Klein, G. (1998) *Sources of Power: How People Make Decisions*. Cambridge, MA: MIT Press.

Kleindorfer, P., Kunreuther, H., & Schoemaker, P. J. H. (1993) *Decision Sciences: An Integrative Perspective*. New York: Cambridge University Press.

Kunreuther, H., Hogarth, R., & Meszaros, J. (1993) Ambiguity and market failure, *Journal of Risk and Uncertainty*, 7, 71–88.

Kunreuther, H., Novemsky, N., & Kahneman, D. (2001) Making low probabilities useful, *Journal of Risk and Uncertainty*, 23, 103–20.

Langer, E. J. (1975) The illusion of control, *Journal of Personality and Social Psychology*, 32, 322–8.

Lawrence, M. J. & O'Connor, M. (1992) Exploring judgmental forecasting, *International Journal of Forecasting*, 8(1), 15–26.

Lichtenstein, S., Fischhoff, B., & Phillips, L. (1982) Calibration of probabilities: The start of the art to 1980. In D. Kahneman, P. Slovic, & A. Tversky (eds.), *Judgment under Uncertainty: Heuristics and Biases*. New York: Cambridge University Press.

Magat, W., Viscusi, K., & Huber, J. (1987) Risk-dollar tradeoffs, risk perceptions, and consumer behavior. In W. Viscusi & W. Magat (eds.), *Learning About Risk* (pp. 83–9), (7). Boston, MA: Harvard University Press.

March, J. G. (1998) *Decisions and Organizations*. Oxford: Basil Blackwell.

Mason, R. & Mitroff, I. (1981) *Challenging Strategic Planning Assumptions*. New York: Wiley.

McGrath, R. G. & MacMillan, I. (1995) Discovery-driven planning, *Harvard Business Review*, (July–August), 4–12.

Meehl, P. (1954) *Clinical Versus Statistical Prediction*. University of Minnesota Press.

Morecroft, J. & Sterman, J. (1994) *Modeling for Learning Organizations*. Portland, OR: Productivity Press.

Murphy, A. H. & Winkler, R. (1984) Probability forecasting in meteorology, *Journal of the American Statistical Association*, 79(Sept.), 489–500.

Myers, D. G. (2002) *Intuition: Its Powers and Perils*. New Haven, CT: Yale University Press.

Nau, R. & Clemen, R. (1996) *Making Hard Decisions: An Introduction to Decision Analysis* (2nd edn.). Boston, MA: PWS-Kent Publishing Co.

O'Connor, M., Remus, W., & Griggs, K. (1993) Judgmental forecasting in times of change, *International Journal of Forecasting*, 9, 163–72.

Perlmuter, L. C. & Monty, R. A. (1977) The importance of perceived control: Fact or fantasy? *American Scientist*, 65 (November–December), 759–65.

Presson, P. & Benassi, V. (1996) Illusion of control: A meta-analytic review, *Journal of Social Behavior and Personality*, 11, 493–510.

Raiffa, H. (1968) *Decision Analysis: Introductory Lectures on Choices Under Uncertainty*. Boston, MA: Addison-Wesley.

Ranyard, R. (1997) *Decision Making: Cognitive Models and Explanations*. London: Routledge.

Ringland, G. (1998) *Scenario Planning*. New York: Wiley.

Russo, J. E. & Schoemaker, P. J. H. (1989) *Decision Traps*. New York: Doubleday Publishing Co.

Russo, J. E. & Schoemaker, P. J. H. (1992) Managing overconfidence, *Sloan Management Review*, Winter, 7–18.

Russo, J. E. & Schoemaker, P. J. H. (2001) *Winning Decisions*. New York: Doubleday Publishing Co.

Schoemaker, P. J. H. (1991) When and how to use scenario planning: A heuristic approach with illustration, *Journal of Forecasting*, 10, 549–64.

Schoemaker, P. J. H. (1992) How to link strategic vision to core capabilities, *Sloan Management Review*, Fall, 67–81.

Schoemaker, P. J. H. (1993) Multiple scenario developing: Its conceptual and behavioral basis, *Strategic Management Journal*, 14, 193–213.

Schoemaker, P. J. H. (1995) Scenario planning: A tool for strategic thinking, *Sloan Management Review*, Winter, 25–40.

Schoemaker, P. J. H. (1998) Twenty common pitfalls in scenario planning. In *Learning from the Future* (pp. 422–31). New York: John Wiley & Sons.

Schoemaker, P. J. H. (2002) *Profiting from Uncertainty*. New York: Free Press.

Schoemaker, P. J. H. & Randall, D. (2002) *Managing Uncertainty: A Guide for Credit Unions.* Madison, WI: Credit Union Executives Society (CUES).

Schoemaker, P. J. H. & Russo, J. E. (2001) Managing frames to make better decisions. In S. J. Hoch, & H. C. Kunreuther, (eds.), *Wharton on Making Decisions* (Chapter 8). New York: Wiley.

Schoemaker, P. J. H. & van der Heijden, K. A. J. M. (1992) Integrating scenarios into strategic planning at Royal Dutch/Shell, *Planning Review*, 20, 41–6.

Schuster, H. G. (1995) *Deterministic Chaos: An Introduction* (3rd edn). New York: Simon & Schuster.

Schwartz, P. (1991) *The Art of the Long View.* New York: Doubleday.

Senge, P. (1990) *The Fifth Discipline.* New York: Doubleday Inc.

Simon, H. (1997) *Models of Bounded Rationality*, Cambridge, MA: MIT Press.

Simon, H. A. & Prietula, M. J. (1989) The experts in your midst, *Harvard Business Review*, Januay–February, 120–4.

Slovic, P. (1987) Perception of risk, *Science*, 236, 280–5.

Sterman, J. D. (1989) Modeling managerial behavior: Misperceptions of feedback in a dynamic decision making environment, *Management Science*, 35(3), 321–39.

Sterman, J. D. (1999) Boom, bust, and failures to learn in experimental markets, *Management Science*, 39(12), 1439–58.

Sterman, J. D. (2000) *Business Dynamics: Systems Thinking and Modeling for a Complex World.* Boston, MA: McGraw-Hill/Irwin.

Sunter, C. (1987) *The World and South Africa in the 1990s.* Cape Town: Human and Rousseau Tafelberg.

Taylor, S. E. & Brown, J. D. (1988) Illusion and well-being: A social psychological perspective on mental health, *Psychological Bulletin*, 193(2), 193–21.

Tiao, G. C. (2001) Vector ARMA models. In D. Peña, G. C. Tiao, & R. S. Tsay (eds.), *A Course in Time Series Analysis.* New York: Wiley.

Thom, R. (1984) *Mathematical Models of Morphogenesis.* London: Ellis Horwood Ltd.

Tversky, A. & Kahneman, D. (1973) Availability: A heuristic for judging frequency and probability, *Cognitive Psychology*, 5(2), 207–32.

Tversky, A. & Kahneman, D. (1974) Judgments under uncertainty: Heuristics and biases, *Science*, 185, 1124–31.

Tversky, A. & Kahneman, D. (1980) Causal schemas in judgements under uncertainty. In M. Fishbein (ed.), *Progress in Social Psychology*, Hillsdale, NJ: Erlbaum.

Tversky, A. & Kahneman, D. (1983) Extensional versus intuitive reasoning: The conjunction fallacy in probability judgment, *Psychological Review*, 90, 293–315.

Van der Heijden, K. (1996) *Scenarios: The Art of Strategic Conversation.* New York: Wiley.

Van der Heijden, K. (2002) Scenarios and forecasting: Two perspectives, *Technological Forecasting and Social Change*, 65, 31–6.

Varela, F. J. (1979) *Principles of Biological Autonomy.* Elsevier North-Holland.

Von Bertalanffy, L. (1976) *General system theory: Foundations, development, applications.* New York: George Braziller.

Wack, P. (1985a) Scenarios: Shooting the rapids, *Harvard Business Review*, November–December, 139–50.

Wack, P. (1985b) Scenarios; Uncharted waters ahead, *Harvard Business Review*, September–October, 73–89.

Wagenaar, W. A. & Timmers, H. (1979) The pond-and-duckweed problem: Three experiments on the misperception of exponential growth, *Acta Psychologica* (43), 239–51.

Wallace, H. A. (1923) What is in the corn judge's mind? *Journal of American Society for Agronomy*, 15.

Weston, H. A. (ed.) (1989) *Intuition in Organizations.* New York: Sage Publications.

Whitecotton, S. M., Sanders, D. E., & Norris, K. B. (1998) Improving predictive accuracy with a combination of human intuition and mechanical decision aids, *Organizational Behavior and Human Decision Processes*, 17(3), 325–48.

Wiener, N. (1961) *Cybernetics* (2nd edn.). Cambridge, MA: MIT Press.

Winkler, R. L. (1981) Combining probability distributions from dependent information sources, *Management Science*, 27(April), 479–88.

Wright, G. (1999) Scenario thinking versus subjective probability forecasting, *Technological Forecasting and Social Change*, 61, 81.

Wright, G. & Goodwin, P. (eds.) (1998) *Forecasting with Judgment.* New York: Wiley.

15

Expertise in Judgment and Decision Making: A Case for Training Intuitive Decision Skills

Jennifer K. Phillips, Gary Klein, and Winston R. Sieck

Introduction

Research on expertise is largely founded on the idea that experts have achieved a rare proficiency in a domain that most of their peers never quite reach. What is the nature of such expertise? How does someone become an expert? How do experts differ from novices? These are questions that have intrigued the vast majority of expertise researchers (e.g., Chi, Glaser, & Farr, 1988; Ericsson & Smith, 1991). Research on expertise within the judgment and decision making (JDM) community has been primarily concerned with quite a different set of issues. What role should experts play in forecasting and decision support systems? Do experts suffer from the same judgmental biases that have been demonstrated in undergraduates? How can experts know so much and predict so badly? (e.g., Camerer & Johnson, 1991; Smith & Kida, 1991; Wright & Bolger, 1993). There may be value in addressing some of these questions. Nevertheless, the stress in this chapter is on the former set of issues as they apply to decision making, with the goal of convincing the reader that such questions deserve a dramatically greater role in JDM research on expertise than they ordinarily receive. First, however, we address the skeptical view of expertise implied in some of the JDM questions above.

There are several programs and approaches in the study of decision making, as illustrated in the first section of this book. Arguably, the dominant program since the 1970s has been the heuristics and biases approach initiated by Daniel Kahneman and Amos Tversky (hereafter K&T; see Chapter 5). The theoretical contribution of K&T was to demonstrate that human judgment arises from qualitatively different processes than suggested by normative theories, and to argue that heuristics would provide a better starting point for the development of psychological theory. K&T's research strategy was to demonstrate sharp departures of human judgment from the normative principles. The uncovered biases were intended to illuminate the heuristic nature of the underlying system (e.g., Gilovich & Griffin, 2002; Kahneman & Tversky, 1972).

Much work on expertise in the JDM literature has also followed the heuristics and biases tradition (e.g., Arkes, Wortmann, Saville, & Harkness, 1981; Bazerman, Loewenstein, & Moore, 2002; Camerer & Johnson, 1991; Koehler, Brenner, & Griffin, 2002; Loftus & Wagenaar, 1988; McNeil, Pauker, Sox, & Tversky, 1982). The goal of such research has been to demonstrate that biases exist outside of normal, laboratory populations. For example, Arkes et al. (1981) demonstrated hindsight bias effects among practicing physicians. Koehler et al. (2002) showed that experts in a variety of domains were poorly calibrated probability assessors. McNeil et al. (1982) illustrated that framing effects can be exhibited in doctors and statistically trained graduate students.

Decision researchers have often been concerned with developing prescriptions for improving decision processes in addition to describing basic mechanisms. A view that has developed out of the heuristics and biases program is that decision making can be improved by striving to eliminate biases (see Chapter 16, this volume). On the whole, efforts to "debias" individuals in lab settings have met with mixed success at best (e.g., Fischhoff, 1982). And beyond lab demonstrations of effectiveness, there are several underlying assumptions that present serious challenges to the utility of such an approach in actual "on the job" decision making. First, the frequency and magnitude of biases studied in laboratory research has not been assessed in natural settings. Second, for debiasing to even have a marginal impact, the procedures have to be accessible or transfer to the situations encountered in natural settings. Finally, the specific recommendation has to fit within the confines of the decision maker's job. This full range of issues must be dealt with in order to demonstrate the value of the debiasing approach, and thus far, progress has been remarkably limited.

Interestingly, despite the general focus of this program and the lack of success of debiasing efforts generally, domain expertise has been found to alleviate biases (e.g., Bornstein, Emler, & Chapman, 1999; Cohen, 1993; Keren, 1987; Shanteau, 1989; Smith & Kida, 1991). For instance, Bornstein et al. (1999) found that medical residents endorse sunk cost reasoning less on medical than on non-medical decisions. Keren (1987) found that expert bridge players rendered extremely well-calibrated predictions that their contracts would win. Smith and Kida (1991) discovered that accountants were less biased on accounting than non-accounting decisions. Expertise undoubtedly offers far more to decision makers than bias reductions. Given that, intensive study of the central questions concerning expertise is clearly warranted.

In this chapter, we cover three topics: (1) the nature of expertise; (2) expertise in decision making; and (3) advancing expertise in a given domain.

The Nature of Expertise

Many researchers have speculated about the nature of expertise, most notably Chi et al. (1988); Ericsson and Smith (1991); Feltovich, Ford, and Hoffman (1997); and Hoffman

(1994). In this section we highlight some of their observations, particularly those that are relevant to decision making. We draw on two research traditions, a laboratory-based examination and a naturalistic investigation of expertise.

The laboratory-based approach to studying expertise attempts to maintain the advantage of precision granted by laboratory settings, but strives to utilize tasks that are highly representative of the experts' domain. The goal of this approach is to approximate the natural performance of experts under controlled conditions (Ericsson & Charness, 1997).

The naturalistic approach to conducting research around expert judgment is exemplified by the Naturalistic Decision Making (NDM) framework (see Flin, Salas, Strub, & Martin, 1997; Klein, Orasanu, Calderwood, & Zsambok, 1993; Lipshitz, Klein, Orasanu, & Salas, 2001; Salas & Klein, 2001; and, Zsambok & Klein, 1997 for a review of NDM). NDM researchers set out to examine expertise in natural settings, instead of in the laboratory. The goal is to study people performing tasks under conditions that are typical for their workplace. NDM researchers have been interested in domains that require high-stakes, time-pressured decision making under conditions of uncertainty and competing goals. Nevertheless, we believe that findings about experts' judgment and decision processes drawn from these domains generalize to domains that are not so crisis-driven.

How should expertise be conceptualized? The term is unfortunately often given a weak connotation in JDM research. For example, Camerer and Johnson (1991, p. 196) offer the following definition:

> For our purposes, an expert is a person who is experienced at making predictions in a domain and has some professional or social credentials. The experts described here are no slouches: They are . . . intelligent, well paid, and often proud. We draw no special distinction between them and extraordinary experts, or experts claimed by their peers (cf. Shanteau, 1988). We suspect that our general conclusions would apply to more elite populations of experts . . .

In our view, these people would be better termed "professionals" who are not necessarily experts. And we strongly disagree with their final conclusion. Words can obviously be used in different ways. However, to attain continuity with the broader research community on expertise, the above definition of "expert" should be dropped by the JDM community (also see Bendor, 2003).

When we speak of expertise we refer to individuals who have achieved exceptional skill in one particular domain. Operationally, peer nomination is essential in determining whether someone has achieved exceptional skill; when searching out experts, we routinely ask "Who is the guy who knows it all?" Furthermore, we are highly selective, and occasionally "cut" those professionals who do not appear to us to be true experts. With respect to domain specificity, there is little evidence that the skill of an expert transfers to an alternate context (Chi et al., 1988; but see Schunn & Anderson, 1999). The primary distinction that separates experts from novices appears to be the breadth and depth of their domain-specific knowledge. These definitional considerations are extremely important in considering the intersection between JDM and expertise. Competence is inherent in the definition of expertise, so questions like "Why do experts predict badly?" do not make sense. A better framing would be, "Why do experienced professionals in some domains not appear to be experts?" This is a complicated question. An important possibility with respect to JDM research is that the researchers have set up judgment tasks that require knowledge outside of the experts' domain, i.e., the specific knowledge that the expert relies upon on the job (e.g., Asare & Wright, 1995). We turn now to review in-depth conceptions of expertise that have emerged from research in that field.

Ericsson and Smith (1991) describe the study of expertise as seeking to understand "what distinguishes outstanding individuals in a domain from less outstanding individuals in that domain, as well as people in general" (p. 2). The term "outstanding" is intentionally vague; it fosters the acceptance of several research approaches to the question of what constitutes expertise.

Some definitions describe changes that occur when expertise is developed. For example, Glaser (1996) describes the following:

- Variable, awkward performance becomes consistent, accurate, complete, and efficient;
- Individual acts and judgments are integrated into overall strategies;
- With perceptual learning, a focus on isolated variables shifts to perception of complex patterns; and
- There is increased self-reliance and ability to form new strategies as needed.

Another perspective on expertise is to view it in terms of representation. Experts seem to represent a problem at a deeper level than do novices, who are relatively superficial in their problem representations (Chi, Feltovich, & Glaser, 1981; Glaser & Chi, 1988; Larkin, McDermott, Simon, & Simon, 1980). For example, experts in the domain of physics were compared with novices in which the task was to represent the topic contained in a physics problem. The experts showed a much deeper, functional understanding of the problem, whereas the novices responded in terms of superficial characteristics of the problem (Anzai, 1991). In a study of battle commanders, Serfaty, MacMillan, Entin, and Entin (1997) found several examples of how higher-expertise commanders saw situations differently than their less-expert counterparts. The high-expertise subjects were able to consider the effects of sequencing and timing of events, as well as the effects of terrain and distances on the battlefield. These are more complex elements of a tactical problem.

We can also discriminate experts from others by describing what experts *know* that others do not, and what experts *can do* that others cannot – the declarative and procedural knowledge described by Anderson (1983). Klein and Militello (in press) suggested several additional categories of knowledge related to expertise, along with the two offered by Anderson:

- *Perceptual skills*: Perceptual skills, in particular the ability to make fine discriminations, seem an essential component of expertise in many settings (e.g., Klein & Hoffman, 1993).
- *Mental models*: Experts have a broader and deeper knowledge and experience base than journeymen and novices. They understand the dynamics of events in their domain. They know how tasks and subtasks are supposed to be performed, how equipment is supposed to function, and how teams are supposed to coordinate. This mental

representation of "how things work" is referred to as a mental model, an internal representation of the external world. Mental models enable the decision maker to describe, explain, and predict (Rouse & Morris, 1986).

- *Sense of typicality and associations*: The knowledge here is often in the form of a repertoire of patterns. Several studies support the assertion that experts can perceive large, meaningful patterns of information (Ericsson & Smith, 1991). One of the classical studies in this area was the work of Newell and Simon (1972) showing expert/novice differences in pattern repertoire for chess positions. Experts can rapidly recognize and interpret complex patterns in a set of information in order to assess the situation more quickly and accurately than non-experts (e.g., Chase, 1983; Dreyfus, 1997; Gentner, 1988). The repertoire of patterns that allows experts to recognize situations as typical, also enables them to spot information that is expected but missing from the picture, and to detect anomalies that are present but not expected.
- *Routines*: This category corresponds to the "knowing how" discussed by Anderson (1983). Experts know a wider variety of tactics for getting things done.
- *Declarative knowledge*: This category corresponds directly to Anderson's (1983) account. Experts simply know more facts, more details. They have command of more explicit knowledge, to use Polanyi's (1966) terminology, to go along with their tacit knowledge. The tacit knowledge of experts would fall in the preceding four categories.

In addition to the different types of knowledge experts possess, Klein and Militello (in press) also describe some of the things experts can do with this knowledge, including:

- *Run mental simulations*: Mental simulation was originally introduced by Einhorn and Hogarth (1981) as an aspect of decision making. They suggested that people use mental simulation to adjust a known value so that it fits a new situation. They imagine various configurations of events by combining what they know to be true with what might be, based on what they see in the new situation. This account of mental simulation comes out of research on anchoring and adjustment strategies.

Other more traditional decision research has also referred to the same process of mental envisioning. For example, Kahneman and Tversky (1982) described a simulation heuristic by which the individual "runs" a mental model of a situation to determine how to react. DeGroot (1965), in his studies of chess players, introduced the concept of progressive deepening to describe how players consider their next move. He observed that skilled players identify a small rather than broad set of plausible moves. Then they simulate the counter-moves their opponent might choose, and the moves they could make in reaction to those.

Experts can use their detailed mental models, coupled with their understanding of the current state of the situation, to construct simulations of how the situation is going to develop in the future, and thereby generate predictions and expectations. For example, Klein (1998) relates studies of firefighter decision making where experienced commanders were able to look at a burning building and know what was happening inside. They could tell from the look and location of the smoke and flames how it was burning and where the fire was probably located. From the exterior of the building they could envision stairways, elevator shafts, and roof supports, and how the fire was impacting each. Mental simulations of how a fire will burn and spread enable them to project into the future.

- *Spot anomalies and detect problems*: Experts spend relatively more time analyzing the situation than deliberating about a course of action, whereas non-experts show the reverse trend; they spend less time on the dynamics of the situation and more determining how to respond (Kobus, Proctor, Bank, & Holste, 2000).

  The richer mental models of experts enable them to identify atypicalities and therefore adjust the story they are developing to explain events. Feltovich, Johnson, Moller, and Swanson (1984) designed an experiment with medical practitioners to test the flexibility of experts versus non-experts on diagnostic tasks. A series of actual clinical cases were presented to the subjects in which the patient information followed a "garden path" structure. That is, early data strongly suggested an incorrect diagnosis, but data that were added to the picture later suggested a different, accurate, diagnosis. The results showed that novices were more rigid and tended to get trapped on the garden path. Experts, on the other hand, were able to identify that the path on which they were headed (toward the incorrect diagnosis) was the wrong one. They were able to detect that a switch needed to be made. The authors attribute this flexibility to a finely discriminated disease schema, where small anomalies that fail to fit the early diagnosis can be detected. In the same study, another clinical case could be successfully diagnosed if the subject interpreted a particular finding correctly. Novices tended to read the finding according to the textbook interpretation and therefore missed the diagnosis. Experts, on the other hand, noticed that the textbook interpretation was not appropriate for this particular patient, and were able to adjust the rules accordingly and generate an accurate diagnosis (Feltovich, Spiro, & Coulson, 1997).

- *Find leverage points*: Klein and Wolf (1998) hypothesized that people can generate novel courses of action by identifying and capitalizing on unapparent opportunities for useful interventions, i.e., leverage points. Mental simulation is a powerful tool for using leverage points to support improvisation, and experts are able to improvise better than non-experts when the situation is novel by forming new, effective strategies (Klein, 1998). We can attribute this to a mental model that provides rich detail around the dynamics of events and a sense of the opportunities that resources provide, in some cases other than their intended use (Lipshitz & Cohen, submitted). As an example, a fireground commander once used a belt intended to secure firefighters while on a ladder to rescue a woman who was dangling on the metal supports of a highway sign. He was able to mentally simulate a series of approaches to rescuing the woman, and eventually determined that the ladder belt would do the trick (Klein, 1998).

- *Manage uncertainty*: Lipshitz and Strauss (1997) and Schmitt and Klein (1996) described a range of strategies for managing uncertainty in field settings. Expert decision makers tend to use their mental models to fill in gaps with assumptions, to mentally simulate and project into the future, to formulate information seeking tactics. The strategies used in the field for managing uncertainty are quite distinct from probability judgment paradigms that are the focus of much research in JDM, and this is very likely an important part of why experts often appear deficient in dealing with uncertainty in such research (e.g., Christensen-Szalanski & Bushyhead, 1981; Loftus & Wagenaar, 1988).

- *Take one's own strengths and limitations into account (i.e., metacognition)*: Several studies indicate that experts are better self-monitors than non-experts. In experiments with physics problems, experts would check their answers more than non-experts (Simon, 1975) and would more frequently abandon a route to a solution before carrying out the calculations (Larkin, 1983). Chi, Feltovich, and Glaser (1980) found that experts were better able to judge the difficulty of a physics problem, and a follow-on study by Chi et al. (1981) noted that the problem features on which the subjects judged difficulty were different for experts and non-experts. The experts in their sample more often considered the underlying principles addressed in the problem, while novices more often considered characteristics unrelated to the problem itself. They suggest that experts' superior self-knowledge is based not only on their greater domain knowledge, but also on the way in which that information can be represented in order to carry more meaning. In studies of chess players, experts were found to have better accuracy than novices when they predicted how many times they would need to see a configuration of pieces on the board before they could reproduce the board (Chi, 1978).

Expertise in Decision Making

In this section we discuss a 15-year research program to understand how experts make good decisions. The fundamental idea is that the first option experts generate is of high quality. The Recognition-Primed Decision (RPD) model (see Figure 15.1) describes how in naturalistic settings, experts rely on an extensive knowledge base to make judgments about situations and decide how to act. While the RPD model is intended to be descriptive with regard to the decision-making process of experts, it also provides a frame within which characteristics of experts can be distinguished from those of novices.

The RPD model (Klein, 1998; Klein, Calderwood, & Clinton-Cirocco, 1986) was originally developed based on observations of firefighter decision making. The researchers set out to show how experienced fireground commanders did not have the luxury of time to compare several options when fighting a fire. Instead, they hypothesized that the commanders would compare two options, one that was their intuitive "favorite" and one that they developed as a comparison to show that the favorite was better. The researchers were surprised by the findings. The subject-matter experts that they interviewed and observed said that they never made decisions. They just acted. In fact, the interview data showed that decisions were made, however, they were perceived by the firefighters to be just actions because multiple options were not directly compared.

The data from this and several other studies of naturalistic decision making, in domains ranging from wildland firefighting to system design to military command and control, indicate that in natural settings, experts typically use a recognition-primed strategy to make decisions. The observational and interview data indicate that 80–90 percent of difficult decisions are made in this fashion (see Klein, 1998, for a review of this research).

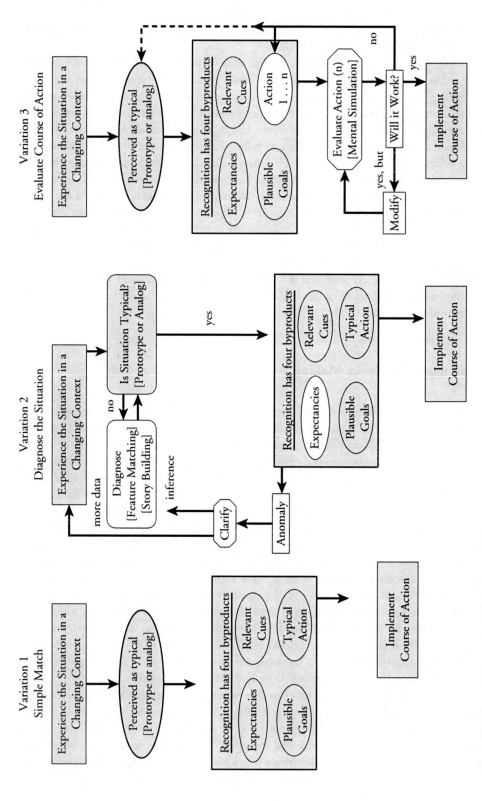

Figure 15.1 Recognition-primed decision model

These general findings have been replicated in several other domains (e.g., Fischhoff, 1996; Flin, Slaven, & Stewart, 1996; Mosier, 1991; Pascual & Henderson, 1997; Randel, Pugh, & Reed, 1996).

The basic explanation is that skilled decision makers make sense of the situation at hand by recognizing it as one of the prototypical situations they have experienced and stored in their long-term memory. This recognition match is usually done without deliberation. Once the decision makers have arrived at a recognition match, an appropriate course of action, or decision, becomes clear. This is Variation 1 of the RPD model. If the situation is familiar and judged to be routine, the decision is intuitive and automatic.

However, not all situations are that straightforward. Sometimes the decision maker runs up against a situation that is ambiguous or unfamiliar. The expert must then deliberate about the nature of the situation, often seeking additional information to round out the picture. In other cases it might be necessary to resolve an anomaly, or a piece of information that was not expected. This is Variation 2 of the RPD – the decision maker must actively work at generating an accurate assessment of the situation, but once that is accomplished, the course of action becomes obvious. Mental simulation may be used to construct a story of how the current situation has arisen, and the most plausible story then is treated as an explanation and as a basis for understanding the current dynamics.

In many cases, the decision maker seeks to evaluate the quality of the initial course of action suggested by a recognition match. This is Variation 3 of the RPD model. In these situations experts envision a plausible course of action and then use mental simulation to mentally "test" its effectiveness. If the first course of action is judged inadequate, then the decision maker develops a second course of action and mentally simulates it. This process continues until the decision maker finds a course of action that passes the test and is implemented.

An important attribute of expert decision makers is that they seek a course of action that is workable, but not necessarily the best or optimal decision. This "satisficing" concept was first described by Simon (1957). In naturalistic settings the time pressures often dictate that the situation be resolved as quickly as possible. Therefore it is not important for a course of action to be the best one; it only needs to be effective. Interestingly, we see satisficing behaviors in situations that are not subject to intense time pressures, such as system developers (Klein & Brezovic, 1986). The time and effort that could be spent generating and contrasting multiple options is instead spent in testing and critiquing and improving the initial options.

As can be seen, our theoretical views on expert decision makers share the basic premise of K&T's heuristics and biases research program. We agree that human decision making is qualitatively different from normative theories, and believe that this is so among experts as well as novices. There are also specific points of connection between the RPD model and the primary heuristics proposed by K&T, especially with respect to the importance of similarity and mental simulation. The RPD further moves beyond lists of heuristics by dealing with issues of representation and process that have largely been ignored in the heuristics program (cf. Smith & Osherson, 1989). From a practical stance, the critical implication is that expert decision makers are not better than novices because their processing literally begins to look more like that of normative theories. Instead, expertise leads to a broader and more refined set of heuristic processes that promote exceptional performance on the specific task domains to which they are attuned.

This broad view of expertise in JDM suggests a counterintuitive approach to improving decision making. The standard methods typically recommend that decision makers strive to develop domain-general decision skills with the goal of following processes that are closer to normative standards, and that eliminate biases (e.g., Hammond, Keeney, & Raiffa, 1999; Hogarth, 2001; Russo, Schoemaker, & Hittleman, 2001). Our proposal is far less radical. Instead of trying to dramatically revise decision processes, we seek merely to improve their quality by facilitating the development of substantive, domain-specific expertise. This is discussed presently.

Acquiring Decision-making Expertise

It has been noted by some that ten years is a sufficient span of time for individuals to acquire expertise in a given domain (e.g., Chase & Simon, 1973; Hayes, 1985). However, mere experience does not produce expertise. Serfaty et al. (1997), in their study of battle command expertise, found clear expert–novice differences in the quality, level of detail, and flexibility of the courses of action generated. Interestingly, high performance on this task was not correlated with years of experience, nor was it correlated with rank. This indicates that experts, more so than their equally experienced counterparts, may make better use of their experience. In a review of the literature, Klein (1998) identified four key ways in which experts learn:

1   engaging in deliberate practice, and setting specific goals and evaluation criteria;
2   compiling extensive experience banks;
3   obtaining feedback that is accurate, diagnostic, and reasonably timely; and
4   enriching their experiences by reviewing prior experiences to derive new insights and lessons from mistakes.

Along with these learning strategies, it is likely that motivational characteristics of the individual also impact the odds of performing at expert levels. For example, we have heard firefighters say that some individuals in their department are passionate about the job. They seek opportunities to learn and improve themselves through whatever means are available. They engage in lively conversations with other firefighters about their experiences. They attend conferences. They read extensively and practice on simulations. These are the people who tend to excel at their jobs. Then there are other firefighters who seem to have less motivation to learn. They seem to be happy clocking in and out and receiving a paycheck. They will never perform at the level of experts.

In addition to personal characteristics, the task domain influences a person's ability to achieve expertise (Shanteau, 1992; Stewart, Roebber, & Bosart, 1997). For example, in weather forecasting, where feedback on one's predictions happens on a daily basis, it is easy to obtain accurate and timely feedback. However, in a domain like clinical psychology, there is likely to be less opportunity for effective feedback (Klein, 1998). It may be impossible to achieve expert predictive or diagnostic ability in such a domain. Perhaps greater reliance on validated scoring rules presents a strategy for improving judgment and acquiring expertise in such high-variability settings (e.g., Sieck, 2003).

Within the confines of the personal and task characteristics presented above, how can people acquire expertise in judgment and decision making? Before we consider specific techniques, we need to distinguish specific versus general intuitions. We define *specific* intuitions as judgments related to a particular task within a domain. For example, contractors must repeatedly generate cost estimates for new projects, and they must estimate the time it will take to complete the project. People often seek to improve their intuitions about key, recurring decisions like these. Because such judgments are relatively discrete, they are amenable to isolation as targets for training. Much of the literature on quantity judgment, multiple-cue probability learning, and judgmental forecasting can be associated with this approach (e.g., Hammond, McClelland, & Mumpower, 1980; Lee & Yates, 1992; Wright & Goodwin, 1998). The advantage to exercising specific intuitions is the ease with which they can be identified – most professionals can articulate which of their decisions are both challenging and important. These intuitions can also be structured within a program of improvement. The disadvantage lies in the practicality of this approach; it is time-consuming and costly to address more than a few judgments in this manner.

We define *general* intuition as knowledge and experience within a particular domain, such as battle command or personnel management. Individuals seek to get better at their jobs, but "getting better" entails improving know-how across a broad range of judgments and actions. The battle commander must read the adversary's intentions and project his course of action, and integrate that with an understanding of his own resources and troop readiness, in order to affect mission accomplishment. And this is a simplistic description of the commander's job. At this broad level it is not realistic to rely on practice and feedback as a training approach due to the difficulty of isolating discrete tasks in order to produce a performance improvement. A different approach must be taken for general intuitions. We have derived six goals from the empirical findings reviewed earlier on expert and novice differences in knowledge and learning strategies, as follows:

1   enhance perceptual skills;
2   enrich mental models about the domain;
3   construct a large and varied repertoire of patterns;
4   provide a larger set of routines;
5   provide a larger experience base of instances; and
6   encourage an attitude of responsibility for one's own learning.

Our ongoing research indicates that a scenario-based instructional approach that addresses these six goals is a promising one for facilitating the development of decision-making expertise in a specific domain. For example, Phillips and Battaglia (2003) showed that a carefully designed series of decision scenarios combined with effective coaching can significantly increase decision quality. Further, Ross, Battaglia, Phillips, Domeshek, and

Lussier (in press) describe a similar training approach that targets and enriches the mental models pertinent to tactical thinking. However, both of these instances took place in single (or two, at most) sessions lasting only a few hours. There is a need to conduct research on the longitudinal development of intuitive decision skills, over a period of months or years, to better understand how to expedite the learning process.

One direct approach to improving specific judgments to facilitate the development of expertise is to establish a regimen of practice and feedback. This approach is the traditional way to strengthen skills that can be defined and for which progress can be monitored. Thus, to strengthen intuitions in a given area the prescription would be to practice the judgments and decisions, and then obtain feedback. While the "practice and feedback" approach sounds reasonable, in fact it is inadequate. It oversimplifies the learning need, and it may even be misleading in some contexts. What is wrong with "practice and feedback"? It is well documented that practice alone cannot affect performance improvement. Salas, Wilson, Burke and Bowers (2002) assert that practice without feedback is usually insufficient. "Task exposure, though beneficial, does not equate to learning" (p. 23). Schneider (1985) explains that many tasks can be identified where practice does not make perfect and may not lead to improvement if the trainee fails to obtain coaching about better strategies.

There are also problems with combining practice and outcome feedback. One issue with outcome feedback is that it is often inconsistent in judgment tasks that are even moderately variable, and many judgment researchers are not optimistic that outcome feedback will be effective in such situations. For example, Hammond, Summers, and Deane (1973) showed that in a multiple-cue probability learning task, providing outcome feedback actually resulted in lower performance compared to a group given no outcome feedback. In a review of the literature, Brehmer (1980) expressed extraordinary pessimism that in probabilistic tasks the provision of outcome feedback would result in substantial improvement in performance.

Fortunately, better forms of feedback can be made available. One form is cognitive feedback, which consists of information about the relations in the environment, relations perceived by the person, and relations between the environment and the person's perceptions. Cognitive feedback has been found to reliably improve performance on judgment tasks (Balzer, Doherty, & O'Connor, 1989). A related form of feedback is process feedback (Cannon-Bowers & Salas, 2001). Process feedback can inform people of necessary changes to their approach, whereas outcome feedback only indicates whether they tend to be improving or not.

Furthermore, to develop intuitive decision-making expertise, we can go beyond practice and feedback. We suggest three additional learning tactics. First, it can be informative for the learner to observe, interview, and/or study subject-matter experts in order to glean insights into why task accomplishment was successful for them. Interview methods exist that identify the heuristics and decision strategies, among other things, used by experts (e.g., Hoffman, Crandall, & Shadbolt, 1998; Klinger & Militello, 2001). The use of case studies is a predominant approach for studying and reflecting on decisions that were made under particular circumstances, and drawing lessons learned from them. Case studies can boost the vicarious experience base and enrich the mental models of the decision maker.

A second approach is to employ coaching as an adjunct to practice. Coaches can provide feedback, but good coaches can go further than that and facilitate the strengthening of the learner's intuitions. Ross et al. (in press) describe skilled tacticians functioning as coaches while the learner engages in a tactical simulation. The coaches in their study were attempting to build the students' mental models of small unit infantry tactics. To do so, they asked questions to direct the student's attention to a pertinent aspect of the simulation, and they asked questions to force the student to describe what was happening, what might happen next, and why. They probed as to how the student envisioned his or her own course of action impacting the situation, in order to reveal potential unintended consequences. All of these techniques contribute to a guided learning strategy whereby the coach facilitates the student in grasping the intricacies and dynamics of the tactical situation.

A third technique for building intuition is to present the learner with advance organizers, or previews of the instructional material, that direct attention to the relevant aspects, declarative information, and descriptions of mental models. However, these tools must be utilized in the context of actual or simulated practice. Feltovich et al. (1997) cautioned about the distortions that enter when people treat continuous processes as discrete, dynamic processes as static, simultaneous events as sequential, organic processes as mechanical, interactive processes as separable, conditional processes as universal, heterogeneous processes as homogeneous, and nonlinear processes as linear. Attempts to provide formal explanations may distort the phenomena, and instill faulty mental models. Schneider (1985) made the additional point that even acquiring an accurate mental model is not sufficient for using it well. Thus, we can obtain a good mental model of a manual transmission, but that will not translate into smooth decision making about when to shift gears while driving. The need is to couple the advanced organizers and documentation of the task with the practice sessions so that the learner can apply the information in context and generate a more accurate mental model around its meaning.

To summarize, we believe it is possible to facilitate the acquisition of decision-making expertise in specific domains with well-structured, scenario-based training sessions. It is prudent at this stage to incorporate what has been learned by judgment researchers with the efforts of naturalistic researchers to assist the acquisition of expertise. By building on the findings from both frameworks we can design additional research to better understand the development of skilled judgment and decision making.

Conclusion

The study of expertise in JDM is important for several reasons. At a theoretical level, we believe that the blending of naturalistic and laboratory-based research can generate a variety of lawful relationships. For example, the RPD model has led to a set of hypotheses about lawful relationships: First, that in most domains handled by experienced decision makers, most decisions will be made using recognitional strategies, rather than an analytic comparison of courses of action (Klein, 1998). Second, as people gain experience, they make more decisions relying on recognitional matches rather than comparison of courses of action (Klein, 1998). Third, for decision makers with even moderate experience, the first option they generate is usually satisfactory (Johnson & Raab, 2003; Klein, Wolf, Militello, & Zsambok, 1995). Fourth, options are more likely to be evaluated using mental simulation than by comparing the options on a generic set of criteria (Klein & Crandall, 1995). Fifth, as decision makers gain experience, they shift from spending most of their time examining options, to spending the majority of their time assessing the situation (Kobus et al., 2000). To date, the supporting evidence for these propositions comes largely from the field. Extensive laboratory research is needed to further test, refine, and possibly reject these and alternative hypotheses.

We also see great practical implications for studying expertise in JDM. It is important to understand the components of expertise to better prepare novices and less experienced individuals to become more expert and build their intuitions. Several researchers and practitioners are applying models of expertise to generate training interventions to help people acquire skill and knowledge more quickly. The goal is to move people up the learning curve at a faster rate by giving them low- and high-fidelity simulations to deliberately practice decisions and judgments. These simulations and their lessons learned help the individual form a base of experience and more complete mental models of the domain (Phillips & Battaglia, 2003; Pliske, Klinger, Hutton, Crandall, Knight, & Klein, 1997; Pliske, McCloskey, & Klein, 2001; Ross et al., 2003; US Army Research Institute, 2001). There are also many implications for Artificial Intelligence (AI) and system designers with regard to what human capabilities can and cannot be replicated by a computer. While systems are good at rule-based tasks, they cannot approximate human judgment when it comes to highly complex cognitive tasks. It is also important to know exactly what humans are capable of and how they do it, so that we can make better choices about how to design effective and acceptable systems to aid human decision making (Hutton, Miller, & Thordsen, 2003; Yates, Veinott, & Patalano, 2003).

Potentially interested JDM laboratory researchers will need to take several steps to make this happen. First, they must push beyond the most dominant experimental paradigms that are currently in fashion. This entails giving up the security and comfort that comes with further replication of old biases or striving to discover new ones. Examination of paradigms from experimental work on expertise outside the JDM area may provide a useful starting point. It also means giving up some of the statistical tightness of results to which most experimental psychologists have become accustomed. Schunn & Anderson (1999) provide guidelines on standards of evidence for research with experts that may facilitate individual thinking, as well as publication decisions. Finally, it is imperative to develop and maintain connections with subject matter experts, and be open to learning about the actual judgment and decision problems that they face. None of this is easy, but we feel strongly that the potential theoretical and practical gains to the JDM field are enormous.

Acknowledgements

This chapter was prepared through participation in the Advanced Decision Architectures Collaborative Technology Alliance sponsored by the US Army Research Laboratory under Cooperative

Agreement DAAD19-01-2-0009. The authors thank Nigel Harvey, Paul Schoemaker, and Steven Salterio for many useful comments.

References

Anderson, J. R. (1983) *The Architecture of Cognition*. Cambridge, MA: Harvard University Press.

Anzai, Y. (1991) Learning and use of representation in physics expertise. In K. A. Ericsson and J. Smith (eds.), *Toward a General Theory of Expertise: Prospects and Limits*. Cambridge: Cambridge University Press.

Arkes, H. R., Wortmann, R. L., Saville, P. D., & Harkness, A. R. (1981) Hindsight bias among physicians weighing the likelihood of diagnoses, *Journal of Applied Psychology*, 66, 252–5.

Asare, S. K. & Wright, A. (1995) Normative and substantive expertise in multiple hypothesis evaluation, *Organizational Behavior and Human Decision Processes*, 64, 171–84.

Balzer, W. K., Doherty, M. E., & O'Connor, R. O. (1989) The effects of cognitive feedback on performance, *Psychological Bulletin*, 106, 410–33.

Bazerman, M., Loewenstein, G., & Moore, D. (2002) Why good accountants do bad audits, *The Harvard Business Review*, 80(11), 97–102.

Bendor, J. (2003) Herbert A. Simon: Political scientist, *Annual Review of Political Science*, 6, 433–71.

Bornstein, B. H., Emler, A. C., & Chapman, G. B. (1999) Rationality in medical treatment decisions: Is there a sunk-cost effect? *Social Sciences & Medicine*, 49, 215–22.

Brehmer, B. (1980) In one word: Not from experience, *Acta Psychologica*, 45, 223–41.

Camerer, C. F. & Johnson, E. J. (1991) The process-performance paradox in expert judgment: How can experts know so much and predict so badly? In K. A. Ericsson and J. Smith (eds.), *Toward a General Theory of Expertise: Prospects and Limits* (pp. 195–217). Cambridge, MA: Cambridge University Press.

Cannon-Bowers, J. A. & Salas, E. (2001) Reflections on shared cognition, *Journal of Organizational Behavior*, 22, 195–202.

Chase, W. G. (1983) Spatial representations of taxi drivers. In D. R. Rogers and J. H. Sloboda (eds.), *Acquisition of Symbolic Skills* (pp. 391–405). New York: Plenum.

Chase, W. G. & Simon, H. A. (1973). The mind's eye in chess. In W. G. Chase (ed.), *Visual Information Processing*. New York: Academic Press.

Chi, M. T. H. (1978) Knowledge structures and memory development. In R. S. Siegler (ed.), *Children's Thinking: What Develops?* (pp. 73–96). Hillsdale, NJ: Lawrence Erlbaum Associates.

Chi, M. T. H., Feltovich, P. J., & Glaser, R. (1980) *Representation of Physics Knowledge by Experts and Novices* (Technical report no. 2). Pittsburgh, PA: University of Pittsburgh: Learning Research and Development Center.

Chi, M. T. H., Feltovich, P. J., & Glaser, R. (1981) Categorization and representation of physics problems by experts and novices, *Cognitive Science*, 5, 121–52.

Chi, M. T. H., Glaser, R. & Farr, M. J. (eds.) (1988) *The Nature of Expertise*. Mahwah, NJ: Lawrence Erlbaum Associates.

Christensen-Szalanski, J. J. J. & Bushyhead, J. B. (1981) Physicians' use of probabilistic information in a real clinical setting, *Journal of Experimental Psychology*, 7, 928–35.

Cohen, M. S. (1993) The naturalistic basis of decision biases. In G. A. Klein, J. Orasanu, R. Calderwood, and C. E. Zsambok (eds.), *Decision Making in Action: Models and Methods* (pp. 51–99). Norwood, NJ: Ablex.

DeGroot, A. D. (1965) *Thought and Choice in Chess*. The Hague: Mouton.

Dreyfus, H. L. (1997) Intuitive, deliberative, and calculative models of expert performance. In C. Zsambok and G. Klein (eds.), *Naturalistic Decision Making* (pp. 17–28). Mahwah, NJ: Lawrence Erlbaum.

Einhorn, H. J. & Hogarth, R. M. (1981) Behavioral decision theory: Processes of judgment and choice, *Annual Review of Psychology*, 32, 53–88.

Ericsson, K. A. & Charness, N. (1997) Cognitive and developmental factors in expert performance. In P. J. Feltovich, K. M. Ford, and R. R. Hoffman (eds.), *Expertise in Context: Human and Machine* (pp. 3–41). Cambridge, MA: MIT Press.

Ericsson, K. A. & Smith, J. (1991) Prospects and limits of the empirical study of expertise: An introduction. In K. A. Ericsson and J. Smith (eds.), *Toward a General Theory of Expertise: Prospects and Limits*. Cambridge, MA: Cambridge University Press.

Feltovich, P. J., Ford, K. M., & Hoffman, R. R. (1997) *Expertise in Context*. Menlo Park, CA: AAAI Press/The MIT Press.

Feltovich, P. J., Johnson, P. E., Moller, J. H., & Swanson, D. B. (1984) LCS: The role and development of medical knowledge in diagnostic expertise. In W. J. Clancey and E. H. Shortliffe (eds.), *Readings in Medical Artificial Intelligence: The First decade* (pp. 275–319). Reading, MA: Addison-Wesley.

Feltovich, P. J., Spiro, R. J., & Coulson, R. L. (1997). Issues of expert flexibility in contexts characterized by complexity and change. In P. J. Feltovich, K. M. Ford, and R. R. Hoffman (eds.), *Expertise in Context* (pp. 125–46). Menlo Park, CA: AAAI/MIT Press.

Fischhoff, B. (1982) Debiasing. In D. Kahneman, P. Slovic, and A. Tverskey (eds.), *Judgment Under Uncertainty: Heuristics and Biases*. Cambridge, MA: Cambridge University Press.

Fischhoff, B. (1996) The real world: What good is it? *Organizational Behavior and Human Decision Processes*, 65, 232–48.

Flin, R., Salas, E., Strub, M., & Martin, L. (eds.) (1997) *Decision Making Under Stress: Emerging Themes and Application*. Aldershot, England: Ashgate Publishing.

Flin, R., Slaven, G., & Stewart, K. (1996) Emergency decision making in the offshore oil and gas industry, *Human Factors*, 38(2), 262–77.

Gentner, D. R. (1988) Expertise in typewriting. In M. T. H. Chi, R. Glaser, and M. J. Farr (eds.), *The Nature of Expertise*. Mahwah, NJ: Lawrence Erlbaum Associates.

Gilovich, T. & Griffin, D. (2002) Introduction – Heuristics and biases: Then and now. In T. Gilovich, D. Griffin, and D. Kahneman (eds.), *Heuristics and Biases: The Psychology of Intuitive Judgment* (pp. 1–18). Cambridge, MA: Cambridge University Press.

Glaser, R. (1996) Changing the agency for learning: Acquiring expert performance. In K. A. Ericsson (ed.), *The Road to Excellence* (pp. 303–11). Mahwah, NJ: Erlbaum.

Glaser, R. & Chi, M. T. H. (1988) Overview. In M. T. H. Chi, R. Glaser, and M. J. Farr (eds.), *The Nature of Expertise*. Mahwah, NJ: Lawrence Erlbaum Associates.

Hammond, J. S., Keeney, R. L., & Raiffa, H. (1999) *Smart Choices: A Practical Guide to Making Better Decisions*. Boston, MA: Harvard Business School Press.

Hammond, K. R., McClelland, G. H., & Mumpower, J. (1980) *Human Judgment and Decision Making: Theories, Methods, and Procedures*. New York: Praeger.

Hammond, K. R., Summers, D. A., & Deane, D. H. (1973) Negative effects of outcome-feedback in multiple-cue probability learning, *Organizational Behavior and Human Decision Processes*, 9, 30–4.

Hayes, J. R. (1985) Three problems of teaching general skills. In J. W. Segal, S. F. Chipman, and R. Glaser (eds.), *Thinking and Learning Skills: Relating Instruction to Research* (vol. 1, pp. 391–405). Hillsdale, NJ: Lawrence Erlbaum Associates.

Hoffman, R. R. (1994) Constructivism versus realism or constructivism and realism? *Journal of Experimental and Theoretical Artificial Intelligence*, 6, 431–5.

Hoffman, R. R., Crandall, B. W., & Shadbolt, N. R. (1998) Use of the critical decision method to elicit expert knowledge: A case study in cognitive task analysis methodology, *Human Factors*, 40(2), 254–76.

Hogarth, R. (2001) *Educating Intuition*. Chicago: University of Chicago Press.

Hutton, R. J. B., Miller, T. E., & Thordsen, M. L. (2003) Decision-centered design: Leveraging cognitive task analysis in design. In E. Holnagel (ed.), *Handbook of Cognitive Task Design* (pp. 383–416). Mahwah, NJ: Lawrence Erlbaum Associates.

Johnson, J. G. & Raab, M. (2003) Take the first: Option generation and resulting choices, *Organizational Behavior and Human Decision Processes*, 91(2), 215–29.

Kahneman, D. & Tversky, A. (1972) Subjective probability: A judgment of representativeness, *Cognitive Psychology*, 3, 430–54.

Kahneman, D. & Tversky, A. (1982) On the study of statistical intuitions, *Cognition*, 11, 123–41.

Keren, G. (1987) Facing uncertainty in the game of bridge: A calibration study, *Organizational Behavior and Human Decision Processes*, 39(1), 98–114.

Klein, G. (1998) *Sources of Power: How People Make Decisions*. Cambridge, MA: MIT Press.

Klein, G. & Militello, L. (in press). The knowledge audit as a method for cognitive task analysis. In H. Montgomery, R. Lipshitz, and B. Brehmer (eds.), *How Professionals Make Decisions*. Mahwah, NJ: Lawrence Erlbaum Associates.

Klein, G. & Wolf, S. (1998) The role of leverage points in option generation, *IEEE Transactions on Systems, Man and Cybernetics: Applications and Reviews*, 28(1), 157–60.

Klein, G., Wolf, S., Militello, L., & Zsambok, C. (1995) Characteristics of skilled option generation in chess, *Organizational Behavior and Human Decision Processes*, 62(1), 63–9.

Klein, G. A. & Brezovic, C. P. (1986) Design engineers and the design process: Decision strategies and human factors literature, *Proceedings of the Human Factors and Ergonomics Society 30th Annual Meeting*, 2, 771–5.

Klein, G. A., Calderwood, R., & Clinton-Cirocco, A. (1986) Rapid decision making on the fireground, *Proceedings of the Human Factors and Ergonomics Society 30th Annual Meeting*, 1, 576–80.

Klein, G. A. & Crandall, B. W. (1995) The role of mental simulation in naturalistic decision making. In P. Hancock, J. Flach, J. Caird, and K. Vicente (eds.), *Local Applications of the Ecological Approach to Human–Machine Systems* (vol. 2, pp. 324–58). Mahwah, NJ: Lawrence Erlbaum Associates.

Klein, G. A. & Hoffman, R. (1993) Seeing the invisible: Perceptual/cognitive aspects of expertise. In M. Rabinowitz (ed.), *Cognitive Science Foundations of Instruction* (pp. 203–26). Mahwah, NJ: Lawrence Erlbaum Associates.

Klein, G. A., Orasanu, J., Calderwood, R., & Zsambok, C. E. (eds.) (1993) *Decision Making in Action: Models and Methods*. Norwood, NJ: Ablex.

Klinger, D. W. & Militello, L. G. (2001). Designing for performance: A cognitive systems engineering and cognitive task analysis approach to the modification of the AWACS weapons director interface. Manuscript submitted 10/2001.

Kobus, D. A., Proctor, S., Bank, T. E., & Holste, S. T. (2000) *Decision-making in a Dynamic Environment: The Effects of Experience and Information Uncertainty*. San Diego, CA: Space and Naval Warfare Systems Center.

Koehler, D. J., Brenner, L., & Griffin, D. (2002) The calibration of expert judgment: Heuristics and biases beyond the laboratory. In T. Gilovich, D. Griffin, and D. Kahneman (eds.), *Heuristics and Biases: The Psychology of Intuitive Judgment* (pp. 686–715). Cambridge, MA: Cambridge University Press.

Larkin, J., McDermott, J., Simon, D. P., & Simon, H. A. (1980) Expert and novice performance in solving physics problems, *Science*, 20, 1335–42.

Larkin, J. H. (1983) The role of problem representation in physics. In D. Gentner and A. L. Stevens (eds.), *Mental Models*. Mahwah, NJ: Lawrence Erlbaum Associates.

Lee, J. W. & Yates, J. F. (1992) How quantity judgment changes as the number of cues increase: An analytical framework and review, *Psychological Bulletin*, 112, 363–77.

Lipshitz, R. & Cohen, M. S. (submitted) Warrants for prescription: Analytically and empirically based approaches to improving decision making. Manuscript submitted for publication-HFES.

Lipshitz, R., Klein, G., Orasanu, J., & Salas, E. (2001) Focus article: Taking stock of naturalistic decision making, *Journal of Behavioral Decision Making*, 14, 331–52.

Lipshitz, R. & Strauss, O. (1997) Coping with uncertainty: A naturalistic decision making analysis, *Organizational Behavior and Human Decision Processes*, 66, 149–63.

Loftus, E. F. & Wagenaar, W. A. (1988) Lawyer's prediction of success, *Jurimetrics Journal*, 437–53.

McNeil, B. J., Pauker, S. G., Sox, H. C., Jr., & Tversky, A. (1982) On the elicitation of preferences for alternative therapies, *New England Journal of Medicine*, 306, 1259–62.

Mosier, K. L. (1991) Expert decision making strategies. In P. Jersen (ed.), *Proceedings of the Sixth International Symposium on Aviation Psychology* (pp. 266–71). Columbus, OH.

Newell, A. & Simon, H. A. (1972) *Human Problem Solving*. Englewood Cliffs, NY: Prentice Hall.

Pascual, R. & Henderson, S. (1997) Evidence of naturalistic decision making in military command and control. In C. E. Zsambok and G. Klein (eds.), *Naturalistic Decision Making*. Mahwah, NJ: Lawrence Erlbaum Associates.

Phillips, J. K. & Battaglia, D. A. (2003) Instructional methods for training sensemaking skills, *Proceedings of the Interservice/Industry Training, Simulation, and Education Conference 2003*, CD-ROM proceedings.

Pliske, R. M., Klinger, D., Hutton, R., Crandall, B., Knight, B., & Klein, G. (1997) *Understanding Skilled Weather Forecasting: Implications for Training and the Design of Forecasting Tools* (Technical Report No. AL/HR-CR-1997-0003 for the Air Force Material Command, Armstrong Laboratory, Human Resources Directorate Brooks AFB, TX). Fairborn, OH: Klein Associates Inc.

Pliske, R. M., McCloskey, M. J., & Klein, G. (2001) Decision skills training: Facilitating learning from experience. In E. Salas & G. Klein (eds.), *Linking Expertise and Naturalistic Decision Making* (pp. 37–53). Mahwah, NJ: Lawrence Erlbaum Associates.

Polanyi, M. (1966) *The Tacit Dimension*. Garden City, NY: Doubleday.

Randel, J. M., Pugh, H. L., & Reed, S. K. (1996) Methods for analyzing cognitive skills for a technical task, *International Journal of Human-Computer Studies*, 45, 579–97.

Ross, K. G., Battaglia, D. A., Phillips, J. K., Domeshek, E. A., & Lussier, J. W. (2003) Mental models underlying tactical thinking skills, *Proceedings of the Interservice/Industry Training, Simulation, and Education Conference 2003*, CD-ROM proceedings.

Rouse, W. B. & Morris, N. M. (1986) On looking into the black box: Prospects and limits on the search for mental models, *Psychological Bulletin*, 100(3), 349–63.

Russo, J. E., Schoemaker, P. J. H., & Hittleman, M. (2001) *Winning Decisions: Getting it Right the First Time*. New York: Doubleday.

Salas, E. & Klein, G. (2001) *Linking Expertise and Naturalistic Decision Making*. Mahwah, NJ: Lawrence Erlbaum Associates.

Salas, E., Wilson, K. A., Burke, C. S., & Bowers, C. A. (2002) Myths about crew resource management training, *Ergonomics in Design*, Fall, 20–4.

Schmitt, J. F. & Klein, G. (1996) Fighting in the fog: Dealing with battlefield uncertainty, *Marine Corps Gazette*, 80, 62–9.

Schneider, W. (1985) Training high-performance skills: Fallacies and guidelines, *Human Factors*, 27, 285–300.

Schunn, C. D. & Anderson, J. R. (1999) The generality/specificity of expertise in scientific reasoning, *Cognitive Science*, 23, 337–70.

Serfaty, D., MacMillan, J., Entin, E. E., & Entin, E. B. (1997) The decision-making expertise of battle commanders. In C. Zsambok and G. Klein (eds.), *Naturalistic Decision Making* (pp. 233–46). Mahwah, NJ: Lawrence Erlbaum Associates.

Shanteau, J. (1988) Psychological characteristics and strategies of expert decision makers, *Acta Psychologica*, 68, 203–15.

Shanteau, J. (1989) Cognitive heuristics and biases in behavioral auditing: Review, comments, and observations, *Accounting Organizations and Society*, 14(1–2), 165–77.

Shanteau, J. (1992) Competence in experts: The role of task characteristics, *Organizational Behavior and Human Decision Processes*, 53, 252–66.

Sieck, W. R. (2003) Effects of choice and relative frequency elicitation on overconfidence: Further tests of an exemplar-retrieval model, *Journal of Behavioral Decision Making*, 16, 127–45.

Simon, H. A. (1957) *Models of Man: Social and Rational*. New York: John Wiley & Sons.

Simon, H. A. (1975) The functional equivalence of problem solving skills, *Psychology*, 7, 268–88.

Smith, E. E. & Osherson, D. N. (1989) Similarity and decision making. In S. Vosniadou and A. Ortony (eds.), *Similarity and Analogical Reasoning* (pp. 60–76). Cambridge, MA: Cambridge University Press.

Smith, J. F. & Kida, T. (1991) Heuristics and biases: Expertise and task realism in auditing, *Psychological Bulletin*, 109(3), 472–89.

Stewart, T. R., Roebber, P. J., & Bosart, L. F. (1997) The importance of the task in analyzing expert judgment, *Organizational Behavior and Human Decision Processes*, 69, 205–19.

US Army Research Institute (2001) *Think like a Commander (Computer CD-ROM and Materials)*. Ft Leavenworth, KS: US Army Research Institute for the Behavioral and Social Sciences.

Wright, G. & Bolger, F. (eds.) (1993) *Expertise and Decision Support: The Language of Science*. New York, NY: Plenum.

Wright, G. & Goodwin, P. (eds.) (1998) *Forecasting with Judgment*. New York: John Wiley & Sons.

Yates, J. F., Veinott, E. S., & Patalano, A. L. (2003) Hard decisions, bad decisions: On decision quality and decision aiding. In S. L. Schneider and J. Shanteau (eds.), *Emerging Perspectives on Judgment and Decision Research*. New York: Cambridge University Press.

Zsambok, C. E. & Klein, G. (eds.) (1997) *Naturalistic Decision Making*. Mahwah, NJ: Lawrence Erlbaum Associates.

16

Debiasing

Richard P. Larrick

The mind has its illusions as the sense of sight; and in the same manner as feeling corrects the latter, reflection and calculation correct the former.

Pierre Simon, Marquis de Laplace

Rationality and Debiasing

That the mind has its illusions is not without dispute. Thirty years of decision research has used rational theories from economics, statistics, and logic to argue that descriptive behavior falls systematically short of normative ideals. But this apparent gap between the normative and the descriptive has provoked many debates: Is there in fact a gap? And, if there is, can it be closed – that is, can biases be "debiased"?

Many economists and philosophers have argued on principle that there is no gap: people are essentially rational, any errors are random and non-systematic, and apparent systematic discrepancies are attributable to improper empirical methods. Stanovich (1999) has aptly termed this group the Panglossians. Early research on debiasing largely served to counter the Panglossian position by demonstrating the robustness of systematic biases to various corrective measures (Fischhoff, 1982). The existence of systematic biases is now largely accepted by decision researchers, and, increasingly, by researchers in other disciplines.

Accepting the existence of a normative–descriptive gap raises the question of how the gap might be closed. One approach has focused on increasing the motivation to perform well. A critical assumption in this approach is that people possess normative strategies and will use them when the benefits exceed the costs. The remaining approaches do not presume this. Instead, they assume that intuitive strategies are imperfect, but that they can be replaced by strategies that approach normative standards (even if falling short).

The identification and dissemination of better strategies is known as prescriptive decision making.

My emphasis will be mainly on prescriptive strategies that individuals themselves can adopt, as opposed to techniques used by external agents to modify the decision environment. An example of the former approach would be increasing retirement savings by training people on the principle of compounding, either abstractly or as a rule of thumb (e.g., "the rule of 72" – an investment that grows at X percent per year will double roughly every 72/X years). An example of the latter approach is Thaler and Benartzi's (2001) highly successful demonstration that organizations can rebias employees to save more by changing the status quo and by exploiting mental accounting. Both rebiasing (using one bias to offset another) and changing the decision environment are viable methods for debiasing. However, I will focus on equipping individuals with strategies because this approach tends to increase their decision skills and their ability to apply those skills to new decision domains (in this example, perhaps, college savings).

One approach to prescription focuses on modifying the *cognitive* strategies of the individual. In this view, optimal prescriptive strategies represent a compromise between a strategy that approximates the normative ideal, but that can be remembered and implemented given ordinary cognitive limitations on memory and computation. Successful implementation also requires an encoding strategy for recognizing when to apply a cognitive strategy (Nisbett, Krantz, Jepson, & Kunda, 1983).

The extent to which purely cognitive strategies can improve reasoning is a source of debate. Stanovich (1999) terms those optimistic about improving cognitive strategies Meliorists, who believe that everyday reasoning falls far short of the ideal, but can be improved through experience and education (Nisbett, 1993). By contrast, the Apologists perceive supposed normative standards to be unattainable for many tasks because of computational constraints and unnatural problem representations (such as the use of Bayes' rule in probabilistic reasoning) and reject the supposed normative standard. They argue that the basic intuitive strategies people follow are evolutionarily well adapted to naturalistic judgment tasks (such as reasoning about frequencies) (see Gigerenzer, Chapter 4, this volume). Each view has different implications for prescription: Meliorists are optimistic about improving cognitive strategies through training, whereas Apologists suggest that decision tasks must be matched to evolutionarily-adapted strategies (I return to an intriguing intermediate position by Sedlmeier, 1999).

The degree to which reasoning can be improved through cognitive strategies has important implications for philosophical debates about rationality. Many philosophers are reluctant to equate rationality with strategies that are not humanly achievable, in which case, the most accurate cognitive strategies that people can use become the standard for rationality. As Stich wryly noted, "it seems simply perverse to judge that subjects are doing a bad job reasoning because they are not using a strategy that requires a brain the size of a blimp" (cited in Stanovich, 1999). Stanovich (1999, in work conducted with West) provides interesting evidence on this point in support of the Meliorists. They observe that, contrary to the Apologist view, there is always a subset of decision makers who give a normative response on a decision task, indicating that at least some people have it in their repertoire. Moreover, the pattern of normative responses across individuals is systematic. Normative responses are correlated positively with general aptitude (see

Jepson, Krantz, & Nisbett, 1983; Larrick, Nisbett, & Morgan, 1993) and with each other across highly diverse decision tasks. These data represent an existence proof that normative cognitive strategies are not unattainable, but are systematically held and used by some individuals.

Although identifying cognitive strategies that individuals are able to implement informs rationality debates, it is not the only means to close the normative–descriptive gap. A second approach to prescription is to expand possible strategies to include techniques external to the decision maker. This represents a Technologist alternative to the Meliorist–Apologist debate: individual reasoning can approach normative standards through the use of tools. Such techniques include using groups in place of individuals, improving information processing through decision aids and information displays, supplementing intuitive decision making with formal decision analysis, and replacing individual judgment entirely with statistical models. Debates about rationality have focused on purely cognitive strategies, obscuring the possibility that the ultimate standard of rationality might be the decision to make use of superior tools.

Despite the different emphases in these approaches, they share a common implication: debiasing requires intervention. Laplace optimistically observed that people recognize and correct their own biases, but there are many reasons to doubt that lone individuals can debias themselves (Kahneman, 2003). In part, this is a matter of which phenomena are declared biases – biases that are difficult for individuals to recognize and correct are selected into the canon of judgment and decision-making research, whereas those that are easily recognized and corrected are not. But there are other reasons why individuals are not able to debias themselves. First, they will often not realize when they have used a poor decision process – feedback on their decision outcome may be delayed, or the causal determinants of the outcome may be ambiguous, making both the existence and source of error difficult to identify (Hogarth, 2001). Second, the tendency to use decision outcomes to evaluate decision processes can lead to faulty conclusions in decisions made under uncertainty. These conclusions may be distorted further by self-serving attributions of ability that lead decision makers to attribute good outcomes to skill and poor outcomes to situational factors.

The study of debiasing, therefore, must go beyond identifying better strategies to identifying methods for *equipping* individual decision makers with those strategies. This is where the traditional study of individuals in isolation may underestimate the potential for improving decision making. Even though lone individuals do not debias themselves, they are surrounded by cultural mechanisms that compensate for their shortcomings (Camerer & Hogarth, 1999; Heath, Larrick, & Klayman, 1998). For example, the evolution of normative models over the last two centuries not only *revealed* intuitive shortcomings, but provided the disciplinary knowledge that could *repair* them (Nisbett et al., 1983). The result is an ongoing race between the identification of biases and the diffusion of tools for reducing them. There is no guarantee, of course, that standard economics and statistics curricula provide the best means for improving intuition (Hogarth, 2001). Part of the research agenda for debiasing, therefore, needs to be identifying methods that promote the acceptance and use of superior decision strategies, which I return to in the final section.

The Nature of Biases

One way of organizing a review of debiasing is by specific bias (Fischhoff, 1982), but the field's success at generating new biases makes this approach impractical. Fortunately, an exhaustive list of biases is not necessary. In a classic article on debiasing, Arkes (1991) argued that a few general causes underlie a wide range of biases, and that understanding these causes facilitates identifying when different debiasing strategies will be effective. His first two categories are errors that are attributable to unconscious, automatic System 1 processes (Kahneman, 2003; Kahneman & Frederick, 2002; Stanovich, 1999). The third category is errors attributable to more conscious and deliberative System 2 strategies (see Table 16.1):

- *Psychophysically-based error (System 1)*: This category includes errors produced by non-linear translations of stimuli in judgment and evaluation. The prototypical examples are reference point effects (see Wu, Zhang, & Gonzalez, Chapter 20, this volume), in which a reference point introduces a kink in slope (due to loss aversion) and curvature (due to diminishing sensitivity) in valuation. Because reference points can shift across contexts – depending on what comparisons are perceptually salient or accessible in memory – the same stimulus can be judged inconsistently (Kahneman, 2003).
- *Association-based error (System 1)*: This category includes errors that are caused by automatic processes that underlie the accessibility of information in memory (Kahneman, 2003). Association-based errors occur when an initial representation, often evoked by a stimulus, leads to the activation of conceptually or semantically associated cognitions and the inhibition of unassociated cognitions. A major consequence of association-based processes is the recruitment of a narrow and often biased information base from which to make judgments and decisions (Payne, Bettman & Schkade, 1999), including narrow framing (Kahneman, 2003).
- *Strategy-based error (System 2)*: The third category includes errors caused by the use of inferior strategies or decision rules. In my use of this category, I will depart from Arkes's (1991) original assumption that strategy-based errors are adaptive – that is, that they reflect a rational benefit–cost calculation. Although there is substantial evidence showing that people adapt their decision strategy to situational demands (Payne, Bettman, & Johnson, 1993), there is little direct evidence that they select strategies optimally or gauge effort and accuracy accurately (Fennema & Kleinmuntz, 1995). Moreover, people simply may not have the normative strategies in their intuitive repertoire, in which case reliance on inferior strategies is not a calculated choice, but a necessity. System 2, in this view, can itself be a major source of error if it contains either flawed strategies or poorly-calibrated strategies that produce under- or overcorrection (Wilson & Brekke, 1994).

Of course, many biases are multiply-determined (see the sunk cost examples in Table 16.1). The implication is that there is unlikely to be a one-to-one mapping of causes

Table 16.1 General causes of bias

	General causes of bias		
	Psychophysical	*Associationistic*	*Strategy*
Description	Non-linear translation of stimuli in judgment and evaluation	Activation of conceptually or semantically associated cognitions	Inappropriate rules
Example biases	• Status quo bias • Preference reversals due to joint vs. separate evaluation • Curvature of the probability weighting function	• Some forms of anchoring • Some forms of confirmation bias • Hindsight bias • Subconscious priming	• Positive test strategies • Lexicographic choice rules
Shortcomings	• Non-linear translation of dimensions that are assumed linear in normative theories (e.g., probability). • Inconsistent judgment of a stimulus	• "Functional fixedness" in problem solving • Overweighting focal outcomes in probability judgment • Narrow recruitment of attributes and alternatives in choice	• Neglect of relevant information in judgment and choice • Improper combination of inputs in judgment and choice
System	System 1	System 1	System 2
Sunk cost example	Diminishing sensitivity (convexity) in losses makes additional losses less painful after initial sunk cost	Cognitions that are consistent with the initial investment decision are accessible, inflating P(success)	Incorrect mental accounting rule: Past costs are kept in current accounts

to bias, or of bias to cure. Different processes may also be interdependent. Processes in the strategy category often rely on the output of the other processes, such as when a combination rule uses non-linear transformations of probabilities as inputs.

I will refer to these categories in discussing when different debiasing approaches are effective. The next sections present arguments and findings on major debiasing approaches. The strategies are organized according to the three approaches outlined in the introduction: Motivational, cognitive, and technological strategies. The final section discusses the major issues underlying the selection, diffusion, and implementation of different debiasing strategies in practice.

Motivational Strategies

Incentives

Economists have often responded to claims about decision errors with a call for better incentives. The assumption is that individuals will expend more effort on "reflection and calculation" – that is, System 2 will kick in – if the stakes are high enough. There is little empirical evidence, however, that incentives consistently improve mean decision performance (see Camerer & Hogarth, 1999, for a selective review). For example, early studies of incentives found that real stakes strengthened preference reversals (see Hsee, Zhang, & Junsong, Chapter 18, this volume). Subsequent studies of other biases found that incentives reduced biases in only a handful of cases. Camerer and Hogarth (1999, p. 33) reached the provocative conclusion that "there is no replicated study in which a theory of rational choice was rejected at low stakes in favor of a well-specified behavioral alternative, and accepted at high stakes."

To understand why incentives are generally ineffective, a second assumption in the incentives approach needs to be recognized. For incentives to improve decision making, decision makers must possess effective strategies that they either fail to apply or apply with insufficient effort when incentives are absent. In the words of Camerer and Hogarth (1999), decision makers must possess the necessary "cognitive capital" to which they can apply additional effort. They note that incentives do improve performance in settings such as clerical and memorization tasks, where people possess the cognitive capital required to perform well but lack the intrinsic motivation. Few decision tasks, however, are analogous to simple clerical work or memorization. Instead, experimental decision-making tasks are either quite complex (e.g., requiring the use of Bayes' rule, which few people intuitively possess); or they are relatively simple, but require that a decision maker possesses both the right strategy (such as the conjunction rule) *and* the ability to recognize when to apply it. When decision makers lack the necessary cognitive capital, incentives may lead them to apply inferior strategies with more determination, producing a pattern I will call the "lost pilot" effect ("I don't know where I'm going, but I'm making good time").

A few decision tasks do benefit from greater effort being applied to simple strategies. In multiattribute choice, accuracy incentives lead people to search more extensively for information and to process information more by alternative than by attribute, resulting in more accurate decisions (Stone & Ziebart, 1995; see also Creyer, Payne, & Bettman, 1990). However, responding to incentives by using more information and by changing strategies can produce a "lost pilot" effect on some tasks, especially *stochastic* tasks. For example, incentives lead decision makers on prediction tasks to rely less on base-rate information and more on imperfect cues that they use inconsistently as they "chase" error, often *reducing* performance on these tasks (Arkes, Dawes, & Christensen, 1986; Hogarth, Gibbs, McKenzie, & Marquis, 1991).

Arkes (1991) has argued that the automatic nature of association-based and psychophysically-based errors should make them largely unresponsive to incentives. This has held true for most biases of these types (e.g., hindsight bias, overconfidence, framing effects). Surprisingly, however, incentives have been shown to reduce the influence of anchors in some instances (see Epley, Chapter 12, this volume). Social psychologists have proposed that people hold intuitive theories about some association-based biases and can recognize and deliberately adjust for them (Wegener & Petty, 1995; Wilson & Brekke, 1994). Thus, incentives can increase the effort decision makers expend in correcting association-based biases – *if* decision makers recognize when they occur (Stapel, Martin, & Schwarz, 1998). A promising area for future research is identifying when people *spontaneously* apply an intuitive theory of association-biased errors.

Although incentives have been ineffective at reducing most biases in laboratory studies, these results may not reflect the true potential of incentives outside the laboratory. First, lack of effort may be a serious problem in some organizational decisions where tasks truly are boring. If the individual has little at stake, he may be satisfied with a superficial search of alternatives, attributes, and cues. In this setting, incentives may be a useful tool to improve decision making and align individual effort with organizational interests. Second, although incentives cannot improve cognitive capital in the course of a brief experiment, they can motivate people to acquire the decision skills they need over longer periods of time (Camerer & Hogarth, 1999).

Accountability

A second motivational approach to debiasing is holding people accountable for their decisions – that is, giving them the expectation that they will later have to explain their decision to others. The logic of accountability is similar to the logic of incentives, except that it depends on the motivational effects of social benefits (such as making a favorable impression and avoiding embarrassment). The principal mechanism by which accountability improves decision making is pre-emptive self-criticism. In preparation for justifying their decisions to others, decision makers anticipate the flaws in their own arguments, thereby improving their decision processes and outcomes.

The popularity of the accountability paradigm has led to many tests of accountability effects on various biases, with notable successes (see Lerner & Tetlock, 1999, for an excellent review). As with monetary incentives, accountability primarily improves performance on tasks for which people already possess the appropriate strategy (Lerner & Tetlock, 1999), such as the sunk cost rule among MBA students (Simonson & Nye, 1992). Just as with monetary incentives, accountability leads to greater effort (e.g., time spent on a task) and use of information (e.g., information searched in an information display) (Huber & Seiser, 2001), which may often lead to improved performance. But, just as with monetary incentives, the use of more information leads to a "lost pilot" effect on prediction tasks if cues are unreliable (Siegel-Jacobs & Yates, 1996, Study 1; Tetlock & Boettger, 1989).

The social nature of accountability makes it different from monetary incentives in several ways. One interesting difference is that accountability evokes a strong social need to look consistent to others. Although rigid consistency is detrimental for many tasks, it does improve prediction tasks, where the inconsistent weighting of reliable cues is a major source of error (Siegel-Jacobs & Yates, 1996). The social nature of accountability also introduces some potential problems. First, accountable decision makers tend to "give the people what they want." If they know their audience's preference for a specific decision *outcome*, decision makers distort their decision process to justify that outcome; if they know their audience's preference for a decision *process*, they are more likely to use that process (Brown, 1999). Consequently, justifying a decision to an audience with *unknown* preferences leads to pre-emptive self-criticism, but justifying a decision to an audience with *known* preferences leads to biased rationale-construction. Second, the focus on justification may have the effect of exacerbating justification-based decision biases (see Shafir and Lebouef, Chapter 17, this volume). For example, both attraction and compromise effects are amplified by accountability (Simonson, 1989). Accountability is likely to strengthen reliance on salient or easily justified dimensions, such as outcome probabilities in choice.

Cognitive Strategies

"Consider the opposite"

By necessity, cognitive strategies tend to be context-specific rules tailored to address a narrow set of biases, such as the law of large numbers or the sunk cost rule. This fact makes the simple but general strategy of "consider the opposite" all the more impressive, because it has been effective at reducing overconfidence, hindsight biases, and anchoring effects (see Arkes, 1991; Mussweiler, Strack, & Pfeiffer, 2000). The strategy consists of nothing more than asking oneself, "What are some reasons that my initial judgment might be wrong?" The strategy is effective because it directly counteracts the basic problem of association-based processes – an overly narrow sample of evidence – by expanding the sample and making it more representative. Similarly, prompting decision makers to consider alternative hypotheses has been shown to reduce confirmation biases in seeking and evaluating new information.

Soll and Klayman (2004) have offered an interesting variation on "consider the opposite." Typically, subjective range estimates exhibit high overconfidence. Ranges for which people are 80 percent confident capture the truth 30 percent to 40 percent of the time. Soll and Klayman (2004) showed that having judges generate 10th and 90th percentile estimates in separate stages – which forces them to consider distinct reasons for low and high values – increased hit rates to nearly 60 percent by both widening and centering ranges.

"Consider the opposite" works because it directs attention to contrary evidence that would not otherwise be considered. By comparison, simply listing reasons typically does not improve decisions because decision makers tend to generate supportive reasons. Also, for some tasks, reason generation can disrupt decision-making accuracy if there is a poor match between the reasons that are easily articulated and the actual factors that determine an outcome (Wilson & Schooler, 1991). Lastly, asking someone to list too many contrary reasons can backfire – the difficulty of generating the tenth "con" can convince a decision maker that her initial judgment must have been right after all (see Roese, Chapter 13, this volume).

Training in rules

An important issue in rationality debates is whether people's inferior strategies can be replaced by better strategies. A practical question then arises: *How* do you replace them? Experience is one possible method, but it is often an inexact and even misleading teacher (Hogarth, 2001). A second method, training, is potentially more precise.

In an extensive program of research, Nisbett (1993) and his colleagues explored the effectiveness of training on normative rules, leading to two sets of implications for debiasing. First, their research identified specific cognitive factors that facilitate the learning and use of normative rules (Fong & Nisbett, 1991; Fong, Krantz, & Nisbett, 1986; Jepson et al., 1983; Nisbett et al., 1983). Second, their research demonstrated that formal training in basic disciplines, such as economics and statistics, is an important cultural mechanism for transmitting effective cognitive strategies (Fong et al., 1986; Larrick, Morgan, & Nisbett, 1990; Lehman & Nisbett, 1990) – although the transmission process can no doubt be improved (Nisbett, 1993).

A basic assumption underlying this work was that people often have a rudimentary understanding of statistical, logical, and economic principles, but have difficulty in knowing how and when to apply them. For example, Nisbett et al. (1983) argued that people have an understanding of basic statistical principles, such as the tendency for sample means to reflect the population mean more accurately as samples get larger. They argued, however, that this understanding is better developed in transparently probabilistic domains than in other domains, but can be improved with experience. When sports novices were told about a new player who had a great performance during a team tryout but performed less well during the season, they often gave deterministic explanations, such as "once the player made the team, he slacked off"; by contrast, sports fans were more likely to attribute the pattern to the small, unreliable sample of evidence provided in the tryout. Fong et al. (1986) went on to demonstrate that principles of sampling and sample variability could be taught in short training sessions either abstractly or with concrete examples, and that a combination of the two was most effective. Finally, Fong and Nisbett (1991) demonstrated that decision makers trained in one type of domain (e.g., sports performance) successfully generalized the rule to other domains (e.g., test taking), although cross-domain transfer diminished over two weeks.

A series of other laboratory studies focused on training in logical and economic principles. In research on logical reasoning, Cheng, Holyoak, Nisbett, and Oliver (1986) successfully trained undergraduates to reason with the material conditional (*if p, then q*), where verification of the relationship requires that a decision maker examine evidence regarding *p* (to test whether *q* is true) and *not-q* (to test that *p* was *not* true) – a pattern of testing that is rarely observed in the Wason selection task. Training was more effective using familiar, pragmatic rules about permission and obligation (if you drink alcohol, you must be at least 18 years of age) than using the purely abstract rule. In addition, combining abstract principles with concrete examples proved particularly important for learning this rule. In research on economic principles, Larrick et al. (1990) demonstrated that students could be trained to ignore sunk costs in financial domains and generalize the rule to time decisions (and vice versa), and that they could correctly distinguish between sunk cost problems for which the normative principle implies opposite actions (discontinuing versus continuing investments, respectively).

Finally, a series of cross-sectional and longitudinal studies demonstrated differential effects of *disciplinary* training. Economics professors were more likely than biology or humanities professors to report abandoning a consumer activity in which they had "sunk" money, such as watching a movie or eating a restaurant meal, despite having the same consumption opportunities (Larrick et al., 1990, 1993). And students majoring in social science and psychology show improved reasoning on statistical problems after three years of related coursework, but no improvement on unrelated logical rules (Lehman & Nisbett, 1990).

Overall, these studies demonstrated that classes of decision rules could be taught effectively, often with relatively brief training. The most effective approaches combined an abstract principle with concrete examples, where experience with examples provided skills at mapping the principle to specific content. Examples-training is important because improvement is not just a matter of enhancing the strategies in System 2, but making their use automatic – in effect, making recognition of when to use them as a System 1 process. The rules that were taught successfully were either relatively simple, such as the sunk cost rule, or familiar, such as the law of large numbers. It is important to note that this rule-training research did not tackle highly complex, unfamiliar, abstract rules, such as Bayes' rule; the assumptions underlying this research would suggest that Bayes' rule would be a poor candidate for training.

Training in representations

A second program of training (Sedlmeier, 1999) was inspired by research showing that people reason more accurately about frequencies than about probabilities (Gigerenzer & Hoffrage, 1995). For example, Tversky and Kahneman (1983) showed that the conjunction fallacy occurs less when reasoning about a set of instances than when judging a single case (see Chapters 1 and 4, this volume; also Griffin & Buehler (1999) on why frequency formats are not a panacea). The relative effectiveness of reasoning about frequencies illustrates a general debiasing principle of "moderator as repair": when a variable is found that moderates accuracy on a decision task, it can become the basis for designing a debiasing strategy. In this case, two strategies are possible. A technological strategy is to present information to decision makers as frequencies rather than as probabilities, thereby debiasing the environment. A cognitive strategy, pursued by Sedlmeier (1999), is to train people to translate probabilistic reasoning tasks into frequency formats.

Through a computer-based set of instructions and illustrations, Sedlmeier trained participants to use a probability-based *or* frequency-based approach to solve a *probability* problem, and then tested performance several weeks later. On the conjunction rule, both probability training (on Venn diagrams) and frequency training (on frequency grids) proved highly effective. For problems that required reasoning about conditional probabilities or Bayes' rule, frequency training (on frequency grids and frequency trees) proved highly effective and durable, surpassing the effects of probability training. The most noteworthy part of this impressive research is that subsequent test problems were always presented in *probability* terms; thus, participants' success on later tests showed that they learned to apply the frequency tools to novel, single-case probability questions. Sedlmeier's training techniques have important implications for making statistics classes useful to everyday decisions.

Training in biases

Research on behavioral decision theory (BDT) is increasingly taught in psychology, law, and management curricula. "Stupid human tricks," as a friend has called them, are often taught in these classes to demonstrate inconsistencies in human reasoning, but with no accompanying instruction in how to overcome them, except a warning such as "beware availability." It would be interesting to perform a controlled experiment to test whether BDT courses reduce decision biases, as statistics courses increase the use of some statistical reasoning (Fong et al., 1986). Just as statistics and economics classes often miss the opportunity to develop people's intuitions through behavioral examples, courses that contain behavioral decision research may miss an opportunity to improve people's intuitions if they do nothing more than demonstrate the flaws. Without accompanying recognition skills and decision tools, it is unlikely that "awareness" alone would be sufficient.

Technological Strategies

Group decision making

Groups are often disparaged as decision-making resources because social influence processes undermine their effectiveness. People in groups often intentionally withhold or misrepresent their private judgments to avoid the social costs of rejection or to "free ride" on the efforts of others. But perhaps the most insidious problem in groups is that people are unknowingly influenced by the public judgments of others. Especially under conditions of uncertainty, people are susceptible to anchoring on the judgments of others in forming their own judgments.

Despite these problems, there are many reasons that groups might be beneficial. First, groups serve as an error-checking system during interaction. Second, "synergies" can emerge when people with complementary expertise interact. But the main benefits of a group may not depend on interaction at all. The third and arguably most important reason that groups improve decision making is statistical. Groups increase the effective sample size of experience used to make a decision. The result is that on tasks that require novel solutions – such as creativity or hypothesis generation tasks – groups hold more diverse perspectives than any one individual. And on tasks that require estimation – such as forecasting or evaluation tasks – the larger sample and diversity of cue-usage in groups makes the combination of individual judgments a powerful way to reduce individual error. The result is that simply averaging individual forecasts has proven a robust method of reducing errors in prediction and estimation (Clemen, 1989; Soll & Larrick, 2004).

However, the statistical benefit of aggregation is fragile. The effective sample size of a group is greatly reduced to the extent that group members' judgments have shared errors (Hogarth, 1978) – in the extreme, each person becomes "redundant" with any other. Shared training, shared experiences, and shared discussions all lead group members to hold a similar view of the world – *and* similar blind spots. Although holding a similar view can foster group cohesion, it reduces the informational benefits of group decision making.

Using groups to improve decisions ultimately depends on assembling a group with diverse experiences and training, and then following a process that preserves the diversity of perspectives. If run effectively, groups generate their own "consider-the-opposite" process. It is interesting that the most popular group decision-making method – brainstorming – comes up wanting on preserving diversity. Brainstorming is designed to encourage diversity of ideas by separating a "no-criticism" idea-generation phase from a selection phase. Despite these helpful rules, the number of unique, high-quality ideas produced in an *n*-person brainstorming group does not come close to matching the output of *n* people working separately for the same period of time (dubbed "nominal groups"). The principal explanations for this deficit have been evaluation apprehension and the sequential rather than simultaneous pooling of information. But an uninvestigated flaw in brainstorming is that early suggestions tend to "contaminate" all members' subsequent ideas. The fundamental requirement of group decision making is that individuals must formulate their own hypotheses, judgments, and estimates *independently* of each other before working in a group; once into the group process, shared ideas can spark new insights.

Linear models, multiattribute utility analysis, and decision analysis

In 1772, Benjamin Franklin proposed to his friend Joseph Priestley a "moral or prudential algebra" for making difficult decisions. It entailed dividing a sheet of paper into two columns – Pro and Con – and then listing examples of each over the course of a few days because "all the reasons pro and con are not present to mind at the same time; but sometimes one set present themselves, and at other times another, the other being out of sight." Once pros and cons are fully enumerated, sets can be compared; when a subset in one column has the same "respective weight" as a subset in the other, both can be struck out, until the decision maker can tell "where the balance lies" (from Dawes & Corrigan, 1974).

Franklin's proposal is celebrated as the forerunner of modern decision analysis because at its core is the basic tenet of decision analysis: "Decompose a complex problem into simpler problems, get one's thinking straight in these simpler problems, [and] paste these analyses together with logical glue . . ." (Raiffa, 1968). For example, a hiring decision can be decomposed into *alternatives* (e.g., candidates under consideration), *attributes* (e.g., characteristics of the candidates, such as teaching experience), and *attribute levels* (e.g., such as three years of teaching experience). Each attribute needs to be weighted and then combined across each alternative. This commonly takes the linear, additive form of $U(A) = wx_1 + wx_2 + wx_3 + \ldots + wx_n$, where w is the weight assigned to an attribute and x is the attribute level.

Proper and improper linear models

The simplest way to derive weights for a linear model is to use a statistical technique such as multiple regression analysis to fit a criterion to a set of predictor variables. In a series of influential reviews, Meehl and Dawes (see Dawes, Faust, & Meehl, 1989) demonstrated that, across scores of studies, statistical models based on past data consistently outperformed the "holistic" estimates of human judges on new cases (even when human judges had access to the same – or more – attribute information as the statistical model). Of course, a "proper" statistical model necessarily captures the true linear relationships in a set of data and therefore represents the upper bound that a perfectly linear, additive human judge could attain. More surprising is that a variety of "improper" models not based on past data also outperform intuitive judgment (Dawes & Corrigan, 1974). These include "bootstrapped" models (see Schoemaker, Chapter 14, this volume), in which a judge's holistic judgments are regressed on a set of attributes, capturing the judge's inevitably flawed attribute weights (or "policy"); and equal-weight models, in which a set of relevant attributes are identified, attribute values are normalized, and then given equal weight in an additive model (Dawes & Corrigan, 1974). Camerer (1981) has shown that bootstrapped models outperform holistic judgment consistently – if not dramatically – and that equal weights perform as well as or better than bootstrapped weights under a wide range of conditions (see also Payne et al., 1993).

Why do blatantly improper models outperform intuitive judgments? One reason is that, in Franklin's terms, relevant attributes are often "out of sight." In tasks that rely on recall, accessibility is likely to make some attributes more salient than others. But even with all relevant attributes available, attention is prone to wander, leading judges to focus on different attributes and to weight them differently as they evaluate specific alternatives, producing cognitive inconsistency (Hammond & Summers, 1972; see Goldstein, Chapter 3, this volume). People may also cope with an overabundance of attributes by using a non-compensatory strategy, such as elimination by aspects, to simplify the task (see Payne and Bettman, Chapter 6, this volume). Thus, even an *improper* linear model is effective because it ensures that *all* the attributes are used, and that they are *weighted* and *combined* consistently. A biased model consistently applied is an improvement over a biased and inconsistent human. Overall, linear models are ideally suited for tasks in which there are a large number of alternatives to review. It is precisely such data-rich but repetitive tasks that prove the most taxing on human information processing and benefit the most from substituting a model for a human.

Multiattribute utility (MAU) analysis

An alternative method for assigning attribute weights in a linear model is to elicit them directly from a decision maker through MAU analysis (see Pidgeon and Gregory,

Chapter 30, this volume). For unique choice problems that have no historical precedent (or accuracy criterion) this is the main alternative to linear models. A variety of methods exist for eliciting weights (Clemen, 1996), and the methods tend to yield similar estimates, indicating reliability (Leon, 1997; Stillwell, Barron, & Edwards, 1983). A practical implication of having multiple methods available is that they can be used simultaneously, and discrepancies examined and reconciled (Payne et al., 1999). For example, by constructing utilities "top down" through MAU analysis (using swing weights, for example) and comparing them to utilities built "bottom up" from choices (through conjoint analysis, a regression technique similar to bootstrapping) one can use discrepancies to reflect on why one's "head" and "heart" disagree.

Few studies have attempted to examine the *validity* of weight-elicitation methods directly because of the lack of a natural accuracy criterion. A commonly used benchmark – holistic judgments of expected satisfaction – is a dubious choice given the weakness of holistic judgments in the linear models literature. The goal is to improve on holistic judgment. Stillwell et al. (1983) provided a clever strategy for overcoming this catch-22: They used output from a formal model that was familiar to the judges as a criterion for evaluating different weight-elicitation methods. More tools for verifying the effectiveness of MAU techniques are desirable.

Decision analysis (DA)

MAU is only one technique in the DA repertoire, which also includes methods for eliciting probabilities and for eliciting utilities under risk. Unfortunately, space does not permit reviewing each of these methods (see Pidgeon and Gregory, Chapter 30, this volume; Clemen, 1996, and Hammond, Keeney, & Raiffa, 1997, for excellent technical introductions; and Payne et al., 1999, for how DA techniques address decision flaws). At an abstract level, however, they share with MAU a set of common features. First, they all rest on an underlying logic of decomposition. D. Kleinmuntz (1990) has argued that all of these decomposition methods gain their effectiveness over holistic judgment by averaging out error in individual components (the same statistical principle that makes group judgments more effective than individual judgments). Second, DA methods rest on important *coherence* assumptions (about additivity, independence, etc.) that must be verified through a series of consistency checks. And, third, sensitivity analyses are important for determining whether conclusions are robust to different estimates of the components.

The quantitative nature of DA has traditionally made it a highly social process in which a technically astute advisor guides a decision maker through these procedures. This may create the impression of DA as complicated, expensive, and obscure. Recent approaches, however, have emphasized the qualitative aspects of *structuring* decisions, including identifying fundamental objectives and generating a broad set of new, creative alternatives (Hammond et al., 1997; Keeney, 2002). In addition, these authors have emphasized giving simpler versions of DA directly to individual decision makers (Hammond et al., 1997). Finally, there is an increasing potential to automate much of DA (discussed in the next section). All of these trends may help make DA more appealing and useful to ordinary decision makers. Unfortunately, perhaps the biggest shortcoming in debiasing research is the lack of empirical evidence on whether DA training actually transfers to and improves everyday decisions – a shortcoming that begs to be addressed. Perhaps these new trends will provide more field and laboratory opportunities for studying decision analysis.

Decision Support Systems (DSS)

Computing technology has vastly enhanced the human ability to calculate and remember. Between the computer's capacity to execute complex algorithms in nanoseconds and to store libraries-worth of data, the computer can dramatically reduce the costs of effort in the *human* "effort–accuracy" tradeoff. In their useful summary of DSS, Edwards and Fasolo (2001, p. 581) speculate that computer-based "decision tools will be as important in the 21st Century as spreadsheets were in the 20th Century." But organizing technology around human tastes and limitations is still essential. As Edwards and Fasolo observe, "The idea of a procedure for making important decisions that does not depend heavily on human inputs seems unlikely as well as unattractive. Selection, training, and elicitation of responses from the person (or, more often, people) . . . become crucial" (p. 588).

DSS has the potential to improve individual decision making in a number of ways (although few systems currently exist that reflect all these possibilities):

1   DSS ensures the use of basic normative algorithms (MAU, Bayesian nets, Subjective Expected Utility Theory) that are otherwise hard for individuals to remember and to implement.
2   DSS can "bury" out of sight algorithms that would otherwise be intimidating to decision makers, making decision analytic tools more palatable.
3   DSS can run consistency checks (e.g., on probabilities or attribute weights) more easily and less obtrusively than a human advisor.
4   DSS can build and show the results of sensitivity analyses.

One of the most promising opportunities for improving decision accuracy through DSS is using information presentation to facilitate information acquisition and processing. Schkade and Kleinmuntz (1994) summarize the important dimensions of information display as:

1   the organization of displays (by alternative, by attribute, or as a matrix);
2   the form of displays (verbal or numeric); and
3   the sequence of information (sorted by preference or randomized).

In an extensive protocol study, they found that organization by alternative, attribute, or matrix led to corresponding differences in information *acquisition*, and that numeric displays yielded more compensatory *processing* than did verbal displays. And displays in which alternatives were sorted by decision maker's utility led decision makers to dwell on the most attractive options and to make faster decisions than did random displays.

Although the information displays did not influence choice quality in Schkade and Kleinmuntz (1994), it is reasonable to expect that factors that facilitate alternative-based acquisition and compensatory decision rules would yield superior decisions under many circumstances. Unfortunately, many current websites are not designed this way. Some websites offer huge data bases that allow a consumer to see a matrix of information and to sort alternatives by individual attributes. However, when there are scores of alternatives and dozens of attributes, consumers are essentially forced to resort to lexicographic decision rules. This is compounded by the fact that few sites provide the option of selecting on *several* attributes simultaneously, either by setting thresholds (a conjunctive decision rule) or by weighting and combining the attributes (in a compensatory way). Ideally, sites would attempt to capture a consumer's weights across attributes to facilitate compensatory tradeoffs in sorting alternatives (Edwards & Fasolo, 2001). The extent to which DSS and information displays can facilitate decision making is a growing area of study (Todd & Benbasat, 2000) that promises to become a central topic for debiasing research.

Adoption and Diffusion of Debiasing Techniques

One of the critical issues in debiasing research is identifying methods for facilitating the adoption of debiasing techniques. People resist being debiased for many reasons (Arkes, 2003; B. Kleinmuntz, 1990). They do not want to be told that they have been "doing it wrong" for all these years. They do not want to relinquish control over a decision process. And, perhaps most importantly, they fail to understand the benefits of many debiasing techniques relative to their own abilities, not just because they are overconfident, but because the techniques themselves are alien and complex, and the benefits are noisy, delayed, or small.

To understand the factors that promote adoption of a practice, it is useful to draw on a social psychological distinction between *compliance* to a behavioral norm and *internalization* of beliefs. Compliance is induced by rewards and coercion, and tends to produce superficial adoption – people mechanically go along with a practice in response to inducements, but abandon it when the inducements are removed. Internalization is fostered when a practice is endorsed by a trusted, expert source and when the acquisition process is active and voluntary, such as participating in the design of the practice (Kaplan, Reneau, & Whitecotton, 2001). Internalization is marked by an understanding of a practice and the intrinsic motivation to use it. Understanding, of course, is important for the successful adoption of cognitive strategies, especially for generalizing them across domains, but also for technological strategies, where ignorance about assumptions underlying DSS can be dangerous and overdependence can retard skills needed for *unaided* decision making (Glover, Prawitt, & Spilker, 1997).

With the exception of interesting research on factors that make decision aids more acceptable (e.g., Kaplan et al., 2001), there have been few studies on the adoption and diffusion of debiasing techniques, especially cognitive strategies. However, there are interesting case examples of the diffusion of similar practices. Every decade or so, a new set of decision-making techniques seems to sweep through organizations, such as Total Quality Management (TQM) in the 1980s and Six Sigma in the late 1990s. Both movements included statistical tools, such as histograms and Pareto charts, in addition to softer tools, such as brainstorming and cause–effect analysis. Perhaps not surprisingly, the statistical tools are the first to be abandoned as practices diffuse through an organization (Zbaracki, 1998). The reasons that management fads die are many – senior management endorses something but does not practice it, engendering cynicism; people are skeptical of outside consultants brought in to train them; and trainees are separated from their coworkers, who put pressure on the trainee to continue with "business as usual" on the trainee's return.

How might an organization overcome these obstacles? In the 1980s, Xerox took great pains to ensure the successful adoption of TQM by its 100,000 employees, including the statistical tools (Kearns & Nadler, 1992). They developed their own week-long training program and teaching materials. Existing organizational units were trained as a "family" and were expected to "learn it, use it, teach it, inspect it," where "using it" included a mandatory "family" project to be done in the group's home setting (thereby transforming declarative into procedural knowledge). The course was initially taught to the most senior managers, who then taught the managers at the next level below them; this process was repeated until the training had been "cascaded" down to the bottom of the organization. And teaching it required a deep understanding (if only to avoid embarrassment) as well as active, public endorsement of the methods. This behaviorally astute training program was perfectly designed to reduce cynicism, to encourage internalization, and to foster group support – not group resistance – for the new practices.

Heath et al. (1998) have argued that, in addition to studying formal training on formal techniques, it is also useful to understand the diffusion of informal debiasing techniques, which they called "cognitive repairs." These feral debiasing strategies include a range of proverbs and procedures that are illustrated in Table 16.2. Examining cognitive repairs suggests several dimensions that affect the tendency for them to be adopted. The dimensions include: simple versus complex; domain-specific versus domain-general; social versus individual; and top-down versus bottom-up (which refers to where in an organization they originate). These dimensions come with inevitable tradeoffs. Many "cognitive repairs" in organizations are quite simple, involving a saying or an acronym, and domain-specific, tied to Wall Street or banks (as in Table 16.2). Together, simplicity and domain-specificity greatly enhance the memorability and applicability of the practices, making them more likely to be adopted in practice. But simple domain-specific repairs come at a cost. They tend not to be very precise (one would prefer a formula for discounting broker performance based on the mean and dispersion of the performance of other brokers) and they do not readily translate to new problems. But professional rules of thumb that point decision makers in the right direction are better than complex, general rules that are never understood, easily distorted, or quickly abandoned.

Heath et al. (1998) also argued that socially administered practices are often more effective than individual practices because individuals are overconfident in their decision-making abilities and fail to recognize when they need help. And, finally, Heath et al. argue that practices that emerge locally (or "bottom-up") tend to have the advantage of

Table 16.2 Examples of "cognitive repairs"

Cognitive repair	Benefits of the repair
Wall Street brokers tell each other "Not to confuse brains with a bull market."	This proverb helps deflate self-serving biases in decision-making ability.
Toyota and other companies encourage their employees to analyze problems by asking the question "Why?" five times.	The Five Whys helps decision makers to arrive at a deeper – rather than a merely accessible – answer for why problems have occurred.
At the Federal Reserve Bank of New York, examiners use an acronym known as CAMEL (capital adequacy, asset quality, management, earnings, and liability) to evaluate loans.	CAMEL ensures that examiners give attention to a full set of relevant attributes.
Motorola breaks up new product teams after the team has completed a project; subsequent new designs are pursued by newly formed teams.	By constantly rotating team members in a seemingly inefficient process, Motorola prevents the problem of shared views and shared errors discussed in the group decision making section.

simplicity, domain-specificity, and a sense of ownership. Combining the two, socially-administered practices that are homegrown, such as local norms of vigorous debate in scientific labs, tend to be more palatable than challenges imposed by superiors or outsiders. Heath et al. conclude that "the most successful repairs will be simple, domain-specific, socially administered, and evolved from bottom-up rather than developed from top-down. We find this conclusion intriguing because it describes repairs that differ sharply from those that are recommended in academic literatures on decision analysis, statistics, and economics" (pp. 30–1).

It is interesting to consider what implications these dimensions hold for the major classes of debiasing techniques reviewed in this chapter. Common socially-administered practices, such as incentives, accountability, and group decision making, guide decision makers to think more deeply than they would left to their own devices. Other practices can be internalized and used individually, such as "consider the opposite" or statistical and economic rules. However, these rules tend to have two strikes against them from an adoption perspective: They are often imposed "top-down" (in mandated statistics classes, for example) and they tend to be domain-general (impeding memorability and applicability). Their domain-generality is why actively applying rules to a broad range of examples is a critical feature of training on such rules. The hope is that they will be transformed from declarative to tacit knowledge – or, alternatively, they will "migrate" from System 2 to System 1 – as recognition of when and how to apply them becomes more automatic (see Kahneman, 2003; Phillips, Klein, & Sieck, Chapter 15, this volume).

The debiasing techniques that pose the greatest problem for adoption, however, are the technological strategies, such as statistical models or decision analysis, which are complex, domain-general, and often imposed "top-down" by managers or consultants. Their logic may be difficult to understand for those less quantitatively trained, and their benefits are difficult to demonstrate in a vivid way, which is a classic obstacle to adoption. The possibility of transforming mysterious technological strategies into simpler, more intuitive, and more acceptable strategies is one of the great opportunities of debiasing research.

The Future of Debiasing

Research on debiasing tends to be overshadowed by research demonstrating biases: It is more newsworthy to show that something is broken than to show how to fix it. (It is tempting to propose that demonstrations of new biases must be accompanied by a debiasing technique, or at least a "moderator as repair" result.) However the sincere desire of many people in this field is to discover flaws not for their own sake, but with the intention of improving decision making. I have reviewed a number of effective debiasing techniques; more are needed. The development of new techniques will continue to be the central issue in debiasing research. But I hope that this chapter has also called attention to a central but neglected question in decision-making research: how do you encourage people to adopt better decision strategies?

I will close by speculating on two future directions for debiasing research. The first comes from the growing focus on how affect, motivation, and self-esteem influence decision making (see Larrick, 1993; Payne & Bettman, Chapter 6, this volume; Rottenstreich & Shu, Chapter 22, this volume). Identifying debiasing techniques for affect-based biases is a promising new area – What interventions help people cope effectively with emotion endogenous to a decision, such as anticipated regret? Or help them recognize and discount emotion that is extraneous to a decision, such as anger from some unrelated experience? The answers may bring decision research surprisingly close to clinical psychology, such as techniques used in cognitive-behavioral therapy. The second direction comes from a growing interest in the robustness of intuitive strategies (Gigerenzer, Chapter 4, this volume; McKenzie, Chapter 10, this volume; Phillips, Klein, & Sieck, Chapter15, this volume). A future challenge for debiasing research will be assessing the benefits and costs of intervention: when is intuition sufficiently reliable that intervention is not worthwhile? Can decision makers be trained to recognize environments when they should trust their intuition and when they should modify or replace it (Hogarth, 2001; Payne & Bettman, Chapter 6, this volume)?

References

Arkes, H. R. (1991) Costs and benefits of judgment errors: Implications for debiasing, *Psychological Bulletin*, 110, 486–98.

Arkes, H. R. (2003) The nonuse of psychological research at two federal agencies, *Psychological Science*, 14, 1–6.

Arkes, H. R., Dawes, R. M., & Christensen, C. (1986) Factors influencing the use of a decision rule in a probabilistic task, *Organizational Behavior and Human Decision Processes*, 37, 93–110.

Brown, C. L. (1999) "Do the right thing": Diverging effects of accountability in a managerial context, *Marketing Science*, 18, 230–46.

Camerer, C. F. (1981) General conditions for the success of bootstrapping models, *Organizational Behavior and Human Performance*, 27, 411–22.

Camerer, C. F. & Hogarth, R. M. (1999) The effects of financial incentives in experiments: A review and capital-labor-production framework, *Journal of Risk and Uncertainty*, 19, 7–42.

Cheng, P., Holyoak, K. J., Nisbett, R. E., & Oliver, L. (1986) Pragmatic versus syntactic approaches to training deductive reasoning, *Cognitive Psychology*, 18, 293–328.

Clemen, R. T. (1989) Combining forecasts: A review and annotated bibliography, *International Journal of Forecasting*, 4, 559–84.

Clemen, R. T. (1996) *Making Hard Decisions: An Introduction to Decision Analysis* (2nd edn.). Pacific Grove: Duxbury Press.

Creyer, E. H., Payne, J. W., & Bettman, J. R. (1990) The impact of accuracy and effort feedback and goals on adaptive decision behavior, *Journal of Behavioral Decision Making*, 3, 1–16.

Dawes, R. M. & Corrigan, B. (1974) Linear models in decision making, *Psychological Bulletin*, 81, 95–106.

Dawes, R. M., Faust, D., & Meehl, P. E. (1989) Clinical versus actuarial judgment, *Science*, 243, 1668–74.

Edwards, W. & Fasolo, B. (2001) Decision technology, *Annual Review of Psychology*, 52, 581–606.

Fennema, M. G. & Kleinmuntz, D. N. (1995) Anticipations of effort and accuracy in multiattribute choice, *Organizational Behavior and Human Decision Processes*, 63(1), 21–32.

Fischhoff, B. (1982) Debiasing. In D. Kahneman, P. Slovic, and A. Tversky (eds.), *Judgment Under Uncertainty: Heuristics and Biases* (pp. 422–44). Cambridge: Cambridge University Press.

Fong, G. T., Krantz, D. H., & Nisbett, R. E. (1986) The effects of statistical training on thinking about everyday problems, *Cognitive Psychology*, 18, 253–92.

Fong, G. T. & Nisbett, R. E. (1991) Immediate and delayed transfer of training effects in statistical reasoning, *Journal of Experimental Psychology*, 120, 34–5.

Gigerenzer, G. & Hoffrage, U. (1995) How to improve Bayesian reasoning without instruction: Frequency formats, *Psychological Review*, 102, 684–704.

Glover, S. M., Prawitt, D. F., & Spilker, B. C. (1997) The influence of decision aids on user behavior: Implications for knowledge acquisition and inappropriate reliance, *Organizational Behavior and Human Decision Processes*, 72, 232–55.

Griffin, D. & Buehler, R. (1999) Frequency, probability, and prediction: Easy solutions to cognitive illusions? *Cognitive Psychology*, 38, 48–78.

Hammond, K. R. & Summers, D. A. (1972) Cognitive control, *Psychological Review*, 79, 58–67.

Hammond, J. S., Keeney, R. L., & Raiffa, H. (1997) *Smart Choices: A Practical Guide to Making Better Life Decisions*. New York: Broadway Books.

Heath, C., Larrick, R. P., & Klayman, J. (1998) Cognitive repairs: How organizations compensate for the shortcomings of individual learners, *Research in Organizational Behavior*, 20, 1–37.

Hogarth, R. M. (1978) A note on aggregating opinions, *Organizational Behavior and Human Performance*, 21, 40–6.

Hogarth, R. M. (2001) *Educating Intuition*. Chicago: University of Chicago.

Hogarth, R. M., Gibbs, B. J., McKenzie, C. R. M., & Marquis, M. A. (1991) Learning from feedback: Exactingness and incentives, *Journal of Experimental Psychology: Learning, Memory, and Cognition*, 17, 734–52.

Huber, O. & Seiser, G. (2001) Accounting and convincing: The effects of two types of justification on the decision process, *Journal of Behavioral Decision Making*, 14, 69–85.

Jepson, D., Krantz, D. H., & Nisbett, R. E. (1983) Inductive reasoning: Competence or skill? *Behavioral and Brain Sciences*, 6, 494–501.

Kahneman, D. (2003). A perspective on judgment and choice: Mapping bounded rationality, *American Psychologist*, 58, 697–720.

Kahneman, D. & Frederick, S. (2002) Representativeness revisited: Attribute substitution in intuitive judgment. In T. Gilovich, D. Griffin, & D. Kahneman (eds.), *Heuristics and biases* (pp. 49–81). New York: Cambridge University Press.

Kaplan, S. E., Reneau, J. H., & Whitecotton, S. (2001) The effects of predictive ability information, locus of control, and decision maker involvement on decision aid reliance, *Journal of Behavioral Decision Making*, 14, 35–50.

Kearns, D. T. & Nadler, D. A. (1992) *Prophets in the Dark: How Xerox Reinvented Itself and Drove Back the Japanese*. New York: Harper Business.

Keeney, R. L. (2002) Common mistakes in making value trade-offs, *Operations Research*, 50, 935–45.

Kleinmuntz, B. (1990) Why we still use our heads instead of formulas: Toward an integrative approach, *Psychological Bulletin*, 107, 296–310.

Kleinmuntz, D. N. (1990) Decomposition and the control of error in decision-analytic models. In R. M. Hogarth (ed.), *Insights in Decision Making* (pp. 107–26). Chicago: University of Chicago Press.

Larrick, R. P. (1993) Self-protective processes in decision making, *Psychological Bulletin*, 113, 440–50.

Larrick, R. P., Morgan, J. N., & Nisbett, R. E. (1990) Teaching the use of cost-benefit reasoning in everyday life, *Psychological Science*, 1, 362–70.

Larrick, R. P., Nisbett, R. E., & Morgan, J. N. (1993) Who uses the normative rules of choice? Implications for the normative status of microeconomic theory, *Organizational Behavior and Human Decision Processes*, 56, 331–47.

Lehman, D. R. & Nisbett, R. E. (1990). A longitudinal study of the effects of undergraduate education on reasoning, *Developmental Psychology*, 26, 952–60.

Leon, O. G. (1997) On the death of SMART and the birth of GRAPA, *Organizational Behavior and Human Decision Processes*, 71, 249–62.

Lerner, J. S. & Tetlock, P. E. (1999) Accounting for the effects of accountability, *Psychological Bulletin*, 125, 225–75.

Mussweiler, T., Strack, F., & Pfeiffer, T. (2000) Overcoming the inevitable anchoring effect: Considering the opposite compensates for selective accessibility, *Personality and Social Psychology Bulletin*, 26, 1142–50.

Nisbett, R. E. (ed.) (1993) *Rules for Reasoning*. Hillsdale, NJ: Erlbaum.

Nisbett, R. E., Krantz, D. H., Jepson, D., & Kunda, Z. (1983) The use of statistical heuristics in everyday reasoning, *Psychological Review*, 90, 339–63.

Payne, J. W., Bettman, J. R., & Johnson, E. J. (1993) *The Adaptive Decision Maker*. Cambridge: Cambridge University Press.

Payne, J. W., Bettman, J. R., & Schkade, D. A. (1999) Measuring constructed preferences: Towards a building code, *Journal of Risk and Uncertainty*, 19, 243–70.

Raiffa, H. (1968) *Decision Analysis*. Reading, MA: Addison-Wesley.

Schkade, D. A. & Kleinmuntz, D. N. (1994) Information displays and choice processes: Differential effects of organization, form, and sequence, *Organizational Behavior and Human Decision Processes*, 57, 319–37.

Sedlmeier, P. (1999) *Improving Statistical Reasoning: Theoretical Models and Practical Implications.* Mahwah, NJ: Erlbaum.

Siegel-Jacobs, K. & Yates, J. F. (1996) Effects of procedural and outcome accountability on judgment quality, *Organizational Behavior and Human Decision Processes*, 65, 1–17.

Simonson, I. (1989) Choice based on reasons: The case of attraction and compromise effects, *Journal of Consumer Research*, 16, 158–74.

Simonson, I. & Nye, P. (1992) The effect of accountability on susceptibility to decision errors, *Organizational Behavior and Human Decision Processes*, 51, 416–46.

Soll, J. B. & Klayman, J. (2004) Overconfidence in interval estimates, *Journal of Experimental Psychology: Learning, Memory, and Cognition*, 30, 299–314.

Soll, J. B. & Larrick, R. P. (2004) Strategies for revising judgment: How, and how well, do people use others' opinions? Unpublished manuscript.

Stanovich, K. E. (1999) *Who is Rational? Studies of Individual Differences in Reasoning.* Mahwah, NJ: Erlbaum.

Stapel, D. A., Martin, L. L., & Schwarz, N. (1998) The smell of bias: What instigates correction processes in social judgments? *Personality and Social Psychology Bulletin*, 24, 797–806.

Stillwell, W. G., Barron, F. H., & Edwards, W. (1983) Evaluating credit applications: A validation of multiattribute utility weight elicitation techniques, *Organizational Behavior and Human Performance*, 32, 87–108.

Stone, D. N. & Zeibart, D. A. (1995) A model of financial incentive effects in decision making, *Organizational Behavior and Human Decision Processes*, 61, 250–61.

Tetlock, P. E. & Boettger, R. (1989) Accountability: A social magnifier of the dilution effect, *Journal of Personality and Social Psychology*, 57, 388–98.

Thaler, R. H. & Benartzi, S. (2001) Save more tomorrow: Using behavioral economics to increase employee saving. Working paper, University of Chicago.

Todd, P. & Benbasat, I. (2000) Inducing compensatory information processing through decision aids that facilitate effort reduction: An experimental assessment, *Journal of Behavioral Decision Making*, 13, 91–106.

Tversky, A. & Kahneman, D. (1983) Extensional vs. intuitive reasoning: The conjunction fallacy in probability judgment, *Psychological Review*, 90, 293–315.

Wegener, D. T. & Petty, R. E. (1995) Flexible correction processes in social judgment: The role of naïve theories in corrections for perceived bias, *Journal of Personality and Social Psychology*, 68, 36–51.

Wilson, T. D. & Brekke, N. (1994) Mental contamination and mental correction: Unwanted influences on judgments and evaluations, *Psychological Bulletin*, 116, 117–42.

Wilson, T. D. & Schooler, J. W. (1991) Thinking too much: Introspection can reduce the quality of preferences and decisions, *Journal of Personality and Social Psychology*, 60, 181–92.

Zbaracki, M. J. (1998) The rhetoric and reality of total quality management, *Administrative Science Quarterly*, 43, 602–36.

PART III

Decisions

17

Context and Conflict in Multiattribute Choice

Eldar Shafir and Robyn A. LeBoeuf

Introduction

People need to evaluate alternatives composed of multiple attributes. The alternatives and their attributes range from alphanumeric characters that come as a hodgepodge of differently oriented lines and curves to job candidates who have good and bad qualities. Normative models posit consistent and appropriate integration over such multiple attributes to reach an overall score for each alternative; the score is then thought to be mapped onto a corresponding response (cf. Birnbaum, 1974; Massaro & Friedman, 1990). In the domain of choice, the alternatives often take the form of competing options composed of a variety of positive and negative attributes. A compelling method for choosing among such options is prescribed by *multiattribute utility theory* (MAUT). The theory, which has its roots in early investigations of multiattribute choice (e.g., Adams & Fagot, 1959; Tverksy, 1967) and in decision analysis (Raiffa, 1968), was developed both as a normative ideal of how difficult decisions *ought* to be made as well as a prescriptive technique meant to guide decision makers through difficult choices (Keeney & Raiffa, 1976). Ideally, MAUT helps decision makers formalize their priorities and make calculated tradeoffs between disparate attributes (Fischer, 1975; Keeney & Raiffa, 1976), thus permitting a more effective, and consistent, maximization of subjective values (Edwards, Guttentag, & Snapper, 1975).

A typical decision, according to MAUT, begins with identification of the choice options and their relevant attributes (or "value dimensions") followed by an assessment of each attribute's relative importance (or "weight"). Each option is then evaluated on each attribute, yielding a set of "single-attribute utilities" or "location measures," which are then aggregated in accord with the corresponding attribute weights (for example, by calculating a weighted sum), yielding the option's overall utility (Edwards & Newman, 1982). Choice then consists simply of selecting the option that yields the greatest utility (Adams & Fagot, 1959; Edwards et al., 1975; Keeney & Raiffa, 1976). As a result of their technically clean formulation, multiattribute utility functions derived in this manner generate consistent and well-ordered preferences (Fischer, 1975; Keeney & Raiffa, 1976; for a recent, highly accessible guide to MAUT-consistent decision making, see Hammond, Keeney, & Raiffa, 1999).

Early research viewed intuitive judgment as generally compatible with MAUT's prescriptions, and attributed departures from those prescriptions predominantly to random error (e.g., Adams & Fagot, 1959; Fischer, 1976; Huber, 1974; see Fischer, 1975, and von Winterfeldt & Fischer, 1975, for reviews). More recent empirical investigations, however, have documented systematic violations of a variety of MAUT's technical requirements, such as independence and additivity. For example, the degree to which change on a particular attribute (e.g., from good to bad) leads to a corresponding change in an option's overall utility was found to depend not just on the changed attribute, but also on related attribute values (Yates & Jagacinski, 1980; see also Miyamoto & Eraker, 1988). More generally, it appears that multiattribute options often are not processed in MAUT-prescribed manners. Instead, behavioral decision studies as well as eye-tracking evidence suggest, for example, that decision makers often compare between options one attribute at a time, eliminating options that perform poorly on certain attributes or selecting options that "win" on others, rather than integrating across attributes to assess each option's overall worth (Russo & Dosher, 1983; cf. "elimination-by-aspects," Tversky, 1972).

Perhaps even more importantly, several of MAUT's fundamental logical requirements appear not to hold in people's decision-making behavior. According to MAUT, an option's attractiveness is a function of its attribute values and their relative importance, which are presumed to be well defined and stable (e.g., Keeney, 1972). However, a wealth of evidence suggests that an option's attractiveness can fluctuate in ways not envisioned by the theory. For example, people's preferences among stable options can reverse depending on the method of preference elicitation. Thus, participants reveal one set of preferences when asked for their maximum willingness to pay for options, but their preference order reverses when they choose between those same options (Lichtenstein & Slovic, 1971). Similarly, as will be shown below, preferences can reverse when participants are asked to select instead of reject one of two alternatives (Shafir, 1993), or when they are asked to evaluate one option at a time instead of being asked to evaluate options concurrently (Hsee, Loewenstein, Blount, & Bazerman, 1999). Such systematically labile preferences among options, with no new information added and in the face of supposedly inconsequential changes in context or presentation, are troubling for MAUT. It is on such preference patterns, which conflict with MAUT and with other theories that assume preference consistency, that this chapter focuses.

The technical developments surrounding MAUT are beyond the purview of this chapter. More extensive explications can be found in Edwards et al. (1975), Edwards and Newman (1982), Keeney and Raiffa (1976), and von Winterfeldt and Fischer (1975), among others. For present purposes, suffice it to note that MAUT, as its name suggests, is, at its core, an extension of utility theory (see Chapter 2, this volume), capturing the same fundamental insights concerning the systematic maximization of subjective value, but specializing in situations in which multiple attributes must be amalgamated.

Perception, Attention, and Other Facts of Psychological Life

The cognitive, social, and emotional processes that guide people's decisions often do not conform to the requirements of consistency imposed by normative accounts such as MAUT. In part because of these processes, preference patterns often violate the assumptions of normative theories; such violations can arise in at least three fundamental ways. First, the psychological scale value assigned to an attribute can change in unforeseen ways. For example, the same $200 change in wealth tends to loom larger when it is viewed as a loss rather than a gain (Kahneman & Tversky, 1979). More generally, because evaluation is often comparative in nature, the perceived value of a change in an attribute (e.g., a $10 discount) can fluctuate as a function of the decision context (e.g., Mellers & Cooke, 1994; Tversky & Kahneman, 1981; Tversky & Simonson, 1993).

Other normative violations arise when attribute values remain constant, but the weights assigned to those attributes fluctuate in normatively unanticipated ways. For example, contrary to the notion of procedure invariance, which requires that logically equivalent ways of eliciting preference yield the same preference ordering, slight variations in the process of elicitation can yield systematic fluctuations in attribute weights (e.g., in how much importance is accorded to price), and consequently in preference.

Finally, people's decision behavior often is guided by motives that simply do not figure in the normative account. For example, the desire to minimize the conflict inherent to difficult decisions can increase the popularity of the "default" option even as more options are added to the choice set, contrary to the normative requirement that a greater number of alternatives not increase the "market share" of an option that was there all along (Tversky & Shafir, 1992a). This pattern is attributable not to a change in attribute values or weights, but rather to the ease or difficulty that people experience in attempting to gauge the comparative advantage of various attributes.

In this chapter, we review studies that document systematic fluctuations in attribute valuations and weights, and we consider the implications of attribute comparisons for decisional conflict and choice. Our review is necessarily selective; we focus on some behavioral patterns more than others, and we are biased towards topics that have been prominent in our own research and that of a few colleagues. We pay special attention to decision patterns that are systematically discrepant with the tenets and predictions of MAUT (and of utility theory more generally, which we sometimes refer to as "the normative theory"). In some of the studies we review, the attributes of options are explicitly itemized; in others, participants are confronted with alternatives that differ on attributes that are not explicitly enumerated. These studies permit investigation of a variety of decision-making processes, many of which are not limited to multiattribute choice. Using a limited number of multiattribute options to examine choice helps induce the observed patterns and organize some of the psychological principles, but the basic lessons often extend to all manner of decisions.

Whereas MAUT and other classical analyses posit clearly defined and well-ordered preferences, we explore empirical studies that show preferences to be often inconsistent and constructed on the fly (for a similar perspective, see Chapter 6, this volume). We conclude that classical analyses such as MAUT provide compelling normative accounts of decision making, but that, descriptively, preferences are sensitive to a host of factors not encompassed by normative analyses. These factors, moreover, are often the outcomes not of distracted shortcuts, but of fundamental aspects of mental life that are central to how people process information when they make decisions.

Fluctuations in Attribute Values

By MAUT's account, the first essential stage in an item's overall evaluation is the gauging of its attributes to derive single-attribute utilities, which then need to be weighted before they are combined. Consider choosing between two cars that differ only in that one has good gas mileage and mediocre acceleration, whereas the other has poor mileage but good acceleration. A decision maker must first determine how much (dis)utility is obtained by the good mileage, the mediocre acceleration, the poor mileage, and the good acceleration, and must then proceed to determine how much each matters before these can be combined. Research suggests, however, that mapping attribute value onto psychological value is not always straightforward, and that minor contextual nuances may alter the perception of values.

A study by Mellers and Cooke (1994) nicely illustrates malleability in value-assessment. Participants rated, for example, the attractiveness of apartments that differed in monthly rent and distance from campus. Participants saw ranges of distances and rents that were either narrow (e.g., rent of $200 to $400) or wide (e.g., rent of $100 to $1,000). Interestingly, the same change on an attribute had a greater impact on overall ratings when the attribute varied over a narrow rather than a wide range. Further analyses showed that the effect arose from changes in perceived attribute values, not weights; thus, $350 was perceived to be substantially greater than $300 when rent range was narrow, but not when it was wide. Notably, these value fluctuations were substantial enough to generate preference reversals. For example, a $200 apartment 26 minutes from campus was judged more attractive than a $400 apartment 10 minutes from campus when rent range was narrow and distance range wide; but the opposite preference obtained when rent range was wide and distance range narrow. Naturally, from the perspective of MAUT, persistent fluctuations in the assignment of attribute values pose difficulties; they show the dependence of perceived value on contextual factors such as scale and range, and call into question the notion that attribute values can be robustly and consistently gauged and combined.

For another pattern of value fluctuation in the face of stable attributes, consider the notion of "evaluability" (Hsee, 1996; see Chapter 18, this volume), which refers to the ease with which attributes can be evaluated. Whereas a change in evaluability can often shift attribute weights (Hsee, 1996; Hsee et al., 1999), occasionally people are unsure about what value to assign to a particular attribute, and may change their evaluation when they gain more insight. When viewed separately, for example, a larger serving of ice cream in an underfilled cup is valued less than a smaller serving in an overfilled cup, but this preference reverses when the two cups are brought together so people can see that the former, though underfilled, contains more ice cream than the latter (Hsee, 1998). Attributes that are hard to evaluate may be gauged with the help of contextual cues (e.g., fullness of the cup) that are ignored when more direct valuation is available. In a similar fashion, a $40,000 salary where colleagues earn more may be valued less than a $35,000 salary when others are paid less. Upon direct comparison, however, most prefer the former over the latter (Bazerman, Schroth, Shah, Diekmann, & Tenbrunsel, 1994; cf., Tversky & Griffin, 1991). Changes in valuation are also observed in framing effects, where the perceived value of an attribute (e.g., fat content in food) fluctuates depending on whether it is described in positive (e.g., percent lean) or negative (e.g., percent fat) terms (Levin, 1987).

Preference malleability is also predicted by prospect theory (Kahneman & Tversky, 1979; see Chapter 20, this volume), a popular behavioral theory of choice, which holds that the psychological valuation of outcomes can change depending on whether they are seen as gains or losses relative to a reference point: losses "loom larger" than corresponding gains, so that a loss of X is more aversive than a gain of X is attractive. Because reference points can be manipulated by factors (such as expectations) that are irrelevant to the decision, the perceived magnitude of a constant attribute change can differ depending upon whether it is seen as a gain or as a loss. This can lead, among other things, to the emergence of framing and endowment effects (e.g., Tversky & Kahneman, 1981; Kahneman, Knetsch, & Thaler, 1990; see Chapter 19, this volume).

While the foregoing effects emerge in many types of decisions, and are not particular to multiattribute options, they are particularly likely to arise in multiattribute choice settings, and are troubling for all models that require stable utility estimates. The findings suggest that decision makers do not have reliable methods by which to evaluate specific attributes and that this is likely to contribute to the persistent emergence of incoherent preferences.

Fluctuations in Attribute Weights

Even when attribute evaluation remains stable, attribute weights can fluctuate in ways not anticipated by normative analyses. People often are unsure how to trade off one attribute relative to another or, for that matter, which attributes matter most. Weight assignment turns out to be a highly malleable process, subject to a variety of incidental influences. The following contextual factors are some that can alter decision weights and, consequently, preferences.

Compatibility

Stimulus attributes often tend to be differentially weighted as a result of trivial changes in procedure. The effects of response elicitation procedures, and particularly of the compatibility between stimulus and response, have long been observed in domains of perception and motor performance. For example, a pointing response is faster than a vocal response if the stimulus is presented visually, but vocalizing is faster than pointing with auditory presentations (Brainard, Irby, Fitts, & Alluisi, 1962; Shafir, 1995). When applied to judgment and choice, the principle of compatibility suggests that the weight given to an attribute will be enhanced by its compatibility with the required response. In line with compatibility, a gamble's potential payoff is weighted more heavily in a pricing task (where both price and payoff are expressed in monetary units) than in choice. Compatibility thus leads to a relative overpricing of high-payoff gambles, and to the preference reversal phenomenon (Lichtenstein & Slovic, 1971; Slovic & Lichtenstein, 1983), wherein subjects choose a lottery that offers a greater chance to win over one that offers a higher payoff, but then price the latter higher than the former. Preference reversals have been observed in numerous experiments, including one involving professional gamblers in a Las Vegas casino (Lichtenstein & Slovic, 1971). Similar reversals are observed between gambles and their certainty equivalents, the amount of money that, if received with certainty, is deemed as attractive as the gamble (von Winterfeldt, 1980). This is particularly problematic since certainty equivalents figure prominently in MAUT (Keeney, 1972; Slovic, Fischhoff, & Lichtenstein, 1977).

For another type of response compatibility, consider choosing one of two options or, alternatively, having to reject one of two options. Logically speaking, the two tasks are interchangeable: people ought to choose the option they prefer, and to reject the option they like less. However, in line with compatibility, people who choose tend to focus on options' positive attributes, which are more compatible with choosing, whereas people who are asked to reject tend to focus on options' negative attributes, compatible with rejection. Shafir (1993) presented people with a hypothetical sole-custody case, in which one parent (the "enriched" option) had a variety of positive and negative attributes, whereas the other (the "impoverished" option) was described in highly neutral terms. Half the respondents were asked which parent to award custody to; the others decided to whom to deny it. Because positive attributes are weighed more heavily in choice and negative attributes matter more during rejection, the enriched parent was the majority choice both for being awarded and denied custody of the child, with combined award and denial rates of 119 percent, significantly more than the expected 100 percent if the two elicitation procedures were complementary. This pattern has been replicated in hypothetical choices between monetary gambles, college courses, and political candidates (Downs & Shafir, 1999; Shafir, 1993). Contrary to classical assumptions of stability, the pattern shows a predictable malleability of attribute weights that leads to systematic preference inconsistencies.

Search for information

Another seemingly irrelevant circumstance that can cause attribute weights to shift is an innocent search for information. Unsure of their preferences, people often look for additional information in hopes that it may facilitate the choice. Tversky and Shafir

(1992b; see also Baron, Beattie, & Hershey, 1988), document instances in which decision makers pursue information about attributes even when the information is unlikely to alter their choices. It is generally assumed that the more information the better; as it turns out, however, information sought often receives more attention (i.e., greater weight) than if it had been simply available from the start.

In one study (Bastardi & Shafir, 1998), respondents assumed the hypothetical role of decision makers evaluating applicants for college admissions. Half of the respondents considered the folder of an applicant who played varsity soccer, had supportive letters of recommendation, and edited the school newspaper. The applicant had a combined SAT score of 1,250 and a high-school average of B. Presented with this information, the majority voted to accept the applicant. Other respondents received similar information. As before, the applicant played varsity soccer, had supportive letters, edited the newspaper, and had a combined SAT score of 1,250. This time, however, there were conflicting reports of the applicant's average grade: The guidance counselor reported a B, whereas the school office reported an A. Records were purportedly being checked, with information about the correct average grade expected shortly. Presented with this scenario, the majority of respondents elected to wait for clarification about the grade before making a decision. Upon being informed that the grade was a B (as in the original version) and not an A, a majority decided to reject the applicant (whereas the original group accepted), presumably due to a greater focus on the "low" average grade after having waited for this information.

As illustrated above, people are inclined to postpone their decisions in order to obtain information about attributes that appear relevant. Attributes about which information is obtained then tend to be weighted more heavily than if the information had simply been known from the start. This process, which can distort subsequent decisions (see also Bastardi & Shafir, 2000; Redelmeier, Shafir, & Aujla, 2001), seems to arise because, when internal attitudes are unclear, people construct their preferences partly on the basis of external cues, including their own behavior (cf. Bem, 1972). Having pursued information that should not have altered the decision, people misconstrue the pursuit as indication that the information ought to prove instrumental, and proceed to make choices they would not have made otherwise. Such behavior, furthermore, appears exceedingly reasonable. People pursue information so as to be thorough and responsible, but then proceed to make choices that endow the pursued information with greater weight, thereby "justifying" the initial pursuit (cf. Sherman, 1980). Attribute weights are thus altered in ways not envisioned by normative analyses, while decision makers rarely suspect any impact on their choices.

Separate versus comparative evaluation

As discussed above, alternative elicitation methods can give rise to differential weighting of attributes. Systematic differences in attribute weights can also be observed between evaluations that occur in isolation, one alternative at a time, compared to those conducted in comparative settings, with two or more alternatives considered simultaneously.

Evaluability

The notion of *evaluability* arose earlier, when attributes that were difficult to gauge in isolation proved easier to evaluate through direct comparison (Hsee, 1996; see Chapter 18, this volume). Manipulations of evaluability can also alter attribute weights, such that attributes that prove relatively unimportant in isolated evaluation often are weighted more heavily in direct comparison. For example, in one study (Hsee, 1996), participants considered two second-hand music dictionaries, one with 20,000 entries but a slightly torn cover; the other with 10,000 entries and a cover in mint condition. Not knowing how many entries to expect in a music dictionary, respondents who saw the options one at a time were willing to pay more for the dictionary with the perfect cover than for the one with a cover slightly torn. When these were evaluated jointly, however, most subjects preferred the dictionary with twice as many entries, despite the inferior cover. In effect, the "entries" attribute was weighted relatively more in joint than in separate evaluation. Such patterns serve to highlight that, though there is a clear conceptual distinction between change in the perceived value of an attribute and change in its weight (cf. Anderson, 1981; Birnbaum & Stegner, 1979; Norman, 1976), such changes may in fact co-occur: joint evaluation can facilitate the valuation of an attribute while also enhancing its importance.

Empathy

Similar reversals between separate and comparative contexts can arise when emotional reactions triggered by a single scenario are discounted in comparative settings. In a study of people's responses to environmental issues, Kahneman and Ritov (1994) presented respondents with statements of problems, along with suggested forms of intervention, such as:

Problem: Skin cancer from sun exposure is common among farm workers.
Intervention: Support free medical checkups for threatened groups.
Problem: Several Australian mammal species are nearly wiped out by hunters.
Intervention: Contribute to a fund to provide safe breeding areas for these species.

One group was asked to choose which of the two interventions they would rather support; a second group was presented with one problem at a time and asked to determine the largest amount they would be willing to pay for the respective intervention. When asked to evaluate each intervention separately, respondents, more moved by the hunted animals' plight than by mundane checkups, were willing to pay more, on average, for the safe breeding of Australian mammals than for free skin cancer checkups. However, when faced with a direct choice between these options, most favored the program for humans over that for animals. As expected, an important attribute (in this case, human safety) acquired greater prominence (i.e., was weighted more heavily) in a direct comparison between issues than in separate evaluation, where a narrower context afforded lesser insight into attributes' relative import. Similar patterns have been observed in other contexts concerning, for example, environmental issues versus consumer commodities (Irwin, Slovic, Lichtenstein, & McClelland, 1993).

Counterfactual thinking

In a study ostensibly intended to establish the amount of compensation that the public considers reasonable, Miller and McFarland (1986) presented respondents with one of two descriptions of a man who lost the use of his right arm as a result of a gunshot wound suffered during a convenience-store robbery. Some respondents were told that the robbery happened at the victim's regular store; others were told that the victim was shot at a store he rarely frequented, which he only went to because his regular store was closed. A higher compensation was predicted in the latter case, because abnormal events strongly evoke a counterfactual undoing, raising the perceived poignancy of outcomes and the sympathy for their victims (see Chapter 13, this volume, for more on counterfactual thinking). Indeed, the man shot at a store he rarely visited was awarded roughly $100,000 more in compensation than was his counterpart shot at the regular store.

The affective impact of events is influenced by the ease with which an alternative event can be imagined (cf., Roese & Olson, 1995). Thus, the death of a soldier on the last day of the war seems more poignant than the death of his comrade six months earlier, and the fate of a plane crash victim who switched to the fatal flight only minutes before take-off is seen as more tragic than that of a fellow passenger who had been booked on that flight for months. But whereas the affective impact of such nuances can be profound, it is sometimes considered irrelevant. When the two versions of the above robbery scenario are presented concurrently, the great majority of people do not think that the victims in the two cases should be awarded different compensations. Certain attributes thus prove easier to detect, gauge, and weigh appropriately in comparative contexts, where one can decide, for example, that the history of visits to the store does not matter, than in separate evaluation, where the relevance of such attributes may remain elusive (see also Sunstein, Kahneman, Schkade, & Ritov, 2002).

To briefly summarize, simple psychological processes can yield systematically discrepant attribute weights in separate versus comparative evaluations. Attributes that predominate in comparative settings can play a lesser role in separate evaluation; attributes that trigger strong sentiments in separate evaluation may be discounted in comparative settings; and attributes that prove hard to assess in separate evaluation are sometimes easier to evaluate, and prove decisive, in direct comparisons. Such fluctuations remain outside the purview of MAUT, where attribute weights are presumed to remain invariant across alternative modes of evaluation. Interestingly, the discrepancies between separate and comparative evaluation may have profound implications for policy and for the role of intuition. Experiences in life are typically had one at a time: a person lives through one scenario or another. Normative intuitions and policies, on the other hand, typically arise from concurrent introspection: we entertain a scenario and its alternatives. To the extent that reactions to an experience stem partly from its occurring alone, important aspects of the experience may be misconstrued by intuitions that arise from concurrent evaluation (Shafir, 2002).

Identity and choice

Not having at their disposal a clear and reliable procedure for assigning values to options, people construct their preferences in the context of decision. As discussed above, attribute weights and the attractiveness of options depend, among other things, on other options available, the nature of the task, and the context of evaluation. However, even when these factors are held constant, attribute weights still change as decision makers experience shifts in the relative salience of their various social identities.

People's social identities stem from a variety of sources, including nationality, race, sex, occupation, family status, and so on (Deaux, 1993; Turner, 1987). The list of potential identities is extensive, with some identities (e.g., "mother") evoking strikingly different values and ideals from others (e.g., "CEO"). Identities can be evoked by contextual and other cues; each identity carries its own set of values and priorities that, in turn, may yield fluctuations in attribute weights. Indeed, some preferences depend on the identity that has momentarily been rendered salient, as described next.

Socialite versus scholar

Consider the preferences of college undergraduates, who are often caught between two conflicting identities. On the one hand, they are novice scholars interested in intellectual pursuits; on the other hand, they are in a milieu that promotes intense socializing and frivolous activities. Capitalizing on this tension, LeBoeuf and Shafir (2004) manipulated the salience of scholar versus socialite identities in undergraduates. One-half of the participants first responded to a brief survey (about co-ed bathrooms and dorm life) designed to bring to mind their socialite identities. Others completed a survey concerning weighty political issues that was expected to evoke a more scholarly identity. All then made hypothetical choices between consumer items, choosing between more serious options and more frivolous alternatives. For example, participants chose between *The Wall Street Journal* and *USA Today*, or between *Before Night Falls* (a serious film) and *Chocolat* (a light comedy). As predicted, scholar-congruent options were selected more often by those whose scholar identity had been rendered salient than by those whose socialite identity was evoked. (Level of identification moderated the effect: those high, but not low, in identification with the evoked identities showed this preference assimilation, suggesting that identity, not mere priming, plays a key role.)

The shifting preferences of Chinese-Americans

Recent research has found differences in cognitive style and values between Eastern and Western cultures (see Markus & Kitayama, 1991; Nisbett, 2003; Nisbett, Peng, Choi, & Norenzayan, 2001; and Chapter 25, this volume, for reviews). East Asian cultures tend to place a greater emphasis on collectivism and social groups than do individualistically oriented Western cultures (Markus & Kitayama, 1991). As part of establishing their individuality, Westerners tend to select unique items from an array of alternatives, whereas East Asian participants tend to prefer non-unique items that "blend in" with the rest (Kim & Markus, 1999). Furthermore, members of Eastern cultures tend to contribute to the common good more often than do members of Western cultures. In prisoners' dilemma games, for example, members of collectivist cultures tend to cooperate more than those from individualistic cultures (Domino, 1992; Hemesath & Pomponio, 1998).

LeBoeuf and Shafir (2004) recruited Chinese-American adults and manipulated the salience of their cultural identities. The prediction was that with their American identities salient, participants would exhibit preferences more stereotypical of the individually oriented American, whereas rendering salient their Chinese identities would lead to preferences reflecting a collectivistic orientation. To evoke the Chinese identity, a randomly selected half received all materials in Chinese and answered questions regarding their birthplace and Chinese landmarks they had visited. To evoke the American identity, the remaining participants received all materials in English and answered parallel questions about their lives in the US, including American landmarks they had visited.

Four multiattribute choice scenarios were used to assess preferences regarding conformity and cooperation. The first asked whether participants preferred a uniquely or a traditionally colored car. The next inquired whether they would depart from the norm and order a new dish at a restaurant over the traditional meal. A third gauged participants' proneness to reciprocate a favor, and the last assessed the desire to cooperate in a prisoners' dilemma game. As predicted, preferences for uniqueness and for non-cooperation were greater (i.e., more "American") when American, as opposed to Chinese, identities had been evoked.

This malleability of preferences has potentially profound implications, since the salience of alternate selves typically does not emerge at random. Ross and Ward (1996), for example, report different rates of cooperation in a prisoners' dilemma-type game depending on whether the game is referred to as the "Wall Street" or the "community" game. This suggests that Wall Street is likely to render salient a highly competitive identity, even among people who, away from that context, may identify with less competitive stances. Generals make strategic decisions in contexts that render their military identities salient; investors make their financial decisions in contexts where notions of money and wealth predominate; and so forth. But, as alternate identities gain salience in other contexts, and give rise to different attribute weights, these same people's preferences may prove less extreme than in the professional milieu. This predicts a systematic "extremity" of decisions by professionals, as well as preference inconsistencies of the kind discussed by Schelling (1984) and other students of inter-temporal choice (cf., Loewenstein & Elster, 1992). More generally, the identity-salience studies illustrate persistent shifts in attribute weighting not subsumed under standard theories of multiattribute choice.

Conflict in Multiattribute Choice

Choices can be hard to make, and people often approach difficult decisions like problem-solving tasks, trying to come up with compelling arguments for choosing one option over another. Contrary to the standard account, according to which each option's worth is assessed independently, people confronting difficult decisions often compare between options on specific attributes, in search of a convincing contrast or a compelling rationale for choosing one option rather than another (cf., Tversky, 1972). Occasionally, such comparisons yield compelling reasons for choice; at other times, the conflict between options is hard to resolve, and the tendency to seek additional alternatives or to maintain the status quo is increased. Such patterns are inconsistent with value maximization, and may produce inconsistent preferences.

Search for options

In many situations, people need to decide whether to opt for an available option or to search for additional alternatives. (This is different from searching for *information* about existing alternatives, discussed earlier.) Seeking new alternatives usually requires additional time and effort, and may involve the risk of losing previously available options. In classical analyses, each option has a value for the decision maker, who is presumed to select the most highly valued option. In particular, a person is expected to search for additional alternatives only if the expected value of searching exceeds that of the best option currently available. Studies of decisional conflict, however, suggest that people are more likely to opt for an available option when they have a compelling rationale that makes the decision easy, and that they are more likely to delay decision and search for additional alternatives when a compelling reason for choice is not readily available and the decision is tough.

Interestingly, what makes choices easy or difficult is often the manner in which the options' attributes interact. In this vein, Tversky and Shafir (1992a) presented participants with pairs of options, such as bets varying in probability and payoff, or student apartments varying in monthly rent and distance from campus. Participants could choose one of the two options or, instead, they could request an additional option, at some cost. Participants first reviewed the entire set of 12 options (gambles or apartments) to familiarize themselves with the available alternatives. In the gamble study half the participants then received the following *conflict* problem:

> Imagine that you are offered a choice between the following two gambles: *x*) 65 percent chance to win $15; and *y*) 30 percent chance to win $35. You can either select one of these gambles or you can pay $1 to add one more gamble to the choice set. The added gamble will be selected at random from the list you reviewed.

The other participants received a *dominance* version, which differed from the above only in that option *y* was replaced by option *x'*, to yield a choice between: *x*) 65 percent chance to win $15; and *x'*) 65 percent chance to win $14.

For each problem, participants indicated whether they wanted to add another gamble or select between the available alternatives. Participants were instructed that the gambles they chose would be played and that their payoffs would correspond to the amount of money they earned minus the fee they paid for any added gambles. They then chose their preferred gamble from the resulting set (with or without the added option).

Note that in the *conflict* condition, choosing between *x* and *y* is nontrivial: *x* is better on one attribute and *y* is better on the other. In the *dominance* condition, in contrast, the choice between *x* and *x'* presents no conflict because the former strictly dominates the latter. While there are reasons for choosing either option in the conflict condition, there is a decisive argument for choosing option *x* in the dominance condition. Of course, were people to evaluate each option independently, all such considerations of conflict and reasons would be beside the point – instead, people would simply select the alternative valued most highly. Because the best alternative offered in the dominance condition (namely, option *x*) is also available in the conflict condition, any value-maximizing agent who chooses to seek an additional alternative (e.g., because *x* is unsatisfactory) in the conflict condition should do so also in the dominance condition. In other words, a true value-maximizing participant cannot be more likely to seek an additional alternative in the conflict than in the dominance condition, since the set of alternatives available in the former is objectively *superior* to the latter (and the expected value of searching is unchanged).

People, however, compare between options along parallel attributes, seeking a compelling rationale to select one option over others (Payne et al., 1993; see Chapter 6, this volume). Having good reasons for choosing a particular option reduces the temptation to look for alternatives, whereas conflicted decisions that are harder to justify yield a greater tendency to search for additional alternatives. On average, subjects paid for an additional alternative 64 percent of the time in the conflict condition, and did so reliably less often – 40 percent of the time – in the dominance condition. (For the specific gambles above, the numbers were 55 percent and 30 percent, respectively.) Thus, the tendency to search for additional alternatives was greater when the choice among options was hard to rationalize than when a compelling reason made the decision easy.

The search for additional alternatives thus depends not only on the value of the best available option, as implied by value maximization, but also on the difficulty of choosing among the options, as determined largely by a comparison of their respective attributes. The observed pattern entails an inconsistent ordering of preferences, since an option (*x*) that was judged inferior to searching in the conflict condition is deemed superior to searching in the dominance condition, after a viable competitor was replaced by an inferior alternative.

Deferred and default decisions

Similar analyses help explain observed violations of the independence of irrelevant alternatives principle, according to which a preference ordering between options should not be altered when additional alternatives are introduced. In particular, for participants who are strict value maximizers, a non-preferred option cannot become preferred when new options are added to the offered set. A value maximizer who prefers an option, *y*, over deferring the choice should not then prefer to defer the choice when both *y* and *x* are available. Similarly, someone who prefers *y* over a default alternative should not then opt for the default when both *x* and *y* are available. The requirement that the "market share" of an option not increase when the offered set is enlarged (so long as the added alternatives do not provide new relevant information) is known as *regularity* (see Tversky & Simonson, 1993). Despite the intuitive appeal of this MAUT-consistent principle, there is evidence that adding and removing options can influence people's preferences among options that were available all along. In particular, adding alternatives can make the decision harder to justify and, consequently, may increase the tendency to defer choice or to choose a default option; conversely, added alternatives may also facilitate attribute comparisons, thus rendering the decision easier.

In one study (Tversky & Shafir, 1992a), 80 students agreed to fill out a brief questionnaire for $1.50. Following the questionnaire, one half of the subjects were offered the opportunity to exchange the $1.50 (the default) for one of two prizes: a metal *Zebra* pen, or a pair of plastic *Pilot* pens. The remaining subjects were only offered the opportunity to exchange the $1.50 for the *Zebra*. The pens were shown to subjects, who were informed that each prize regularly costs just over $2.00 and that they could keep the chosen prize. Twenty-five percent opted for the payment when *Zebra* was the only alternative offered, but a reliably greater 53 percent chose the payment when both the *Zebra* and the *Pilot* pens were available. Faced with a tempting alternative, the majority took advantage of the opportunity to obtain an attractive prize; the conflict generated by competing alternatives, on the other hand, increased the tendency to retain the default option, contrary to regularity and value maximization.

Similar effects of decisional conflict have been shown in everyday settings and among experts. Iyengar and Lepper (2000) set up booths in a grocery store, offering the opportunity to taste any of 6 jams in one condition, or any of 24 jams in another. In the 6-jam condition, 40 percent of shoppers stopped to taste and, of those, 30 percent proceeded to purchase a jam. In the 24-jam ("high conflict") condition, a full 60 percent stopped to taste, but only 3 percent of them purchased. In another study (Redelmeier & Shafir, 1995), 287 experienced physicians were presented with a description of a hypothetical patient suffering from chronic hip pain and about to be referred to orthopedics. Half had to decide whether or not to assign this patient a particular medication (Motrin); the other half were presented with two alternative medications (Motrin and Feldene). The percentage of physicians who refrained from assigning any new medication was 53 percent in the former group and 72 percent in the latter. Thus, the availability of a second medication reduced the tendency to assign either.

Whereas adding competing alternatives can increase the tendency to delay decision, as in the examples above, the level of conflict and its ease of resolution depend not simply on the number of options available, but also on how their attributes interact. If an added option is such that its attributes are distinctly inferior, the tendency to choose one of the original options increases and the temptation to defer decision diminishes (e.g., Shafir, Simonson, & Tversky, 1993). This tendency of a dominated or relatively inferior alternative, when added to a set, to increase the preference for the dominating option is known as the asymmetric dominance effect (Huber, Payne, & Puto, 1982). This effect has been replicated in numerous marketing contexts, with both hypothetical and actual goods (e.g., Simonson & Tversky, 1992; Wedell, 1991). The presence of an option with clearly inferior attributes provides a compelling rationale for choosing the dominating alternative. Indeed, verbal protocols from participants making such choices often mention clear advantages along specific attributes. It is noteworthy that such attribute-based comparisons entail a markedly distinct process from the presumed evaluation of options one at a time.

To summarize, standard normative accounts do not deny the existence of conflict, nor, however, do they assume any influence of conflict on choice. Interestingly, to the extent that people are guided by utility, there does not appear to be much room for internal conflict: either differences in utility are large and the decision is easy, or they are small, and the decision matters little. On the other hand, a psychology of conflict and indecision yields predictable patterns that violate normative expectations. Among other things, when a comparison of options' attributes fails to yield a clear preference, people feel conflicted and, consequently, are more likely to keep on searching than when conflict is low. Conflict among a subset of options is likely to benefit alternatives with distinct attributes, and conflict about new options tends to benefit the default option, or the status quo. Conflict is often a function not of the *number* of options, or even of their attractiveness, but rather of the manner in which the various attributes compare and contrast to yield what appears like the right choice.

Concluding Remarks

A variety of studies show systematic inconsistencies in preferences for multiattribute options in settings ranging from students' hypothetical choices among consumer goods to medical decisions made by experts. Not having at their disposal a clear and reliable procedure for assigning values to options, people need to construct (not merely "reveal") their preferences in the process of making a decision. As a result, preference depends on various contextual nuances, such as the description of the options, the nature of the task, the other options in the set, and the perspective of the decision maker. These contextual factors tend systematically to alter attribute values and weights, generating patterns of choice behavior that conflict with standard, normative expectations.

Normative theories, such as MAUT, are often acknowledged to have limited descriptive validity. Whereas some early studies explored the extent to which "natural" decisions adhered to MAUT's criteria (e.g., Fischer, 1975; von Winterfeldt & Fischer, 1975), and although some were optimistic about MAUT's predictive abilities (see, e.g., Beattie & Baron, 1991), MAUT's roots are in decision analysis, which explicitly attempts to improve on unaided human decision making (Raiffa, 1968). Recent treatments (e.g., Hammond et al., 1999) recognize that decision makers are unlikely to apply MAUT-like procedures, and, more generally, students of decision making acknowledge that people's behavior tends not to be quite as well ordered, consistent, and elegant as that envisioned by the classical treatment.

In their best-selling economics textbook, Samuelson and Nordhaus (1992) write, "We consumers are not expected to be wizards . . . What is assumed is that consumers are fairly *consistent* in their tastes and actions – that they do not flail around in unpredictable ways, making themselves miserable by persistent errors of judgment or arithmetic." In contrast with these authors' rather modest assumptions, the studies reviewed above document preferences that are often inconsistent. At the same time, the studies do not paint a picture of people flailing around; they capture behavior that is neither erratic nor unpredictable, nor is it fraught with errors of judgment or arithmetic. Indeed, preferences can be predictably malleable, context-dependent, and inconsistent while the decision maker is thoughtful, serious, and engaged. (LeBoeuf & Shafir, 2003, for example, find that those who do and who do not engage in effortful thought are equally likely to exhibit standard framing effects.) The inconsistencies reviewed above are typically the outcome not of imperfect shortcuts, fallible computation, carelessness, or distraction, but rather of a number of fundamental perceptual and computational aspects of our mental lives. In particular, preferences between multidimensional options are often inconsistent because our evaluation mechanisms trigger comparisons, weights, and evaluations that are systematic and often even reasonable, but that fail to conform to the sort of requirements that would guarantee consistent choices. Common to many of these effects is a failure to generate a canonical representation of the decision situation or to conduct a context-independent evaluation of the options, both of which are normally assumed in classical treatments. Of course, upon reflection, most people would endorse and appreciate the dictates of normative accounts such as MAUT. But the psychological processes that generate choices often are neither privy to, nor governed by, these wishes.

When making multiattribute choices, people systematically ignore critical requirements imposed by theories such as MAUT, while honoring other considerations largely ignored, or outright dismissed, by normative accounts. This may have important implications for occasions when theories such as MAUT are used as decision aids (see Chapter 16, this volume). For, although people can be methodically guided through decision processes in accord with the requirements of MAUT, they may also be predictably disappointed with the prescribed decision. Rather than serving to crystallize people's wishes, the application of such criteria may often feel foreign, if not forced. For, as we have seen in this chapter, people fail to conform to MAUT-like requirements not due to carelessness, but because their preferences are of a different nature. In fact, it may generally help to conceive of individual decision makers not as faulty maximizing agents, but as fundamentally different creatures. Creatures, who are, to be sure, interested in improving their lot and who have their preferences, but who, at the same time, are a different kind of information processors from those envisioned by classical analyses. Rather than deducing options' values from their attributes, people make their multiattribute choices in the midst of decisional conflict and in heavily context-dependent ways.

References

Adams, E. W. & Fagot, R. (1959) A model of riskless choice, *Behavioral Science*, 4, 1–10.

Anderson, N. H. (1981) *Foundations of Information Integration Theory*. New York: Academic Press.

Baron, J., Beattie, J., & Hershey, J. (1988) Heuristics and biases in diagnostic reasoning: II. Congruence, information and certainty, *Organizational Behavior and Human Decision Processes*, 42, 88–110.

Bastardi, A. & Shafir, E. (1998) On the pursuit and misuse of useless information, *Journal of Personality and Social Psychology*, 75, 19–32.

Bastardi, A. & Shafir, E. (2000) Nonconsequential reasoning and its consequences, *Current Directions in Psychological Science*, 9, 216–19.

Bazerman, M. H., Schroth, H. A., Shah, P. P., Diekmann, K. A., & Tenbrunsel, A. E. (1994) The inconsistent role of comparison others and procedural justice in reactions to hypothetical job descriptions: Implications for job acceptance decisions, *Organizational Behavior and Human Decision Processes*, 60, 326–52.

Beattie, J. & Baron, J. (1991) Investigating the effect of stimulus range on attribute weight, *Journal of Experimental Psychology: Human Perception and Performance*, 17, 571–85.

Bem, D. J. (1972) Self-perception theory. In L. Berkowitz (ed.), *Advances in Experimental Social Psychology* (vol. 6, pp. 2–61). New York: Academic Press.

Birnbaum, M. H. (1974) The nonadditivity of personality impressions, *Journal of Experimental Psychology*, 102, 543–61.

Birnbaum, M. H. & Stegner, S. E. (1979) Source credibility in social judgment: Bias, expertise, and the judge's point of view, *Journal of Personality and Social Psychology*, 37, 48–74.

Brainard, R. W., Irby, T. S., Fitts, P. M., & Alluisi, E. (1962) Some variables influencing the rate of gain of information, *Journal of Experimental Psychology*, 63, 105–10.

Deaux, K. (1993) Reconstructing social identity, *Personality and Social Psychology Bulletin*, 19, 4–12.

Domino, G. (1992) Cooperation and competition in Chinese and American children, *Journal of Cross Cultural Psychology*, 23, 456–67.

Downs, J. S. & Shafir, E. (1999) Why some are perceived as more confident and more insecure, more reckless and more cautious, more trusting and more suspicious, than others: Enriched and impoverished options in social judgment, *Psychonomic Bulletin and Review*, 6, 598–610.

Edwards, W., Guttentag, M., & Snapper, K. (1975) A decision-theoretic approach to evaluation research. In E. L. Struening and M. Guttentag (eds.), *Handbook of Evaluation Research* (vol. 1, pp. 139–81). Beverly Hills, CA: Sage.

Edwards, W. & Newman, J. R. (1982) *Multiattribute Evaluation*. Beverly Hills, CA: Sage.

Fischer, G. W. (1975) Experimental applications of multi-attribute utility models. In D. Wendt and C. Vlek (eds.), *Utility, Probability, and Human Decision Making* (pp. 7–46). Dordrecht, Holland: D. Reidel Publishing Company.

Fischer, G. W. (1976) Multidimensional utility models for risky and riskless choice, *Organizational Behavior and Human Decision Processes*, 17, 127–46.

Hammond, J. S., Keeney, R. L., & Raiffa, H. (1999) *Smart Choices: A Practical Guide to Making Better Decisions*. Boston: Harvard Business School Press.

Hemesath, M. & Pomponio, X. (1998) Cooperation and culture: Students from China and the United States in a prisoners' dilemma, *Cross Cultural Research: The Journal of Comparative Social Science*, 32, 171–84.

Hsee, C. K. (1996) The evaluability hypothesis: An explanation of preference reversals between joint and separate evaluations of alternatives, *Organizational Behavior and Human Decision Processes*, 67, 247–57.

Hsee, C. K. (1998) Less is better: When low-value options are valued more highly than high-valued options, *Journal of Behavioral Decision Making*, 11, 107–21.

Hsee, C. K., Loewenstein, G. F., Blount, S., & Bazerman, M. H. (1999) Preference reversals between joint and separate evaluations of options: A review and theoretical analysis, *Psychological Bulletin*, 5, 576–90.

Huber, G. P. (1974) Multi-attribute utility models: A review of field and field-like studies, *Management Science*, 20, 1393–402.

Huber, J., Payne, J. W., & Puto, C. (1982) Adding asymmetrically dominated alternatives: Violations of regularity and the similarity hypothesis, *Journal of Consumer Research*, 9, 90–8.

Irwin, J., Slovic, P., Lichtenstein, S., & McClelland, G. H. (1993) Preference reversals and the measurement of environmental values, *Journal of Risk and Uncertainty*, 6, 5–18.

Iyengar, S. & Lepper, M. (2000) When choice is demotivating: Can one desire too much of a good thing? *Journal of Personality and Social Psychology*, 79, 995–1006.

Kahneman, D., Knetsch, J. L., & Thaler, R. (1990) Experimental tests of the endowment effect and the Coase theorem, *Journal of Political Economy*, 98, 1325–48.

Kahneman D. & Ritov I. (1994) Determinants of stated willingness to pay for public goods: A study in the headline method, *Journal of Risk and Uncertainty*, 9, 5–38.

Kahneman, D. & Tversky, A. (1979) Prospect theory: An analysis of decision under risk, *Econometrica*, 47, 263–91.

Keeney, R. L. (1972) Utility functions for multiattributed consequences, *Management Science*, 18, 276–87.

Keeney, R. L. & Raiffa, H. (1976) *Decisions with Multiple Objectives: Preferences and Value Tradeoffs*. Cambridge: Cambridge University Press.

Kim, H. & Markus, H. R. (1999) Deviance or uniqueness, harmony or conformity? A cultural analysis, *Journal of Personality and Social Psychology*, 77, 785–800.

LeBoeuf, R. A. & Shafir, E. (2003) Deep thoughts and shallow frames: On the susceptibility to framing effects, *Journal of Behavioral Decision Making*, 16, 77–92.

LeBoeuf, R. A. & Shafir, E. (2004) Alternating selves and conflicting choices. Manuscript under review.

Levin, I. P. (1987) Associative effects of information framing, *Bulletin of the Psychonomic Society*, 25, 85–6.

Lichtenstein, S. & Slovic, P. (1971) Reversals of preference between bids and choices in gambling decisions, *Journal of Experimental Psychology*, 89, 46–55.

Loewenstein, G. & Elster, J. (eds.) (1992) *Choice Over Time*. New York: Russell Sage Foundation.

Markus, H. R. & Kitayama, S. (1991) Culture and the self: Implications for cognition, emotion, and motivation, *Psychological Review*, 98, 224–53.

Massaro, D. W. & Friedman, D. (1990) Models of integration given multiple sources of information, *Psychological Review*, 97, 225–52.

Mellers, B. A. & Cooke, A. D. J. (1994) Trade-offs depend on attribute range, *Journal of Experimental Psychology: Human Perception and Performance*, 20, 1055–67.

Miller, D. T. & McFarland, C. (1986) Counterfactual thinking and victim compensation: A test of norm theory, *Personality and Social Psychology Bulletin*, 12, 513–19.

Miyamoto, J. M. & Eraker, S. A. (1988) A multiplicative model of the utility of survival duration and health quality, *Journal of Experimental Psychology: General*, 117, 3–20.

Nisbett, R. E. (2003) *The Geography of Thought: How Asians and Westerners Think Differently . . . and Why*. New York: Free Press.

Nisbett, R. E., Peng, K., Choi, I., & Norenzayan, A. (2001) Culture and systems of thought: Holistic versus analytic cognition, *Psychological Review*, 108, 291–310.

Norman, K. L. (1976) A solution for weights and scale values in functional measurement, *Psychological Review*, 83, 80–4.

Payne, J. W., Bettman, J. R., & Johnson, E. (1993) *The Adaptive Decision Maker*. New York: Cambridge University Press.

Raiffa, H. (1968) *Decision Analysis: Introductory Lectures on Choices Under Uncertainty*. Reading, MA: Addison-Wesley.

Redelmeier, D. & Shafir, E. (1995) Medical decision making in situations that offer multiple alternatives, *Journal of the American Medical Association*, 273, 302–5.

Redelmeier, D., Shafir, E., & Aujla, P. (2001) The beguiling pursuit of more information, *Medical Decision Making*, 21, 376–81.

Roese, N. J. & Olson, J. M. (eds.) (1995) *What Might Have Been: The Social Psychology of Counterfactual Thinking*. Mahwah, NJ: Erlbaum.

Ross, L. & Ward, A. (1996) Naive realism in everyday life: Implications for social conflict and misunderstanding. In E. S. Reed, E. Turiel, and T. Brown (eds.), *Values and Knowledge* (pp. 103–35). Mahwah, NJ: Erlbaum.

Russo, J. E. & Dosher, B. A. (1983) Strategies for multiattribute binary choice, *Journal of Experimental Psychology: Learning, Memory, and Cognition*, 9, 676–96.

Samuelson, P. A. & Nordhaus, W. D. (1992) *Economics* (14th edn.). New York: McGraw-Hill.

Schelling, T. C. (1984) Self-command in practice, in policy, and in a theory of rational choice, *American Economic Review*, 74, 1–11.

Shafir, E. (1993) Choosing versus rejecting: Why some options are both better and worse than others, *Memory and Cognition*, 21, 4, 546–56.

Shafir, E. (1995) Compatibility in cognition and decision. In J. R. Busemeyer, R. Hastie, and D. L. Medin (eds.), *Decision Making from the Perspective of Cognitive Psychology* (pp. 247–74). New York: Academic Press.

Shafir, E. (2002) Cognition, intuition, and policy guidelines. In R. Gowda and J. Fox (eds.), *Judgments, Decisions, and Public Policy*, (pp. 71–88). Cambridge: Cambridge University Press.

Shafir, E., Simonson, I., & Tversky, A. (1993) Reason-based choice, *Cognition*, 49, 11–36.

Sherman, S. J. (1980) On the self-erasing nature of errors of prediction, *Journal of Personality and Social Psychology*, 2, 211–21.

Simonson, I. & Tversky, A. (1992) Choice in context: Tradeoff contrast and extremeness aversion, *Journal of Marketing Research*, 29, 281–95.

Slovic, P., Fischhoff, B., & Lichtenstein, S. (1977) Behavioral decision theory, *Annual Review of Psychology*, 28, 1–39.

Slovic, P. & Lichtenstein, S. (1983) Preference reversals: A broader perspective, *American Economic Review*, 73, 596–605.

Sunstein, C. R., Kahneman, D., Schkade, D., & Ritov, I. (2002) Predictably incoherent judgments, *Stanford Law Review*, 54, 1153–215.

Turner, J. C. (1987) A self-categorization theory. In J. C. Turner, M. A. Hogg, P. J. Oakes, S. D. Reicher, & M. S. Wetherell (eds.), *Rediscovering the Social Group* (pp. 42–67). Oxford and New York: Basil Blackwell.

Tversky, A. (1967) Additivity, utility, and subjective probability, *Journal of Mathematical Psychology*, 4, 175–201.

Tversky, A. (1972) Elimination by aspects: A theory of choices, *Psychological Review*, 76, 281–99.

Tversky, A. & Griffin, D. (1991) Endowment and contrast in judgments of well-being. In F. Strack, M. Argyle, and N. Schwarz (eds.), *Subjective Well-Being: An Interdisciplinary Perspective* (pp. 101–18). New York: Pergamon Press.

Tversky, A. & Kahneman, D. (1981) The framing of decisions and psychology of choice, *Science*, 211, 453–8.

Tversky, A. & Shafir, E. (1992a) Choice under conflict: The dynamics of deferred decision, *Psychological Science*, 3, 358–61.

Tversky, A. & Shafir, E. (1992b) The disjunction effect in choice under uncertainty, *Psychological Science*, 3, 305–9.

Tversky, A. & Simonson, I. (1993) Context-dependent preferences, *Management Science*, 39, 1178–89.

von Winterfeldt, D. (1980) Additivity and expected utility in risky multiattribute preferences, *Journal of Mathematical Psychology*, 21, 66–82.

von Winterfeldt, D. & Fischer, G. W. (1975) Multi-attribute utility theory: Models and assessment procedures. In D. Wendt and C. Vlek (eds.), *Utility, Probability, and Human Decision Making* (pp. 47–85). Dordrecht, Holland: D. Reidel Publishing Company.

Wedell, D. H. (1991) Distinguishing among models of contextually induced preference reversals, *Journal of Experimental Psychology: Learning, Memory, and Cognition*, 17, 767–78.

Yates, J. F. & Jagacinski, C. M. (1980) Reference effects in multiattribute evaluations, *Organizational Behavior and Human Decision Processes*, 24, 400–10.

18

Internal and Substantive Inconsistencies in Decision Making

Christopher K. Hsee, Jiao Zhang, and Junsong Chen

Introduction

Most effects that have intrigued students of behavioral decision theories can be characterized as "inconsistencies." These inconsistencies fall into two general categories: internal and substantive inconsistencies (Kahneman, 1994). Most existing research on judgment and decision making concerns internal inconsistency. An internal inconsistency occurs when people's decisions violate one or several basic axioms of rational decision theory, such as procedure invariance, descriptive invariance, cancellation, and transitivity. A prime example of internal inconsistency is the preference-reversal phenomenon, that the preference elicited using one method differs from the preference elicited using a different – but normatively equivalent – method. This constitutes a violation of procedure invariance. Students of preference-reversals are interested in why decisions made under normatively equivalent conditions contradict each other and not in whether the decision in either condition is "good" or "bad" according to an external criterion.

Inspired by Kahneman and his coauthors' work on decision, predicted, and experienced utilities (e.g., Kahneman, 1994, 2000; Kahneman & Snell, 1990, 1992; Kahneman, Wakker, & Sarin, 1997), a new direction in judgment-and-decision research has emerged. It concerns the substantive inconsistency of decisions. A substantive inconsistency occurs when one's decision is suboptimal according to some external substantive criterion, such as the maximization of (predicted) hedonic experience (Kahneman, 1994). The criterion requires decision makers to choose the option that brings the greatest (predicted) experienced utility.

This chapter consists of two parts. The first part focuses on internal inconsistency and reviews research on preference-reversal. The second part focuses on substantive inconsistency and reviews recent research showing inconsistency between decision and (predicted) experience. The review in this chapter is not meant to be comprehensive, but is thematic and reflects what we consider to be representative.

Internal Inconsistency: The Case of Preference-Reversal

Broadly defined, any systematic change in preference order between normatively equivalent conditions can be called a preference-reversal (e.g., Slovic & Lichtenstein, 1983). However, preference-reversal has a more restricted meaning. It usually refers to situations where the choice options, including their descriptions, remain the same but the preference elicitation methods differ. For the purpose of this review, we divide preference elicitation methods into three classes: (a) choice versus pricing; (b) choice versus matching; and (c) joint versus separate evaluations. The first two are about types of responses, and the last is about mode of evaluation. All these preference-reversals are violations of procedure invariance. Procedure invariance, an important pillar of rational choice, demands that "strategically equivalent methods of elicitation will give rise to the same preference order" (Tversky, 1996, p. 185). We now review these three classes of preference-reversals in turn (for other reviews, see Seidl, 2002; Chapter 17, this volume; Slovic, 1995).

Preference-reversal between choice and pricing

Lichtenstein and Slovic (1971) and Lindman (1971) demonstrated the preference-reversal phenomenon by showing that the preference elicited through a direct choice differs from the preference elicited through a pricing task. Consider the following pair of lotteries from Lichtenstein and Slovic (1971):

A: 0.95 Win $2.50; 0.05 Lose $.75
B: 0.40 Win $8.50; 0.60 Lose $1.50.

Lottery A (called a P-bet) gave a large probability of winning a small amount of money; lottery B (called a $-bet) gave a smaller probability of winning a larger amount of money. Participants were either asked to pick the lottery they wanted to play (the choice condition) or to price the two lotteries (the pricing condition).

Normatively, these two elicitation methods should yield the same preference order. But Lichtenstein and Slovic documented a robust preference-reversal: In the choice condition, most participants chose the P-bet, but in the pricing condition, most assigned a higher price to the $-bet. The choice–pricing preference-reversal has been replicated by many other researchers (e.g., Grether & Plott, 1979; Pommerehne, Schneider, & Zweifel, 1982; Reilly, 1982), and also replicated in casinos with real gamblers and real money (e.g., Lichtenstein & Slovic, 1973).

The most widely accepted explanation for the choice–pricing preference-reversal is the compatibility hypothesis. This compatibility hypothesis states that an attribute will have a greater weight on the required response if the attribute is compatible in scale or units with the response than if it is not (e.g., Slovic & MacPhillamy, 1974). Because monetary payoffs are compatible with the pricing response and not with the choice response, monetary payoffs receive more weight in the pricing task (Lichtenstein & Slovic, 1973). Some researchers suggest that choice–pricing reversals are mediated by anchoring and adjustment (e.g., Lichtenstein & Slovic, 1971, 1973; Schkade & Johnson, 1989).

Slovic, Griffin, and Tversky (1990) showed that the compatibility hypothesis also applies to riskless options. For example, in choice, people prefer an option with a shorter time delay over an option with a higher payoff, but in pricing, the preference reverses. Irwin (1994) and Irwin and Baron (2001) secured evidence for the compatibility hypothesis involving moral judgments. For example, Irwin and Baron found that when people evaluate different desks, the prices of the desks (monetary considerations) receive greater weight in willingness to pay (monetary responses), and whether the desks are made of rainforest wood (non-monetary considerations) receives greater weight in attractiveness ratings (non-monetary responses).

Goldstein and Einhorn (1987) identified a confounding factor in previous studies on choice-pricing reversal. They argued that the choice task is comparative and is not about money, and the pricing task is non-comparative and is about money. They unconfounded these two factors and found preference-reversals both between monetary and non-monetary responses and between comparative and non-comparative responses. We will review preference-reversals between comparative and non-comparative responses later. Mellers and her coauthors (Mellers, Chang, Birnbaum, & Ordonez, 1992; Mellers, Ordonez, & Birnbaum, 1992) proposed a change-of-process theory to account for preference-reversals between rating and pricing: probabilities and payoffs are integrated additively in rating but multiplicatively in pricing.

Preference-reversal between choice and matching

Another important type of preference-reversal concerns the inconsistency between choice and matching. This effect was first discovered by Slovic (1975), and was studied extensively by Tversky, Sattath, and Slovic (1988). In a classic study showing the effect (Tversky et al., 1988), participants were presented with information about two hypothetical job candidates applying for a production engineer position who differed on two attributes, technical knowledge and human relations, as follows:

	Technical knowledge	Human relations
Candidate A	86	76
Candidate B	78	91

Both attributes were evaluated on a scale ranging from 40 (very weak) to 100 (superb). One group of participants (the choice condition) was asked to choose between the two candidates. Another group of participants (the matching condition) was presented with the same two alternatives, with one of the four scores missing, and were asked to fill in that missing score so that the two candidates were equally attractive. The result revealed a choice-matching preference-reversal: In choice, most people chose Candidate A (the one with the better technical knowledge), but in matching, the score most people filled in implied a preference for Candidate B (the one with better human relations). This finding suggests a *prominence effect* – that the more important attribute in a choice set (e.g., technical knowledge in the study) receives greater weight in choice than in matching.

Tversky et al. (1988) explained the prominence effect with a new compatibility hypothesis that concerns the compatibility between the qualitative/quantitative nature of the response and the qualitative/quantitative nature of the strategies people use to provide the response. A qualitative response, such as choice, evokes a qualitative decision strategy, such as the lexicographic rule; a quantitative task, such as matching, evokes a quantitative decision strategy, such as the weighted average rule.

Fischer and Hawkins (1993) referred to this new compatibility hypothesis as strategy compatibility, and referred to the original compatibility hypothesis as scale compatibility, and showed that strategy compatibility can operate independently of scale compatibility. These authors also demonstrated that the more prominent attribute in a choice set not only weights more in choice than in matching, but also weights more in other qualitative tasks (e.g., strength of preference) than in other quantitative tasks (e.g., rating).

Nowlis and Simonson (1997) studied the compatibility between the comparative/non-comparative nature of responses and the comparable/non-comparable nature of stimuli. For example, they found that in choice, poor-brand/low-price products are favored over good-brand/high-price products, but in ratings of purchase intention, the preference reverses. Presumably, price is a comparable attribute and choice is a comparative response; brand is a non-comparable and enriched attribute and rating is a non-comparative response. Therefore, price looms larger in choice and brand looms larger in rating.

Compatibility between stimuli and responses can take other forms than scale and strategy: Tversky (1977) showed that common features of alternative options weight more heavily in similarity judgments and distinctive features weight more heavily in dissimilarity judgments. Slovic et al. (1990) proposed the notion of valence compatibility between stimuli and responses. Supporting this idea, Shafir (1993) found that people are both more likely to accept and more likely to reject enriched options (which have more positive and more negative features) over impoverished options (which have fewer positive and fewer negative features). Chapman and Johnson (1995) identified a compatibility effect due to the semantic relationship between attributes and responses. For example, they found that health items such as products that improve one's eye-sight are preferred to commodities when evaluations are expressed in life expectancy, and that the preference reverses when evaluations are expressed in monetary terms.

In summary, the preference-reversals reviewed so far exist between different types of responses. Different types of responses accentuate different aspects of the stimuli and lead to different preferences. This is the essence of the compatibility idea. In the next section we review a different kind of preference-reversal.

Preference-reversal between joint and separate evaluations

Arguably, any judgment or decision is made in one or some combination of two basic modes – joint and separate. In the joint evaluation (JE) mode, people are exposed to multiple options simultaneously and evaluate them comparatively. In the separate or single evaluation (SE) mode, people are exposed to only one option and evaluate it in isolation. For example, when shopping for a TV in an electronics store, consumers are in JE, because usually there are many models for them to compare. On the other hand, when consumers are debating whether to bid for a TV at an estate auction where there are no other TVs, they will probably consider this particular TV alone and are therefore in SE. JE and SE are not a dichotomy, but a continuum.

Recent research has documented systematic reversals between JE and SE. In a typical study (Hsee, 1996), participants were asked to indicate their willingness to pay (WTP) for two second-hand music dictionaries in either JE or SE. The dictionaries involved a tradeoff along two attributes – number of entries and cosmetic condition, as below:

	Number of entries	Cosmetic condition
Dictionary A:	20,000	A torn cover
Dictionary B:	10,000	Intact cover

In JE, WTP was higher for the 20,000-entry/torn-cover dictionary; but in SE, WTP was higher for the 10,000-entry/intact-cover dictionary.

JE/SE reversals have been documented in other contexts, such as compensations and job offers (e.g., Bazerman, Loewenstein, & White, 1992; Bazerman, Schroth, Shah, Diekmann, & Tenbrunsel, 1994; Hsee, 1993), consumer products (e.g., Nowlis & Simonson, 1994), and hiring (e.g., Hsee, 1996). For example, Bazerman et al. (1992) found that between an option that entailed a high payoff to oneself and looked unfair (e.g., $600 to self and $800 to other) and an option that entailed a lower payoff to oneself and looked fair (e.g., $500 to both sides), the former option was favored in JE and the latter favored in SE. Hsee (1993) found that between a salary stream with a higher total amount and a decreasing trend, and one with a lower total amount and an increasing trend, the former was favored in JE and the latter favored in SE.

JE/SE reversals are different from the traditional choice–pricing and choice–matching reversals. In the traditional preference-reversals, the tasks that produce the reversal always involve different types of responses; whether they involve different evaluation modes is not essential. For example, in the choice–matching preference-reversal, both choice and matching are in JE. In the JE/SE reversals, the tasks that produce the reversal involve different evaluation modes (JE versus SE); whether they involve different types of responses is not essential. For example, in the dictionary study, the response is always willingness to pay.

Hsee (1996; Hsee, Loewenstein, Blount, & Bazerman, 1999) proposed the *evaluability hypothesis* to account for JE/SE reversals. According to this hypothesis, a JE/SE reversal occurs because some attributes are more difficult to evaluate independently than others and these attributes exert greater impact on JE than on SE. For example, in the dictionary study, number of entries is difficult to evaluate independently; most people in SE would not know how good a dictionary with 10,000 entries or a dictionary with 20,000 entries is, and would not evaluate the two dictionaries much differently. Conversely, whether the cover of a dictionary is intact or defective is easier to evaluate independently; even in SE people would find a defective cover undesirable and an intact cover desirable, and would evaluate the intact-cover dictionary more favorably. In JE, people could recognize that 20,000 entries are considerably better than 10,000 entries and would favor the 20,000-entry dictionary.

The evaluability hypothesis suggests that in SE, an objectively dominated option may be valued more highly than an objectively dominating option. For instance, Hsee (1998) asked students to indicate their willingness to pay for one or both of two servings of Haagen Daz ice cream: Serving A featured 8 oz of ice cream in a 10 oz cup (underfilled), and Serving B featured 7 oz of ice cream in a 5 oz cup (overfilled). Objectively, Serving A dominated Serving B, because Serving A contained more ice cream (and offered a larger cup!). Not surprisingly, in JE Serving A received a higher WTP. But in SE, Serving B received a higher WTP. This result supports the evaluability hypothesis: Whether the serving contains 7 or 8 oz of ice cream is independently difficult to evaluate and makes little difference in SE; in contrast, whether a serving is underfilled or over-filled is independently easy to evaluate and makes a difference in SE.

A similar violation of dominance was obtained in a study involving two sets of din-nerware: one containing 24 intact pieces and the other containing 40 pieces, of which 32 were intact and eight were broken (Hsee, 1998). In JE the 40-piece set was valued more. But in SE, the 24-piece was valued more, presumably because whether a dinnerware set contained 24 or 32 intact pieces was a difficult-to-evaluate cue and whether a dinnerware set contained broken pieces or not was an easy-to-evaluate cue. This result has been replicated in a study involving real financial consequences to the respondents (List, 2002).

Besides what we have reviewed above, there are other types of JE/SE reversals. For example, Irwin, Slovic, Lichtenstein, and McClelland (1993) found that in JE people were willing to pay more for improving the air quality in Denver than for improving a consumer product such as a VCR, but that in SE WTP values were higher for improving the consumer product. Kahneman and Ritov (1994) found that in JE people would contribute more to programs that save human lives (e.g., farmers with skin cancers) but in SE they would contribute more to programs that save endangered animals (e.g., dolphins) (see also Sunstein, Kahneman, Schkade, & Ritov, 2002). Unlike the stimuli used in the studies previously reviewed, the options in Irwin et al.'s and Kahneman & Ritov's studies were of different categories (e.g., air quality versus consumer products) and shared no common attributes. Explanations for these results require a combination of norm theory (Kahneman & Miller, 1986) and the evaluability hypothesis and are beyond the scope of this chapter (cf. Hsee et al., 1999).

Internal inconsistency: Summary

In this section, we have concerned ourselves with internal inconsistencies of decisions, and have focused on the case of preference-reversals. We have reviewed the literature on two general classes of preference-reversals, those involving different types of responses (choice versus pricing or choice versus matching) and those involving different evalu-ation modes (JE versus SE).

Despite their theoretical differences, these two classes of preference-reversals are often confounded in reality. In particular, a choice task typically involves JE, requiring people to compare the alternative options simultaneously. On the other hand, a judgment task often entails SE or some combination of JE and SE, allowing people to evaluate one object at a time. Consequently, preference-reversals in reality often exist between "JE choice" and "SE judgment," and these reversals can potentially be accounted for either by evaluability, compatibility, or both.

The preference-reversal literatures reviewed in this section refute a basic assumption of rational choice model, that preferences are stable, and support an important proposition of behavioral decision theory, that preferences are constructed and labile (e.g., Bettman, Luce, & Payne, 1998; Payne, 1982; Chapter 6, this volume; Payne, Bettman, & Johnson, 1992; Slovic, 1995).

Substantive Inconsistency: The Case of Decision–Experience Inconsistency

Behavioral decision researchers have devoted much of their effort to the study of internal inconsistency of decisions, where seemingly inconsequential manipulations lead to marked different responses. The preference-reversals we have reviewed are examples of such internal inconsistencies.

A potentially more important topic is substantive inconsistency of decisions – people's failure to choose the best option according to some external, substantive criterion (e.g., Hammond, 1996; Kahneman, 1994; Kahneman & Snell, 1990, 1992; Chapter 1, this volume; Sen, 1993). What would be a reasonable substantive criterion for decisions? The answer depends on the decision. The present review focuses on decisions about choice options that have a well-defined consumption period and do not differ systematically in aspects other than their experienced utility during this period. For such decisions, we follow Kahneman (1994, 2000; Kahneman et al., 1997) and consider the maximization of consumption experience (i.e., experienced utility during the consumption period) as the substantive criterion. If one fails to choose the option that delivers the best consumption experience, we say that an inconsistency between decision and experience occurs. In what follows, we review several major causes for such inconsistencies.

Impact bias

An important prerequisite for consistency between decision and experience is that the decision maker accurately predicts which option will bring the best experience. In the past several decades, psychologists and behavioral decision theorists have accumulated ample evidence showing that people often overpredict the intensity or duration of their future affective reaction, a phenomenon called the impact bias (Gilbert, Driver-Linn, & Wilson, 2002; Wilson & Gilbert, 2003). Here, we follow Wilson and Gilbert (2003) to use "impact bias" to refer to both intensity bias (e.g., Buehler & McFarland, 2001) and durability bias (Gilbert, Pinel, Wilson, Blumberg, & Wheatley, 1998).

The impact bias may arise when people fail to predict the power of adaptation or change in aspiration (e.g., Brickman, Coates, & Janoff-Bulman, 1978; Frederick &

Loewenstein, 1999; Kahneman, 2000; Loewenstein & Schkade, 1999). For example, when a person moves from a small apartment to a bigger one, she may predict lasting increased happiness. In reality, her happiness will increase initially but over time it will dwindle, because she has hedonically adapted to the larger home, or because she develops an aspiration for an even bigger home, or both.

The impact bias may also occur because of focalism, that predictors focus too much on the target event and overlook other factors that may influence their experience (e.g., Schkade & Kahneman, 1997). For example, after the defeat of their favorite team, sports fans predicted that they would be very unhappy for a long time, but in reality the memory of a lost game was just one of myriad things that affected their experience and had little impact only a few days after the game (Wilson, Wheatley, Meyers, Gilbert, & Axsom, 2000). A variation of focalism is that people overpredict the impact of features unique to the target event and underpredict the impact of features shared by both the target event and alternative events (e.g., Dunn, Wilson, & Gilbert, 2003).

For negative events, there is another cause for misprediction: People fail to anticipate the power of their psychological immune system to moderate the impact of a negative event (Gilbert et al., 1998). For instance, Gilbert et al. (1998) asked participants to predict how they would feel a few minutes after receiving negative personality feedback from either an experimental computer program or a team of seasoned clinicians. The participants predicted that they would feel equally bad in the two conditions. However, they actually felt less bad when the negative feedback was delivered by the computer program than by the clinicians. Presumably, when the negative feedback was conveyed by a computer program, it was easier for the immune system to set in and reduce its impact by dismissing the validity of the feedback.

Failure to appreciate the power of one's own immune system may lead to a decision–experience inconsistency. In one study (Wilson, Wheatley, & Gilbert, 2000), the participants were asked to imagine that they were playing a hypothetical dating game in which they were competing with another same-sex participant. In one condition, the "predictors" were asked to select a dosage of a mood-enhancing drug they would like to take if they lost the game before predicting how bad they would feel if they lost the game. The "experiencers" were asked to make the same decision and to indicate how bad they felt after they were told that they had lost the game. Interestingly, the predictors selected a significantly higher dosage than did the experiencers. As in the typical immune neglect studies (e.g., Gilbert et al., 1998), the predictors also predicted that they would feel worse than the experiencers actually felt. It seems that the predictors chose too high a dosage because they predicted that they would feel worse than they actually would.

Mispredictions due to biased memory, incorrect theory or wrong state

Our choice of future events is often based on our memory of past events, but our memory of past events may be biased (e.g., Karney & Coombs, 2000; Levine, 1997; Mather, Shafir, & Johnson, 2000). One particular bias in memory is duration neglect (e.g., Fredrickson & Kahneman, 1993). The following study illustrates duration neglect and its implication for decision–experience inconsistency. Kahneman, Fredrickson, Schreiber,

& Redelmeier (1993) asked research participants to go through two aversive episodes, one short and one long. The short episode required the participants to submerge their hands in very cold water for 60 seconds. The long episode required the participants to submerge their hands in very cold water for 60 seconds and then in mildly cold water for another 30 seconds. Objectively, the long episode was worse than the short one. Yet the participants remembered the long episode as less aversive, because (a) they were insensitive to the duration of the episode and (b) their memory of the overall aversiveness of an episode was dictated by the aversiveness of the final moment of the episode. Consequently, when the participants were asked to repeat one of the two episodes, most chose to repeat the long one.

Misprediction may also result from inaccurate lay theories of adaptation, contrast, and other psychological effects (e.g., Kahneman & Snell, 1992; Novemsky & Ratner, 2003; Robinson & Clore, 2002). In a study by Kahneman and Snell (1992), participants predicted decreasing enjoyment from repeated consumption of the same yogurt over several days but in reality their enjoyment increased. In a study by Novemsky and Ratner (2003), participants predicted that their enjoyment of a good-tasting jellybean would increase after consuming a bad-tasting jellybean, but in reality they did not experience such contrast effects.

Another potential contributor to misprediction is what Loewenstein (1996) called empathy gap. People are said to be in a "hot" state when under the influence of visceral factors, such as hunger and sexual arousal, or in a "cold" state when not under such visceral influences. Poor predictions may occur when people in a hot (cold) state predict their experiences in a cold (hot) state. For example, Read and van Leeuwen (1998) found that currently hungry people are more likely than currently satiated people to choose an unhealthy snack even though the snack will only be consumed in the future (see also Gilbert, Gill, & Wilson, 2002).

Distinction bias

Another source of failure to make accurate affective forecasting or experience-maximizing choices is evaluation mode, joint (JE) versus separate (SE). Extending the evaluability hypothesis, Hsee and Zhang (2004) proposed that the evaluation (utility) function of most attributes differ systematically between JE and SE. In JE, people can compare alternative values of an attribute, and through such comparisons, can differentiate the desirability of these values. Consequently, the evaluation function in JE will be relatively steep (the solid curve in Figure 18.1). In SE, people see only one value on the attribute. Generally speaking, people are able to tell whether a value is good or bad, but unable to tell precisely how good or how bad it is. For example, in SE most people would find winning $10 good and losing $10 bad, but would not find winning $10 much different from winning $30. Thus, the evaluation function in SE will be steep around zero (or a reference point) and relatively flat elsewhere (the dashed line in Figure 18.1) See Willemsen & Keren, in press, for a similar analysis of the evaluation functions.

More often than not, decisions, and their accompanying affective predictions, are made in JE, but the consequence of a decision is experienced in SE. For example, when

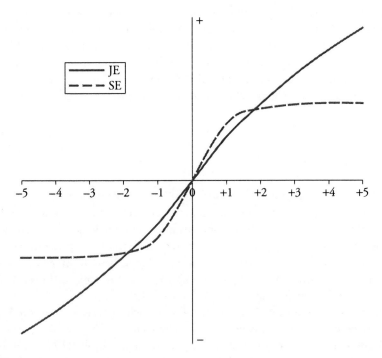

Figure 18.1 The "utility" (evaluation) function of an attribute can differ systematically depending on whether utility is elicited in joint evaluation (JE) or in separate evaluation (SE)

a person shops for a house, she typically compares the houses on the market with each other or with her current house (JE). When the person lives in the new house she has bought, she is mostly in SE of that house alone. In other words, experience follows the SE curve, but predictions and decisions follow the JE curve.

The mismatch in evaluation mode between predictions and experience may lead to mispredictions. Specifically, if two values of an attribute differ only quantitatively or far from the reference point (e.g., losing $10 versus losing $30, and living in a 2,000 ft² versus living in a 3,000 ft² house), people in JE are likely to exhibit a distinction bias, i.e., overpredict the difference these values will make to SE experience. If two values differ qualitatively or on two sides of the reference point (e.g., winning $10 versus losing $10, and being employed versus being unemployed), people in JE are unlikely to overpredict the difference these values will make to SE experience. These propositions have been confirmed empirically (see Hsee & Zhang, 2004).

The misprediction discussed above can also lead to mischoice. The following story, adapted from Hsee (2000), illustrates the point. A person shopping for a pair of audio speakers in an audio store was debating between two equally expensive models. One looked attractive and the other ugly. He then compared the sounds of the two systems by playing a CD back and forth. Through the comparisons he found the sound of the ugly model *slightly* but *distinctively* better, and decided to buy it. But soon after he had brought the speakers home, he found their appearance annoying and relegated them to the basement. The moral of the story is that in comparing the two models, the protagonist exhibited a distinction bias: he overpredicted the difference in sound quality between the two models – something that was salient in JE but would be inconsequential in SE (see Kahneman, Knetsch, & Thaler, 1986 for a similar observation concerning fairness perception). For empirical demonstrations of this type of mischoice, see the task-reward experiment in Hsee and Zhang (2004) and the noise-picture experiment in Hsee and Zhang (2003).

Lay rationalism

In order to choose the experientially optimal option, people not only need to accurately predict future experience, but also need to base their decision on their prediction. The research we have reviewed above concerns inaccurate prediction of experiences. The research we review in this section shows failure to base decisions on predicted experiences. One cause of this failure is *lay rationalism*, a tendency to base decisions on rationalistic factors rather than on the overall predicted experience of the options (Hsee, Zhang, Yu, & Xi, 2003; see also Shafir, Simonson, & Tversky, 1993).

Lay rationalism manifests itself in different forms, including lay economism, lay scientism, and lay functionalism. *Lay economism* is the tendency to base decisions on economic values of the options. In a classic study by Tversky and Griffin (1991), for example, respondents were presented with two job options, one with a lower salary to self ($33,000) and an even lower salary to their colleague ($30,000), and one with a higher salary to self ($35,000) and an even higher salary to their colleague ($38,000). Most respondents predicted higher overall happiness from the first job, but most chose the latter. In a more recent study (Hsee, Zhang et al., 2003), participants were given two consumption sequences – one entailing an improving temporal pattern but a smaller total monetary value and the other entailing a decreasing temporal pattern but a larger total monetary value. Most people predicted greater overall enjoyment from the former sequence, but most chose the latter.

Another manifestation of lay rationalism is *lay functionalism*, a tendency to base decisions on functions and objectives rather than on overall enjoyment. For example, in a study reported in Hsee, Zhang et al. (2003), respondents were asked to assume that they had won a $1,000 cash prize from a department store and could claim the money in one of two ways: (a) go to the store and receive a beautifully-printed check with their name on it; or (b) have the store wire the money to their bank without seeing the check. Most respondents predicted greater happiness doing (a), but most respondents chose to do (b). This is consistent with previous research showing that people have both consummatory and instrumental needs (e.g., Pham, 1998); compared with experience-predictors, decision makers are more concerned with non-consummatory, instrumental aspects of the choice options.

A third manifestation of lay rationalism is *lay scientism*, a tendency to base decisions on hard and objective attributes rather than on soft and subjective attributes. In a study by Hsee, Zhang et al. (2003), respondents considered two hypothetical stereo systems varying in power and sound richness. In one condition, power was described as an objective attribute and sound richness a subjective experience; in the other condition, power was described as a subjective experience and sound richness an objective attribute. A choice/ predicted-experience inconsistency occurred in both conditions, but in the opposite directions. When power was the "hard" attribute, power received greater weight in choice than in predicted experience; when sound richness was the "hard" attribute, sound richness received greater weight in choice than in predicted experience.

Traditional economists are sometimes faulted for their obsession with money and tangible goods (e.g., Frey & Stutzer, 2002; Rabin, 2002). The preceeding review suggests that this materialistic and objectivist position is not invented by economists, but rooted in the lay public.

We wish to note that an inconsistency between predicted experience and decision is not always an error. For example, suppose that a restaurant patron predicts greater enjoyment from eating a high-cholesterol steak, but orders a low-cholesterol pasta instead. This may simply reflect the person's willingness to sacrifice (predicted) enjoyment for health benefits. Hsee, Zhang et al. (2003) suggest that lay rationalism is an antidote to impulsive behavior, a way to sacrifice pleasure for other benefits. The problem, however, is that people do not (sufficiently) distinguish situations where the sacrifice of pleasure will bring about other benefits and situations where it will not, and that people follow lay rationalism even in the latter situations. In these situations, following lay rationalism and making decisions that are inconsistent with predicted experiences *are* errors.

Decisions based on rules

Lay rationalism implies that decision makers do not base their choice strictly on predicted consequences of the choice options. This implication is shared by research on *rule-based decisions* (e.g., Amir & Ariely, 2003; Prelec & Herrnstein, 1993; Simonson, 1989; Simonson & Nowlis, 2000). Examples of decision rules (broadly defined) include "don't waste" (Arkes & Ayton, 1999; Arkes & Blumer, 1985), "seek variety" (e.g., Simonson, 1990), "don't choose the same dish as your friends" (Ariely & Levav, 2000), "don't pay for delays" (Amir & Ariely, 2003), to name just a few.

Research on variety-seeking has also revealed inconsistencies between decision and (predicted) experience. In one of the original studies on variety-seeking, Simonson (1990) asked one group of students to make simultaneous choices of candies for several future consumption occasions, another group to make sequential choices of candies right before each consumption occasion, and a third group to make predictions for candy preferences in those occasions. The result is intriguing: Both the sequential choosers and the preference-predictors preferred low variety, but the simultaneous choosers sought high variety.

In a more recent study on variety-seeking, Ratner, Kahn and Kahneman (1999) asked participants to construct a song sequence from one of two sets of songs. One set contained more songs than the other, but the additional songs were less enjoyable. Ratner et al. found that those who were given the larger set constructed sequences with greater variety but enjoyed them less. In a study on group variety-seeking, Ariely and Levav (2000) found that restaurant goers tend to order different items than their friends order, but enjoy the resulting items less.

In a study exploring the "don't waste" rule, Arkes and Blumer (1985) asked participants to imagine that they purchased a $100 ticket for a weekend ski trip to Michigan and a $50 ticket for a weekend ski trip to Wisconsin. They later found out that the two trips were for the same weekend. They could not return either of the two tickets and had to pick one to use. Although the participants were told that they thought the Wisconsin trip was more enjoyable, most of them chose the trip that cost them more money – the Michigan trip (see Chapter 16, this volume, for strategies to minimize such biases).

Medium maximization

Another potential cause of decision–experience inconsistency is medium maximization. Oftentimes, when people exert effort in order to obtain a desired outcome, the immediate reward they receive is not the outcome per se, but a medium – an instrument with which they can trade for the desired outcome (e.g., Kivetz & Simonson, 2002; van Osselaer, Alba, & Manchanda, 2001). For example, points in consumer loyalty programs and miles in frequent flyer programs are both media. Suppose that an individual is faced with different courses of actions, each corresponding to a certain level of effort, a certain level of medium and a certain outcome, as follows:

Action A ➔ effort level A ➔ medium level A ➔ outcome A
Action B ➔ effort level B ➔ medium level B ➔ outcome B
Action C ➔ effort level C ➔ medium level C ➔ outcome C
. . . .

Assume also that the action that yields the best effort-to-outcome return (i.e., the utility of outcome minus the disutility of effort) is not the action that yields the highest effort-to-medium return.

Ideally, when people are faced with such options, they should ignore the medium and choose the outcome that yields the best effort-to-outcome return. In reality, decision makers often choose the option that yields the best effort-to-medium return (see Hsee, Yu, Zhang, & Zhang, 2003 for theory and evidence). This finding has important implications for life. The money people earn for their work is a medium and the experience derived from consuming the things they obtain with the money is the outcome. The finding that people maximize medium suggests that when people choose between different jobs, they may choose the job with the greatest effort-to-money return rather than the job with the best effort-to-experience return.

Substantive inconsistency: Summary

In this section we have reviewed selected research on inconsistencies between decision and (predicted) experience. Theoretically the different causes we reviewed are separable. Practically they often co-exist. To illustrate, let us consider the following two-society problem, adapted from Frank (1999):

> There are two societies, A and B. Each resident in Society A earns an equivalent of $60,000 a year and has ample time to spend with his or her friends. Each resident in Society B earns an equivalent of $80,000 a year but has little time to spend with his or her friends.

We predict that residents in Society A are generally happier, but that when presented with a choice between the two societies, many will choose Society B. In fact, most countries in the world are moving toward the direction of Society B and this may be an indication that people are choosing Society B over Society A.

People may choose Society B for several of the reasons we reviewed above. One is lay rationalism: People may find it more rational or defensible to base their choice on concrete economic gains than on non-economic concerns. A second reason is impact bias. People may fail to predict that they will adapt to either level of income and that the difference in income will make little difference in the long run. A third reason is the medium effect. People may base their choice on the face value of the income rather than the utility of the income; the difference between $80,000 and $60,000 seems large in face value, but may be tiny in utility. A fourth reason is distinction bias: Whether one earns $60,000 or $80,000 is only a matter of degree and would make little difference in SE, but whether or not one has time with their friends is a matter of valence and would make a greater difference in SE. Experience with each society is in SE, and this is why people in Society A are likely to be happier. But a choice between the two societies requires JE, and this explains why people are likely to choose Society B.

Conclusion

Much of the early and now-classic behavioral decision research is designed to identify and explain internal inconsistencies in decisions between normatively equivalent conditions. Internal inconsistency is important because it implies that the decision in at least some condition is substantively suboptimal, but it does not tell us in which condition the decision is substantively suboptimal.

Some recent behavioral decision research focuses more directly on substantive suboptimality of decisions, particularly on inconsistencies between decisions and predicted or real experiences. Arguably, the optimization of experience is the ultimate goal of our decisions (e.g., Kahneman, 1994; see also Frey & Stutzer, 2002; Chapter 1, this volume). The emerging interest in the experienced utility of decisions gives behavioral decision research a new significance, and motivates it to join forces with other areas of psychology and with economics (e.g., Diener & Biswas-Diener, 2002; Easterlin, 2001; Frank, 1999; Frey & Stutzer, 2002) to develop an interdisciplinary science of happiness.

References

Amir, O. & Ariely, D. (2002) Decision by rules: disassociation between preferences and willingness to act. Unpublished manuscript, Massachusetts Institute of Technology.

Ariely, D. & Levav, J. (2000) Sequential choice in group settings: Taking the road less traveled and less enjoyed, *Journal of Consumer Research*, 27, 279–90.

Arkes, H. R. & Ayton, P. (1999) The sunk cost and Concorde effects: Are humans less rational than lower animals? *Psychological Bulletin*, 125, 591–600.

Arkes, H. R. & Blumer, C. (1985) The psychology of sunk cost, *Organizational Behavior and Human Decision Processes*, 35, 124–40.

Bazerman, M. H., Loewenstein, G. F., & White, S. B. (1992) Reversals of preference in allocation decisions: Judging an alternative versus choosing among alternatives, *Administrative Science Quarterly*, 37, 220–40.

Bazerman, M. H., Schroth, H. A., Shah, P. P., Diekmann, K. A., & Tenbrunsel, A. E. (1994) The inconsistent role of comparison others and procedural justice in reactions to hypothetical job descriptions: Implications for job acceptance decisions, *Organizational Behavior and Human Decision Processes*, 60, 326–52.

Bettman, J. R., Luce, M. F., & Payne, J. W. (1998) Constructive consumer choice processes, *Journal of Consumer Research*, 25, 187–217.

Brickman, P., Coates, D., & Janoff-Bulman, R. (1978) Lottery winners and accident victims: Is happiness relative? *Journal of Personality and Social Psychology*, 36, 917–27.

Buehler, R. & McFarland, C. (2001) Intensity bias in affective forecasting: The role of temporal focus, *Personality and Social Psychology Bulletin*, 27, 1480–93.

Chapman, G. B. & Johnson, E. J. (1995) Preference-reversals in monetary and life expectancy evaluations, *Organizational Behavior and Human Decision Processes*, 62, 300–17.

Diener, E. D. & Biswas-Diener, R. (2002) Will money increase subjective well-being? *Social Indicators Research*, 57, 119–69.

Dunn, E. W., Wilson, T. D., & Gilbert, D. T. (2003) Location, location, location: The misprediction of satisfaction in housing lotteries, *Personality and Social Psychology Bulletin*, 29, 1421–32.

Easterlin, R. (2001) Income and happiness: Towards a unified theory, *Economic Journal*, 111, 465–84.

Fischer, G. W. & Hawkins, S. A. (1993) Strategy compatibility, scale compatibility, and the prominence effect, *Journal of Experimental Psychology: Human Perception and Performance*, 19, 580–97.

Frank, R. (1999) *Luxury Fever: Why Money Fails to Satisfy in an Era of Excess.* New York: Free Press.

Frederick, S. & Loewenstein, G. F. (1999) Hedonic adaptation. In D. Kahneman, E. Diener, and N. Schwartz (eds.), *Well-being: The Foundations of Hedonic Psychology* (pp. 302–29). New York: Russell Sage Foundation.

Fredrickson, B. L. & Kahneman, D. (1993) Duration neglect in retrospective evaluations of affective episodes, *Journal of Personality and Social Psychology*, 65, 45–55.

Frey, B. S. & Stutzer, A. (2002) What can economists learn from happiness research? *Journal of Economic Literature*, 40, 402–35.

Gilbert, D. T., Driver-Linn, E., & Wilson, T. D. (2002) The trouble with Vronsky: Impact bias in the forecasting of future affective states. In L. F. Barrett and P. Salovey (eds.), *The Wisdom in Feeling: Psychological Processes in Emotional Intelligence* (pp. 114–43). New York: Guilford.

Gilbert, D. T., Gill, M. J., & Wilson, T. D. (2002) The future is now: Temporal correction in affective forecasting, *Organizational Behavior and Human Decision Processes*, 88, 430–44.

Gilbert, D. T., Pinel, E. C., Wilson, T. D., Blumberg, S. J., & Wheatley, T. P. (1998) Immune neglect: A source of durability bias in affective forecasting, *Journal of Personality and Social Psychology*, 75, 617–38.

Goldstein, W. M. & Einhorn, H. J. (1987) Expression theory and the preference-reversal phenomena, *Psychological Review*, 94, 236–54.

Grether, D. M. & Plott, C. R. (1979) Economic theory of choice and the preference-reversal phenomenon, *American Economic Review*, 69, 623–38.

Hammond, K. R. (1996) How convergence of research paradigms can improve research on diagnostic judgment, *Medical Decision Making*, 16, 281–7.

Hsee, C. K. (1993) When trend of monetary outcomes matters: Separate versus joint evaluation and judgment of feelings versus choice, working paper.

Hsee, C. K. (1996) The evaluability hypothesis: An explanation for preference-reversal between joint and separate evaluations of alternatives, *Organizational Behavior and Human Decision Processes*, 67, 247–57.

Hsee, C. K. (1998) Less is better: When low-value options are judged more highly than high-value options, *Journal of Behavioral Decision Making*, 11, 107–21.

Hsee, C. K. (1999) Value-seeking and prediction-decision inconsistency: Why don't people take what they predict they'll like the most? *Psychonomic Bulletin and Review*, 6, 555–61.

Hsee, C. K. (2000) Attribute evaluability and its implications for joint-separate evaluation reversals and beyond. In D. Kahneman and A. Tversky (eds.), *Choices, Values and Frames*. Cambridge University Press.

Hsee, C. K., Loewenstein, G. F., Blount, S., & Bazerman M. H. (1999) Preference-reversals between joint and separate evaluations of options: A review and theoretical analysis, *Psychological Bulletin*, 125, 576–91.

Hsee, C. K., Yu, F., Zhang, J., & Zhang, Y. (2003) Medium maximization, *Journal of Consumer Research*, 30, 1–14.

Hsee, C. K. & Zhang, J. (2003) Choice-consumption inconsistency, unpublished manuscript.

Hsee, C. K. & Zhang, J. (2004) Distinction bias: Mis-prediction and mis-choice due to joint evaluation, *Journal of Personality and Social Psychology*, 86, 680–95.

Hsee, C. K., Zhang, J., Yu, F., & Xi, Y. (2003) Lay rationalism and inconsistency between predicted experience and decision, *Journal of Behavioral Decision Making*, 16, 257–72.

Irwin, J. R. (1994) Buying/selling price preference-reversals: Preference for environmental changes in buying versus selling modes, *Organizational Behavior and Human Decision Processes*, 60, 431–57.

Irwin, J. R. & Baron, J. (2001) Response mode effects and moral values, *Organizational Behavior and Human Decision Processes*, 84, 177–97.

Irwin, J. R., Slovic, P., Lichtenstein, S., & McClelland, G. H. (1993) Preference-reversals and the measurement of environmental values, *Journal of Risk and Uncertainty*, 6, 5–18.

Kahneman, D. (1994) New challenges to the rationality assumption, *Journal of Institutional and Theoretical Economics*, 150, 18–36.

Kahneman, D. (2000) Experienced utility and objective happiness: A moment-based approach. In D. Kahneman and A. Tversky (eds.), *Choices, Values and Frames*. Cambridge: Cambridge University Press.

Kahneman, D., Fredrickson, B. L., Schreiber, C. A., & Redelmeier, D. A. (1993) When more pain is preferred to less: Adding a better end, *Psychological Science*, 4, 401–05.

Kahneman, D., Knetsch, J. L., & Thaler, R. H. (1986) Fairness and the assumptions of economics, *Journal of Business*, 59, 285–300.

Kahneman, D. & Miller, D. T. (1986) Norm theory: Comparing reality with its alternatives, *Psychological Review*, 93, 136–53.

Kahneman, D. & Ritov, I. (1994) Determinants of stated willingness to pay for public goods: A study in the headline method, *Journal of Risk and Uncertainty*, 9, 5–38.

Kahneman, D. & Snell, J. (1990) Predicting utility. In R. M. Hogarth (ed.), *Insights in Decision Making* (pp. 295–311). Chicago, IL: University of Chicago Press.

Kahneman, D. & Snell, J. (1992) Predicting a changing taste: Do people know what they will like? *Journal of Behavioral Decision Making*, 5, 187–200.

Kahneman, D., Wakker, P., & Sarin, R. (1997) Back to Bentham, *Quarterly Journal of Economics*, 11, 375–401.

Karney, B. R. & Coombs, R. H. (2000) Memory bias in long-term close relationships: Consistency or improvement? *Personality and Social Psychology Bulletin*, 26, 959–70.

Kivetz, R. & Simonson, I. (2002) Earning the right to indulge: Effort as a determinant of customer preferences towards frequency program rewards, *Journal of Marketing Research*, 39, 155–70.

Levine, L. J. (1997) Reconstructing memory for emotions, *Journal of Experimental Psychology: General*, 126, 165–77.

Lichtenstein, S. & Slovic, P. (1971) Reversal of preference between bids and choices in gambling decisions, *Journal of Experimental Psychology*, 89, 46–55.

Lichtenstein, S. & Slovic, P. (1973) Response-induce reversals of preference in gambling: An extended replication in Las Vegas, *Journal of Experimental Psychology*, 101, 16–20.

Lindman, H. R. (1971) Inconsistent preferences among gamblers, *Journal of Experimental Psychology*, 89, 390–7.

List, J. A. (2002) Preference-reversals of a different kind: The "more is less" phenomenon, *American Economic Review*, 92, 1636–43.

Loewenstein, G. (1996) Out of control: visceral influences on behavior, *Organizational Behavior and Human Decision Processes*, 65, 272–92.

Loewenstein, G. & Schkade, D. (1999) Wouldn't it be nice? Predicting future feelings. In D. Kahneman, E. Diener, and N. Schwartz. (eds.), *Well-being: The Foundations of Hedonic Psychology*. New York, NY: Russell Sage Foundation.

March, J. (1994) *A Primer on Decision Making: How Decisions Happen*. New York: The Free Press.

Mather, M., Shafir, E., & Johnson, M. K. (2000) Misremembrance of options past: Source monitoring and choice, *Psychological Science*, 11, 132–8.

Mellers, B. A., Chang, S., Birnbaum, M. H., & Ordonez, L. D. (1992) Preferences, prices and ratings in risky decision making, *Journal of Experimental Psychology: Human Perception and Performance*, 18, 347–61.

Mellers, B. A., Ordonez, L. D., & Birnbaum, M. H. (1992) A change-of-process theory for contextual effects and preference-reversals in risky decision making, *Organizational Behavior and Human Decision Processes*, 52, 331–69.

Novemsky, N. & Ratner, R. N. (2003) The time course and impact of consumers' erroneous beliefs about hedonic contrast effects, *Journal of Consumer Behavior*, 29, 507–16.

Nowlis, S. M. & Simonson, I. (1994) The context-dependency of attributes as a determinant of preference-reversals between choices and judgments of purchase likelihood. Unpublished manuscript, Stanford University.

Nowlis, S. M. & Simonson, I. (1997) Attribute-task compatibility as a determinant of consumer preference-reversals, *Journal of Marketing Research*, 34, 205–18.

Payne, J. W. (1982) Contingent decision behavior, *Psychological Bulletin*, 92, 382–402.

Payne, J. W., Bettman, J. R., & Johnson, E. J. (1992) Behavioral decision research: A constructive processing perspective, *Annual Review of Psychology*, 43, 87–131.

Pham, M. T. (1998) Representativeness, relevance, and the use of feelings in decision making, *Journal of Consumer Research*, 25, 144–59.

Pommerehne, W. W., Schneider, F., & Zweifel, P. (1982) Economic theory of choice and preference-reversal phenomenon: A reexamination, *American Economic Review*, 72, 569–74.

Prelec, D. & Herrnstein, R. (1993) Preferences or principles: Alternative guidelines for choice. In R. J. Zeckhauser (ed.), *Strategy and Choice*. Cambridge, MA: MIT Press.

Rabin, M. (2002) A perspective on psychology and economics, *European Economic Review*, 46, 657–85.

Ratner, R. K., Kahn, B. E., & Kahneman, D. (1999) Choosing less-preferred experiences for the sake of variety, *Journal of Consumer Research*, 26, 1–15.

Read, D. & van Leeuwen, B. (1998) Predicting hunger: The effects of appetite and delay on choice, *Organizational Behavior and Human Decision Processes*, 76, 189–205.

Reilly, R. J. (1982) Preference-reversal: Further evidence and some suggested modifications in experimental design, *American Economic Review*, 72, 576–84.

Robinson, M. D. & Clore, G. L. (2002) Belief and feeling: Evidence for an accessibility model of emotional self-report, *Psychological Bulletin*, 128, 934–60.

Schkade, D. A. & Johnson, E. J. (1989) Cognitive processes in preference-reversals, *Organizational Behavior and Human Decision Processes*, 44, 203–31.

Schkade, D. A. & Kahneman, D. (1997) Does living in California make people happy? A focusing illusion in judgments of life satisfaction, *Psychological Science*, 9, 340–6.

Seidl, C. (2002) Preference-reversal, *Journal of Economic Surveys*, 16, 621–55.

Sen, A. (1993) Internal consistency of choice, *Econometrica*, 61, 495–521.

Shafir, E. (1993) Choosing versus rejecting – why some options are both better and worse than others, *Memory and Cognition*, 21, 546–56.

Shafir, E., Simonson, I., & Tversky, A. (1993) Reason-based choice, *Cognition*, 49, 11–36.

Simonson, I. (1989) Choice based on reasons – the case of attraction and compromise effects, *Journal of Consumer Research*, 16, 158–74.

Simonson, I. (1990) The effect of purchase quantity and timing on variety-seeking behavior, *Journal of Marketing Research*, 27, 150–62.

Simonson, I. & Nowlis, S. M. (2000) The role of explanations and need for uniqueness in consumer decision making: Unconventional choices based on reasons, *Journal of Consumer Research*, 27, 49–68.

Slovic, P. (1975) Choice between equally valuable alternatives, *Journal of Experimental Psychology: Human Perception and Performance*, 1, 280–7.

Slovic, P. (1995) The construction of preference, *American Psychologist*, 50, 364–71.

Slovic, P., Griffin, D., & Tversky, A. (1990) Compatibility effects in judgment and choice. In R. M. Hogarth (ed.), *Insights in Decision Making: Theory and Applications*. Chicago: University of Chicago.

Slovic, P. & Lichtenstein, S. (1968) Relative importance of probabilities and payoffs in risk taking, *Journal of Experimental Psychology*, 78, 1–18.

Slovic, P. & Lichtenstein, S. (1983) Preference-reversals: A broader perspective, *American Economic Review*, 73, 596–605.

Slovic, P. & MacPhillamy, D. (1974) Dimensional commensurability and cue utilization in comparative judgment, *Organizational Behavior and Human Performance*, 11, 172–94.

Sunstein, C. R., Kahneman, D., Schkade, D., & Ritov, I. (2002) Predictably incoherent judgments, *Stanford Law Review*, 54, 1153–215.

Tversky, A. (1977) Features of similarity, *Psychological Review*, 84, 327–52.

Tversky, A. (1996) Rational theory and constructive choice. In K. J. Arrow, E. Colombatto, M. Perlman, and C. Schmidt (eds.), *The Rational Foundations of Economic Behavior* (pp. 185–202). London and New York: Macmillan and St. Martin's Press.

Tversky, A. and Griffin, D. (1991) Endowment and contrast in judgments of well-being. In F. Strack, M. Argyle, and N. Schwartz (eds.), *Subjective Well-being: An Interdisciplinary Perspective* (vol. 21, pp. 101–18). Oxford: Pergamon Press.

Tversky, A., Sattath, S., & Slovic, P. (1988) Contingent weighting in judgment and choice, *Psychological Review*, 95, 371–84.

van Osselaer, S. M. J., Alba, J. W., & Manchanda, P. (2001) Loyalty programs and process in mediated intertemporal choice. Unpublished manuscript, University of Chicago, Chicago, IL 60637.

Willemsen, M. G. & Keren, G. (in press) The role of negative features in joint and separate evaluation, *Journal of Behavioral Decision Making*.

Wilson, T. D. & Gilbert, D. (2003) Affective forecasting, *Advances in Experimental Social Psychology*, 35, 345–411.

Wilson, T. D., Wheatley, T., & Gilbert, D. T. (2000) Unpublished raw data, University of Virginia.

Wilson, T. D., Wheatley, T., Meyers, J., Gilbert, D. T., & Axsom, D. (2000) Focalism: a source of durability bias in affective forecasting, *Journal of Personality and Social Psychology*, 78, 821–36.

19

Framing, Loss Aversion, and Mental Accounting

Dilip Soman

Every fact has two sides to it. What is seen as good can also be bad, a loss can be seen as a gain, sorrow may have some pleasure, and bad news can be delivered to make it good. No glass is ever fully full or fully empty, it is what one makes of it that matters.

(Anonymous)

The frames we use to view the world determine what we see, locking us into certain ideas and shutting out new possibilities.

(Schoemaker and Russo, 2001)

Introduction

Consider a decision maker, Mr. A, who is faced with a choice between two options. In one option, he will earn $100 for sure. In the other option, there is a 50 percent chance of earning $200 and a 50 percent chance of earning nothing.

Traditional normative theories of choice typically assume that people are rational and that they have clear and stable preferences, based on some utility function (von Neumann & Morgenstern, 1947). Choice theory assumes description invariance (Tversky & Kahneman, 1986) – the manner in which the information is presented to the decision maker should not change the decision; and procedure invariance (Tversky & Kahneman, 1986; Shafir, 1993) – the method of eliciting preference should not change the decision.

Our hypothetical decision maker, Mr. A, may well be guided by his utility function in a laboratory setting if he were presented with the above choice problem devoid of any context. However, real-world decision makers bring other perspectives to the table in making decisions like these. For instance, Mr. A might consider the worst-case scenario (earning nothing) as a benchmark, and treat all outcomes as an improvement over this benchmark. Alternately, he could treat the best outcome as a benchmark and treat everything else as an unsatisfactory outcome in relation. In a similar vein, he might consider this choice as a one-shot decision – a choice he might make only once, or as one choice in a series of decisions he needs to make. And he may undertake the task of deciding which of the two options to select, or alternately, which of the two to reject. In the language of this chapter, Mr. A might use different frames to view the problem. Interestingly, the use of these different frames may result in a difference in choice.

What is a Frame?

A frame refers to a mental model (Johnson-Laird, 1983) of the decision problem that individuals use to solve the problem, and includes details about the elements of the decision problems (i.e., information) as well as a context. While the information from a particular problem may remain the same, it may be perceived, organized, and interpreted differently; it may be structured differently; and the problem may be solved in a different context, by different people or at different times. Collectively, we refer to any of these different ways of looking at the same problem as a different frame (cf. Kahneman & Tversky, 1984; Schoemaker & Russo, 2001).

The implication of a personal and situation specific mental model is that two individuals who might be presented with the same problem stimulus might actually be solving different "mental" problems (see Figure 19.1). Importantly, the true objects of evaluation and choice are not real objects, nor their verbal descriptions; but rather their mental representations. This idea is relatively novel in decision-making research and has gathered momentum over the past 30 years. However, cognitive psychologists have realized this principle for a very long time. As Kahneman writes, "Anyone who has taken a course in perception has learnt to distinguish objective reality from the proximal stimulus, and to distinguish both reality and the stimulus from the mental representation that the observer eventually constructs" (Kahneman, 2000, p. xiv).

While the term "frame" has its origins in cognitive science and artificial intelligence (Johnson-Laird, 1983; Minsky, 1975), an analogy with window frames is appropriate. Architects have demonstrated that a window plays a crucial role in the final appearance, view and get-up of a room, and that the same room appears to have a very different personality with seemingly subtle changes in windows (O'Gorman, 1998). There are two

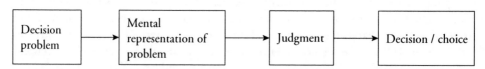

Figure 19.1 The role of mental representations in judgment and decision making

important sets of factors that underlie the critical role of a window. The location and type of the window frame of the window can change the perspective and clarity of the view. And the size of a window determines the extent of the view that can be seen. In much the same way, the manner in which the elements of a decision are structured can influence the decision maker's perspective and hence his decision. In this chapter, the different representations of the decision problem are referred to as *Outcome Framing*. And the size of the decision maker's view – whether he views the decision narrowly, or as part of a broader set of tasks can also influence the decision. In this chapter, we refer to this as *Structure Framing*. We also consider a third type of framing, *Task Framing* to refer to the manner in which the decision maker interprets the task (or the problem definition) that is involved in making a decision.

To Frame, or To Be Framed

The particular frame that is generated in any given decision-making situation depends on a number of factors – previous patterns and experience, norms and expectations, the desire for simplicity, and habit (cf. Johnson-Laird, 1983; Schoemaker & Russo, 2001). Framing is typically spontaneous and subconscious, but decision makers can also be deliberative in creating frames. However, in addition to creating their own frames, decision-makers can also be "framed" (i.e., the problem can be presented to them in a specific structure) by clever experimenters. In particular, the concreteness principle (Slovic, 1972; Thaler & Johnson, 1990) suggests that decision makers will use information in the context of the frame that is presented to them without making any attempts to reframe it. In early research on framing, researchers took the same information and presented it differently to two groups of subjects (Kahneman & Tversky, 1979; Tversky & Kahneman, 1981). They were able to demonstrate significant differences in choices across these groups of subjects, and were able to attribute these differences solely to presentation differences that presumably resulted in differences in the mental representation.

This early wave of research in framing effects was restrictive in the sense that it "framed" the decision maker rather than studied processes that these decision makers use to generate frames. Framing effects generated through the type of experiments described above do not study what individuals do; rather they showed what individuals did not do. In particular, consistent with the concreteness principle, "decision makers are generally quite passive and therefore inclined to accept any frame that they are presented with" (Kahneman, 2000, p. xv). However, the strength of the early findings on framing effects was quite surprising, even to the researchers who first uncovered them. As Kahneman (2000, p. xv) writes, "We were surprised by how easy it was to construct different versions of a decision problem that were transparently equivalent when considered together but evoked different preferences when considered separately."

While research in the "framing effects" paradigm has continued over the years, a new stream of work emerged through the writings of Richard Thaler (1980, 1985, 1999). In particular, Thaler proposed that individuals follow a cognitive version of cost accounting to organize and interpret information as the basis for making a decision. Thaler dubbed this cognitive structure as a mental accounting system, and broadly defined mental accounting as the study of the processes used by individuals to record, summarize, and analyze their expenses and consumption with the objective of making a decision. Thaler's early work was an example of research in which the experimenter did not specifically provide subjects with frames, but instead provided contexts that provoked subjects to frame the same problem differently.

As a specific example of mental accounting, consider Mr. B who invests a certain sum of money to buy a ticket to a basketball game. When investing in (or prepaying for) a particular endeavor, Mr. B creates a mental account for that endeavor (in this instance, the basketball game) and allocates the disutility of the payment to this account. This account will stay open until Mr. B has completed the endeavor and obtained some benefit (i.e., watched the basketball game). The mental account can then be closed after being credited with the value of this benefit (Prelec & Loewenstein, 1998; Thaler, 1980, 1999).

One important ingredient of mental accounting is the manner in which the monetary outcome is framed. Another ingredient relates to the scope and the life of the mental account (Read, Loewenstein & Rabin, 1999). Mental accounts can be defined narrowly (at the level of a single transaction) or can be more broadly defined at the level of a spending category (Heath & Soll, 1996; Soman, 2001). In the case of Mr. B, the expense and consumption of the basketball game was narrowly framed in one account. More generally, expenses are divided into different spending categories (e.g., food, entertainment), and spending in each category is constrained by budgets. It might also be possible for Mr. B to classify his expense under the "entertainment" frame. Finally, mental accounts can be defined with a fixed temporal life (e.g., monthly budgets, Heath & Soll, 1996), or can extend over a period of time (Gourville & Soman, 1998).

The study of mental accounting is a study of the mental representation of information. In particular, individuals faced with a specific decision of whether or not to make a particular purchase do not make such a decision in isolation (Soman, 2001). The decision might depend on the availability of budgets (Heath & Soll, 1996), the nature of the expense and the amount of similar expenses incurred (Soman, 2001), the manner in which the price is presented (Gourville, 1998), and the scope of the mental account under which the expense is categorized (Cheema & Soman, 2003).

Outcome Framing

In many decision-making situations, outcomes are often defined in terms of numerical quantities. As such, numerical quantities can be described in a number of ways. In particular, three methods of framing outcomes have been studied in the literature:

1   Framing as gains or losses;
2   Framing as aggregate or disaggregate quantities; and
3   Framing by scaling the outcome in a different currency.

Framing as gains or losses

Outcomes are commonly perceived as either gains or losses relative to a neutral reference state. The following two Asian disease problems (from Tversky & Kahneman 1981) provide an example of such a framing effect, and illustrate a violation of the invariance principle. In this example and all others that follow, the numbers in parentheses against each option denote the percent of subjects choosing that option.

> *Problem 1 (N = 152)*: Imagine that the US is preparing for the outbreak of an unusual Asian disease, which is expected to kill 600 people. Two alternative programs to combat the disease have been proposed. Assume that the exact scientific estimates of the consequences of the programs are as follows:
> If program A is adopted, 200 people will be saved.   [72 percent]
> If program B is adopted, there is a one-third probability that 600 people
>   will be saved and a two-thirds probability that no people will be saved.   [28 percent]
> Which of the two programs would you favor?

It is clear that most of the respondents are risk-averse in this frame of problem. Now consider another problem in which the same cover story is followed by a different frame of the outcomes:

> *Problem 2 (N = 155)*:
> If program C is adopted, 400 people will die.   [22 percent]
> If program D is adopted, there is a one-third probability that nobody
>   will die and a two-thirds probability that 600 people will die.   [78 percent]
> Which of the two programs would you favor?

Programs A and B in Problem 1 are objectively identical with programs C and D in Problem 2, respectively. The results of Problem 2, however, indicate that the majority of respondents are risk-seeking, rather than risk-averse, in this frame of the decision problem. Thus, different framing of the outcomes for a decision problem shifts people's choice from risk-averse to risk-seeking behavior.

Kahneman & Tversky (1979) have proposed a descriptive model of choices, called "Prospect Theory" to accommodate these observations that are anomalous with respect to the normative theory. They argue that the outcomes of risky prospects, or gambles, are evaluated by a value function that has three essential characteristics. First, *reference dependence* suggests that values are coded as gains and losses relative to a reference point. Second, *diminishing sensitivity* suggests that the value function is concave in the domain of gains and convex in the domain of losses. Third, *loss aversion* implies the value function is steeper in the loss than in the gain domain. This property implies that losses loom larger than corresponding gains. These three properties give rise to an asymmetric S-shaped value function as illustrated in Figure 19.2.

Under the prospect theory framework, the frame can dramatically change the perceived reference point of the question. In Problem 1, the outcomes are framed in terms of saving lives; the potential disaster of losing all the lives becomes the neutral reference

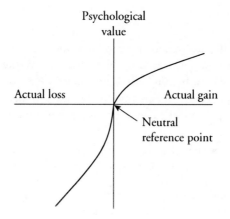

Figure 19.2 The prospect theory value function

Source: Adapted with permission from "Prospect theory: An analysis of decision under risk" [D. Kahneman and A. Tversky, *Econometrica*, 47(2), 263–91. Copyright © 1979, The Econometric Society].

point. The two alternative programs A and B are then evaluated on the upper part of the value function, and risk-averse behavior results. That is, since the gain function is concave, the value placed on saving 600 lives is viewed as not being three times as great as saving 200 lives. As a result, most (72 percent) respondents chose program A. In Problem 2, the outcomes are framed in terms of losing lives. The current position of having 600 lives forms the reference point. The choice between programs C and D is evaluated on the lower part of the value function and risk-seeking behavior results. That is, since the loss function is convex, the negative value placed on the loss of 600 lives is perceived as not being one and a half times as high as losing 400 lives. Consequently, most (78 percent) respondents chose program D.

Framing as aggregate or disaggregate quantities

The prospect theory value function can also be used to make predictions about whether individuals would prefer to frame outcomes in an aggregate (integrated) or segregated manner. Imagine a person who has to evaluate a joint outcome (x, y), where x and y are two outcomes. The evaluation will depend on the manner in which the problem is framed; either jointly as $v(x + y)$ or separately as $v(x) + v(y)$. Thaler (1985) suggests that people selectively choose one rule of the two depending on which rule can generate higher value for the joint outcome under question. That is, people employ "hedonic editing" as follows:

$$v(x \& y) = Max[v(x + y), v(x) + v(y)]$$

where "&" denotes the psychological representation of the combination of the two outcomes.

He then derives the following principles of hedonic editing for people who follow a prospect theory value function and wish to evaluate joint outcomes in a way that can maximize the value to them. Let $x > 0$ and $y > 0$:

1 For multiple gains, the concavity of the gain curve indicates that segregation is preferred, since $v(x) + v(y) > v(x + y)$.
2 For multiple losses, the convexity of the loss curve indicates that integration is preferred, since $v(-x) + v(-y) < v(-(x + y))$.
3 For a large gain and a small loss: Concavity of the gain curve predicts that $v(y) + v(x - y) > v(x)$, and loss aversion indicates that $v(-y) < -v(y)$. Thus, $v(x) + v(-y) < v(x) - v(y) < v(x - y)$. Integration is preferred.
4 For a large loss and a small gain. Consider outcomes x and $-y$ where $x < y$ so there is a net loss. In this case we cannot determine without further information whether integration or segregation is preferred. When facing a large loss and a small gain, e.g., ($\$40$, $-\$6,000$), segregation is preferred which is referred to as the "silver lining" principle. On the other hand, for a ($\$40$, $-\$50$) mix, integration may be preferred.

Intuitively, these principles seem compelling. That is, people are happier winning two lotteries that pay $\$50$ and $\$30$ separately, than winning a single lottery that pays $\$80$. Also, people would like to identify, or segregate, small silver linings from a big loss as small comfort in times of a big loss.

One implication of the silver lining principle is in the domain of marketing. Retailers often offer discounts on high-price items to make them appear more attractive. However, when individuals are already spending a lot of money (i.e., incurring a loss), a small reduction in that loss will not have a very large impact. However, if the discount amount were instead segregated and offered as either a rebate or a free gift, it would have a greater impact (see Johnson, Hershey, Meszaros & Kunreuther, 1993).

Gourville (1998) noticed that marketers frequently reframe a transaction from an aggregate expense to a series of small daily expenses using what he calls a Pennies-a-Day (PAD) strategy. For example, Sally Struthers advertises that for "Only 72 cents a day" we can feed a starving child, and a mattress retailer claims that you can sleep comfortably for "Only 10 cents a night." Prospect theory and the hedonic editing principle predict that the PAD framing strategy will backfire since consumers should prefer an aggregate framing of losses as one large loss rather than segregating framing that emphasizes a series of small losses. But the widespread use of PAD strategy in industry suggests that it can be effective in influencing consumers' product evaluations.

In a study of donation behavior, 60 subjects were asked a hypothetical question of whether they would donate 85 cents per day (PAD framing) over a one year period to a worthy cause; another 60 subjects were requested the aggregate framing of $\$300$ per year. The data show that the percentage of subjects agreeing to donate was significantly higher under the PAD framing than under the aggregate framing (52 vs. 30 percent). In another study on long-distance telephone carriers, subjects in the PAD condition required a mean saving of $\$11.75$ per month to switch carriers, or an equivalent of $\$141$ per year. But the subjects in the aggregate condition required a mean saving of only $\$56$ per year.

With a series of subsequent studies, Gourville (1998, 1999) concludes that a PAD framing can increase the attractiveness of transactions involving monetary losses and decrease the attractiveness of transactions involving monetary gains. But this PAD effect is moderated by the size of the monetary request in that a large daily dollar amount may actually exaggerate the perceived monetary magnitude, thereby causing PAD strategy to backfire. Gourville argues that the temporal framing of price for a transaction systematically influences the nature of expenses that a consumer retrieves as comparison standard. A PAD framing will foster the retrieval of daily or ongoing expenses whereas an aggregate framing will foster the retrieval of large infrequent expenses. However, the retrieved category width will also be influenced by the monetary magnitude. As a result, while the PAD framing of a low-cost transaction fosters comparisons to palatable expenses (e.g., "$3 a day is what I spend on coffee each day"), the PAD framing of a high-cost transaction may actually hinder comparison (e.g., "I don't really spend $30 each day on anything").

Framing by scaling in a different currency

A third way of framing outcomes is by scaling the numerical quantities in different currencies. It has been long noticed in economics that people focus on the nominal face value of a given amount of money, rather than its real value, when making economic decisions. Fisher (1928) coined the term "money illusion" to describe this phenomenon. Using experimental data, Shafir, Diamond and Tversky (1997) showed that the face value of an amount of money (in dollars) exerts greater impact on consumer preferences than its purchasing power (taking account of interest and inflation rates).

More recently, Soman, Wertenbroch and Chattopadhyay (2003) invited subjects to participate in a gamble in a fictitious foreign currency (PI$). The gamble had a one-third chance of a win, and the resulting payoff was 5 times the amount gambled (zero for a loss). All subjects were given the same gambling budget in Hong Kong dollars (HK$20), but received either PI$ 200 or PI$ 2 as a function of the exchange rate which was clearly specified to subjects. Subjects could bet any amount between zero and this endowment, and at the end of the experiment, all their PI$ were fully convertible to HK$ at the specified exchange rate. Results showed that subjects who had PI$200 wagered an average amount equivalent to HK$ 12.06 as compared to HK$ 6.17 for subjects who had PI$ 2. When the exact same amount was framed as PI$ 200 rather than PI$ 2, individuals seemed to be willing to take a greater risk with the amount!

There have been two explanations for the currency framing effect. Raghubir and Srivastava (2002) propose an anchoring and adjustment process (see Chapter 12, this volume; Tversky & Kahneman 1974) in which consumers anchor on the nominal value, then adjust using exchange rate to convert the unknown currency price into the home currency price. This adjustment process is cognitively consuming and therefore is often inadequate. A second explanation offered by Soman et al. (2003) is based on the numerosity effect in making quantity judgments (Pelham, Sumarta, & Myaskovsky, 1994). People use numerosity (i.e., the number of units in which the stimulus is divided) as a heuristic to make judgments of quantity.

Loss Aversion and Related Phenomena as Outcome Framing Effects

Loss aversion refers to the phenomenon that the prospect theory value function is steeper in the loss domain than in the gain domain, i.e., losses loom larger than gains in decision making (Kahneman & Tversky, 1979). It is reflected in the fact that people are often reluctant to bet on a fair coin toss for equal stakes. The attractiveness derived from the possible gain is not high enough to compensate for the aversion of the possible loss. Similarly, reframing a "gain" gamble as a "loss" gamble will change choice, as shown in this classroom demonstration based on Kahneman and Tversky's experiments.

Problem 3: Choose between:
Option A: A coin toss with 50 percent chance of getting $3,000,
    50 percent chance of getting nothing   [35 percent]
Option B: Get $1,500 for sure   [65 percent]

Problem 4: Suppose you are given $3,000. You then have to choose between:
Option A: A coin toss with 50 percent chance of losing $3,000,
    50 percent chance of losing nothing   [72 percent]
Option B: Lose $1,500 for sure   [28 percent]

While it is easy to see that Option A and Option B in both problems are functionally identical to each other, the difference in choice patterns is explained by loss aversion. In Problem 4, the framing of Option B makes it a certain loss, which is aversive to subjects. Hence, in the loss frame, choices shift towards the risky option because it has the potential to avoid loss completely. The result of this study can be interpreted to say that loss aversion results in a reduction in risk aversion.

The endowment effect

Consider the following scenario adapted from Thaler (1980):

Mr. R. bought a case of good wine in the late 1950s for about $5 a bottle. A few years later his wine merchant offered to buy the wine back for $100 a bottle. He refused, although he has never paid more than $35 for a bottle of wine.

This is an illustration of the fact that people often demand much more to give up an object than they would be willing to pay to acquire it. Thaler (1980) coined a term "endowment effect" to describe this discrepancy between the willingness to accept (WTA) and willingness to pay (WTP). Endowment effect is an immediate consequence of loss aversion, since the value loss associated with giving up an object is greater than the value gain associated with getting the same object (see Kahneman, Knetsch & Thaler, 1990).

The sunk-cost effect

Consider again the example of Mr. B who had spent, say $40 in advance purchasing a ticket to a basketball game. This individual sets up an account for the game, and this account can only be closed satisfactorily on consuming $40 "worth" of benefit. Suppose there is a snowstorm on the day of the game and it is dangerous to drive. Rationally speaking, Mr. B should go only if the anticipated benefit from the game is greater than the risk and costs of driving. However, Mr. B is also averse to losing the $40 and having to close his mental account with a loss, so he trudges through the snow. The frame imposed by the game-specific mental account drives Mr. B's consumption behavior. Had he paid $80, he would have been even more determined to attend, had he been given the ticket for free, he would have chosen to stay at home in front of a fire and watch the game on TV. The increased tendency to continue an endeavor because some past investment has been made is called the sunk-cost effect (Arkes and Blumer, 1985). In marketing, it can be thought of as a person's increased likelihood of consuming a product simply because of the price they paid to acquire that product (Gourville and Soman, 2002). The greater the price paid, the greater the "sunk cost" pressure to not let that product go to waste.

In another well-known example, Thaler (1980) notes:

> A man joins a tennis club and pays a $300 yearly membership fee. After two weeks of playing he develops a tennis elbow. He continues to play (in pain) saying, "I don't want to waste the $300!"

In a similar vein, Arkes and Blumer (1985) asked 61 college students to assume that they had mistakenly purchased tickets for both a $50 ski trip and a $100 ski trip for the very same weekend. These students also were told that they thought that they would have more fun on the $50 trip than on the $100 trip. Finally, they were told that they had to choose one of the two trips and let their ticket to the other trip go to waste. In response, more than half of all the students reported that they would choose the less-enjoyable $100 trip. Amazingly, the greater "sunk" cost of the $100 trip had a greater impact on the students' choices than the greater expected enjoyment of the $50 trip!

Advantages and disadvantages in choice

Loss aversion implies that a given difference between two options will have greater impact if it is viewed (or, framed) as a difference between two disadvantages (relative to a reference point) than if it is viewed (or, framed) as a difference between two advantages. That is, advantages and disadvantages may not be mirror images. For example, consider the following question (from Tversky & Kahneman, 1991):

> *Problem 5 (N = 106)*: Imagine that as part of your professional training you were assigned to a part-time job. The training is now ending, and you must look for employment. You consider two possibilities. They are like your training job in most respects except for the

amount of social contact and the convenience of commuting to and from work. To compare the two jobs to each other and to the present one, you have made up the following table:

Job	Social contact	Daily travel time (min)
Present job	Isolated for long stretches	10
Job x	Limited contact with others	20
Job y	Moderately sociable	60

Problem 6 involves the same Job x and Job y, but a different reference job, which is described as "much pleasant social interaction and 80 minutes of daily commuting time."

Since both options (Job x and Job y) are framed as losses in the second version of the problem, the difference in the social contact aspect of the jobs was highlighted in Problem 6. As a result, 70 percent of respondents chose Job x in Problem 5, but only 33 percent chose it in problem 6.

More generally, the composition of the choice set offered to the decision maker also influences the frame, and hence the resulting outcome. A complete review of this literature is beyond the scope of the present chapter (see Chapter 18, this volume, for a review).

Status quo bias

Loss aversion naturally induces a bias that favors the status quo over other options. Samuelson and Zeckhauser (1988) introduce the term "status quo bias" to describe people's tendency to remain at the status quo. In a field study, they found that a new medical plan was chosen more by new Harvard employees, who were recruited after the plan was introduced, than by employees recruited before the plan was introduced. The existing employees had to lose some benefits in exchange for gaining others, and since the loss loomed larger than the gain, they decided to stay on with the status quo option. In another study by Knetsch (1989), students were randomly gifted with either a mug or a chocolate bar, and then allowed to trade. Given the random nature of the initial allocation and low transaction costs, one would have expected to see a substantial number of trades. However, consistent with the endowment effect, approximately 90 percent of the students retained the gifts they were given.

Reluctance to choose

Suppose a decision maker is choosing between two options that involve a tradeoff (e.g., suppose Option A is superior on attribute 1, but not on attribute 2; while Option B is superior on attribute 2, but not on 1). As long as this individual is still in the process of choosing, she will not experience a loss along either dimension. However, as soon as she chooses one option (say, A), she might experience a loss (say, along attribute 2), as a result of which the rejected option may start appearing more valuable. In a recent paper,

Carmon, Wertenbroch, and Zeelenberg (2003) suggest that loss aversion causes foregone alternatives to be evaluated more highly after the consumer has decided to purchase the chosen alternative, thus making the consumer feel worse after the decision as compared to before it.

Structure Framing

The framing of structure (i.e., the *size* and *arrangement* of the decision maker's view of the problem) can be done in different ways:

1   The integration or segregation of information;
2   Sequential framing of contingent events; and
3   The scope of the frame, specifically whether the specific decision is viewed in isolation, or as part of a larger set of decisions.

The integration and segregation of information

As one example of structure framing, consider the following problems (from Tversky & Kahneman, 1981):

> *Problem 7 (N = 86)*: Choose between:
> E: 25 percent chance to win $240 and 75 percent chance to lose $760   [0 percent]
> F: 25 percent chance to win $250 and 75 percent chance to lose $750   [100 percent]

It is obvious that F dominates E and indeed all the respondents chose accordingly. Now consider another problem.

> *Problem 8 (N = 150)*: Imagine that you face the following pair of concurrent decisions.
> First examine both decisions, then indicate the options you prefer.
> Decision 1 choose between:
> A: A sure gain of $240   [84 percent]
> B: 25 percent chance to gain $1,000 and 75 percent chance to
>   gain nothing   [16 percent]
> Decision 2 choose between:
> C: A sure loss of $750   [13 percent]
> D: 75 percent chance to lose $1,000 and 25 percent chance to
>   lose nothing   [87 percent]

A majority of the respondents were risk-averse in decision 1 but risk-seeking in decision 2. More importantly, 73 percent of them chose A and D and only 3 percent chose B and C. Since the respondents considered the two decisions in problem 8 simultaneously, they expressed a conjunctive preference for A and D over B and C. However, if we examine the two pairs carefully, we can see that the conjunction of A and D yields exactly option E in problem 7, and the conjunction of B and C yields exactly the option F in problem 7. In other words, the preferred pair of A and D is actually dominated by the rejected pair of B and C. Thus, structurally reframing a problem by separating the actions produces violation of the dominance principle underlying the theory of rational choice.

The discrepancy between Problems 7 and 8 was labeled elsewhere by Read et al. (1999) as the "bracketing effect." They propose that when facing a group of choices, a decision maker may bracket them together into one compound choice by taking into account the effect of each choice on all the other choices in the group, which is referred to as "broad bracketing." On the other hand, the decision maker may simply consider the choices one by one, which is referred to as "narrow bracketing." The subjects in Problem 10 apparently treated the two choices separately, i.e., they bracketed narrowly. Had they been able to broadly bracket the two choices together, they should have chosen B and C that connectively yield option F in Problem 7.

Sequential framing of contingent events

Another type of structural framing is illustrated in Problems 9 and 10 (from Tversky & Kahneman, 1981):

> *Problem 9 (N = 85):* Consider the following two-stage game. In the first stage, there is a 75 percent chance to end the game without winning anything, and a 25 percent chance to move into the second stage. If you reach the second stage, you have a choice between:
> A: A sure win of $30 (74 percent); and
> B: 80 percent chance to win $45 (26 percent)

Your choice must be made before the game starts, i.e., before the outcome of the first stage is known. Please indicate the option you prefer.

> *Problem 10 (N = 81):* Which of the following options do you prefer?
> C: 25 percent chance to win $30 (42 percent); or
> D: 20 percent chance to win $45 (58 percent).

Problems 9 and 10 are identical in terms of both actual probabilities and outcomes. In the two-stage game in Problem 9, option A offers a probability of 25 percent to win $30, which is exactly option C in Problem 10; option B offers a probability of 25 percent × 80 percent = 20 percent to win $45 that is exactly the option D in Problem 10. However, the choice patterns are strikingly different.

The contrast between these problems was labeled as the pseudocertainty effect by Tversky and Kahneman (1981). The prospect that offers $30 seems more attractive in the two-stage version because respondents wrongly take entering into the second stage of the game as granted. The "certainty" associated with option A, however, is merely an illusion. It is contingent on entering into the second stage that has only 25 percent chance.

The scope of the frame

A third aspect of structure framing relates to the scope and breadth of the frame. In the earlier example of Mr. B who purchases a basketball game ticket for $40, the decision is framed narrowly in a transaction specific mental account. Mr. B paid one price ($40) and will receive one benefit (the consumption of the basketball game). In the language of Prelec and Loewenstein (1998), the cost and benefit in a narrowly framed mental account are "coupled." However, a broader framing of the situation can facilitate decoupling (Prelec & Loewenstein, 1998; Soman, 2001).

One way in which individuals are influenced to adopt broad frames is through the commonplace marketing practice of price bundling. Consider the following scenario adopted from Soman and Gourville (2001):

> Ernie and Bert are serious skiers who have each prepurchased four days' worth of lift tickets. Ernie paid $40 for each of four one-day lift tickets, and Bert paid $160 for a four-day ski pass. After three days of skiing in perfect conditions, each wakes up on the fourth day to find that ski conditions have deteriorated considerably. Who is more likely to ski in spite of the poor conditions?

From an economic perspective, the format of the payment shouldn't matter. The sunk-cost effect suggests that each man will consider the sunk cost of his ticket, increasing his likelihood of skiing on the fourth day. But given the fact that each has paid an identical amount of money, the two men face the same sunk costs and should, again, be equally likely to ski on the fourth day.

Soman and Gourville (2001) demonstrate in a series of studies that the sunk-cost effect is moderated in this case by the ambiguity inherent in a bundled transaction. In bundled transaction, the link between a specific cost and benefit is ambiguous and open to interpretation. Given the format of his payment, Ernie will frame each day of skiing separately while Bert will frame the four days as one bundle. In deciding whether to forego the last day of skiing, Ernie will explicitly realize that it cost him $40, and his decision will be influenced by the desire to not lose that amount. Bert, on the other hand will treat the $160 as the cost of the total bundle and ask himself whether he has derived enough benefit from the first three days to offset this cost. If yes, he will forego the fourth day. Note that because of his narrow framing, Ernie cannot reallocate the benefit from the first three days over the total $160.

Reducing loss aversion through broad framing
As the above example illustrates, one of the important implications of choice bracketing is that "loss aversion would have little impact on decision making if people aggregated multiple decisions together" (Read et al., 1999, p. 193). Cheema and Soman (2003) presented visitors to a travel agency with promotional material for a vacation package comprising airfare, hotel, and sightseeing. They were then presented with an event (either attractive or unattractive) that conflicted with the sightseeing tour and asked for their willingness to forego the tour. Two versions of materials were used – one version gave only the bundled price, while a second version gave the bundled price, but also decomposed it into prices for airfare, hotel, and sightseeing. They found that subjects who

knew the (decomposed) price of the sightseeing tour were the most reluctant to forego it – the tour was expensive, and foregoing it would have seemed like a waste. On the other hand, subjects who saw a bundled price were more willing to forego the sightseeing tour in favor of an attractive alternative. Open-ended responses suggested that subjects were framing the situation in order to justify foregoing the sightseeing tour. The broad frame they adopted allowed these participants to reallocate costs and benefits across the various components of the package.

An individual who is given the option of playing a gamble will also choose differently in a narrow frame and a broad frame. Perhaps the earliest example of this principle is offered by Samuelson (1963), who asked a colleague if he would accept equal odds on winning $200 or losing $100. The colleague refused in the narrow frame, but added that he would be only too happy to accept 100 such bets. The loss aversion that was apparent in the narrow frame disappeared in the broad frame. Similarly, Benartzi and Thaler (1995) suggested that loss-averse individuals dislike stocks because of their volatility, and hence overinvest in fixed income securities over equity (this is the so called Equity Premium Puzzle). However, volatility over longer time periods is lower, and hence if individuals did not scrutinize their portfolios on an ongoing basis, they would be less likely to fall prey to loss aversion.

Broad temporal brackets can also serve to dampen the psychological impact of payment, and hence reduce the perception of loss. Gourville and Soman (1998) experimentally show when the cost significantly precedes benefits (e.g., advanced purchased match tickets), consumers will gradually adapt to the upstream costs as time passes by to the point where the benefit takes on the characteristics of a free good. Specifically, "payment depreciation" takes effect in one of two ways depending on whether the benefit can be inventoried (i.e., the consumer has discretion on when to consume) or not (i.e., if the benefit is not consumed in a specific timeframe, it lapses and is not available). First, if a benefit cannot be inventoried (e.g., a ticket to a sport match), payment depreciation will lead to an increased likelihood of forgoing the pending benefit. Second, if the pending benefit can be inventoried (e.g., a bottle of wine), payment depreciation will lead to an increased likelihood of consuming the pending benefit.

Task Framing

Decisions are often made by focusing on considerations that justify the selection of one alternative over others (Simonson, 1989). Different methods of framing the task can highlight different aspects of the alternatives, and therefore bring forth different considerations, which give rise to different decisions. One common method of task framing is to frame the task as a decision to choose one option from a given set, or a decision to reject options from the set. Shafir (1993) proposes that positive and negative features of an option are weighted differently, depending on whether the options are being chosen or rejected. Positive features of an option provide good reasons to choose it and thus are given heavier weights when people are asked to choose among options. Negative features of the option, on the other hand, provide good reasons to reject it, and thus receive heavier weights when people are asked to reject among alternatives. Such differences in the relative weighting of features can make decision problems easy to settle and justify to oneself and others. When one option apparently dominates another, a slight change in the relative weighting is unlikely to have significant effect on people's choices. However, when the decision problem is difficult and options are comparable with each other, framing of choosing versus rejecting can have significant effects. Consider the following problem (from Shafir, 1993):

Problem 11 (N = 170): Imagine that you serve on the jury of an only-child sole-custody case following a relatively messy divorce. The facts of the case are complicated by ambiguous economic, social, and emotional considerations, and you decide to base your decision entirely on the following few observations. [To which parent would you *award* sole custody of the child? / Which parent would you *deny* sole custody of the child?]

		Award	Deny
Parent A	Average income	[36 percent]	[45 percent]
	Average health		
	Average working hours		
	Reasonable rapport with the child		
	Relatively stable social life		
Parent B	Above-average income	[64 percent]	[55 percent]
	Very close relationship with the child		
	Extremely active in social life		
	Lots of work-related travel		
	Minor health problems		

The only difference between the two versions (award versus deny) is the question in the brackets. Half the subjects received the award (or, choice) version. The other half received the deny (or, rejection) version. Parent A is the "impoverished" option with no striking positive or negative features. Parent B is the "enriched" option with more positive *and* more negative features.

Normative choice theory would predict that in a choice set of two options, choosing and rejecting are complementary, or the percentages of subjects who awarded to and who denied a particular option should sum up to one. According to the previous reasoning, however, the enriched option (parent B) with both more positive and more negative features is expected to be chosen and rejected more often than the impoverished option. Indeed, the results support Shafir's notion of the compatibility effect and indicate inconsistency in preferences (64 percent + 55 percent > 1, and 36 percent + 45 percent < 1). In fact, the data indicate an even stronger pattern of compatibility effect in that parent B was chosen and rejected at the same time by the majority of two groups of presumably homogeneous subjects (64 percent and 55 percent, respectively).

Framing Matters

Research reviewed in this chapter argues that framing matters, and presents studies from a program of research that conclusively demonstrate effects of framing. When individuals are presented with a decision problem, they form a mental representation of that problem using a particular frame, and it is this representation that they solve. Hence, a study of decision making is incomplete without studying the process used by individuals to frame problems, and the factors that influence framing.

Research on framing effects originated primarily in an effort to provide counter-examples to the dominant theme of rational choice that pervaded the field at the time (Kahneman, 2000). For a long time, the paradigm of interest was to present the same information in two different formats to two different groups of people, and to demonstrate differences in choice. More recently, however, attention has shifted to understanding how people organize decisions, and how this organization in turn influences the decision making process. From a methodological standpoint, this latter approach involves going beyond crisp manipulations and simple choice tasks, and into richer forms of data and more complex stimuli.

Framing matters not only in experimental investigations, but also in the real world. Soman and Gourville (2001) present data from a summer theater festival in which patrons could buy tickets at different points in time, in different forms (i.e., in a bundle or singly), and using different payment mechanisms (e.g., checks vs. credit cards). Each of these factors can influence the manner in which patrons might frame their purchase, and hence the effects on consumption decisions. For example, consider a patron who is faced with a last minute conflict for a particular play to which he has a ticket. One factor that might drive his framing is the nature of ticket he has – a single ticket might trigger off a narrow frame that fosters loss aversion and hence drives consumption, while a season ticket might trigger off a broad frame that weakens loss aversion and hence the pressure to consumer. Indeed, Soman and Gourville (2001) find that 99.4 percent of single tickets were consumed, while only 78.5 percent of four-play bundled tickets were used. In an earlier experiment not reported in their (2001) paper, they find that even the physical form of otherwise identical tickets matters. Season tickets in the form of a booklet with a number of coupons for each performance foster narrow framing and hence a greater likelihood of consumption, while the same ticket in the form of a single card weakens loss aversion and reduces the likelihood of consumption.

While relatively more seems to be known about how external factors (including information presentation effects) drive framing, relatively less is known about how frames are internally generated. In the domain of mental accounting, Henderson and Peterson (1992) show that principles of similarity and categorization drive the formation of mental accounts. More recently, O'Curry (2001) showed that spending decisions are framed in the context of the source of the income that may be used to fund the expense (see also Soman & Cheema, 2001). However, broader questions remain. Research suggests that mental accounting frames are constructed in response to a particular decision task and are not retrieved (Soman, 2001), but more research is needed to address this issue. Early researchers in framing effects were surprised by the fact that subjects passively accepted any frame that was presented to them (Kahneman, 2000). Is this always the case, and under what conditions do people actively reframe decision problems? Recent evidence also supports past work on reasons-based choice (Simonson, 1989) by showing that when there is ambiguity in the environment and when they are motivated to choose a particular option, individuals reframe the task to justify their choice (Cheema & Soman, 2003). Again, further research is needed to address this question.

Finally, can decision makers be trained to reframe? Researchers in creativity and innovative thinking certainly think so (DeBono, 1990), and research in the area of debiasing provides recommendations on a number of cognitive strategies for reframing (see Chapter 16, this volume). The importance of the decision and the level of involvement are certainly potential drivers that may prompt reframing. However, future research needs to address these and other factors in order to paint a more comprehensive picture of how individuals frame simple decision problems.

Ackowledgments

I thank Amar Cheema, Prithviraj Chattopadhyay, John Gourville, Nigel Harvey, Derek Koehler, Renna Jiang and Teesta Soman for many helpful discussions and comments on previous drafts. I am especially indebted to Renna Jiang for research assistance, and to Teesta Soman for editorial advice in preparing this chapter.

References

Arkes, H. & Blumer, C. (1985) The psychology of sunk cost, *Organizational Behavior and Human Decision Processes*, 35(1), 124–40.

Bernartzi, S. & Thaler, R. (1995) Myopic loss aversion and the equity premium puzzle, *Quarterly Journal of Economics*, 110(1), 73–92.

Carmon, Z., Wertenbroch, K., & Zeelenberg, M. (2003) Option attachment: When deliberating makes choosing feel like losing, *Journal of Consumer Research*, 30(3), 15–29.

Cheema, A. & Soman, D. (2003) Malleable mental accounting. Unpublished working paper, St. Louis, MO: Washington University, Olin School.

DeBono, E. (1990) *Lateral Thinking for Management: A Handbook*. Harmondsworth: Penguin.

Fisher, I. (1928) *The Money Illusion*. New York: Adelphi.

Gourville, J. (1998) Pennies-a-day: The effect of temporal reframing on transaction evaluation, *Journal of Consumer Research*, 24, 395–408.

Gourville, J. (1999) The effect of implicit versus explicit comparisons on temporal pricing claims, *Marketing Letters*, 10(2), 113–24.

Gourville, J. & Soman, D. (1998) Payment depreciation: The behavioral effects of temporally separating payments from consumption, *Journal of Consumer Research*, 25(2), 160–74.

Gourville, J. & Soman, D. (2002) Pricing and the psychology of consumption, *Harvard Business Review*, (September), 90–6.

Heath, C. & Soll, J. B. (1996) Mental budgeting and consumer decisions, *Journal of Consumer Research*, 23, 40–52.

Henderson, P. & Peterson, R. (1992) Mental accounting and categorization, *Organizational Behavior and Human Decision Processes*, 51, 92–117.

Johnson, E., Hershey, J., Meszaros, J., & Kunreuther, H. (1993) Framing, probability distortions and insurance decisions, *Journal of Risk and Uncertainty*, 7, 35–51.

Johnson-Laird, P. (1983) *Mental Models*. Cambridge, MA: Harvard University Press.

Kahneman, D. (2000) Preface to choices, values, frames. In D. Kahneman and A. Tversky (eds.), *Choices, Values and Frames* (pp. ix–xvii). New York: Russell Sage Foundation & Cambridge University Press.

Kahneman, D., Knetsch, J. L., & Thaler, R. (1990) Experimental tests of the endowment effect and the Coase theorem, *Journal of Political Economy*, 98, 1325–48.

Kahneman, D. & Tversky, A. (1979) Prospect theory: An analysis of decision under risk, *Econometrica*, 47, 263–91.

Kahneman, D. & Tversky, A. (1984) Choices, values, and frames, *American Psychologist*, 39, 341–50.

Knetsch, J. (1989) The endowment effect and the evidence of nonreversible indifference curves, *American Economic Review*, 79, 1277–84.

Minsky, M. (1975) A framework for presenting knowledge. In P. Winston (ed.), *The Psychology of Computer Visions*. New York, NY: McGraw-Hill.

O'Curry, S. (2001) Income source effects. Unpublished working paper, DePaul University.

O'Gorman, J. (1998) *ABC of Architecture*. Philadelphia: University of Pennsylvania Press.

Pelham, B., Sumarta, T., & Myaskovsky, L. (1994) The easy path from many to much: The numerosity heuristic, *Cognitive Psychology*, 26, 103–33.

Prelec, D. & Loewenstein, G. (1998) The red and the black: Mental accounting of savings and debt, *Marketing Science*, 17, 4–28.

Raghubir, P. & Srivastava, J. (2002) Effect of face value on product valuation in foreign currencies, *Journal of Consumer Research*, 29(3), 335–47.

Read, D., Loewenstein, G., & Rabin, M. (1999) Choice bracketing, *Journal of Risk and Uncertainty*, 19, 171–97.

Samuelson, P. (1963) Risk and uncertainty: A fallacy of large numbers, *Scientia*, 98, 108–13.

Samuelson, W. & Zeckhauser, R. (1988) Status quo bias in decision making, *Journal of Risk and Uncertainty*, 1, 7–59.

Schoemaker, P. & Russo, J. (2001) Managing frames to make better decisions. In S. Hoch and H. Kunreuther (eds.), *Wharton on Making Decisions* (pp. 131–55). New York: John Wiley & Sons.

Shafir, E. (1993) Choosing versus rejecting: Why some options are both better and worse than others, *Memory and Cognition*, 21(4), 546–56.

Shafir, E., Diamond, P., & Tversky, A. (1997) Money illusion, *Quarterly Journal of Economics*, 112, 342–74.

Simonson, I. (1989) Choice based on reasons: The case of attraction and compromise effects, *Journal of Consumer Research*, 16, 158–74.

Slovic, P. (1972) From Shakespeare to Simon: Speculations and some evidence about man's ability to process information, *Oregon Research Institute Monograph*, 12(2), Eugene, OR.

Soman, D. (2001) Effects of payment mechanism on spending behavior: The role of rehearsal and immediacy of payments, *Journal of Consumer Research*, 27, 460–74.

Soman, D. & Cheema, A. (2001) The effect of windfall gains on the sunk cost effect, *Marketing Letters*, 12(1), 51–62.

Soman, D. & Gourville, J. (2001) Transaction decoupling: How price bundling affects the decision to consume, *Journal of Marketing Research*, 38, 30–44.

Soman, D., Wertenbroch, K., & Chattopadhyay, A. (2003) Currency numerosity effects on the perceived value of transactions. Unpublished working paper, Hong Kong University of Science and Technology.

Thaler, R. (1980) Toward a positive theory of consumer choice, *Journal of Economic Behavior and Organization*, 1, 39–60.

Thaler, R. (1985) Mental accounting and consumer choice, *Marketing Science*, 4, 199–214.

Thaler, R. (1999) Mental accounting matters, *Journal of Behavioral Decision Making*, 12, 183–206.

Thaler, R. & Johnson, E. (1990) Gambling with the house money and trying to break even: The effects of prior outcomes on risky choice, *Management Science*, 36, 643–60.

Tversky, A. & Kahneman, D. (1974) Judgment under uncertainty: Heuristics and biases, *Science*, 185(4157), 1124–31.

Tversky, A. & Kahneman, D. (1981) The framing of decisions and the psychology of choice, *Science*, 211(4481), 453–8.

Tversky, A. & Kahneman, D. (1986) Rational choice and the framing of decisions, *Journal of Business*, 59, 251–78.

Tversky, A. & Kahneman, D. (1991) Loss aversion in riskless choice: A reference-dependent model, *Quarterly Journal of Economics*, 106, 1039–61.

von Neumann, J. & Morgenstern, O. (1947) *Theory of Games and Economic Behavior* (2nd edn.). Princeton, NJ: Princeton University Press.

20

Decision Under Risk

George Wu, Jiao Zhang, and Richard Gonzalez

Introduction

Most decisions, whether choices to purchase flood insurance, invest overseas, pursue an experimental medical treatment, or steal a base, involve risk. Purchasing insurance is sensible if you believe a flood will happen, but a bad idea if you are convinced it won't. The study of risky decision making has addressed two broad questions. How *should* individuals behave when faced with a risky choice like the ones above? How *do* individuals behave when faced with a risky choice? The first question is *normative*; the second, *descriptive*.[1] Although the first question is clearly important, our aim in this chapter is to provide answers to the second question.

The study of risky decision making has a long, distinguished, and interdisciplinary history. The list of contributors include some of the most prominent figures in economics and psychology, including several Nobel Prize-winners in Economics, and these ideas have in turn been applied with great success to business, law, medicine, political science, and public policy. We hope to give the reader an overview of the exciting developments made by these researchers and others. In particular, the goals of this chapter are fourfold:

1 survey the evolution of questions asked by researchers of risky decision making;
2 review the major intellectual contributions;
3 summarize the present state of knowledge; and
4 offer a research agenda for the next generation of research in the field.

We first distinguish between *risk* and *uncertainty* (Knight, 1921). Risk defines decision situations in which the probabilities are *objective* or given, such as betting on a flip of a fair coin, a roll of a balanced die, or a spin of a roulette wheel. Uncertainty defines situations in which the probabilities are *subjective* (i.e., the decision maker must estimate or infer the probabilities), like the decision to invest overseas and the other examples given above. Although most important decisions clearly involve uncertainty rather than risk, we focus primarily on risk in this chapter. We do so, first, because risk is the simpler case and because there is considerably more empirical evidence on risk than uncertainty. But more importantly, we argue that our understanding of the simpler situation of risk readily extends to the more realistic case of uncertainty. In the latter sections of this review, we discuss how research on risk helps us understand decisions under uncertainty.

Before we begin, we point to the many excellent reviews of this sort that have been written over the years (e.g., Camerer, 1995; Edwards, 1954, 1961; Fox & See, 2003; Luce, 2000; Machina, 1987; Mellers, Schwartz, & Cooke, 1998; Schoemaker, 1982; Starmer, 2000). We encourage those interested in the field to read these reviews; they provide a perspective of how the field has evolved over the years, and also highlight the differences and similarities between how economists and psychologists have approached this field.

Expected Utility

We begin by reviewing the classical model of decision under risk, *expected utility* (EU) theory. Consider a gamble that gives p_i chance at x_i, which we represent $(p_1, x_1; \ldots; p_n, x_n)$. The expected utility of this gamble is $\sum p_i u(x_i)$, where $u(x_i)$ captures the "utility" of receiving outcome x_i. In expected utility, the burden of explaining risk attitudes falls completely on the shape of the utility function. Risk-averse behavior, such as the purchase of insurance, requires that the utility function be concave, while risk-seeking behavior, such as buying a lottery ticket, is explained by convexity of the utility function. Thus, it is difficult for EU to explain why an individual simultaneously purchases insurance and lottery tickets. This individual's utility function must be concave for some wealth levels and convex for other wealth levels (Friedman & Savage, 1948). Nevertheless, economics usually assumes that decision makers are risk-averse, the primary justification being diminishing marginal utility: a dollar to a pauper is considerably more useful than a dollar to Bill Gates (e.g., Varian, 1992).

Bernoulli (1738) proposed expected utility in the eighteenth century as a resolution of the famous St. Petersburg Paradox. The St. Petersburg gamble is a prospect that offers a $1/2^n$ chance at $\$2^n$ for $n = 1, \ldots, \infty$. Although this gamble has an infinite expected value, most people would pay less than $10 for this gamble. Many concave utility functions, including logarithmic and power utility functions, impose finite bounds on the maximum an individual would pay for the St. Petersburg bet. The contribution of Bernoulli, however, went far beyond reconciling this example. Bernoulli rejected expected value as a criterion for making risky choices, arguing more generally that two people with different desires and different wealth levels should not necessarily value the identical gamble equally. Although it is unclear whether Bernoulli was making a descriptive argument or normative argument, the generalization of expected value to expected utility was introduced and has remained important to this day.

Expected utility took off in the 1940s and 1950s when von Neumann and Morgenstern axiomatized the model in their *Games and Economic Behavior* (von Neumann & Morgenstern, 1947). Whereas Bernoulli assumed the EU representation, von Neumann and Morgenstern provided an axiomatic system: a set of conditions that were necessary and sufficient for expected utility. Axioms have a descriptive as well as normative benefit: they decompose a complex theory into smaller pieces, each of which can be tested empirically or scrutinized as normative principles. The most important axiom became known as the *Independence Axiom* or *Substitution Axiom*, and was reformulated by Marschak (1950) and Samuelson (1952). The basic idea of the axiom is straightforward. If you like gamble A more than gamble B, then you should prefer the mixture of A and some other gamble C (in some probabilistic proportion) to the mixture of B and C (in the same probabilistic proportion). The Independence Axiom can be stated formally: if $A > B$ then $pA + (1 - p)C > pB + (1 - p)C$, where ">" stands for the binary relation "is preferred to" and $pA + (1 - p)C$ denotes a probabilistic mixture of A and C. To illustrate, suppose you prefer a 0.50 chance at \$100 (A) to a 0.80 chance at \$50 (B). The independence axiom requires that you prefer a 0.25 chance at \$100 to a 0.40 chance at \$50, since these gambles are derived by mixing the antecedent gambles with \$0 for sure (C) in equal proportions.

In the early 1950s, there was considerable debate about the normative status of EU and the Independence Axiom and how to interpret EU's utility function (Ellsberg, 1954; Friedman & Savage, 1952). When this debate finished, it was widely believed that EU was a compelling normative model (Savage, 1954). Indeed, in its abstract form, the Independence Axiom is intuitively compelling. Given a choice between $pA + (1 - p)C$ and $pB + (1 - p)C$, the decision maker receives A or B if an unfair coin comes up heads, and C if the unfair coin comes up tails. If the coin comes up tails, it doesn't matter what you chose. If the coin comes up heads, you should choose A if you like A more than B, and B otherwise. Thus, this logic argues that choosing between A and B is the same as choosing between $pA + (1 - p)C$ and $pB + (1 - p)C$.

Subjective Expected Utility

In 1954, Savage published the influential *The Foundations of Statistics*. The major contribution was an axiomatic system that extended expected utility from risk to uncertainty. In uncertain situations, probabilities are not given, and outcomes depend on which event obtains. Consider a prospect, $(E_1, x_1; \ldots; E_n, x_n)$, that offers x_i if event E_i occurs. The *subjective expected utility* (SEU) of this prospect is given by $\sum \rho(E_i)u(x_i)$, where $u(\cdot)$ is a utility function as in standard expected utility and $\rho(\cdot)$ is a *subjective probability measure* that obeys the standard axioms of probabilities. Thus, SEU is the natural generalization of EU from risk to uncertainty.

The critical axiom is Savage's "Sure Thing Principle." The sure thing principle shares the same basic intuition as the Independence Axiom, which we illustrate with the following example. Consider a choice between A and B in Table 20.1, where the outcome of the prospects depends on what event is realized:

Table 20.1

	E_1	E_2	E_3
A	100	0	0
B	0	100	0

A preference for A over B can be interpreted as a belief that E_1 is more likely to occur than E_2. Since E_3 shares a common outcome, 0, this event is irrelevant for the choice between A and B. Thus, a decision maker should have the same preferences if, as in Table 20.2, we substitute 50 (or any other outcome) for 0 in E_3:

Table 20.2

	E_1	E_2	E_3
A'	100	0	50
B'	0	100	50

Despite the normative appeal of the independence axiom and the sure thing principle, EU and SEU would soon be challenged as reasonable descriptive models of decision under risk and uncertainty.

The Pre-prospect Theory Era

Edwards' review paper

Are the elegant normative frameworks of Savage and von Neumann and Morgenstern descriptively accurate models? In a remarkable review of the decision-making literature written only seven years after von Neumann and Morgenstern axiomatized EU, Edwards (1954) summarized the empirical and theoretical literature. There was already mounting empirical evidence that the normative theory of expected utility was descriptively inadequate. One pressure point came from the field, a need to explain the simultaneous purchase of insurance and lottery tickets. There were some impressive attempts to salvage the expected utility framework so that it could conform to this observation. For example, in a famous paper, Friedman and Savage (1948) attempted to account for the simultaneous purchase of insurance and gambling by introducing a utility function that had regions of convexity and regions of concavity (the former accounting for the risk-seeking behavior of gambling and the latter accounting for the risk-averse behavior of insurance purchase).

Another set of attacks came from the laboratory. Preston and Baratta (1948) found preliminary evidence that people distort given probabilities: small probabilities are over-weighted and large probabilities are underweighted. This study, as well as other early empirical endeavors (e.g., Mosteller & Nogee, 1951; Davidson, Suppes, & Siegel, 1957) had various methodological problems, making it difficult to make inferences about the underlying mechanisms. These experiments were the best of the lot, leading Edwards (1954, p. 403) to remark of the others: "Such experiments are too seldom adequately controlled, and are almost never used as a basis for larger-scale, well-designed experiments."

Looking back, it is surprising how much was already known both empirically and the-oretically by 1954. It is also surprising how far away researchers and theoreticians were from a comprehensive model of decision making under risk and uncertainty. Many of the major empirical results that characterized research in the 1980s were already known, but the lack of a proper theoretical framework kept researchers from fully understanding these results. As a child may misunderstand the clues given to her about where the last Easter egg is hidden, the researchers at the time were misled by many of the empirical results that were available – not merely because of the methodological deficiencies, but also because of the limited types of inferences the existing theoretical models permitted.

Edwards identified the fundamental problem of decision-making research, "[the] development of a satisfactory scale of utility of money and of subjective probability" (p. 403). Indeed, Edwards also anticipated the theoretical problem that would character-ize much research in the last 15 years: the composition rule that combines utility with distorted probabilities. In Edwards' words, "it seems very difficult to design an experi-ment to discover that law of combination" (p. 400).

The Allais and Ellsberg Paradoxes

Allais (1953) posed the first major direct challenge to expected utility. He collected data at a Paris Colloquium in 1952 that was attended by a number of distinguished researchers interested in the foundations of decision theory. One of the problems Allais presented in-volved two choice pairs. The first pair was a choice between (A) $1 million for sure, and (B) a 0.10 chance at $5 million and 0.89 chance at $1 million. (For simplicity, the 0.01 chance at $0 with B is implicit.) The second pair involved a choice between (C) a 0.11 chance at $1 million, and (D) a 0.10 chance at $5 million. The modal choices of A and D are inconsistent with EU. This example became famously known as the *Allais paradox*.

The intuition behind these two choices is the following. In the first choice, the sure thing of $1 million is highly attractive, thus it is not worth risking a chance of nothing for the possibility of winning $5 million. In the second choice, the two probabilities (0.10 and 0.11) appear indistinguishable relative to the difference between $5 million and $1 million (e.g., Slovic & Tversky, 1974). Choosing A and D violates the independence condition. Note that A and B share a "common consequence" (a 0.89 chance at winning $1 million), while C and D share a different common consequence (a 0.89 chance at winning $0). Expected utility requires that a change in a common consequence not alter preference. So, if a decision maker chooses A over B, she should choose C over D. It is interesting that no careful empirical evidence for this choice pattern was collected for over 10 years. MacCrimmon (1965) collected data for his PhD thesis (see also MacCrimmon, 1968), and replications were conducted by others (e.g., Morrison, 1967; Slovic & Tversky, 1974).

There was an analogous violation of the sure thing principle in the domain of uncertainty. Ellsberg (1961) proposed a famous problem that became known as the *Ellsberg paradox*. Ellsberg did not publish data in that paper (although data appeared in his Harvard PhD thesis), but the violation was soon empirically verified by Becker and Brownson (1964) and then many others (see the review by Camerer & Weber, 1992).

Imagine an urn with 90 balls, 30 of which are red, and 60 of which are black or yellow in an unknown proportion (i.e., perhaps 0 black and 60 yellow, 60 black and 0 yellow, or any combination in between). Prospects link payments to whether a red, black, or yellow ball is drawn. Option *A* pays $100 for red (and $0 for black or yellow), while *B* pays $100 for black (and $0 for red or yellow). Now consider a variation on the above problem where the winnings for the yellow ball in both options are converted to $100 instead of $0. You win $100 with *C* on red or yellow, and $100 with *D* on black or yellow.

The predominant choice in the first pair is *A*, while the modal choice in the second pair is *D*. In both cases, subjects prefer betting on known probabilities to unknown or vague probabilities (*A* offers $100 with a known chance of 1/3, while the chance of $100 with *B* may be anywhere between 0 and 2/3). However, these choices are incompatible with the sure thing principle. As Ellsberg described the pattern, "The first pattern, for example, implies that the subject prefers to bet 'on' red rather than 'on' black; and he also prefers to bet 'against' red rather than 'against' black" (p. 654).

Prospect Theory

Kahneman and Tversky's (1979) "Prospect theory: An analysis of decision under risk" is the second most cited paper in economics during the period, 1975–2000 (Coupé, in press; Laibson & Zeckhauser, 1998).[2] The paper's success is probably due to its unique combination of simplicity and depth. Kahneman and Tversky presented convincing empirical demonstrations that highlighted some general descriptive deficiencies with expected utility, as well as a powerful formal theory for organizing these demonstrations. Although the Allais paradox was now 25 years old, very little data existed challenging expected utility, and there were no theoretical alternatives to the classic model.

The classic model of decision under risk assumes that individuals are generally risk-averse (perhaps because of diminishing marginal utility). However, Kahneman and Tversky demonstrated that people are risk-averse *and* risk-seeking and that the pattern of risk attitudes can be organized in a remarkably simple manner. They found that 84 percent of subjects preferred $500 for sure to a 0.50 chance at $1,000, but 72 percent preferred a 0.001 chance at $5,000 to $5 for sure. The first choice demonstrates risk aversion for moderate probabilities, the second risk seeking for small probabilities. When choices involve losses, the pattern reversed: 69 percent chose a 0.50 chance at losing $1,000 to losing $500 for sure, and 83 percent chose losing $5 for sure over a 0.001 chance at

Table 20.3

	Small probabilities	*Medium to large probabilities*
Gains	Risk-seeking	Risk-averse
Losses	Risk-averse	Risk-seeking

losing $5,000. For losses, subjects were risk-seeking for moderate probabilities and risk-averse for small probabilities.

These data are typical of a more general pattern, called the *reflection effect*: preferences tend to reverse when the sign of the outcomes is changed. This pattern has become known as the *four-fold pattern of risk attitudes* and can be summarized as in Table 20.3 (Tversky & Kahneman, 1992).

Kahneman and Tversky also presented two direct violations of expected utility, the common-consequence effect and common-ratio effect. Expected utility can explain the four-fold pattern by positing a specific utility function, but doing so would strain the theory (Rabin, 2000). The common-consequence and common-ratio effects are examples of a different approach: a direct test of one of the axioms underlying expected utility. A violation of any of the EU axioms falsifies the EU model – there can be no utility function that can accommodate the pattern.

We begin with the *common consequence effect*, an example that follows the same basic schema as Allais' original demonstration. Most subjects preferred $2,400 for sure to a 0.33 chance $2,500, a 0.66 chance at $2,400, and a 0.01 chance at $0, but preferred a 0.33 chance at $2,500 to a 0.34 chance to $2,400. To show that no utility function can reconcile this pattern, it suffices to observe that the first choice under EU reduces to $0.34u(2,400) > 0.33u(2,500)$, while the second choice simplifies to $0.34u(2,400) < 0.33u(2,500)$. Indeed, this example was constructed to test the independence axiom directly. One pair is derived from the other pair by substituting a 0.66 chance at $2,400 for a 0.66 chance at $0 (hence the name common-consequence effect).

Why do the majority of subjects violate expected utility? The reasoning may go something like this: "In the first choice, it is not worth sacrificing a sure thing for a chance at getting a slightly better outcome. In the second choice, neither gamble is a sure thing. Since 0.33 and 0.34 are very similar, it is worth going for the better outcome, $2,500." This pattern demonstrates the *certainty effect*: subjects are willing to pay a large premium to avoid a small chance of receiving nothing.

In the *common-ratio effect*, subjects chose $3,000 for sure to a 0.80 chance at $4,000, but a 0.20 chance at $4,000 to a 0.25 chance at $3,000. This pattern also contradicts expected utility, since the first choice implies $u(3,000) > 0.8u(4,000)$, but the second implies $0.25u(3,000) < 0.2u(4,000)$. The independence axiom is violated in this example as well since the second pair is constructed by mixing a 25 percent chance of the first pair with a 75 percent chance of receiving $0. The effect gets its name because the ratio of the probability of winning $4,000 to the probability of winning $3,000 is the same for both choices.

Kahneman and Tversky proposed a formal theory to explain the four-fold pattern, common-consequence effect, common-ratio effect, and a slew of other demonstrations. The major components were a *value function* and a *probability weighting function*. In expected utility theory, the utility function is defined over final wealth states, an assumption that is known as asset integration. In contrast, the value function in prospect theory, $v(\cdot)$, is defined over changes in wealth rather than absolute wealth levels. The function is concave for gains, convex for losses, and exhibits "loss aversion", i.e., the function is steeper for losses than gains (see Chapter 19, this volume).

The probability weighting function, $\pi(\cdot)$, captures how different probability levels contribute to the evaluation of a gamble. Tversky and Kahneman presented a schematic weighting function that overweights small probabilities, and underweights medium and large probabilities. They also suggested that there might be a discontinuity at the end points of 0 and 1: differences between 0 and 1 either would be ignored, or there would be a categorical distinction between 0 ("impossibility") and some small probability ("possibility") and a distinction between 1 ("certainty") and some large probability close to 1 ("uncertainty"). The weighting function also exhibits *subcertainty*, $\pi(p) + \pi(1 - p) < 1$. Roughly speaking, the weighting function is more below the identity line (for moderate and high probabilities) than it is above the identity line (for low probabilities).

Prospect theory combines the two functions as follows. Consider a gamble $(p, x; q, y; 1 - p - q, 0)$, where $p + q < 1$ and x and y may both be positive, both negative, or one positive and one negative. The value of such a gamble is given by $U(p, x; q, y) = \pi(p)v(x) + \pi(q)v(y)$. This functional form explains the four-fold pattern of risk attitudes, common-consequence effect, and common-ratio effect in terms of the qualitative properties on $v(\cdot)$ and $\pi(\cdot)$ discussed above. This form also has the same basic structure as expected value and expected utility. Expected utility is the sum of utility values weighted by probabilities. Prospect theory generalized this notion by summing utility values weighted by transformed probabilities or *decision weights*.

Recall that EU had a hard time reconciling simultaneous purchasing of insurance and gambling because the utility function had to do all the heavy lifting. The burden of explaining risk attitudes now falls on the value function and the probability weighting function. In prospect theory, insurance purchasing and gambling are explained by the overweighting of small probabilities. Insurance purchasing is risk-averse behavior: thus overweighting of small probabilities has to be large enough to overcome the convexity of the value function in losses. Similarly, gambling represents risk seeking, which is predicted if overweighting of small probabilities is sufficient to overcome the concavity of the value function in gains.

We return to Edwards' (1954) question about how to separate distortions of value from distortions of probabilities. The prospect theory representation permits independent inferences about the value and weighting function. For example, restrictions on the weighting function can be inferred from the common-consequence effect problems, and restrictions on the value function (i.e., concavity and loss aversion) can be inferred from other examples presented in their paper.[3]

It is a surprise to many people that many of the ideas from prospect theory existed in previous literatures. In a remarkable paper, Markowitz (1952, p. 154) proposed a utility function that defined utility as changes from present wealth as an attempt to capture the observation that individuals at just about every wealth were insurance buying gamblers. Preston and Baratta (1948) investigated choices involving varying probability levels and found a pattern remarkably similar to that captured by prospect theory's weighting function (see also Mosteller & Nogee, 1951; Davidson et al., 1957). Edwards (1953) documented probability preferences, preferences to bet on certain probabilities when faced with bets of equal expected value, and argued that descriptive models needed to take account of the nonlinear impact probabilities have on decisions. Finally, MacCrimmon (1968) and MacCrimmon and Larsson (1979) presented similar demonstrations of the common-ratio and common-consequence violations, and Williams (1966) documented rejection of fair gambles, consistent with loss aversion (see, also, Mosteller & Nogee, 1951; Slovic & Lichtenstein, 1968, p.10).

Thus, many of the pieces of prospect theory, taken alone, were not novel. However, the reputation of prospect theory as one of the most important papers in social science is nevertheless completely deserved. The paper took ideas that had been around, some for as long as 30 years, scattered in different literatures and thought to be unrelated, and constructed a formal model in which all the elements worked together. The paper also produced compelling demonstrations (some extensions of old findings and some new predictions such as the isolation and pseudo-certainty effects, and the rejection of probabilistic insurance). Even those with no interest in formal theory could nevertheless understand why expected utility was an unsuitable descriptive model and what was required of an adequate descriptive model. Most importantly, the view that the Allais paradox was an isolated problem for expected utility was no longer tenable.

The Post-prospect Theory Era

An overview

Kahneman and Tversky attacked the independence axiom and expected utility in an elegant, coherent, and convincing manner. Since the Allais paradox could no longer be considered an isolated anomaly, prospect theory forced economists to consider EU violations seriously. In this section, we review the quarter-century of research following prospect theory. The phase can best be understood as an ongoing dialogue between alternative models to EU and ingenious tests conducted to discriminate among these alternative models.

In hindsight, the post-prospect theory models appear to be motivated by two different concerns, those of economists and those of psychologists. In general, economists strove for a descriptive theory of decision under risk that was elegant, general, and mathematically tractable. This strategy was practical, as much as aesthetic. Expected utility had been applied with great success to many important areas of economics, such as game theory and information economics (e.g., Pratt, 1964; Rothschild & Stiglitz, 1970). The new models relaxed the independence axiom and hence are "generalizations" of EU in the sense that EU is a special case of these models. The common-consequence and common-ratio effect violations presented in the last section posed a minimum standard for a set of new models.

Why did theorists need an alternative to prospect theory when prospect theory explained the basic violations just fine? There are at least three reasons. Many theorists disliked the prospect theory representation since it admitted possible violations of stochastic dominance: $(p, x; q, x - \varepsilon)$ could exceed $(p + q, x)$, even though the second gamble stochastically dominates the first gamble (Fishburn, 1978).[4] To avoid this problem, Kahneman and Tversky proposed an editing operation where subjects spotted dominated alternatives. Second, theorists wanted to have a model that included EU as a special case. Finally, prospect theory was limited to two non-zero outcomes.

In contrast, psychologists were generally more concerned with explaining the underlying psychological process. Some alternative models were cognitive, while others considered personality and motivational factors (e.g., Birnbaum & Stegner's (1979) configural weight theory and Lopes' (1987) aspiration-level theory). These models tended to have more free parameters than prospect theory, and therefore were more flexible but less tractable and parsimonious.

At the end of these 25 years of research, prospect theory stands out as the best descriptive model. However, prospect theory, too, evolved as part of this dialogue. One important fruit of this stream of theoretical and empirical work was a refinement of prospect theory, cumulative prospect theory (CPT; Tversky & Kahneman, 1992). Although original prospect theory (OPT) was groundbreaking, it had clear limitations, some of which were acknowledged in the original paper (for a historical perspective, see Kahneman, 2000). Not only did cumulative prospect theory overcome the potential violations of dominance that some saw as a flaw of OPT, CPT generalized prospect theory to apply to an arbitrary number of outcomes, and uncertainty as well as risk. We discuss details of CPT later.

One simple device greatly facilitated the dialogue, the probability triangle or simplex, used originally by Marschak (1950) and later adopted by Machina (1982). The unit triangle provided a common "language" and platform for understanding the implications of different models and visualizing and organizing empirical findings. Models could be understood in terms of restrictions placed on the curvature, slope, and fanning property of the indifference curves in the triangle.[5] Figure 20.1 illustrates indifference curves for some of the major theories.

Alternatives to prospect theory

Since the common-consequence and common-ratio effects violate the independence axiom, an adequate descriptive model of decision under risk needs to "relax" the independence axiom in some respect. Many generalized EU models took the strategy of replacing the independence axiom with a weaker form. We discuss several different families of model that were advanced in the 1980s.

Machina (1982) took a non-axiomatic approach. EU requires that indifference curves be linear and parallel. Machina suggested an ingenious hypothesis called the *fanning-out*

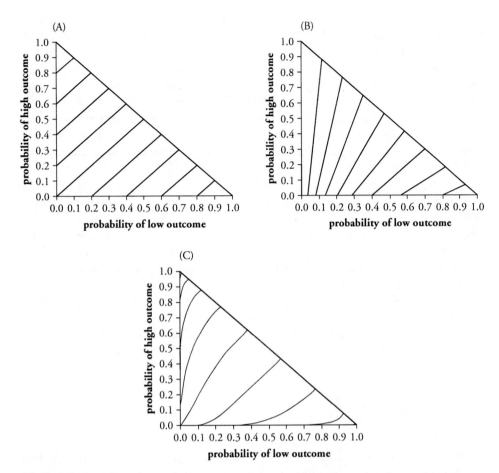

Figure 20.1 The probability triangle is used to depict gambles with at most three outcomes

The *x* axis captures the probability of the lowest outcome, the *y* axis the probability of the highest outcome. Shown are indifference curves for (A) expected utility theory; (B) weighted utility with indifference curves that "fan out"; (C) rank-dependent utility. All gambles on an indifference curve yield the same utility.

hypothesis. Indifference curves no longer had to be linear or parallel, but just needed to "fan out". Fanning out requires that decision makers became more risk-averse as lotteries improve in the sense of first-order stochastic dominance. Graphically, fanning-out hypothesis posits that the indifference curves in the unit triangle become steeper when moved in the northwest direction (see Figure 20.1b). Fanning out of indifference curves is consistent with the basic common-consequence and common-ratio effects.

One family of models replaced the independence axiom with a weaker form called *betweenness*. Betweenness requires that a probabilistic mixture of two lotteries should be in the middle of the two lotteries in preference, i.e., for any two lotteries A and B: if $A \geq B$ then $A \geq pA + (1 - p)B \geq B$. Betweenness is intuitively appealing as well as pragmatic: some important economic applications only require betweenness and not the full force of the independence axiom (Crawford, 1990).

A number of betweenness models were proposed, including weighted utility theory (Chew & MacCrimmon, 1979; Chew, 1983), implicit weighted utility theory (Dekel, 1986), skew-symmetric bilinear utility theory (Fishburn, 1984), Neilson's (1992) boundary effect hypothesis, and disappointment-aversion theory (Gul, 1991). Graphically, betweenness requires that indifference curves in the probability triangle be straight lines (as with EU), but not necessarily parallel (as required by EU) (see Figures 20.1a and 20.1b). With appropriate parameters, these models can accommodate the basic common-consequence and common-ratio effects. These models mainly differ in the fanning properties of the indifference curves, either imposing uniform fanning (all fanning in or all fanning out) or mixed fanning.

Rank-dependent models are variants of prospect theory. In prospect theory, there is a nonlinear transformation of outcomes, as well as probabilities. Original prospect theory permits violations of dominance or monotonicity, a problem that Kahneman and Tversky recognized and dealt with in the editing phase (but see Tversky & Kahneman, 1986). *Rank-dependent* utility (RDU) was an ingenious way of allowing probability distortions, like prospect theory, while prohibiting violations of dominance. The basic idea is to transform *cumulative* probabilities instead of individual probabilities (Quiggin, 1982; see also, Luce, 1988; Yaari, 1987). A prospect, $(p, x; q, y)$, where $x > y$, would be valued by $\pi(p)v(x) + [\pi(p + q) - \pi(p)]v(y)$. The *decision weight*, the amount that a particular outcome is weighted, depends on the probability of that outcome as well as the rank of that outcome in the gamble. More generally, the value of a prospect, $(p_1, x_1; \ldots; p_n, x_n)$, where $x_i > x_{i+1}$, is given by:

$$\sum_{i=1}^{n} \left(\pi \left(\sum_{j=1}^{i} p_j \right) - \pi \left(\sum_{j=1}^{i-1} p_j \right) \right) v(x_i).$$

In this general form, the decision weight for an outcome x_i is the probability weighting function applied to the probability of receiving at least outcome x_i minus the weighting function applied to the probability of receiving at least outcome x_{i-1} (for a useful introduction, see Diecidue & Wakker, 2001).[6,7]

Regret theory took a different approach to generalizing EU. One carrier of value is *regret*, the comparison between the outcome received and the outcome that would have been received under some other choice. Bell (1982) and Loomes and Sugden (1982) independently demonstrated how particular forms of regret theory could explain a wide range of phenomena, including purchasing of insurance and lotteries, the reflection effect, the Allais paradox, probabilistic insurance, and preference reversals. (We do not review tests of regret theory here, however see Starmer, 2000.)

Critical empirical evidence

A slew of tests were designed to discriminate between the various models. The most discerning tests either tested general axioms such as betweenness or general features of preferences such as the fanning-out hypothesis. This approach was efficient: choice patterns inconsistent with these axioms or features ruled out a whole family of models.

Machina's (1982) hypothesis that indifference curves fan out everywhere in the unit triangle stimulated many empirical tests. Conlisk (1989) generalized the Allais paradox and the common-consequence effect. He found that subjects preferred (0.10,$5M;0.89,$1M) over (0.20,$5M;0.78,$1M), but preferred (0.98,$5M) over (0.88,$5M;0.11,$1M). This pattern violates fanning out, since preferences become more risk-seeking as gambles are improved. This particular problem generalizes the common-consequence effect in the following sense. In Allais' example and Kahneman and Tversky's (1979) original demonstration, probability mass is shifted from the lowest to the middle outcome, which corresponds to a horizontal movement of gamble pairs in the unit triangle. Here, the shift is from the middle to the highest outcome, corresponding to vertical movement of gambles pairs. Similar results showing that indifference curves that fan in vertically are found in a variety of studies (Battalio, Kagel, & Jiranyakul, 1990; Camerer, 1989; Starmer & Sugden, 1989; Wu & Gonzalez, 1998). Prelec (1990) demonstrated fanning in in a very different part of the triangle. His subjects preferred (0.02,$20,000) to (0.01, $30,000) but (0.01,$30,000;0.32,$20,000) to (0.34,$20,000). Wu and Gonzalez (1996) found similar patterns of fanning-in along the bottom edge.

Empirical evidence showing mixed fanning within the unit triangle ruled out models assuming uniform fanning out or uniform fanning in, such as weighted utility theory, implicit weighted utility theory, and Machina's (1982) fanning-out hypothesis. Other models allowed mixed fanning, such as Gul's disappointment aversion theory (1991), Neilson's (1992) boundary effect hypothesis, rank-dependent utility, and prospect theory.

Another set of studies investigated betweenness. If betweenness is violated, all betweenness models are falsified. Prelec (1990) documented a stunning violation of betweenness. He found that 94 percent of subjects preferred $A = (0.17,$20,000)$ to $C = (0.17,$30,000)$ but 82 percent of subjects preferred $B = (0.01,$30,000;0.32,$20,000)$ to $A = (0.34,$20,000)$. Since $B = \frac{1}{17}C + \frac{16}{17}A$, betweenness requires that B should lie between A and C in preference. Other empirical tests with gambles located in the southeast corner found similar patterns (Battalio et al., 1990; Camerer, 1989, 1992; Camerer & Ho, 1994). Prelec offered a very intuitive way of interpreting his finding. People may find trading a 2 percent chance of $20,000 for a 1 percent chance of $30,000 attractive, thus choose B over A. However, they do not like taking 17 such trades, which means exchanging a 34 percent chance of $20,000 for a 17 percent chance of $30,000.

The direction of violations is also useful for distinguishing between models. Violation of betweenness could be due to either quasi-concave preferences (i.e., convexity of indifference curves) or quasi-convex preferences (i.e., concavity of indifference curves), indicating a preference for or against randomization, respectively (Camerer, 1992). Prelec's example constitutes quasi-concave preferences. Quasi-convex preferences have been found for gambles located in the northwest corner (Battalio et al., 1990; Camerer, 1989, 1992; Camerer & Ho, 1994), while both quasi-concavity (Chew & Waller, 1986; Gigliotti & Sopher, 1993) and quasi-convexity (Conlisk, 1989) are found in the southwest corner of the triangle. Finally, betweenness violations tend to be weaker for gambles located inside the unit triangle than for gambles on the boundary.

Are any of the models described above consistent with the pattern of mixed fanning and quasi-concave and quasi-convex preferences? An appropriate model needs to be "nonlinear in probability" in order to capture betweenness violations. It turns out that

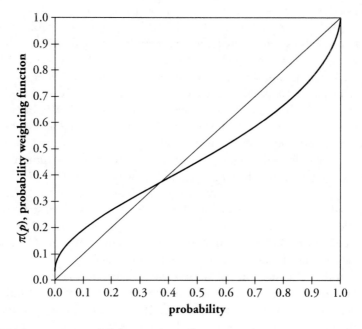

Figure 20.2 A characteristic probability weighting function

betweenness data are consistent with both prospect theory and rank-dependent utility models, assuming an inverse S-shaped weighting function (see Camerer & Ho, 1994). Consider the weighting function depicted in Figure 20.2. The weighting function is concave for small probabilities and convex for medium and large probabilities. This shape generates indifference curves that are convex in the southeast corner, concave in the north corner, and mixed in the south corner (Camerer & Ho, 1994), consistent with the general findings. It also predicts the fanning-in patterns found by Prelec (1990) and Conlisk (1989), located in very different regions (Wu & Gonzalez, 1998). Finally, these models capture the diminished EU violations in the interior of the triangle (see Camerer, 1992).

Refinements of prospect theory

In 1992, Tversky and Kahneman proposed cumulative prospect theory. The new prospect theory used the same basic building blocks as original prospect theory: a value function, defined over gains and losses, and a weighting function that captured probability distortions. The major technical innovation was to use the rank-dependent form to extend prospect theory to an arbitrary number of outcomes and to uncertainty as well as risk. For risk, a separate rank-dependent transformation was applied to the gain and loss portions of a prospect. The weighting function for gains and losses is also possibly sign-dependent. For uncertainty, CPT used a related model that had been developed for uncertainty, Choquet Expected Utility (Gilboa, 1987; Schmeidler, 1989).

The new theory unified the basic shape of the value and weighting function according to one psychophysical principle. Consider the probability weighting function depicted in Figure 20.2. This particular form of the weighting function explains the betweenness violations as well as the fanning patterns discussed in the previous section. For outcomes, concavity of gains and convexity of losses reflects diminishing sensitivity away from the reference point of 0. Concavity of the weighting function for small probabilities and convexity of the weighting function for large probabilities reflects the same principle applied to different reference points: diminishing sensitivity away from the boundaries of 0 (impossibility) and 1 (certainty). Consider three individuals endowed with a 0 chance to win 100, a 0.33 chance to win 100, and a 0.99 chance to win 100. How might these three individuals view a 0.01 chance improvement in the chance of winning? An inverse S-shaped weighting function suggests that individuals are most sensitive to changes near the extremes and relatively insensitive to changes in the middle. Thus, the individuals endowed with a 0 chance to win, and a 0.99 chance to win will view the change much more favorably than the person with a 0.33 chance to win. In weighting function terms, $\pi(0.01) - \pi(0) > \pi(0.34) - \pi(0.33)$, and $\pi(1) - \pi(0.99) > \pi(0.34) - \pi(0.33)$.

Tversky and Kahneman (1992) presented a comprehensive empirical test of the model. Subjects provided cash equivalents for a number of gambles, differing in the probability and magnitude of the highest outcome, and involving gains and losses. The vast majority of subjects exhibited the four-fold pattern of risk attitudes: risk aversion for most gains and low probability losses, and risk seeking for most losses and low probability gains. A parametric regression analysis of the cash equivalents produced an S-shaped value function, and a weighting function of the form of Figure 20.2. Many other studies, using a variety of methodologies, find a similar inverse S-shape (e.g., Abdellaoui, 2000; Bleichrodt & Pinto, 2000; Camerer & Ho, 1994; Tversky & Fox, 1995; Wu & Gonzalez, 1996, 1998). The weighting function is found to intersect the identity line somewhere between $0.30 < p < 0.40$. It is noteworthy that Kahneman and Tversky's original common-consequence effect demonstration used values that approximately maximize the size of the EU violation.

Wu and Gonzalez used a common-consequence schema to produce a non-parametric trace of the weighting function. They started with a choice between (p, x) and (q, y), where $x > y$. Both gambles were improved in increments by the common consequence (r, y), with r increasing throughout the probability range. Consistent with an inverse S-shaped weighting function, they found the percentage of subjects choosing the risky gamble increases and then decreases. For example, 38 percent of subjects preferred (0.05,$240) to (0.07,$200), 65 percent preferred (0.05,$240;0.30,$200) to (0.37,$200), and 39 percent preferred (0.05,$240;0.90,$200) to (0.97,$200).

There have been numerous efforts to parameterize the weighting function. Tversky and Kahneman (1992) assumed a one-parameter form of the weighting function,

$$\pi(p) = \frac{p^\gamma}{\left(p^\gamma + (1-p)^\gamma\right)^{1/\gamma}},$$ and fit this form to cash equivalent data. The fitted form

had the characteristic inverse S-shape, with a crossover point of around $p = 0.39$. Other exercises have produced similar parameter estimates, even though these exercises varied considerably in terms of the data used (choice versus cash equivalent) estimation techniques (nonlinear regression of cash equivalents versus fitting stochastic choice functionals) (see Abdellaoui, 2000; Camerer & Ho, 1994; Tversky & Fox, 1995; Wu & Gonzalez, 1996).

More recently, Gonzalez and Wu (1999) fit a two-parameter weighting function to median data and individual subject data, $\pi(p) = \dfrac{\delta p^{\gamma}}{\delta p^{\gamma} + (1 - p)^{\gamma}}$. The estimated function for median data resembled previous analyses, but there was considerable heterogeneity at the level of individual subjects. This weighting function has two parameters to capture the relative flatness or steepness of the weighting function ("curvature" through γ) and the relative level ("elevation" through δ) of the weighting function. Adding a second parameter did not appreciably improve the fit for the median data, but both parameters were needed to model the heterogeneity of individual subjects. Although all 10 subjects had inverse S-shaped weighting functions, there was considerable variation along the two dimensions. While the majority of subjects exhibited sub-certainty $(\pi(p) + \pi(1 - p) < 1)$, some subjects exhibited super-certainty $(\pi(p) + \pi(1 - p) > 1)$. Some subjects had weighting functions that were close to the identity line, while others had weighting functions that approximated step functions.

The two-parameter weighting function has also proved useful for understanding how literally the reflection effect holds. Tversky and Kahneman (1992) estimated weighting and value functions for gains and losses. The value function had the same coefficient for both gains and losses, $v(x) = x^{.88}$. The weighting function had nearly identical coefficients for gains and losses, $\gamma = 0.61$ for gains and $\gamma = 0.69$ for losses, leading Tversky and Kahneman to conclude that: "the weighting functions for gains and losses are quite close, although the former is slightly more curved than the latter." In a different study using a very different elicitation methodology, Abdellaoui (2000) estimated nearly identical parameters, $\gamma = 0.60$ for gains and $\gamma = 0.70$ for losses. However, Abdellaoui also fitted the two-parameter function used by Gonzalez and Wu (1999) and found significant differences between losses and gains: the weighting function was significantly more elevated for losses $(\delta = 0.84)$ than gains $(\delta = 0.65)$, whereas the curvature parameters were nearly identical. Similar results have been found by Abdellaoui, Vossmann, and Weber (2002). Indeed, a re-analysis of Tversky and Kahneman's (1992) data found the same sign-dependence in elevation. We used Tversky and Kahneman's (1992) median data (Table 20.3) and assumed the two-parameter weighting function and $v(x) = x^{.88}$ for gains and losses. A nonlinear regression produced estimates of $\delta = 0.79$ and $\gamma = 0.60$ for losses and $\delta = 0.88$ and $\gamma = 0.67$ for gains.

Extension to uncertainty

The Allais and Ellsberg Paradoxes led researchers to treat decision under risk and decision under uncertainty differently for many years. More recent evidence suggests a unification of these results. Many of the principles underlying decision under risk apply directly to decision under uncertainty. For example, Tversky and Fox (1995) tested two conditions, lower- and upper-subadditivity conditions, for both risk and uncertainty. Roughly, these conditions can be thought of as capturing the possibility and certainty effects. They found strong support for lower- and upper-subadditivity in both domains, but more subadditivity for uncertainty than risk. The main reason that individuals were less sensitive to uncertainty than risk is that probability judgments were subadditive as well, consistent with support theory (Tversky & Koehler, 1994). This led Tversky and Fox (1995) (see also Fox & Tversky, 1998) to suggest a two-stage model, in which an uncertain prospect (E, x) is valued by $W(E)v(x) = \pi(p(E))v(x)$, where $\pi(\cdot)$ is the probability weighting function for risk, and $p(E)$ is the subjective probability of E.

Tversky and Kahneman (1992) generalized the common consequence effect from risk to uncertainty and found qualitatively identical results. More recently, Wu and Gonzalez (1999) extended concavity and convexity conditions from risk to uncertainty and found a nearly identical U-shaped pattern of risk preferences as Wu and Gonzalez (1996). Thus, it seems that the same general principles apply to risk and uncertainty. Below, however, we discuss some ways that risk and uncertainty differ.

Future Research

In the past ten years, a relatively clear picture of risky decision making and prospect theory has emerged. Violations of expected utility are robust and systematic, and prospect theory seems to explain these violations with the most ease. Basic properties of the value and weighting function, qualitatively as well as quantitatively, can organize these violations, and these basic principles readily extend from risk to uncertainty. Parsimonious parametric forms of prospect theory fit choice data well, at both the aggregate level and at the level of individual subjects.

However, the picture is somewhat incomplete, as some parts of prospect theory have received very little empirical attention. We highlight two of these "loose threads" and suggest some avenues for future research in these areas.

Simplification and evaluation

Kahneman and Tversky (1979) proposed an editing phase, which was designed "to organize and reformulate the options so as to simplify subsequent evaluation and choice" (p. 274). They proposed six operations: coding, combination, segregation, cancellation, simplification, and detection of transparent dominance. Discussion of editing does not appear until the conclusion of Tversky and Kahneman's (1992) revision of prospect theory, and it is tempting to conclude that rank-dependent representation obviates the need for editing operations. However, Tversky and Kahneman conclude with an apt quote: "Theories of choice are at best approximate and incomplete . . . When faced with a complex problem, people employ a variety of heuristic procedures in order to simplify the representation and evaluation of prospects" (p. 317). Below, we discuss some open issues in the processes of simplification and evaluation.

Almost no research exists on how decision makers code and represent gambles. Research on managerial decision making has found that managers tend to focus on the best and worst outcomes (the "upside" and "downside") with almost no attention to the probability of the outcomes (March and Shapira, 1987). Beyond this, while decision makers almost certainly use operations to simplify gambles, it is not well-understood when individuals use within-gamble operations such as combination, or across-gamble operations such as cancellation. Some theories that evoke similarity as an across-gambles operation exist (e.g., Leland, 1998; Rubinstein, 1988), but a more comprehensive theory of editing is out-of-sight at the moment. We suspect that this sort of theorizing is probably the wrong strategy. Instead, we hope that researchers document violations of EU that can be plausibly explained by some editing operation (Wu, 1994). When an ample set of findings have been assembled, it might then be possible to build a more comprehensive theory of editing.

In terms of evaluation of gambles, more research needs to be conducted in two areas: mixed gambles and composition rules. The little research on mixed gambles is particularly surprising since most real-world gambles involve some possibility of gain and some possibility of loss, at least relative from the status quo. Prospect theory and other bilinear models have problems explaining some of the mixed gamble data collected to date (Chechile & Butler, 2000). We hope to see more data of this sort collected, particularly data collected to test axioms that permit separability between gains and losses, such as Tversky and Kahneman's (1992) "double matching axiom."

Finally, original and cumulative prospect theory differ in terms of how the weighting and value functions are combined, i.e., the composition rule used. The overall evidence is mixed about which prospect theory is better in explaining the empirical results. The two prospect theories are identical for prospects with one non-zero outcome, and thus provide the same explanation for the common-ratio effect. The models however diverge for more complicated gambles. Both models can explain the original common-consequence violations, as well as generalizations of the common-consequence violations (e.g., Wu & Gonzalez, 1996, 1998), albeit with different restrictions on the weighting function. Beyond that, there are some patterns that cannot be explained by CPT (Wu, 1994), and some patterns that CPT fits better than OPT (Fennema & Wakker, 1997; Wakker, 2003). In goodness of fit tests using particularly parametric forms of the value and weighting function, the pattern is mixed. OPT sometimes fits aggregate data better (Camerer & Ho, 1994; Wu & Gonzalez, 1996), but CPT fits particular patterns better (Wu & Gonzalez, 1996). Birnbaum and McIntosh (1996) and Birnbaum, Patton, and Lott (1999) present choice patterns that cannot be explained by CPT, although some can be explained by OPT. Gonzalez and Wu (2003) used parameters estimated from two-outcome gambles, where CPT and OPT coincide, to predict three-outcome gambles, where the models diverge. Neither model did particularly well predicting the cash equivalents from the three-outcome gamble holdout sample. OPT tended to overpredict, while CPT tended to underpredict three-outcome gamble cash equivalents. Finally, Wu, Zhang, and Abdellaoui (2004) adapt Abdellaoui's (2002) tradeoff consistency conditions to create a critical test of the two prospect theories. They find that CPT is violated for critical test gambles that do not involve a sure thing, while OPT is violated for gambles that involve a sure thing.

Which composition rule is better is an open question. The mixed results suggest that there may be no general answer. The answer probably ultimately depends on a number of factors, including the components of the choice set (Stewart, Chater, Stott, & Reimers, 2003), and whether editing rules can be applied. Gonzalez and Wu (2003) offer some suggestions about how composition rules may be related to areas of cognition, including attention, information processing, and similarity.

Source preference

How does the evaluation of a gamble that pays $100 with 0.7 chance differ from the evaluation of a prospect that offers $100 if the Yankees win tomorrow's game? The difference between these gambles captures the difference between risk and uncertainty. The research reviewed above suggests that these two choices are qualitatively similar. However, we suggest that there are some differences. Of course, uncertainty is more complicated than risk: decision makers faced with the sports bet must assess the likelihood of a Yankee victory. Tversky and Fox's (1995) two-stage model suggests that individuals judge the probability of a particular event and then transform this judgment via a probability weighting function. Under this simple form, a decision maker who judges the likelihood of a Yankee win to be 0.7 will value the risky gamble and the uncertain gamble the same.

Although the two-stage model is a useful simplification, it fails systematically in some situations. Decision makers may prefer to bet on one source over another, even when the subjective likelihood is equated for the two sources. The clearest example is the Ellsberg paradox (Ellsberg, 1961). In the two-urn problem, most subjects assign a probability of 0.5 to both of the two urns, yet nevertheless prefer betting on the objective 0.5 to the subjective 0.5 (see Camerer & Weber, 1992, for a review).

Numerous empirical studies have demonstrated some sort of source preference. Heath and Tversky (1991) found that individuals prefer to bet on domains in which they felt particularly competent to domains in which they felt less competent, even when subjective probabilities for the two domains were matched. Fox and Tversky (1995) found that the Ellsberg paradox was reduced or disappeared in between-subject tests. Evidently, subjects are not averse to ambiguity per se, but only when they feel comparatively ignorant (see also, Frisch & Baron, 1988). More recently, Kilka and Weber (2001) measured the degree of source preference directly. German students valued prospects based on a familiar source, the price of Deutsche Bank, a German bank, and an unfamiliar source, the price of Dai-Icho Kangyo Bank, a Japanese bank. The weighting function for the familiar source was significantly more elevated than the weighting function for the more unfamiliar source.

The few studies to date suggest that source dependence acts on the elevation of the weighting function, rather than on the curvature. Illusion of control (Langer, 1975) can be seen as working through elevation of the weighting function. We suspect, however, that there may be effects that work through curvature of the weighting function as well. A decision maker who does not feel particularly knowledgeable about a source, such as politics, may judge one event to be more likely than another, but may attach the same value to a gamble based on the first event compared to a gamble based on the second event. Thus, we hypothesize a flatter weighting function for sources in which subjects feel comparably ignorant.

Source preference complicates matters in one other respect. Decision theorists have assumed that beliefs can be inferred from actions (Ramsey, 1931). For example, suppose that you are indifferent between a risky bet, $100 with a 0.7 chance, and an uncertain event, $100 if the Yankees win tomorrow's game. Under the standard interpretation, indifference means that you judge the probability of the event in question to be 0.7. However, a decision-based definition of probability is elusive if decision makers prefer to bet on one source over another (Wakker, 2004).

Final Thoughts

This chapter has taken the reader through a tour of the many phases in the history of risky decision-making research. We also have tried to provide some preview of what the future holds in store. We close by suggesting two additional fertile research areas. First, we suspect that the study of decision under risk and uncertainty will increasingly consider the role of affect and emotion. Initial investigations in this area have proven quite promising (e.g., Mellers, Schwartz, Ho, & Ritov, 1997; Rottenstreich & Hsee, 2001; Chapter 22, this volume). Second, we see researchers in economics and finance importing these theories and models at an increasing rate. This trend includes research that uses these models to generate more general theoretical predictions (Barberis, Huang, & Santos, 2001), as well as work that uses functional specifications in more flexible structural models (cf. Barberis & Thaler's (2003) review of behavioral economics).

Notes

1   A third category is *prescriptive*: how to get ordinary people to act more normatively? This particular question motivates decision analysis (e.g., Raiffa, 1968). Many decision analysts see the divergence between descriptive and normative models as an argument why decision analysis is needed (e.g., Bell, Raiffa, & Tversky, 1988).
2   Kahneman and Tversky originally envisioned a theory of regret, but "abandoned this approach because it did not elegantly accommodate the pattern of results that we labeled 'reflection' ..." (Kahneman, 2000).
3   The common-consequence effect demonstration reveals subcertainty of $\pi(\cdot)$, while rejection of an asymmetric fair gamble, $(x,0.50; -x,0.50)$ reveals loss aversion, $v(x) < -v(-x)$, and a preference for $(p, x; p, y)$ over $(p, x + y)$ reveals concavity of $v(\cdot)$: $v(x) + v(y) > v(x + y)$.
4   A stochastically dominates B if it has at least as high a probability of any outcome x, and a strictly better probability of some outcome y.
5   However, the unit triangle method is limited to lotteries having at most three outcomes. More complex lotteries therefore cannot be studied within the unit triangle paradigm. For more details on the probability triangle, see Camerer (1989) and Machina (1987). For reviews and details of non-expected utility models, see Camerer (1992) and Fishburn (1988).
6   We do not discuss the axioms underlying rank-dependent utility models, since they tend not to be transparent or easily tested. There are at least two exceptions, axiom systems based on ordinal independence (Green & Jullien, 1988) and tradeoff consistency (Abdellaoui, 2002).

7   Note that the rank-dependent form appeared in Kahneman and Tversky (1979) for two-outcome gambles, $(p, x; 1 - p, y)$, where $x > y > 0$.

References

Abdellaoui, M. (2000) Parameter-free elicitation of utility and probability weighting functions, *Management Science*, 46, 1497–512.

Abdellaoui, M. (2002) A genuine rank-dependent generalization of the Von Neumann-Morgenstern expected utility theorem, *Econometrica*, 70, 717–36.

Abdellaoui, M., Vossman, F., & Weber, M. (2002) Choice-based elicitation and decomposition of decision weights for gains and losses under uncertainty. Working paper.

Allais, M. (1953) Le comportement de l'homme rationel devant le risque, critique des postulates et axiomes de l'école Américaine, *Econometrica*, 21, 503–46.

Barberis, N., Huang, M., & Santos, T. (2001) Prospect theory and asset prices, *Quarterly Journal of Economics*, 116, 1–53.

Barberis, N. & Thaler, R. (2003) A survey of behavioral finance. In G. M. Constantinides, M. Harris, and R. M. Stulz (eds.), *Handbook of the Economics of Finance* (pp. 1053–123). Elsevier.

Battalio, R. C., Kagel, J., & Jiranyakul, K. (1990) Testing between alternative models of choice under uncertainty: Some initial results, *Journal of Risk and Uncertainty*, 3, 25–50.

Becker, S. W. & Brownson, F. O. (1964) What price ambiguity? Or the role of ambiguity in decision-making, *Journal of Political Economy*, 72, 62–73.

Bell, D. E. (1982) Regret in decision making under uncertainty, *Operations Research*, 30, 961–81.

Bell, D. E., Raiffa, H., & Tversky, A. (1988) Descriptive, normative, and prescriptive interactions in decision making. In D. E. Bell, H. Raiffa, and A. Tversky (eds.), *Decision Making: Descriptive, Normative, and Prescriptive Interactions*. New York: Cambridge University Press.

Bernoulli, D. (1738) Specimen theoriae novae de mensura sortis, *Commentarii Academiae Scientiarum Imperialis Petropolitanae*, 5, 175–92. Translated by L. Sommer as New expositions of on the measurement of risk, *Econometrica*, 22, 23–6.

Birnbaum, M. H. & McIntosh, W. R. (1996) Violations of branch independence in choices between gambles, *Organizational Behavior and Human Decision Processes*, 67, 91–110.

Birnbaum, M. H., Patton, J. N., & Lott, M. K. (1999) Evidence against rank-dependent utility theories: Tests of cumulative independence, interval independence, stochastic dominance, and transitivity, *Organizational Behavior and Human Decision Processes*, 77, 44–83.

Birnbaum, M. H. & Stegner, S. E. (1979) Source credibility in social judgment: Bias, expertise, and the judge's point of view, *Journal of Personality & Social Psychology*, 37, 48–74.

Bleichrodt, H. & Pinto, J. L. (2000) A parameter-free elicitation of the probability weighting function in medical decision analysis, *Management Science*, 46, 1485–96.

Camerer, C. F. (1989) An experimental test of several generalized utility theories, *Journal of Risk and Uncertainty*, 2, 61–104.

Camerer, C. F. (1992) Recent tests of generalizations of expected utility theory. In W. Edwards (ed.), *Utility: Theories, Measurement, and Applications* (pp. 207–51). Norwell, MA: Kluwer.

Camerer, C. F. (1995) Individual decision making. In J. H. Kagel and A. E. Roth (eds.), *The Handbook of Experimental Economics* (pp. 587–703). Princeton: Princeton University Press.

Camerer, C. F. & Ho, T. H. (1994) Violations of the betweenness axiom and nonlinearity in probability, *Journal of Risk and Uncertainty*, 8, 167–96.

Camerer, C. F. & Weber, M. W. (1992) Recent developments in modelling preferences: Uncertainty and ambiguity, *Journal of Risk and Uncertainty*, 5, 325–70.

Chechile, R. A. & Butler, S. F. (2000) Is "Generic utility theory" a suitable theory of choice behavior for gambles with mixed gains and losses? *Journal of Risk and Uncertainty*, 20, 189–211.

Chew, S. H. (1983) A generalization of the quasilinear mean with applications to the measurement of income inequality and decision theory resolving the Allais Paradox, *Econometrica*, 51, 1065–92.

Chew, S. H. & MacCrimmon, K. R. (1979) Alpha-nu choice theory: An axiomatization of expected utility. Working paper no. 669, University of British Columbia Faculty of Commerce.

Chew, S. H. & Waller, W. S. (1986) Empirical tests of weighted utility theory, *Journal of Mathematical Psychology*, 30, 55–72.

Conlisk, J. (1989) Three variants on the Allais example, *American Economic Review*, 79, 392–407.

Coupé, T. (in press) Revealed performances: Worldwide rankings of economists and economics departments, 1990–2000, *Journal of the European Economic Association*.

Crawford, V. P. (1990) Equilibrium without independence, *Journal of Economic Theory*, 50, 127–54.

Davidson, D., Suppes, P., & Siegel, S. (1957) *Decision Making: An Experimental Approach*. Stanford, CA: Stanford University Press.

Dekel, E. (1986) An axiomatic characterization of preferences under uncertainty: Weakening the independence axiom, *Journal of Economic Theory*, 40, 304–18.

Diecidue, E. & Wakker, P. P. (2001) On the intuition of rank-dependent utility, *Journal of Risk and Uncertainty*, 23, 281–98.

Edwards, W. (1953) Probability-preferences in gambling, *American Journal of Psychology*, 66, 349–64.

Edwards, W. (1954) The theory of decision making, *Psychological Bulletin*, 51, 380–417.

Edwards, W. (1961) Behavioral decision theory, *Annual Review of Psychology*, 12, 473–98.

Ellsberg, D. (1954) Classic and current notions of "measurable utility," *Economic Journal*, 64, 528–56.

Ellsberg, D. (1961) Risk, ambiguity, and the Savage axioms, *Quarterly Journal of Economics*, 75, 643–99.

Fennema, H. & Wakker, P. P. (1997) Original and new prospect theory: A discussion and empirical differences, *Journal of Behavioral Decision Making*, 10, 53–64.

Fishburn, P. C. (1978) On Handa's "New Theory of Cardinal Utility" and the maximization of expected return, *Journal of Political Economy*, 86, 321–4.

Fishburn, P. C. (1984) SSB utility theory: An economic perspective, *Mathematical Social Science*, 8, 63–94.

Fishburn, P. C. (1988) *Nonlinear Preference and Utility Theory*. Baltimore, Johns Hopkins University Press.

Fox, C. R. & See, K. E. (2003) Belief and preference in decision under uncertainty. In D. Hardman and L. Macchi (eds.), *Thinking: Psychological Perspectives on Reasoning, Judgment, and Decision Making* (pp. 273–314). New York: Wiley.

Fox, C. R. & Tversky, A. (1995) Ambiguity aversion and comparative ignorance, *Quarterly Journal of Economics*, 110, 585–603.

Fox, C. R. & Tversky, A. (1998) A belief-based account of decision under uncertainty, *Management Science*, 44, 879–95.

Friedman, M. & Savage, L. J. (1948) The utility analysis of choices involving risk, *Journal of Political Economy*, 56, 279–304.

Friedman, M. & Savage, L. J. (1952) The expected utility hypothesis and the measurability of utility, *Journal of Political Economy*, 60, 463–74.

Frisch, D. & Baron, J. (1988) Ambiguity and rationality, *Journal of Behavioral Decision Making*, 1, 149–57.

Gigliotti, G. & Sopher, B. (1993) A test of generalized expected utility theory, *Theory and Decision*, 35, 75–106.

Gilboa, I. (1987) Expected utility with purely subjective nonadditive probabilities, *Journal of Mathematical Economics*, 16, 65–88.

Gonzalez, R. & Wu, G. (1999) On the shape of the probability weighting function, *Cognitive Psychology*, 38, 129–66.

Gonzalez, R. & Wu, G. (2003) Composition rules in original and cumulative prospect theory. Unpublished paper.

Green, J. & Jullien, B. (1988) Ordinal independence in nonlinear utility theory, *Journal of Risk and Uncertainty*, 1, 355–87.

Gul, F. (1991) A theory of disappointment in decision making under uncertainty, *Econometrica*, 59, 667–86.

Heath, C. & Tversky, A. (1991) Preference and belief: Ambiguity and competence in choice under uncertainty, *Journal of Risk and Uncertainty*, 4, 5–28.

Kahneman, D. (2000) Preface. In D. Kahneman and A. Tversky (eds.), *Choices, Values, and Frames* (pp. ix–xvii). Cambridge: Cambridge University Press.

Kahneman, D. & Tversky, A. (1979) Prospect theory: An analysis of decision under risk, *Econometrica*, 47(2), 263–91.

Kilka, M. & Weber, M. (2001) What determines the shape of the probability weighting function? *Management Science*, 47, 1712–26.

Knight, F. H. (1921) *Risk, Uncertainty, and Profit*. New York: Houghton Mifflin.

Laibson, D. & Zeckhauser, R. (1998) Amos Tversky and the ascent of behavioral economics, *Journal of Risk and Uncertainty*, 16, 7–47.

Langer, E. J. (1975) The illusion of control, *Journal of Personality and Social Psychology*, 32, 311–28.

Leland, J. (1998) Similarity judgments in choice under uncertainty: A reinterpretation of the prediction of regret theory, *Management Science*, 44, 659–72.

Loomes, G. & Sugden, R. (1982) Regret theory: An alternative theory of rational choice under uncertainty, *Economic Journal*, 92, 805–25.

Lopes, L. L. (1987) Between hope and fear: The psychology of risk. In L. Berkowitz (ed.), *Advances in Experimental Social Psychology* (vol. 20, pp. 255–95). New York: Academic Press.

Luce, R. D. (1988) Rank-dependent, subjective expected utility representations, *Journal of Risk and Uncertainty*, 1, 305–22.

Luce, R. D. (2000) *Utility of Gains and Losses: Measurement – Theoretical and Experimental Approaches*. Mahwah, NJ: Lawrence Erlbaum.

MacCrimmon, K. R. (1965) An experimental study of the decision making behavior of business executives. PhD thesis, UCLA.

MacCrimmon, K. R. (1968) Descriptive and normative implications of the decision-theory postulate. In K. H. Borch and J. Mossin (eds.), *Risk and Uncertainty* (pp. 3–23). New York: St. Martin's Press.

MacCrimmon, K. R. & Larsson, S. (1979) Utility theory: Axioms versus paradoxes. In M. Allais and O. Hagen (eds.), *The Expected Utility Hypothesis and the Allais Paradox* (pp. 333–409). Dordrecht, Holland: D. Riedel.

Machina, M. J. (1982) "Expected utility" analysis without the independence axiom, *Econometrica*, 50, 277–323.

Machina, M. J. (1987) Choice under uncertainty: Problems solved and unsolved, *Journal of Economic Perspectives*, 1, 121–54.

March, J. & Shapira, Z. (1987) Managerial perspectives on risk and risk taking, *Management Science*, 33, 1404–18.

Markowitz, H. (1952) The utility of wealth, *Journal of Political Economy*, 60, 151–8.

Marschak, J. (1950) Rational behavior, uncertain prospects, and measurable utility, *Econometrica*, 18, 111–41.

Mellers, B. A., Schwartz, A., & Cooke, A. D. J. (1998) Judgment and decision making, *Annual Review of Psychology*, 49, 447–77.

Mellers, B. A., Schwartz, A., Ho, K., & Ritov, I. (1997) Decision affect theory: Emotional reactions to the outcomes of risky options, *Psychological Science*, 8, 423–9.

Morrison, D. G. (1967) On the consistency of preferences in Allais' Paradox, *Behavioral Science*, 12, 373–83.

Mosteller, F. & Nogee, P. (1951) An experimental measurement of utility, *Journal of Political Economy*, 59, 371–404.

Neilson, W. S. (1992) A mixed fan hypothesis and its implications for behavior towards risk, *Journal of Economic Behavior and Organization*, 19, 197–211.

Pratt, J. W. (1964) Risk aversion in the small and in the large, *Econometrica*, 32, 122–36.

Prelec, D. (1990) A "Pseudo-endowment" effect, and its implications for some recent nonexpected utility models, *Journal of Risk and Uncertainty*, 3, 247–59.

Preston, M. G. & Baratta, P. (1948) An experimental study of the auction-value of an uncertain outcome, *American Journal of Psychology*, 61, 183–93.

Quiggin, J. (1982) A theory of anticipated utility, *Journal of Economic Behavior and Organization*, 3, 323–43.

Rabin, M. (2000) Risk aversion and expected-utility theory: A calibration theorem, *Econometrica*, 68, 1281–92.

Raiffa, H. (1968) *Decision Analysis: Introductory Lectures on Choice Under Uncertainty*. Reading, MA: Addison-Wesley.

Ramsey, F. P. (1931) Truth and probability. In *The Foundations of Mathematics and Other Logical Essays* (pp. 156–98). London: Routledge & Kegan Paul.

Rothschild, M. and Stiglitz, J. (1970) Increasing risk. I: A definition, *Journal of Economic Theory*, 2, 225–43.

Rottenstreich, Y. & Hsee, C. K. (2001) Money, kisses, and electric shocks: On the affective psychology of risk, *Psychological Science*, 12, 185–90.

Rubinstein, A. (1988) Similarity and decision-making under risk (Is there a utility theory resolution to the Allais paradox?), *Journal of Economic Theory*, 46, 145–53.

Samuelson, P. (1952) Probability, utility, and the independence axiom, *Econometrica*, 20, 670–8.

Savage, L. J. (1954) *The Foundations of Statistics*. New York: Wiley.

Schmeidler, D. (1989) Subjective probability and expected utility without additivity, *Econometrica*, 57, 571–87.

Schoemaker, P. J. H. (1982) The expected utility model: Its variants, purposes, evidence and limitations, *Journal of Economic Literature*, 20, 529–63.

Slovic, P. & Lichtenstein, S. (1968) The importance of variance preferences in gambling decisions, *Journal of Experimental Psychology*, 78, 646–54.

Slovic, P. & Tversky, A. (1974) Who accepts Savage's axiom? *Behavioral Science*, 19, 368–73.

Starmer, C. (2000) Developments in non-expected utility theory: The hunt for a descriptive theory of choice under risk, *Journal of Economic Literature*, 38, 332–82.

Starmer, C. & Sugden, R. (1989) Probability and juxtaposition effects: An experimental investigation of the common ratio effect, *Journal of Risk and Uncertainty*, 2, 159–78.

Stewart, N., Chater, N., Stott, H. P., & Reimers, S. (2003) Prospect relativity: How choice options influence decision under risk, *Journal of Experimental Psychology: General*, 132, 23–46.

Tversky, A. & Fox, C. R. (1995) Weighing risk and uncertainty, *Psychological Review*, 102, 269–83.

Tversky, A. & Kahneman, D. (1986) Rational choice and the framing of decisions, *Journal of Business*, 59, S251–S278.

Tversky, A. & Kahneman, D. (1992) Advances in prospect theory: Cumulative representation of uncertainty, *Journal of Risk and Uncertainty*, 5, 297–323.

Tversky, A. & Koehler, D. J. (1994) Support theory: A nonextensional representation of subjective probability, *Psychological Review*, 101, 547–67.

Varian, H. R. (1992) *Microeconomic Analysis* (3rd edn.). New York: Norton.

Von Neumann, J. & Morgenstern, O. (1947) *Theory of Games and Economic Behavior* (2nd edn.). Princeton: Princeton University Press.

Wakker, P. P. (2003) The data of Levy and Levy (2002), "Prospect theory: Much ado about nothing?" support prospect theory, *Management Science*, 49, 979–81.

Wakker, P. P. (2004) On the composition of risk preference and belief, *Psychological Review*, 111, 236–41.

Williams, C. A. Jr. (1966) Attitudes toward speculative risks as an indicator of attitudes toward pure risks, *Journal of Risk and Insurance*, 33, 577–86.

Wu, G. (1994) An empirical test of ordinal independence, *Journal of Risk and Uncertainty*, 9, 39–60.

Wu, G. & Gonzalez, R. (1996) Curvature of the probability weighting function, *Management Science*, 42, 1676–90.

Wu, G. & Gonzalez, R. (1998) Common consequence conditions in decision making under risk, *Journal of Risk and Uncertainty*, 16, 115–39.

Wu, G. & Gonzalez, R. (1999) Nonlinear decision weights in choice under uncertainty, *Management Science*, 45, 74–85.

Wu, G., Zhang, J., & Abdellaoui, M. (2004) Testing prospect theories using probability tradeoff consistency. Unpublished paper.

Yaari, M. E. (1987) The dual theory of choice under risk, *Econometrica*, 55, 95–117.

21

Intertemporal Choice

Daniel Read

Introduction

The term "intertemporal choice" is used to describe any decision that requires tradeoffs among outcomes that will have their effects at different times. This definition is broad, as reflected by the range of choices and activities that are embraced by it. These include:

- whether or not to have a flu shot;
- the choice between fruit salad or tiramisu;
- when to get down to work on a promised paper;
- whether to invest in a pension plan or buy a widescreen TV; and
- (for a pigeon) one food pellet in one second, or two pellets in two seconds.

In every case, the agent is called on to decide between an earlier and usually smaller penalty or reward (e.g., a flu shot, a TV) and a later and usually larger one (the flu, comfortable retirement). The goal of research into intertemporal choice is to understand how these choices are made, and how they should be made.

This chapter introduces the major issues in the study of intertemporal choice from the perspective of behavioral decision making. The first section describes some basic concepts, including both the terms used and the basic mathematical notation and calculations. This is followed by a discussion of normative issues, which highlights the fact that we cannot easily determine whether the weight people put on future outcomes is due to delay discounting, or to rational utility maximization. Next, I consider the assumptions that underpin (usually implicitly) the interpretation of experimental findings. After these foundations are in place, I survey the major findings – those usually classified as "anomalies" – in intertemporal choice, and discuss some psychological theories that have been developed to explain them. My primary goal is less to provide a broad survey of what is now a voluminous body of research, than to highlight major issues that have sometimes been given too little weight.

The Terminology of Intertemporal Choice

The conventional analysis of intertemporal choice takes the view that the effect of delay on the subjective value of future outcomes can be captured by a *discount function*, which plays the same role in intertemporal choice as the probability weighting function does in risky choice. Just as outcomes should receive less weight the lower their probability, so it is usually assumed they should receive less weight the longer they are delayed.

The discount function can be denoted as $F(d)$, where d is delay, the time intervening between the present and the time of consumption. According to *discounted utility theory*, the utility obtained from a series of future consumption occasions occurring at regular intervals is given by:

$$\sum_{d=0}^{n} F(d)u(c(d)), \qquad (21.1)$$

where $F(0) = 1$, $c(d)$ refers to the resources consumed at delay d, and $u(c(d))$ is the instantaneous utility derived from that consumption. If $F(d)$ is a declining function of delay, the decision maker is *impatient*, and the rate at which $F(d)$ changes is the *pure rate of time preference*.

The discount function is often given as a *discount rate* (r), which is the proportional change in $F(d)$ over a standard time period (usually one year), or as a *discount factor* (δ), which is the proportion of value that remains after delaying an outcome by that standard period. At a given delay $d \geq 1$ the discount rate is:

$$r(d) = -\frac{F(d) - F(d-1)}{F(d-1)}, \qquad (21.2)$$

and the discount factor is:

$$\delta(d) = \frac{F(d)}{F(d-1)} = 1 - r(d). \qquad (21.3)$$

In Table 21.1, $F(d)$, $r(d)$ and $\delta(d)$ are illustrated for four widely used discount functions. As will be explained shortly, the exponential function, in which the discount rate is the same for all future time periods, is the economic gold-standard. The other functions in Table 21.1 are often called "hyperbolic," meaning only that delay is in the *denominator* of the discount function so that the impact of an increase in delay of one period, from d to $d + 1$, is greater the shorter the original delay d (Ainslie, 1975). Hyperbolic functions have been widely adopted because they appear to better reflect

Table 21.1 Four frequently discussed discount functions and their corresponding discount rates (*r*) and discount factors (δ)

	Exponential	Hyperbolic discounting		
		One-parameter (Mazur, 1984)	Generalized (Loewenstein & Prelec, 1992)	Proportional discounting (Harvey, 1994)
$F(d)$	$\left(\dfrac{1}{1+r}\right)^{d}$	$\dfrac{1}{1+kd}$	$(1+\alpha d)^{-\beta/\alpha}$	$\dfrac{h}{h+d}$
$r(d)$	$\dfrac{r}{1+r}$	$\dfrac{k}{1+kd}$	$\dfrac{\beta}{1+\alpha d}$	$\dfrac{1}{h+d}$
$\delta(d)$	$\dfrac{1}{1+r}$	$\dfrac{1+k(d-1)}{1+kd}$	$\left(\dfrac{1+\alpha(d-1)}{1+\alpha d}\right)^{\beta/\alpha}$	$\dfrac{h+d-1}{h+d}$

In financial terms, exponential discounting is equivalent to *compound* interest, while one-parameter hyperbolic discounting is *simple* interest.

how people (and even animals) value future outcomes (Laibson, 1997; Rachlin & Green, 1972).

Normative Analysis of the Discount Rate

The modal strategy in behavioral decision research is to compare observed behavior with a normative model. Intertemporal choice has an uncontroversial normative principle, due to Irving Fisher (1930), that dictates the rate at which money should be discounted – rational decision makers will borrow or lend so that their marginal rate of substitution between present and future money (i.e., the rate at which it can be exchanged while keeping utility constant) will equal the market interest rate.[1]

One implication of this is that the pure rate of time preference will be independent of the willingness to trade off monetary amounts available at different times. To see why, I will discuss a "5 percent market" in which borrowing and lending can be done at 5 percent. Consider an impatient individual who is indifferent between consuming $100 now or $120 in a year. What should he choose if offered a choice between $100 now and $110 in one year? The answer is he should wait for the $110. Then, he should borrow $100 on the capital market and pay back $105 in one year when he receives the $110, thereby earning $5 for his troubles. A similar argument holds for someone who is very patient and is indifferent between consuming $100 now or $102 in one year. If given a choice between £100 now and $104 in a year she should take the $100 and lend it for a year, at which point she will be paid back at $105 including interest. In short, all rational decision makers will make identical choices between delayed money. This does not mean they will make the same *consumption* decisions: the impatient man will probably spend his $100 immediately, while the patient woman will lend hers. But their intertemporal tradeoffs for money will not tell us how impatient they are (cf., Mulligan, 1996).

More generally, discounting can have two bases. The first is that *opportunity costs* grow over time, and discounting compensates for this. The interest lost from delaying the receipt of money or paying it out too soon is one example of an opportunity cost: in the 5 percent world, for example, waiting one year for $104 instead of taking $100 immediately would cost the decision maker $1 in interest. The second basis is *impatience* or pure time preference, meaning that a given amount of utility is preferred the earlier it arrives. I will consider these two bases in turn.

First, delays are costly in almost every productive activity, and so it is rational to prefer more now rather than later. For the farmer, seed grain (like all capital goods), can be transformed into more grain next year, and so the farmer prefers one bushel now to one next year. Likewise, a taxicab driver waiting for the delivery of his cab is missing fares, and the businessman waiting for a cab is losing quality time at home. In general, most people grow wealthier over time, and therefore a given quantity of almost any resource brings more benefit now than in the future. In addition, delays are desirable for losses, and for much the same reason as they are undesirable for gains. A given amount lost will be worth less in the future (as in the farmer who would rather lose one bushel next year than this year), and time enables us to prepare or prevent future losses, so we should want to defer them. Discounting for these reasons is rational, because delay is the medium in which value, risk and uncertainty grow.

A well-developed example of rational discounting is found in evolutionary theory (e.g., Rogers, 1994; Sozou & Seymour, 2003). Theoretically, intertemporal choices are made to maximize Darwinian fitness, meaning the expected reproductive capacity of organisms and their kin (weighted by the degree of kinship). The organism reaches an economic equilibrium when the marginal rate of substitution between present and future fitness is held constant. To give a simple example, imagine you could produce one child now, or more in ten years, but that the probability that you will be able to implement any future reproduction plan is only 0.5. For instance, you might be unable to find a partner, dead, or infertile. Then you should wait only if by doing so, and if you can implement your plan, you will get more than two offspring. The marginal rate of substitution between now and then is 0.5, since you will trade one child in the future for half a child now. This evolutionary account rationalizes discounting, but only because a given amount of resource usually contributes more to Darwinian fitness the earlier it is consumed. Therefore, taking an opportunity now rather than later is an example of taking the option with the lowest opportunity cost.

The second kind of discounting, properly denoted as pure time preference or impatience, involves putting more weight on expected utility the earlier it comes. The concept of utility is notoriously difficult to define, but it is best thought of as "whatever we ultimately care about." Perhaps it is Darwinian fitness, perhaps it is happiness or feelings of mastery, or perhaps a combination of these and other things besides (see Chapter 2, this volume). Whatever utility is, impatience means that someone who currently expects to experience equal utility at two future times will want to increase the earlier utility by one unit, in exchange for a decrease in the later utility of more than one unit. The overall consequence is that, under the assumption of diminishing marginal utility to consumption, impatience will result in a reduction of total lifetime utility.

Because impatience will reduce lifetime utility, there have been few attempts to justify it, and it is often met with disapproval (Peart, 2000). It is, indeed, difficult to explain why we should care less about future than current utility, in the sense that we would take less utility now over more later. One who has tried to justify it is Parfit (1984), who has argued for a position earlier proposed (and rejected) by Sidgwick (1874). The argument begins with the very old idea that we can be described as a sequence of "selves" distributed over time: you will not be (entirely) the same person tomorrow as you are today. Moreover, it is ethically justifiable to care less about the utility of other people than about ourselves. For the same reason, the argument concludes, we can justifiably value the utility of our future selves less than that of our current selves. It is clear that even if we agree with the premises, we need not agree with the conclusion since it requires that we see no relevant differences in our relationship to our future selves and other people. Nonetheless, this argument may be the only way to justify true impatience. Curiously, Frederick (2003a) has tested whether the discount rate is correlated with how much people identify with their future selves, and has found no relationship, suggesting that the Parfitian notion of identity does not underlie discounting.

Time Consistency

Strotz (1955) proposed an additional normative principle for intertemporal choice: if we make plans for future consumption, we should stick to them unless we have a good reason to do otherwise. This is called *time consistency*, and can be illustrated with a commonplace example. If you currently prefer £1,010 in 13 months to £1,000 in 12 months, then – unless you have an unexpected need for immediate money – in 12 months you should prefer £1,010 in 1 month to £1,000 immediately. This may not occur. Indeed, we see *time inconsistency* every day: many smokers *plan* to quit, but light up when the urge hits; many dieters *plan* to have an apple for dessert but end up with bread-and-butter pudding; and many academics *plan* to work on the promised chapter but find other things to do when the time comes.

Because exponential discounting is the only way to avoid time inconsistency, it is widely held to be the only rational way to discount. In contrast, the *hyperbolic* discount function, which can produce time inconsistency, has been widely adopted as a more-realistic way of describing how people (and animals) value future outcomes. The crucial properties of hyperbolic functions are shown in Figure 21.1. The choice is between two alternatives, a smaller-sooner (x_1) and a larger-later (x_2) one. While the larger-later alternative is preferred when both are substantially delayed, when the smaller-sooner alternative becomes imminent it undergoes a rapid increase in value and is briefly preferred. The smaller-sooner reward might be the pleasure from a cigarette, the larger-later reward might be good health: one week in advance, you prefer the prospect of good health, but as time passes the desire for the cigarette grows faster than the desire for good health, until, for what may be a very brief period, the cigarette is preferred. Unfortunately, it is

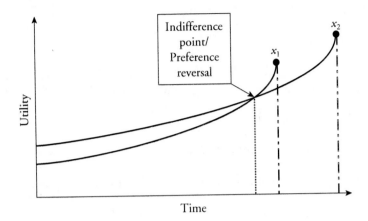

Figure 21.1 Hyperbolic discount function, showing how preferences can briefly change from a larger-later (x_2) to a smaller-sooner (x_1) reward

during this brief period that irreversible decisions can usually be made, and a lifetime's resolve can be sometimes overcome by a moment's weakness.

Exponential discounting means discounting at a *constant* rate. This constancy can be divided into a weak and a strong form: both forms are delay-independent, but the strong form (called *stationarity*; Koopmans, 1960) is also *date-independent*, while the weak form is *date-dependent*. *Date-independence* means that not only can decision makers make consistent plans, but also that they can advance or delay a sequence without changing their preferences. This means, for instance, that if you prefer the sequence $A = \{20,10,22\}$ to $B = \{20,20,10\}$, where the numbers represent utility in successive time periods, you will also prefer $\hat{A} = \{10,22\}$ to $\hat{B} = \{20,10\}$. That is, dropping a common outcome in one time period and advancing the remainder of the sequence by one period will not change the preference order. I call this *cross-sectional* time consistency, since it means that preferences for different sequences evaluated *at the same time* are consistent with one another.

The weaker version of constant time discounting allows *date-dependence* which means that you might, for example, have different discount rates for the different years of your life (as proposed by Rogers, 1994; Trostel & Taylor, 2001, and many others), but that these remain unchanged as you get older. Date-dependent discounting will not necessarily lead to cross-sectional time consistency, but it does entail *longitudinal* time consistency, which means that once you have made a plan, you will not change it with the passage of time. To illustrate with the above sequences, imagine someone who has the following discount factors for three periods: $\delta(1) = 0.9$, $\delta(2) = 0.7$, $\delta(3) = 0.9$. He prefers A to B:

$$u(A: 20,10,22) = (0.9{*}20) + (0.9{*}0.7{*}10) + (0.9{*}0.7{*}0.9{*}22) \cong 37$$

$$u(B: 20,20,10) = (0.9{*}20) + (0.9{*}0.7{*}20) + (0.9{*}0.7{*}0.9{*}10) \cong 36.$$

The passage of one year will not change this preference, because he will still evaluate the second and third period outcomes using $\delta(2)$ and $\delta(3)$:

$u(\hat{A}$:-, 10,22$) = (0.7*10) + (0.7*0.9*22) \cong 21$

$u(\hat{B}$:-, 20,10$) = (0.7*20) + (0.7*0.9*10) \cong 20.$

This is longitudinal dynamic consistency. On the other hand, if the sequences are advanced by one period and the first period outcome dropped, then $\delta(1)$ and $\delta(2)$ will be used:

$u(\hat{A}$: 10,22$) = (0.9*10) + (0.9*0.7*22) \cong 23$

$u(\hat{B}$: 20,10$) = (0.9*20) + (0.9*0.7*10) \cong 24.$

Now, $\hat{B}$ is preferred to $\hat{A}$, and cross-sectional time consistency is violated.

Empirical Research into Time Preference

There are two broad approaches to the study of intertemporal choice. One is to observe consumption in different periods, and to infer from this consumption what the person's discount rate must be (e.g., Trostel & Taylor, 2001). For example, if someone with $1,000 spends $550 in the first period and $450 in the second, they are showing positive time preference.

In judgment and decision-making research, however, the usual method is to estimate the discount rate r or discount factor δ by obtaining choices or matching judgments. This typically involves finding pairs of outcomes x_1 and x_2 that occur at delays d_1 and d_2 such that $u(x_1) = u(x_2)$. Then r and δ can be derived in the following way:

$$\delta = \left(\frac{u(x_1)}{u(x_2)}\right)^{\frac{1}{d_2-d_1}} \qquad (21.4)$$

$$r = \left(\frac{u(x_2)}{u(x_1)}\right)^{\frac{1}{d_2-d_1}} - 1 \qquad (21.5)$$

In most experiments the outcomes are monetary, although there are many exceptions, including a growing literature on trading off health outcomes (reviewed in Chapman, 2003; see Chapter 29, this volume). In these studies, the interpretation of results depends on a set of untested and sometimes implausible assumptions. These are described in the first section below. In the next section, a set of results that appear to be at variance with various normative principles – called anomalies – are summarized.

Assumptions

Most reported studies of intertemporal choice make at least a few, and sometimes all, of the assumptions described in this section.

1   *Outcomes will occur with certainty*: The term $u(c)$ in equation 21.1 represents the expected utility from consumption at a given time. If consumption cannot be assumed to occur with certainty, its value should be discounted for uncertainty as well as its delay. Since the future is always uncertain, with uncertainty increasing as a function (not necessarily linear) of delay, observed discounting should always involve a combination of the effects of risk and delay. Experimental results are usually interpreted on the assumption that participants assume future outcomes will occur with certainty. Yet any expected risk will increase apparent discounting and, moreover, nonlinearities in the rate at which risk increases with time could well lead to behavior consistent with hyperbolic or other varieties of non-constant time discounting (Benzion, Rapoport, & Yagil, 1989; Sozou, 1998).

2   *Outcomes are consumed instantly*: The results of studies are usually interpreted as if c, in the expression $u(c)$ from equation 21.1, is identical to whatever is received at that moment. This assumption will rarely be true for any good that can be stored or traded. The consumption of money, for instance, will be spread over time, and may even have occurred *before* it has been received. Even spending money does not mean that its consumption is achieved at that moment – the utility from the purchase of durable goods extends far beyond the moment of purchase. A similar argument holds for any outcome that need not be consumed at once, or whose consumption has distributed consequences. Indeed, even the least fungible of outcomes – including specific experiences such as headaches or kisses – can have lasting consequences.

3   *Target outcomes are not evaluated in the context of other possibilities*: This means that participants choose without thinking about their other opportunities. As already discussed, because rational decisions involve minimizing opportunity costs, most observed decisions should reflect market forces rather than pure time preference. It is only when there is no market (such as with health outcomes) that rational choices will reflect pure time preference. This assumption is a particularly tough nut to crack. If a person's observed δ deviates from what it *should* be based on their market opportunities, this means they are behaving "irrationally." But what form does this irrationality take? One suggestion is that if people do not behave as they would if they were economic maximizers, then their choices must reflect their true rate of impatience (Coller & Williams, 1999). But this is a problematic view, since if people are irrational, what justification can there be for assuming that their irrationality takes a specific, albeit analytically convenient, form?

4   *The utility of a good is related to the quantity of that good by a multiplicative constant*: In most studies, δ or r is computed by substituting x_1 and x_2 for $u(x_1)$ and $u(x_2)$ in equations 21.4 and 21.5, but this may not be valid. This is best illustrated with an example: Suppose I observe that you are indifferent between $100 today and $121 in one year, and I am willing to make Assumptions 1, 2 and 3. I still cannot conclude that this represents your pure rate of time preference because to do so I must still assume that $u(\$100)/u(\$121) = 100/121 = \delta$. If we take the usual view that marginal utility (or value) is a decreasing function of amount, treating utility as linear in amount will generally lead to overestimates of the true discount rate. For instance, if $u(c) = c^{1/2}$, then for this example δ would be 10/11, so that if we make the linearity assumption we would overestimate discounting. In general, if we are

not sure about the utility function, then any given value of δ for money is compatible with any value of δ for utility.

5   *The utility from outcomes is timing-independent*: Just as ice is more valuable in the summer than the winter, so it is generally true that the utility from a given kind of consumption will depend on its timing. Therefore, if people make intertemporal tradeoffs between outcomes that differ in value at different times, these differences will influence measured discount rates. If the good being evaluated has less per-unit value earlier rather than later, then we will underestimate discount rates, and if it is less valuable later we will overestimate them. To give an example relevant to research practice, college and university students perceive themselves as poor when in school, yet expect to be well off in the near future, after they graduate. Any moderate time-horizon is likely to involve both sides of this divide. These students will *appear* more impatient than they really are, because a given amount of money means more to them now than later.

Although these five assumptions are rarely discussed in the context of empirical reports, data are frequently interpreted in a way that is only warranted if they are all true. I suggest that we, as researchers, should focus more attention on these assumptions. We should make sure they are justified and, if not, attempt to vitiate their effects.

Anomalies

The goal of much intertemporal choice research has been to test the economic model, and to demonstrate how it fails. Usually, the economic principle tested is not the first (least-controversial) one which states that money should be discounted at the prevailing market rate, although it is well known that people do not do this (Benzion et al., 1989; Frederick, Loewenstein, & O'Donoghue, 2002; Thaler, 1981). The focus has rather been on whether each person can be characterized by a stationary discount rate, regardless of what that rate is. The consensus is that people do not apply a single rate to all decisions. Rather, their implied discount rate is highly domain dependent (Chapman & Elstein, 1995; Madden, Bickel, & Jacobs, 1999), and even within domains it depends on the choice context. Consequently several "anomalies," or systematic deviations from constant discounting, have been identified. These are described and briefly discussed in this section.

1   *Time inconsistency*: The concept of time inconsistency was introduced earlier. *Cross-sectional* time inconsistency, involving variations of delay within a single session, has been demonstrated in several domains (Green, Fristoe, & Myerson, 1994; Kirby & Herrnstein, 1995). Kirby and Herrnstein (1995) offered people a choice between a small prize immediately and a large prize later. They first established that the smaller-sooner prize was preferred to the larger-later one, and then delayed both prizes by a constant amount. Participants almost invariably changed to the larger, later prize, usually after a very small increase in delay.

   Longitudinal time inconsistency, or impulsivity, which means that the preference for smaller-sooner over larger-later options increases as they become closer in time, is the prototypical phenomenon of intertemporal choice. Yet there have been no studies showing results like those implied by Figure 21.1 – in which preferences change in the direction of a smaller-sooner x_1 after a period of favoring larger-later x_2. Rather, the few demonstrations of longitudinal time inconsistency have shown that when there are two non-monetary outcomes available at the same time, but one is more immediately beneficial than the other, preference will often switch in the direction of the more tempting alternative at the moment of consumption (Read & Van Leeuwen, 1998). This pattern *is* often explained using hyperbolic discounting along with assumptions about how the utility from different options is distributed over time (see Read, 2003), but this may not be the best explanation (as we will discuss below). It remains a puzzle why such a widely discussed phenomenon as longitudinal dynamic inconsistency has not been properly tested.

2 *Delay effect*: If we elicit the present-value of a delayed outcome, or the future-value of an immediate outcome, then the obtained value of δ will be larger (and r will be smaller) the longer the delay. To illustrate, Thaler (1981) obtained the future value of amounts of money available now, if they were delayed by times varying from 3 months to 10 years. If the amount now was $15, the discount rate varied from 277 percent for a three-month delay to 19 percent for a ten-year delay. Similar results have been reported in dozens of subsequent studies (e.g., Benzion et al., 1989; Green & Myerson, 1996; Raineri & Rachlin, 1993; Kirby, 1997). As in the example, most demonstrations of the delay effect concern money, although it has been shown for other domains, including health and holidays (Chapman, Brewer, Coups, Brownlee, Leventhal, & Leventhal, 2001; Chapman & Elstein, 1995). The delay effect is generally attributed to some form of hyperbolic discounting, although it could equally be due to the *interval effect*.

3 *Interval effect*: The difference between the delays to two outcomes is the *interval* between them. Discounting depends strongly on the length of this interval, with longer intervals leading to smaller values of r or larger values of δ. To illustrate, consider two intervals of equal length: one from d_1 to d_2; the other from d_2 to d_3. A decision maker equates pairs of outcomes available at the beginning and end of each interval:

$$u(x_1) = u(x_2),$$

$$u(x_2) = u(x_3).$$

He also equates the outcome available at the beginning of the first interval with one at the end of the second interval:

$$u(x_1) = u(\hat{x}_3).$$

The interval effect means that, in general, $x_3 > \hat{x}_3$. Or, in other words, shorter intervals lead to more discounting per-time-unit (Read, 2001a; Read & Roelofsma, 2003).

The interval effect provides an alternative account for the delay effect. If $d_1 = 0$, meaning x_1 is received immediately, then the delay and the interval are confounded, and the two effects can be confused. This was suggested by Read (2001b), who reported equal discount rates for intervals of equal size, regardless of when they occurred (that is, $x_1/x_2 = x_2/x_3$). More recent work (Read & Roelofsma, 2003), however, suggests that there is both a delay and interval effect, although the interval plays the largest role. A systematic analysis of the relative contributions of delay and interval to discounting is yet to be done.

4 *Magnitude effect*: This means that the discount rate is higher for smaller amounts. The magnitude effect is the most robust of the "classic" anomalies, and is obtained whenever discounting is measured for differing amounts under otherwise identical conditions. The effect is greatest for smaller amounts and short delays: Kirby (1997) obtained strong magnitude effects when comparing discounting of $10 and $20 over 30 days; Shelley (1993) observed magnitude effects for values between $40 and $200, and almost no effect for larger amounts; Green, Myerson and McFadden (1997) found negligible effects for amounts above $200. The magnitude effect has also been generalized to other domains (Chapman, 1996b) and, moreover, Chapman and Winquist (1998) have shown that something similar happens in other contexts – people give smaller (proportional) tips the larger the restaurant bill.

5 *Direction effect*: The discount rate obtained by increasing the delay to an outcome is greater than that from reducing it (Loewenstein, 1988). In one study, Loewenstein gave participants a gift certificate worth $7 for a local record shop, available in either 1, 4 or 8 weeks. They then chose between the gift certificate they had, and differently valued gift certificates available earlier or later. For example, someone who received an 8-week gift certificate could choose between that and (say) a $6 certificate in 4 weeks. The value put on a given delay was much greater when the certificate was delayed than when it was expedited. Loewenstein (1988) interpreted this using prospect theory. Expediting or delaying an outcome means losing something at one time and gaining it at another. Because of loss aversion, the substitute outcome must be disproportionately large to compensate for the loss. For delay, the substitute outcome is the later amount and so this effect increases the discount rate, while for expediting the substitute comes earlier, thus decreasing the discount rate.

6 *Sign effect*: The discount rate is lower for losses than gains. This has proved a relatively robust effect (Antonides & Wunderink, 2001; Thaler, 1981). Indeed, people often show zero or even negative discount rates for losses – in many studies people will want to take even monetary losses immediately rather than defer them (Yates & Watts, 1975) and are very likely to want to experience bad health outcomes immediately (Van der Pol & Cairns, 2000).

The sign effect is not, however, uncontroversial. Shelley (1994) found more discounting for losses and gains, as well as an interaction between the sign effect and the direction effect: The discount rate from delaying a loss is greater than that from delaying a gain, while that from expediting a gain is greater than that from expediting a loss (Shelley, 1993). Moreover, the tendency to discount losses less contradicts studies of approach-avoidance conflicts, which found that the avoidance gradient is steeper than the approach gradient – implying that losses will be discounted more rapidly than gains (Miller, 1959). This idea was developed into a theory of intertemporal choice by Mowen and Mowen (1991), but evidence of a sign effect appeared to contradict it. More recently, however, studies of the discounting of mixed (positive and negative) outcomes suggest that their negative parts receive more weight with delay. For example, Soman (1998) showed that when people evaluate rebates, which have a positive component (amount to be received) and a negative one (effort required to redeem them), the negative component receives much less weight the longer the outcome is delayed.

7   *Sequence effects*: A sequence is a set of dated outcomes all of which are expected to occur, such as one's salary or mortgage payments. In a wide variety of choice contexts, people usually (although not always) prefer constant or increasing sequences to decreasing ones, even when the total amount in the sequence is held constant. To illustrate, given a choice between three ways to distribute $300 over three months – increasing = {90, 100, 110}, constant = {100,100,100}, or decreasing = {110,100,90} – most will choose constant over increasing, and increasing over decreasing (Barsky, Juster, Kimball, & Shapiro, 1997; Chapman, 1996a; Gigliotti & Sopher, 1997; Loewenstein & Prelec, 1993; Loewenstein & Sicherman, 1991; Read & Powell, 2002). Such a preference is puzzling for two reasons. First, it shows poor economic judgment because under any positive interest rate a decreasing *monetary* sequence has a higher present value than an increasing one. Second, it is difficult to reconcile with other studies of time preference, since anyone with a positive discount rate will prefer a decreasing income distribution.

Theories of Time Discounting

There are two main theoretical approaches to the anomalies in intertemporal choice. The first is to *rationalize* the anomalies by showing that they are what we would expect rational actors to do in the environment in which they find themselves. Such explanations are usually behavioral or economic, based on finding a fit between actions and choices. Many cases of such rationalizing were described above: a positive event in the future might be valued less than it is now because it is more uncertain, because it will lead to less evolutionary fitness, or because we will be richer in the future and so want it less than we do now. The second approach is to *mechanize* phenomena by describing processes that will produce the anomalies, without committing ourselves to whether the output of that process is rational or not. The current section offers a brief review of some proposed mechanisms. As will be seen, no theory accounts for all observed phenomena, and the theories are not necessarily even rivals. Intertemporal choice is a complex phenomenon, and probably determined by many mechanisms.

Value function approaches

The earlier discussion of Assumption 4 showed that the discount rate could be over- or under-estimated by treating outcome magnitude as proportional to outcome utility. In fact, some intertemporal-choice anomalies can be explained in terms of a non-linear utility or value function with special properties.

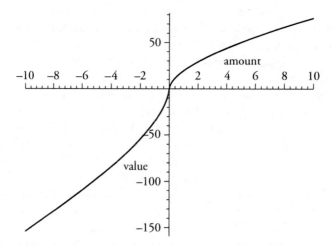

Figure 21.2 Value function having the three properties described by Loewenstein and Prelec (1992) to account for magnitude, sign, and direction effects

One such approach was reported by Loewenstein and Prelec (1992), who proposed a value function, like the one in Figure 21.2, having three properties: Steeper for losses than gains; more elastic for losses than gains; and more elastic the larger the absolute value of the option.[2] This function will produce magnitude, sign, and direction effects. For example, the sign effect occurs because the proportional change in value from −$5 to −$10 is smaller than the change from $5 to $10 (more elastic for losses than gains), and the magnitude effect occurs because the proportional change in value from $50 to $100 is greater than that from $5 to $10 (more elastic the larger the amount).

The value function cannot be the only explanation for intertemporal choice anomalies. One reason is that it cannot account for time-specific effects, such as the delay effect and time inconsistency, as shown by the fact that Loewenstein and Prelec's (1992) complete model also includes the generalized hyperbolic discount function from Table 21.1. A more general issue is that the value-function approach assumes alternative-based choice, which is incompatible with many intertemporal choice phenomena.

Attribute-comparison models

In *alternative-based choice* each option is first evaluated, as in equation 21.1, by summing up the discounted utility of each unit of consumption, and then the option with the highest utility is chosen. In *attribute-based choice*, on the other hand, options are compared attribute-by-attribute, and choice is based on some transformation of attribute differences. Such attribute-based choice leads to anomalous intertemporal choices whenever the decision weight put on delay or outcome magnitude depends on the choice context. This can occur when the weight assigned to attribute values depends on the magnitudes being compared, or when some differences are non-compensatory, as in lexicographic or threshold-based choice. Many studies have shown that attribute-based models are both sufficient to account for many familiar anomalies, and necessary to explain some patterns of intertemporal choices.

Intransitive choice cannot come from alternative-based choice processes, so evidence for systematic intransitivity is also evidence for attribute-based choice. Roelofsma and Read (2000) showed that intransitive intertemporal choice is easy to produce, and attributed this to the use of a lexicographic-like procedure with interval evaluated first and amount evaluated second. According to their model, and within the range of choices they studied, when the interval is large enough then the smaller-sooner option is taken, but otherwise the larger-later one is. The interval effect, described above, also reveals alternative-based decision processes – because the interval is a difference between delays, the fact that intervals and not delays determine choice means that the delays are being compared *prior* to choice (Read, 2001b).

Rubinstein (2003) and Leland (2002) have both argued that many classic anomalies arise from an attribute-based process based on what they call *similarity* relations between option attributes. According to Rubinstein, when the levels for an attribute are very similar, that attribute is given little or no weight in choice. So, for instance, 101 and 111 days are very similar, while 1 and 11 days are not. This can explain the delay effect and time inconsistency, because a given interval is given little weight when the delays are long, but a lot of weight when the delays are short. Rubinstein showed that when the similarity and hyperbolic discounting hypotheses conflict, the similarity hypothesis wins out. One of his many examples used the following pair of choices:

A   In 60 days you expect delivery of a stereo costing $960. You must pay on receipt. Will you accept a delivery delay of 1 day for a discount of $2?
B   Tomorrow you expect delivery of a stereo costing $1,080. You must pay on receipt. Will you accept a delivery delay of 60 days for a discount of $120?

Hyperbolic discounting predicts that nobody who accepts A will refuse B,[3] yet more people agree to B than to A. Rubinstein argues that in Option A the two payments are very similar ($958; $960), and so they receive almost no decision weight. On the other hand, the two payments of Option B are very dissimilar ($960; $1,080) and so receive much more weight.

Attribute-based models account for delay and interval effects in an intuitively appealing manner, and also predict new phenomena such as intransitivity and Rubinstein's antihyperbolic effects. Their shortcoming, however, is that they are primarily applicable to rudimentary choices involving delayed amounts of money – there is no clear way, for instance, to use the theory of similarity to explain intertemporal choices between a sports car and a sedan, or between smoking and a stick of gum. This is the goal of the richer psychological theories reported next.

Cognitive/representation theories

These theories explain intertemporal choice in terms of how we represent future outcomes as a function of delay. Böhm-Bawerk, for example, suggested that one reason for discounting was that "we limn a more or less incomplete picture of our future wants and especially of the remote distant ones" (cited in Loewenstein, 1992, p. 14). This general approach – viewing the problem of discounting as being due to how we represent and think about future outcomes – has wide currency. One model has been proposed by Becker and Mulligan (1997), who argue that the discount rate is a function of the resources invested in imagining the future. In their model, decision makers maximize lifetime utility subject to difficulties in envisioning exactly how rewarding the future will be. Hence, they will expend resources to make their image of the future vivid and clear. To cite one example, we might spend time with our parents to remind ourselves of what our needs will be when we are their age.

One influential cognitive approach is Trope and Liberman's (2000, 2003) *temporal construal theory*. They begin by asserting that option attributes vary in their centrality, with "high-level" attributes being more central to the option than "low-level" ones. The definition of high- and low-level is broad, but typically low-level attributes are more concrete and mundane than high-level ones. Trope and Liberman argue that as options are delayed, their representation becomes increasingly dominated by high-level attributes, and so their present-value also becomes more influenced by those attributes. For example, the act of "writing a book chapter" has high-level attributes that might be "obtaining a publication" or "informing the field," while its low-level attributes include "several difficult days of writing." When the decision to write it is made (and the deadline is remote) the low-level attributes are much less important than when the deadline is near. This can lead to time inconsistency between options differing in the value of their high- and low-level attributes. An option that has relatively unattractive low-level attributes but relatively attractive high-level ones can go from being desirable when still delayed (and the high-level attributes are most important), to undesirable when available immediately (when the low-level attributes dominate). This can explain Soman's (1998) rebate study, mentioned earlier. He showed that a mail-in rebate is a more effective selling strategy if both the effort from applying for the rebate and the payoff are delayed than if they both occur immediately. To put this in the terms of temporal construal theory, the high-level attribute is the reward amount, while the low-level attribute is the effort involved, and the importance of the high-level attribute relative to the low-level one is greater when both are delayed than when they are imminent.

Emotion-based theories

Becker and Mulligan (1997) suggest that imagining the future more vividly can decrease our discount rate for that future. This depends, however, on what is being imagined. Imagining something can increase our desire for it along with our impatience (Mischel, Ayduk, & Mendoza-Denton, 2003). For example, if we focus our attention on the wonderful meal waiting for us when we get home we might become hungrier, and therefore more likely to snack between meals. Our desire for food, triggered by the vivid image, becomes a strong impetus for action.

This idea forms the basis for a major re-examination of time preference by Loewenstein (1996). He argues that the temporal and *physical* proximity of options that can reduce aversive arousal states (hunger, sexual arousal, withdrawal symptoms) leads to a dispro-portionate but transient increase in the attractiveness of those options. Indeed, they can even create a feeling of deprivation – we get hungry when we see a steak, and sexually aroused when we see a potential partner.

While visceral factors can explain impulsive choices, the arousal that is produced is not caused by delay, but rather by the presence of the aggravating stimulus. If you cannot see or smell food the temporal proximity of possible consumption might not lead to impulsive preferences; while if you can see and smell it, even if you cannot consume it, the strong and overwhelming desire can still arise. The bacon in your own fridge (which you can eat right now) has much less effect than the smell of bacon from your neighbour's skillet (which you cannot). Usually the presence of the visceral good is confounded with delay-to-consumption, but when visceral arousal is unaccompanied by temporal proximity it nonetheless has the expected effect. To illustrate, Read and Van Leeuwen (1998) reported that people who chose a snack they would not get for a week were more likely to choose an unhealthy snack if they were hungry when choosing than if they were not (cf., Loewenstein, Nagin, & Paternoster, 1997).

Although impulsivity from visceral states cannot account for all findings in intertemporal choice, it might account for most of those that interest us most – the weakness of resolve in the face of temptation. Indeed, the ultimate goal of the study of intertemporal choice is to help us overcome this weakness of will, the lack of which contributes to a vast number of major social problems, including under-saving, obesity, and addictions of all sorts.

Conclusion

This chapter is not a comprehensive account of research into intertemporal choice. The field is now so large, and growing so rapidly, that it will soon warrant a handbook of its own. To give an idea of how true this is, consider the following *important* topics that are largely missing from this chapter: the physiology of intertemporal choice (Manuck, Flory, Muldoon, & Ferrell, 2003); application of non-constant discounting models in economics (Laibson, 1998); formal models of self-control (Benabou & Pycia, 2002; O'Donoghue & Rabin, 2000, 2001); individual differences in discounting (Green, Myerson, & Ostaszewski, 1999; Trostel & Taylor, 2001); pathologies of discounting such as addiction and criminality (Bickel & Marsch, 2001; Wilson & Herrnstein, 1985); intergenerational discounting (Chapman, 2001; Frederick, 2003b; Schelling, 1995); discounting of health outcomes (Bleichrodt & Gafni, 1996; Chapman, 2003); and applications to marketing (Wertenbroch, 2003) and public policy (Caplin, 2003). The list could continue. My goal has been to provide enough background to permit readers to engage in a critical exploration of this field, as well as to prepare them to make contributions of their own.

Notes

1   Fisher's analysis assumes a perfect capital market, in which borrowing and lending can freely be carried out at the same rate, and that one can borrow as much or as little as desired subject to the constraint that total income is held constant. In a real market, people will differ in their borrowing opportunities. Some will have credit cards offering 0 percent interest rates, some will not be able to borrow at all. To anticipate the future discussion, if they are fully rational it is these opportunities that will constrain their intertemporal decision making about money.
2   Elasticity is the percentage change in amount divided by the percentage change in value. For instance, if $v = A^2$, then when A is 10 $v = 100$. If A is increased by 10 percent to 11, v would increase to 121 – a 21 percent change. The elasticity would be $21/10 = 2.1$.
3   Hyperbolic discounting will say that the penalty for each day of delay will be less than its successor. If the delay from the first to the sixty-first day can be compensated for by $120, then the sixty-first day alone can certainly be compensated for by $2.

Acknowledgements

Thanks to Marc Scholten for improving my understanding of discount functions, and to Burcu Orsel and N. L. Read for very helpful comments and criticism. Work on this chapter was partially funded by ESRC Award RES-000-22-0201. A longer version of this chapter is available on the LSE OR web site: http://www.lse.ac.uk/collections/operationalResearch/research/workingPapers.htm

References

Ainslie, G. (1975) Specious reward: A behavioral theory of impulsiveness and impulse control, *Psychological Bulletin*, 82, 463–9.
Antonides, G. & Wunderink, S. R. (2001) Subjective time preference and willingness to pay for an energy-saving durable good, *Zeitschrift Für Sozialpsychologie*, 32(3), 133–41.
Barsky, R. B., Juster, F. T., Kimball, M. S., & Shapiro, M. D. (1997) Preference parameters and behavioral heterogeneity: An experimental approach in the health and retirement study, *Quarterly Journal of Economics*, 112(2), 537–79.
Becker, G. S. & Mulligan, C. B. (1997) The endogenous determination of time preference, *Quarterly Journal of Economics*, 112(3), 729–58.
Benabou, R. & Pycia, M. (2002) Dynamic inconsistency and self-control: A planner-doer interpretation, *Economics Letters*, 77(3), 419–24.
Benzion, U., Rapoport, A., & Yagil, J. (1989) Discount rates inferred from decisions – an experimental study, *Management Science*, 35(3), 270–84.
Bickel, W. K. & Marsch, L. A. (2001) Toward a behavioral economic understanding of drug dependence: Delay discounting processes, *Addiction*, 96(1), 73–86.
Bleichrodt, H. & Gafni, A. (1996) Time preference, the discounted utility model and health, *Journal of Health Economics*, 15(1), 49–66.
Caplin, A. (2003) Fear as a policy instrument. In G. Loewenstein, D. Read, and R. F. Baumeister (eds.), *Time and Decision: Economic and Psychological Perspectives on Intertemporal Choice*. New York: Russell Sage Foundation.
Chapman, G. B. (1996a) Expectations and preferences for sequences of health and money, *Organizational Behavior and Human Decision Processes*, 67(1), 59–75.

Chapman, G. B. (1996b) Temporal discounting and utility for health and money, *Journal of Experimental Psychology-Learning Memory and Cognition*, 22(3), 771–91.

Chapman, G. B. (2001) Time preferences for the very long term, *Acta Psychologica*, 108(2), 95–116.

Chapman, G. B. (2003) Time discounting of health outcomes. In G. Loewenstein, D. Read, and R. F. Baumeister (eds.), *Time and Decision: Economic and Psychological Perspectives on Intertemporal Choice*. New York: Russell Sage Foundation.

Chapman, G. B., Brewer, N. T., Coups, E. J., Brownlee, S., Leventhal, H., & Leventhal, E. A. (2001) Value for the future and preventive health behavior, *Journal of Experimental Psychology – Applied*, 7(3), 235–50.

Chapman, G. B. & Elstein, A. S. (1995) Valuing the future – temporal discounting of health and money, *Medical Decision Making*, 15(4), 373–86.

Chapman, G. B. & Winquist, J. R. (1998) The magnitude effect: Temporal discount rates and restaurant tips, *Psychonomic Bulletin & Review*, 5(1), 119–23.

Coller, M. & Williams, M. B. (1999) Eliciting individual discount rates, *Experimental Economics*, 2, 107–27.

Elster, J. (1979) *Ulysses and the Sirens*. Cambridge: Cambridge University Press.

Fisher, I. (1930) *The Theory of Interest*. New York: Macmillan.

Frederick, S. (2003a) Time preference and personal identity. In G. Loewenstein, D. Read, and R. F. Baumeister (eds.), *Time and Decision: Economic and Psychological Perspectives on Intertemporal Choice*. New York: Russell Sage Foundation.

Frederick, S. (2003b) Measuring intergenerational time preference: Are future lives valued less? *Journal of Risk and Uncertainty*, 26(1), 39–53.

Frederick, S., Loewenstein, G., & O'Donoghue, T. (2002) Time discounting and time preference: A critical review, *Journal of Economic Literature*, 40(2), 351–401.

Gigliotti, G. & Sopher, B. (1997) Violations of present-value maximization in income choice, *Theory and Decision*, 43(1), 45–69.

Green, L., Fristoe, N., & Myerson, J. (1994) Temporal discounting and preference reversals in choice between delayed outcomes, *Psychonomic Bulletin & Review*, 1(3), 383–9.

Green, L. & Myerson, J. (1996) Exponential versus hyperbolic discounting of delayed outcomes: Risk and waiting time, *American Zoologist*, 36(4), 496–505.

Green, L., Myerson, J., & McFadden, E. (1997) Rate of temporal discounting decreases with amount of reward, *Memory & Cognition*, 25(5), 715–23.

Green, L., Myerson, J., & Ostaszewski, P. (1999) Discounting of delayed rewards across the life span: Age differences in individual discounting functions, *Behavioural Processes*, 46(1), 89–96.

Harvey, C. M. (1994) The reasonableness of nonconstant discounting, *Journal of Public Economics*, 53(1), 31–51.

Kirby, K. N. (1997) Bidding on the future: Evidence against normative discounting of delayed rewards, *Journal of Experimental Psychology – General*, 126(1), 54–70.

Kirby, K. N. & Herrnstein, R. J. (1995) Preference reversals due to myopic discounting of delayed reward, *Psychological Science*, 6(2), 83–9.

Koopmans, T. C. (1960) Stationary ordinal utility and impatience, *Econometrica*, 28, 287–309.

Laibson, D. (1997) Golden eggs and hyperbolic discounting, *Quarterly Journal of Economics*, 112, 443–77.

Laibson, D. (1998) Life-cycle consumption and hyperbolic discount functions, *European Economic Review*, 42(3–5), 861–71.

Leland, J. W. (2002) Similarity judgments and anomalies in intertemporal choice, *Economic Inquiry*, 40(4), 574–81.

Loewenstein, G. F. (1988) Frames of mind in intertemporal choice, *Management Science*, 34(2), 200–14.

Loewenstein, G. (1992) The fall and rise of psychological explanations in the economics of intertemporal choice. In G. Loewenstein & J. Elster (eds.), *Choice Over Time*. Russell Sage Foundation: New York.

Loewenstein, G. (1996) Out of control: Visceral influences on behavior, *Organizational Behavior and Human Decision Processes*, 65(3), 272–92.

Loewenstein, G., Nagin, D., & Paternoster, R. (1997) The effect of sexual arousal on expectations of sexual forcefulness, *Journal of Research in Crime and Delinquency*, 34(4), 443–73.

Loewenstein, G. & Prelec, D. (1992) Anomalies in intertemporal choice – evidence and an interpretation, *Quarterly Journal of Economics*, 107(2), 573–97.

Loewenstein, G. F. & Prelec, D. (1993) Preferences for sequences of outcomes, *Psychological Review*, 100(1), 91–108.

Loewenstein, G. & Sicherman, N. (1991) Do workers prefer increasing wage profiles? *Journal of Labor Economics*, 9(1), 67–84.

Madden, G. J., Bickel, W. K., & Jacobs, E. A. (1999) Discounting of delayed rewards in opioid-dependent outpatients: Exponential or hyperbolic discounting functions? *Experimental and Clinical Psychopharmacology*, 7(3), 284–93.

Manuck, S. B., Flory, J. D., Muldoon, M. F., & Ferrell, R. E. (2003) A neurobiology of intertemporal choice. In G. Loewenstein, D. Read, and R. F. Baumeister (eds.), *Time and Decision: Economic and Psychological Perspectives on Intertemporal Choice*. New York: Russell Sage Foundation.

Mazur, J. E. (1984) Tests of an equivalence rule for fixed and variable delays, *Journal of Experimental Psychology: Animal Behavior Processes*, 10, 426–36.

Miller, N. E. (1959) Liberalization of basic S-R concepts: Extension to conflict behavior, motivation and social learning. In S. Koch (ed.), *Psychology: A Study of a Science*. New York, McGraw-Hill.

Mischel, W., Ayduk, O., & Mendoza-Denton, R. (2003) Sustaining delay of gratification over time: A hot-cool systems perspective. In G. Loewenstein, D. Read, and R. F. Baumeister (eds.), *Time and Decision: Economic and Psychological Perspectives on Intertemporal Choice*. New York: Russell Sage Foundation.

Mowen, J. C. & Mowen, M. M. (1991) Time and outcome valuation – implications for marketing decision-making, *Journal of Marketing*, 55(4), 54–62.

Mulligan, Casey B. (1996) A logical economist's argument against hyperbolic discounting. Working paper, University of Chicago.

O'Donoghue, T. & Rabin, M. (2000) The economics of immediate gratification, *Journal of Behavioral Decision Making*, 13(2), 233–50.

O'Donoghue, T. & Rabin, M. (2001) Choice and procrastination, *Quarterly Journal of Economics*, 116(1), 121–60.

Parfit, D. (1984) *Reasons and Persons*. Oxford: Oxford University Press.

Peart, S. J. (2000) Irrationality and intertemporal choice in early neoclassical thought, *Canadian Journal of Economics-Revue Canadienne D'Economique*, 33(1), 175–89.

Rachlin, H. and Green, L. (1972) Commitment, choice and self-control, *Journal of the Experimental Analysis of Behavior*, 17, 15–22.

Raineri, A. & Rachlin, H. (1993) The effect of temporal constraints on the value of money and other commodities, *Journal of Behavioral Decision Making*, 6, 77–94.

Read, D. (2001a) Intrapersonal dilemmas, *Human Relations*, 54, 1093–117.

Read, D. (2001b) Is time-discounting hyperbolic or subadditive? *Journal of Risk and Uncertainty*, 23(1), 5–32.

Read, D. (2003) Time and the marketplace. Working paper, London School of Economics.

Read, D. & Powell, M. (2002) Reasons for sequence preferences, *Journal of Behavioral Decision Making*, 15(5), 433–60.

Read, D. & Roelofsma, P. H. M. P. (2003) Subadditive versus hyperbolic discounting: A comparison of choice and matching, *Organizational Behavior and Human Decision Processes*, 91, 140–53.

Read, D. & Van Leeuwen, B. (1998) Predicting hunger: The effects of appetite and delay on choice, *Organizational Behavior and Human Decision Processes*, 76(2), 189–205.

Roelofsma, P. & Read, D. (2000) Intransitive intertemporal choice, *Journal of Behavioral Decision Making*, 13(2), 161–77.

Rogers, A. R. (1994) Evolution of time preference by natural-selection, *American Economic Review*, 84(3), 460–81.

Rubinstein, A. (2003) Economics and psychology? The case of hyperbolic discounting, *International Economic Review*, 44, 1207–16.

Schelling, T. C. (1995) Intergenerational discounting, *Energy Policy*, 23(4–5), 395–401.

Shelley, M. K. (1993) Outcome signs, question frames and discount rates, *Management Science*, 39(7), 806–15.

Shelley, M. K. (1994) Gain loss asymmetry in risky intertemporal choice, *Organizational Behavior and Human Decision Processes*, 59(1), 124–59.

Sidgwick, H. (1874) *Methods of Ethics*. Indianapolis: Hackett.

Soman, D. (1998) The illusion of delayed incentives: Evaluating future effort–money transactions, *Journal of Marketing Research*, 35(4), 427–37.

Sozou, P. D. (1998) On hyperbolic discounting and uncertain hazard rates, *Proceedings of the Royal Society of London Series B-Biological Sciences*, 265(1409), 2015–20.

Sozou, P. D. & Seymour, R. M. (2003) Augmented discounting: Interaction between ageing and time-preference behaviour, *Proceedings of the Royal Society of London Series B-Biological Sciences*, 265, 1047–53.

Strotz, R. H. (1955) Myopia and inconsistency in dynamic utility maximization, *Review of Economic Studies*, 23, 165–80.

Thaler, R. (1981) Some empirical evidence of dynamic inconsistency, *Economics Letters*, 8, 201–7.

Trope, Y. & Liberman, N. (2000) Temporal construal and time-dependent changes in preference, *Journal of Personality and Social Psychology*, 79(6), 876–89.

Trope, Y. & Liberman, N. (2003) Construal level theory of intertemporal judgment and decision. In G. Loewenstein, D. Read, & R. F. Baumeister (eds.), *Time and Decision: Economic and Psychological Perspectives on Intertemporal Choice*. New York: Russell Sage Foundation.

Trostel, P. A. & Taylor, G. A. (2001) A theory of time preference, *Economic Inquiry*, 39(3), 379–95.

Van der Pol, M. M. & Cairns, J. A. (2000) Negative and zero time preference for health, *Health Economics*, 9(2), 171–5.

Wertenbroch, K. (2003) Self-rationing: Self-control in consumer choice. In G. Loewenstein, D. Read, & R. F. Baumeister (eds.), *Time and Decision: Economic and Psychological Perspectives on Intertemporal Choice*. New York: Russell Sage Foundation.

Wilson, J. Q. & Herrnstein, R. J. (1985) *Crime and Human Nature*. New York: Simon & Schuster.

Yates, J. F. & Watts, R. A. (1975) Preferences for deferred losses, *Organizational Behavior and Human Performance*, 13, 294–306.

22

The Connections between Affect and Decision Making: Nine Resulting Phenomena

Yuval Rottenstreich and Suzanne Shu

Introduction

The psychological study of decision making has long drawn on the tension between normative and descriptive considerations. Because normative accounts, such as expected utility, predate descriptive inquiry, this approach has produced a research program that is to some extent inherently conservative. First, the experimental agenda has often been molded by a desire to improve upon the older normative theories. A common tactic is to isolate some normative requirement that seems likely to fail empirically and to conduct experiments corroborating this failure. Second, descriptively-inspired theories have avoided sweeping changes in favor of maintaining agreement with the broad themes of normative accounts. Kahneman and Tversky's *prospect theory*, which is the best-known descriptively-inspired theory, provides an example. Recently, Kahneman remarked:

> The theory that we constructed was as conservative as possible . . . We did not challenge the philosophical analysis of choices in terms of beliefs and desires that underlies utility theory, nor did we question the normative [status of] models of rational choice . . . The goal . . . was to assemble the minimal set of modifications of expected utility theory that would provide a descriptive account . . .
>
> (Kahneman & Tversky, 2000)

The conservative bias has been one of decision-making research's greatest assets. Indeed, prospect theory has been highly influential in large part exactly because differences between it and antecedent normative theories were kept to a minimum. By maintaining most of the established approach, the theory made plain and stark the insights it was intended to convey.

One unfortunate consequence of the conservative bias has been neglect of affective phenomena. Because emotional experience does not figure prominently in normative theories, as long as normative perspectives molded research agendas, the connection between affect and decision making was overlooked. Happily, however, recent years have seen a flurry of interest in the connections between emotions and decision making. Because emotions clearly shape many decisions, it was perhaps inevitable that the interplay of affect and choice would eventually become a topic of interest. Nevertheless, the emergence of this topic also reflects an evolution of research programs. After long being shaped by normative theories, research agendas have begun to place greater emphasis on topics emerging from the field's own inherent interests.

In this chapter, we review recent research concerning the interplay of affect and decision making. We organize our comments in a manner highlighting the newer form of research agendas. Rather than contrasting findings about affect with normative standards, we analyze these findings with respect to prospect theory. Just as earlier work built on the relationship between the descriptive and the normative, we attempt to build on the relationship between prospect theory and affective concerns.

We address two types of questions. First, what affective phenomena are highlighted by prospect theory or suggested by modifications to it? Second, on the flip side, what affective phenomena cannot be incorporated into a prospect theory framework? In the course of our discussion, we highlight nine empirical patterns of decision making that appear to be closely related to affective experience.

Prospect Theory Preliminaries

The insights uncovered by prospect theory are meant to apply to any risky choice, from the prosaic, such as whether to carry an umbrella, to the profound, such as whether to overthrow a despotic regime. Nevertheless, the actual formulation of the theory is highly schematic: the theory depicts each option faced by a decision maker as a gamble that can yield various outcomes with different probabilities. In the simplest version of the theory, the utility of an option having i different potential outcomes, each with probability p_i, is given by $\Sigma w(p_i)v(i)$. Here, the subjective value function v indexes the decision maker's assessments of the attractiveness of possible outcomes, and the weighting function w quantifies the decision maker's reactions to probabilities. The overall utility of an option is a weight-based linear combination of the values of potential outcomes. The decision maker is presumed to choose the available option of highest utility. Phenomena uncovered by prospect theory largely correspond to properties of v or w or of the way these functions are combined to form an overall utility. We assume that the reader is familiar with these phenomena, which include reference-dependence, diminishing sensitivity, and loss aversion, all of which concern v, and certainty and impossibility effects, which concern w. For thorough explications of prospect theory see Kahneman and Tverksy (1979) and Tversky and Kahneman (1992).

The remainder of this chapter is organized as follows. The next two sections concern phenomena associated with the value and weighting function, respectively. The subsequent section differentiates among various types of emotional experience and largely focuses on affective phenomena that prospect theory seems incapable of handling.

The Value Function

We begin with the subjective value function, *v*. To illustrate the notion of "subjective value," consider how long someone who is willing to work one hour for $10 would be willing to work for $30 and how much someone who is willing to donate $10 to save one endangered animal would be willing to donate to save four endangered animals. To gauge how long someone would work for $30 rather than $10, one must assess how much "satisfaction" or "value" the person accrues from either amount. If the satisfaction accrued from $30 is not much larger than that from $10, the individual will not work appreciably longer for the larger amount. Making a charitable donation presumably gives one moral satisfaction (e.g., Kahneman & Knetsch, 1992). Thus, to gauge how much more someone would donate to save four endangered animals rather than one, one must assess the extent to which an increase in the number of animals saved increases the amount of moral satisfaction.

As these examples suggest, subjective value sometimes has emotional determinants. Even if money earned from work is not evaluated in a highly affective manner it seems clear that the warm glow one receives from charitable donations reflects some form of emotional experience. In sum, at least in some circumstances, emotional experience influences subjective value.

Dual-process theories of valuation

Prospect theory is agnostic about the processes used to assess value; the theory does not differentiate between any determinants of value, let alone affective and non-affective determinants. Thus, one important avenue for research includes analyses of valuation that differentiate between affective and non-affective processes.

Hsee and Rottenstreich (2003) have distinguished two psychological processes by which people might assess subjective value: valuation by calculation and valuation by feeling. To illustrate these concepts, consider decisions of how much to pay for a second-hand box set composed of either five or ten Madonna compact discs. Valuation by calculation might appeal to the typical cost of a single used CD (e.g., $3) and then account for the number of discs, perhaps coming to a willingness-to-pay of approximately $15 for the five-CD set and $30 for the ten-CD set. In contrast, valuation by feeling might focus on feelings evoked by Madonna songs and images. Because such feelings are independent of the number of discs available, using them as a cue for value might lead to roughly equal willingness-to-pay for either set.

More generally, Hsee and Rottenstreich define valuation by calculation as a process that relies on some algorithm (e.g., involving the typical cost of a disc) that takes into account the nature of the stimulus (e.g., the box set consists of Madonna discs) and its scope (e.g., there are five discs in the collection). They define valuation by feeling as a process that reacts to one's gut feeling toward the stimulus (e.g., one's liking of Madonna).

In the domain of multiattribute choice, many authors have similarly contrasted valuations that proceed by "reason" with valuations that proceed by "feeling." When valuing by reason, decision makers weigh and combine individual attributes into an overall assessment; alternatively, decision makers may ignore an option's components and assess value by asking the higher-level question "how do I feel about this option?" Noteworthy distinctions between reason and feeling are provided by Damasio (1994), Pham (1998), Sloman (1996), and Zajonc (1980).

In much the same vein as calculation versus feeling or reason versus feeling dichotomies, Baron (1992) distinguishes between decisions based on logical rules and decisions based on anticipated emotional reactions. These modes of thoughts sometimes agree (e.g., people may consider some action logically appropriate and may simultaneously anticipate feeling guilty were they to avoid it) but are often in conflict (e.g., people may consider some action logically appropriate yet anticipate feeling guilty for taking it).

Frederick's (2002) dichotomy of "deliberate" and "automatic" valuation processes is also in line with the distinctions between calculation and feeling and between reason and feeling. Deliberate valuations arise when people have no immediate "sense" of their subjective value for some target. This is most often the case when people are confronted with abstract, multiattribute information that does not evoke intuitive impressions. Consider a consumer who is looking for an apartment. When asked to select either a cheaper apartment that is a bit older and smaller and entails a shorter commute or a more expensive apartment that is more modern and larger but entails a longer commute, the consumer may have to ponder the issue and search for his or her personal answer. In this case, he or she must consciously select some type of analytical approach (i.e., a calculation such as x minutes of commute are worth y dollars and z square feet) to gauge the subjective values of the apartments.

Automatic valuations arise when people do have an immediate awareness of their subjective value for some target. This is, almost by definition, most often the case when people confront evocative stimuli that elicit strong feelings. For instance, imagine that the consumer tours an apartment offering a breathtaking view. In this case the determination of subjective value may not require conscious deliberation, because the consumer may rely on automatic affective evaluations of what he or she likes (e.g., "I'll take this apartment because the view is breathtaking").

Valuation by feeling is closely related to Finucane, Alhakami, Slovic and Johnson's (2000) notion of an "affect heuristic." These authors argue that affective reactions are often used as cues for value, much as assessments of availability or representativeness are used as cues for likelihood. For example, perceived risk and perceived benefit are often negatively correlated (see Ganzach, 2000). Activities toward which people have negative feelings (e.g., nuclear power generation) are judged as high risk and low benefit while activities toward which people have positive feelings (e.g., use of cellular phones) are judged as low risk and high benefit. Put differently, unfavorable affective reactions form the basis for judgments of high risk and low benefit, while favorable affective reactions form the basis for judgments of low risk and high benefit. That risk and benefit are, in reality, typically positively correlated may be obscured by reliance on feelings. Evidently, affective reactions towards risks shape perceptions of associated costs and benefits, rather than vice versa.

Schwarz and Clore's (1983, 1996) notion of feelings-as-information asserts that affect is sometimes used as a cue for decision making and that when it is used, it may often be confused with other cues. In particular, these authors argue that people frequently value a target essentially by asking themselves: "How do I feel about this?"; they emphasize that, because it is difficult to distinguish one's pre-existing mood from one's feelings about a target, people are likely to answer this question more positively when in a happy rather than sad mood. From our perspective, the feeling-as-information account posits that people often engage in valuation by feeling, and that this valuation process is prone to systematic errors concerning the source of experienced affect.

So far, we have focused on defining or describing affective and non-affective processes for the assessment of subjective value. We now discuss three empirical patterns that appear to reflect differences between affective and non-affective valuation processes.

Pattern 1: Valuation processes as a source of preference malleability

Researchers have long been interested in framing effects, price–choice preference-reversals, and other phenomena that highlight the extent to which people's preferences are malleable. Indeed, the malleability of preferences – and the fact that such malleability is systematic and reflects various psychological processes rather than random error – may be considered as the "central finding" of decision-making research. In our opinion, much preference malleability reflects the operation of different valuation processes. Certain targets may facilitate automatic valuation by feeling while others may facilitate deliberate valuation by calculation, but many targets are amenable to different types of processing. The selection of a particular valuation process for such targets will often depend on the specific circumstances in which valuation happens to occur and will thus be a primary contributor to preference malleability.

An experiment by Shiv and Fedorikhin (1999) provides one example. These authors had participants memorize either a two-digit or seven-digit number. Participants were then instructed to walk to another room to report this number. On the way, they were offered a choice between two snacks, chocolate cake (more favorable feelings – tasty, less favorable cognitions – unhealthy) or fruit salad (less favorable feelings – less tasty, more favorable cognitions – healthy). Shiv and Fedorikhin predicted that high-memory load (seven digits) would reduce the capacity for deliberation, thus increasing the likelihood that the affectively favorable option (cake) would be selected. Indeed, chocolate cake was favored more often when memory load was high than when it was low (see also Ward & Mann, 2000). It appears that the value of chocolate cake was greater when feelings were automatically used to establish preferences than when cognitions were deliberately used to calculate preferences.

Valuations influenced by criteria such as "is this useful?" or "is this what I am supposed to do?" also illustrate how different mechanisms may "compete" for influence of the valuation process. Gilbert, Gill, and Wilson (1998) provide an especially compelling example contrasting preferences constructed by feeling with preferences constructed by deliberate consideration of what one is supposed to do. These authors had grocery shoppers list the items they intended to purchase. Only some shoppers were allowed to retain their list during their actual shopping trip. Furthermore, some shoppers were asked to eat a quarter pound of muffins just before shopping. Among list-less shoppers, those who were unfed bought more unlisted items than those who were well fed. But, among shoppers retaining their lists, those who were unfed did not buy more unlisted items. Presumably, list-less shoppers experienced more positive affective reactions to unlisted items when unfed ("those cookies look delicious!") than when well fed ("I never want to eat again"). Shoppers with lists surely had the same affective reactions, but evidently decided whether to purchase an appealing item by checking their list to see if they were "supposed" to buy it, rather than by following their affective reactions.

To reiterate, in our opinion the experiments of Shiv and Fedorihkin and of Gilbert et al. demonstrate how the malleability of preferences may in part reflect the extent to which different circumstances facilitate different valuation processes. The same person may prefer chocolate cake when his or her circumstances engender automatic valuation by feeling but prefer fruit salad when his or her circumstances engender deliberate valuation by calculation.

Pattern 2: Different valuation processes yield different functional forms for v

As suggested by the Madonna example, Hsee and Rottenstreich find that when people rely on feeling, value varies with the presence or absence of a stimulus (i.e., the difference between zero and some scope) but does not much vary with further variation of scope. In contrast, when people rely on calculation, value reveals relatively constant sensitivity to any variation in scope. That is, Hsee and Rottenstreich find that v is nearly a step-function of scope when feeling predominates and closer to linear when calculation predominates.

Researchers interested in valuations of non-market goods have also observed nearly step-function value functions that appear to reflect the role of feelings. In a representative experiment, Desvousges, Johnson, Dunford, Hudson, Wilson, & Boyle (1993) asked (separate groups of) participants how much they would donate to save 2,000, 20,000, or 200,000 migrating birds from drowning in oil ponds. The mean responses, $80, $78, and $88, showed astounding scope-insensitivity (see also Baron & Greene, 1996; Carson & Mitchell, 1993; Frederick & Fischhoff, 1998).

Kahneman, Ritov, and Schkade (1999) explain these results by arguing that Desvousges et al.'s questions evoke "a mental representation of a prototypical incident, perhaps an image of an exhausted bird, its feathers soaked in black oil, unable to escape" and that participants decided how much to donate on the basis of their affective reactions to this image. More generally, Kahneman et al. use the term "affective valuation" for assessments of preference on the basis of "the sign and intensity of the emotional response to objects" and stress that affective valuations are scope-insensitive because "the attitude to a set of similar objects is often determined by the affective valuation of a prototypical member of that set . . ."

Baron and Spranca (1997; Baron & Ritov, 1994) observed step-function like value functions for issues to which people have meaningful moral and emotional attachments. For instance, when asked to consider programs for genetic engineering intended to make children more intelligent or for forcing women to be sterilized because they are retarded, people established very similar values across very different scope-levels (i.e., the number of children or the number of women).

Building on the observation that many targets are amenable to more than one valuation process, Hsee and Rottenstreich propose a model of valuation in which people are portrayed as relying on a mix of calculation and feeling. In this model, subjective value follows the equation $v = A^\alpha S^{1-\alpha}$. Here, A represents the intensity of affective or automatic reactions to a target, S denotes the target's scope, and α is an "affective focus coefficient" bounded by 0 and 1. The form $v = A^\alpha S^{1-\alpha}$ is equivalent to the Cobb–Douglas utility function often invoked in economics; for a given (A, α) pair, it reduces to the power law of psychophysics. When α is small, valuation depends mostly on deliberate calculations that consider scope; in this case v is nearly a linear function of scope. When α is large, valuation depends mostly on automatic affective reactions and neglects scope; in this case v is nearly a step function, equaling zero when scope is zero and A otherwise.

Any intermediate α corresponds to some mix of calculation and feeling and, moreover, yields a curved value function. The notion of mixes of calculation and feeling may thus provide a novel interpretation for why value functions are typically curved: concave in the domain of gains and convex in the domain of losses. Historically, curvature of value has been attributed to satiation or diminishing sensitivity. Presumably, the more units of a good one consumes (e.g., in the domain of gains: the more pandas are saved; in the domain of losses: the more pandas are lost), the less one desires (in the domain of gains) or is averse to (in the domain of losses), and thus the less one values, additional units of this good. By this view, the faster the rate of satiation, the more pronounced is the curvature of value.

Although satiation is surely an important influence, the model of Rottenstreich and Hsee suggests that the particular mix of valuation processes relied upon, and not just the nature of satiation, may determine the curvature of value. In particular, the model predicts that as the reliance on affect grows, in other words as α gets larger, the observed curvature should become more pronounced. This greater curvature implies greater risk aversion in the domain of gains and greater risk seeking in the domain of losses. Several studies support this prediction, revealing greater risk aversion with positive affect and greater risk seeking with negative affect, which in turn suggests that there is indeed greater curvature of value in affect-rich settings. First, Hsee and Weber (1997) observed that most people believed that others were less risk-averse than they themselves were and suggested that this belief had affective underpinnings. People may think they are more risk-averse than others if: (a) while contemplating their options they experience a feeling along the lines of a "desire to wimp out" and they then follow that feeling; while (b) they do not appreciate that others experience the same kind of feelings.

Second, in an important series of studies, Isen and colleagues have found that people in a positive mood are more risk-averse than people in a neutral state (for a review see Isen, 1993). Likewise, it appears that people in a negative mood are more risk-seeking (Mano, 1992, 1994). These observations are often explained by the mood-maintenance hypothesis according to which happy people are reluctant to gamble, because a loss would eliminate their good mood, whereas sad people are willing to gamble, because a win would alleviate their bad mood. In addition to their influence on mood-maintenance, it may be that positive and negative moods encourage greater reliance on valuation by feeling, which in turn engenders greater curvature of value.

Pattern 3: Affect-richness yields pronounced loss aversion

One of the best-known findings in decision-making research is that a loss relative to the status quo has more impact than a corresponding gain relative to the status quo. This pattern, known as loss aversion, is often summarized by Kahneman and Tversky's famous tag line "losses loom larger than gains." It is accommodated in prospect theory by a value function that is steeper in the domain of losses than in the domain of gains. To distinguish loss aversion and steepness on the one hand from curvature on the other hand, note that in terms of the equation $v = A^{\alpha}S^{1-\alpha}$ greater curvature corresponds to larger values of α, whereas greater steepness corresponds to larger (absolute) values of A.

Recently, Dhar and Wertenbroch (2000) observed that hedonic goods, which induce pronounced affective reactions, are associated with greater loss aversion than utilitarian goods, which induce muted affective reactions. As we have mentioned, affect-rich items presumably facilitate automatic valuation by feeling whereas affect-poor items presumably facilitate deliberate valuation by calculation. Thus, it may be that the nature of the valuation process, and in particular the relative reliance on affect in valuation, may influence not only the curvature of v but also the magnitude of loss aversion it displays.

Consistent with Dhar and Wertenbroch's findings, Luce (1998; Luce, Bettman, & Payne, 1997; Luce, Payne, & Bettman, 1999) reports that the tendency to stick with the status quo increases as the content of a decision elicits greater negative emotion. Similarly, it appears that people are extremely reluctant to accept losses involving moral, safety, or health considerations that are likely tinged with strong emotional considerations (Baron, 1986, 1992; Beattie & Barlas, 1993).

Isen, Nygren, and Ashby (1988) observed that people presented with a gamble when in a positive mood have more thoughts about losing than do controls (Isen and Geva, 1987) and self-report a greater negative utility for a given loss (Nygren, Isen, Taylor, & Dulin, 1996). These results suggest that positive affect gamblers have value functions that show a great deal of loss aversion.

Section summary

In this section we have reviewed work on valuation. Several researchers have contrasted two processes of valuation, one more deliberate and calculative, the other more automatic and affective. There may be systematic differences in the values assessed by these processes. In particular, three phenomena appear to reflect the influence of different valuation processes. First, the use of different valuation processes may contribute to preference malleability. Second, valuation by feeling is relatively scope-insensitive yielding step-function value functions, whereas valuation by calculation is relatively scope-sensitive yielding more linear value functions; moreover, curvature of the value function may be attributed to reliance on feeling rather than calculation. Third, valuation by feeling appears to yield greater loss aversion than valuation by calculation.

The Weighting Function

Prospect theory suggests that people overemphasize certainty and impossibility. To illustrate, suppose you had some chance to win $1,000,000. For most people, a change in the probability of winning from, say, 0.30 to 0.31 seems minor, but a change from 0 to 0.01 or from 0.99 to 1.00 seems extremely impactful (Tversky & Kahneman, 1992). Such "possibility effects" and "certainty effects" are captured in prospect theory by a weighting function w that has pronounced slope near probabilities of zero and one and very mild slope at intermediate probabilities. The pronounced slope near zero is such that w overweights small probabilities, $w(p) > p$; given that $w(0) = 0$, $w(p) > p$ for small probabilities models the possibility effect. Likewise, the pronounced slope near one is such that w underweights large probabilities, $w(p) < p$ which, given that $w(1) = 1$, $w(p) < p$ for large probabilities models the certainty effect.

Rottenstreich and Hsee (2001) proposed an affective interpretation of w meant to explain the certainty and possibility effects. They suggested that the steep slope on the left-hand side of w differentiates situations in which some hope exists (whenever the probability of winning a positive prize is greater than zero) from situations in which there is no hope (whenever the probability of winning a positive prize is equal to zero). Likewise, the steep slope on the right-hand side of w differentiates situations in which some fear exists (whenever the probability of winning is less than one) from situations in which there is no fear (whenever the probability of winning is equal to one). In contrast, altering the degree of possibility from one intermediate probability to another should have relatively little affective impact, so that w will have a mild slope in the interior of the probability scale. In sum, Rottenstreich and Hsee's affective approach holds that the over- and under-weighting displayed by w can be attributed, at least in part, to affective reactions (cf. Tversky & Fox, 1995).

The role of affect in probability weighting raises questions about *probability–outcome independence*, one of the most fundamental implications of the prospect theory representation $\sum w(p_i)v(i)$. By positing separate functions for the evaluation of outcomes and probabilities, prospect theory assumes that the impact of a given probability is a function of that probability but not of the outcome to which it is attached. In contrast, Rottenstreich and Hsee's analysis implies that probability–outcome independence is unlikely to hold across outcomes having different affective intensities. Indeed, their analysis implies probability–outcome dependence: because they yield stronger emotional reactions, affect-rich outcomes should elicit both more pronounced overweighting of small probabilities and more pronounced underweighting of large probabilities than affect-poor outcomes (see Lopes, 1987 for an additional hypothesis of probability–outcome dependence).

Pattern 4: Affect-richness yields pronounced certainty and impossibility effects

Consistent with this prediction, Rottenstreich and Hsee found that the certainty and possibility effects were larger for affect-rich outcomes than for affect-poor outcomes. In one experiment, participants were presented with $500 coupons that could be used either for tuition payments (affect-poor) or towards expenses associated with a vacation to Paris, Venice, and Rome (affect-rich). Given a 1 percent chance of winning a coupon, people preferred the vacation coupon; that is, the possibility effect was more pronounced for the vacation than tuition coupon. However, given a 99 percent of winning a coupon, people preferred the tuition coupon; thus, the certainty effect was also more pronounced for the vacation than tuition coupon. In other words, the slope of the weighting function is steeper at the endpoints of 0 and 1 for the affect-rich item than for the affect-poor item. This leads to a crossover, in which weighting of small probabilities is greater for the affect-rich item but weighting of large probabilities is greater for the affect-poor item, inconsistent with probability–outcome independence.

Pronounced certainty and possibility effects for affect-rich targets imply pronounced insensitivity to intermediate probability variations for those same targets. Psychophysical studies of anxiety and fear demonstrate exactly such insensitivity. People's physiological responses to impending electric shocks appear essentially uncorrelated with the probability of receiving the shock, as long as this probability is greater than zero (Bankhart & Elliott, 1974; Elliott, 1975; Monat, Averill, & Lazarus, 1972; Snortum & Wilding, 1971). This result can be restated as follows: evidently, feelings (of fear or worry or of any other kind) are scope-insensitive – they depend on the mere possibility rather than the probability of outcomes (cf. Loewenstein, Weber, Hsee, & Welch, 2001; Loewenstein & Lerner, 2003).

The notion that hope and fear underlie the certainty and impossibility effects is consistent with a model of the weighting function as $w = p^{1-\alpha}/[p^{1-\alpha} + (1-p)^{1-\alpha}]$. Here, α is an "affect index," bounded by 0 and 1, with larger values indicating greater affect-richness. When $\alpha = 0$, w reduces to the identity; as α grows larger, w becomes more curved, indicating more pronounced overweighting and underweighting.

Pattern 5: Savoring and dread influence elevation of w

Several researchers have distinguished between curvature and elevation of w (e.g., Gonzalez & Wu, 1999). Formally, consider the family of functions $w = (1+a)p/[(1+a)p + (1-p)]$. When $a = 0$, w again reduces to the identity; but as a grows larger, w does not become more curved, it becomes more elevated at all probability levels.

Variations in elevation are consistent with an account emphasizing not hope and fear, but savoring and dread (see Loewenstein, 1987; Elster & Loewenstein, 1992).

Compared to affect-poor outcomes, affect-rich outcomes might give rise to more savoring (positive prizes) or dread (negative prizes). More pronounced savoring and dread would elevate the (absolute) value of affect-rich lotteries at every probability.

The hope-and-fear and savoring-and-dread accounts may be seen as complementary. By this view, more pronounced savoring of a European vacation rather than a tuition coupon may contribute to the greater allure of the vacation at low probabilities, while the preference for the tuition coupon at high probabilities would suggest that, at least in this circumstance, the fear of losing has greater impact than the savoring of a high-likelihood prize (Brandstatter, Kuhberger, & Schneider, 2002 and Wu, 1999 present additional affective hypotheses about w).

Furthermore, formally mixing the two accounts yields the function $w = (1 + a)p^{1-\alpha}/[(1 + a)p^{1-\alpha} + (1 - p)^{1-\alpha}]$. Here, α captures the intensity of hope and fear and a captures the intensity of savoring and dread. Although they did not emphasize an affective interpretation of the weighting function, this form of w is closely related to the form proposed by Tversky and Kahneman (1992). When both a and α equal zero, the proposed form reduces to $w = p$; it could be said that $\alpha = a = 0$ yields "weighting by calculation" that depends directly on probabilities themselves, whereas $\alpha > 0$ or $a > 0$ yield "weighting by feeling."

Pattern 6: The role of affect-laden imagery

The influence of emotions on w may often operate through affect-laden imagery, both for hope and fear and savoring and dread. To appreciate how hope, fear, and imagery may interact to yield hypersensitivity near probabilities of zero and one and intermediate insensitivity, consider a thought experiment by Elster and Loewenstein (1992). Picture a fatal car crash involving your closest friend. The harrowing image that emerges might make you drive more carefully. In other words, the possibility of a terrible crash may lead to an affective reaction to a salient image, and this feeling (not explicit consideration of the scenario's probability) may guide behavior. Such feelings will be hypersensitive to departures from probabilities of zero or one, because the difference between no chance and some chance or some chance and certainty "activates" either an image of the potential outcome or a counter-image accentuating its absence. In contrast, such feelings will be independent of intermediate probability variations (whether chances of a crash are 1 in 1,000 or 100,000), because intermediate variations will not alter the associated image.

An experiment by Slovic, Monahan, and MacGregor (2000; see also Yamagishi, 1997) reveals the role that imagery may play in the elicitation of dread. These authors had clinicians judge the risk that various patients hospitalized with mental disorders posed of harming someone after discharge. At any given level of likelihood, a patient was judged as posing greater risk if that likelihood was presented as a frequency (e.g., 10 out of 100) rather than a probability (e.g., 10 percent). Slovic et al. suggest that a probability format naturally creates an image of a single individual. Because this individual may or may not be violent, the image of him or her might appear relatively benign. The assessed risk in this case might therefore be relatively low. On the other hand, a frequency format suggests an image that necessarily includes a number of violent patients and is thus frightening and affectively loaded, in short: dreadful. The assessed risk in this case might be relatively high.

Pattern 7: Systematic biases in judgments of likelihood

The formulation of prospect theory as $\Sigma w(p_i)v(i)$ implicitly presumes that numerical probabilities p_i are provided to a decision maker. In many instances, however, the decision maker is not confronted with numerical probabilities but with a situation in which each outcome is contingent on some event e_i. In such instances, most applications of prospect theory presume that the decision maker judges the likelihood of each e_i and then weights these judgments in forming a decision. In this framework the judged likelihoods are denoted $p(e_i)$ and the relevant model becomes $\Sigma w(p(e_i))v(i)$.

The certainty and impossibility effects concern w or the weighting of probability, and we have seen that this weighting is susceptible to affective influences. Much research suggests that affect also operates at the next level down – judgments of probabilities or the function p. In particular, many studies indicate that positive and negative moods bias people's probability and frequency judgments of valenced events. Compared to controls, people in a positive mood appear to judge desirable events as more likely and undesirable events as less likely; people in a negative mood judge desirable events less likely and undesirable events more likely (Bower, 1981; Nygren et al., 1996; Wegener, Petty, & Klein, 1994).

In a seminal study, Johnson and Tversky (1983) observed that the influence of negative mood is general; that is, negative mood increases the perceived likelihood of any undesirable event, irrespective of the degree to which that event is related to the particular causes of the negative mood. For example, a negative mood induced by reading an article about a disease (e.g., AIDS) increases estimates of the frequency of fatalities due to natural disasters just as it increases estimates of fatalities due to other diseases (e.g., cancer). The effect of positive mood also appears to be general (Mayer, Gaschke, Braverman, & Evans, 1992).

Recent work has focused on qualifications to another aspect of generality, concerning the nature of the elicited emotion rather than the nature of the eliciting or judged events. In particular, many researchers have found that even specific emotions of the same valence (e.g., sadness and fear) may have distinct effects on judgments of likelihood (DeSteno, Petty, Wegener, & Rucker, 2000; Lerner & Keltner, 2000, 2001; Raghunathan & Pham, 1999).

Section summary

In this section we have reviewed work on affect and the impact of uncertainty. Four phenomena appear to reflect affective reactions to uncertainty. First, by engendering hope and fear, affect-richness may yield pronounced certainty and impossibility effects and extreme insensitivity to intermediate probability variations. These patterns correspond to properties of the slope of w. Second, by engendering savoring and dread, affect-richness may contribute to the elevation of w. Third, the influence of affect is likely to depend on the imagery evoked. Fourth, affect, especially in the form of mood, appears to bias judgments of likelihood.

Different Varieties of Affective Experience

So far, we have not carefully differentiated between different types of affective experiences. One way to distinguish emotional experiences is by when in the decision-making process they occur. This consideration suggests a tripartite partition. First, emotions may be experienced at the time that a decision is being made (decision time). Second, emotions may be experienced after a decision has been made but before the consequences of those decisions have been realized (post-decision but pre-resolution of uncertainty). Third, emotions may be experienced in reaction to receipt of an outcome (post-resolution).

Most of our attention has been on the study of emotions experienced at decision time. These emotions have different sources including mood, the affect-richness of outcomes and events under consideration (e.g., as captured by A in the model $v = A^{\alpha}S^{1-\alpha}$), and the extent to which the process used to assess the relevant outcomes and events focuses on affective considerations (e.g., as captured by α in the model $v = A^{\alpha}S^{1-\alpha}$). Furthermore, decision-time affect may be subdivided into two varieties: emotions anticipated to arise as a consequence of the decision (either pre- or post-resolution) and that are thus used in forming one's decision (e.g., one might choose the option that is expected to make one happiest – or one might choose not to do so) versus emotions directly connected to having to make a decision or with the process of deciding (e.g., having to decide may be unpleasant; one might be in a positive mood while deciding). There has recently been much important work concerning post-decision but pre-resolution affect (Trope & Liberman, 2003; Lovallo & Kahneman, 2000). The study of post-resolution emotion has also garnered much attention (Gilovich & Medvec, 1995). However, in the remainder of this section, we will largely be concerned with discussing research concerning the two subvarieties of decision-time affective experience that we will label *anticipatory* versus *process* experiences (cf. Loewenstein et al., 2001). The principal conclusion that will emerge is that some forms of decision-time affect cannot be easily accommodated within the framework of prospect theory.

Anticipatory feelings

A growing body of research documents the extent to which decision making is shaped by the anticipation of post-decision emotions. Damasio and colleagues (Damasio, 1994; Bechara, Damasio, Tranel, & Damasio, 1997) studied brain-damaged patients who were normal with respect to basic intelligence and memory but impaired in emotional experience: these patients appeared incapable of associating feelings with anticipated consequences. In one experiment, Damasio had participants make successive selections of cards from any of four available decks. Turning each card resulted in the gain or loss of a sum of money. Some decks included a favorable distribution of wins and losses; others interspersed attractive large payoffs with occasional huge losses. Normal subjects quickly learned to avoid troublesome decks, but brain-damaged patients did not and thus lost a great deal of money. The patients responded appropriately to gains and losses when they occurred (e.g., they showed normal skin-conductance responses just after an outcome was experienced) but did not seem to learn to anticipate future outcomes (e.g., they did not show normal skin-conductance responses when considering choosing from a bad deck).

Peters and colleagues (Peters & Slovic, 2000; Peters & Mauro, 2000) extended the work of Damasio. Studying a similar card task, they found that normal participants' self-reported assessments of affective reactivity were good predictors of choices. Greater self-reported reactivity to negative outcomes was associated with fewer selections from decks with large losing payoffs. On the other hand, greater self-reported reactivity to positive outcomes was associated with more selections from high-gain decks.

Mellers and colleagues (Mellers, 2000; Mellers, Schwartz, & Ritov, 1999) studied people's predictions of their emotional reactions to potential outcomes of a risky choice and observed that people tended to pick the risky option for which they expected to feel better on average (i.e., across all possible events). Relatedly, many researchers have pursued the notion that aversion to post-decision regret or disappointment shapes choice (Bell, 1982, 1985; Gul, 1991; Josephs, Larrick, Steele, & Nisbett, 1992; Loomes & Sugden, 1982, 1986, 1987; Zeelenberg, van Dijk, Manstead, & van der Pligt, 2000).

Taken together, Damasio's, Peters', and Mellers' work and the work on regret and disappointment underscore the intuitive observation that people make decisions in part by anticipating their potential, subsequent feelings. However, we wish to emphasize that there may be an inherent discrepancy between these important studies and the dual process theories of valuation discussed earlier. Dual process theories essentially predict that anticipated emotions guide decisions in certain circumstances (when automatic valuation by feeling predominates) but not in others (when deliberate valuation by calculation predominates). Indeed, Hsee (1999) presents situations in which people seem to choose options that they do not expect will yield the best emotional reactions. Understanding the boundary conditions for the type of results provided by studies of anticipated emotion provides an important avenue for further research.

Pattern 8: People have to cope with choice

We now turn to the issue of process-induced feelings. In an important series of studies Luce (1998), Luce et al. (1997), and Luce et al. (1999) investigate people's motivation to cope with negative emotions that arise from the process of making a decision. These authors note that decisions entailing a conflict between valued goals often evoke negative affective reactions (cf. Baron & Spranca, 1997; Beattie & Barlas, 1993). For instance, the parent of a young baby may experience a discomfiting feeling when mulling an automobile purchase which requires a tradeoff between his or her family's safety and a car's cost. Luce and colleagues propose that decision makers often try to cope with or minimize such negative emotions during the decision-making process. Consistent with this proposition, they observe that avoidant responses become more common as the content of the decision elicits greater negative emotion. Avoidant responses, such as maintaining the status quo or prolonging search, satisfy coping goals by minimizing explicit confrontation of negative consequences and aversive tradeoffs.

In prospect theory and all related theories, the act of choosing is not in and of itself viewed as troublesome. Thus, observations that it can be suggest numerous paradoxical phenomena. For instance, from a theoretical perspective adding options to an available set should always improve the decision maker's well-being (the new options may be better than the old, and if they are not then they can be ignored). Yet, adding options to a choice set may make the process of choosing harder to cope with, and may thus discourage decision makers or even leave them worse off. Consistent with this observation, Iyengar and Lepper (2000), Tversky and Shafir (1992) and Dhar (1996) found that adding options to a choice set often increased the selection of an avoidant response. Botti and Iyengar (2003) posit that negative emotions arising from the process of choosing may contaminate post-resolution evaluations of options; consistent with this prediction, they find that in certain circumstances people who are simply given some outcome are happier with that outcome than people who obtained the same outcome by choice.

Pattern 9: Affective influences incompatible with prospect theory

Some recent studies isolate situations in which objective or judged probabilities are the same across experimental conditions, yet participants' feelings about the relevant uncertainty appear to be different. For instance, in their study of the "alternative-outcome effect," Windschitl and Wells (1998; Windschitl & Weber, 1999) found that people preferred to participate in a raffle in which they held 21 of 88 tickets and five other players held 15, 14, 13, 13, and 12 tickets, respectively, rather than a raffle in which they held 21 of 88 tickets and five other players held 52, 6, 5, 2, and 2 tickets, respectively. Participants asked to assess the probability of winning returned the same estimates in either condition. Nevertheless, the comparison with the most salient outcome evidently yielded uncomfortable feelings in the latter condition, because 21 tickets is a lot less than 52, but not in the former condition, because 21 is slightly better than 15.

The notion that objective or judged probabilities may be the same across two situations, yet feelings in the two situations may diverge, suggests that such situations may yield different preferences – because of different feelings – when prospect theory requires that they yield equivalent preferences. This line of thought guides Loewenstein, Weber, Hsee, and Welch's (2001) "risk-as-feelings" hypothesis, which contends that emotional reactions to uncertainty may diverge from assessments focusing on value and weight, and, critically, that when such divergence occurs, emotional reactions will often drive decision making. Loewenstein et al. write that "although emotional reactions are also sensitive to probability and outcome valence, the functional relationships are quite different . . ." An extreme interpretation of this argument would imply that there are two separate systems – an affective system and a perhaps more cognitive system compatible with prospect theory – and that when affect guides behavior it may do so in a manner entirely incompatible with prospect theory or related formulations. Exploring the possibility of this kind of divergence between affect and prospect theory forms an important avenue for future research.

Section summary

In this section we distinguished between different types of affective experience. Emotional reactions may occur at decision time, after decision but before consequences are realized, or after consequences are realized. We have largely focused on decision-time affect, subvarieties of which are anticipatory and process emotion. Process emotions yield two important patterns. First, the need to cope with choice yields many paradoxical phenomena. Second, the effects of emotion may be separate from and incompatible with assessments of value and weight and may thus be difficult to reconcile with prospect theory.

Conclusion

One unfortunate consequence of the historical conservative bias in decision-making research was neglect of affective phenomena. In recent years, this neglect has been remedied by an outpouring of interest in this topic. Just as earlier work used the juxtaposition of descriptive and normative accounts, we have attempted to review recent research on the connections between affect and decision making by using a juxtaposition of findings on emotion with earlier findings on prospect theory. We hope that the merits of this approach outweigh its own inherent conservative bias.

References

Bankhart, C. & Elliott, R. (1974) Heart rate and skin conductance in anticipation of shocks with varying probability of occurrence, *Psychophysiology*, 11, 160–74.

Baron, J. (1986) Capacities, dispositions, and rational thinking. In R. J. Sternberg and D. K. Detterman (eds.), *What is Intelligence? Contemporary Viewpoints on its Nature and Definition*. Norwood, NJ: Ablex.

Baron, J. (1992) The effect of normative beliefs on anticipated emotions, *Journal of Personality and Social Psychology*, 63, 320–30.

Baron, J. & Greene, J. (1996) Determinants of insensitivity to quantity in valuation of public goods: Contribution, warm glow, budget constraints, availability, and prominence, *Journal of Experimental Psychology: Applied*, 2, 107–25.

Baron, J. & Ritov, I. (1994) Protected values and omission bias, *Organizational Behavior and Human Decision Processes*, 79, 79–94.

Baron, J. & Spranca, M. (1997) Protected values, *Organizational Behavior and Human Decision Processes*, 70, 1–16.

Beattie, J. & Barlas, S. (1993) Predicting perceived differences in tradeoff difficulty. In E. U. Weber, J. Baron et al. (eds.) (2001) *Conflict and Tradeoffs in Decision Making. Cambridge Series on Judgement and Decision Making* (pp. 25–64). New York: Cambridge University Press.

Bechara, A., Damasio, H., Tranel, D., & Damasio, A. (1997) Deciding advantageously before knowing the advantageous strategy, *Science*, 275, 1293–5.

Bell, D. (1982) Regret in decision making under uncertainty, *Operations Research*, 30, 961–81.

Bell, D. (1985) Disappointment in decision making under uncertainty, *Operations Research*, 33, 1–27.

Botti, S. & Iyengar, S. (2003) The psychological pleasure and pain of choosing: When people prefer choosing at the cost of subsequent well-being. Working paper, University of Chicago.

Bower, G. (1981) Mood and memory, *American Psychologist*, 36, 129–48.

Brandstatter, E., Kuhberger, A., & Schneider, F. (2002) A cognitive-emotional account of the shape of the probability weighting function, *Journal of Behavioral Decision Making*, 15, 79–100.

Carson, R. & Mitchell, R. (1993) The issue of scope in contingent valuation, *American Journal of Agricultural Economics*, 75, 1263–7.

Damasio, A. (1994) *Descartes' Error: Emotion, Reason, and the Human Brain.* New York: Putnam.

DeSteno, D., Petty, R., Wegener, D., & Rucker D. (2000) Beyond valence in the perception of likelihood: The role of emotion specificity, *Journal of Personality and Social Psychology*, 78, 397–416.

Desvousges, W., Johnson, F., Dunford, R., Hudson, S., Wilson, K., & Boyle, K. (1993) Measuring resource damages with contingent valuation: Tests of validity and reliability. In *Contingent Valuation: A Critical Assessment.* Amsterdam: North Holland.

Dhar, R. (1996) The effect of decision strategy on the decision to defer choice, *Journal of Behavioral Decision Making*, 9(4), 265–81.

Dhar, R. & Wertenbroch, K. (2000) Consumer choice between hedonic and utilitarian goods, *Journal of Consumer Research*, 27, 60–71.

Elliott, R. (1975) Heart rate in anticipation of shocks which have different probabilities of occurrences, *Psychological Reports*, 36, 923–31.

Elster, J. & Loewenstein, G. (1992) Utility from memory and anticipation. In G. Loewenstein and J. Elster (eds.), *Choice Over Time* (pp. 213–34). New York: Russell Sage.

Finucane, M., Alhakami, A., Slovic, P., & Johnson, S. (2000) The affect heuristic in judgments of risks and benefits, *Journal of Behavioral Decision Making*, 13, 1–17.

Frederick, S. (2002) Automated choice heuristics. In T. Gilovich, D. Griffin, and D. Kahneman (eds.) *Heuristics and Biases: The Psychology of Intuitive Judgment.* New York: Cambridge University Press.

Frederick, S. & Fischhoff, B. (1998) Scope (in)sensitivity in elicited valuations, *Risk, Decision, and Policy*, 3, 109–23.

Ganzach, Y. (2000) Judging risk and return of financial assets, *Organizational Behavior and Human Decision Processes*, 83, 353–70.

Gilbert, D., Gill, M., & Wilson, T. (1998) How do we know what we will like? The informational basis of affective forecasting. Unpublished manuscript, Harvard University.

Gilovich, T. & Medvec, V. (1995) The experience of regret: What, why, and when, *Psychological Review*, 102, 379–95.

Gonzalez, R. & Wu, G. (1999) On the shape of the probability weighting function, *Cogntive Psychology*, 38, 129–66.

Gul, F. (1991) A theory of disappointment aversion, *Econometrica*, 59, 667–86.

Hsee, C. K. (1999) Value-seeking and prediction-decision inconsistency, *Psychonomic Bulletin and Review*, 6, 555–61.

Hsee, C. K. & Rottenstreich, Y. (2003) Music, pandas, and muggers: On the affective psychology of value. Working paper, University of Chicago.

Hsee, C. K. & Weber, E. (1997) A fundamental prediction error: Self–other discrepancies in risk preference, *Journal of Experimental Psychology: General*, 126, 45–53.

Isen, A. (1993) Positive affect and decision making. In M. Lewis and J. M. Haviland (eds.), *Handbook of Emotions* (pp. 261–77). New York: Guilford Press.

Isen, A. & Geva, N. (1987) The influence of positive affect on acceptable level of risk: The person with a large canoe has a large worry, *Organizational Behavior and Human Decision Processes*, 39, 145–54.

Isen, A., Nygren, T., & Ashby, F. (1988) Influence of positive affect on the subjective utility of gains and losses: It is just not worth the risk, *Journal of Personality and Social Psychology*, 55, 710–17.

Iyengar, S. & Lepper, M. (2000) When choice is demotivating: Can one desire too much of a good thing? *Journal of Personality and Social Psychology*, 76, 995–1006.

Johnson, E. & Tversky, A. (1983) Affect, generalization, and the perception of risk, *Journal of Personality and Social Psychology*, 45, 20–31.

Josephs, R., Larrick, R., Steele, C., & Nisbett, R. (1992) Protecting the self from the negative consequences of risky decisions, *Journal of Personality and Social Psychology*, 62, 26–37.

Kahneman, D. & Knetsch J. (1992) Valuing public goods – the purchase of moral satisfaction, *Journal of Environmental Economics and Management*, 22, 57–70.

Kahneman, D., Ritov, I., & Schkade, D. (1999) Economic preferences or attitude expressions? An analysis of dollar responses to public issues, *Journal of Risk and Uncertainty*, 19, 203–37.

Kahneman, D. & Tversky, A. (1979) Prospect theory, *Econometrica*, 47, 263–92.

Kahneman, D. & Tversky, A. (2000) *Choices, Values, and Frames*. New York: Russell Sage Foundation, Cambridge University Press.

Lerner, J. & Keltner, D. (2000) Beyond valence: Toward a model of emotion-specific influences on judgment and choice, *Cognition and Emotion*, 14, 473–94.

Lerner, J. & Keltner, D. (2001) Fear, anger, and risk, *Journal of Personality & Social Psychology*, 81, 146–59.

Loewenstein, G. (1987) Anticipation and the valuation of delayed consumption, *Economic Journal*, 97, 666–84.

Loewenstein, G. & Lerner, J. (2003) The role of emotion in decision making. In R. J. Davidson, H. H. Goldsmith, & K. R. Scherer (eds.), *The Handbook of Affective Science*. Oxford: Oxford University Press.

Loewenstein, G., Weber, E., Hsee, C., & Welch, E. (2001) Risk as feelings. *Psychological Bulletin*, 127(2), 267–86.

Loomes, G. & Sugden, R. (1982) Regret theory: An alternative of rational choice under uncertainty, *Economic Journal*, 92, 805–24.

Loomes, G. & Sugden, R. (1986) Disappointment and dynamic consistency in choice under uncertainty, *Review of Economic Studies*, 53, 271–82.

Loomes, G. & Sugden, R. (1987) Testing for regret and disappointment in choice under uncertainty, *Economic Journal*, 97, 118–29.

Lopes, L. (1987) Between hope and fear: The psychology of risk, *Advances in Experimental Social Psychology*, 20, 255–95.

Lovallo, D. & Kahneman, D. (2000) Living with uncertainty: Attractiveness and resolution timing, *Journal of Behavioral Decision Making*, 13, 179–90.

Luce, M. (1998) Choosing to avoid: Coping with negatively emotion-laden consumer decisions, *Journal of Consumer Research*, 24, 409–31.

Luce, M., Bettman, J., & Payne, J. (1997) Choice processing in emotionally difficult decisions, *Journal of Experimental Psychology: Learning, Memory, and Cognition*, 23, 384–405.

Luce, M., Payne, J., & Bettman, J. (1999) Emotional tradeoff difficulty and choice, *Journal of Marketing Research*, 26, 143–59.

Mano, H. (1992) Judgments under distress: Assessing the role of unpleasantness and arousal in judgment formation, *Organizational Behavior and Human Decision Processes*, 52, 216–45.

Mano, H. (1994) Risk taking, framing effects, and affect, *Organizational Behavior and Human Decision Process*, 57, 28–58.

Mayer, J., Gaschke, Y., Braverman, D., & Evans, T. (1992) Mood-congruent judgment is a general effect, *Journal of Personality and Social Psychology*, 63, 119–32.

Mellers, B. (2000) Choice and the relative pleasure of consequences, *Psychological Bulletin*, 126, 910–24.

Mellers, B., Schwartz, A., & Ritov, I. (1999) Emotion-based choice, *Journal of Experimental Psychology: General*, 128, 332–45.

Monat, A., Averill, J., & Lazarus, R. (1972) Anticipatory stress and coping reactions under various conditions of uncertainty, *Journal of Personality and Social Psychology*, 24, 237–53.

Nygren, T., Isen, A., Taylor, P., & Dulin, J. (1996) The influence of positive affect on the decision rule in risk situations, *Organizational Behavior and Human Decision Processes*, 66, 59–72.

Peters, E. & Mauro, R. (2000) Feeling our way through a complex world: Affective reactivity, physiology, and choice. Decision Research working paper.

Peters, E. & Slovic, P. (2000) The springs of action: Affective and analytical information processing in choice, *Personality and Social Psychology Bulletin*, 26, 1465–75.

Pham, M. (1998) Representativeness, relevance, and the use of feelings in decision making, *Journal of Consumer Research*, 25, 144–59.

Raghunathan, R. & Pham, M. (1999) All negative moods are not equal: Motivational influences of anxiety and sadness on decision making, *Organizational Behavior and Human Decision Processes*, 79, 56–77.

Rottenstreich, Y. & Hsee, C. K. (2001) Money, kisses, and electric shocks: On the affective psychology of risk, *Psychological Science*, 12, 185–90.

Schwarz, N. & Clore, G. (1983) Mood, misattribution, and judgments of well-being: Information and directive functions of affective states, *Journal of Personality and Social Psychology*, 45, 513–23.

Schwarz, N. & Clore, G. (1996) Feelings and phenomenal experiences. In E. T. Higgins and A. Kruglanski (eds.), *Social Psychology: A Handbook of Basic Principle* (pp. 433–65). New York: Guilford Press.

Shiv, B. & Fedorikhin, A. (1999) Heart and mind in conflict: The interplay of affect and cognition in consumer decision making, *Journal of Consumer Research*, 26, 278–92.

Sloman, S. (1996) The empirical case for two systems of reasoning, *Psychological Bulletin*, 119, 3–22.

Slovic, P., Monahan, J., & MacGregor, D. (2000) Violence risk assessment and risk communication: The effects of using actual cases, providing instruction, and employing probability versus frequency formats. *Law and Human Behavior*, 24, 271–96.

Snortum, J. & Wilding, F. (1971) Temporal estimation of heart rate as a function of repression-sensitization score and probability of shock, *Journal of Consulting and Clinical Psychology*, 37, 417–22.

Trope, Y. & Liberman, N. (2003) Temporal construal, *Psychological Review*, 110, 403–21.

Tversky, A. & Fox, C. (1995) Weighing risk and uncertainty, *Psychological Review*, 102, 269–83.

Tversky, A. & Kahneman, D. (1992) Advances in prospect theory: Cumulative representation of uncertainty, *Journal of Risk and Uncertainty*, 5, 297–323.

Tversky, A. & Shafir, E. (1992) Choice under conflict: The dynamics of deferred decision, *Psychological Science*, 3, 358–61.

Ward, A. & Mann, T. (2000) Don't mind if I do: Disinhibited eating under cognitive load, *Journal of Personality and Social Psychology*, 78, 753–63.

Wegener, D. T., Petty, R. E., & Klein, D. J. (1994) Effects of mood on high elaboration attitude change: The mediating role of likelihood judgments, *European Journal of Social Psychology*, 24, 25–43.

Windschitl, P. & Weber, E. (1999) The interpretation of likely depends on context, but 70% is 70%, right? The influence of associative processes on perceived certainty, *Journal of Experimental Psychology: Learning, Memory, and Cognition*, 25, 1514–33.

Windschitl, P. & Wells, G. (1998) The alternative-outcomes effect, *Journal of Personality and Social Psychology*, 75, 1411–23.

Wu, G. (1999) Anxiety and decision making with delayed resolution of uncertainty, *Theory and Decision*, 46, 159–98.

Yamagishi, K. (1997) When a 12.86% mortality is more dangerous than 24.14%: Implications for risk communication, *Applied Cognitive Psychology*, 11, 495–506.

Zajonc, R. (1980) Feeling and thinking: Preferences need no inference, *American Psychologist*, 35, 151–75.

Zeelenberg, M., van Dijk, W., Manstead, A., & van der Pligt, J. (2000) On bad decisions and disconfirmed expectancies: The psychology of regret and disappointment, *Cognition and Emotion*, 14, 521–42.

23

Group Decision and Deliberation: A Distributed Detection Process

Robert D. Sorkin, Shenghua Luan, and Jesse Itzkowitz

Introduction

Imagine for a moment that you are the acquisitions director of a small but prestigious museum in Charleston, South Carolina. While attending a conference in Rouen, France, you are approached by a local art dealer. He has a small sketch that he believes was drawn by an early French impressionist. The sketch is not listed in any known collection and its provenance is unclear. You ask the members of your acquisitions committee to examine the drawing, but there is no time for physical tests of authenticity. The committee must make a decision soon about purchasing the drawing, before word of its availability becomes public and its price inflates dramatically. You need to be prudent because some of your recent acquisitions have proven to be fakes, and your reputation may be affected by another error of that sort.

Your committee has four members: Louise, Louis, Terrence, and Olivia. Louise is a genuine expert on impressionist works, but is usually quite liberal about valuations; she is always finding "valuable" works in attics and garage sales. Louis is married to Louise and usually agrees with her recommendations. Terrence is just the opposite – quite conservative about saying a work is genuine, but not quite up to Louise's level of expertise. Your own expertise is about equal to Terrence's. Olivia is less expert than Terrence, but she usually adopts a middle-of-the-road criterion for authenticity. Although the ultimate responsibility is yours, the committee recommendation is the main basis for your decision.

The committee deliberates during a hurried conference call. Before the call, you believe the work authentic, but realize the risk of forgery is high. Louis begins the call with an evaluation of *fake*. Louise follows by pronouncing the drawing *authentic*. Olivia next weighs in with *authentic*, followed by Terrence with *fake*. You momentarily withhold your opinion. Now Louis changes his mind and says the piece is *authentic*. Next, Olivia switches to *fake*, and no one speaks for several minutes. You finally respond *fake*, then Louis switches back to *fake*, and the call ends with a four-to-one consensus against acquisition. Is it possible to formally describe this decision process? How did the personal properties of the members affect the final decision?

For more than 50 years, the general issues about group decision raised in this example have been a topic of consideration by scientists in economics, engineering, psychology, statistics, and other fields. A review by Clemen and Winkler (1999) provides an excellent summary of many of the mathematical and behavioral issues. The mathematical issues are often complex, and perhaps it is not surprising that papers on group decision making often avoid consideration of these core issues. The behavioral side of group decision making is perhaps even more difficult to model and predict. Here, social factors such as acceptance and team cohesion and individual factors such as biases for confirmation and consistency all play a role. Davis (1992) offers a fascinating review of the history (and fashions) of behavioral research on group decision making between 1950 and 1990.

In their review, Clemen and Winkler (1999) argue that we need new approaches to modeling and improving group decision making. These new models should be able to predict the effects of the group's composition and aggregation rules on the accuracy and bias of the group's decisions. The models should show groups how they can maximize the accuracy of their performance. This chapter reviews a methodology and some recent experiments that attempt to fulfill those goals. The present approach, which derives from electrical engineering analyses of signal detection, has generally not received attention in the judgment and decision literature. Not surprisingly, the mathematical issues to be considered are basically the same as those discussed by Clemen and Winkler (1999) and Genest and Zidek (1986) in their earlier reviews. However, it is hoped that by viewing the problem from a signal detection perspective, decision scientists will gain an improved understanding of the interacting mathematical and behavioral issues involved in the group decision problem and, as a side benefit, will acquire a powerful method for characterizing the accuracy and bias of group performance.

The present approach rests on several assumptions: group performance is assumed to depend not only on the members' individual expertise, but also on how well member information is communicated, aggregated, and converted to the group decision. An additional assumption is that the communication of member information is inherently imperfect: member information is categorical or finite-valued, thus resulting in information loss. In the extreme case, member communication may be limited to binary or dichotomous messages. Finally, the group decision situations considered in this chapter will be limited to dichotomous decisions (under risk and uncertainty) and it is assumed that there are no conflicts between the group's and the members' outcome goals.

In the electrical engineering literature, dichotomous decision making by groups is referred to as *distributed (or decentralized) signal detection*. The problem concerns the optimal detection of signals in noise by a detector array. Figure 23.1 shows a diagram of such a system. The group of detectors must decide about the occurrence of a probabilistic event, either signal s_0 or signal s_1. The task is made difficult by noise (input variances, σ^2_i and σ^2_{common}) and by the detectors' having a limited response vocabulary (finite-valued output). We shall refer to the group members as Local Decision Makers (LDMs). After receiving the input, each LDM estimates the likelihood of signal occurrence and converts that estimate to a categorical response $r_{i,j}$. That response is communicated to the

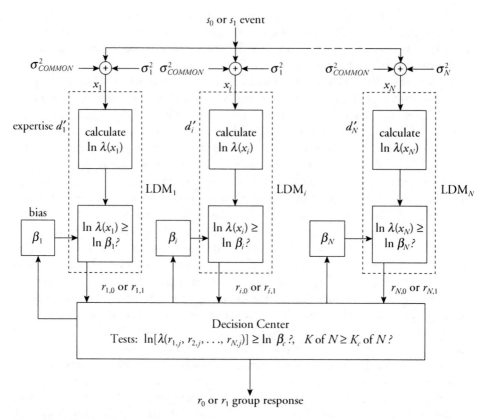

Figure 23.1 The distributed detection model

The input is s_0 or s_1; independent and shared noise is present at each input, producing observation x_i. LDMi has detection ability d_i' and bias β_i. If $\ln \lambda(x_i) \geq \ln(\beta_i)$ LDMi responds r_1 otherwise r_0. Responses go to DC for final decision or may feed back to LDMs for iterated β_i and response (see text).

Decision Center (DC) where the group's final decision is made. The DC may use an algorithm to aggregate the LDM information and then test the result against a preset criterion. Alternatively, the DC's decision may be based on a process that involves additional interaction with the LDMs, as in the interaction of the art acquisitions committee. Subsequent sections of this chapter will expand on this brief description. The major goal is to introduce the distributed detection approach and demonstrate its power to provide formal descriptions and quantitative predictions about group decision making. An additional goal is to show the relationships between distributed detection theory and traditional approaches to describing group decision making.

The application of statistical decision theory to signal detection has a 50 year history in electrical engineering and sensory psychology (Tanner & Swets, 1954; Swets, Tanner, & Birdsall, 1961). During the past 20 years, the basic theory has been extended to the important problem of signal detection using arrays of detectors (Reibman & Nolte, 1987a, b; Pete, Pattipati, & Kleinman, 1993a, b; Viswanathan & Varshney, 1997). The original theory is now referred to as *centralized* or *classical* signal detection and more recent applications to group detection are called *distributed* or *decentralized* signal detection. This chapter will briefly review the classical detection case in order to introduce the reader to the problem of normative information aggregation and to the detection-theoretic measures of accuracy and bias. Subsequent sections will discuss the distributed signal detection model and its application to decision making and deliberation by human groups.

Classical (Centralized) Detection Model

The classical signal detection problem can be framed as follows: the decision maker (DM) is presented with an input, x, drawn from one of two possible signal events, s_0 or s_1. These events have been identified as the "noise-alone" event (s_0) and the "signal-plus-noise" event (s_1). The input, x, is statistical in nature; otherwise, DM would perform without error. Then, $f(x \mid s_0)$ and $f(x \mid s_1)$ define the probability distributions of the signal and noise events on x. DM uses x to compute a decision statistic, z, and then bases her decision on the magnitude of z. In the art acquisition example, s_1 designates "authentic," s_0 designates "fake," and z corresponds to the judge's (continuous) estimate of authenticity.

For the moment (see Figure 23.2), assume z is normally (Gaussian) distributed given s_0 or s_1, with distributions $f(z \mid s_0)$ and $f(z \mid s_1)$. Let these distributions have equal variance but different means, with $\sigma_0^2 = \sigma_1^2$ and $\mu_1 > \mu_0$ as illustrated in the figure. DM's ability to discriminate between the two signal events is related to the difference between the means of the distributions on z divided by their standard deviation, $(\mu_1 - \mu_0)/\sigma$. This normalized separation between the means is termed the detection index, d' (Tanner & Birdsall, 1958).

After observing the input and computing a value for the statistic, z, DM makes response r_0 or r_1. The goal is to achieve the largest number of correct decisions $r_1 \cdot s_1$ and $r_0 \cdot s_0$ (correct identifications of s_1, "hits," and correct identifications of s_0, "correct

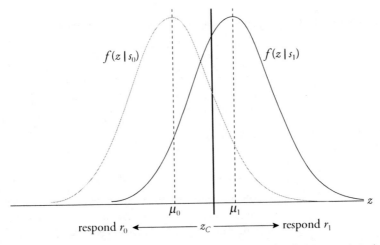

Figure 23.2 Hypothesis distributions (and response criterion) on the decision statistic (see text)

rejections"), and the smallest number of incorrect decisions $r_1 \cdot s_0$ and $r_0 \cdot s_1$ (incorrect r_1 responses, "false alarms," and incorrect r_0 responses, "misses"). The number of hits plus correct rejections divided by the number of trials is the percent correct performance, $p(C)$. The $p(C)$ provides a simple measure of accuracy but fails to capture whether the DM has exhibited a bias favoring one response over the other.

The vertical line in Figure 23.2 shows one response strategy: respond r_1 if $z \geq z_c$ else respond r_0. If the parameters of the distributions are known, the hit and false alarm probabilities are specified by:

$$p(r_1 | s_1) = \int_{z_C}^{\infty} f(z | s_1)dz = 1 - F(z_c, \mu_1, \sigma) \tag{23.1}$$

and

$$p(r_1 | s_0) = \int_{z_C}^{\infty} f(z | s_0)dz = 1 - F(z_c, \mu_0, \sigma) \tag{23.2}$$

where $F(z)$ is the cumulative normal function (the integral from $-\infty$ to z_c).

Table 23.1 shows the four possible outcomes on a trial. If the decision behavior is independent across trials, the frequency of hits and false alarms completely specify DM's performance. If the hypothesis distributions on z are normally distributed, we can calculate the *observed* index of detection, $d'_{observed}$, and response criterion, $z_{c\text{-}observed}$, from:

$$z_{c\text{-}observed} = F^{-1}[1 - p(r_1 | s_0)] \tag{23.3}$$

and

$$d'_{observed} = F^{-1}[p(r_1 | s_1)] - F^{-1}[p(r_1 | s_0)] \tag{23.4}$$

Table 23.1 The possible decision outcomes on an experiment trial (see text)

		Decision (response)		
		r_0	r_1	
Input event (signal)	s_0	correct rejection (payoff V_{00})	false alarm (payoff V_{01})	number of s_0 events
	s_1	miss (payoff V_{10})	hit (payoff V_{11})	number of s_1 events
		number of r_0 decisions	number of r_1 decisions	number of trials

where $F^{-1}(p)$ is the inverse cumulative normal function of the probability p. Thus, $d'_{observed}$ characterizes the expertise of the art judge and $z_{c\text{-}observed}$ indicates her criterion or bias. Values of d' equal to 1.0 and 2.0 correspond, respectively, to percent correct performance of approximately 69 percent and 84 percent. Table 23.1 also shows the possible gain (or cost) to the DM, V_{ij}, associated with the four possible decision outcomes.

How should the decision statistic, z, be computed? It can be shown that a decision based on a likelihood ratio calculation, $\lambda(x)$, on the observation, x, where

$$\lambda(x) = \frac{f(x|s_1)}{f(x|s_0)} \tag{23.5}$$

will be *optimal* under a number of different criteria including: (1) maximum hit rate at fixed false alarm rate (Neyman-Pearson); (2) maximum expected value; (3) maximum information; and (4) maximum difference between posterior distributions (Hoballah & Varshney, 1989a, b; Viswanathan & Varshney, 1997). So the normative rule prescribes that DM calculate $\lambda(x)$ and respond r_1 if $\lambda(x) \geq \beta$ and r_0 if $\lambda(x) < \beta$, where β is a criterion determined by the payoff and prior probability conditions and other factors. A maximum expected value setting for β is

$$\beta = \frac{(V_{00} + V_{01})}{(V_{11} + V_{10})} \cdot \frac{p(s_0)}{p(s_1)} = V \cdot \frac{p(s_0)}{p(s_1)} \tag{23.6}$$

where $p(s_0)$ and $p(s_1)$ are the prior probability of the signals, and $\{V_{ij}\}$ are the payoffs for the possible trial outcomes. The decision statistic can be any monotonic transformation of likelihood ratio, such as the natural log. A decision statistic having convenient properties is $z = \ln[\lambda]$; the decision rule is respond r_1 if $\ln[\lambda] \geq \ln \beta$.

An important concept in the sensory literature, d'_{ideal}, specifies the expertise of the normative or "ideal" observer, a DM who bases her decision on a likelihood ratio test and adds no additional noise to the process (Tanner & Birdsall, 1958; Green & Swets, 1966). If the distributions on x are normal and have parameters μ_{S_1}, μ_{S_0}, and σ, [i.e., $X_{S_1} \sim Normal(\mu_{S_1}, \sigma)$ and] $X_{S_0} \sim Normal(\mu_{S_0}, \sigma)$], then d'_{ideal} is equal to $(\mu_{S_1} - \mu_{S_0})/\sigma$.

Consider the outcome of a detection experiment as a point in a plot of hit probability, $p(r_1|s_1)$, versus false alarm probability, $p(r_1|s_0)$, as shown by point A in Figure 23.3. The Receiver Operating Characteristic (ROC) curve (Swets, 1973, 1986a, b; 1988) is the locus of all operating points that may be produced by a DM who operates at different values of $z_{c\text{-}observed}$ but with a fixed value of $d'_{observed}$. Swets (1986b) has shown that when the physical conditions of the task (task "difficulty") are fixed, people will operate at different points on one ROC curve, depending on their preferences for the choice alternatives. Practically, we desire juries to employ a conservative decision criterion (point A) that would free ten guilty people before convicting one innocent person. Conversely, when designing an alarm to alert us to the presence of a dangerous condition, it is desirable for the alarm to have a liberal criterion (point C) that would produce a high number of false alarms rather than one missed signal.

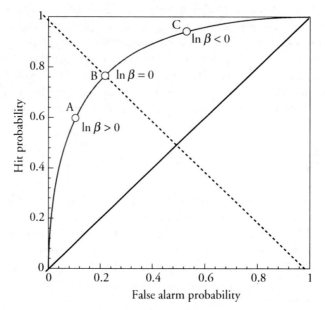

Figure 23.3 A plot of hit probability versus false alarm probability

The Receiver Operating Characteristic (curved line) specifies all outcomes for a system operating with constant expertise ($d' = 1.5$) and different response criteria; A reflects a conservative bias ($\ln \beta > 0$), B a neutral bias ($\ln \beta = 0$), and C a liberal bias ($\ln \beta < 0$). The diagonal line (0,0 to 1,1) indicates chance performance. Points on the dotted diagonal have neutral bias.

Multiple observations

Consider the visual decision task shown in Figure 23.4. For the moment, imagine that the task only involves the left-most display element. DM must decide which of two distributions led to the displayed value: was the horizontal line sampled from the normal distribution (signal-plus-noise) having a mean equal to the higher of the two marks shown to the left of the display, or sampled from the distribution (noise-alone) having a mean equal to the lower mark? We would expect DM to choose some criterion display value above which she would report "signal"; else she would report "noise." Her performance will depend on the mean separation and standard deviation of the distributions, as well as on physical factors such as the display size, luminance, duration, and possible visual limitations. The obtained value for $d'_{observed}$ would be less than d'_{ideal} because of variability in the DM's visual perception. Tanner and Birdsall (1958) defined the difference between the performance of the human and ideal DM in terms of the efficiency, η, where

$$\eta = (d'_{observed} / d'_{ideal})^2 \tag{23.7}$$

Suppose that instead of a single element, the stimulus consists of all nine independent display elements shown in Figure 23.4. The same two distributions are associated with

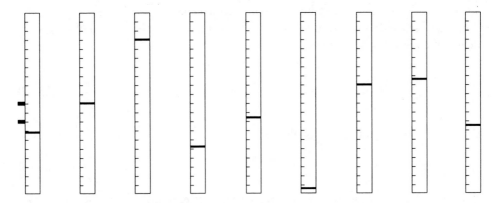

Figure 23.4 Example of a nine-element visual display

On each trial, the values on the nine gauges are drawn from either the signal or the noise distribution.

each of the elements, $x_1, x_2 \ldots x_9$. On any given trial, values for all elements are drawn from either one distribution or the other. Let the difficulty of discriminating the ith display element be:

$$d'_i = (\mu_{i,1} - \mu_{i,0})/\sigma_i \qquad (23.8)$$

In order for the DM to decide whether the signal or noise distribution was sampled on a trial, she must calculate the likelihood ratio on the nine-element observation

$$\lambda(x_1, x_2, \ldots x_N) = \frac{f((x_1, x_2, \ldots x_N)|s_1)}{f((x_1, x_2, \ldots x_N)|s_0)} \qquad (23.9a)$$

If the elements of the display are independent,

$$\frac{f((x_1, x_2, \ldots x_N)|s_1)}{f((x_1, x_2, \ldots x_N)|s_0)} = \frac{f(x_1|s_1)f(x_2|s_1)\ldots f(x_N|s_1)}{f(x_1|s_0)f(x_2|s_0)\ldots f(x_N|s_0)} = \prod_{i=1}^{N} \lambda(x_i) \qquad (23.9b)$$

and

$$\ln\left[\prod_{i=1}^{N} \lambda(x_i)\right] = \sum_{i=1}^{N} \ln[\lambda(x_i)] \qquad (23.10)$$

If the distributions on x are normally distributed, the optimal decision statistic, z, is

$$z = \sum_{i=1}^{N} \ln[\lambda(x_i)] = \sum_{i=1}^{N} a_i x_i \qquad (23.11)$$

where $a_i = d_i'$ and z is normally distributed with equal variance given s_0 or s_1. The normalized separation between the means of the decision statistic, $\Sigma(d_i' x_i)$ given s_0 or s_1, defines the ideal detection index for the task:

$$d'_{ideal} = \sqrt{\sum_{i=1}^{N} (d_i')^2}$$

(23.12)

If the elements have identical distributions,

$$d'_{ideal} = d' \sqrt{N}$$

(23.13)

We have performed experiments with human DMs using visual stimuli like that shown in Figure 23.4 and independent elements (Sorkin, Mabry, Weldon, & Elvers, 1991). The observed d's were consistent with expectations from a slightly degraded ideal; detection efficiencies were approximately 0.8. If a task parameter such as the element mean difference, standard deviation, or number of elements was varied, performance was predicted by Equation 23.12 so long as the display duration was sufficiently long and the display's size, contrast, and luminance were not changed. In a subsequent experiment, participants gave higher weights to elements that had lower variances (Montgomery & Sorkin, 1996). Similar questions about how people aggregate information from multiple continuous sources have been addressed from a number of perspectives in the judgment and decision literature (see, e.g., Genest & Zidek, 1986; Sniezek & Henry, 1989; Gigone & Hastie, 1997; Wallsten, Budescu, Erev, & Diederich, 1997; Clemen & Winkler, 1999).

What if the display elements were not independent? Using an approach based on a multichannel signal detection analysis by Durlach, Braida, and Ito (1986), Sorkin and Dai (1994) considered the situation when the elements in the display had the uniform pair-wise correlation, ρ. They produced that correlation by having elements share variance from a common source. They showed that the ideal index is:

$$d'_{ideal} = \sqrt{N} \left[\frac{\sigma_{d'}^2}{1 - \rho} + \frac{\mu_{d'}^2}{1 + \rho(N - 1)} \right]^{1/2}$$

(23.14)

where $\mu_{d'}$ and $\sigma_{d'}^2$ are the mean and variance of the element d_i' values. Ideal detection accuracy increases with N and decreases as ρ increases from zero. Suppose that the elements' values were *estimates* generated by *members of a group*. Equation 23.14 would then prescribe how the group decision accuracy should depend on the correlation among the group members' judgments.

Group experiments

We have used visual stimuli similar to Figure 23.4 to study decision making by groups of up to 10 participants (Sorkin, Hays, & West, 2001). Participants observed independently generated nine-element displays and then had to decide, as a group or individually, which signal had occurred on that trial. Each member of the group viewed a display and then estimated the likelihood of signal occurrence. This estimate was a rating from 0 to 100, where 0 represented an observation that was definitely noise and 100 was definitely signal. These initial estimates were shown to all members and one member was designated to make the group decision. In some conditions we asked for an initial response and then polled the group for a final vote. In other cases, we allowed full discussion prior to a vote. We also ran conditions in which we manipulated the task difficulty of some of the group members (by increasing the variance of their display elements) and the correlation between the judgments of group members (in a manner similar to that described for generating correlated display elements). All participants were highly trained and monetary payoffs were determined by the accuracy of the individual and group responses.

In general, group performance was consistent with Equation 23.14; that is, percent correct and $d'_{observed\text{-}group}$ increased with group size, N, and decreased with ρ. However, performance increased with N at a slower rate than predicted by the model. In fact, group detection *efficiency* decreased as group size was increased from three to ten members, indicating a decreasing marginal advantage of increasing size. This increased deviation from optimal with increasing group size has often been reported in the group literature (Clemen & Winkler, 1985; Ferrell, 1985).

Because we had recorded the actual stimuli presented, as well as each member's estimate of signal likelihood, we could compute their individual detection efficiency. We could also separately calculate the efficiency with which members aggregated the estimates of the other members into a final decision. The overall efficiency of performance can be factored into two independent components:

$$\eta_{overall\text{-}for\text{-}DM} = \left(\frac{d_{based\text{-}on\text{-}member\text{-}estimate}}{d_{based\text{-}on\text{-}actual\text{-}stimulus}} \right)^2 \cdot \left(\frac{d_{based\text{-}on\text{-}final\text{-}response}}{d_{based\text{-}on\text{-}member\text{-}estimates}} \right)^2$$

$$= \eta_{member\ detection} \cdot \eta_{aggregation\ of\ member\ estimates} \tag{23.15}$$

where the first component, *member detection efficiency*, is a measure of how well DM performed her *individual* detection relative to the difficulty (mean-to-sigma ratio) of her display, and the second component, the *aggregation efficiency*, summarizes how accurately DM *aggregated* the team estimates to form her final decision.

When we performed these calculations, we found a surprising result. The efficiency in aggregating information from other members remained constant in groups of from four to ten members, even when there were differences in the detection abilities of the members. However, *individual* detection efficiency decreased with increasing group size. The decrease in overall efficiency with group size was therefore attributable to a decrease in individual detection effort rather than to a decrease in the efficiency of aggregating information from other members. We (Sorkin, Hays, & West, 2001) attributed the reduction to a kind of social loafing effect (e.g., Latané, Williams, & Harkins, 1979; Kerr, 1983; Shepperd & Taylor, 1999).

Interestingly, this effect was not replicated when we ran a similar experiment with individual subjects playing a computer game-like version of the task (Sorkin, Luan, & Itzkowitz, 2001). In that experiment, participants were run individually and given estimates generated by virtual group members. Again, we measured the efficiency of each participant's individual effort and their efficiency at aggregating the virtual estimates. There was no drop in either efficiency measure as the number of virtual estimates was increased to 17! This result suggests that under the right conditions people can aggregate information effectively from multiple sources. Because the efficiency measure is related to $(d')^2$ rather than d', the efficiency measure exaggerates the small reduction in group d' produced by the members' decreased individual efforts. The actual effect on group percent correct is small. An advantage of that small reduction is that each member can share some attention with other demands, such as might be needed for group interaction or communication (see Hinsz, Tindale, & Vollrath, 1997). Such attention sharing may not be relevant in the individual computer game-like situation, where the participant appears to attend only to the computer display.

A number of investigators have studied similar group situations and observed that participants' overall behavior is generally below the normative predictions (i.e., Clement & Schiereck, 1973; Hinsz, 1990). In some experiments, the correlation between participants' judgments may be greater than that assumed by the experimenter or there may be other deviations from the normative assumptions. Another explanation is that people may make their decision based on a simple heuristic that deviates from the normative procedure (Gigerenzer, Chapter 4, this volume). Still other explanations include inappropriate weightings for some information sources (e.g., Einhorn, Hogarth, & Klemperer, 1977). For example, people may have a bias to weigh their own estimates higher than others' (Sorkin, Hays, & West, 2001; Harvey & Harries, in press). Clemen and Winkler (1999) propose that this is due to an anchoring bias where the primacy of the group member's own observation causes it to be more "sticky" and resist the appropriate influence of other members' decisions. Some of these effects are discussed further in the distributed detection section of this chapter. The classical detection analysis is also similar to analyses based on a pooling model proposed by Wallsten and his colleagues (see Wallsten et al., 1997; Johnson, Budescu, & Wallsten, 2001) and to Lens Model analyses (see Gigone and Hastie, 1997; Goldstein, Chapter 3, this volume); and some of the efficiency measures that we have described have counterparts in those analyses.

Distributed Detection Systems

What would happen if the values of the nine display elements in the individual visual experiment were binary indications or if the responses by the group members in the group experiment were binary rather than continuous ratings? The non-continuous nature of the LDMs' responses constitutes the key feature of the distributed detection situation. This requires the assumption of category boundaries on each LDM's responses; in the dichotomous case, each LDM has a single response threshold. This situation is characterized as a distributed detection system because the response criteria of all members of the detection system – including the DC who aggregates the multiple LDM responses – are involved in the decision. Hence, the decision is *distributed* between the central decision center and the local DMs.

Consider the distributed detection system shown in Figure 23.1. Each LDM makes a binary response and these responses flow to the DC. We characterize the general case when information can flow *back and forth* between the DC and the LDMs as group deliberation, and we discuss this process in a later section. How should the DC make its decision in the simpler, non-deliberation case? Since the LDM responses are binary, there are 2^N possible patterns of LDM responses $(r_{1,j}, r_{2,j}, \ldots r_{N,j})$ where each pattern is a binary string corresponding to the sequence of responses from each LDM. The DC's task is to partition these 2^N patterns into an r_0 or r_1 decision. An optimal strategy is to use the likelihood ratio test:

$$\text{if } \ln \lambda(r_{1,j}, r_{1,j}, \ldots, r_{N,j}) \geq \ln(\beta_{DC}) \text{ respond } r_1 \text{ else respond } r_0 \qquad (23.16)$$

where $\ln(\beta_{DC})$ is the DC's criterion.

The likelihood ratio calculation could depend on complicated combinations of the responses, calling for specific decisions to particular conjunctions of the LDM votes ("decide yes if and only if LDM1 and LDM2 vote r_1 and LDM3 votes r_0"). Why might a simple count of LDM's responses not be appropriate for a group decision? First, some of the LDMs might have very low expertise – their votes should be weighed less than LDMs having higher ds. Second, some LDMs might have biased response criteria. An r_0 vote from an extremely conservative LDM contains little useful information and can be safely ignored – that LDM tends to make that response, regardless of the input. However, an r_1 vote from that same LDM would be evidence she had received a strong observation favoring the signal. Third, suppose that two LDMs share common sources of noise, resulting in correlated estimates of likelihood, as did Louise and Louis in the scenario at the beginning of the chapter. The impact of their two votes on a decision should be less than two independent votes. Finally, suppose that two correlated LDMs have different and known response criteria. Depending on the situation, a 01 or 10 pattern of responses could provide a more accurate estimate of their observations than a 00 or 11 pattern.

The correlated-member situation could be complicated further. Suppose that one member speaks after the other and can set her criterion to optimize the information obtained from her response *in combination with* the preceding response. Let Louis answer first with r_0 and criterion β. Assume that, once made, Louise's criterion (and response) will be known; therefore after hearing Louis's response, Louise could set her criterion so as to convey the maximum information to the next member. Person-by-person setting of the LDM criteria is a technique for obtaining a globally optimal set of local and central response criteria (Viswanathan & Varshney, 1997). Optimizing the response criteria and aggregation rule for a system can be very difficult if the LDMs are correlated, if the LDMs or the signals have unknown properties, or if the structure is not a simple parallel array (Reibman & Nolte, 1987a, b; Hoballah & Varshney, 1989a, b; Pete et al., 1993a, b; Viswanathan & Varshney, 1997; Willett, Swaszek, & Blum, 2000). However, in spite of the complexity of the general distributed detection problem, it is often possible to arrive at a strategy that will produce very good performance. In some situations, for example, a decision based on the simple majority vote of the LDMs may approach optimal performance.

Suppose that the DC responds r_1 if and only if K or more LDMs have responded r_1. This situation resembles the classical Condorcet case, except that the group members have different probabilities of making a correct decision, p_i. This situation has been analyzed by many researchers (Nitzan & Paroush, 1982; Grofman, Owen, & Feld, 1983; Grofman, Feld, & Owen, 1984; Shapley & Grofman, 1984; Grofman & Feld, 1986). Pete et al. (1993b) show that the linear weight method of combining the local responses (e.g., Nitzan & Paroush, 1982; Shapley & Grofman, 1984) is a special case of the likelihood ratio test and depends on the empirically questionable assumption that all LDMs operate on the neutral bias point on their ROC (the point on the negative diagonal; point B in Figure 23.3). Traditional methods ignore the need to separately specify the LDMs' levels of expertise, d'_i, and criterion, β_i. Pete et al. show that under the more general assumption of LDM differences in expertise and criterion (and assuming independence), the optimal aggregation rule is a K of N majority in which the LDM responses are weighted by both their expertise and criterion parameters. The DC decision statistic is:

$$\ln \lambda(r_{1,j}, r_{2,j}, \ldots, r_{N,j}) = \sum_{i=1}^{N} \ln\left(\frac{p(r_i \mid s_1)}{p(r_i \mid s_0)}\right) = \sum_{i=1}^{N} w_i(r_i) \tag{23.17}$$

where the LDM weights are given by

$$w_i(r_1) = \ln[(1 - p(r_{i,1} \mid s_1)/(1 - p(r_{i,1} \mid s_0)] \tag{23.18a}$$

and

$$w_i(r_0) = \ln[p(r_{i,1} \mid s_1)/p(r_{i,1} \mid s_0)] \tag{23.18b}$$

Experiments with Distributed Groups

People often make decisions that conform to the opinions of those around them. One argument says this behavior is caused by fulfilling positive expectations of others or compliance to social pressure. However, some have argued the contrary view that conforming behavior exists not because of social pressure, but because conforming usually leads to better decisions (statistical or "informational" influence; Deutsch & Gerard, 1955; Penner & Davis, 1969). Statistically, the majority choice will tend to be the more accurate choice (assuming independence), so agreeing with the majority of one's neighbors usually produces better decisions. It is sometimes difficult to differentiate the informational from the social influences in a group decision-making situation (Turner, 1991). Techniques developed from the signal detection approach may provide an opportunity to clarify this issue and gain insight into why conforming behaviors are so widely observed.

It is often the case in group experiments that the members' response biases are unknown or assumed neutral (Hinsz, 1990). However, suppose the group members' responses were known to be biased. What would be the effect on performance and would members still exhibit conforming behavior? We repeated some of the visual display experiments discussed earlier but asked for binary responses from each group member (Sorkin, Hays, & West, 2001; Luan, Sorkin, & Itzkowitz, 2004). Participants observed the display and then made an r_1 or r_0 vote. These were displayed to everyone and then one member made the team's decision. Payoffs were based on the accuracy of both the individual and team votes. We ran the task under conditions where there were different monetary penalties for misses or false alarms on the first response, which produced different degrees of either conservative or liberal bias toward one decision alternative. The display of initial votes was accompanied by a reminder of the payoff condition for each LDM so that each member knew what criterion was associated with each response. Following the display of the votes, the acting DC (who was randomly selected from the group) made the final vote.

We evaluated the predictions of two models of the DC: (a) a rational detection strategy that aggregated the first votes in a way that maximized the information and minimized the detrimental impact of the biased information and (b) a conforming strategy that simply went along with the majority of the first votes. The detection model assumed fixed LDM criteria (based on the first vote payoff matrix), a likelihood-ratio decision rule, and a neutral final criterion. The second model simply based a decision on the majority of the first vote. Results indicated that most participants deviated from the rational strategy: their decision was determined by a simple majority of the known first votes. Even though the participants knew that the LDM responses were highly biased – and therefore not informational – they still gave significant weight to those biased responses in their decisions. As a result, their final vote performance was below the achievable level.

The majority heuristic also describes the results of other manipulations (Luan et al., 2004). We gave participants continuous estimates from two different LDM sources: one source consisted of one LDM estimate and the other source consisted of from one to six LDM estimates. The participants had been informed that these sources had equal (aggregate) information value regardless of the number of component estimates provided. Normatively, the weights that people assign to each source should be equal, but our participants assigned greater decisional weight to the sources having multiple components. The weight increased with the number of components, consistent with earlier experiments by Harkins and Petty (1981, 1987) and the use of a majority rule heuristic.

Although the majority rule heuristic used by our participants produced less than optimum performance, in most cases that performance was far superior to that if the LDM had responded without knowing the other LDMs' votes. This advantage may have made participants reluctant to adopt a more complicated decision strategy that would not have produced very much better performance. Given the simplicity of the majority heuristic and the potential complexity of other strategies, perhaps it is no surprise that conforming behavior is so common in group decision making (Stasser, Kerr, & Davis, 1989; Hinsz, 1990), although it may be more common in tasks that lack clearly demonstrable outcomes (Laughlin & Ellis, 1986).

Distributed Detection with Deliberation

Social scientists have long pondered the question of how groups reach decisions (e.g., Penrod & Hastie, 1979; Davis, 1992). Davis (1973) coined the term *social decision scheme* to describe the process by which group decisions are achieved and how the final decision depends on the initial preferences of the group's members. A major interest is the relationship between the distribution of the initial (binary) positions of the members and the final group position. In this section, we describe a distributed detection model of the deliberation process. We assume that, upon hearing other members' positions, a member employs a normative rule to revise her own position. The model is easily modified by an assumption of member anonymity as in the Delphi model. We show that the model specifies the effects of key variables on the accuracy and bias of the group decision, such as the type of majority rule, the correlations between member judgments, the expertise and bias of the group's members, and the degree of knowledge of member information.

Consider again the system in Figure 23.1, this time noting that information about local responses can flow *back* to the LDMs, allowing members to communicate their responses (and response criteria) *to each other*. This information allows LDMs to modify their individual response criteria (or likelihood estimates) with an updated estimate of signal likelihood based on the responses of the other LDMs. This process can be iterative, as in a standard American jury. Jury members take repeated ballots, communicating their votes and updating their positions until a consensus is achieved via a majority rule. The jurors may be characterized by a set of expertise levels $\{d_i'\}$ and initial criteria $\{\ln \beta_i\}$ known to the other jurors. Each juror makes an internal estimate of guilt $\{\ln \lambda(x_i)\}$ and an initial binary response $\{r_{i,j}\}$. These responses are communicated to everyone. Each juror then uses Bayes' rule to incorporate the information gained from the other jurors' responses and votes again.

As an example of this process, suppose that juror number three on a four-person jury has an initial criterion, β_3, equal to her estimated prior odds ratio, $p(s_0)/p(s_1)$, multiplied by some pay-off ratio, V, (as in Equation 23.6)[1]

$$\beta_3 = V \cdot \frac{p(s_0)}{p(s_1)} \tag{23.19}$$

The other members of that four-member jury provide their votes $\{r_{1,1}, r_{2,0}, r_{4,0}\}$ to member number three (i.e., juror 1 votes "guilty" and jurors 2 and 4 vote "not guilty"). Juror 3 uses Bayes' theorem to update her initial estimate of the prior odds ratio (i.e., now a *posterior* odds ratio). Her updated criterion is

$$\beta_3 = V \cdot \frac{p(s_0 | r_{1,1}, r_{2,0}, r_{4,0})}{p(s_1 | r_{1,1}, r_{2,0}, r_{4,0})} = V \cdot \frac{p(r_{1,1}, r_{2,0}, r_{4,0} | s_0) p(s_0)}{p(r_{1,1}, r_{2,0}, r_{4,0} | s_1) p(s_1)} \tag{23.20}$$

If the jurors' responses are independent,

$$\beta_3 = V \cdot \frac{p(r_{1,1}, r_{2,0}, r_{4,0} \mid s_0)p(s_0)}{p(r_{1,1}, r_{2,0}, r_{4,0} \mid s_1)p(s_1)} = V \cdot \frac{p(r_{1,1} \mid s_0)p(r_{2,0} \mid s_0)p(r_{4,0} \mid s_0)p(s_0)}{p(r_{1,1} \mid s_1)p(r_{2,0} \mid s_1)p(r_{4,0} \mid s_1)p(s_1)} \tag{23.21}$$

The values for $p(r_{i,j} \mid s_1)$, $p(r_{i,j} \mid s_0)$ in Equation 23.21 can be calculated from the values of d_i' and β_i for each juror (using Equations 23.1 and 23.2). This process can be iterated until a required consensus is reached. Swaszek and Willett (1995) term this iteration process a *parley* and show that it always reaches a consensus; they also show that the process usually converges in two or three ballots.

We have attempted to quantify the relative advantages of different majority rules (such as a simple majority, 2/3, 3/4, and unanimous) for the standard American jury, given assumptions about the distributions of juror expertise and bias (Sorkin, Luan, & Itzkowitz, 2003; Sorkin, Luan, Itzkowitz, & Crandall, submitted). Using Monte Carlo simulations of the jury model, we evaluated the accuracy and bias of the jury's final decision, the probability that the jury hung (failed to decide within m ballots), and the relative behavior of several non-optimal rules for updating the juror's criterion. Our simulations evaluated juries of from 3 to 12 members, with 25 Monte Carlo runs per condition and 500 trials per run; voting was terminated after 6 full jury ballot iterations.

Figure 23.5 shows some typical results (parameter values, $\rho = 0$, $\mu_{d'} = 1$, $\sigma_{d'} = 0.33$, and $\sigma_{\ln \beta} = 0.33$) from our analysis. The top three curves show the percent correct jury performance when the jurors began with a neutral mean criterion ($\ln \beta = 0$) and using unanimous, three-quarters, and simple majority rules, respectively. A unanimous majority

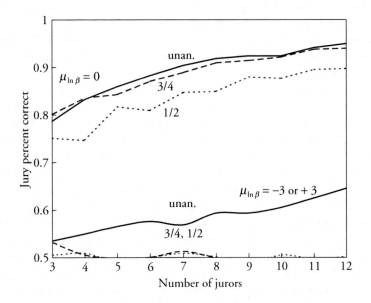

Figure 23.5 Percent correct as a function of jury size for six simulated juries

In the top three curves, the juries begin deliberation with an average neutral bias. The three curves shown are for a unanimous, three-quarters, and simple majority rule (see text). In the bottom three curves, the juries begin deliberation with an extreme negative or positive bias.

rule resulted in jury performance closest to the ideal, non-distributed case (not plotted) and was successively poorer under less stringent majority rules. The function that results from the simple majority rule is the same as that produced by a jury that votes *without deliberation.* More stringent rules without deliberation produce even worse performance, consistent with Sorkin, West, and Robinson (1998) and Feddersen and Pesendorfer (1998); see also Guarnaschelli, McKelvey, and Palfrey (2000).

Performance dropped greatly as the initial bias differed from zero, but the magnitude of the drop also depended on the majority rule; the unanimous rule was the most resistant to the negative effect of a biased jury. The lower three curves shown in Figure 23.5 were produced by deliberating juries that employed unanimous, three-quarters, and simple majority rules, respectively, but with an extreme initial mean juror criterion of +3 or −3. A plot (not shown) of the bias of the final decision (rather than the accuracy) showed that the stricter the majority rule, the closer the final bias approached zero. So the model clearly demonstrates the mediating effect on decision bias produced by a stringent majority rule.

We have also evaluated other updating rules, including a Delphi rule and a simple criterion shift rule. The Delphi rule (anonymous voting) assumes that the jurors' individual d' and β values are not known; an average d' and β value is used for the calculations in Equation 23.21 (Gustafson, Shukla, Delbecq, & Walster, 1973; Hillman, Hessel, Swensson, & Herman, 1977). The simple criterion shift rule assumes a fixed shift in criterion toward the majority position, similar to a SDS rule (Kerr, MacCoun, & Kramer, 1996). In other words, if most of the juror votes (excluding your own vote) are for guilty, you would move your response criterion in a direction that would require less evidence for you to vote for the guilty option on the next ballot. In the simple version of the model tested, large majorities were assumed to produce the same magnitude shift as small majorities. This rule produced performance almost as good as the Delphi rule, depending on the magnitude of the criterion shift. Neither rule produced performance as good as the Bayes' rule.

It should be obvious that this analysis ignores many facts about how people incorporate information from other sources and from other group members. For example, groups may adopt more extreme positions than their individual members (Stoner, 1968). A distributed detection approach may clarify the process that underlies a group's putative criterion shift, its boundary conditions, and the factors or rules that may mediate such shifts (see also Bordley, 1983). A distributed detection approach also addresses the question of how the initial distribution of LDM votes affects the deliberation process and the accuracy and bias of the final decision (see Kerr et al., 1996). Finally, our model assumes that jurors share their votes simultaneously. In real-life deliberation, LDM information probably arrives sequentially rather than simultaneously, and the order of arrival of information could have an effect on the accuracy and bias of the decision. One of us (J. I.) is studying the effect of different rules for determining who speaks next, such as the member with the greatest expertise, most extreme bias, or largest difference $|\ln \lambda_i - \ln \beta_i|$. The goal is to discover the effects of such structural factors on the performance of hypothetical and human groups. So far, the results confirm the expectation that response protocols that give priority to the members with the best information, produce the highest performance.

Conclusions

We hope we have demonstrated the usefulness of the distributed detection model for describing group performance and for gaining insight into the process of group deliberation. The detection theoretic perspective (including use of the ROC concept) enables one to achieve some understanding of the effects of group structure, member expertise and criteria, and group aggregation rule, on group decision accuracy and bias. The distributed detection analysis also highlights the computational complexity of the decision situation when the members' observations are correlated.

Given the potential complexity of the optimal model and the abundant evidence for human variation from optimal behavior, is the distributed detection approach irrelevant for describing human groups? We believe that the complexity of the optimal detection rule – and the simplicity and near-optimum performance of the K of N majority rule – argue strongly for the latter description of human group behavior. What could be more "rational" than for the human DM to use a simple heuristic that is near optimal in many different situations? Finally, by adding a Bayesian updating procedure, the detection analysis provides a formal description of the process of group deliberation and consensus. Future research will show how well the model describes the deliberation process of human groups.

Acknowledgment

The preparation of this chapter was partially supported by the Air Force Office of Scientific Research.

Note

1   The initial β does not have to be optimal. Updating the criterion simply involves updating the prior probability component. The same response would be produced by updating the likelihood estimate while keeping the criterion fixed. An interesting empirical question is what actually changes under majority influence – a person's opinion (likelihood estimate) or their response criterion?

References

Bordley, R. F. (1983) A Bayesian model of group polarization, *Organizational Behavior & Human Decision Processes*, 32(2), 262–74.

Clemen, R. T. & Winkler, R. L. (1985) Limits for the precision and value of information from dependent sources, *Operation Research*, 33, 427–42.

Clemen, R. T. & Winkler, R. L. (1999) Combining probability distributions from experts in risk analysis, *Risk Analysis*, 19(2), 187–203.

Clement, D. E. & Schiereck, J. J., Jr. (1973) Sex composition and group performance in a visual signal detection task, *Memory & Cognition*, 1(3), 251–5.

Davis, J. H. (1973) Group decision and social interaction: A theory of social decision schemes, *Psychological Review*, 80(2), 97–125.

Davis, J. H. (1992) Some compelling intuitions about group consensus decisions, theoretical and empirical research, and interpersonal aggregation phenomena: Selected examples, 1950–1990, *Organizational Behavior and Human Decision Processes*, 52, 3–38.

Deutsch, M. & Gerard, H. B. (1955) A study of normative and informational social influences upon individual judgment, *International Journal of Psychology*, 51, 629–36.

Durlach, N. I., Braida, L. D., & Ito, Y. (1986) Towards a model for discrimination of broadband signals, *Journal of the Acoustical Society of America*, 80, 60–72.

Einhorn, H. J., Hogarth, R. M., & Klempner, E. (1977) Quality of group judgment, *Psychological Bulletin*, 84(1), 158–72.

Feddersen, T. & Pesendorfer, W. (1998) Convicting the innocent: The inferiority of unanimous jury verdicts under strategic voting, *American Political Science Review*, 92, 23–36.

Ferrell, W. R. (1985) Combining individual judgments. In G. Wright (ed.), *Behavioral Decision Making* (pp. 111–45). New York: Plenum.

Genest, C. & Zidek, J. V. (1986) Combining probability distributions: A critique and annotated bibliography, *Statistical Science*, 1, 114–48.

Gigone, D. & Hastie, R. (1997) Proper analysis of the accuracy of group judgments, *Psychological Bulletin*, 121, 149–67.

Green, D. M. & Swets, J. A. (1966) *Signal Detection Theory and Psychophysics*. New York: Wiley.

Grofman, B. & Feld, S. (1986) Determining optimal weights for expert judgment. In B. Grofman and G. Owen (eds.) *Decision Research* (vol. 2, pp. 167–72). Greenwich, CT: JAI Press.

Grofman, B., Feld, S., & Owen, G. (1984) Group size and the performance of a composite group majority: Statistical truths and empirical results, *Organizational Behavior and Human Performance*, 33, 350–9.

Grofman, B., Owen, G., and Feld, S. (1983) Thirteen theorems in search of the truth, *Theory and Decision*, 15, 261–78.

Guarnaschelli, S., McKelvey, R. D., & Palfrey, T. R. (2000) An experimental study of group decision rules, *American Political Science Review*, 94, 407–23.

Gustafson, D. H., Shukla, R. K., Delbecq, A., & Walster, G. W. (1973) A comparative study of differences in subjective likelihood estimates made by individuals, interacting groups, Delphi groups, and nominal groups, *Organizational Behavior and Human Performance*, 9, 280–91.

Harkins, S. & Petty, R. (1981) The multiple source effect in persuasion: The effect of distraction, *Personality and Social Psychology Bulletin*, 7, 627–35.

Harkins, S. & Petty, R. (1987) Information utility and the multiple source effect, *Journal of Personality and Social Psychology*, 52, 260–8.

Harvey, N. & Harries, C. (2003, in press) Effect of judges' forecasting on their later combination of forecasts for the same outcomes, *International Journal of Forecasting*.

Hillman, B. J., Hessel, S. J., Swensson, R. G., & Herman, P. G. (1977) Improving diagnostic accuracy: A comparison of interactive and Delphi consultations, *Investigative Radiology*, 12(2), 112–15.

Hinsz, V. B. (1990) Cognitive and consensus processes in group recognition memory performance, *Journal of Personality and Social Psychology*, 59(4), 705–18.

Hinsz, V. B., Tindale, R. S., & Vollrath, D. A. (1997) The emerging conceptualization of groups as information processors, *Psychological Bulletin*, 121, 43–64.

Hoballah, I. Y. & Varshney, P. K. (1989a) An information theoretic approach to the distributed detection problem, *IEEE Transactions on Information Theory*, 35(5), 988–94.

Hoballah, I. Y. & Varshney, P. K. (1989b) Distributed Bayesian signal detection, *IEEE Transactions on Information Theory*, 35(5), 995–1000.

Johnson, T. R., Budescu, D. V., & Wallsten, T. S. (2001) Averaging probability judgments: Monte Carlo analyses of asymptotic diagnostic value, *Journal of Behavioral Decision Making*, 14, 123–40.

Kerr, N. L. (1983) Motivation losses in task-performing groups: A social dilemma analysis, *Journal of Personality and Social Psychology*, 45, 819–28.

Kerr, N. L., MacCoun, R. J., & Kramer, G. P. (1996) Bias in judgment: Comparing individuals and groups, *Psychological Review*, 103(4), 687–719.

Latané, B., Williams, K., & Harkins, S. (1979) Many hands make light the work: The causes and consequences of social loafing, *Journal of Personality and Social Psychology*, 37, 822–32.

Laughlin, P. R. & Ellis, A. L. (1986) Demonstrability and social combination processes on mathematical intellective tasks, *Journal of Experimental Social Psychology*, 22, 177–89.

Luan, S., Sorkin, R. D., and Itzkowitz, J. (2004) Weighing information from outside sources: A biased process, *Journal of Behavioral Decision Making*, 17, 95–116.

Montgomery, D. A. & Sorkin, R. D. (1996) Observer sensitivity to element reliability in a multi-element visual display, *Human Factors*, 38, 484–94.

Nitzan, S. & Paroush, J. (1982) Optimum decision rules in uncertain dichotomous choice situations, *International Economic Review*, 23(2), 289–97.

Penner, L. A. & Davis, J. H. (1969) Conformity and the "rational" use of unanimous majorities, *Journal of Social Psychology*, 78, 299–300.

Penrod, S. & Hastie, R. (1979) Models of jury decision making: A critical review, *Psychological Bulletin*, 86(3), 462–92.

Pete, A., Pattipati, K. R., & Kleinman, D. L. (1993a) Distributed detection in teams with partial information: A normative-descriptive model, *IEEE Transactions on Systems, Man, and Cybernetics*, 23(6), 1626–48.

Pete, A., Pattipati, K. R., & Kleinman, D. L. (1993b) Optimal team and individual decision rules in uncertain dichotomous situations, *Public Choice*, 75, March, 205–30.

Reibman, A. R. & Nolte, L. W. (1987a) Optimal detection and performance of distributed sensor systems, *IEEE Transactions on Aerospace and Electronic Systems*, AES-23(1), 24–30.

Reibman, A. R. & Nolte, L. W. (1987b) Design and performance comparison of distributed detection networks, *IEEE Transactions on Aerospace and Electronic Systems*, AES-23(6), 789–97.

Shapley, L. & Grofman, B. (1984) Optimizing group judgmental accuracy in the presence of interdependencies, *Public Choice*, 43, 329–32.

Shepperd, J. A. & Taylor, K. M. (1999) Social loafing and expectancy-value theory, *Personality & Social Psychology Bulletin*, 25(9), 1147–58.

Sniezek, J. A. & Henry, R. A. (1989) Accuracy and confidence in group judgment, *Organizational Behavior and Human Decision Processes*, 43, 1–28.

Sorkin, R. D. & Dai, H. (1994) Signal detection analysis of the ideal group, *Organizational Behavior and Human Decision Processes*, 60, 1–13.

Sorkin, R. D., Hays, C. J., & West, R. (2001) Signal detection analysis of group decision making, *Psychological Review*, 108, 183–203.

Sorkin, R. D., Luan, S., & Itzkowitz, J. (2001) Rational models of social conformity and social loafing. Paper presented at the European Association for Decision Making (SPUDM-18), Amsterdam, Netherlands, August 2001.

Sorkin, R. D., Luan, S., and Itzkowitz, J. (2003) Effect of majority rule and initial bias on information aggregation by groups. Paper presented at AFOSR, EADM, and NSF Workshop on Information Aggregation in Decision Making, Silver Spring, MD, May 2003.

Sorkin, R. D., Luan, S., Itzkowitz, J. & Crandall, C. (submitted for publication) Signal detection theory of group deliberation: Jury decision making.

Sorkin, R. D., Mabry, T. R., Weldon, M., & Elvers, G. (1991) Integration of information from multiple element displays, *Organizational Behavior and Human Decision Processes*, 49, 167–87.

Sorkin, R. D., West, R., & Robinson, D. E. (1998) Group performance depends on the majority rule, *Psychological Science*, 9, 456–63.

Stasser, G., Kerr, N. L., & Davis, J. H. (1989) Influence processes and consensus models in decision-making groups. In P. Paulus (ed.), *Psychology of Group Influence* (2nd edn.). Hillsdale, NJ: Erlbaum.

Stoner, J. A. (1968) Risky and cautious shifts in group decisions: The influence of widely held values, *Journal of Experimental Social Psychology*, 4(4), 442–59.

Swaszek, P. E. & Willett, P. (1995) Parley as an approach to distributed detection, *IEEE Transactions on Aerospace and Electronic Systems*, 31(1), 447–57.

Swets, J. A. (1973) The relative operating characteristic in psychology, *Science*, 182(7), 990–1000.

Swets, J. A. (1986a) Indices of discrimination or diagnostic accuracy: Their ROCs and implied models, *Psychological Bulletin*, 99(1) 100–17.

Swets, J. A. (1986b) Form of empirical ROCs in discrimination and diagnostic tasks: Implications for theory and measurement of performance, *Psychological Bulletin*, 99(2) 181–98.

Swets, J. A. (1988) Measuring the accuracy of diagnostic systems, *Science*, 240(3), 1285–93.

Swets, J. A., Tanner, W. P., Jr., & Birdsall, T. G. (1961) Decision processes in perception, *Psychological Review*, 68, 301–40.

Tanner, W. P. Jr. & Birdsall, T. G. (1958) Definition of d' and η as psychophysical measures, *Journal of the Acoustical Society of America*, 30, 922–8.

Tanner, W. P., Jr., & Swets, J. A. (1954) A decision-making theory of visual detection, *Psychological Review*, 61, 401–09.

Turner, J. C. (1991) *Social Influence*. Milton Keynes: Open University Press.

Viswanathan, R. & Varshney, P. K. (1997) Distributed detection with multiple sensors: Part I – fundamentals, *Proceedings of the IEEE*, 85, 54–63.

Wallsten, T. S., Budescu, D. V., Erev, I., & Diederich, A. (1997) Evaluating and combining subjective probability estimates, *Journal of Behavioral Decision Making*, 10, 243–68.

Willett, P., Swaszek, P. F., & Blum, R. S. (2000) The good, bad and ugly: Distributed detection of a known signal in dependent Gaussian noise, *IEEE Transactions on Signal Processing*, 48(12), 3266–79.

24

Behavioral Game Theory

Simon Gächter

Introduction

Game theory is a mathematical tool to describe and analyze situations of conflict, cooperation, and coordination. In rational player models it is typically assumed that players are highly rational beings who completely understand the strategic situation and who always maximize their consistent preferences given their rationally formed beliefs about the behavior of their opponents. At the opposite extreme, in evolutionary models, players have no cognition and therefore "no choice" but are "programmed strategies" that survive or go extinct in an evolutionary contest.

By contrast, the approach of behavioral game theory (BGT) is to seek empirical information about how *human* beings – as opposed to highly rational beings or programmed strategies – behave in strategic situations. Thus, BGT takes the middle ground between these two extremes but builds on the great advances of formal game theory, without which BGT would not exist. BGT aims to answer the following research questions:

- To what extent is standard game theory a useful approximation to the strategic behavior of real people?
- If we observe deviations from what standard theory predicts, can we disentangle the reasons for the discrepancies?
- What are the players' preferences and their strategic reasoning processes?
- How do people learn in games?

In the long run, the goal of BGT is to discover theories that rest on plausible psychological foundations. BGT has this approach in common with the field of behavioral finance (see Chapter 26, this volume). Thus, BGT is not about "disproving" game theory but rather about making it a more powerful tool for the analysis of strategic situations. The most important research tool of BGT is incorporating insights from psychology and conducting controlled laboratory experiments.

In this chapter I will discuss some seminal experiments and recent developments in BGT. Lack of space makes my approach selective. This chapter is structured as follows. In the next section, I will discuss the most important concepts of standard game theory, as they are relevant for understanding the goals of BGT. I then review some classic findings on classic games. This sets the stage for the following section, which concentrates on three building blocks of modern game theory – preferences, strategic reasoning, and equilibration. The final section provides my concluding remarks.

For those who want to dig deeper, Camerer (2003) provides the most comprehensive overview available of the field of BGT. Crawford (1997) is a very useful shorter survey. Kagel and Roth (1995) provide an extensive overview of research in experimental economics. Selten (1998) offers a bounded rationality perspective on BGT.

What is (Behavioral) Game Theory?

Game theory is a branch of applied mathematics that provides a framework for modeling and predicting behavior in social situations of cooperation, coordination, and conflict. The famous book by John von Neumann and Oskar Morgenstern (1944), *Theory of Games and Economic Behavior*, founded the field of game theory. While in the first two decades after the publication of von Neumann and Morgenstern's book game-theoretical research was mainly confined to small mathematical communities, it entered the intellectual discourse in the social and biological sciences in the 1960s and 1970s. Two decision theorists, Duncan Luce and Howard Raiffa wrote one of the first textbooks in game theory (Luce and Raiffa, 1957). In his classic book, *The Strategy of Conflict*, Thomas Schelling introduced game-theoretic arguments to political science (Schelling, 1960). Game-theoretic reasoning also has had a great impact on evolutionary theories in the biological sciences. There are also applications of game theory in anthropology and sociology. In economics, game theory is a cornerstone in all curricula, and an essential element of modern economic theory.

Before I discuss the goals of BGT in more depth, it is useful to introduce some important game-theoretical concepts. I will confine myself to rational player models and to concepts that are relevant for our discussion of BGT. A full account of modern game theory can be found in Colman (1995), or Gintis (2000) who both frequently refer to experimental findings on the various games they discuss. The latter book also covers recent evolutionary models.

There are two ways of describing strategic situations – the normal form and the extensive form. I will start with the normal form and introduce the extensive form later. The *normal form* of a game consists of a specification of (1) a set of n players, (2) their actions or strategies, and (3) their payoffs. Examples may help to fix ideas. To keep things simple, I will concentrate on two-person games where each player has just two strategies. Of course, everything can be extended to n-player games with m actions.

	Mary			Mary			Mary	
	C	D		C	D		C	D
John C	2, 2	0, 3	C	2, 2	0, 1	C	3, –3	–1, 1
John D	3, 0	1, 1	D	1, 0	1, 1	D	–9, 9	3, –3

| (a) Prisoners' dilemma | (b) "Stag hunt"/"Weak link" | (c) Zero-sum game |

Figure 24.1 Classic games of (a) cooperation, (b) coordination, and (c) conflict in normal form

Figure 24.1 depicts three classic games in normal form. These games describe generic social situations of cooperation, coordination and conflict. The chosen games are also interesting for the solution concepts needed to solve them.

In all games of Figure 24.1, there are two players, Mary and John. Both of them have two actions they can choose, C and D. It is assumed that John and Mary choose simultaneously, i.e., without knowing about their opponent's choice. In all games, there are four strategy combinations: (C, C); (D, C); (C, D); and (D, D). The numbers in each matrix refer to the payoffs each player receives as a result of the possible strategy combinations. The first number in each cell refers to John and the second to Mary. For example, if in game (a) John plays D and Mary plays C, then John's payoff will be 3 and Mary will get 0. Payoffs are numerical representations (called "utilities") of players' preference orderings over possible outcomes. For instance, game (a) is a situation where John prefers the outcome (D, C) over (C, C), over (D, D), over (C, D). The utilities reflect this preference ordering.

Solution concepts predict how people will play the game. As in other domains of rational decision making (compare Chapters 2 and 20, this volume) the behavioral assumption about rational play in games is that players maximize their expected utilities. The most basic solution concept is *dominance*, i.e., the assumption that rational players will not play strategies that are dominated by other strategies that a player has at his or her disposal. Look at game (a). In this game, both John and Mary are better off by choosing D than C regardless of what the opponent chooses, i.e., C is a dominated strategy for both players. Thus, dominance as a solution concept predicts outcome (D, D). This game is the famous prisoners' dilemma, the prototype game to study issues of *cooperation*.

Not all games are dominance-solvable. In games (b) and (c) no solution in dominant strategies exists. An appropriate solution concept for these games is the *Nash equilibrium*. A Nash equilibrium prevails if players choose mutually best responses, i.e., each player chooses the strategy that maximizes his or her utility given the strategies played by the opponents. In other words, in a Nash equilibrium, no player has an incentive to choose another strategy than the one he or she is currently playing. If we apply this reasoning to game (a) then we find that only (D, D) is a Nash equilibrium. Game (b) has two Nash equilibria (in so-called "pure strategies"): (C, C) and (D, D). Game (b) is a so-called coordination game, because the fact that it has multiple equilibria requires *coordination* on one of the equilibria.

If we apply the solution concept of Nash equilibrium to game (c), we find that no solution in pure strategies exists. Yet, in a seminal paper John Nash (1950) proved that any game with finite player and strategy sets has an equilibrium at least in mixed strategies. A mixed strategy is a probability distribution over pure strategies. *A mixed-strategy Nash equilibrium* requires that the mixed strategies are mutual best responses. In the unique mixed-strategy Nash equilibrium of game (c) both John and Mary will play C with probability $^3/_4$. Game (c) is a prototypical example of pure *conflict*, because it is a zero-sum game: John's gains are Mary's losses, and vice versa.

We are now in a position to take a first look at three issues of BGT that are closely linked to conceptual building blocks of modern game theory that I will discuss more thoroughly in the fourth part of this chapter. One important recent issue concerns the players' preferences. In theory, payoffs are utilities and just represent the players' preferences. These utilities can accommodate almost every taste, as long as some basic consistency axioms are met. Yet, in (economic) applications of game theory it is often presumed that the utilities represent material payoffs. For instance, firms maximize profits and employees their income. In experiments, participants earn money. Players are then viewed as selfish maximizers, who only care for their own payoff. Yet, as we will see below, this assumption is frequently at odds with the facts. A second task of BGT is to understand human strategic reasoning. Many models assume that players possess infinite reasoning powers and form rational beliefs about how their opponents will behave and thereby take into account the belief formation of their opponent players, including beliefs about beliefs ... ad infinitum. In an equilibrium these beliefs will be mutually consistent. Equilibrium play may look like an innocuous assumption, in particular if each player has a dominant strategy, like in the prisoners' dilemma game. Yet, in games where a number of iterations are necessary to eliminate dominated strategies (see section on "Measuring and modeling cognitions"), or in games with multiple equilibria such an assumption is far less innocuous. With multiple equilibria, it is an empirical question which equilibrium is played. A third issue of BGT therefore is to investigate how players learn in games and how an equilibrium might emerge. I will set the stage for a discussion of these issues by first looking at some classic results in classic games.

Classic Games of Cooperation, Coordination, and Conflict

Laboratory experiments are the best-suited tool to study behavior in games. A game with its decision rules can be directly implemented in the lab. The most difficult part is "controlling" the preferences. When behavioral game theorists run experiments, participants are paid according to their decisions. Practices in psychology often differ here (see Hertwig and Ortmann, 2001). An important argument in favor of paying is that it is safe to assume that all people, regardless of their preferences, are non-satiated in money. Thus, paying subjects for their decisions ensures that at least the subjects' monetary preferences are controlled. Decisions will have true opportunity costs and are not just hypothetical statements.

Games of cooperation

In a sense, BGT started right after game theory was invented. The prisoners' dilemma, for instance, was conceived in 1950. At about this time the first experiments on the prisoners' dilemma were conducted. Rapoport and Chammah (1965) report one of the first series of systematic experiments on the prisoners' dilemma. Several hundred studies followed. The striking result is that people cooperate much more than is compatible with a simple dominance argument that underlies the prediction in the prisoners' dilemma (if we assume that players maximize only their monetary payoffs). This result also holds for "social dilemma games" and "public goods games", which are both generalized *n*-person prisoners' dilemmas (see, e.g., Dawes, 1980; and Ledyard, 1995).

Coordination games

Many situations in social life require the coordination of activities. Examples abound. Language is an obvious case. A further prominent example of a solved coordination game is on which side of the road to drive. At an abstract level, any game with multiple equilibria is a coordination game. Which equilibrium, if any, will people play? This is fundamentally an empirical question and an important task of BGT to understand how people actually solve coordination problems. Important issues concern the role of "saliency" (e.g., Mehta, Starmer, & Sugden, 1994) or communication (e.g., Cooper, DeJong, Forsythe, & Ross, 1990) as coordination devices. The literature is large and I therefore concentrate on one class of coordination games, namely "stag-hunt" games. See Camerer (2003) for a more complete discussion.

Stag-hunt games are interesting because the equilibria in these games differ according to their "riskiness" and efficiency. Game (b) in Figure 24.1 illustrates this nicely. Think of John and Mary who can cooperate in hunting big game or defect and hunt a rabbit. If they both go for the stag they earn two payoff units; if John defects and goes for the rabbit, he catches a rabbit, worth one payoff unit, but Mary will be unable to catch a stag, and earn nothing. If both defect and go for the rabbit they both will catch a rabbit and get a payoff of 1. This game has three equilibria: the pure strategy equilibria (C, C), (D, D), and an equilibrium in mixed strategies. The stag-hunt game captures a situation where cooperation pays but is risky. Choosing D is safe because it yields a secure payoff of 1. In the language of game theory, the (C, C) equilibrium is "payoff-dominant," but (D, D) is "risk-dominant." Experiments by Cooper et al. (1990) and Van Huyck, Battalio, & Beil (1990) show that, after some initial miscoordination, play converges to an equilibrium. Yet, unless the players can communicate, they almost invariably end up playing the risk-dominant instead of the payoff-dominant equilibrium.

Games of conflict

Zero-sum games, for which game (c) in Figure 24.1 is an example, are interesting because of their purely competitive nature that implies the absence of pure strategy equilibria.

Players want to be "unpredictable" (for instance, a tennis player doesn't want to be predictable about whether she serves the ball left or right). Being unpredictable requires playing a mixed strategy.

In any mixed-strategy equilibrium players will choose probability distributions such that their opponent will be indifferent in choosing his or her pure strategies. For instance, in the mixed-strategy equilibrium of game (c), John will play C with probability $3/4$ and D with probability $1/4$.

Yet, behaviorally, there are at least three problems. First, in equilibrium, players have to accurately guess the exact probabilities with which the opponents will play their mixed strategies. Second, players should really randomize their choices. However, it is well known from psychological research that people are not very good in producing random sequences (Rapoport and Budescu, 1997). Third, learning is difficult, because in equilibrium people are indifferent between their choices. This implies that there are no positive incentives for playing a particular strategy. Yet, the degree to which human players display behavior that is consistent with the mixed-equilibrium prediction is an empirical question and an important task for BGT.

Malcolm and Lieberman (1965) report one of the first tests of game (c). The mixed-strategy equilibrium prediction is that C will be played with frequency 0.75. Yet, the actual frequency of plays of C of pairs of subjects who repeated this game 200 times, is only 0.57. Results from other studies are ambiguous. Maybe for this discouraging reason, research on mixed-strategy play stalled for many years. It was rejuvenated by a paper by O'Neill (1987), who reported more favorable results in an improved design. New experiments with further improved designs and data analysis by Binmore, Swierzbinski, & Proulx (2001) and Shachat (2002) report results that are favorable for mixed-strategy equilibrium in the sense that the observed frequencies are close to the theoretical frequencies. These results are quite surprising and good news for the mixed-equilibrium prediction, given that there are sound psychological reasons to assume that the concept is behaviorally rather demanding.

Preferences, Strategic Thinking, and Learning

The results from the previous section provide the backdrop for my discussion of recent advances in BGT. The topics I will touch concern three conceptual building blocks of modern game theory, the players' preferences, their strategic reasoning, and the process of learning.

Measuring and modeling motivations – social preferences

To appreciate the recent advances in BGT research on preferences, remember that payoffs in games are utilities that reflect the players' preferences over the outcome profiles. In theory, provided they are consistent, preferences can encompass any motivation. Yet, most applications of game theory make the assumption that the players are purely selfish.

An important contribution of BGT in recent years concerns our understanding of human players' actual social preferences, i.e., to what extent people take the well-being of other players into account in their preferences. The results from the cooperation games suggest that many players are not purely selfish. Yet, simultaneous-move games of cooperation are rather blunt tools to measure social preferences because it is very hard to distinguish altruism, reciprocity, and selfishness. Therefore, games in so-called "extensive form," where players move sequentially, are more apt to measure social preferences than simultaneous-move games. Before I discuss social preferences, I introduce the extensive form as a tool to describe situations that require sequential decisions, and the most important solution concept, the subgame-perfect equilibrium.

A digression: Extensive form and subgame-perfect equilibrium
The *extensive form* depicts the sequence of moves, the information and actions players have when it is their turn to make a move, and the final payoffs as a function of the moves of all players in the game. Figure 24.2 is a very simple example. It shows the extensive form of a simplified ultimatum game, called the "mini-ultimatum game." Next to the prisoners' dilemma, the ultimatum game, invented by Güth, Schmittberger, & Schwarze (1982), is probably the most researched game in BGT. As I will show below, this game is ideally suited to measure reciprocal preferences.

In this simple game John moves first. He has the choice between two allocations of $10, offer A or B. After John has made his offer, Mary is informed about it. She has two actions: she can either accept or reject the proposed allocation. If Mary accepts offer A, for instance, then John will receive $8 and Mary will get $2. If she turns it down, both receive nothing. This simple game is called the "ultimatum game" because Mary gets only one offer that she can either take or leave. It is a "mini-ultimatum game" because its "big brother" is a game where John can split $10 as he likes.

To find the solution, we will apply the principle of backward induction, i.e., we will start at the second stage first. Surely, Mary will accept any offer because in either case she ends up with more than 0. Since John anticipates this, he will propose A and Mary will

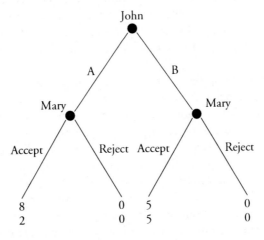

Figure 24.2 The extensive form of the mini-ultimatum game

accept. Yet, it is easy to verify that there is another Nash equilibrium, where John offers B and Mary accepts B, but threatens to reject offer A. While this is a Nash equilibrium, it does not satisfy sequential rationality. In the subgame after offer A, Mary would reject an offer that gives her more than 0, which is an incredible threat and hence not "subgame perfect" (Selten, 1975). Thus, a subgame-perfect equilibrium is a Nash equilibrium that is also sequentially rational. Next to the concept of Nash equilibrium, the subgame-perfect Nash equilibrium is a cornerstone of game theory.

Measuring social preferences with simple games

I now discuss the most important social preferences as they have been investigated in hundreds of experiments. The games are deliberately simple to avoid cognitive complexities that might interfere with the measurement of social preferences. Likewise, most games are one-shot, in the sense that the experimental subjects play only once against a particular opponent. This excludes strategic incentives that come from repeated interactions with the same opponents. Moreover, all games contain induced monetary incentives that allow a straightforward prediction if people are solely motivated by monetary returns. Deviations from this prediction can be interpreted as a willingness to pay (a "revealed social preference") for implementing the preferred action.

Negative reciprocity

Because the subgame-perfect equilibrium concept looks so compelling in simple games like the ultimatum game, the results of the first experiments by Güth et al. (1982) came as a shock and surprise to many economists and game theorists. Güth et al.'s (1982) version of the game is the same as in Figure 24.2, except that John can split $10 in any way he wants. Under the assumption that both players only care about their own monetary payoffs, subgame perfection predicts that John will offer the smallest money unit, say 1 cent, and pocket $9.99. Mary will accept the cent.

This is not what happened in Güth et al.'s (1982) experiment. The average offer was roughly 35 percent and offers below 50 percent were increasingly likely to be rejected. This result has been replicated dozens of times under various conditions, including "high stakes." One very remarkable study is by a group of anthropologists who ran experiments in 15 remote small-scale societies (see Henrich, Boyd, Bowles, Camerer, Fehr, & McElreath, 2001). They showed that unfair offers are likely to be rejected almost everywhere.

Most researchers today agree that rejecting a positive offer in the ultimatum game indicates negative reciprocity. A person has negatively reciprocal preferences, if she is willing to pay some price to punish an opponent for behavior that is deemed unfair or inappropriate. The observation of negative reciprocity is not confined to ultimatum games. It has also been observed in social dilemma and public goods games where players had the opportunity to punish their opponents. Many cooperators were willing to incur costs to punish the defectors, even in one-shot games without any future interaction (e.g., Fehr and Gächter, 2002). Rejecting a positive offer in a one-shot ultimatum game or punishing defectors means to forgo money without any material benefit. Many people have a willingness to punish even in the absence of any present or future rewards. This kind of behavior is fundamentally different from punishment strategies in repeated games (like "tit-for-tat" – see e.g., Axelrod, 1984), where punishment can be motivated by future returns.

Positive reciprocity

The friendly version of reciprocity is called positive reciprocity. Positive reciprocity means that people are prepared to pay a price to reward a friendly or a generous action by an opponent player. They are willing to pay this price even in the absence of any present and future material benefits. Thus, a purely self-interested individual would never exhibit positive reciprocity. And yet, positive reciprocity is quite common. One of the first demonstrations of positive reciprocity in an experimental game is from Fehr, Kirchsteiger, & Riedl (1993) in the so-called "gift-exchange game." This game mimics a labor relation where an employer pays a wage to an employee, who then chooses his or her effort level. In the game, incentives are set such that the employee always has a strict incentive to provide the lowest effort level, because effort is increasingly costly. The results are not consistent with this clear-cut prediction. Most employees respond with a high effort level if their employer pays them a generous wage. This result has been replicated under various institutional conditions (see Fehr and Gächter, 2000, for an overview). Positive reciprocity has also been demonstrated in a game related to the gift-exchange game, the so-called trust game (Berg, Dickhaut, & McCabe, 1995).

Altruism

There is a lot of evidence that many people are prepared to make anonymous donations to charities or to spontaneously help others who are in need. A person has altruistic preferences if her utility increases with the well-being of others. The experimental tool to study this is the "dictator game" (Kahneman, Knetsch, & Thaler, 1986). A player (the "dictator") is endowed with some money, say $10, and can then decide how much to pocket, and how much to pass on to a passive recipient, who cannot veto the offer. Of course, under standard assumptions, the dictator will keep everything. Under double-blind conditions, roughly two-thirds of the people give nothing and one third gives amounts between 10 and 50 percent of the pie. Offers are significantly lower than in the ultimatum game, because the dictators do not have to fear rejections (see, e.g., Forsythe, Horowitz, Savin, & Sefton, 1994). The significance of the results from the dictator games is that many people, even under complete anonymity, are willing to share their wealth with others.

Attributions

The implicit assumption made in almost all of rational choice analysis and regardless whether people are selfish or other-regarding is that decision makers only care about outcomes. Yet, casual evidence and daily experience suggest that not only outcomes but also the "intentions" (the attribution of motivations) behind a decision matter for our evaluation of outcomes. To fix ideas, look again at Figure 24.2. In this game, John can choose between offer A, which, if Mary accepts it, gives John $8 and Mary $2. Offer B gives both players $5. Now imagine another game where the rejection payoffs and offer A stay the same, but offer B gives John $2 and Mary $8, instead of ($5, $5). If Mary just cares about final payoffs, the rejection probability of *offer A* should not be influenced by the unchosen offer B. Yet, experimental evidence shows that unchosen alternatives matter a lot for the rejection probability of offer A. For instance, Falk, Fischbacher, & Fehr (2003) who implemented this game, found that the rejection probability of offer A, when the alternative offer B is (5,5) is 44.4 percent, and only 26.7 percent if offer B amounts to (2,8). An explanation is that in case (5,5) is available, to offer A signals a greedy intention, whereas this is not the case if offer B is (2,8) and therefore as unequal as offer A. Rejections are also lower if a computer, which has no intentions, generates the unfair offers (e.g., Sanfey, Rilling, Aronson, Nystrom, & Cohen, 2003).

Modeling social preferences

How can we theoretically account for the empirical results? My interpretation of the results is that they show us people's apparent willingness to pay to achieve fairness or to punish unfair behavior. In other words, their behavior reveals a preference. Yet, many social scientists, most fervent the economists, traditionally have been very hostile against using preference explanations to rationalize social phenomena, because almost every result can be "explained" this way. This is a very strong argument if preferences are unobservable. However, the simple experiments and the more refined tools of neuroscientific research (see, e.g., Sanfey et al., 2003) are instruments to gather the necessary empirical evidence. Thus, the challenge now is to find a utility function that is psychologically plausible, can explain a wide variety of games and can be subjected to further experimental tests. Meanwhile a large literature has developed that has made a start on this issue. Camerer (2003) provides a comprehensive overview. In the following I will focus on models of inequity aversion (Fehr and Schmidt, 1999; Bolton and Ockenfels, 2000) because they are now used in applied work.

The idea of these models is to assume that individuals have a higher utility the more material resources they possess but, in addition to this self-centered motivation, people also care for the fairness of the allocation, i.e., they are inequity averse. To make this precise, let us assume (following Fehr and Schmidt, 1999) that Mary has the utility function U_M, which depends on the allocation of material resources to her and John:

$$U_M(x_M, x_J) = x_M - \alpha_M \max[x_J - x_M, 0] - \beta_M \max[x_M - x_J, 0]. \tag{24.1}$$

Mary's utility increases with her own resources x_M, and decreases with the inequity of the allocation. If John gets more than Mary ($x_J - x_M > 0$), Mary experiences a disutility because of unfavorable inequity, provided $\alpha_M > 0$. If Mary also dislikes inequity that favors her ($x_M - x_J > 0$), β_M is positive as well. A typical assumption is that $\alpha_M > \beta_M$, i.e., Mary's disutility is larger in case of unfavorable than favorable inequity. This utility function also contains selfish preferences (that characterize a significant group of subjects in almost all experiments) as a special case. If Mary is selfish, she only cares for x_M and not about the inequity of the allocation, i.e., $\alpha_M = \beta_M = 0$. Various combinations of α and β allow us to model the observations that people are heterogeneous with respect to their social preferences.

How can inequity aversion explain, for instance, rejections in the mini-ultimatum game depicted in Figure 24.2? Assume John proposes allocation A, which gives him $8 and leaves $2 for Mary. If Mary does not care about the inequity of this offer, she will surely accept, because $2 > $0. If, however, Mary is sufficiently inequity-averse, she will reject the offer and thereby restore equity. A similar logic holds in the public goods game with punishment, because a free rider has a payoff advantage that can be reduced by punishment. Aversion against favorable inequity ($\beta > 0$) can also explain why some people reject offers that give them more than the opponent player. This approach that is only sketched here can also explain the results from dictator games, public goods games, and a variety of market games.

A drawback of models like this is that they cannot explain that often the set of alternatives and the intentions behind a choice, and not just final outcomes, matter for decision makers. For instance, when people reject offers in the ultimatum game or punish defectors in the public goods game, they often do this not only because they are inequity averse, but they also want to punish the greedy intention.

Models that incorporate intentions by modeling them as beliefs that are part of the utility function (so-called "psychological games" – see Geneakoplos, Pearce, & Stacchetti, 1989) do a better job here. A seminal model is Rabin (1993) who shows how the perceived "kindness" of a choice can, e.g., explain why cooperation in the prisoners' dilemma can be a "fairness equilibrium." Dufwenberg and Kirchsteiger (2004) and Falk and Fischbacher (1999) generalize Rabin's (1993) approach from normal form games to extensive form games. Falk and Fischbacher (1999) and Charness and Rabin (2002) merge inequity aversion and intention-based reciprocity.

Except for changing the utility function the models retain all assumptions about rationality and optimal strategic play that characterize solution concepts in rational choice game theory. This assumption might be approximately correct for describing very simple games, but in more complex games it is certainly doubtful to assume away cognitive costs and bounded rationality. In the next section I will therefore look at the insights gained on people's cognitions, when they play (strategically complex) games.

Measuring and modeling cognitions – strategic thinking

Backward induction

Backward induction is an important rationality principle because it ensures sequential rationality. To put backward induction to a test requires separating it from social preferences. The observation that people deviate from subgame-perfect play can have two reasons – people have social preferences and/or they do not behave sequentially rationally. The fact that recent theories of social preferences can rationalize observed play in deliberately simple games where backward induction is probably not an important issue does not mean that people really obey the principle of backward induction. While backward induction surely is a very convincing principle of rational behavior, it is psychologically demanding and may be deemed unnatural, at least by untrained subjects. Backward induction requires looking forward to the end of the game tree and thinking about subgames that are possibly never reached in the game.

Johnson, Camerer, Sen, & Rymon (2002) conducted a psychologically rich experiment on backward induction that controls for social preferences. The experimental subjects play a three-stage alternating bargaining game (where John makes the first proposal how to split that is followed by Mary's counteroffer if Mary rejects John's first offer and where John can make a final offer if he rejects Mary's offer). After each rejection the pie shrinks. There are two novel features in Johnson et al.'s (2002) experiments. First, to control for social preferences, participants in one treatment know that they play against a payoff-maximizing computer, which excludes payoff comparisons to another human being. In another treatment, the opponent is another human player. Second, in both treatments Johnson et al. (2002) apply a so-called "Mouselab" procedure used in decision research, to infer thinking processes from observed information acquisition. Specifically, subjects see on a computer screen the covered boxes of the pie sizes in each of the three rounds. They also see the covered boxes that contain the information of the role of a subject in a given round. By moving the cursor to a box the box automatically uncovers and reveals the corresponding information (moving away the cursor re-covers the box). The software records the time the subject spends looking at a specific box, how often this box is visited and how a subject switches back and forth between the boxes. If people backward induct, they should start by looking at the third-round boxes.

There are two main results. First, offers were closer to the standard equilibrium predictions when subjects played against the computer, which suggests that payoff comparisons to other human players matter. Second, most subjects spent most of their time looking at the first-round boxes instead of the third-round boxes, as required by backward induction reasoning. There are a number of subjects who never looked at the third-round boxes. When subjects were told about backward induction, their information acquisition became more rational. The significance of these results is twofold: First, they nicely demonstrate that both social preferences and limited cognitions determine bargaining behavior. Second, the patterns of information acquisition tell us something about principles of strategic reasoning of people who are less than fully rational. In the following section I will return to normal form games and take another look at principles of strategic thinking.

Strategic sophistication

Strategic thinking in games requires players to form beliefs about what opponents will do. The issues that are involved can most easily be demonstrated with the concept of *dominance*, which is a very basic rationality principle. For instance, if in game (a) of Figure 24.1 numbers reflect the player's real utilities, then strategy D dominates C for both players. This game is the simplest example of a dominance-solvable game. Yet, most games that are dominance-solvable require the *iterated* elimination of dominated strategies. If this process allows the elimination of all but one strategy combination the game is dominance-solvable. In rational game theory the iterated elimination of dominated strategies is a mental exercise that rational players will entertain under the assumption of common knowledge of rationality. Yet, empirically, it might be that a particular player avoids playing a dominated strategy but is not sure that other players are doing the same.

The following game, known as the "beauty contest game" nicely illustrates the issues that are involved in strategic reasoning. All players in a group of n players simultaneously write down a real number between 0 and 100. The average of these numbers is multiplied by a factor $p < 1$. The player whose stated number is closest to this statistic is the winner and gets the prize. The others receive nothing. In case of ties the prize is randomly given to one of the tied winners. Assume, for instance, that $p = 0.7$. Applying iterated elimination of dominated strategies immediately eliminates all numbers larger than 70, because they can never be winning numbers. Given that all numbers above 70 are eliminated, the winning number cannot be larger than $70 \times 0.7 = 49$, and so on. The only number that survives the iterated elimination of weakly dominated strategies is 0. Yet, even if players understand this logic, zero is most likely not the winning number (at least not when this game is played for the first time). Nagel (1995) was the first study on this game. In her experiments with $p = 2/3$, the average number was 35 in the first round and quickly converged to zero after a few further plays of the game. The game has been replicated many times (see Nagel 1999).

The beauty of this simple game is that it can be used to measure depths of strategic reasoning, which might differ between people. For instance, all studies report that some subjects choose their number more or less randomly. Following Stahl and Wilson (1995) these people might be called "level-0 players," because they do not think strategically. Level-1 players make one step of iterated reasoning. They believe that others are level-0 types who choose randomly (with an average of 50). Level-1 types best-respond by picking 35. Level-2 players anticipate that there are level-1 players around and choose a number in the vicinity of 25. Thus, a level-k player assumes that all others are one level below him or her, and best responds to this belief by choosing a number $50p^k$. Only a level $k = \infty$ would choose zero. Yet, choosing zero is "too smart" a choice. Estimations from first-round data of various experiments show that most people are level-3 or lower-level types, i.e., they use up to three steps of iterated reasoning. The trick is to be one step ahead of the opponents, but not further.

One drawback of the beauty contest games to measure levels of strategic thinking is that just one single choice is observed and the player is then classified on the basis of this choice. To circumvent this problem, Costa-Gomes, Crawford, & Broseta (2001) designed a series of normal form games and also used the "Mouselab" technique to see how players use payoff information. They confirm that most players are level-2 or level-1 types (see also Stahl and Wilson, 1995). These results are important information for any theory of boundedly rational strategic play. In the following section I will briefly discuss two models that aim at explaining people's behavior in one-shot games.

Models of strategic play

I concentrate on two aspects: First, when people play games, they make errors. Second, people differ in their levels of iterated reasoning.

A sensible assumption is that the likelihood of playing a particular strategy is a function of the strategy's expected payoff, but people make mistakes. A desirable property of a choice rule is that the probability of choosing a particular strategy increases with the expected payoff of the strategy and decreases with the errors people make. The logit function is a frequently used rule that has these desirable properties. Assume that we want to explain the choices in the games of Figure 24.1. The probability $p_M(C)$ that Mary plays her strategy C, given Mary's expected utility of playing C, $EU_M(C)$, is:

$$p_M(C) = \frac{e^{EU_M(C)/\mu}}{e^{EU_M(C)/\mu} + e^{EU_M(D)/\mu}}. \qquad (24.2)$$

The parameter μ is an error rate. If $\mu \to 0$, the strategy with the higher expected payoff is played with probability 1. If $\mu \to \infty$, then Mary chooses randomly between her strategies (i.e., in the games of Figure 24.1 the probability of choosing C approaches 0.5). Thus, this logit choice rule has the desired properties. Imposing the assumption that in equilibrium the choice probabilities have to be consistent, leads to the solution concept of the "Quantal Response Equilibrium" (QRE, see McKelvey and Palfrey, 1995), which generalizes the concept of a Nash equilibrium by allowing for errors. QRE does a surprisingly good job in explaining both small and large deviations from the Nash equilibrium in a variety of one-shot games (Goeree and Holt, 1999). QRE can also be adopted to incorporate iterated reasoning with errors ("noisy introspection" – see Goeree and Holt, 1999).

The "cognitive hierarchy" model (Camerer, Ho, & Chong, 2003) assumes that level-k players believe that all other players are level-k-1 players and that for reasons of memory constraints more thinking steps are increasingly rare. Camerer et al. (2003) show that the frequency distribution of level-k types follows a Poisson distribution with mean and variance τ, where τ is the number of thinking steps. They fit a great many games and find that the average τ is 1.5. Data from the "beauty contest" experiments with various student and non-student subjects pools show that τ varies from 3.8 (computer scientists and game theorists) to 0 (some college students).

The noisy introspection model and the cognitive hierarchy model have primarily been developed to explain strategic thinking in games that people play only once, i.e., where there are no learning opportunities. These models can explain how people start playing a game. Learning models, to which I turn next, explain how people change their strategies as a function of their experience in playing the game and give us a hint how equilibration may come about empirically.

Learning

How does an equilibrium arise in a game? One theoretical interpretation is that players reason their way to an equilibrium, as, for example, in dominance-solvable games. Yet, in all but the simplest games this is psychologically not very plausible. Instead, people will play an equilibrium only after some process of trial-and-error, i.e., after some learning. Thus, a psychologically convincing interpretation is to see an equilibrium as the possible limit point of a learning process.

Learning models aim to explain the learning process, i.e., to understand how people change their strategies with experience. There exist plenty of learning models. For lack of space I will concentrate in this section on three frequently used models. See Camerer (2003) for an extensive overview of the experimental literature and Fudenberg and Levine (1998) for a theoretical account of learning in games.

Reinforcement learning
The learning models I look at typically assume that a particular strategy has a certain propensity, or initial attraction with which this strategy will be played. This attraction

may come from the experiences of having played a similar game in the past, strategic considerations like the ones discussed in the previous section, or some other analysis. Learning rules then model how these attractions get updated as a function of experience. One simple rule, rooted in behaviorist psychology, is "choice reinforcement," which says that the attraction of a strategy is increased by its previous payoff. The attraction of a strategy that has not been played stays the same. The attractions then determine via a probabilistic choice rule how likely a particular strategy will be played. The more successful a strategy the more frequently it will be chosen (which is also known as the "law of effect"). Erev and Roth (1998) looked at normal form games with mixed-strategy equilibria and Roth and Erev (1995) applied this model to explain behavior in ultimatum games and two further games with similar subgame perfect equilibria. The simulations showed that the reinforcement-learning rule tracks the observed choices.

Belief learning
A cognitively more demanding approach, traditionally mostly used by game theorists, is belief learning. The most frequently used model is "fictitious play." It assumes that players play best responses given the beliefs they have about their opponents' strategies. Players are assumed to have a good memory – beliefs are formed by observing the whole history of strategy choices. Players play a best response to the relative frequency with which their opponents have played their strategies in the past. A special case of "fictitious play" is Cournot learning, where players best respond just to the most recent strategy choice of their opponents. Cheung and Friedman (1997) provide a general framework, called "weighted fictitious play" that contains both fictitious play and Cournot learning as special cases. Specifically, the main idea is that beliefs are formed by weighting past choices of opponent players by a discount factor γ, such that the most recent choices get more weight than historical choices. If $0 < \gamma < 1$, then people learn adaptively. If $\gamma = 1$, then all past choices are equally weighted – this is the case of fictitious play. If $\gamma = 0$, only the most recent choice is considered, i.e., we have Cournot learning. Cheung and Friedman (1997) test their model on 2×2 normal form games. The estimated median γs do not strongly differ between games and are closer to 0 than to 1, i.e., people are closer to Cournot learning than to fictitious play.

Experienced-weighted attraction learning (EWA)
The final model I look at is EWA, invented by Camerer and Ho (1999). EWA is a hybrid model that combines belief and reinforcement learning and contains their pure forms as special cases. Camerer and Ho (1999) show that belief learning and reinforcement models are closely related, despite their very different appearances. The crucial feature of all learning models is how the attractions get updated. In EWA both actually chosen and unchosen strategies are reinforced. The chosen strategies are reinforced by the payoff they actually yield. For instance, if both Mary and John in game (b) of Figure 24.1 choose C, then Mary's strategy C is reinforced by the payoff $\pi_M(C,C) = 2$. The unchosen strategies are reinforced by the payoff they could have yielded, weighted by a so-called "imagination factor" δ. In the example, Mary's unchosen strategy D is reinforced by $\delta\pi_M(D,C) = \delta$. If the imagination factor $\delta = 0$, forgone payoffs are ignored

and only the actually chosen strategy is reinforced; if $\delta = 1$, actual and forgone payoffs equally determine the attractions. The experience-weighted attractions then determine via a probabilistic choice rule the actual choice probabilities.

The ambition of EWA is that all important parameters have a natural psychological interpretation and can be measured empirically. The interpretation of the most important parameter, the imagination factor δ, is that it captures two important aspects of human learning, which Camerer and Ho (1999) aptly call the "law of actual effect" and the "law of simulated effect," respectively.

Camerer and Ho (1999) evaluate their model econometrically and compare it to reinforcement and belief learning with data from constant sum games with unique mixed-strategy equilibria, dominance-solvable beauty contest games, and a coordination game with Pareto-rankable pure-strategy Nash equilibria. Estimations show that EWA outperforms reinforcement learning in all three games and is better than belief learning in most cases. On average, across all the data sets that Camerer and Ho (1999) study, the imagination factor $\delta = 0.50$, which says that people weigh forgone payoffs about half as much as actual payoffs. People not only learn from their successful strategies (as in reinforcement learning) but also from simulating what they could have earned had they chosen another strategy.

Concluding Remarks

What will the future of BGT be? The ultimate goal of BGT should be to predict behavior not only in lab experiments but in real-world strategic situations. A couple of steps are probably necessary to get there. One direction is to study more systematically how the results from individual judgment and decision research, and bounded rationality apply in games (compare Hastie and Dawes, 2001; and Chapters 4, 5, and 20, this volume). Knowing how groups, compared to individuals, behave in strategic decisions certainly would be fruitful for many practical purposes (see also Chapter 23, this volume). One important observation from many experiments is that people are heterogeneous both with respect to their social preferences and their strategic sophistication. A better understanding of motivational and cognitive heterogeneity, and their interplay, is surely necessary. One of the biggest payoffs for all these questions may come from paying more attention to the "mental models" people apply, how people reason in games, what determines players' social preferences, and the role of emotions in strategic reasoning and behavior (see also Chapter 22, this volume). "Mouselab" and neuroscientific techniques have already been successfully employed. These instruments, along with standard experiments and belief elicitation, certainly are very apt tools for further increasing our understanding of strategic thinking and behavior.

Acknowledgment

I am grateful to Derek Koehler, Nigel Harvey, and Jean-Robert Tyran for helpful comments.

References

Axelrod, R. (1984) *The Evolution of Cooperation*. New York: Basic Books.

Berg, J., Dickhaut, J., & McCabe, K. (1995) Trust, reciprocity, and social history, *Games and Economic Behavior*, 10, 122–42.

Binmore, K., Swierzbinski, J., & Proulx, C. (2001) Does minimax work? An experimental study, *Economic Journal*, 111, 445–64.

Bolton, G. & Ockenfels, A. (2000) ERC – a theory of equity, reciprocity, and competition, *American Economic Review*, 100, 166–93.

Camerer, C. (2003) *Behavioral Game Theory: Experiments in Strategic Interaction*. Princeton: Princeton University Press.

Camerer, C. & Ho, T. (1999) Experience-weighted attraction learning in normal form games, *Econometrica*, 67, 827–74.

Camerer, C., Ho, T., & Chong, K. (2003) Models of thinking, learning, and teaching in games, *American Economic Review*, 93(2), 192–5.

Charness, G. & Rabin, M. (2002) Understanding social preferences with simple tests, *Quarterly Journal of Economics*, 116, 817–69.

Cheung, Y.-W. & Friedman, D. (1997) Individual learning in normal form games: Some laboratory results, *Games and Economic Behavior*, 19, 46–76.

Colman, A. M. (1995) *Game Theory and its Applications in the Social and Biological Sciences*. London and New York: Routledge.

Cooper, R., DeJong, D., Forsythe, R., & Ross, T. (1990) Selection criteria in coordination games: Some experimental results, *American Economic Review*, 80, 218–33.

Costa-Gomez, M., Crawford, V., & Broseta, B. (2001) Cognition and behavior in normal form games: An experimental study, *Econometrica*, 69, 1193–235.

Crawford, V. (1997) Theory and experiment in the analysis of strategic interaction. In D. Kreps and K. Wallis (eds.), *Advances in Economics and Econometrics* (vol. I, pp. 206–42). Cambridge: Cambridge University Press.

Dawes, R. M. (1980) Social dilemmas, *Annual Review of Psychology*, 31, 169–93.

Dufwenberg, M. & Kirchsteiger, G. (2004) A theory of sequential reciprocity, *Games and Economic Behavior*, 47, 268–98.

Erev, I. & Roth, A. E. (1998) Predicting how people play games: Reinforcement learning in experimental games with unique, mixed-strategy equilibria, *American Economic Review*, 88, 848–81.

Falk, A. & Fischbacher, U. (1999) A theory of reciprocity, working paper no. 6, Institute for Empirical Research in Economics, University of Zurich.

Falk, A., Fischbacher, U., & Fehr, E. (2003) On the nature of fair behavior, *Economic Inquiry*, 41, 20–6.

Fehr, E. & Gächter, S. (2000) Fairness and retaliation: The economics of reciprocity, *Journal of Economic Perspectives*, 14, 159–81.

Fehr, E. & Gächter, S. (2002) Altruistic punishment in humans, *Nature*, 415, 137–40.

Fehr, E., Kirchsteiger, G., & Riedl, A. (1993) Does fairness prevent market clearing? *Quarterly Journal of Economics*, 108, 437–60.

Fehr, E. & Schmidt, K. M. (1999) A theory of fairness, competition, and cooperation, *Quarterly Journal of Economics*, 114, 817–68.

Forsythe, R. L., Horowitz, J., Savin, N. E., Sefton, M. (1994) Fairness in simple bargaining games, *Games and Economic Behavior*, 6, 347–69.

Fudenberg, D. & Levine, D. (1998) *The Theory of Learning in Games*. Cambridge, MA: MIT Press.

Geneakoplos, J., Pearce, D., & Stacchetti, E. (1989) Psychological games and sequential rationality, *Games and Economic Behavior*, 1, 60–79.

Gintis, H. (2000) *Game Theory Evolving*. Princeton: Princeton University Press.

Goeree, J. K. & Holt, C. A. (1999) Stochastic game theory: For playing games, not just for doing theory, *Proceedings of the National Academy of Sciences*, 96, 10564–7.

Güth, W., Schmittberger, R., & Schwarze, B. (1982) An experimental analysis of ultimatum bargaining, *Journal of Economic Behavior and Organization*, 3, 367–88.

Hastie, R. & Dawes, R. M. (2001) *Rational Choice in an Uncertain World. The Psychology of Judgment and Decision Making*. Thousand Oaks, CA: Sage Publications.

Henrich, J., Boyd, R., Bowles, S., Camerer, C., Fehr, E., & McElreath, R. (2001) In search of homo economicus: Behavioral experiments in 15 small-scale societies, *American Economic Review*, 91(2), 73–8.

Hertwig, R. & Ortmann, A. (2001) Experimental practices in economics: A methodological challenge for psychologists? *Behavioral and Brain Sciences*, 24, 383–451.

Johnson, E. J., Camerer, C., Sen, S., & Rymon, T. (2002) Detecting failures of backward induction: Monitoring information search in sequential bargaining, *Journal of Economic Theory*, 104, 16–47.

Kagel, J. H. & Roth, A. E. (eds.) (1995) *Handbook of Experimental Economics*. Princeton: Princeton University Press.

Kahneman, D., Knetsch, T., & Thaler, R. (1986) Fairness and the assumptions of economics, *Journal of Business*, 59, S285–S300.

Ledyard, J. (1995) Public goods: A survey of experimental research. In J. H. Kagel and A. E. Roth (eds.), *Handbook of Experimental Economics* (pp. 111–94). Princeton: Princeton University Press.

Luce, D. & Raiffa, H. (1957) *Games and Decisions. Introduction and Critical Survey*. New York: Dover Publications.

Malcolm, D. & Lieberman, B. (1965) The behavior of responsive individuals playing a two-person zero-sum game requiring the use of mixed strategies, *Psychonomic Science*, 12, 373–4.

McKelvey, R. & Palfrey, T. (1995) Quantal response equilibria for normal form games, *Games and Economic Behavior*, 10, 6–38.

Mehta, J., Starmer, C., & Sugden, R. (1994) The nature of salience: An experimental investigation of pure coordination games, *American Economic Review*, 84, 658–73.

Nagel, R. (1995) Unraveling in guessing games: An experimental study, *American Economic Review*, 85, 1313–26.

Nagel, R. (1999) A survey on experimental beauty contest games: Bounded rationality and learning. In D. V. Budescu, I. Erev, and R. Zwick (eds.), *Games and Human Behavior*. Mahwah, NJ: Lawrence Erlbaum.

Nash, J. F. (1950) Equilibrium points in n-person games, *Proceedings of the National Academy of Sciences*, 36, 48–9.

O'Neill, B. (1987) Nonmetric test of the minimax theory of two-person zerosum games, *Proceedings of the National Academy of Sciences*, 84, 2106–9.

Rabin, M. (1993) Incorporating fairness into game theory and economics, *American Economic Review*, 83, 1281–302.

Rapoport, A. & Budescu, D. V. (1997) Randomization in individual choice behavior, *Psychological Review*, 104, 603–17.

Rapoport, A. & Chammah, A. M. (1965) *Prisoners' Dilemma. A Study in Conflict and Cooperation*. Ann Arbor: The University of Michigan Press.

Roth, A. E. & Erev, I. (1995) Learning in extensive-form games: Experimental data and simple dynamic models in the intermediate term, *Games and Economic Behavior*, 8, 164–212.

Sanfey, A. G., Rilling, J. K., Aronson, J. A., Nystrom, L. E., & Cohen, J. D. (2003) The neural basis of economic decision-making in the ultimatum game, *Science*, 300, 1755–8.

Schelling, T. C. (1960) *The Strategy of Conflict*. Cambridge, MA: Harvard University Press.

Shachat, J. (2002) Mixed strategy play and the minimax hypothesis, *Journal of Economic Theory*, 104, 189–226.

Selten, R. (1975) Re-examination of the perfectness concept for equilibrium points in extensive games, *International Journal of Game Theory*, 4, 25–55.

Selten, R. (1998) Features of experimentally observed bounded rationality, *European Economic Review*, 42, 413–36.

Stahl, D. O. & Wilson, P. W. (1995) On players' models of other players: Theory and experimental evidence, *Games and Economic Behavior*, 10, 218–54.

Van Huyck, J., Battalio, R., & Beil, R. (1990) Tacit coordination games, strategic uncertainty, and coordination failure, *American Economic Review*, 80, 234–48.

Von Neumann, J. & Morgenstern O. (1944) *Theory of Games and Economic Behavior*. Princeton: Princeton University Press.

25

Culture and Decisions

Incheol Choi, Jong An Choi, and Ara Norenzayan

Introduction

Recent years have seen a rebirth of cultural research in psychology. Although the cultural foundations of the human mind have been recognized from very early years in psychology (e.g., Wundt, 1916), the attempt to explore the interplay between culture and mind has rarely received the level of recognition and popularity that it does now. In social psychology, for example, a growing amount of recent published research about topics such as self, self-esteem, attribution, and motivation, includes either cross-cultural data directly or, at least, some discussions and speculations about the cross-cultural implications of their findings (Fiske, Kitayama, Markus, & Nisbett, 1998; Heine, Lehman, Markus, & Kitayama, 1999; Markus & Kitayama, 1991; Nisbett, Peng, Choi & Norenzayan, 2001). The cultural zeitgeist in social psychology is significant, not because all social psychologists study cross-cultural issues but because they are all expected to have a cultural perspective (Miller, 2001).

Such a great success of "culture" in social psychology contrasts sharply with the limited recognition of it in the area of judgment and decision making (JDM). Historically, social psychology and JDM have mutually benefited by exchanging theories, research findings, and methodologies. Hence, we would have expected that the recognition of culture in social psychology would result in a comparable outcome in JDM. However, although we are seeing an increasing number of studies dealing with culture in JDM, the number of such studies is still very limited (Weber & Hsee, 1999). We do not mean, however, to imply that culture and JDM have not made any significant progress. In fact, several fascinating cross-cultural findings have been reported, which will be summarized later, and some systematic models have been offered as theoretical frameworks of culture and JDM (e.g., Palmer, 1996; Weber & Hsee, 1999; Yates, Lee, & Bush, 1997). Nonetheless, the pace of progress in culture and JDM has been quite slow and cross-cultural research in JDM is still "in its infancy" (Markman & Medin, 2002). Why is this the case? What has been lacking? And what will facilitate cultural research in JDM?

Why Cross-cultural Differences in JDM Have Been Overlooked

The most critical reason for the limited role of culture in JDM may be the lack of guiding theories for cross-cultural research in JDM. Cross-cultural research in other areas of psychology, notably in social psychology, has been guided by some well-grounded theoretical frameworks, best represented by individualism–collectivism (Hofstede, 1980; Triandis, 1995) and independent–interdependent self (Markus & Kitayama, 1991). These conceptual frameworks have contributed to a burgeoning literature on culture and psychology in two significant ways.

First, these theories have been the sources of endless intuitions, conjectures, speculations, and hypotheses about culture and social behavior. Armed with these theories, cultural social psychologists were able to reinterpret nearly every important phenomenon and principle of social behavior discovered among Western populations and created a set of testable hypotheses about not only cultural differences but also cultural similarities. Even those researchers who did not have intimate familiarity with other cultures were able to launch their own cross-cultural research with the aid of these theories. Ultimately, these theories created a consensus among researchers on "what questions are to be addressed."

Second, these guiding theories provided an integrative conceptual framework. Cross-cultural studies about social behavior were conducted even before those theories were formulated, but they were mostly driven by atheoretical empiricism. Therefore, even when they reported some intriguing patterns of cultural differences, researchers were not able to fully understand those differences and integrate them into existing frameworks. But now with the models of individualism–collectivism and independent–interdependent self, cultural social psychology offers a package of systematic and integrative knowledge, not just a list of scattered findings.

Unfortunately, the area of JDM did not seem to have actively embraced those cultural models in social psychology as guiding theoretical models for cross-cultural research. Most cross-cultural research in JDM was driven by empiricism rather than theoretically guided frameworks, with the notable exceptions of the program of research on overconfidence by Yates and his colleagues (for a review, see Yates, Lee, Sieck, Choi, & Price, 2002), and the studies on risk perception by Weber and Hsee (1999). Moreover, even those models offered by Yates and Weber and Hsee explain cultural differences only in specific areas of JDM. They do not work as a unifying theory that covers all or even most of the major areas of JDM. Therefore, the cross-cultural findings in one area (for example, probability judgment) do not predict or relate to similar findings in other areas. This lack of a unifying theory is a major obstacle for culture and decision making to become a major force in JDM.

Another important contributor to the slow pace of cultural research in JDM is related to the strong universalist assumption cognitive psychologists and decision scientists have long entertained, asserting that cognitive process and cognitive content are independent of each other and that cognitive content (that is the particular beliefs that individuals hold) can vary with cultures but cognitive process must be the same among all human groups. This universalist position regards observed cultural differences in JDM as variations in the parameters of a single theory, not as something that should be explained by "different theories" underlying decisions in different cultures (Markman & Medin, 2002). The popularity of the heuristics and biases research in JDM over the past few decades strengthened this universalist stance to a certain degree. The cognitive heuristics and biases discovered in JDM seem so robust that few would doubt their generality across cultures. Therefore, most decision researchers who have long dreamed of discovering "their own" heuristics and biases became indifferent to the role of culture in JDM.

However, recent developments in cultural psychology of cognition strongly challenge such universalist assumptions. Nisbett and his colleagues (Nisbett et al., 2001; see also Nisbett & Norenzayan, 2002) argued that cognitive content and cognitive process may not be as distinct as psychologists have assumed and that cognitive content can affect cognitive process. The essence of their argument is that differences in social practices and meanings exist among cultures and these in turn create differences in ontological beliefs (i.e., cognitive content), and, therefore, create differences in cognitive process. We will examine this theory later in the chapter.

In summary, we have considered two major theoretical obstacles in the integration of cross-cultural research to JDM research: a lack of guiding theories, and the universality assumption of cognitive processes. We believe that the models of independent–interdependent self and individualism–collectivism, and the related model of analytic versus holistic thinking by Nisbett and his colleagues (2001) can address these two problems substantially and, consequently, when taken together, these models offer an integrated, guiding framework for systematic cross-cultural research in JDM.

Chapter Overview

This chapter does not attempt to offer a comprehensive, state-of-the-discipline portrait of everything we know about culture and JDM because several excellent reviews on culture and JDM already exist (e.g., McDaniels & Gregory, 1991; Weber & Hsee, 2000; Yates & Lee, 1996; Yates et al., 2002). Besides, this chapter does not cover all "cultures" and instead focuses exclusively on "East vs. West."

Since Weber and Hsee (2000) published their review on culture and individual decision-making, the most comprehensive one to date, few new studies on culture and decision-making have been published. Readers are advised to read Weber and Hsee (2000) for a comprehensive review of cross-cultural differences in JDM in general and Yates et al. (2002) for understanding cultural differences in probability judgment in particular.

The present chapter has three major goals. First, instead of providing a comprehensive summary of the past research, we will selectively present some "surprises" in culture and JDM because the discovery of such unexpected, counterintuitive cross-cultural findings has been the primary force for the development of the field of culture and JDM. Second, we will introduce a new framework, that of holistic-analytic thinking (Nisbett et al.,

2001) and discuss how this model can explain some previous findings and stimulate future research. In particular, we will focus on the questions of how and why holistic versus analytic modes of thinking can influence the earliest processes of decision making, which has been relatively ignored: information search and information integration. Finally, we will discuss recent developments in cultural psychology, in particular studies on the extent to which cultural thinking styles can be dynamically switched on and off, studies on the boundary conditions of cultural differences, and finally discuss the implications of these lines of research for culture and JDM.

Surprises in Cross-cultural Research in JDM

Although the history of culture and JDM is very short, we have seen at least a couple of surprising and meaningful findings in the area of probability judgment and risk perception. These surprises stimulated a degree of curiosity and renewed enthusiasm toward cultural research in JDM.

Probability judgment

Perhaps the most prolific area in cross-cultural research in JDM has been probability judgment. Research on culture and probability judgment was sparked by a counterintuitive finding by Wright and Phillips that Southeast Asians (Malaysian, Indonesian, and Hong Kong Chinese) were more overconfident than British in probability judgment (Phillips & Wright, 1977; Wright & Phillips, 1980; Wright, Phillips, Whalley, Choo, Ng, Tan, & Wisudha, 1978). Wright and Phillips, along with their collaborators, asked participants a number of two-alternative forced-choice general knowledge questions, with each followed by a probability estimation judgment, such as:

Which is longer?
(a) Panama Canal
(b) Suez Canal
Now indicate the probability (50–100%) that your chosen answer is correct: _____%

In general, probability judgments are "well calibrated" to the extent that the judgments attached to various events match the relative frequencies with which those events actually occur. In general knowledge tests like the one above, people's judgments are typically miscalibrated in an overconfident direction: participants' average probability estimate is greater than the average percent of correct answers.

What Wright and Phillips found in their series of cross-cultural studies on probability judgment was that, surprisingly enough, Southeast Asian judgments were more overconfident than British probability assessments. Furthermore, the numerical probabilities provided by Southeast Asians were more extreme and less realistic than those provided by British. For example, Asian participants used the "100 percent sure" response overconfidently. In contrast, British participants used that assessment relatively less frequently and more accurately. Consistent with this finding, Lau and Ranyard (1999) examined the linguistic expression of probability and probabilistic thinking in Chinese and English and found that in Chinese, the lexicon for describing probabilities was quite restricted and that Chinese students showed less probabilistic thinking than British students in games of chance. This pattern of cultural difference was obtained regardless of whether questions were posed in English or in participants' native languages. Moreover, it was replicated not only among college students but also among managerial and clerical workers.

The findings of Wright and Phillips are at odds with common cultural stereotypes as well as with the robust cross-cultural difference in self-esteem. Asians are believed to be more modest and less confident than Westerners. Indeed, social psychological research indicates that Asians' self-esteem scores are significantly lower than Westerners' self-esteem scores (for a review, see Heine et al., 1999). Moreover, Asians are less likely than Westerners to hold to a sense of control (Peng & Nisbett, 1999). All these taken together predict that if there were any cultural difference in overconfidence in probability judgment, it might well be Westerners, not Asians, that are more overconfident. In fact, when lay people were provided with a detailed introduction of overconfidence bias, including how it is measured, and were asked directly to predict who would be more overconfident between Taiwanese and Americans, both Taiwanese and Americans picked Americans to be more overconfident (Yates, Lee, & Shinotsuka, 1996). Yet, Wright and Phillips' data showed exactly the opposite.

This initial surprising finding was expanded by a more systematic program of research by Yates and his colleagues (Lee, Yates, Shinotsuka, Singh, Onglatco, Yen, Gupta, & Bhatnagar, 1995; Yates et al., 1997; Yates, Lee, Shinotsuka, Patalano, & Sieck, 1998; Yates, Lee, Shinotsuka, & Sieck, 2000; Yates, Zhu, Ronis, Wang, Shinotsuka, & Toda, 1989) that resulted in several major contributions. First, Yates and his colleagues generalized Wright and Phillips' findings into other Asian nations, including mainland China, Taiwan, India, and Korea. Although the exact magnitude of overconfidence displayed by Asian participants varied across studies, the main effect that Asians were more overconfident than Westerners was robust. In nearly all studies, the participants from these Asian nations were markedly more overconfident than those from the United States with the notable exception of Japanese, which will be discussed later.

Second, Yates and his colleagues tested and ruled out several alternative explanations for cultural difference in probability judgment. For example, Yates et al. (1989) demonstrated that the difference between Chinese and Americans in overconfidence was not due to the "difficulty" effect. The difficulty effect (Lichtenstein & Fischhoff, 1977) refers to the pattern that overconfidence tends to be stronger for difficult items than for easy items. If the test items were more difficult for Chinese participants than for American participants, then the difference between Chinese and Americans in overconfidence with Chinese being more overconfident is nothing but a manifestation of the difficulty effect, not a genuine cultural effect. To test the validity of the difficulty effect explanation, Yates et al. (1989) controlled for the item difficulty for Chinese and Americans, yet they still found the same pattern of cultural difference.

Third, Yates and his colleagues extended this line of research beyond the two-alternative forced-choice general knowledge judgment. For example, Yates et al. (1989)

sought to examine whether "distribution overconfidence" was also stronger for Chinese than for Americans. They also examined the cultural difference in overconfidence in a more realistic task domain (e.g., "medical diagnosis"). Participants from Taiwan, Japan, and the United States assumed the role of a physician who was confronted with two (fictional) diseases. They were provided with a set of symptoms for each patient and asked to make a choice between the two diagnoses. Participants also reported their probability judgment of their diagnosis being correct. The results showed again that Taiwanese participants were significantly more overconfident than either American or Japanese participants (Yates et al., 1998).

Fourth, very interestingly, Yates and his colleagues repeatedly discovered that participants from Japan were different from those of other Asian nations in probability judgments. Japanese were similar to and sometimes less overconfident than Americans. In one study (Lee et al., 1995), the overconfidence index was 7 percent for Americans but only about 3 percent for Japanese. In a sense, Japanese judgments are consistent with cultural stereotypes of Asians, but they are an exception in the literature of culture and overconfidence.

Finally, and perhaps most significantly, Yates offered an explanation that could simultaneously explain why Chinese were more overconfident and why Japanese were (sometimes) less overconfident than Westerners. Following Koriat, Lichtenstein, and Fischhoff (1980) and Griffin and Tversky (1992), Yates argued that the main reason for overconfidence would be people's cognitive tendency to selectively seek or recruit confirming arguments or evidence for their judgment. For instance, suppose a participant chose "Suez Canal" as the correct answer to the question presented earlier. When asked to assess the probability of his or her answer being correct, he or she will gather reasons for why "Suez Canal" must be the correct answer and why "Panama Canal" must not be the correct answer (both are confirming reasons). However, he or she tends to neglect to recruit disconfirming arguments (i.e., why Suez Canal might not be the correct answer and why Panama Canal might be the correct answer). This imbalance in argument-recruitment causes overconfidence in probability judgment. What Yates argued and proved was that this imbalance was greater for Chinese than for Americans and Japanese.

In Yates et al. (2000), participants were asked to list arguments for and against each of the alternative answers to general knowledge questions posed to them. American and Japanese participants were almost twice as likely as Chinese participants to list arguments that disagreed with the alternatives they chose as the correct one. Yates et al. attributed such differences in imbalance between confirming and disconfirming reasons to cultural differences in educational practices. Specifically, Yates et al. argued that students in American and Japanese classrooms are actively encouraged to think critically and to consider both pros and cons simultaneously. In contrast, in the Chinese educational tradition, students are encouraged to consider "precedence" and the classics as the foundations of learning. Whereas the Western tradition values a critical approach that involves public questioning of widely accepted wisdom, the Chinese tradition values effortful, respectful, and absorptive learning and discourages the cognitive habit of considering disconfirming evidence (Tweed & Lehman, 2002).

The argument that most East Asians except for Japanese tend to consider disproportionately confirming evidence for one's judgment is in line with cross-cultural findings regarding the hindsight bias, or the mistaken tendency to believe in retrospect that one could have predicted some outcome. The hindsight bias, a special case of overconfidence, was more pronounced for Korean participants than for Americans (Choi & Nisbett, 2000), although it did not differ between Americans and Japanese (Heine & Lehman, 1996). However, it is not clear at this point whether the greater tendency to seek confirming evidence by East Asians except for Japanese, is really robust and can be applicable to the confirmation bias in general (Klayman & Ha, 1989). Future research should address this issue.

Risk preference

Another JDM area that produced a surprising pattern of cultural difference is risk preference. Again, anecdotal observation would predict that Americans would be more adventurous and risk-taking than Chinese. However, a series of studies by Hsee and Weber showed that the opposite was the case. That is, Chinese were more willing to take risks than Americans in financial decisions (Hsee & Weber, 1999; Weber & Hsee, 1999; Weber, Hsee, & Sokolowska, 1998). Confronted with a series of choices between a sure option (e.g., sure gain of $400) and a risky option (e.g., flip coin; receive $2,000 if head or receive $0 if tail), Chinese were more likely to opt for risky options than were Americans.

Hsee and Weber offered "the cushion hypothesis" to account for this counterintuitive finding. This hypothesis basically states that Chinese, because of the collective nature of their society, form and maintain very large social networks and that they use their social networks as a cushion in case they are in trouble financially. Therefore, they can afford to take greater financial risks than those from a more individualistic culture, such as the United States.

The cushion hypothesis specifically predicts that social networks can function as a cushion only for risky financial decision situations. Social networks are not able to protect their members from failing in other risky situations, such as the academic situation. When an individual has to decide whether to write a term paper on a conventional topic so that a certain level of grade is obtainable with little difficulty or to write a paper on a provocative topic so that the grade could be either very high or very low (i.e., risky), his or her social networks can do little. Hsee and Weber tested and indeed confirmed their hypothesis that Chinese would be more risk-taking in financial decisions, but not in academic or medical decisions (Hsee & Weber, 1999). In further support of their hypothesis, Hsee and Weber showed that the cultural difference in risk preference was statistically mediated by the larger size and better quality of the social networks of Chinese participants.

Although the cushion hypothesis can account for what Hsee and Weber found, more research is warranted to see if the same findings can be found in other collectivistic cultures as well. Nonetheless, the finding reported by Hsee and Weber is very important in that it demonstrated that differences in socio-cultural variables could explain cognitive differences.

Thus far, we have briefly summarized the research findings in two of the most prolific areas of cross-cultural research in JDM. Now we turn to the recent theoretical framework of culture and cognition developed by Nisbett and his colleagues and then discuss how this model can explain some empirical findings, especially cross-cultural differences in the earliest stage of judgment and decision making: information search and information combination.

Analytic versus Holistic Modes of Thinking

Scholars in history, philosophy of science, and ethnography have long maintained that East Asian and Western cultures favor different modes of thinking (e.g., Cromer, 1993; Lloyd, 1991; Logan, 1986; Moore, 1967; Nakamura, 1985; Needham, 1962). Building on these claims, Nisbett and his colleagues launched a series of empirical studies in which they compared East Asians (Chinese, Japanese, and Koreans) with Westerners (mostly Americans) on various cognitive tasks. Based on their empirical findings, Nisbett and his colleagues offered a model of the two distinct modes of thinking by Westerners and East Asians, referred to as analytic thinking and holistic thinking, respectively (Nisbett et al., 2001). Analytic thinking involves a detachment of the object from its context, a preference to focus on attributes of the object and to assign the object to categories based on these attributes, and a tendency to use rules about the categories to predict and explain the object's behavior. Holistic thinking involves an orientation to the context as a whole, attention to relationship between the object and the context, and a preference for explaining the behavior of the object based on such relationships. Holistic thinking relies on experience rather than logic, and includes a "dialectical" orientation, meaning that there is an emphasis on change and a tolerance for contradiction. The model covers cultural differences in a very diverse range of cognitive activities and has the potential to function as a guiding theory in culture and decision research. We will summarize the model, albeit briefly, and its implications on culture and JDM.

   The following are some cognitive differences between analytic and holistic thinkers observed by Nisbett et al. that we believe have implications for culture and decision making.

1   East Asians have a more holistic, field-dependent attention mode and Westerners have a more focused analytic, field-independent attention mode. In other words, East Asians pay attention more to the field than to the object per se, and are more attuned to the relationship between the object and the field (Abel & Hsu, 1949; Ji, Peng, & Nisbett, 2000; Masuda & Nisbett, 2001; Park, Nisbett, & Hedden, 1999).

2   Westerners possess a sense of control to a greater degree than East Asians. When a sense of control is induced, Westerners' confidence and performance in a cognitive task increase, but that is not the case for East Asians (Ji et al., 2000; Yamagushi, Gelfand, Mizuno & Zemba, 1997).

3   Westerners tend to explain behavior in terms of internal attributes, whereas East Asians explain behavior in terms of the interaction between internal attributes and situational factors. As a consequence, East Asians are less susceptible to the fundamental attribution error, or the tendency to overattribute behavior to dispositions internal to a person rather than to situational factors. Another major difference in

causal understanding between East Asians and Westerners is that the former group has a more complex idea of causality than the latter group (Choi & Nisbett, 1998; Lee, Hallahan, & Herzog, 1996; Morris & Peng, 1994; Norenzayan, Choi, & Nisbett, 2002; Norenzayan & Nisbett, 2000).

4   Westerners tend to use deterministic rules when categorizing objects, whereas East Asians use similarities and relationships among objects (Chiu, 1972; Ji & Nisbett, 2001; Norenzayan, Smith, Kim, & Nisbett, 2002).

5   Westerners are likely to confront conceptual conflicts or contradictions and "polarize" their decision, that is, make a principled choice between opposing positions. In contrast, East Asians opt to avoid conflicts or contradictions and are quick to find a compromise solution between opposing positions (Briley, Morris, & Simonson, 2000; Peng & Nisbett, 1999).

6   Westerners and East Asians differ in their beliefs about change. Westerners have a linear perspective toward the future, believing that a certain trend will stay the same in the future. However, East Asians have a more dialectical perspective toward the future and believe that a certain trend will change in the future (Ji, Nisbett, & Su, 2001).

Although the analytic versus holistic distinction has rich implications for many areas of JDM, we focus here on information search because it has been largely overlooked in cross-cultural research despite its critical role in judgment and decision making.

Implications of Analytic versus Holistic Thinking for Information Search

The initial phase of judgment and decision making involves information search in which an individual must decide which information is relevant, where to locate the information, and how to combine the acquired relevant information. The analytic-holistic distinction predicts several differences in the stage of information search between East Asians and Westerners.

Amount of information

The first prediction concerns the amount of information decision makers collect before making final decisions. According to the model of analytic versus holistic thought by Nisbett et al. (2001) as well as other scholars in philosophy of science (e.g., Munro, 1985; Nakamura, 1985; Needham, 1962), East Asians have holistic assumptions about the universe, dictating that, for example, all elements in the universe are somehow interconnected and, consequently, an event or object cannot be understood in isolation from the whole. In stark contrast, Westerners hold that the universe consists of separate objects that can be understood in isolation from one another. Therefore, it would seem to follow that compared to Westerners, East Asians consider a multitude of information in order to explain a certain event. Choi, Dalal, Kim-Prieto and Park (2003) conducted a series of studies to test this prediction.

Choi and his colleagues (2003) provided American, Asian-American and Korean participants with a short scenario of a murder incident, adapted from an actual newspaper headline, in which a graduate student killed his advisor (Study 1). The participants were also provided with a list of 97 items of information that might or might not be relevant to the explanation of the incident. The following is a sample of the items:

- the graduate student's history of mental disorders;
- whether or not the graduate student had a history of violence;
- the graduate student's favorite color;
- whether or not the graduate student had a web page;
- the way the professor dressed; and
- whether the professor preferred to use IBM or Macintosh computers.

Participants were asked to either choose only the relevant information (inclusion) or eliminate the irrelevant information from the list (exclusion). Previous research that examined the consequences of the inclusion and the exclusion strategy on information-narrowing process repeatedly found that by the exclusion strategy people ended up with a larger set of information for further consideration than by the inclusion strategy, a phenomenon called "subcomplementarity" (Heller, Levin, & Goransson, 2002; Levin, Huneke, & Jasper, 2000; Levin, Jasper, & Forbes, 1998; Yaniv & Schul, 1997, 2000).

Consistent with the prediction of the analytic-holistic thinking, Korean participants wanted to consider more information than did either Asian Americans or European Americans. Interestingly, this cultural difference was more pronounced in the exclusion strategy than in the inclusion strategy. Korean participants, compared to American participants, seemed to experience a particularly high level of difficulty in throwing out a piece of information from further consideration. Choi et al. (2003) explained this pattern by proposing that it would be particularly difficult for holistic reasoners who believed the wholeness of the universe to judge a given piece of information irrelevant and "not connected."

Then, will holistic thinkers always consider more information than analytic thinkers in making decisions? Not necessarily. The judgment of causality is heavily influenced by one's implicit theories about human behavior that are in turn culturally shaped. Hence, the findings of Choi et al. might not be that surprising because it is now well established that East Asians and Americans have different theories about social causality. What if the judgmental task does not require one's implicit theory about a particular domain and instead requires a systematic, algorithm-type procedure of rule discovery in context-free problems?

Kernan and Schkade (1972) provide suggestive evidence related to this issue, although they compared Americans with Mexicans, instead of East Asians. Since cross-cultural research indicates that Mexican culture is collectivistic rather than individualistic, it is plausible to assume that Mexicans are less analytic and more holistic than Americans. Kernan and Schkade reasoned that a cultural difference would appear in the amount of information an individual uses in non-social decisions in which the operation of one's cultural implicit theory is limited. In order to test their hypothesis, the experimenters provided American and Mexican participants with five containers, each of which held a number of chips that were red, blue, or white. Participants were asked to draw one chip at a time, without replacing any, and as many as they liked. Their job was to ascertain the predominant color makeup of the chip population of all five containers. Participants were further instructed that points would be given for a correct appraisal of the majority color but that the greater the number of chips drawn, the less would be the number of points they receive for a correct appraisal. Simply put, participants had to correctly guess the majority color based on the drawing of as few chips as possible.

There is little reason to believe that Americans and Mexicans have different *a priori* theories about the distribution of different colored chips. Therefore, the task offers an ideal opportunity to examine the role of culture in the amount of information people consider before making judgments. What Kernan and Schkade found was that the number of chips drawn indeed differed between the two cultural groups. Specifically, American participants sampled significantly more chips than their Mexican counterparts. Kernan and Schkade attributed this cultural difference to American "optimizing" culture in which costs and benefits are carefully scrutinized and little is left to chance. Kernan and Schkade contrasted this analytic tendency of Americans with Mexicans' more instantaneous mode of thinking that utilizes one's intuition and heuristics.

Although a more systematic program of future research is needed, it seems that culture can play a significant role in the information search stage and that the distinction between analytic versus holistic thinking may be useful in understanding cultural differences in the amount of information a decision maker considers.

Type of information searched

According to the model of analytic versus holistic thinking, cultural differences may exist not only in the amount of information but also in the type of information a decision maker deems important. Culture determines what is and what is not important and consequently directs one's attention to the important pieces of information and away from the "not important" ones. For example, Masuda and Nisbett (2001) presented underwater scenes through computer animation to Japanese and American participants. Each scene included "focal fish" along with other small fish, inert animals, plants, and rocks. Then, participants were asked to describe what they had seen. The results showed that Japanese were more likely than Americans to refer to the entire field. Unlike American participants, most Japanese participants began their descriptions by referring to the context.

Since differential weights are given to different types of information by different cultural groups, the presence of a particular piece of information may boost one's judgmental confidence in one culture but not necessarily in other cultures. Consider the following situation (Gelfand, Spurlock, Sniezek, & Shao, 2000), which involves reliance on information regarding independence-interdependence:

> Imagine that you are working at an organization. One of your coworkers is leaving the organization, and another person whom you do not know has been chosen to replace your

coworker. You have always had a good relationship with your present coworkers and you want to know about the new coworker. You will be meeting your new coworker to have lunch so the two of you can get acquainted. On your way to meet this person, you meet another employee who worked closely with your new coworker.

In one condition (relational), participants were told that the other employee gave them some information about social relational aspects of the new coworker such as family and social class. In the other condition (individuating), participants were told that they obtained from the other employee information about personal aspects of the new coworker such as personal interests, beliefs and accomplishments. Then, participants were asked to rate the usefulness of the information they received and the degree to which the information could increase their confidence in predicting the behavior of the new coworker. As expected, Chinese participants judged relational information more useful than individuating information, while the reverse was true for American participants. In addition, Chinese expected that their confidence in predicting the new coworker's behavior would increase more with relational than individuating information, but the reverse was true for Americans.

Combination of information

Cultures can also differ in the way a decision maker combines various information, especially in dealing with conflicting information. In particular, the model of analytic versus holistic thinking predicts that East Asians, compared to Westerners, will avoid contradictory information.

The ways of combining information are roughly classified as either compensatory or noncompensatory. In noncompensatory rules, strength on one dimension (e.g., quality) cannot compensate for weakness on another (e.g., price). In other words, if an alternative has a lower value than a threshold for a certain dimension, the alternative is eliminated from further consideration no matter how good it is on other dimensions. The elimination-by-aspect by Tversky (1972) is a good example of noncompensatory rules. In contrast, compensatory rules involve tradeoffs between attributes, thus allowing compensation for weakness on one dimension by strength on another. Compensatory rules are conflict-confronting, whereas noncompensatory rules are conflict-avoiding (Hogarth, 1974) because compensatory rules entail "computational and emotional difficulties of making trade-offs" (Kottemann & Davis, 1991, p. 919). Because noncompensatory rules focus on only a few attributes and usually only one attribute, a decision maker is less likely to experience cognitive and emotional difficulties of making tradeoffs.

East Asians strive for harmony, not conflict, in interpersonal relations, and this conflict-avoidance tendency in social domains has transformed into a tendency of conflict avoidance in cognitive domains (Nisbett et al., 2001; Peng & Nisbett, 1999). So, for example, when confronted with a set of two conflicting pieces of information, Chinese are more likely to simply make a compromise between them, rather than scrutinizing each of them carefully and making a principled choice between them, which is characteristic of Westerners. Therefore, it would seem to follow that East Asians would prefer

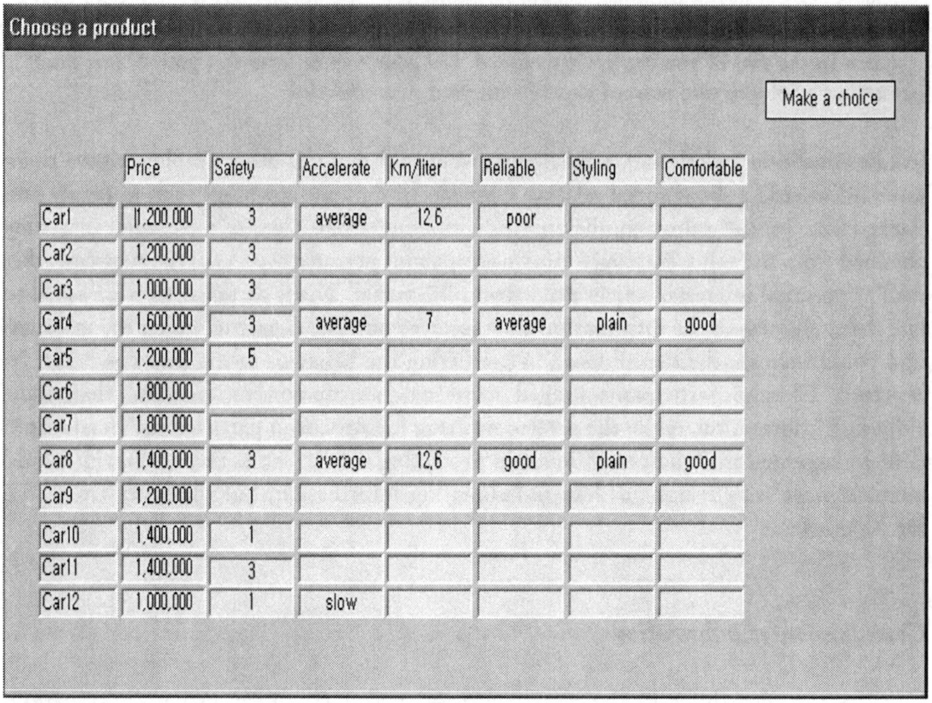

Choose a product

Make a choice

	Price	Safety	Accelerate	Km/liter	Reliable	Styling	Comfortable
Car1	1,200,000	3	average	12,6	poor		
Car2	1,200,000	3					
Car3	1,000,000	3					
Car4	1,600,000	3	average	7	average	plain	good
Car5	1,200,000	5					
Car6	1,800,000						
Car7	1,800,000						
Car8	1,400,000	3	average	12,6	good	plain	good
Car9	1,200,000	1					
Car10	1,400,000	1					
Car11	1,400,000	3					
Car12	1,000,000	1	slow				

Figure 25.1 The matrix form of choice problem in a computer window

noncompensatory rules to compensatory rules whereas the opposite would be true for Westerners. Chu, Spires, and Sueyoshi (1999) tested this hypothesis by comparing Japanese and Americans.

Participants in Chu et al. (1999) were asked to select a new compact car for purchase. The choice problem was displayed in a computer window in matrix form, as shown in Figure 25.1. The rows of the matrix were alternative cars, and the columns of the matrix were the values of each attribute. Some attributes had three levels. For example, safety had three levels of good (5), average (3), and poor (1). Some other attributes had five levels. For instance, acceleration had five levels of very fast (5), fast (4), average (3), slow (2), and very slow (1). Participants were told that they could click a cell in order to see the value of a particular attribute for a particular alternative. If they click a cell once, the value comes in a text format (e.g., "good," "average," "poor"), and if they click it again, the value format changes into a numeric one (e.g., "5," "3," "1,"). If they click the cell a third time, the attribute value will be hidden. Participants were asked to collect as much information as they wanted by clicking cells in order to make a final choice.

In this task, whether the subject used a compensatory rule or non-compensatory rule can be detected in several ways, including the following two. One is to analyze the proportion of cells explicitly accessed in numeric format. The reason is that the use of a compensatory rule requires such numeric transformation so that a final value can be computed for each alternative. Although it is not entirely impossible to calculate a certain score for an alternative after considering text formats for each attribute, it would be extremely difficult. Therefore, it is safe to assume that numeric transformation is required for a compensatory rule to be implemented. Another way would be to calculate the proportion of the alternative-based search. In the alternative-based search, an individual clicks attribute cells for a given alternative. In contrast, in the attribute-based search, an individual clicks alternative cells for a given attribute. The attribute-based search is noncompensatory because one can make a choice by focusing on only one attribute and comparing all or some alternatives of that attribute.

When Chiu et al. (1999) computed these two indices for Japanese and American participants, both indices were significantly higher for American participants than for Japanese participants, supporting the hypothesis that Americans use a compensatory rule more than Japanese. Moreover, when participants were provided with a decision aid, so that a numeric score for a given alternative could be automatically calculated by a computer (i.e., a compensatory search was supported by the aid – "compute" function), American participants were more likely than their Japanese counterparts to use the "compute" function.

However, more research seems warranted to take the finding of Chiu et al. (1999) seriously. Above all, future research should address whether compensatory rule is indeed conflict-confronting and noncompensatory rule is indeed conflict-avoiding. Besides, the finding needs to be replicated among other cultural groups. Nonetheless, the finding of Chiu et al. (1999) is very significant in that it suggested the possibility that the way people combine information may be affected by culture.

In summary, we have linked some cross-cultural findings in information search to the model of analytic versus holistic thinking. As may be apparent to the readers, the studies considered are still preliminary and more research is warranted to draw firmer conclusions. Nevertheless, we would like to propose that systematic cultural differences exist in the earliest phase of decision making and that the distinction between analytic and holistic thinking can work as a useful framework for future research on this area.

Future Direction: A Dynamic Approach to Culture and JDM

Several scholars of culture and psychology have proposed that cultural influence on cognition is not static in that cultural differences do not occur in all conditions (Chiu, Morris, Hong, & Menon, 2000; Hong, Chiu, & Kung, 1997; Hong, Morris, Chiu, & Benet-Martinez, 2000). For example, whether the typical attributional difference between Chinese and Americans occurs depends on certain factors, including one's cognitive needs. Chiu et al. (2000) demonstrated that the typical attributional difference between Hong Kong Chinese and Americans was more likely to occur when the need for closure was high. Therefore, when exploring cultural influence on cognition including JDM, we need to take a more dynamic approach in the future and consider the mediating variables. The work of Briley et al. (2000) is a good example of such an approach.

Briley et al. (2000) studied the consumer choices of East Asians and European Americans, aiming to examine cultural difference in the compromise effect. All consumer choices were among a triad of objects that differed on two dimensions. Object A was superior to both Object B and C on one dimension and Object C was superior to both Object A and B on the other dimension. Object B was always intermediate between A and C on both dimensions. Interestingly enough, across the range of choices, Americans and East Asians in a control condition were about equally likely to choose intermediate Object B. In other words, the magnitude of the compromise effect differed little between the two cultural groups. The model of analytic-holistic thinking would have predicted that the compromise effect, or choosing the middle way, would be greater for Chinese than for Americans.

However, in another condition, Briley et al. had participants give reasons for their choice. They anticipated that this would remind participants of their cultural norms and that participants' choices would become more in line with what the model would predict. Specifically, Briley and his colleagues expected that this "justification" manipulation would prompt Americans to look for a simple rule that would justify a given choice (e.g., "RAM is more important than hard drive space") but would prompt people of Asian cultures to seek a compromise ("both RAM and hard drive space are important"). That was indeed the case: Americans in the justification condition moved to a preference for one of the extreme objects whose choice could be justified with reference to a simple rule, whereas Asian participants moved to a preference for the compromise object. Justifications given by participants were consistent with their choices, with Americans being more likely to give rule-based justifications and Chinese being more likely to give compromise-based justifications. This result demonstrates the "dynamic" quality of cultural differences in choice, as they are more likely to emerge in some conditions than others.

One's own choice of the past can also bring cultural norms to the fore and thereby makes the predicted cultural difference more likely to occur than otherwise. Kim and Drolet (2003) provided American and Korean participants with a set of alternatives for a consumer product such that an intermediate alternative would more likely be chosen than an extreme one. In fact, a comparable number of American and Korean participants selected the intermediate compromise alternative. This procedure was repeated for two products. Then, participants were offered a set of alternatives for a different product, but this time the alternative values were arranged such that the intermediate alternative and the extreme ones were equally likely to be chosen. The question was whether participants from the two cultures would continue to choose the intermediate one or choose an extreme one. Kim and Drolet expected that having made a compromise choice twice beforehand might pressure American, but not Korean, participants to follow a cultural norm against compromise and seek a variety by choosing an extreme alternative in the critical trial. Indeed, this was what they found.

Justification or accountability may not be the only boundary condition for cultural differences in choice. As mentioned earlier, the state of need for cognitive closure may be another important variable in JDM. Need for cognitive closure is naturally strong in a situation where one has to make a decision quickly. In everyday life, people often have to make quick decisions. According to Chiu et al. (2000), under high time pressure or high need for cognitive closure, people are likely to fall back on their cultural scripts to make rapid judgments. Hence, cultural differences may be more likely in decisions that need to be made quickly, and among people with high need for closure, a possibility that deserves further exploration in the future.

Recent studies with the priming technique suggest that there exist abundant cues in everyday contexts that prime people to think in a particular way. These cues remind people from a certain cultural group of their cultural knowledge and behavioral scripts so that they behave according to their cultural norms. Cultural icons are among those cues. An exposure to icons of one's own culture may evoke in an individual a particular frame of mind that will induce or force the individual to think and act in a culturally consistent fashion. Hong and her colleagues (Hong et al., 1997) provided convincing evidence for this reasoning. They exposed some Hong Kong Chinese participants to American icons (e.g., the American flag, Superman, the Capitol Building) and other Hong Kong Chinese participants to Chinese icons (e.g., a Chinese dragon, Stone Monkey, the Great Wall). After the exposure, all participants were given an attribution task. What Hong et al. found was that participants primed with American icons displayed a more American-like attribution (i.e., more internal attribution) than the control group and those primed with Chinese icons showed a more Chinese-like attribution (i.e., more external attribution) than the control group.

A series of studies by Kühnen (Kühnen, Hannover, & Schubert, 2001; Kühnen & Oyserman, 2002) are also fascinating in that they demonstrate that priming a particular construal of self (i.e., independent versus interdependent self) induces an individual to adopt a particular mode of thinking (i.e., analytic versus holistic thinking). In one study, Kühnen and others (Kühnen et al., 2001) asked some participants to think about differences between themselves and their family and friends (i.e., priming independent self), and other participants to think about what they had in common with their family and friends (i.e., priming interdependent self). Then, participants received a version of the Embedded Figures Test (Witkin, Oltman, Raskin, & Karp, 1971) in which a simple figure was embedded in a complex figure. Participants had to isolate the simple figure. Previous research on EFT has shown that doing well in EFT requires a decontextualized, field-independent and analytic mode of thinking. A holistic (and field-dependent) thinker is more likely to perform poorly in the EFT than an analytic thinker. What Kühnen et al. found was that priming an independent self induced participants to perform better than priming an interdependent self. These studies suggest a promising line of research in which temporarily activated self-construal patterns may affect a host of decision processes, such as the amount and type of information searched, the relative weight given to different types of information, as well as decision processes involving the assessment and use of contradictory information.

Concluding Remarks

In recent years, it has become increasingly evident that the cultural context in which people live not only affects their beliefs and values but also shapes the very cognitive processes by which people think about and respond to the world. Novel theoretical frameworks such as independent–interdependent self-construals, as well as analytic-holistic modes of thought, promise to synthesize a broad array of cross-cultural findings as well as guide future research in fruitful directions. To the extent that decision scientists integrate cultural variables in their work, the field of JDM will be enriched by such work in two ways. First, cross-cultural examination of decision making will broaden the empirical knowledge base to include a wider range of populations that have been previously overlooked. This in turn will encourage decision scientists to engage in more comprehensive and intricate theorizing to account for decision processes. Second, as cultural diversity and intercultural contact increasingly define the fabric of everyday life in societies around the world, the cognitive implications of human cultural diversity can be ignored only to our peril. Decision scientists are in a unique position to learn about the cultural bases of a central human activity – decision making – and to contribute to our knowledge of the cognitive roots of intercultural conflict.

Acknowledgment

We thank Derek Koehler and Karl Teigen for their helpful comments on earlier versions of this chapter. Writing of this chapter was supported by Korea Research Foundation Grant (KRF-2002-042-H00017).

References

Abel, T. M. & Hsu, F. I. (1949) Some aspects of personality of Chinese as revealed by the Rorschach Test, *Journal of Projective Techniques*, 13, 285–301.

Briley, D. A., Morris, M. W., & Simonson, I. (2000) Reasons as carriers of culture: Dynamic versus dispositional models of cultural influence on decision making, *Journal of Consumer Research*, 27, 157–78.

Chiu, C.-Y., Morris, M. W., Hong, Y.-Y., & Menon, T. (2000) Motivated cultural cognition: The impact of implicit cultural theories on dispositional attribution varies as a function of need for closure, *Journal of Personality and Social Psychology*, 78, 247–59.

Chiu, L.-H. (1972) A cross-cultural comparison of cognitive styles in Chinese and American children, *International Journal of Psychology*, 7, 235–42.

Choi, I., Dalal, R., Kim-Prieto, C., & Park, H. (2003) Culture and judgment of causal relevance, *Journal of Personality and Social Psychology*, 84, 46–59.

Choi, I. & Nisbett, R. E. (1998) Situational salience and cultural difference in the correspondence bias and actor–observer bias, *Personality and Social Psychology Bulletin*, 24, 949–60.

Choi, I. & Nisbett, R. E. (2000) The cultural psychology of surprise: Holistic theories and recognition of contradiction, *Journal of Personality and Social Psychology*, 79, 890–905.

Choi, I., Nisbett, R. E., & Norenzayan, A. (1999) Causal attribution across cultures: Variation and universality, *Psychological Bulletin*, 125, 47–63.

Chu, P. C., Spires, E. E., & Sueyoshi, T. (1999) Cross-cultural differences in choice behavior and use of decision aids: A comparison of Japan and the United States, *Organizational Behavior & Human Decision Processes*, 77, 147–70.

Cromer, A. (1993) *Uncommon Sense: The Heretical Nature of Science*. New York: Oxford University Press.

Fiske, A., Kitayama, S., Markus. H. R., & Nisbett, R. E. (1998) The cultural matrix of social psychology. In D. T. Gilbert, S. T. Fiske, and G. Lindzey (eds.), *The Handbook of Social Psychology* (pp. 915–81). New York: McGraw-Hill.

Gelfand, M. J., Spurlock, D., Sniezek, J. A., & Shao, L. (2000) Culture and social prediction: The role of information in enhancing confidence in social predictions in the United States and China, *Journal of Cross-Cultural Psychology*, 31, 498–516.

Griffin, D. & Tversky, A. (1992) The weighing of evidence and the determinants of confidence, *Cognitive Psychology*, 24, 411–35.

Heine, S. J. & Lehman, D. R. (1996) Hindsight bias: A cross-cultural analysis, *Japanese Journal of Experimental Social Psychology*, 35, 317–23.

Heine, S. J., Lehman, D. R., Markus, H. R., & Kitayama, S. (1999) Is there a universal need for positive self-regard? *Psychological Review*, 106, 766–94.

Heller, D., Levin, I. P., & Goransson, M. (2002) Selection of strategies for narrowing choice options: Antecedents and consequences, *Organizational Behavior & Human Decision Processes*, 89, 1194–213.

Hofstede, G. (1980) *Culture's Consequence: International Difference in Work-related Values*. Beverley Hills, CA: Sage.

Hogarth, R. M. (1974) Process tracing in clinical judgment, *Behavioral Science*, 19, 298–313.

Hong, Y.-Y., Chiu, C.-Y., & Kung, T. M. (1997) Bringing culture out in front: Effects of cultural meaning system activation on social cognition. In K. Leung, Y. Kashima, U. Kim, and S. Yamaguchi (eds.), *Progress in Asian Social Psychology* (vol. 1, pp. 135–46). Singapore: Wiley.

Hong, Y.-Y., Morris, M. W., Chiu, C.-Y., & Benet-Martinez, V. (2000). Multicultural minds: A dynamic constructivist approach to culture and cognition, *American Psychologist*, 55, 709–20.

Hsee, C. K. & Weber, E. U. (1999) Cross-national differences in risk preference and lay predictions, *Journal of Behavioral Decision Making*, 12, 165–79.

Ji, L. & Nisbett, R. E. (2001) Culture, language and categories. Unpublished manuscript, University of Michigan.

Ji, L., Nisbett, R. E., & Su, Y. (2001) Culture, change, and prediction, *Psychological Science*, 12, 450–56.

Ji, L., Peng, K., & Nisbett, R. E. (2000) Culture, control, and perception of relationships in the environment, *Journal of Personality and Social Psychology*, 78, 943–55.

Kernan, J. B. & Schkade, L. L. (1972) A cross-cultural analysis of stimulus sampling, *Administrative Science Quarterly*, 17, 351–8.

Kim, H. S. & Drolet, A. (2003), Choice as self-expression: The effect of cultural assumptions of choice and uniqueness on variety seeking, *Journal of Personality & Social Psychology*, 85, 373–82.

Klayman, J. & Ha, Y.-W. (1989) Hypothesis testing in rule discovery: Strategy, structure, and content, *Journal of Experimental Psychology: Learning, Memory, & Cognition*, 15, 596–604.

Koriat, A., Lichtenstein, S., & Fischhoff, B. (1980) Reasons for confidence, *Journal of Experimental Psychology: Human Learning & Memory*, 6, 107–18.

Kottemann, J. E. & Davis, F. D. (1991) Decisional conflict and user acceptance of multicriteria decision-making aids, *Decision Sciences*, 22, 918–26.

Kühnen, U., Hannover, B., & Schubert, B. (2001) The semantic-procedural interface model of the self: The role of self-knowledge for context-dependent versus context-independent modes of thinking, *Journal of Personality & Social Psychology*, 80, 397–409.

Kühnen, U. & Oyserman, D. (2002) Thinking about the self influences thinking in general: Cognitive consequences of salient self-concept, *Journal of Experimental Social Psychology*, 38, 492–99.

Lau, L. Y. & Ranyard, R. (1999) Chinese and English speakers' linguistic expression of probability and probabilistic thinking, *Journal of Cross Cultural Psychology*, 30, 411–21.

Lee, F., Hallahan, M., & Herzog, T. (1996) Explaining real life events: How culture and domain shape attribution, *Personality and Social psychology Bulletin*, 22, 732–41.

Lee, J. W., Yates, J. F., Shinotsuka, H., Singh, R., Onglatco, M. L. U., Yen, N. S., Gupta, M., & Bhatnagar, D. (1995) Cross-national difference in overconfidence, *Asian Journal of Psychology*, 1, 63–9.

Levin, I. P., Huneke, M. E., & Jasper, J. D. (2000) Information processing at successive stages of decision making: Need for cognition and inclusion-exclusion effect, *Organizational Behavior & Human Decision Processes*, 82, 171–93.

Levin, I. P., Jasper, J. D., & Forbes, W. S. (1998) Choosing versus rejecting at different stages of decision-making, *Journal of Behavioral Decision Making*, 11, 193–210.

Lichtenstein, S. & Fischhoff, B. (1977) Do those who know more also know more about how much they know? *Organizational Behavior & Human Decision Processes*, 20, 159–83.

Lloyd, G. E. R. (1991) The Invention of nature. In G. E. R. Lloyd (ed.), *Methods and Problems in Greek Science* (pp. 417–34). Cambridge: Cambridge University Press.

Logan, R. F. (1986) *The Alphabet Effect*. New York: Morrow.

Markman, A. & Medin, D. L. (2002) Decision making. In H. Pashler and D. Medin (eds.), *Stevens' Handbook of Experimental Psychology* (3rd edn.), *vol. 2: Memory and cognitive processes* (pp. 413–66). New York: John Wiley & Sons.

Markus, H. R. & Kitayama, S. (1991) Culture and the self: Implication for cognition, emotion and motivation, *Psychological Review*, 98, 224–53.

Masuda, T. & Nisbett, R. E. (2001) Attending holistically versus analytically: Comparing the context sensitivity of Japanese and Americans, *Journal of Personality & Social Psychology*, 81, 922–34.

McDaniels, T. L. & Gregory, R. S. (1991) A framework for structuring cross-cultural research in risk and decision making, *Journal of Cross-Cultural Psychology*, 22, 103–28.

Miller, J. G. (2001) The cultural groundings of social psychological theory. In A. Tesser and N. Schwarz (eds.), *Blackwell Handbook of Social Psychology: Intraindividual Processes* (pp. 22–43). Oxford: Blackwell.

Moore, C. A. (1967) *The Chinese Mind: Essentials of Chinese Philosophy and Culture*. Honolulu: University of Hawaii Press.

Morris, M. W. & Peng, K. (1994) Culture and cause: American and Chinese attributions for social and physical events, *Journal of Personality and Social Psychology*, 67, 949–71.

Munro, D. J. (1985) Introduction. In D. Munro (ed.), *Individualism and Holism: Studies in Confucian and Taoist Values* (pp. 1–34). Ann Arbor: Center for Chinese Studies, University of Michigan.

Nakamura, H. (1985) *Ways of Thinking of Eastern People*. Honolulu: University of Hawaii Press, (first published 1964).

Needham, J. (1962) *Science and Civilization in China, vol. 4: Physics and Physical Technology*. Cambridge: Cambridge University Press.

Nisbett, R. E. & Norenzayan, A. (2002) Culture and cognition. In H. Pashler and D. L. Medin (eds.), *Stevens' Handbook of Experimental Psychology: Cognition* (3rd edn., vol. 2, pp. 561–97). New York: John Wiley & Sons.

Nisbett, R. E., Peng, K., Choi, I., & Norenzayan, A. (2001) Culture and systems of thought: Holistic vs. analytic cognition, *Psychological Review*, 108, 291–310.

Norenzayan, A., Choi, I., & Nisbett, R. E. (2002) Cultural similarities and differences in social inference: Evidence from behavioral predictions and lay theories of behavior, *Personality and Social Psychology Bulletin*, 28, 109–20.

Norenzayan, A. & Nisbett, R. E. (2000) Culture and causal cognition, *Current Directions in Psychological Science*, 9, 132–5.

Norenzayan, A., Smith, E., Kim, B. J., & Nisbett, R. E. (2002) Cultural preferences for formal versus intuitive reasoning, *Cognitive Science*, 26, 653–84.

Palmer, C. G. S. (1996) Risk perception: An empirical study of the relationship between worldview and the risk construct, *Risk Analysis*, 16, 717–24.

Park, D. C., Nisbett, R. E., & Hedden, T. (1999) Culture, cognition, and aging, *Journal of Gerontology*, 54B, 75–84.

Peng, K. & Nisbett, R. E. (1999) Culture, dialectics, and reasoning about contradiction, *American Psychologist*, 54, 741–54.

Phillips, L. D. & Wright, G. N. (1977) Cultural differences in viewing uncertainty in assessing probabilities. In H. Jungermann and G. de Zeeuw (eds.), *Decision Making and Change in Human Affairs* (pp. 507–19). Dordrecht, The Netherlands: Reidel.

Triandis, H. C. (1995) *Individualism and Collectivism*. Boulder, CO: Westview Press.

Tversky, A. (1972) Elimination by aspects: A theory of choice, *Psychological Review*, 79, 281–99.

Tweed, R. & Lehman, D. (2002) Learning considered within a cultural context: Confucian and Socratic approaches, *American Psychologist*, 57, 89–99.

Weber, E. U. & Hsee, C. K. (1999) Models and mosaics: Investigating cross-cultural differences in risk perception and risk preference, *Psychonomic Bulletin & Review*, 611–17.

Weber, E. U. & Hsee, C. K. (2000) Culture and individual judgment and decision making, *Applied Psychology*, 49, 32–61.

Weber, E. U., Hsee, C. K. & Sokolowska, J. (1998) What folklore tells us about risk and risk taking: Cross-cultural comparisons of American, German, and Chinese proverbs, *Organizational Behavior & Human Decision Processes*, 75, 170–86.

Witkin, H. A., Oltman, P. K., Raskin, E., & Karp. S. A. (1971) *Manual for the Embedded Figures Test. Children's Embedded Figures Test, and Group Embedded Figures Test*. Palo Alto, CA: Consulting Psychologists Press.

Wright, G. M. & Phillips, L. D. (1980) Cultural variation in probabilistic thinking: Alternative ways of dealing with uncertainty, *International Journal of Psychology*, 15, 239–57.

Wright, G. M., Phillips, L. D., Whalley, P. C., Choo, G. T., Ng, K. O., Tan, I., & Wisudha, A. (1978) Cultural differences in probabilistic thinking, *Journal of Cross-Cultural Psychology*, 9, 285–99.

Wundt, W. (1916) *Elements of Folk Psychology: Outlines of a Psychological History of the Development of Mankind*. London: Allen & Unwin.

Yamagushi, S., Gelfand, M., Mizuno, M., & Zemba, Y. (1997) Illusion of collective control or illusion of personal control: Biased judgment about a chance event in Japan and the US. Paper presented at the Second Conference of the Asian Association of Social psychology, Kyoto, Japan.

Yaniv, I. & Schul, Y. (1997) Elimination and inclusion procedures in judgment, *Journal of Behavioral Decision Making*, 10, 211–20.

Yaniv, I. & Schul, Y. (2000) Acceptance and elimination procedures in choice: Noncomplementarity and the role of implied status quo, *Organizational Behavior & Human Decision Processes*, 82, 293–313.

Yates, J. F. & Lee, J.-W. (1996) Chinese decision-making. In B. M. Harris (ed.), *The Handbook of Chinese Psychology*. New York: Oxford University Press.

Yates, J. F., Lee, J.-W., & Bush, J. G. (1997) General knowledge overconfidence: Cross-national variations, response style, and "reality," *Organizational Behavior & Human Decision Processes*, 70, 87–94.

Yates, J. F., Lee, J.-W., & Shinotsuka, H. (1996) Beliefs about overconfidence, including its cross-national variation, *Organizational Behavior & Human Decision Processes*, 65, 138–47.

Yates, J. F., Lee, J.-W., Shinotsuka, H., Patalano, A. L., & Sieck, W. R. (1998) Cross-cultural variations in probability judgment accuracy: Beyond general knowledge overconfidence? *Organizational Behavior & Human Decision Processes*, 74, 89–117.

Yates, J. F., Lee, J.-W., Shinotsuka, H., & Sieck, W. R. (2000) The argument recruitment model: Explaining general knowledge overconfidence and its cross-cultural variations. Working paper, Department of Psychology, University of Michigan, Ann Arbor.

Yates, J. F., Lee, J.-W., Sieck, W. R., Choi, I., & Price, P. C. (2002) Probability judgment across cultures. In T. Gilovich, D. Griffin, and D. Kahneman (eds.), *Heuristics and Biases*. Cambridge: Cambridge University Press.

Yates, J. F., Zhu, Y., Ronis, D. L., Wang, D. F., Shinotsuka, H., & Toda, W. (1989) Probability judgment accuracy: China, Japan, and the United States, *Organizational Behavior & Human Decision Processes*, 43, 147–71.

PART IV

Applications

26

Behavioral Finance

Markus Glaser, Markus Nöth, and Martin Weber

Traditional and Behavioral Finance

Behavioral finance as a subdiscipline of behavioral economics is finance incorporating findings from psychology and sociology into its theories. Behavioral finance models are usually developed to explain investor behavior or market anomalies when rational models provide no sufficient explanations. To understand the research agenda, methodology, and contributions, it is necessary to review traditional finance theory first. Then, we will show how modifications (e.g. incorporating market frictions) can rationally explain observed individual or market behavior. In the second section, we will explain the behavioral finance research methodology – how biases are modeled, incorporated into traditional finance theories, and tested empirically and experimentally – using one specific subset of the behavioral finance literature, the overconfidence literature.

Traditional Finance and Empirical Evidence

Traditional finance theory assumes that agents are rational and the law of one price holds. Important aspects of agents' rationality are maximization of expected utility and Bayesian learning (see Chapter 2, this volume). This implies, for example, that choices are time-consistent (see Chapter 21, this volume). From a market perspective, traditional finance theory rests on the law of one price, which states that securities with the same payoff have the same price. Arbitrageurs eliminate instantaneously any violations of the law of one price by simultaneously buying and selling these securities at advantageously different prices. Consider, for example, the shares of DaimlerChrysler AG. They are traded simultaneously on the New York Stock Exchange (NYSE) and in Frankfurt (Xetra) between 1:30 p.m. and 6:00 p.m. UTC. During these 4.5 hours, shares should trade for the same prices on both exchanges adjusted for the current EUR–USD exchange rate. If these adjusted prices are different from each other, an arbitrageur would sell shares at the higher price at one exchange and would buy the same number of shares at the other exchange and would thus realize a risk-less profit (see Shleifer &Vishny (1997) for another example of arbitrage).

The key question is whether agents' irrationalities affect market outcomes – otherwise, finance researchers would not care. Even if some or even all market participants are irrational, it may be possible that the market absorbs (at least to some degree) these individual irrationalities and thus prevents their impact on prices and allocation. Whether the market can average out irrationalities depends on the structure of the observed behavior: unsystematic irrationalities can be absorbed more easily than systematic deviations from rational behavior.

Market efficiency and security return patterns
If agents are rational and the law of one price holds, market efficiency may exist. Fama (1970, p. 83) defines an efficient market as a "market in which prices always 'fully reflect' available information." Different forms of market efficiency exist due to the amount of information that is assumed to be "available." If the current price contains only the information consisting of past prices, the market is "weak-form" efficient. If prices reflect all publicly available information (historical prices and, for example, earnings announcements), the market is "semi-strong form" efficient. Finally, if prices reflect all private information (i.e. including all insider information), the market is "strong-form" efficient.

It is unlikely that market prices contain *all* private information. One explanation for this inefficiency is the existence of noise traders who trade randomly and not based on information. For example, they trade to match their own liquidity requirements because of inherited money (= buy stocks) or because they want to buy a new car or house (= sell stocks). As a consequence, it is no longer possible to identify private information completely based on buying or selling activity by observing market prices because noise traders' orders jam the trading signal generated by insiders.

But even the original "weak-form" efficiency did not survive empirical tests. "Weak-form" market efficiency in connection with the assumption of constant expected returns had long been successful in explaining security return patterns. Studies as discussed in Fama (1970) show that stock returns are typically unpredictable based on past returns. However, empirical studies over the past 25 years demonstrated that future returns are predictable to some extent. Several studies document positive autocorrelation of short-term stock returns, as well as a negative autocorrelation of short-term returns separated by long lags. In addition, the current dividend yield predicts subsequent returns. Fama (1991) surveys studies on the abovementioned time-series predictability of returns.

Furthermore, trading strategies exist, which are based on past returns and which earn statistically significant profits. One specific example is the momentum strategy in which stocks with high returns over the last three to 12 months ("winner") are bought and stocks with low returns over the same period ("loser") are sold. The short-selling of "losers" finances the buying of "winners," i.e. there is no need to invest your own money. After a holding period of up to 12 months, the "losers" are bought back and the "winners" are sold. Jegadeesh and Titman (1993, 2001) showed for US stocks that this strategy results in significant positive profits. This strategy has been successful in other stock markets as well (see Rouwenhorst, 1998, 1999; as well as Glaser & Weber, 2003a; for international evidence on the profitability of momentum strategies).

Closely related are the following cross-sectional return patterns. Returns of stocks with low market capitalization have been on average higher than returns of stocks with high market capitalization (= size effect; see, e.g., Banz, 1981; Dimson & Marsh, 2000). Returns of value stocks, i.e. stocks with a high dividend yield, a low price/earnings ratio and/or a high book-to-market ratio have been on average higher than returns of growth stocks, i.e. stocks with a low dividend yield, a high price/earnings ratio and/or a low book-to-market ratio (see, e.g., Fama & French, 1992; Lakonishok, Shleifer, & Vishny, 1994). Moreover, specific events may predict subsequent security returns (event-based return predictability). Such events are, for example, earnings announcements or stock splits (see Daniel, Hirshleifer, & Subrahmanyam, 1998; Fama, 1991, 1998).

The question is now whether these findings are real profit opportunities and thus a violation of market efficiency or just a proper reward for risk. Some researchers argue that the observed security return regularities are rational and can be explained by time-varying expected returns (Fama, 1991). Other researchers argue that securities are mispriced (see, e.g., Lakonishok et al., 1994). Resolving this conflict is at least difficult if not impossible because market efficiency can only be tested using a specific asset pricing model, i.e. a test of market efficiency is always a joint test of market efficiency and the assumed correctness of the asset pricing model. Thus, a security market anomaly can either result from market inefficiency or from the wrong asset pricing model. As the above-presented empirical evidence is still, for this reason, inconclusive, we will show in the next subsection that some securities are obviously mispriced.

Law of one price

Recently, some puzzles have been discovered proving that the law of one price is violated. This violation is so severe that prices are inconsistent with all valuation models. One example is security prices of "Siamese twin" shares, such as Royal Dutch Petroleum and Shell Transport and Trading. Twin shares trade at different places or in different countries and the division of current and future cash flows is fixed to each twin. Shares of Royal Dutch are primarily traded in the US and in the Netherlands whereas Shell is primarily traded in the UK. Future cash flows are split in the proportion of 60:40 in favor of Royal Dutch. Even if we do not know the correct fundamental value of Royal Dutch and Shell, we know that the market value of Royal Dutch has to be 1.5 times as large as the market value of Shell if prices reflect fundamental value.

However, Froot and Dabora (1999) find that Royal Dutch is sometimes more than 40 percent underpriced and sometimes 10 percent overpriced relative to the share prices of Shell. Thus, market prices are clearly wrong and this mispricing persists for several years. Possible rational explanations such as exchange rate risks, different liquidity due to the market microstructure, and asynchronous trading as a result of different trading hours are not sufficient to account for the apparent mispricing.

Another example of non-rational market prices that are not compatible with the law of one price is presented by Lamont and Thaler (2003). They study equity carve-outs by analyzing the spin-off of Palm which was owned by 3Com. In March 2000, 3Com sold

5 percent of its Palm shares in an initial public offering and kept the remaining 95 percent of the shares. 3Com announced that its shareholders would eventually receive 1.5 shares of Palm for every 3Com share they owned. Accordingly, the stock price of 3Com has to be at least 1.5 times as high as the stock price of Palm, as long as the value of the whole 3Com company is positive. However, the stock price of Palm was far above the stock price of 3Com implying a value of −22 billion US dollars of 3Com's non-Palm business.

Rational explanations of why arbitrage is not sufficient to avoid violations of the law of one price, are looked at in the next subsection.

Limits of arbitrage
In addition to the evidence presented in the previous subsection, bubbles and crashes occur from time to time and seem to reject the notion of efficient markets and the positive effect of arbitrage, too. For example, the NASDAQ Index rose from about 1,000 in late 1997 to more than 4,500 in March 2000 before declining to 1,000 in March 2003. In Germany, the New Market index (Nemax50) rose to more than 9,000 (March 2000) and stood at about 310 (three hundred and ten!) by the end of March 2003. These huge changes of market indices are difficult to explain using a standard finance model. Moreover, the question arises why arbitrage cannot dampen these swings which are, as common sense suggests, not only due to new information.

Several models within the rational framework were developed to explain limits of arbitrage. If the investment horizon is shorter than the time until the fundamental value of an asset is reached with certainty, severe mispricing will not necessarily be eliminated by arbitrage (Dow & Gorton, 1994). Moreover, mispricing can occur because of noise traders who create additional risk by trading randomly. This additional risk is priced by the market. If these noise traders take this additional risk, they can earn higher returns than rational investors (DeLong, Shleifer, Summers, & Waldmann, 1990b). In other words, irrational investors are not necessarily eliminated from the market due to their losses.

DeLong, Shleifer, Summers, and Waldmann (1990a) and Shleifer and Vishny (1997) show that noise trader risk can worsen the mispricing in the short run. If arbitrageurs have short investment horizons, noise trader risk will prevent them from exploiting this mispricing. Kogan, Ross, Wang, and Westerfield (2003) show that survival and price impact of irrational traders are two independent concepts: They find that the price impact of irrational traders does not rely on their survival in the long run and that they can even influence prices when their wealth becomes negligible.

Finally, other market frictions such as short-sale constraints or non-tradable future labor income may limit arbitrage, too. Summing up, limits of arbitrage exist and may lead to severe mispricing even with fully rational market participants and unsystematic irrational behavior of noise traders.

Agents' rationality
So far, we have discussed theoretical and empirical issues concerning market outcomes. However, recently a wide range of studies deal with another central pillar of standard finance, i.e. agents' rationality. These studies try to examine how agents in

financial markets – professional and individual investors – actually behave. This research usually demonstrates investor behavior that is difficult to reconcile with rationality or predictions of standard finance models. In this handbook, all kinds of deviations from rationality of judgment and decision making are surveyed. In this subsection we present a few examples from the finance literature that deal with some of these problems.

One example is naïve diversification or the $1/n$ heuristic. Benartzi and Thaler (2001) analyze 401(k) retirement savings plans. Each savings plan offers a fixed number of investment options that varies across firms. Benartzi and Thaler (2001) find that some individuals spread their savings evenly across the investment alternatives and do not take into account the riskiness of the investment options. As a consequence, the asset allocation of individuals is influenced by the percentage of stock funds offered. The higher the number of stock funds, the higher the allocation to equities, a finding that is difficult to reconcile with agents' rationality.

Another aspect of non-rational behavior is that market behavior of investors is influenced by framing. Depending on the framing of gains and losses, the behavior of market participants changes as Weber, Keppe, and Meyer-Delius (2000) have demonstrated in an experimental asset market. Traders are willing to pay more for assets if they have a short position at the beginning of a trading period compared to situations with a long position even though the expected value of both portfolios is the same. In the first case, trading is driven by loss aversion whereas in the second case diversification is the main reason for trading.

Furthermore, agents' rationality requires that all available information is evaluated using Bayes' rule. However, if investors use specific heuristics that put too much weight on recent information, this systematic bias has an impact not only on the price reaction to new information but also on the price reaction afterwards when this error becomes obvious. Barberis, Shleifer, and Vishny (1998) model investors who make systematic errors when evaluating public information. Investors are prone to a conservatism bias, the underweighting of new evidence when updating probabilities, and to a particular manifestation of the representative heuristic, the tendency of people to expect even short sequences of realizations of a random variable to reflect the properties of the parent population from which the realizations are drawn.

Behavioral finance and remaining puzzles

In principle, there are two different approaches towards behavioral finance. Both approaches have the same goal, i.e. to explain observed prices, market trading volume, and individual behavior better than traditional finance models. In the first approach, the starting points are results from psychology describing human behavior in certain economic circumstances. These results are used to build new models to explain market observations. In the second approach, empirical deviations from predictions based on traditional finance theory are observed. Then, psychological results of individual behavior are screened to find an explanation for the observed market phenomena. Figure 26.1 shows the two approaches.

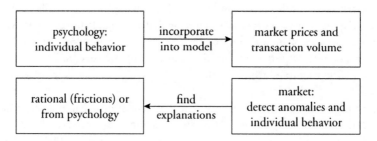

Figure 26.1 Two approaches of behavioral finance

Table 26.1 Relative and absolute trading volume in major stock markets (2002)

	US	UK	Japan	Germany	France
Trading volume in US$ trn	10.31	4.00	1.57	1.21	1.10
% market capitalization	100	215	70	180	115

This table contains the absolute trading volume (in US$ trillions) and the relative trading volume in percent of market capitalization (turnover) for five stock markets in 2002.

One important puzzle is the high trading volume in all capital markets. Table 26.1 shows the absolute trading volume and the relative trading volume in percent of market capitalization (turnover) for some stock markets in 2002.

Given that a significant number of shares are owned by long-term-oriented institutional investors like pension funds, large mutual funds, or index funds, a turnover of 100 percent, as observed in the US, implies that every available share is traded more than once per year. This trading volume appears to be high. Why do rational investors trade at all? Rational investors only trade when they are heterogeneous, i.e. when they differ with regard to tastes (such as the degree of risk aversion), endowments (such as liquidity shocks due to, for example, accidents or unexpected bequests), or information. But even differences in information do not necessarily lead to trading. Consider investors who have common prior beliefs about the value of an asset and the initial allocation of the risky asset is pareto-optimal, i.e. it is not possible to make an investor better off without making another investor worse off by changing the allocation (= trading). If these investors receive different pieces of private information about the uncertain value of the risky asset, there is heterogeneity between investors and thus a potential for trade. However, when an investor wants to sell us a security, we can conclude that he has received a bad signal about the value of this security. So why should we buy this security? Therefore, it is possible that even differences in private information do not lead to trading volume (no trade theorem; see Milgrom and Stokey, 1982). Pagano and Röell (1992) provide further details about rational motives for trading.

Common sense suggests that these rational motives for trade are not sufficient to explain the high trading volume observed in financial markets. Recent theoretical work in finance suggests that different beliefs or different opinions across people (e.g. about the value of a risky asset in the future or about how to interpret public news) may explain high levels of trading volume (see the next section and Glaser & Weber, 2003b). But why do people have differing beliefs or opinions? Are their expectations biased? Are differences of opinion a result of overconfidence? Insights from psychology may provide answers to these questions.

The equity premium puzzle, i.e. stocks have a higher risk-adjusted return than bonds (see Mehra & Prescott, 1985), may be another problem requiring a behavioral explanation. Risk aversion is not sufficient to explain the empirical findings. Benartzi and Thaler (1995) provide a behavioral explanation based on (myopic) loss aversion – if an investor is loss-averse and evaluates his portfolio at least every year, he faces a high probability of observing losses and thus requests a higher risk premium compared to the fully rational investor who is not influenced by short-term fluctuations. Barberis, Huang, and Santos (2001) provide a refined explanation for the equity premium puzzle. They study asset prices in an economy with investors deriving utility not only from consumption but also from the value of their financial wealth. Furthermore, they assume investors are loss-averse over these changes. Barberis et al. (2001) thus incorporate central ideas of prospect theory (Kahneman & Tversky, 1979). Loss aversion is captured by a piecewise linear function that is steeper for losses than for gains relative to a reference point. Thus, the model does not capture the feature of the original version of prospect theory with risk aversion in the domain of gains and risk seeking in the domain of losses. In addition, it is assumed that prior outcomes affect the degree of loss aversion. Losses are less painful after gains whereas they are more painful after losses. This assumption is consistent with the house money effect (Thaler & Johnson, 1990), gamblers' increased willingness to bet after gains. Barberis and Huang (2001) extend this model by additionally incorporating a further form of mental accounting (besides the house money effect) – investors either care about the value of their whole stock portfolio or about the value of each single security in their portfolio and thus ignore correlations. Note however that there is some doubt that the equity premium puzzle is (still) existing given the burst of the stock market bubble in recent years and the performance of stocks in Japan over the past 20 years.

Before we concentrate on the overconfidence literature, it is important to stress that behavioral finance research is either focused on individual behavior (e.g. asset allocation within a 401(k) plan) or on the implications for financial market outcomes. In the first case it is obvious that psychological research has to be adapted to a different context. In the second case, psychological results are needed to explain interactions between investors.

Behavioral finance models

In this subsection, we will briefly survey recent theoretical behavioral finance literature. The goal is not to discuss every model that has been published in recent years. Rather, the aim is to present a representative selection of recent behavioral finance theories to show which, and how, findings of psychology research are incorporated into standard finance models. We restrict our focus on the theoretical behavioral finance literature as recent behavioral finance surveys offer an in-depth discussion of various empirical findings (see Daniel, Hirshleifer, & Teoh, 2002; Shiller, 1999).

Table 26.2 Behavioral finance models

Year	Authors	Journal[1]	Evidence from psychology	Important findings and model predictions
2001	Barberis & Huang	JF	Mental accounting (individual stock vs. portfolio accounting), prospect theory	Equity premium, excess volatility, value/growth effect
2001	Barberis, Huang, & Santos	Q JE	Prospect theory, house money effect	Equity premium, excess volatility, time-series predictability of stock returns
2001	Daniel, Hirshleifer, & Subrahmanyam	JF	Overconfidence	Cross-sectional return predictability
2001	Gervais & Odean	RFS	Overconfidence, biased self-attribution	High trading volume, higher trading volume after investment successes
2001	Hirshleifer & Luo	JFM	Overconfidence	Survival of overconfident investors in competitive security markets
1998	Barberis, Shleifer, & Vishney	JFE	Conservatism, representativeness heuristic	Positive short-lag autocorrelation, negative long-lag autocorrelation, value/growth effect, event-based return predictability
1998	Benos	JFM	Overconfidence	High trading volume, excess volatility
1998	Daniel, Hirshleifer, & Subrahmanyam	JF	Overconfidence, biased self-attribution	Positive short-lag autocorrelation, negative long-lag autocorrelation, excess volatility, event-based return predictability
1998	Odean	JF	Overconfidence	High trading volume
1998	Wang	JFM	Overconfidence	High trading volume

[1] JF: *Journal of Finance*; JFE: *Journal of Financial Economics*; JFM: *Journal of Financial Markets*; Q JE: *Quarterly Journal of Economics*; and RFS: *Review of Financial Studies*.
The table shows the psychological finding that is incorporated into the model as well as the empirical findings that these models are able to explain.

Table 26.2 presents a summary of recent behavioral finance models that have been published in some of the leading finance and economics journals (*Journal of Finance, Review of Financial Studies, Journal of Financial Economics, Journal of Financial Markets, Quarterly Journal of Economics*) and lists the psychological biases that are modeled. The last column contains empirical findings that are explained by the respective model.

Table 26.2 shows that the models can be classified in two ways: belief-based and preference-based models. Belief-based models incorporate findings such as overconfidence, biased self-attribution, conservatism, and representativeness. Preference-based models use prospect theory, house money effect, and other forms of mental accounting.

Most of the models shown in Table 26.2 study how overconfident investors affect market outcomes. Overconfidence is modeled as overestimation of the precision of information or, stated equivalently, underestimation of the variance of information signals. Some dynamic models assume that the degree of overconfidence changes over time in the way that it increases as a function of past investment success due to biased self-attribution. As overconfidence is the most studied bias in the theoretical and empirical behavioral finance literature, we will focus on the overconfidence literature in finance to demonstrate the behavioral finance research methodology. Even though we focus on one particular research area within behavioral finance, research is not restricted to the aggregate stock market, asset pricing, or investor behavior. Other applications are, for example, corporate finance, financial contracting, or banking.

Overconfidence

In this section, we will discuss in more depth recent behavioral finance theories that incorporate overconfident investors. In the first subsection, we describe the way overconfidence is modeled and motivated in finance, especially the *implicit* assumptions behind the particular way of modeling overconfidence. The discussion of the theoretical overconfidence literature in finance in the second subsection will point out the most important results of these models. In the last subsection, we present various endeavors to empirically and experimentally test these theories.

We do not attempt to provide a comprehensive overview of the psychological overconfidence literature. Chapter 9, in this volume, surveys psychological literature on subjective probability calibration. We only mention the main psychological findings that are discussed in the finance literature.

Modeling and motivating overconfidence in theoretical finance

Overconfidence is usually modeled as overestimation of the precision of private information. In finance models, the uncertain liquidation value of a risky asset is modeled as a realization of a random variable. Assume, the liquidation value v is a realization of a normal distribution with mean 0 and variance $\sigma_{\tilde{v}}^2$, i.e. $\tilde{v} \sim N(0, \sigma_{\tilde{v}}^2)$. Some or all investors receive private information signals s. These signals contain information but the signals are noisy, i.e. they contain a random error ε as well. Assuming that random variables (the distribution of the liquidation value, $\tilde{v}$, and the distribution of the error term, $\tilde{\varepsilon} \sim N(0, \sigma_{\tilde{\varepsilon}}^2)$ are independent, the signal s is usually written as a realization of the random variable $\tilde{s}$, which is the sum of the random variables $\tilde{v}$ and $\tilde{\varepsilon}$, i.e. $\tilde{s}(= \tilde{v} + k \cdot \tilde{\varepsilon}) \sim N(0, \sigma_{\tilde{v}}^2 + k^2 \cdot \sigma_{\tilde{\varepsilon}}^2)$. The parameter k captures the finding of overconfidence. Psychological studies show that people are miscalibrated in the way that their probability distributions or confidence intervals for uncertain quantities are too tight (Lichtenstein, Fischhoff, & Phillips, 1982; and Chapter 9, this volume). If the parameter k is in the interval $(0,1)$, an investor underestimates the variance of the signal s (or, stated equivalently, underestimates the variance of the error term). If $k = 0$, an investor even believes that he knows the value of the risky asset with certainty. Thus, this way of modeling overconfidence captures the idea that people overestimate the precision of their knowledge, or stated equivalently, underestimate the variance of signals or the uncertain liquidation value of an asset, i.e. their confidence intervals are too tight.

Although other psychological research results concerning (mis)calibration (see Chapter 9, this volume) are not ignored in the finance literature, as can be seen in several introductions of finance articles (see, e.g., Odean, 1998, p. 1892), the above way of modeling overconfidence is justified in the following way:

> The foremost reason is that people usually *are* overconfident. . . . Most of those who buy and sell financial assets try to choose assets that will have higher returns than similar assets. This is a difficult task and it is precisely in such difficult tasks that people exhibit the greatest overconfidence. . . . Learning is fastest when feedback is quick and clear, but in securities markets the feedback is often slow and noisy.
>
> (Odean, 1998, p. 1896)

Some models assume that the degree of overconfidence, i.e. the degree of the underestimation of the variance of signals, is a stable individual trait and is thus constant over time. However, other models assume that overconfidence dynamically changes over time. This assumption is motivated by psychological studies that find biased self-attribution (Wolosin, Sherman, & Till, 1973; Langer & Roth, 1975; Miller & Ross, 1975; Schneider, Hastorf, & Ellsworth, 1979). People overestimate the degree to which they are responsible for their own success. In the finance literature, overconfidence and biased self-attribution are sometimes regarded as static and dynamic counterparts (Hirshleifer, 2001). In overconfidence models with biased self-attribution, the degree of overconfidence, i.e. the degree of overestimation of the precision of private information, is a function of past investment success.

Although overconfidence is almost exclusively modeled as overestimation of the precision of private information, overconfidence models are usually motivated by a richer set of findings that are often summarized as overconfidence in the finance literature (although psychologists treat these as distinct concepts). Under this view, overconfidence can manifest itself, besides various findings subsumed as miscalibration, in the following forms: People believe that their abilities are above average (better than average effect; Svenson, 1981; Taylor & Brown, 1988); they think that they can control random tasks, and they are excessively optimistic about the future (illusion of control and unrealistic optimism; Langer, 1975; Langer & Roth, 1975; Weinstein, 1980). In a finance journal, Kahneman and Riepe (1998, p. 54), summarize this motivation of overconfidence as follows: "The combination of overconfidence and optimism is a potent brew, which causes people to overestimate their knowledge, underestimate risks, and exaggerate their ability to control events."

However, whether the abovementioned facets of overconfidence are related, is by no means clear. Some argue that these manifestations are related (e.g., Taylor & Brown, 1988, p. 194), others argue that this need not to be the case (e.g., Biais, Hilton, Mazurier, & Pouget, 2002, p. 9), or even deny a logical link (e.g., Hvide, 2002, p. 19). Empirical evidence on this issue is still limited. Glaser and Weber (2003b) correlate scores that measure individual differences in the degree of miscalibration, the better than average effect, illusion of control, and unrealistic optimism for a group of individual investors. They find that most of the correlations are insignificant. Some correlation coefficients are even negative. The results of this study cast doubt on whether overconfidence, as it is used as a motivation in the finance literature, is a stable concept or a general valid phenomenon and that the abovementioned manifestations of overconfidence are related. But these are preliminary results that need further investigation. Evidence on this issue is important, as theoretical models often incorporate only one facet of overconfidence, miscalibration, whereas the motivation of this use is based on a variety of possibly unrelated findings and it is unclear which manifestation of overconfidence actually drives economic behavior.

At this point of the survey, we want to stress the following explicit and implicit assumptions of the way overconfidence is modeled in theoretical finance. Static models or models with constant overconfidence over time assume that there are stable individual differences in the degree of overconfidence, i.e. miscalibration. In contrast to these explicit and implicit assumptions, there is a large debate in the psychological literature over whether miscalibration is domain or task dependent or even a statistical illusion (see, e.g., Gigerenzer, Hoffrage, and Kleinbölting, 1991; Klayman, Soll, González-Vallejo, & Barlas, 1999; Juslin, Winman, & Olson, 2000; Erev, Wallsten, & Budescu, 1994) or if there are stable individual differences in reasoning or decision-making competence (see Parker & Fischhoff, 2001; Stanovich & West 1998, 2000).

Important results and predictions of overconfidence models

In this subsection, we discuss the most important results of models that incorporate overconfident market participants. Due to the page constraints in this survey, we omit a comprehensive presentation of the precise mechanism of how overconfidence affects the model predictions. Such a presentation would require a discussion of, for example, the following details: market environment, number of trading periods, or number of assets traded. Investors in a competitive market environment do not influence the price of assets whereas other investors in a strategic market environment take into account that their trading behavior might influence the market price. Moreover, some models are static in the way that there is only one trading round whereas dynamic models analyze several periods. Furthermore, models have either one or multiple risky assets that are traded. The interested reader will find a presentation of various overconfidence models and other behavioral finance models in the survey of Hirshleifer (2001).

Table 26.2 shows that most of the overconfidence models predict high trading volume in the market in the presence of overconfident traders. Moreover, at the individual level, overconfident investors will trade more aggressively: The higher the degree of overconfidence of an investor, the higher her or his trading volume. Odean (1998) calls this finding "the most robust effect of overconfidence." DeBondt and Thaler (1995) note that the high trading volume observed in financial markets "is perhaps the single most embarrassing fact to the standard finance paradigm" and that "the key behavioral factor needed to understand the trading puzzle is overconfidence." Apart from the ability to explain high levels of trading volume, the models of Benos (1998), Caballé and Sákovics (2003), Kyle and Wang (1997), Odean (1998), and Wang (1998) make further predictions as well. Odean (1998) finds that overconfident traders have lower expected utility than rational traders and hold underdiversified portfolios. In contrast, Kyle and Wang (1997) find that overconfident traders might earn higher expected profits or have higher expected utility than rational traders as overconfidence works like a commitment device to aggressive trading. Benos (1998) finds similar results. However, higher profits of overconfident investors are a result of a first mover advantage in his model. Benos (1998), Caballé and Sákovics (2003), and Odean (1998) show that the presence of over-confident traders helps explain excess volatility of asset prices, i.e. the fluctuation of asset prices is higher than the fluctuation of the fundamental value. This presentation shows that some predictions are common results of all models (the effect of overconfidence on trading volume) whereas other predictions depend on further assumptions (e.g. the effect of overconfidence on expected utility).

Hirshleifer and Luo (2001), Kyle and Wang (1997), Wang (2001) show that over-confident traders may survive in security markets. Daniel et al., (1998) show that over-confidence might present an explanation for the momentum effect and for long-run reversals of returns whereas the model of Daniel, Hirshleifer, and Subrahmanyam (2001) is able to generate the value/growth effect and the size effect. Gervais and Odean (2001) analyze how overconfidence dynamically changes through time as a function of past investment success due to a self-attribution bias.

Empirical and experimental tests of overconfidence models

There are two points of departure to test the empirical validity of an overconfidence model: model assumptions and model predictions. In the following two subsections we will discuss empirical and experimental tests of model assumptions and model predictions in turn.

Empirical and experimental tests of model assumptions

Model assumptions can be evaluated by experiments and questionnaire studies that analyze whether individual and institutional investors do underestimate the variance of stock returns, overestimate the precision of their knowledge, or how they react to re-leases of private or public information. In this subsection we present a few studies that show that investors are miscalibrated in the context of financial markets.

Kirchler and Maciejovsky (2002) is an example of an experiment that analyzes whether investors overestimate the precision of their knowledge or give too tight confidence intervals in a market environment. They experimentally investigate individual overconfid-ence in the context of an experimental asset market with several trading periods. Before each period, overconfidence was measured via subjective confidence intervals and via the comparison of objective accuracy and subjective certainty. Subjects' confidence intervals were too tight indicating overconfidence whereas according to the comparison of object-ive accuracy and subjective certainty the same people can sometimes even be classified as underconfident.

Hilton (2001) surveys questionnaire studies that analyze exchange rate and stock price predictions. These studies find too narrow confidence intervals. Another example of a questionnaire study that analyzes whether financial markets participants or financial pro-fessionals underestimate the variance of stock returns is by Graham and Harvey (2002). They study expectations of stock market risk premium as well as their volatility estimates in a panel survey. On a quarterly basis, Chief Financial Officers of US corporations are asked to provide their estimates of the market risk premium as well as upper and lower bounds of 80 percent confidence intervals of this premium. Graham and Harvey (2002) find that, compared to historical standard deviations of one-year stock returns, Chief Financial Officers underestimate the variance of stock returns and are thus very confid-ent in their assessments.

Summing up, the abovementioned studies show that it is a reasonable modeling assumption that investors are miscalibrated by underestimating stock variances or equival-ently by overestimating the precision of their knowledge. Note that this is the way how overconfidence is modeled in the finance literature.

Empirical and experimental tests of model predictions
Model predictions can be tested in several ways. We structure these various endeavors as follows:

1   Predictions concerning trading behavior and investment performance of (individual and institutional) investors.
2   Predictions concerning market outcomes.

Predictions concerning behavior and performance of investors
The most important prediction in category 1 is that trading volume increases with an increasing degree of overconfidence. The abovementioned predictions can be tested by analyzing the following data from the field or from experiments:

a)   analysis of market level data, such as returns and trading volume;
b)   analysis of trading behavior of investors; and
c)   correlation of proxies or measures of overconfidence on the one hand and economic variables such as trading volume on the other hand.

We will discuss these three possibilities in turn while focusing on the abovementioned hypothesis concerning overconfidence and trading volume.

Statman, Thorley, and Vorkink (2003) and Kim and Nofsinger (2002) are examples of group a). Statman et al. (2003) use US market data to test the hypothesis that over-confidence leads to high trading volume. They test dynamic models predicting that after high returns subsequent trading volume will be higher as investment success increases the degree of overconfidence. They find that high current stock trading volume is associated with high stock returns in the previous weeks. Statman et al. (2003) argue that this finding supports the hypothesis as high returns make investors overconfident and they will, as a consequence, trade more subsequently. Kim and Nofsinger (2002) confirm these findings using Japanese market level data. They identify stocks with varying degrees of individual ownership to test the hypothesis and discover higher monthly turnover in stocks held by individual investors during the bull market in Japan. Moreover, high past returns in both studies might be interpreted as a proxy of overconfidence as stated in group c).

Odean (1999) is an example of group b). He analyzes the trades of 10,000 individuals with discount brokerage accounts. He finds that these investors reduce their returns by trading and thus concludes that trading volume is excessive – a finding that is consistent with overconfidence models and thus indirect evidence in favor of the abovementioned hypothesis.

The Barber and Odean (2001) study is a further example of group c). Their proxy for overconfidence is gender. In the paper, they summarize psychological studies that find a higher degree of overconfidence among men than among women. Consequently, they partition their data set which consists of 35,000 households from a large discount brokerage house on gender and find that men trade more than women which is consistent with overconfidence models.

All the abovementioned studies share the shortcoming that overconfidence is never directly observed. The evidence in favor of overconfidence models is either indirect, as in Odean (1999), or uses only crude proxies for overconfidence (past returns, gender). A direct test of the hypothesis that a higher degree of overconfidence leads to higher trading volume is the correlation of measures of overconfidence and measures of trading volume as mentioned in c). In the following, we will discuss two recent studies that use this approach.

Glaser and Weber (2003b) directly test the hypothesis that overconfidence leads to high trading volume by analyzing trades of individual investors who have online broker accounts. These investors were asked to answer an Internet questionnaire, which was designed to measure various facets of overconfidence (miscalibration, the better-than-average effect, illusion of control, unrealistic optimism). They test the hypothesis by correlating individual overconfidence scores with several measures of trading volume of these individual investors (number of trades, turnover). The measures of trading volume were calculated by the trades of 215 individual investors who answered the questionnaire. Glaser and Weber (2003b) find that investors trade more if they believe that they are above average in terms of investment skills or past performance. When realized returns are used as a proxy for investment skills, investors overestimate their relative position within the group of investors. Measures of miscalibration are, contrary to theory, unrelated to measures of trading volume. This result is striking as theoretical models that incorporate overconfident investors model overconfidence as underestimation of the variance of signals, i.e. miscalibration. The results hold even when several other determinants of trading volume are controlled for in a cross-sectional regression analysis.

Biais et al. (2002) analyze experimentally if psychological traits and cognitive biases affect trading. Based on the answers of 184 subjects (students) to a psychological questionnaire they measured, among other psychological traits, the degree of overconfidence via calibration tasks. The subjects also participated in an experimental asset market afterwards. Biais et al. (2002) find that overconfident subjects have a greater tendency to place unprofitable orders. However, their overconfidence measure – the degree of miscalibration – is unrelated to trading volume. Contrary to predictions of overconfidence models, overconfident subjects do not place more orders.

Why is miscalibration not positively related to trading volume, as predicted by overconfidence models? One important point to remember is that the link between miscalibration and trading volume has never been shown or even analyzed empirically or experimentally. Overconfidence models are motivated by psychological studies that show that people are generally miscalibrated or by empirical findings that are consistent with miscalibrated investors, such as high trading volume. But there might be other biases that are able to explain the same empirical findings when implemented in a theoretical model. This shows the importance of analyzing the link or correlation between judgment biases and economic variables such as trading volume as the only way to test which bias actually influences economic behavior. Furthermore, there are other reasons that might explain the failure of miscalibration scores in explaining volume. In the psychological literature, there is a debate over whether miscalibration is domain- or task-dependent or even a statistical illusion (see Chapter 9, this volume). If miscalibration is not a stable individual trait or if the degree of miscalibration depends on a specific task then it is no surprise that the abovementioned studies are unable to empirically confirm the hypothesis that a higher degree of miscalibration leads to higher trading volume. Glaser and Weber (2003b) contains an enlarged discussion of these points and further possible explanations and interpretations of the result that miscalibration scores are unrelated to measures of trading volume.

Predictions concerning market outcomes

In the remainder of this section, we discuss how predictions of overconfidence models in group 2 can be tested. For example, in the model of Daniel et al. (1998) the momentum effect is a result of the trading activity of overconfident traders. One implication of their model is that momentum is strongest among stocks that are difficult to evaluate by investors. One example for such stocks is growth stocks with hard-to-value growth options in the future. Daniel and Titman (1999) confirm this implication. They find that momentum is stronger for growth stocks. If disagreement of investors about future performance is stronger among hard-to-value stocks and if trading volume is a measure of this disagreement then a further implication of the Daniel et al. (1998) model is a stronger momentum effect among high-volume stocks. This finding is confirmed by Lee and Swaminathan (2000) and Glaser and Weber (2003a) using turnover, the number of shares traded divided by the number of shares outstanding, as a measure of trading volume – momentum is stronger among high-turnover stocks.

Summary and Open Questions

Behavioral finance has become widely accepted among finance academics. It is neither a minor subdiscipline nor a new paradigm of finance. Behavioral finance tries to improve existing models via more realistic assumptions. Thus, behavioral finance follows the traditional way of financial modeling that incorporates real-world imperfections such as transaction costs, taxes, or asymmetric information on the one hand or observed traits of individuals such as risk aversion on the other hand into finance models.

Naturally, behavioral finance has drawn some criticism. As Fama (1998, p. 291) writes:

> My view is that any new model should be judged . . . on how it explains the big picture. The question should be: Does the new model produce rejectable predictions that capture the menu of anomalies better than market efficiency? For existing behavioral models, my answer to this question (perhaps predictably) is an emphatic no.

In other words, behavioral finance models are currently not able to replace traditional finance theory. One reason for this conclusion is given by Frankfurter and McGoun (2002, pp. 375–6):

> Even the supposed proponents of behavioral finance, however, are marginalizing themselves by clinging to the underlying tenets, forms, and methods of the dominant paradigm . . . . Although "'behavioral finance'" sounds as if it would be a new methodology or even a significant new paradigm for research in financial economics, behavioral finance has never been, and looks as if it may never be, either.

Thaler (1999, p. 16) predicts the end of behavioral finance as *all* financial theorists will sooner or later incorporate realistic assumptions:

> I predict that in the not-too-distant future, the term "behavioral finance" will be correctly viewed as a redundant phrase. What other kind of finance is there? In their enlightenment, economists will routinely incorporate as much "behavior" into their models as they observe in the real world. After all, to do otherwise would be irrational.

Behavioral finance as a field is a rather young enterprise that has proved its usefulness by first results but which still has some way to go. On the level of individual decision making in markets, e.g. individual or professional investors' behavior, we have quite a large amount of knowledge. A large part of this knowledge stems from psychological research that tries to answer similar questions. On the level of aggregate variables, like market prices or trading volume, we know less. As these variables are central for research in finance, ultimately, behavioral finance will have to prove its usefulness here as well. To make further progress, it will be necessary to develop financial models that are based on alternative, behavioral assumptions of decision making. The challenge will be to show that these new models come up with predictions different from standard financial models and that these alternative predictions win over predictions from standard theory.

We conclude with some thoughts on how research in behavioral finance might become even more successful. From the perspective of psychology, it would be helpful to extend the research program beyond individual decision making by investigating problems or open questions that are central to a financial (or economic) context. Examples are: strategic and dynamic interaction of economic agents in markets, decision making in organizations or principle–agents situations.

For research in finance, it would be helpful to read more carefully what psychologists have found. As we demonstrated in the case of overconfidence, researchers in finance want truths from psychologists that are as simple as possible. The truths have to be simple, because otherwise financial models get too complex. By studying the psychological literature, researchers in finance have to extract those findings that are robust as well as useful for modeling purposes. Clearly, it would be best to join forces from both disciplines to further enhance behavioral finance, which, after all, is an interdisciplinary field of research.

References

Banz, R. (1981) The relationship between return and market value of common stocks, *Journal of Financial Economics*, 9, 3–18.

Barber, B. M. & Odean, T. (2001) Boys will be boys: Gender, overconfidence, and common stock investment, *Quarterly Journal of Economics*, 116, 261–92.

Barberis, N. & Huang, M. (2001) Mental accounting, loss aversion, and individual stock returns, *Journal of Finance*, 56, 1247–92.

Barberis, N., Huang, M., & Santos, T. (2001) Prospect theory and asset prices, *Quarterly Journal of Economics* 116, 1–53.

Barberis, N., Shleifer, A., & Vishny, R. (1998) A model of investor sentiment, *Journal of Financial Economics*, 49, 307–43.

Benartzi, S. & Thaler, R. (1995) Myopic loss aversion and the equity premium puzzle, *Quarterly Journal of Economics*, 110, 73–92.

Benartzi, S. & Thaler, R. (2001) Naïve diversification strategies in defined contribution saving plans, *American Economic Review*, 91, 79–98.

Benos, A. V. (1998) Aggressiveness and survival of overconfident traders, *Journal of Financial Markets*, 1, 353–83.

Biais, B., Hilton, D., Mazurier, K., & Pouget, S. (2002) Psychological traits and trading strategies. CEPR discussion paper no. 3195.

Caballé, J. & Sákovics, J. (2003) Speculating against an overconfident market, *Journal of Financial Markets*, 6, 199–225.

Daniel, K., Hirshleifer, D., & Subrahmanyam, A. (1998) Investor psychology and security market under- and overreactions, *Journal of Finance*, 53, 1839–85.

Daniel, K., Hirshleifer, D., & Subrahmanyam, A. (2001) Overconfidence, arbitrage, and equilibrium asset pricing, *Journal of Finance*, 56, 921–65.

Daniel, K., Hirshleifer, D., & Teoh, S. H. (2002) Investor psychology in capital markets: Evidence and policy implications, *Journal of Monetary Economics*, 49, 139–209.

Daniel, K. & Titman, S. (1999) Market efficiency in an irrational world, *Financial Analysts Journal*, 55, 28–40.

DeBondt, W. F. M. & Thaler, R. H. (1995) Financial decision making in markets and firms: A behavioral perspective. In R. A. Jarrow, V. Maksimovic, and W. T. Ziemba (eds.), *Handbooks in Operations Research and Management Science*, vol. 9, *Finance* (pp. 385–410). Amsterdam: North-Holland Elsevier.

DeLong, J. B., Shleifer, A., Summers, L. H., & Waldmann, R. J. (1990a) Noise trader risk in financial markets, *Journal of Political Economy*, 98, 703–38.

DeLong, J. B., Shleifer, A., Summers, L. H., & Waldmann, R. J. (1990b) Positive feedback investment strategies and destabilizing rational speculation, *Journal of Finance*, 45, 379–95.

Dimson, E. & Marsh, P. (2000) The demise of size. In G. Hawawini, D. B. Keim, and W. T. Ziemba (eds.), *Security Market Imperfections in World Wide Equity Markets* (pp. 116–43). Cambridge: Cambridge University Press.

Dow, J. & Gorton, G. (1994) Arbitrage chains, *Journal of Finance*, 49, 819–49.

Erev, I., Wallsten, T. S., & Budescu, D. V. (1994) Simultaneous over- and underconfidence: The role of error in judgment processes, *Psychological Review*, 101, 519–28.

Fama, E. F. (1970) Efficient capital markets: A review of theory and empirical evidence, *Journal of Finance*, 25, 383–417.

Fama, E. F. (1991) Efficient capital markets II, *Journal of Finance*, 46, 1575–617.

Fama, E. F. (1998) Market efficiency, long-term returns, and behavioral finance, *Journal of Financial Economics*, 49, 283–306.

Fama, E. F. & French, K. (1992) The cross-section of expected returns, *Journal of Finance*, 47, 427–66.

Frankfurter, G. M. & McGoun, E. G. (2002) Resistance is futile: The assimilation of behavioral finance, *Journal of Economic Behavior and Organization*, 48, 375–89.

Froot, K. A. & Dabora, E. M. (1999) How are stock prices affected by the location of trade, *Journal of Financial Economics*, 53, 189–216.

Gervais, S. & Odean, T. (2001) Learning to be overconfident, *Review of Financial Studies*, 14, 1–27.

Gigerenzer, G., Hoffrage, U., & Kleinbölting, H. (1991) Probabilistic mental models: A Brunswikian theory of confidence, *Psychological Review*, 98, 506–28.

Glaser, M. & Weber, M. (2003a) Momentum and turnover: Evidence from the German stock market, *Schmalenbach Business Review*, 55, 108–35.

Glaser, M. & Weber, M. (2003b) Overconfidence and trading volume, CEPR discussion paper no. 3941.

Graham, J. R. & Harvey, C. R. (2002) Expectations of equity risk premia, volatility, and asymmetry. Working paper, Duke University.

Hilton, D. J. (2001) The psychology of financial decision-making: Applications to trading, dealing, and investment analysis, *Journal of Psychology and Financial Markets*, 2, 37–53.

Hirshleifer, D. (2001) Investor psychology and asset pricing, *Journal of Finance*, 56, 1533–97.

Hirshleifer, D. & Luo, G. Y. (2001) On the survival of overconfident traders in a competitive securities market, *Journal of Financial Markets*, 4, 73–84.

Hvide, H. K. (2002) Pragmatic beliefs and overconfidence, *Journal of Economic Behavior and Organization*, 48, 15–28.

Jegadeesh, N. & Titman, S. (1993) Returns to buying winners and selling losers: Implications for stock market efficiency, *Journal of Finance*, 48, 65–91.

Jegadeesh, N. & Titman, S. (2001) Profitability of momentum strategies: An evaluation of alternative explanations, *Journal of Finance*, 56, 699–720.

Juslin, P., Winman, A., & Olson, H. (2000) Naive empiricism and dogmatism in confidence research: A critical examination of the hard-easy effect, *Psychological Review*, 107, 384–96.

Kahneman, D. & Riepe, M. W. (1998) Aspects of investor psychology, *Journal of Portfolio Management*, 24(4), 52–65.

Kahneman, D. & Tversky, A. (1979) Prospect theory: An analysis of decision under risk, *Econometrica*, 47, 263–92.

Kim, K. A. & Nofsinger, J. R. (2002) The behavior and performance of individual investors in Japan. Working paper.

Kirchler, E., & Maciejovsky, B. (2002) Simultaneous over- and underconfidence: Evidence from experimental asset markets, *Journal of Risk and Uncertainty*, 25, 65–85.

Klayman, J., Soll, J. B., González-Vallejo, C., & Barlas, S. (1999) Overconfidence: It depends on how, what, and whom you ask, *Organizational Behavior and Human Decision Processes*, 79, 216–47.

Kogan, L., Ross, S., Wang, J., & Westerfield, M. (2003) The price impact and survival of irrational traders. NBER working paper 9434.

Kyle, A. S. & Wang, F. A. (1997) Speculation duopoly with agreement to disagree: Can overconfidence survive the market test? *Journal of Finance*, 52, 2073–90.

Lakonishok, J., Shleifer, A., & Vishny, R. W. (1994) Contrarian investment, extrapolation, and risk, *Journal of Finance*, 49, 1541–78.

Lamont, O. A. & Thaler, R. H. (2003) Can the market add and subtract? Mispricing in tech stock carve-outs, *Journal of Political Economy*, 111, 227–68.

Langer, E. J. (1975) The illusion of control, *Journal of Personality and Social Psychology*, 32, 311–28.

Langer, E. J. & Roth, J. (1975) Heads I win, tail it's chance: The illusion of control as a function of the sequence of outcomes in a purely chance task, *Journal of Personaliy and Social Psychology*, 32, 951–5.

Lee, C. M. C. & Swaminathan, B. (2000) Price momentum and trading volume, *Journal of Finance*, 55, 2017–69.

Lichtenstein, S., Fischhoff, B., & Phillips, L. D. (1982) Calibration of probabilities: The state of the art to 1980. In D. Kahneman, P. Slovic, and A. Tversky (eds.), *Judgment Under Uncertainty: Heuristics and Biases* (pp. 306–34). Cambridge: Cambridge University Press.

Mehra, R. & Prescott, E. C. (1985) The equity premium puzzle, *Journal of Monetary Economics*, 15, 145–61.

Milgrom, P. & Stokey, N. (1982) Information, trade and common knowledge, *Journal of Economic Theory*, 26, 17–27.

Miller, D. T. & Ross, M. (1975) Self-serving biases in attribution of causality: Fact or fiction? *Psychological Bulletin*, 82, 213–25.

Odean, T. (1998) Volume, volatility, price, and profit when all traders are above average, *Journal of Finance*, 53, 1887–934.

Odean, T. (1999) Do investors trade too much? *American Economic Review*, 89, 1279–98.

Pagano, M. & Röell, A. (1992) Trading volume. In P. Newman, J. Eatwell, and M. Milgate (eds.), *The New Palgrave Dictionary of Money and Finance* (pp. 679–83). London: Macmillan.

Parker, A. M. & Fischhoff, B. (2001) An individual difference measure of decision making competence. Working paper, Carnegie Mellon University.

Rouwenhorst, K. G. (1998) International momentum strategies, *Journal of Finance*, 53, 267–84.

Rouwenhorst, K. G. (1999) Local return factors and turnover in emerging markets, *Journal of Finance*, 54, 1439–64.

Schneider, D. J., Hastorf, A. H., & Ellsworth, P. C. (1979) *Person Perception*. Reading, MA: Addison-Wesley.

Shiller, R. J. (1999) Human behavior and the efficiency of the financial system. In John B. Taylor and Michael Woodford (eds.), *Handbook of Macroeconomics* (pp. 1305–40). Amsterdam: Elsevier Science.

Shleifer, A. & Vishny, R. W. (1997) The limits of arbitrage, *Journal of Finance*, 52, 35–55.

Stanovich, K. E. & West, R. F. (1998) Individual differences in rational thought, *Journal of Experimental Psychology*, 127, 161–88.

Stanovich, K. E. & West, R. F. (2000) Individual differences in reasoning: Implications for the rationality debate, *Behavioral and Brain Sciences*, 23, 645–726.

Statman, M., Thorley, S., & Vorkink, K. (2003) Investor overconfidence and trading volume, working paper.

Svenson, O. (1981) Are we all less risky and more skillful than our fellow drivers? *Acta Psychologica*, 47, 143–8.

Taylor, S. E. & Brown, J. D. (1988) Illusion and well-being: A social psychology perspective on mental health, *Psychological Bulletin*, 103, 193–210.

Thaler, R. H. (1999) The end of behavioral finance, *Financial Analysts Journal*, 55, 12–17.

Thaler, R. H. & Johnson, E. J. (1990) Gambling with the house money and trying to break even: The effects of prior outcomes on risky choices, *Management Science*, 36, 643–60.

Wang, F. A. (1998) Strategic trading, asymmetric information and heterogeneous prior beliefs, *Journal of Financial Markets*, 1, 321–52.

Wang, F. A. (2001) Overconfidence, investor sentiment, and evolution, *Journal of Financial Intermediation*, 10, 138–70.

Weber, M., Keppe, H.-J., & Meyer-Delius, G. (2000) Framing effects in experimental markets, *Journal of Economic Behavior and Organization*, 41, 159–76.

Weinstein, N. D. (1980) Unrealistic optimism about future life events, *Journal of Personality and Social Psychology*, 39, 806–20.

Wolosin, R. J., Sherman, S. J., & Till, A. (1973) Effects of cooperation and competition on responsibility attribution after success and failure, *Journal of Experimental Social Psychology*, 9, 220–35.

27

Judgment and Decision-making Accounting Research: A Quest to Improve the Production, Certification, and Use of Accounting Information

Natalia Kotchetova and Steven Salterio

Introduction

Judgment and decision-making (hereafter JDM) research in accounting traces its roots back to the mid-1970s as a part of a wave of accounting researchers who started to scientifically examine the phenomenon of accounting. While most of these researchers embraced economics as their base discipline (Beaver, 1998), a significant group of accounting researchers chose judgment and decision making as the scientific foundation for their research. The JDM accounting researchers recognized that while the content of accounting originated in economic transactions, the preparation, certification, and interpretation of accounting information was strongly affected by the human information processing characteristics of professional accountants and other users of accounting information such as managers.

Many excellent reviews have been published about various aspects of JDM research in accounting and its various sub-disciplines (e.g., Solomon & Trotman (2003) for auditing; Sprinkle (2003) for managerial accounting; Libby, Bloomfield, & Nelson (2002) for financial accounting; and Davis (1995) for tax) but they are writing for a predominantly accounting research audience. Our review concentrates on JDM accounting research that has been published since 1994, since the last review that was targeted at the more general JDM community was published (Ashton & Ashton, 1995). In order to provide context for the non-accounting reader, we first describe the domain of accounting and a brief overview of the major themes in JDM accounting research from 1974 to 1995. Second, we document the breadth and depth of JDM accounting research in the period from 1995 to 2002. Finally, we qualitatively identify the main JDM themes in recent accounting research and discuss the directions for future JDM research in accounting.

Accounting, Accountants and Accounting Information Users

Accounting can be broadly thought of as the measurement and the communication of relevant economic information to decision makers (Beaver, 1998). The best known form of accounting information is the financial statement included in the annual report to public company shareholders (e.g. Microsoft, IBM, British Airways, and other similar companies). The annual report includes various management reports about the company's business activities as well as a complete set of financial statements (i.e., an income statement, a balance sheet, a statement of cash flows and normally 10 to 20 pages of explanatory notes) prepared by management in accordance with "generally accepted accounting principles (GAAP)."

Closely associated with the production of the financial statements are three related sub-fields: auditing, accounting information systems, and taxation. The auditor's (or independent accountant's) report provides assurance (or certification in many countries) about the reliability (and potentially the relevance) of the accounting information to decision makers, normally interpreted as investors and creditors.

Accounting information systems provide the means of collecting, organizing, and summarizing data about economic transactions. These data are then transformed into accounting information by accounting judgments, practices, and application of rules. While state-of-the-art computerized accounting information systems make the processing of routine transaction data generally easy and error-free (e.g., how many dollars in sales last evening at your local McDonald's), there are many accounting activities that may require estimates (e.g., how much your university needs to expense for your pension, a pension which will not be paid until retirement, but a benefit you earned this year) or projections of future event (non)occurrence. These estimates and projections may be subject to both bias and noise (random error).

The tax users of accounting information modify it to suit the requirements of various governmental taxation authorities. Issues studied in the tax realm can be as simple as individual taxpayers' desires for a tax refund (even though a refund represents an interest free loan to the government) to complex judgments made by tax professionals about tax minimization strategies for international corporations.

A Brief History of JDM Accounting Research

JDM accounting research started with the publication in the *Journal of Accounting Research* (the top accounting journal for over three decades (Brown & Huefner, 1994)), of the two dissertation articles by PhD graduates of the University of Illinois at Urbana-

Champaign and the University of Minnesota (Libby, 1975; Ashton, 1974). Both of these articles were motivated by the early JDM research on clinical judgments (e.g., Goldberg, 1968) that used a form of Brunswik's lens model (Brunswik, 1940; Hammond, 1955; Chapter 3, this volume). These JDM accounting researchers used the lens model as a means of capturing the judgments of auditors and bank loan officers. As noted above, auditors examine evidence, on a test basis, that underlies the published financial statements of companies to arrive at an opinion as to whether the financial statements are in accordance with generally accepted accounting principles (GAAP). GAAP is a combination of written rules set by accounting standard setters (such as the Financial Accounting Standards Board in the United States) and generally accepted practices and principles found in textbooks and employed in practice. Bank loan officers employ these GAAP-based financial statements or information that is based on these statements in making judgments about the creditworthiness of a company seeking loans.

The judgments examined in these two articles would resonate with JDM researchers of that era as they examined judgment consensus among participants, judgment consistency of the same participant over time, and the self-insight of participants into the cues that most affect their judgments. Furthermore, Libby (1975) introduced the issue of relative expertise into accounting research. Early findings indicated that these accounting experimental participants had a higher degree of consistency (both test-retest and over time) within subjects as well as a higher degree of consensus between subjects than was indicated by the results from other domains (e.g., Peterson, Hammond and Summers, 1965). Consistent with the basic JDM findings, accounting participants had limited self-insight into what cues were important to their judgments. The follow-up studies showed an increased understanding of underlying JDM theory and employed stronger research designs (see Libby, 1981 and Ashton, 1982 for reviews).

The next major development in JDM accounting research was the incorporation of the heuristics and biases JDM paradigm (e.g., Tversky & Kahneman, 1974) into the accounting setting (e.g., Joyce & Biddle, 1981a, 1981b). The 1980s' JDM accounting research was dominated by documenting that auditors, management accountants, and managers who used accounting information were subject to the various heuristics and biases documented in JDM research. Furthermore, JDM accounting researchers found that increasing the years of general domain work experience of accountants/managers did not result in the biases being substantially reduced (e.g., Wright, 1988). Smith and Kida (1991) reexamined this literature and pointed out that the closer the experimental accounting task came to a realistic accounting task that participants normally performed, the less likely the biases were to manifest themselves, and when they did they were of smaller magnitude. This analysis suggested that experimental tasks that had appropriate accounting content matched to professional accountants or managers who normally carried out the task would invoke the domain-specific expertise leading to better JDM performance (Libby & Luft, 1993). This was a critical breakthrough in JDM accounting research as it provided a direct means of examining what made an "expert" professional accountant or user of accounting information given the previous proxy, years of experience, was found to have little or no explanatory power (Wright, 1988).

JDM accounting research in the 1990s, or the era of expertise research, was dominated by examining how professional accountants developed the expertise that they brought to their tasks and how experience, knowledge, ability, and the accounting environment interacted to affect accountants' judgment and decision performance on accounting tasks (Libby & Luft, 1993). For the first time, accounting researchers thought they had a competitive advantage over JDM researchers who also studied expertise (e.g., Shanteau, 1992; Einhorn, 1974; Chi, Glaser, & Farr, 1988) as the accounting researcher most often had substantive expertise about the subject matter, accounting, whereas JDM psychology researchers struggled with having to develop substantive expertise in a domain prior to examining expert judgment (Hogarth, 1991). Hence, the JDM accounting researchers developed and tested hypotheses at the intersection of the substantive domain (i.e. some aspect of the accounting domain) and JDM theory to predict what expertise was needed and what the effects would be of the lack of such expertise on the accountant's judgment performance.

To summarize, the first 20 years of JDM accounting research (1974 to 1995) documented that: (a) accounting judgments could be formally studied (something that was very controversial among professional accountants and managers – see Ashton (1974)); (b) in general, accountants and managers using accounting information used the same heuristics and were susceptible to the same biases as other JDM subjects; and (c) in general, domain-specific expertise in a specific professional accounting task improved judgment performance. Next, we briefly survey the depth and breadth of JDM research approaches and theories used in the accounting domain during the period 1995 to 2002.

Breadth and Depth of JDM Research Approaches and Theories Employed in Accounting Research: 1995–2002

In order to quantify the breadth and depth of JDM accounting research published in leading accounting journals during 1995 to 2002, we identified JDM accounting articles employing two criteria. First, the article was published in one of the following leading nine accounting journals (these journals include four of the top five accounting journals as defined in Brown and Huefner (1994) as well as the five journals of the various interest groups in the American Accounting Association (an academic professional body equivalent to the American Psychological Association): *Journal of Accounting Research*; *The Accounting Review*; *Contemporary Accounting Research*; *Accounting, Organizations, and Society*; *Auditing: Journal of Practice & Theory*; *Journal of American Taxation Association*; *Journal of Information Systems*; *Journal of Management Accounting Research*; and *Behavioral Research in Accounting*. Second, the article had to include an experimental task(s) that involved a judgment, decision, or both in one or more accounting contexts. Our sample of articles does not include articles that report results of surveys, field studies, cases studies, and economic theory based experiments.

Using this data, we determined that 264 JDM accounting articles were published during the seven-year period between 1995 and 2002. This represents roughly 18 percent of all accounting research articles published in those nine journals during the period and 12 percent of the articles published in the top four accounting journals.

We classified our JDM accounting articles by JDM approach over the seven-year period (see Table 27.1). The overwhelming majority of JDM accounting articles adopt

Table 27.1 JDM accounting articles by JDM approach: 1995–2002

JDM approach	JDM accounting articles	
	Total	*(%)*
Information processing	230	87.1
Heuristics and biases	36	13.6
Bounded rationality/satisficing	14	5.3
Rational actor models	7	2.7
Computational modeling	4	1.5
Rationality and the normative–descriptive distinction	3	1.1
Brunswik's lens model approach	3	1.1
Einhorn and Hogarth's ambiguity model	1	0.4
Total JDM accounting articles*	264	

* Some JDM accounting articles used more than one JDM approach thus leading the total reported approaches to be 298.

the human information processing framework (see Chapter 6, this volume). We find such a strong emphasis on information processing, including knowledge and memory, somewhat expected due to the substance of the accounting domain, that is, the process of recording, classifying, and summarizing economic events for the purpose of providing information for decision makers. Similarly, the foci of many accounting sub-disciplines consist of data classification, evaluation, verification, and other types of information processing. The second most popular JDM approach used by accounting researchers is that of heuristics and biases (see Chapter 5, this volume). Again, emphasis on biases in JDM accounting research is expected given the JDM accounting researcher's objective of describing and, ideally, improving the processes that accountants and/or managers use to make accounting estimates, risk assessments, and other complex judgments or decisions.

The majority of JDM accounting studies focuses on judgments (136 or 51.5 percent), followed by choices/decisions (81 or 30.7 percent) and both judgments and choices/decisions in combination (47 or 17.8 percent). We examine the accounting articles by judgment and decision theories employed by JDM accounting researchers. The three most frequently employed judgment theories employed are: expert judgment (192 articles or 72.7 percent), forecasting and scenario planning (59 articles or 22.3 percent), and hypothesis testing and information search (37 articles or 14 percent). Emphasis on these three judgment theories is consistent with the focus on, respectively, (a) judgments made by professional accountants, who are viewed as experts; (b) the use of accounting information for decisions about future events; and (c) the process of auditors gathering evidence to support their opinion on the compliance of financial statements with GAAP. Note that JDM accounting researchers use multiple judgment theories within individual articles to motivate the hypotheses of interest to JDM accounting researchers.

The most frequently studied decision theories by accounting researchers are decisions under risk and uncertainty (139 articles or 52.7 percent), multiattribute choice and

Table 21.2 Number of JDM accounting experimental articles by participant background and average years of relevant work experience: 1995–2002

Accounting sub-discipline	Undergraduate students		MBA and other graduate students		Auditors/professional accountants		Company managers		Financial analysts		Other*		Total articles
	no. of articles	average years experience	no. of articles	average years experience	no. of articles	average years experience	no. of articles	average years experience	no. of articles	average years experience	no. of articles	average years experience	
Auditing	15	n/a	10	3.11	140	4.97	7	7.09	1	0	13	n/a	186
Financial accounting	5	n/a	13	1.43	1	6.77	5	7.70	8	8.80	5	n/a	37
Information systems and accounting	17	n/a	4	1.53	0	–	1	18.70	1	0	2	n/a	25
Management accounting	22	n/a	10	2.09	1	12.00	7	5.87	1	8.00	1	n/a	42
Taxation	7	n/a	7	0.81	13	4.57	2	2.02	0	–	2	n/a	31
Average years of experience**		n/a		1.79		5.66		8.28		3.36		n/a	
Total number of JDM accounting articles***	66		44		155		22		11		23		264
% of JDM accounting articles	25.00		16.70		58.70		8.30		4.20		8.70		

* Other participants include jurors, judges, accounting managers in financial service firms, bank branch managers, customers, tax payers, senior citizens, police officers, and investigators.
** Average years of experience is normally not reported for undergraduate students or, if it is reported, it is normally less than 1 year. Years of experience for the "Other" category does not provide any meaningful information when aggregated over so many different types of participants.
*** Some JDM accounting articles featured more than one type of participant background.

conflict/context (75 articles or 28.4 percent), and group and interactive decision making (42 articles or 15.9 percent). Accounting decisions are almost always made under conditions of risk and uncertainty, involve tradeoffs among multiple desired goals, and can involve groups in the decision-making process. Again note that multiple decision theories can be employed in any single JDM accounting study as well as that judgment theory and decision theory are often used in combination to study an accounting phenomenon of interest.

Table 27.2 provides summary data on the number of articles by participant background and where relevant, their years of relevant professional work experience. During the past seven years auditors/professional accountants were employed as participants in at least some of the experiments reported in the article in over half all the JDM accounting articles published. Other large groups of participants in JDM accounting experiments include company managers, financial analysts, as well as a miscellaneous compendium of jurors, judges, bank branch managers, customers, taxpayers, senior citizens, police officers, and government investigators. Undergraduate and graduate students also participate in JDM accounting experiments as a proxy for experienced participants (e.g., junior auditors, relatively naïve investors, middle- to low-level managers). Overall, undergraduate students appeared in at least some experiments in about one quarter of the articles published, with MBA and other Masters students participating about 15 percent of the time. It is noteworthy that some accounting sub-disciplines are much more likely to employ participants with relevant work experience than others, with information systems employing the fewest and auditing employing the most.

Current JDM Accounting Research

This section describes current themes in JDM accounting research. Three judgment theories are of particular current interest to JDM accounting researchers: hindsight or outcome effects (see Chapter 13, this volume); hypotheses testing (see Chapter 10, this volume); and the effects of presentation format. The effect of the decision frame is the main decision theory (see Chapter 19, this volume) emphasized in recent JDM accounting research. We discuss why these particular judgments and decisions are of interest to JDM accounting researchers via an examination of recently published articles. We also discuss how JDM approaches and theories have been adapted, extended and modified to be useful to study accounting judgments and decisions.

Hindsight and outcome effects

As noted above, the largest area of JDM accounting research is the sub-discipline of auditing. The auditor provides an opinion, based on selected tests, of the conformity of accounting information with GAAP. Auditors, in examining whether client management financial statements are in accordance with GAAP, have to make *ex ante* judgments about the conformity of these statements; however, they are judged by regulatory bodies, jurors, or judges *ex post*, often years later. These various regulatory and legal parties have to determine if the auditor exercised "due professional care" in the conduct of an audit, or whether with better auditing the auditor might have discovered that the financial statements were not in accordance with GAAP. This definition of "hindsight" is different than that employed in typical JDM studies (see Chapter 13, this volume) where a typical participant is attempting to reflect on what their own original judgment would have been in light of knowledge of the outcome. In the case of litigation against an auditor, judges and juries face a hindsight task where they must evaluate the case facts from the auditor's perspective before the problem that resulted in litigation was known. However, they may be unable to make an assessment of the auditor's negligence in the light of accounting problems that were not discovered at the time of the audit which left the plaintiff with, for example, a large loss of his/her investment, resulting in a judge or juror hindsight bias-like phenomenon.

In the early 1990s the largest international public accounting firms reported that 10 percent of gross firm revenue was being spent on defending lawsuits from investors alleging audit failure when audit clients became financially distressed or bankrupt (Arthur Andersen et al., 1992). JDM research in psychology and law (see Chapter 28, this volume) documented that the jurors' judgments of liability for punitive damages (e.g., Hastie, Schkade, & Payne, 1999) and search and seizure cases (e.g., Casper, Benedict, & Kelly, 1988) exhibit hindsight effects. These JDM researchers found that increasing participant awareness of alternative outcomes (e.g. having the participants list possible alternative medical diagnoses) resulted in a reduction in the influence of outcome knowledge on participants' judgments (Arkes, Faust, Guilmette, & Hart, 1988).

In attempting to apply these findings to the audit trial, Anderson et al. (1997, p. 22) used judges as experimental participants because in many cases involving auditors the case is litigated before a judge alone. They demonstrated that in a hypothetical auditor negligence case, alternative outcome awareness (e.g., by providing the judge with different interpretations of what could have caused the bankruptcy of an auditor's client) by itself was not effective in reducing the judge's hindsight bias. Anderson et al. (1997) employed ethical utilitarianism, a philosophy of judicial review well known to judges, as a debiaser. Ethical utilitarianism requires an individual to consider potential alternative actions and outcomes, as well as alternative stakeholders and how they will be (dis)advantaged by these actions and outcomes (Anderson et al., 1997, p. 24). They found that when judges received information that clarified auditors' responsibilities to a variety of stakeholders (including societal groups other than the plaintiffs), they were better able to understand the auditors' decision-making process and the potential damage to other stakeholders as a result of possible actions the auditor might have pursued. Andersen et al. (1997) found that in this condition the hindsight bias was reduced.

Anderson et al. (1997) demonstrate that the nature of the issue studied, negligence lawsuits against auditors, involves serious economic consequences for auditors. Second, basic JDM research identified a potential judgment bias and JDM accounting researchers replicated it employing experienced participants who would be making the actual judgments. Third, the proposed JDM debiasing technique was found not to be effective on these experienced participants (i.e., the judges). Fourth, using domain knowledge from law and accounting, the JDM accounting researchers were able to modify the proposed JDM debiasing method to make it an effective debiaser. It is predominantly the last aspect where the JDM accounting researchers' domain-specific knowledge comes into play.

Confirmation bias

Confirmation bias, the search for and interpretation of evidence in a manner that is consistent with one's existing beliefs (see Chapter 10, this volume), has been examined in tax, audit, and financial accounting environments (e.g., Anderson & Koonce, 1995; Cloyd & Spilker, 1999, 2000). In a tax scenario, a professional accountant searches applicable tax statutes and authorities to provide assessments to clients of the authoritative support for client-favored accounting that affects their tax liability. Tax professionals are expected to be client advocates, however, basic professionalism (and in the USA professional tax standards) require that tax professionals communicate accurately the degree of risks associated with client-favored tax accounting positions to the taxpayer.

Cloyd and Spilker (1999) tested the relationship between client preferences, tax professional information search, tax professional likelihood assessments of judicial success, and the strength of their recommended tax advice. Their results suggested that tax professionals' search strategies emphasized judicial cases with conclusions consistent with client preferences. They also found that the biased search strategy indirectly affected the tax professionals' judgments and recommendations to the point of making their recommendations overly aggressive and unsupportable if challenged by the tax officials.

Cloyd and Spilker (1999) demonstrate another unique application of JDM research by JDM accounting researchers. In JDM research confirmation bias is normally construed as closely associated with the individual's own position, indeed the very definition of the bias includes the terms "personal beliefs." Cloyd and Spilker (1999) show that the tax professional accountant trained in a profession that exhorts them to be unbiased appears to act as if they adopt the personal preferences of the clients that come to them for advice even at the stage where the professional is just gathering the facts upon which to base a recommendation.

Presentation format

Presentation format, that is, the form and organization of information cues, has been shown to affect the quality of judgment and decision making, including those in the accounting sub-disciplines (e.g., Dilla & Stone, 1997a, 1997b; Hirst, Koonce, & Miller, 1999; Sedor, 2002). Dilla and Stone (1997a) examined the effects of three scale characteristics on auditors' risk judgments: presentation format (numeric versus linguistic), fineness (discrete versus continuous scales), and user choice (assignment of a scale versus participant's choice of a scale). The testing of these factors was motivated by conflicting findings with respect to scale formats in psychology (e.g., Wallsten, Budescu, & Zwick, 1993) and auditing (e.g. Reimers, Wheeler, & Dusenbury, 1993). While research in psychology (e.g., Wallsten, 1990) suggested that numeric scales do not lead to better quality risk judgments, auditors' risk judgments expressed in numbers were more conservative (Reimers et al., 1993), consistent, and exhibited greater consensus (Stone & Dilla, 1994). However, auditors who were allowed to choose their own scales were more likely to choose linguistic scales. Those who *chose* scales, either linguistic or numeric, had higher agreement on cue weights and judgment consensus than participants who were *assigned* to response scales. In addition, allowing auditors to choose their own scales reduced the time spent acquiring decision cues and expressing risk judgments.

Dilla and Stone (1997a) proposed that benefits of numeric risk judgments in auditing could be resulting from scale fineness (e.g., finer distinctions on continuous scales that are more likely to be numeric versus discrete scales that are more likely to be linguistic), and not from scale representation. They found that increasing scale fineness improved judgment consistency and consensus, but also increased effort required to express risk judgments. However, scale representation did *not* affect judgment quality.

Dilla and Stone's (1997a, 1997b) research identified the boundary conditions of JDM research and extended JDM findings in a novel way. With respect to boundary conditions, they documented that auditors' judgments, in contrast to the judgments of participants used in prior psychology-based studies (e.g., Wallsten et al., 1993), are more consistent and conservative when expressed in numbers instead of words, despite the auditors' preference for linguistic scales documented above. An implication of this finding is that auditor training and expertise may result in the preferences for presentation formats that are different from participants normally studied by JDM researchers. Dilla and Stone (1997a) extend basic JDM research by offering an enhanced specification of the relation between dimensions of presentation format (scale representation, scale fineness) and judgment quality.

Decision

The main focus of JDM accounting researchers has been on judgment formulation as opposed to a decision (choice). Nonetheless, there is a robust JDM accounting literature that focuses on decisions (often in combination with judgments).

Framing

Accounting studies on framing and loss aversion (see Chapter 19, this volume) tend to have one of the following two objectives: (a) explaining framing effects found in an accounting setting using prospect theory (e.g., Emby & Finley, 1997) and/or other descriptive theories (e.g., Chang, Yen, & Duh, 2002); and (b) documenting that decision framing in a specific context biases the decision in a normatively unacceptable manner and attempting to eliminate (debias) the effects of the decision frame (e.g., Emby & Finley, 1997).

Emby and Finley (1997) provided auditors with descriptions of internal controls within a company, and then asked one group of auditors to individually make decisions about which audit tests to use based on *strength* of internal controls, while the other auditors made the same decision but after they were asked about the *weaknesses or risks* associated with the internal controls. They found a significant difference between the numbers of audit tests that participants suggested in the two conditions. When researchers asked a subset of each group of participants to consider individually the direction and relevance of information cues before making the choice, the difference between the number audit tests disappeared. This simple manipulation mitigated the framing bias among this group of auditors.

Emby and Finley (1997) demonstrated that the Tversky and Kahneman's (1981) rather robust finding of loss/gain framing effects cannot be easily transferred into the accounting domain. If, as Emby and Finley (1997) assume, risk/strength frames are equivalent to loss/gain, their results are opposite to those of Tversky and Kahneman (1981). They found that the risk frame (equivalent to negative or loss frame) was associated with risk-averse behavior (i.e., greater number of audit tests), whereas the strength frame (equivalent to positive or gain frame) led to risk-seeking behavior (i.e., fewer audit tests). However, one may argue that risk and strength in the context of internal controls are not opposite frames; rather, they represent objectively different tasks (Boritz, 1997). Nonetheless, this research demonstrated that audit context and auditor domain-specific knowledge interact to produce novel results (both as to the nature of biases and types of debiasers) that would not be predicted from JDM research.

Improving Judgments and Decisions

While most JDM research is carried out with the goal of improving human judgment and decision making, this issue has always been central to JDM accounting research. Even in the early years of JDM accounting research, where the initial research goal was simply to prove that professional accountants' judgments (e.g., Ashton, 1974) and the effects of accounting information on other decision makers could be rigorously studied (e.g., Libby, 1975), judgment improvement was always the main goal. JDM accounting researchers spent the 1980s trying to show (unsuccessfully) that general years of accounting experience would enable professional accountants to overcome various judgment heuristics and consequent biases (e.g., Wright, 1988). JDM accounting researchers in the early 1990s focused on matching the accounting task to the accountant's/decision maker's expertise and succeeded in documenting that when the task–skill set matched the judgments were better then for those whom the task–skill set did not match (Chapters 3, 4 and 15 of this volume present analogous arguments from other perspectives).

JDM research has a rich history of documenting biases and then attempting various interventions as attempts to debias those judgments (see Chapter 16, this volume). JDM accounting researchers reasoned that if professional accounting firm management acted as adaptive decision makers (cf. Payne, Bettman, & Johnson, 1993) the structures they set up might indicate effective debiasers in accounting judgment settings and hence began to explore these structures. Building on the research in the early 1990s that showed superior expert judgment across a range of accounting tasks by professional accountants (Libby, 1995), JDM accounting researchers also began to systematically study settings where non-accountants (frequently managers or investors) made judgments based on accounting information.

Improving judgments via debiasing

Accountability

Since the mid-1980s, social judgment researchers have demonstrated that accountability affects people's judgments (e.g., Tetlock, 1985). The professional accounting environment is one ripe with conflicting accountabilities. For example, management of the company hires the public accounting firm to carry out the audit of management's accounting, but the auditors report to the shareholders who do not determine the auditor's hiring or compensation. Furthermore, individual members of the public accounting firm have accountabilities to auditors at higher levels in the firm and those at the highest level of the firm (i.e. partners) have accountability to each other. There are conflicting accountability pressures within the firm, such as ensuring engagement profitability while at the same time carrying out an audit that complies with professional standards (Gibbins & Newton, 1994).

Turner (2001) examines part of this complex environment as she studies the pressure from more senior auditors on more junior auditors. She examines three conditions:

1   pressure by a senior auditor on junior auditors to minimize engagement costs by seeking only evidence to confirm the client's explanation;
2   pressure on more junior auditors by a more skeptical senior auditor who may prefer a careful evidence search to evaluate the client's explanation; and
3   pressure on junior auditors by a senior auditor whose preference is not known to the junior auditors.

Turner (2001) finds that the preferences of the senior auditor affected both the amount of evidence examined as well as the amount of time the junior auditor spent on the evidence task. Those junior auditors who had a senior auditor focused on engagement profitability examined less evidence and took less time to perform the task than those junior auditors who had a senior auditor who was concerned about whether the client explanation was correct. Furthermore, the junior auditors responded as if the senior auditor whom they did not know the preference of was a more skeptical senior interested in careful evidence evaluation. Hence, in this audit environment, junior auditors automatically defaulted to a skeptical information search strategy in the absence of explicit senior auditor preferences to the contrary.

Turner (2001) demonstrates that accountability pressures in the professional accounting setting can provide both negative and positive motivation to accounting decision makers (i.e., junior auditors). This finding also demonstrates that the general tendency of JDM subjects towards searching for confirming information is not the default strategy of auditors, indeed, their default strategy is to look for disconfirming information. Hence, Turner (2001) provides yet another demonstration of how accounting JDM researchers found a boundary condition for results documented by JDM researchers. Note, however, the difference in the conclusion with the professional tax accountant research discussed previously (e.g. Cloyd & Spilker, 1999). To the non-accounting JDM researcher this difference in default strategy of disconfirming evidence search versus confirming evidence search might seem puzzling. However, a JDM accounting researcher understands that in the audit context professional skepticism is emphasized from the earliest undergraduate course whereas in the tax environment the educational and social emphasis is on minimizing client taxes payable. This illustrates again that the domain expertise of the JDM researcher is important to understanding the implications of the research.

Decision aids

The use of decision aids to improve judgments has long been advocated by JDM researchers as a potential response to tasks where biases arise (see Chapter 16, this volume). Decision aids of various types, from simple checklists to expert systems, are pervasive in the accounting setting. Decision aids have been extensively studied in professional accounting setting due to the incentives that public accounting firms have to ensure judgment consistency and to minimize engagement costs by making routine those judgments and decisions that can be so structured.

Prior accounting research had identified that auditors tended to "game" the decision aids in a variety of settings (e.g., Kachelmeier & Messier, 1990). One classic JDM finding is the relative insensitivity to population size of experimental participants when making judgments about the appropriateness of sample size even when supported by a decision aid (Kleinmuntz, 1990). Kachelemeier and Messier (1990) documented that auditors, by determining what their desired sample size was for a particular audit test, worked backward to determine the value for the decision aid inputs that resulted in the desired size produced by the aid. This "gaming" resulted in sample sizes well below what were recommended for an audit of the given risk level as well as considerable inconsistency between auditor judgments.

In light of this research, professional auditing standard setters revised their guidance on how to select sample size as well as revising the decision aid. JDM accounting researchers sought to determine if the new guidance and decision aid overcame this tendency to "game" previous aids (Messier, Kachelmeier, & Jensen, 2001). Messier et al. (2001) documented that the "working backward" phenomenon continued to characterize the process of auditor judgment even after the revised guidance. The revised decision aid, however, reduced the difference between the decision aid's suggested sample size and the intuitive sample size the auditor selected unaided, to a statistically insignificant amount. In addition, judgment consistency was much higher using the new decision aid than under the previous aid or with unaided judgment. This increased consistency is cited as a benefit of the decision aid.

As opposed to JDM research that has to create artificial decision aids for solving artificial problems (e.g., Dawes, 1979), JDM accounting researchers were able to test decision aids in contexts where the experimental participant would normally encounter such an aid. Hence, one is not as worried about artifactual results in tests of decision aids in the audit environment. Furthermore, this specific example demonstrates the interaction between JDM accounting research and professional auditing standard setters whereby research led to a revision in professional guidance and the revised professional guidance led to more research. Hopefully, such interaction creates a virtuous circle whereby research and normative practice lead to improved judgments.

Expanding JDM accounting research to accounting users

Table 27.2 shows that the most common subject matter studied by JDM accounting researchers in recent years is auditing. The tendency to study auditors is even more pronounced when examining the JDM accounting literature of the 1980s and early 1990s. Such emphasis on auditors may be surprising given the fact that in the 1970s we found that users of financial statements (e.g., bank loan officers) were prominently featured in the JDM accounting research literature (Libby, 1975). While there are numerous reasons for the emphasis on auditors (e.g., significant research funding available from public accounting firms) the period from 1995 to 2002 witnessed a flowering of research on preparers (e.g., management accountants, see Dearman & Shields, 2001) and users (e.g., financial analysts, see Hopkins, 1995; and less sophisticated investors, see Hirst et al., 1999).

One issue that JDM accounting researchers had to contend with in rediscovering research on accounting information preparers and users was how much of the accumulated JDM accounting knowledge about auditors would apply to accountants in other domains (e.g., tax) or to non-accountant managers, investors, and other participants in the corporate governance web (e.g., Beasley & Salterio, 2001; Cohen, Krishnamoorthy, & Wright, 2002). One example of this expansion of decision-maker focus is in the area of audit committees. Concerns about corporate governance issues (e.g. Levitt, 1998; NACD, 1999) led to research being conducted on the judgments of audit committee members. Audit committees are composed of board of director members who received delegated power from the board to oversee the company's financial reporting process. The members of the board represent the shareholders of public companies and are required by law to ensure the integrity of the financial statements that are reported to the public and filed with the Securities and Exchange Commission in the United States (or equivalent bodies in other countries). Boards of directors are made up of a wide variety of individuals, from sports stars and movie stars, to prominent academics, lawyers, doctors, Chief Executive Officers of other companies, as well as a limited number of managers of the firm (always the Chief Executive Officer and sometimes other corporate officers such as the Chief Financial Officer). All members, except for the management member, serve on a part-time basis while often holding down other full-time jobs and/or other board memberships. Indeed, most boards have only one member (out of the 8 to 12 members that make up the average board) who has accounting expertise and for many boards that is a recent development.

DeZoort and Salterio (2001) sought to extend research from the professional accounting domain that examined the roles of auditor experience and knowledge on auditor judgment performance to the judgments of audit committee members. Whereas prior audit research had related domain-specific experience/knowledge to specific audit task performance, DeZoort and Salterio (2001) studied audit committee members' tendency to support either management's or the auditor's opinion in a situation where they could not agree on correct accounting. DeZoort and Salterio (2001) found that audit committee members who were more knowledgeable about the audit process and had more experience as an independent board member were more likely to support the auditor in disputes with client management about accounting policy selection issues. It remains to be seen whether it is the common knowledge of auditing or that this knowledge increases the member's confidence in their own independent judgment that results in them being more willing to oppose management's position.

Research on such corporate governance issues expands the domain of JDM accounting research as well as increases the likelihood that new factors must be taken into account by JDM accounting researchers (versus those considered in the audit environment). Furthermore, with less specialized knowledge bases to draw on, and with fewer institutional practices developed in an attempt to reduce judgment biases, we may be more likely to see the results of the basic JDM research generalize to these settings. On the other hand, it may be that the age and the experience of these participants in addition to their relative success in the business world may well lead them to find adaptive strategies that overcome these biases (e.g., Payne et al., 1993).

Team decision making

While much basic JDM research is focused on the individual, audits (and indeed other important decisions made by users of accounting information) are carried out by hierarchical teams. Many important audit decisions result from a hierarchical review process whereby a more senior auditor reviews the proposed judgments and decisions of a more junior auditor. While there is a robust JDM literature in group decision making (see Chapter 23, this volume), the accounting environment does not feature group decisions as the norm for decision making. Furthermore, audit teams are increasingly specialized on an industry basis. Hence, they are not as ad hoc as groups frequently studied in the basic JDM literature (e.g., Dawes, van de Kragt, & Orbel, 1988).

Basic JDM research found that nominal teams generally outperform real teams (e.g., Dawes et al., 1988). Recent JDM accounting research (Owhoso, Messier, & Lynch, 2002) examines this phenomenon in the context of industry specialized audit teams. Owhoso et al. (2002) find that the basic JDM finding of a nominal team's superior performance held when the real team documented simple mechanical errors and for all errors only when the real team was working in an industry outside their area of specialization. However, Owhoso et al. (2002) also found that serious conceptual errors of the type that could result in serious mistakes in audit decisions were discovered as frequently by real within-industry specialized teams as with nominal within-industry specialized teams.

This research demonstrates that application of basic JDM research findings can face boundary conditions (in the case of within-industry specialized audit teams and conceptual errors) in their application to accounting phenomena. Furthermore, the results may be more reliable as the real teams were teams of auditors that worked together on a regular basis, i.e., not artificially formed in the laboratory. In addition, this JDM accounting research studies a different type of group decision making, hierarchical team based decisions, as opposed to the norm in basic JDM research of studying groups that have members of equal status (however, see Stewart & Stasser (1995) as an exception).

The Future of JDM Accounting Research

Based on our examination of publications in top accounting research journals, JDM accounting research continues to thrive into the twenty-first century; quantitatively impacting the larger body of accounting research and qualitatively affecting our understanding of judgment and decision-making approaches and theories. JDM accounting researchers continue to refine basic JDM theories, determine the boundary conditions of such theories, examine settings and situations that occur naturally in the work place, and place a strong emphasis on improving judgment and decision-making practice.

Recent JDM accounting research (e.g., Gibbins, Salterio, & Webb, 2001; Fisher, Frederickson, & Peffer, 2000) is incorporating the findings from the behavioral negotiation literature that are based, at least in part, on JDM research (see Bazerman, 2002; Chapters 8 and 9, this volume), to study such issues as how auditors and client management negotiate what is presented in the financial statements when GAAP is unclear. JDM accounting researchers have used, and continue to use, combinations of JDM theories in their attempts to improve judgments of producers, certifiers, and users of accounting information (e.g., Vera-Muñoz, Kinney, & Bonner, 2001). Furthermore, in an effort to explain accounting phenomena of interest, and to improve accounting related judgments, JDM accounting researchers are at the forefront of combining research from other psychology areas with JDM research. Recent trends in JDM accounting research include combining social psychology research (e.g. affect, motivated reasoning) with basic JDM findings (e.g., Moreno, Kida, & Smith, 2002; Wilks, 2002) to a much greater extent than basic JDM research has done.

JDM accounting researchers continue to expand the nature of the accounting phenomenon studied to areas such as corporate governance, management accounting, and investing. Bazerman (2002, p. vi) has called one logical extension of JDM financial accounting research, behavioral finance (see Chapter 26, this volume), as one of the most exciting developments in JDM research. While researchers from finance are principal researchers in that field, the research done by JDM accounting researchers over the past 30 years, when most finance researchers were uninterested in JDM (see Thaler, 1992 as an exception) laid the foundation for the rapid progress of that field (see Chapter 7, this volume; Bazerman, 2002).

JDM accounting researchers also continue to publish as well in journals familiar to readers of this handbook, thus contributing back to their base discipline new theoretical insights gleaned from their research on more applied tasks. Overall, JDM accounting research and researchers are a vibrant part of the mosaic that makes up JDM research in the first decade of the twenty-first century.

References

Anderson, J. C., Jennings, M. M., Lowe, J. D., & Reckers, P. M. J. (1997) The mitigation of hindsight bias in judges' evaluation of auditor decisions, *Auditing: Journal of Practice & Theory*, 16, 20–39.

Anderson, U. & Koonce, L. (1995) Explanation as a method for evaluating client-suggested causes in analytical procedures, *Auditing: Journal of Practice & Theory*, 14, 124–32.

Arkes, H. R., Faust, D., Guilmette, T. J., & Hart, K. (1998) Eliminating the hindsight bias, *Journal of Applied Psychology*, 73, 305–17.

Arthur Andersen & Co., Coopers & Lybrand, Deloitte & Touche, Ernst & Young, KPMG Peat Marwick, & Price Waterhouse. (1992) *The Liability Crisis in the United States: Impact on the Accounting Profession, A Statement of Position*. Press release August 6.

Ashton, A. & Ashton, R. H. (eds.) (1995) *Judgment and Decision-making Research in Accounting and Auditing*. New York: Cambridge University Press.

Ashton, R. H. (1974) An experimental study of internal control judgments, *Journal of Accounting Research*, 12, 143–57.

Ashton, R. H. (1982) *Human Information Processing in Accounting: Studies in Accounting Research no. 17*. Sarasota FL: American Accounting Association.

Bazerman, M. (2002) *Judgment in Managerial Decision Making* (5th edn.). New York: John Wiley & Sons.

Beasley, M. S. & Salterio, S. E. (2001) The relationship between board characteristics and voluntary improvements in audit committee composition and experience, *Contemporary Accounting Research*, 18, 539–70.

Beaver, W. H. (1998) *Financial Reporting: An Accounting Revolution*. Upper Saddle River, NJ: Prentice Hall.

Boritz, J. E. (1997) Discussion of "Debiasing framing effects in auditor's internal control judgments and testing decisions," *Contemporary Accounting Research*, 14, 79–90.

Brown, L. D. & Huefner, R. F. (1994) The familiarity with and perceived quality of accounting journals, *Contemporary Accounting Research*, 11, 223–51.

Brunswik, E. (1940) Thing constancy as measured by correlation coefficients, *Psychological Review*, 47, 69–78.

Casper, J. D., Benedict, K., & Kelly, J. R. (1988) Cognitions, attitude, and decision-making in search and seizure cases, *Journal of Applied Social Psychology*, 18, 93–113.

Chang, C. J., Yen, S. J., & Duh, R. R. (2002) An empirical examination of competing theories to explain the framing effect in accounting-related decisions, *Behavioral Research in Accounting*, 14, 35–64.

Chi, M., Glaser, R., & Farr, M. (1988) *The Nature of Expertise*. Hillsdale NJ: Lawrence Erlbaum Associates.

Cloyd, C. B. & Spilker, B. (1999) The influence of client preferences on tax professionals' search for judicial precedents, subsequent judgments, and recommendations, *The Accounting Review*, 74, 299–322.

Cloyd, C. B. & Spilker, B. (2000) Confirmation bias in tax information search: A comparison of law students and accounting students, *Journal of American Taxation Association*, 22, 60–71.

Cohen, J., Krishnamoorthy G., & Wright, A. (2002) Corporate governance and the audit process, *Contemporary Accounting Research*, 19, 573–94.

Davis, J. S. (1995) *Behavioral Tax Research: Prospects and Judgment Calls*. Sarasota, FL: American Accounting Association.

Dawes, R. M. (1979) The robust beauty of improper linear models, *American Psychologist*, 34, 571–82.

Dawes, R. M., van de Kragt, A. J. C., & Orbel, J. M. (1988) Not me or thee but we: The importance of group identity in eliciting cooperation in dilemma situations, *Acta Psychologica*, 68, 83–97.

Dearman, D. & Shields, M. (2001) Cost knowledge and cost-based judgment performance, *Journal of Management Accounting Research*, 13, 1–18.

DeZoort, F. T. & Salterio, S. E. (2001) The effects of corporate governance experience and financial-reporting and audit knowledge on audit committee members' judgments, *Auditing: Journal of Practice & Theory*, 20, 31–48.

Dilla, W. D. & Stone, D. N. (1997a) Response scales in risk judgments: The effects of representation, fineness and user choice, *Journal of Information Systems*, 11, 75–96.

Dilla, W. D. & Stone, D. N. (1997b) Representations as decision aids: The asymmetric effects of words and numbers on auditors' inherent risk judgments, *Decision Sciences*, 28, 709–44.

Einhorn, E. (1974) Expert judgment – some necessary conditions and an example, *Journal of Applied Psychology*, 59, 562–71.

Emby, C. & Finley, D. (1997) De-biasing framing effects in auditors' internal control judgments and testing, *Contemporary Accounting Research*, 14, 55–77.

Fisher, J. G., Frederickson, J. A., & Peffer, S. A. (2000) Budgeting: An experimental investigation of the effects of negotiation, *The Accounting Review*, 75, 93–115.

Gibbins, M. & Newton, J. D. (1994) An empirical exploration of complex accountability in public accounting, *Journal of Accounting Research*, 32, 165–87.

Gibbins, M., Salterio, S., & Webb, A. (2001) Evidence about auditor-client management negotiation concerning client's financial reporting, *Journal of Accounting Research*, 39, 535–63.

Goldberg, L. R. (1968) Simple models or simple processes? Some research on clinical judgments, *American Psychologist*, July, 483–96.

Hammond, K. (1955) Probabilistic functioning and the clinical method, *Psychological Review*, 62, 255–62.

Hastie, R., Schkade, D. A., & Payne, J. W. (1999) Juror judgments in civil cases: Hindsight effects on judgments of liability for punitive damages, *Law and Human Behavior*, 23, 597–614.

Hirst, D. E., Koonce, L., & Miller, J. (1999) The joint effect of management's prior forecast accuracy and the form of its financial forecasts on investor judgment, *Journal of Accounting Research*, 37, 101–24.

Hogarth, R. M. (1991) A perspective on cognitive research in auditing, *The Accounting Review*, 66, 277–90.

Hopkins, P. (1995) The effect of financial statement classification of hybrid financial instruments on financial analysts' stock price judgments, *Journal of Accounting Research*, 34, 33–50.

Joyce, E. & Biddle, G. (1981a) Anchoring and adjustment in probabilistic inference in auditing, *Journal of Accounting Research*, 19, 120–45.

Joyce, E. & Biddle, G. (1981b) Are auditors' judgments sufficiently regressive? *Journal of Accounting Research*, 19, 323–49.

Kachelmeier, S. J. & Messier, Jr., W. F. (1990) An investigation of the influence of a nonstatistical decision aid on auditor sample size decisions, *The Accounting Review*, 65, 209–26.

Kleinmuntz, B. (1990) Why we still use our heads instead of formulas: Toward an integrative approach, *Psychological Bulletin*, 107, 296–310.

Levitt, A. (1998) The numbers game. Speech delivered at NYU Center for Law and Economics, September 28.

Libby, R. (1975) Accounting ratios and the prediction of failure – some behavioral evidence, *Journal of Accounting Research*, 13, 150–61.

Libby, R. (1981) *Accounting and Human Information Processing: Theory and Applications*. Englewood Cliffs, NJ: Prentice Hall.

Libby, R. (1995) The role of knowledge and memory in audit judgment. In A. Ashton and R. H. Ashton (eds.), *Judgment and Decision-making Research in Accounting and Auditing* (pp. 176–206). New York: Cambridge University Press.

Libby, R., Bloomfield, R., & Nelson, M. W. (2002) Experimental research in financial accounting, *Accounting, Organizations and Society*, 27, 775–810.

Libby, R. & Luft, J. (1993) Determinants of judgment performance in accounting settings: Ability, knowledge, motivation, and environment, *Accounting, Organizations and Society*, 18, 425–51.

Messier, W. F., Jr., Kachelmeier, S. J., & Jensen, K. L. (2001) An experimental assessment of recent professional developments in nonstatistical audit sampling guidance, *Auditing: Journal of Practice & Theory*, 20, 81–96.

Moreno, K., Kida, T., & Smith, J. F. (2002) The impact of affective reactions on risky decision making in accounting contexts, *Journal of Accounting Research*, 40, 1331–45.

NACD (National Association of Corporate Directors) (1999) *Report and Recommendations of the Blue Ribbon Committee on Improving the Effectiveness of Corporate Audit Committees*. New York: NACD.

Owhoso, V. E., Messier, Jr., W. F., & Lynch, Jr., J. G. (2002) Error detection by industry-specialized teams during sequential audit review, *Journal of Accounting Research*, 40, 883–900.

Payne, J. W., Bettman, J. R., & Johnson, E. J. (1993) *The Adaptive Decision Maker*. New York: Cambridge University Press.

Peterson, C. R., Hammond, K. R., & Summers, D. A. (1965) Optimal responding in multi-plecue probability learning, *Journal of Experimental Psychology*, 70, 270–6.

Reimers, J., Wheeler, S., & Dusenbury, R. (1993) The effect of response mode on auditors' control risk assessments, *Auditing: A Journal of Practice & Theory*, 12, 62–78.

Sedor, L. M. (2002) An explanation for unintentional optimism in analysts' earnings forecasts, *The Accounting Review*, 77, 731–53.

Shanteau, J. (1992) Competence in experts: The role of task characteristics, *Organizational Behavior and Human Decision Processes*, 53, 95–106.

Smith, J. F. & Kida, T. (1991) Heuristics and biases: Expertise and task realism in auditing, *Psychological Bulletin*, 109, 472–89.

Solomon, I. & Trotman, K. T. (2003) Experimental judgment and decision research in auditing: The first 25 years of AOS, *Accounting, Organizations and Society*, 28, 395–412.

Sprinkle, G. B. (2003) Perspectives on experimental research in managerial accounting, *Accounting, Organizations and Society*, 28, 287–318.

Stewart. D. & Strasser, G. (1995) Expert role assignment and information sampling during collective recall and decision making, *Journal of Personality and Social Psychology*, 69, 619–28.

Stone, D. & Dilla, W. N. (1994) When numbers are better than words: The joint effects of response representation and experience on inherent risk judgments, *Auditing: A Journal of Practice & Theory*, 13 (supplement), 1–19.

Tetlock, P. E. (1985) Accountability: The neglected social context of judgment and choice, *Research in Organizational Behavior*, 7, 297–332.

Thaler, R. (1992) *The Winner's Curse: Paradoxes and Anomalies of Economic Life*. New York: Free Press.

Turner, C. W. (2001) Accountability demands and the auditor's evidence search strategy: The influence of reviewer preferences and the nature of the response (belief vs. action), *Journal of Accounting Research*, 39, 683–707.

Tversky, A. & Kahneman, D. (1974) Judgment under uncertainty: Heuristics and biases, *Science*, 185, 1124–31.

Tversky, A. & Kahneman, D. (1981) The framing of decisions and the psychology of choice, *Science*, 211, 453–8.

Vera-Muñoz, S. C., Kinney, W. R., & Bonner, S. E. (2001) The effects of domain experience and task presentation format on accountants' information relevance assurance, *The Accounting Review*, 76, 405–29.

Wallsten, T. S. (1990) The costs and benefits of vague information. In R. Hogarth (ed.), *Insights in Decision Making: Theory and Applications* (pp. 28–43). Chicago, IL: University of Chicago Press.

Wallsten, T. S., Budescu, D. V., & Zwick, R. (1993) Comparing the calibration and coherence of numerical and verbal probability judgments, *Management Science*, 39, 176–90.

Wilks, T. J. (2002) Predecisional distortion of evidence as a consequence of real-time audit review, *The Accounting Review*, 77, 51–67.

Wright, W. F. (1988) Audit judgment consensus and experience. In K. R. Ferris (ed.), *Behavioral Accounting Research: A Critical Analysis* (pp. 305–28). Columbus, OH: Century VII Publishing.

28

Heuristics, Biases, and Governance

Jeffrey J. Rachlinski

Introduction

Good judgment is essential to any well-functioning legal system. A legal system must avoid erroneously convicting the innocent, assigning arbitrary civil or criminal penalties, and adopting misguided laws. Greed, corruption, or ignorance can produce such unjust outcomes, but even well-intentioned, well-informed decision makers can make mistakes. The decision makers in the legal system – whether they are judges, juries, legislators, or bureaucrats – rely on the same kinds of cognitive processes common to all human beings. Whether cognitive processes serve legal decision makers well depends largely on whether legal processes are designed to facilitate good judgment. To produce good judgment, a well-functioning legal process must present the underlying questions to decision makers in a way that takes advantage of the virtues of human cognition and respects its limitations.

The lawmakers who design procedures governing courts, legislatures, and administrative agencies are, at best, intuitive psychologists. They operate in ignorance of the latest work in the psychology of judgment and choice and would benefit from an understanding of human psychology. Nevertheless, even without a direct understanding of cognitive psychology, courts and legislatures, just as many social institutions (Heath, Larrick, & Klayman, 1998), identify processes that produce erroneous choices and alter them to improve their judgment. Review of the self-conscious design of many legal processes, in fact, reveals a surprising attention to many of the concerns that cognitive psychologists have expressed about human judgment.

Cognitive Errors in Assigning Legal Blame

Assigning blame is a fundamental purpose of the courts. Courts must determine which criminal and civil defendants must be punished and which exonerated. The trial process, however, is an inherently difficult environment in which to make good judgments. Judges and juries must make intricate judgments about the meaning of complicated sets of evidence. Critical information needed to make an informed choice is often absent or deliberately withheld from the process. The information that is available to decision makers is presented in question-and-answer format, one witness at a time, one party at a time. Jurors especially find themselves in an unnatural setting, but even judges commonly face unfamiliar issues. The helpful mental shortcuts that both judges and juries develop to guide them through their lives outside the courtroom might lead them astray in the trial process. Rather than reflecting a careful, deliberative procedure, adjudication might consist of nothing more than "trial by heuristic" (Saks & Kidd, 1986).

Several well-known cognitive processes play a role in the assignment of culpability in the courtroom: the fundamental attribution error, the hindsight bias, and the representativeness heuristic. Although this is by no means an exhaustive list, these processes have received close attention from both psychologists and legal scholars and illustrate both how cognitive limitations can produce erroneous judgments and how procedures might respond.

The fundamental attribution error

The attribution processes common to social life likely play a central role in the assignment of responsibility at any trial. Consequently, fundamental attribution error, the tendency to over-attribute conduct to dispositional traits, rather than situational cues (Ross, 1977), can undermine the law's efforts to assess culpability. Generally, the fundamental attribution error will harm defendants, who commonly attempt to demonstrate that they are not responsible for any adverse outcome or are not responsible for their actions. The natural tendency of judges and juries, however, will be to blame people for bad outcomes, even if they could not avoid them, and to hold people responsible for their conduct, even if it was the product of duress or other situational pressures.

For example, consider the problem of coerced confessions. The failure to appreciate the power of police pressures to overwhelm an individual's volition can lead judges and juries to attribute improperly coerced confessions to a defendant's willingness to own up to a crime. Most people do not accurately recognize the circumstances that would induce innocent people to confess (Kassin, Goldstein, & Savitsky, 2003). People look for physical torture when, in fact, subtle deprivations (food, water, sleep, bathroom privileges) and aggressive questioning can also induce the innocent to confess. Many people even believe that an innocent person would never confess. This confusion can produce erroneous convictions of defendants who have falsely confessed to crimes. In fact, a number of death-row inmates who confessed their crimes have recently been exonerated through DNA evidence (Kassin et al., 2003).

Similarly, the fundamental attribution error can lead judges and jurors to judge a defendant's mental state more harshly than is appropriate (Ross & Shestowsky, 2003). Defendants who acted only negligently might be judged to have committed intentional torts. Defenses that rely on a diminished capacity to act, such as duress and insanity, might fail, even under circumstances in which the defendant should not be held responsible.

Jurors might also pay more attention to evidence concerning the character of the accused than to direct evidence of the crime and convict defendants because of a belief in their criminal proclivity rather than because of the actual evidence (Saks & Kidd, 1986).

The error can affect civil cases as well. In most accident cases, for example, a court must determine whether an ordinary person, behaving with care to avoid injury to others, would have been able to avoid causing an injury (Korobkin & Ulen, 2000). This determination requires ascribing responsibility to an unavoidable situation, or to an individual's behavior. The fundamental attribution error suggests that judges and juries will start with the presumption that an individual is responsible for their conduct, and not for situations, thereby skewing trial outcomes.

The hindsight bias

The hindsight bias (see Chapter 13, this volume) plays a pervasive role in the legal system (Rachlinski, 1998). A wide range of legal actors, from medical doctors to corporate managers, must make judgments in foresight that are assessed as reasonable or unreasonable in hindsight (Arkes & Schipani, 1994). Consider Kamin and Rachlinski's (1995) demonstration of how the bias can affect legal judgments. In their study, subjects in foresight judged whether or not undertaking an expensive safety precaution against a flood was reasonable. The participants in their study were told that the expected damage from the flood was ten times the cost of a precaution that would avoid damage from the flood. The participants were also told that the precaution was reasonable only if the likelihood of a flood in any given year exceeded ten percent. After reviewing evidence on the likelihood of the flood, 75 percent of these participants determined that the precaution was unnecessary. Participants judging in hindsight reviewed similar information, except that they were told that the defendant had declined to take the precaution and a flood had occurred, thereby costing the plaintiff ten times as much in damage as the precaution would have cost the defendant. These participants were also told that taking the precaution was reasonable only if the defendant determined that the likelihood of a flood exceeded ten percent. In hindsight, 57 percent of the subjects determined that the failure to undertake the precaution was unreasonable. Actions that seem reasonable in foresight are frequently deemed unreasonable (and negligent) in hindsight (Hastie, Schkade, & Payne, 1999a).

Not only does the bias affect jurors, it affects judges (Guthrie, Rachlinski, & Wistrich, 2001; Reckers, Jennings, & Lowe, 1997; Viscusi, 1999). Judges sometimes even display an overt reliance on hindsight in their published opinions. For example, in *First Alabama Bank v. Martin* (1982), the Alabama supreme court found evidence that a trustee had negligently managed assets in the fact that he had sold stocks "at the bottom of the market." This court failed to explain how it is that the trustee could have known that the market had bottomed out. In one infamous case in 1931, *In re Estate of Chamberlain*, a judge held a trustee liable for failing to foresee the stock market crash of 1929. The judge wrote that, "it was common knowledge, not only amongst bankers and trust companies, but the general public as well, that . . . [in early 1929, stock prices] were very much inflated and that a crash was almost sure to occur."

The hindsight bias potentially affects all kinds of legal judgments (Rachlinski, 1998). Contracting parties are only responsible for the foreseeable damages arising from a breach of contract; courts determine forseeability after the damage is done. Inventors may only patent innovations that are not "obvious"; courts assess obviousness after the invention is described. Corporate managers are liable for failing to disclose potential problems that might materially affect a company's revenue; courts determine "materiality" after events unfold. Managers of trusts are liable if they fail to invest the trust's assets in ways that are "prudent"; courts assess prudence after it becomes known how well the trustees investment strategy performed. In criminal cases, police can justify having conducted a search if they face exigent circumstances and they had "probable cause"; courts determine probable cause after the outcome of the search is known. All of these areas present opportunities for the hindsight bias to influence a court's judgment.

The representativeness heuristic and base-rate neglect

Many legal contexts require decision makers to account for the base rate at which events occur. The basic concept of "circumstantial evidence" refers to evidence that provides statistical support for an underlying proposition. Scholars have even argued that "all evidence is probabilistic" (Allen, 1986, p. 402), and that all legal factfinders implicitly rely on Bayesian analysis (Koehler, 2002). To be sure, many legal decisions are characterized by categorical, reason-based inference processes, rather than explicitly statistical reasoning (Pennington & Hastie, 1986). Nevertheless, many legal disputes explicitly require fact finders to make statistical inferences. Forensic evidence, such as hair samples, blood-type, DNA evidence, ballistics and even fingerprints, all inherently require an assessment of probabilities. If judges and juries are incapable of conducting Bayesian analysis properly (see Chapter 8, this volume), then many trials will be fraught with mistakes.

Judges and juries seem to lack the cognitive abilities necessary to make proper statistical inferences. Research on the evaluation of DNA evidence, in particular, suggests that people confuse the probability that a randomly selected sample would match the target sample with the probability that the defendant is innocent (Thompson, 1989). For example, if a DNA sample known to be from the perpetrator would match one in one million randomly selected individuals, and it matches the defendant, a factfinding committing this fallacy would conclude that the odds that the defendant is innocent are one in one million (and presumably convict). This reasoning process has been termed the "prosecutor's fallacy," not only because the prosecution would benefit from it, but also because prosecutors would tend to encourage this kind of thinking in the arguments that they might make to juries (Thompson & Schumann, 1987). Such efforts might not always be successful, however. Similar research reveals that many people commit a "defense attorney's fallacy," concluding that since there are clearly a number of innocent people who would match the sample, the statistical forensic evidence is irrelevant (Thompson & Schumann, 1987).

Other difficulties undermine people's evaluation of probabilistic evidence. In evaluating forensic evidence, people are remarkably insensitive to the probability that an innocent sample would match a perpetrator. In one study, participants found evidence that a sample would match one in one million randomly selected individuals to be equally persuasive as a sample that would match one in one billion randomly selected people and one that would match one in one trillion randomly selected people (Koehler, 1997). People are also sensitive to subtle changes in the format in which probabilistic evidence is presented. Evidence presented in subject format (e.g., 0.1 percent of a randomly selected person matching) leads mock jurors to be more certain of the defendant's guilt than the same evidence presented in a frequentist format (e.g., one in one thousand randomly selected people would match) (Koehler, 2001). Identifying a specific sample (e.g., one in one thousand people in Houston would match at random), further increases confidence in the defendant's guilt (Koehler, 2001). In a similar study, evidence of the likelihood that a mentally disturbed offender will commit a violent act presented in frequentist format (e.g., "20 in 100 such patients commit a violent act") leads both psychiatrists and judges to be more willing to involuntarily commit such a patient than the same evidence presented in subjective probability format (e.g, "20 percent of such patients commit a violent act") (Monahan & Slovic, 1995). Thus, when evaluating probabilistic evidence, people both ignore important aspects of the evidence (such as the probability of a random match) and attend to irrelevant aspects (such as the presentation format).

Judges also seem unable to evaluate statistical evidence properly. For example, for decades, in accident cases, courts would presume that a defendant's conduct was negligent upon a showing that the plaintiff's injury is of the type that does not occur when reasonable care is taken (Dobbs, 2000). This doctrine, known as *res ipsa loquitur*, incorporates a logical fallacy into accident law. Showing that an injury does not occur when reasonable care is taken does not provide evidence of negligence unless such a showing is also accompanied by evidence that negligent conduct is more likely to produce the injury than non-negligent conduct. Even then, the mere fact of an injury does not mean that the injury is more likely than not the product of negligence. In circumstances in which negligence is uncommon, the more likely conclusion is that the injury was the unusual result of a common occurrence (non-negligence) than the usual result of a very uncommon occurrence (Kaye, 1979). The situation resembles that of the well-known "rare disease problem," in which the appropriate conclusion to draw from a positive result from a highly diagnostic test for a rare disease is that the patient is unlikely to have the disease (Casscells, Schoenberger, & Greyboys, 1978). Recent reform efforts from the American Law Institute (a group of distinguished academics, judges, and practitioners) have led to a correction of the doctrine's formulation (ALI, 1998). Before this effort, however, courts in both the United States and England maintained and applied this fallacious formulation of *res ipsa loquitur* for well over a century.

Cognitive Errors in Measuring the Extent of Harm

In addition to assigning culpability, the legal system must also measure the degree of liability. In civil cases, judges and juries must commonly convert ephemeral assessments of qualitative harms into quantitative damage awards. Judges and juries must convert non-economic damages for pain and suffering into dollars. Similarly, in cases in which a jury determines that conduct is sufficiently reckless, it must determine a dollar amount of punitive damages that adequately expresses the outrage of a community to punish the reckless conduct. In criminal cases, judges must translate a community's outrage at a crime into a numeric prison sentence. Recent research on the subject has revealed the process to be quite difficult, and subject to several deleterious influences.

Most people are familiar with translating preferences into dollars. All consumers must make such determinations as to whether a slice of pizza is worth $2.50, or whether a new car is worth $25,000. Only rarely, however, must people translate their outrage at a corporation's misconduct into a dollar damage award, or their sense of wrong into a prison term. As Sunstein, Kahneman, and Schkade (1998) have observed, translating legally relevant concepts into dollars is similar to that observed in any psychometric case in which people must translate any quantitative sensation into a numeric scale. For such translations to produce reliable results, people need a fixed referent, or a modulus. Courts, however, do not provide juries with a fixed referent or a modulus.

Translating legal judgments into dollars without a fixed modulus can produce erratic dollar awards. Without having access to a sensible means of converting pain into dollars, jurors who vary only slightly in their sense of how distressing a broken arm might be are as likely to award $5,000 as $50,000 (Sunstein et al., 1998). The erratic nature of this translation is evident in the ubiquitous finding that jury damage awards are positively skewed (Eisenberg, Goerdt, Ostrum, Rottman, &Wells, 1997). It also produces damage awards that are unreliable. In a demonstration of this, Sunstein et al. (1998) asked jury-eligible adults to assess 20 different fact patterns. The participants were to identify an appropriate damage award and assess the relative outrageousness of the underlying conduct. The assessments of the outrageousness of the conduct were well ordered; particip-ants' ratings correlated highly with those of other participants. The correlation coefficient of damage awards among participants, however, was essentially zero.

Studies of real damage awards by real juries support these conclusions. In a study involving the results from hundreds of actual trials, Eisenberg and his colleagues (1997) found that even though the log of punitive damage awards correlated highly with the log of compensatory awards, raw dollar awards were still unpredictable. For example, the authors note that in a case with a compensatory award of $1 million, the ninety-five percent confidence interval for a predicted punitive damage award is $15,000 to $10.7 million. This result demonstrates that punitive damages are a direct, logarithmic func-tion of the amount of harm that jurors feel that the defendant has inflicted. Jurors, it seems, have a strong ordinal sense of physical harm and outrageous conduct, but trans-late this sense into dollars in an erratic fashion.

The cognitive difficulties associated with translating qualitative judgments into quan-titative ones also leave judges and juries vulnerable to potentially undesirable cognitive influences, particularly anchoring (see Chapter 12, this volume). Several studies of mock juries show a strong tendency for these juries to rely on numeric anchors to guide their determination of damage awards (Chapman & Bornstein, 1996; Hastie, Schkade, & Payne, 1999b; Hinsz & Indahl, 1995; Malouff & Schutte, 1989). In one study, the mean award depended heavily on the damage request made by the plaintiff's attorney, even though the researchers used everything from an implausibly low anchor ($100) to an implausibly high anchor ($1 billion) (Chapman & Bornstein, 1996). The high requests made mock jurors view the plaintiff as greedy and unreasonable, but these requests nevertheless increased the award. The title of this paper says it all: "The more you ask for, the more you get."

The trial process itself can generate misleading anchors other than just a request by a self-serving plaintiff's attorney. Many states have adopted statutory maximum damages, referred to as "damage caps" (Sunstein, Kahneman, Schkade & Ritov, 2002). Damage caps generally apply to non-economic awards, such as pain and suffering or punitive damages, and are often specific to one or more types of lawsuit – most commonly, medical malpractice. Legislatures create damage caps to facilitate predictability in damage awards by creating an outer boundary for awards, but damage caps might also have the unintended effect of introducing a cognitive anchor. Absent anchoring, the addition of a damage cap to jury instructions should truncate awards abruptly at the cap, but leave most of the distribution of damage awards unaffected. Mock-jury studies, however, show that the addition of a damage cap affects the entire distribution of awards (Robbennolt & Studebaker, 1999). A damage cap that is low relative to the uncapped awards compresses the distribution of awards down. A damage cap that is high relative to the uncapped awards stretches the distribution of awards up.

In a quest for some sort of information to ground a sensible conversion of qualitative judgments into dollars, legal factfinders look for meaningful contrasts. Consider the following example from a recent study by Sunstein et al. (2002). These researchers asked individuals to assign an appropriate punitive damage award in a case involving either financial fraud or physical injury caused by a defective product. The cases also varied in the degree of outrageousness of the conduct that led to the injury, although the authors kept the amount of harm done constant. The outrageous fraud case, evaluated on its own, presented conduct that seemed much more outrageous to the participants in the study than they would have expected for a fraud case, thereby inducing them to penalize the conduct heavily. In contrast, the less egregious personal-injury case, evaluated on its own, presented conduct that seemed much less outrageous to the participants than they would have expected for a personal-injury case, thereby inducing them to assign lenient penalties. When participants evaluated the cases together, however, they recognized that causing physical injuries is generally more outrageous than committing fraud, and so they assigned higher damage awards to the personal injury case than to the fraud case. The study thus suggests that when people generate numeric damage estimates, they look for some sort of fixed reference to which to compare their case. Consequently, switching the natural reference class changed the award (see also, Chapter 18, this volume). Similar phenomena have been identified both in real cases (Eisenberg, Rachlinski, & Wells, 2002) and in criminal sentences (Rachlinski & Jourden, 2003).

The lack of a fixed reference point can render legal judgments vulnerable to other manipulations as well, such as compromise effects. Kelman, Rottenstreich, and Tversky (1996) showed that in determining a defendant's criminal culpability, judgments depend heavily upon the range of available alternatives. In a series of studies, these researchers found that people deciding whether a defendant's conduct constituted murder or manslaughter were influenced by whether a more harsh verdict (murder with special circumstances) was available. Making a more serious sentence category available increased the proportion of subjects who selected murder as the appropriate verdict, relative to the number who selected manslaughter. In effect, increasing the range of available verdict alternatives stretched the scale upon which subjects measured defendants' conduct, causing them to judge it more harshly. Similar results were obtained by Koch and Devine (1999), although these authors found that giving jurors detailed instructions as to how to decide the case mitigated the effect.

These cognitive difficulties also support the folk intuition that juries have a good sense of what an appropriate award might be, but can get led astray in the actual calculation. One study showed that mock-juries provide higher damage awards when jury instructions break up the elements of an award into separate components (Poser, Bornstein, & McGorty, 2003). In the study, all jurors were instructed to include "loss of enjoyment of life" as part of a damage award, but when jurors had to separately identify the amount for this element, the overall award increased. Similarly, several studies show that mock jurors conflate determinations of fault and determinations of the extent of damages (Darley & Huff, 1990; Greene, Johns, & Bowman, 1999). Consequently, when jurors cannot award punitive damages, they award greater compensatory damages, especially in the face of outrageous conduct by the defendant (Anderson & MacCoun, 1999; Greene, Coon, & Bornstein, 2001; Robbennolt, 2002).

Translating qualitative legal judgments into quantitative amounts thus seems to be one of the most difficult aspects of the trial process. Jurors seem to be engaged in a search for any means of making the process tractable, whether it is finding anchors or identifying referent cases. Even though these efforts reveal conscientious and rational efforts to make sense of the task, they also leave the trial process vulnerable to undesirable influences.

Cognitive Errors in the Democratic Process

Cognitive processes also influence the creation and development of law. As the development of the *res ipsa loquitur* doctrine indicates, judges can rely on misleading cognitive processes when developing law. Absent safeguards, legislatures and administrative agencies might do the same. In a democratic system, this can occur either because cognitive processes influence public demand for regulation (see also, Chapter 30, this volume) or because the regulators themselves suffer from cognitive errors.

In a democratic system, it should not be surprising that the demand for legislative action reflects how people think about social problems. The cognitive processes that guide how people assess problems and legislative responses produce the policy preferences that shape the political process. Because many social problems are vastly complicated and most citizens have limited time and interest in their resolution, people's political preferences are apt to be heavily influenced by simple heuristics. Simple heuristics might influence choice in the voting booth, decisions on campaign contributions, and lobbying efforts, all of which put pressure on legislatures. Although people doubtless adopt a variety of mental shortcuts when evaluating social choices, legal scholars have worried most about the role of cognitive availability and framing effects in how public opinion shapes the demand for law.

Availability and public policy

The availability heuristic plays a central role in modern political life (Kuran & Sunstein, 1999). To estimate the extent to which social problems are widespread and in need of redress, people rely on cognitive availability. As Slovic, Fischhoff, and Lichtenstein (1982) documented, news media coverage of risks increases public perception of the degree of danger associated with those risks. In turn, the public perception that a crisis exists drives legislative and regulatory responses, even when evidence of a crisis is uncertain and even when the responses are of questionable benefits.

For example, the perception that jury verdicts are out of control arises largely from widespread reports of exorbitant jury awards. The case in which an elderly woman won a \$4 million damage award for a burn she sustained after spilling hot McDonalds' coffee on herself has achieved almost legendary status for proponents of tort reform (Eisenberg, 2001). Doctors and legislators also frequently cite exorbitant awards as causing increases in insurance premiums. Support for these efforts comes from the perception that jury damage awards are out of control. Public opinion on this issue, however, seems unaffected by the underlying facts and statistics. Studies of the tort system in general show that extremely high awards are rare exceptions from the sobering mass of sane and sensible jury verdicts (Eisenberg, 2001). Nevertheless, people assume that exorbitant awards are the norm, and not the exception.

Similar processes affect public perception of all manner of social risks. When a memorable event grabs the attention of the public, it drives legislative efforts (Kuran & Sunstein, 1999). For example, although the United States Congress had considered adopting legislation to address the problem of abandoned hazardous-waste dumps for many years, it took the publicity of the events at Love Canal, New York, before Congress finally acted (Kuran & Sunstein, 1999). At Love Canal, a school and a residential neighborhood had been constructed on an abandoned waste-disposal site containing a huge volume of hazardous chemicals. Dramatic media coverage of the events created a public sense that abandoned hazardous waste-disposal facilities were widespread, thereby making a legislative response to the problem irresistible.

To be sure, cognitive availability might play a constructive role by directing public attention to issues that need greater public attention. For example, the mismanagement and fraud at the Enron Corporation properly highlighted a real need for legislative reform of the corporate accounting system. The availability heuristic can also create legislative pressures that overcome the power of entrenched interest groups and a stubbornly slow legislative process. Arguably, the events at Love Canal produced a positive outcome by breaking a legislative logjam that had held up needed reforms.

The net influence of the availability heuristic on legislative action, however, is probably negative. Widespread reliance on the availability heuristic by the general public makes public opinion easy to manipulate. Interest groups might act as "availability entrepreneurs," working to make certain anecdotes salient (Kuran & Sunstein, 1999). Availability entrepreneurs try to make news events salient so as to mobilize public opinion in favor of legislation that furthers their own ends. Politicians and news reporters might also work to convince the public that an issue is a problem, solely to direct attention to themselves. Furthermore, cognitive availability is fleeting. Even in instances in which the salience of a health or safety risk reflects a serious underlying hazard, the public's attention might drift off the topic long before social institutions can craft and adopt a coherent regulatory response. As the public loses interest in the problem, well-heeled lobbyists serving special interests can coopt a lengthy legislative drive for reform, and "strike while the iron is cold" (Noll & Krier, 1991). Finally, the underlying story that drives public beliefs might simply be wrong, thereby misdirecting legislative effort. Erroneous anecdotes can persist for surprising periods in public life (Heath, Bell, & Sternberg, 2001). Even the facts in the McDonalds case are misleading – the plaintiff ultimately settled for a mere $40,000. Thus, the availability heuristic has more potential for harm than good in a democratic process.

Framing and legislation

The character of public choices as involving gains or losses also influences legislative activity (see Chapter 19, this volume). Individuals or corporations affected by legislative decisions treat lost opportunities as less costly than incurred losses. Consequently, they can be expected to fight harder against legislation that imposes losses on them than in favor of legislation that would provide benefits.

Perhaps no other aspect of public decision making illustrates the role of framing in legislation more than revenue policies. Individuals react more negatively to tax increases than positively to tax decreases (McCaffery, 1994). This can make it difficult for the government to increase its revenue stream to accommodate new missions and new mandates. Often, the only way that the government can increase revenue is through a refusal to update the tax code to reflect inflation. In an inflationary economy, unless the government raises the tax bracket cutoffs to match increases in wages and prices, the actual tax rate will rise. Furthermore, the revenue code is filled with caps and phase-outs on deductions for wealthier taxpayers. If the income level at which these restrictions apply does not rise with inflation, it will also produce "hidden" tax increases. Changes in public revenue end up determined more by the interaction of inflation with quirks in the tax code than by informed legislative discussion over the appropriate size of government programs.

Numerous laws outside of the tax code evidence an unwillingness to impose new costs on existing individuals and corporations. In the 1970s, as Congress began passing tough environmental regulations requiring compliance with strict new pollution permits, it simultaneously exempted existing polluters from such regimes (Salzman & Thompson, 2003). For example, those who would build new electric-generating facilities must incorporate the most stringent pollution-control technologies available, while little is required of existing plants. Similarly, even as new pesticide regulations simultaneously imposed careful restrictions on the sale of new forms of pesticides, the same regulations made it nearly impossible for regulators to ban the sale of pesticides already in use. The aversion to losses among polluters might have made such compromises an essential part of modern environmental law, but these compromises have had the effect of "freezing" technology in place and placing new pollution-saving innovations at an extreme competitive disadvantage against existing technologies (Salzman & Thompson, 2003).

Biases Among Public Officials

Erroneous judgment is not exclusive to the general public. Legislators and bureaucrats might also be prone to rely excessively on misleading heuristics. Although neither group has received much direct study by psychologists, the conditions under which they operate are ripe for producing certain predictable errors in judgment.

Legislators, in particular, face a cognitively difficult job that almost certainly forces them to rely on mental shortcuts. Legislators must take positions on hundreds of pieces of legislation each year, each of which might address issues of staggering complexity. The annual Federal budget alone requires 13 separate appropriations requests, each thousands of pages long. At the same time, legislators must balance the desires of a bewildering diversity of demands from their constituents, voters, and contributors. They could not help but rely on mental shortcuts.

This process might exacerbate the effect of errors among the general public on legislation. Legislators rely on polls or focus groups, which can be inaccurate barometers of public opinion, to identify the public's beliefs and concern. Focus groups produce results based on extremely small samples, and polls produce results that can be extremely sensitive to the form of the question or to recent events. These methods can magnify the biases among the general public, leading legislators to react in an exaggerated fashion to public mistakes. In a kind of "base-rate neglect," legislators might fail to appreciate that they should discount the results of surveys and focus groups as somewhat unreliable. This process thereby magnifies the impact of transient or erroneous attitudes among the public on legislative policy.

Bureaucrats working in administrative agencies have an easier cognitive mission than legislators. They tend to be experts who can focus their attention on a narrow problem, rather than generalists who must adopt a position on all public issues. Delegating public decisions to expert bureaucratic bodies, however, will not avoid erroneous judgment (Camerer & Johnson, 1991). Experts know more than lay persons, but expertise can introduce its own biases (see Chapter 15, this volume). First, experts tend to be overconfident in their judgment (see Chapter 9, this volume). The literature on overconfidence predicts that experts' estimates of outcomes will be more accurate than those of lay persons, but that experts' confidence interval around such estimates will be too narrow (Koehler, Brenner, & Griffin, 2002). Many heath, safety, and environmental statutes require experts to build caution into their predictions, and overconfidence might undermine this process. For example, the Clean Air Act directs the Environmental Protection Agency (EPA) to protect the public health with an adequate margin of safety (Salzman & Thompson, 2003). To fulfill this mandate, the EPA must estimate the harms that ambient levels of air pollutants might cause as well as identify the functional equivalent of a confidence interval around this estimate, so as to ensure that most people are not adversely affected by air pollution.

Second, expertise can create myopia (Camerer & Johnson, 1991). All disciplines adopt their own goals that focus attention on some aspects of a problem at the expense of others. For example, doctors rarely worry about a patient's financial condition, and accountants spend little energy determining their client's health. Government bureaucrats are thought to suffer from similar problems. Developing an expertise sometimes can dictate the types of solutions that bureaucrats adopt, limiting the kinds of solutions Federal agencies might pursue (Rachlinski & Farina, 2002). For example, in the 1970s engineers in the EPA adopted regulations that required the installation of expensive pollution-control technology to reduce sulfur dioxide emissions among power plants, even though adopting better economic incentives to alter production processes would have reduced emissions more and cost less (Ackerman & Hassler, 1981).

In one of the few attempts by psychologists to study bureaucratic choice directly, Sunstein and his colleagues identified another manifestation of regulatory myopia (Sunstein et al., 2002). Just as individual juries fail to see the case before them in a broader context, so too might regulators. Agencies that set civil and criminal penalties for violations of the regulations that they enforce might create penalty schedules that fail to match the violations well. For example, the Fish and Wildlife Service probably views a deliberate, illegal killing of a grizzly bear as a more serious crime than the public at large. For the Fish and Wildlife Service, such an act would be among the most serious crimes within its jurisdiction. While most people would likely view the act as less serious than a minor violation of food-safety regulations that leads to severe illness among a few consumers, the Food and Drug Administration might view the food-safety violation as among the less serious crimes it reviews. Consequently, the deliberate killing of the bear might be penalized more heavily than the food-safety violation. In a preliminary assessment of this issue, Sunstein and his coauthors have found some indication that inter-agency myopia creates exactly these kinds of inconsistencies (Sunstein et al., 2002).

Adaptations in the Law

The courts, legislatures, and administrative agencies have had extensive experience with human judgment and how it might go astray. It would be surprising if these entities have failed to make some adjustments in their decision-making processes to accommodate the strengths and weaknesses of human cognition and "debias" the process (see Chapter 16, this volume). For example, it would be astonishing if, after centuries of decisions made in hindsight, courts had failed to notice the influence of the hindsight bias (Rachlinski, 1998). Careful review of legal decision-making processes, in fact, reveals that many such accommodations exist.

Adaptations in the courts

Courts have adopted several rules meant to avoid the undesirable influence of several of the cognitive processes that could lead to erroneous decisions in the courts. In several contexts, the courts have identified the influence of the fundamental attribution error and the hindsight bias. Several aspects of the trial process are also designed to address some of the difficulties associated with converting qualitative into quantitative judgments.

Courts seem to have recognized the influence of the fundamental attribution error on judgment, in at least some limited contexts. For example, courts severely limit the admissibility of evidence that might encourage erroneous judgments concerning a party's character (Korobkin & Ulen, 2000). These rules include limitations on the admissibility of a party's past criminal convictions, especially in criminal cases, and restrictions on the admissibility of victims' sexual history in rape cases. Similarly, in products liability cases, manufacturers are responsible for the foreseeable misuse of their products; in effect, courts impose greater responsibility on manufacturers, who control the environment in which a product gets used, than on consumers, who might be mistakenly perceived as clumsy by juries (Rachlinski, 2003).

The existence of an "entrapment" defense in criminal law shows a particularly astute accommodation of concerns about the fundamental attribution error into legal doctrine (Borgida & Park, 1988). In cases in which the police have lured a defendant into committing the crime, the defendant may argue that the police arrangement was unduly coercive. The defense arises from a concern that, given sufficient resources, the police could induce almost anyone to commit a crime. To defend ordinarily innocent citizens from this potential for police excess, the courts exonerate a defendant who can show that his or her illegal conduct was largely the product of the circumstances that the police had arranged and the defendant's proclivity to commit crime. The entrapment defense thus prevents the police from targeting ordinary citizens unlikely to break the law. The existence of such a defense demonstrates the ability of courts to recognize the power of situations to make otherwise law-abiding individuals into criminals.

A review of several areas of law reveals numerous legal doctrines that attempt to correct for the hindsight bias (Rachlinski, 1998). In civil cases, even though the standard for liability is generally one of reasonableness judged by the court, courts try to judge civil defendants' conduct by standards available before the adverse event occurred. For example, in medical malpractice cases, judges and jurors do not assess the reasonableness of a doctor's treatment. Rather, they assess whether the doctor provided treatment consistent with customary medical care. Similarly, in patent cases, courts do not assess whether an invention is "obvious" on its face. Rather, courts look for other factors that are less subject to hindsight problems, such as whether an invention enjoyed immediate commercial success, or fulfilled a long-felt, unresolved need. Concern with the hindsight bias might be so extreme in some circumstances, that the courts completely distrust their own judgment. For example, courts will not hold corporate managers liable for negligent mismanagement, because they are concerned about the effects of hindsight on judging business decision in hindsight.

The legal system also incorporates some limited measures to correct for the cognitive difficulty a jury might have translating its qualitative judgments into a quantitative damage award. Jury damage awards are subject to review, and are frequently overturned when they exceed ten times the compensatory award (Eisenberg & Wells, 1999). In criminal cases, in which a judge must translate a sense of justice into a prison term, legislatures and prosecutors provide narrow guidelines (which are, in some cases, mandatory)

(Guthrie et al., 2001). The end product of the legal system might be more coherent than the underlying cognitive processes suggest.

Adapting to errors in public perception

In some cases, the erroneous judgments that people make as part of a democratic system might be sufficiently troublesome that the democratic process has to be shielded from itself. If availability cascades predictably sweep away good judgment for inflamed passions, then it would be best not to cement public misconceptions into legislative actions. Sound, stable governmental systems, in fact, incorporate mechanisms designed to slow or re-direct legislative processes when the public seems misinformed (Rachlinski & Farina, 2002). For example, the American Constitution requires the assent of two separate legislative houses plus the President (or a super-majority of the legislature) before legislation can be adopted. This takes time, allowing for public passions to settle, and it means that several different perspectives play a role in any legislative effort.

Many legislative actions only have effect to the extent to which they are administered by agencies. This delay provides several other safeguards against misguided legislation (Rachlinski & Farina, 2002). First, the bureaucratic agencies are filled with experts, who might override the judgment of the public (Sunstein, 2000). Second, some agencies operate as "independent" agencies, which are run by people who have some measure of tenure. If the public misunderstands risk and demands misguided regulation, then arguably, regulatory choices should be as removed from the representative structure of the government as possible. Thus, locating regulatory choices in independent agencies might produce more rational regulation than locating these choices in the politically accountable agencies, as is now the case.

Limiting errors in legislatures and bureaucratic agencies

The concern that agency experts suffer from myopia has motivated a number of reforms of the regulatory state. The adoption of the National Environmental Policy Act in the United States in 1970 is a prime example. This statue requires every Federal agency to submit major projects to a review intended to identify their environmental impact. These reviews are meant to break agencies out of a myopic focus on their principle mission and force them to factor environmental harms into their actions. Although the success of this statute is uncertain, the adoption of this measure demonstrates government's concern with agency myopia. Furthermore, it is among the most widely copied American environmental statute among other countries, thereby suggesting that many nations have similar problems with their own bureaucracies.

Similar concerns with agency myopia have motivated the rise of centralized review of agency action within the executive branch by a specialized agency – the Office of Regulatory Impact Assessment within the Office of Management and Budget (Sunstein, 2000). Pursuant to executive orders issued by a series of Presidents, this office conducts cost–benefit analyses of regulatory initiatives, with the goal of forcing agencies to consider the impact of their actions on the economy at large. Centralized review, whether conducted through statutory mandates or supervision by the executive branch, is meant to combat agency myopia.

Judicial review of the decisions administrative agencies make can also be characterized as a means of combating cognitive error (Seidenfeld, 2002). In the United States, courts review agency decisions to ensure that they are not "arbitrary and capricious." In practice, this review means that agencies must be able to explain their actions to judges. Because judges typically lack expertise in the area of regulation, this review essentially means that the agency experts must be able to support their position with arguments acceptable to lay persons, in an adversarial setting. Although many scholars and judges have criticized this review, arguing that it substitutes the judgments of lay persons for experts, the review process has virtues. Arguably, judicial review of agencies simulates some of the common strategies psychologists have developed to counteract overconfidence. Forcing oneself to explain one's beliefs to others while reviewing alternative arguments provides some means of combating overconfidence (Seidenfeld, 2001). Thus, in developing the process of reviewing administrative agencies, courts have essentially mimicked a common debiasing procedure.

Conclusion

Society must design its legal institutions so as to respect the strengths and the limitations of human cognition. The procedures by which legal decisions get made can either accommodate human cognition or produce erroneous choices. Understanding contemporary cognitive psychology thus provides an important link in understanding the operation of law. In particular, understanding the circumstances that are likely to produce erroneous or misleading conclusions also identifies aspects of the legal system that are likely to produce undesirable outcomes. To a surprising extent, courts, legislatures, and bureaucratic agencies have identified sources of erroneous judgment and made some correction for them. But the corrections are incomplete. Many areas of law could benefit from incorporating the less obvious lessons of cognitive psychology. Without attention to cognitive psychology, any society will be governed by heuristic, rather than by the rule of law.

References

Ackerman, B. A. & Hassler, W. T. (1981) *Clean Coal/Dirty Air: Or How the Clean Air Act Became a Multibillion-dollar Bail-out for High-sulfur Coal Producers and What Should Be Done About It.* New Haven: Yale University Press.

Allen, R. J. (1986) A reconceptualization of civil trials, *Boston University Law Review,* 66, 401–37.

American Law Institute (1998) *Restatement (Third) of Torts (Council Draft No. 1, Sept. 25, 1998).* Philadelphia: American Law Institute.

Anderson, M. C. & MacCoun, R. J. (1999) Goal conflict in juror assessment of compensatory and punitive damages, *Law and Human Behavior,* 23, 313–30.

Arkes, H. R. & Schipani, C. A. (1994) Medical malpractice v. the business judgment rule: Differences in hindsight bias, *Oregon Law Review*, 73, 587–638.

Borgida, E. & Park, R. (1988) The entrapment defense: Juror comprehension and decision making, *Law and Human Behavior*, 12, 19–40.

Camerer, C. F. & Johnson, E. J. (1991) The process–performance paradox in expert judgment: How can experts know so much and predict so badly? In K. A. Ericsson and J. Smith (eds.), *Toward a General Theory of Expertise: Prospects and Limits* (pp. 195–217). New York: Cambridge University Press.

Casscells, W., Schoenberger, A., & Greyboys, T. (1978) Interpretation by physicians of clinical laboratory results, *New England Journal of Medicine*, 299, 999–1000.

Chapman, G. B. & Bornstein, B. H. (1996) The more you ask for the more you get: Anchoring in personal injury verdicts, *Applied Cognitive Psychology*, 10, 519–40.

Darley, J. M. & Huff, C. W. (1990) Heightened damage assessment as a result of the intentionality of the damage-causing act, *British Journal of Social Psychology*, 29, 181–8.

Dobbs, D. B. (2000) *The Law of Torts*. St. Paul: West.

Eisenberg, T. (2001) Damage awards in perspective: Behind the headline-grabbing awards in *Exxon Valdez* and *Engle*, *Wake Forest Law Review*, 36, 1129–55.

Eisenberg, T., Goerdt, J., Ostrum, B., Rottman, D., & Wells, M. T. (1997) The predictability of punitive damages, *The Journal of Legal Studies*, 26, 623–61.

Eisenberg, T., Rachlinski, J. J., & Wells, M. T. (2002) Reconciling experimental incoherence with real-world coherence in punitive damages, *Stanford Law Review*, 54, 1239–71.

Eisenberg, T. & Wells, M. T. (1999) The predictability of punitive damages awards in published opinions, the impact of *BMW v. Gore* on punitive damages awards, and forecasting which punitive awards will be reduced, *The Supreme Court Economic Review*, 7, 59–86.

Greene, E., Coon, D., & Bornstein, B. (2001) The effects of limiting punitive damage awards, *Law and Human Behavior*, 25, 217–34.

Greene, E., Johns, M., & Bowman, J. (1999) The effects of injury severity on jury negligence decisions, *Law and Human Behavior*, 23, 675–94.

Guthrie, C., Rachlinski, J. J., & Wistrich, A. J. (2001) Inside the judicial mind, *Cornell Law Review*, 86, 777–830.

Hastie, R., Schkade, D. A., & Payne, J. W. (1999a) Hindsight effects on judgments of liability for punitive damages, *Law & Human Behavior*, 23, 597–614.

Hastie, R., Schkade, D. A., & Payne, J. W. (1999b) Juror judgments in civil cases: Effects of plaintiff's requests and plaintiff's identity on punitive damage awards, *Law & Human Behavior*, 23, 445–70.

Heath, C., Bell, C., & Sternberg, E. (2001) Emotional selection in memes: The case of urban legends, *Journal of Personality and Social Psychology*, 81, 1028–41.

Heath, C., Larrick, R. P., & Klayman, J. (1998) Cognitive repairs: How organizational practices can compensate for individual shortcomings, *Research in Organizational Behavior*, 20, 1–37.

Hinsz, V. B. & Indahl, K. E. (1995) Assimilation to anchors for damage awards in a mock civil trial, *Journal of Applied Social Psychology*, 25, 991–1026.

Kamin, K. A. & Rachlinski, J. J. (1995) Ex ante ≠ ex post: Determining liability in hindsight, *Law and Human Behavior*, 19, 89–104.

Kassin, S. M., Goldstein, C. C., & Savitsky, K. (2003) Behavioral confirmation in the interrogation room: On the dangers of presuming guilt, *Law and Human Behavior*, 27, 187–203.

Kaye, D. (1979) Probability Theory meets res ipsa loquitur, *Michigan Law Review*, 77, 1456–84.

Kelman, M., Rottenstreich, Y., & Tversky, A. (1996) Context-dependence in legal decision making, *Journal of Legal Studies*, 25, 287–318.

Koch, C. M. & Devine, D. J. (1999) Effects of reasonable doubt definition and inclusion of a lesser charge on jury verdicts, *Law and Human Behavior*, 23, 653–74.

Koehler, D. J., Brenner, L., & Griffin, D. (2002) The calibration of expert judgment: Heuristics and biases beyond the laboratory. In T. Gilovich, D. Griffin, & D. Kahneman (eds.), *Heuristics and Biases: The Psychology of Intuitive Judgment* (pp. 686–715). Cambridge: Cambridge University Press.

Koehler, J. J. (1997) One in millions, billions and trillions: Lessons from *People v. Collins* (1968) for *People v. Simpson* (1995), *Journal of Legal Education*, 47, 214–23.

Koehler, J. J. (2001) The psychology of numbers in the courtroom: How to make DNA match statistics seem impressive or insufficient, *Southern California Law Review*, 74, 1275–306.

Koehler, J. J. (2002) When do courts think base-rate statistics are relevant? *Jurimetrics Journal*, 42, 373–402.

Korobkin, R. B. & Ulen, T. S. (2000) Law and behavioral science: Removing the rationality assumption from law and economics, *California Law Review*, 88, 1051–144.

Kuran, T. & Sunstein, C. R. (1999) Availability cascades and risk regulation, *Stanford Law Review*, 51, 683–768.

Malouff, J. & Schutte, N. S. (1989) Shaping juror attitudes: Effects of requesting different damage amounts in personal injury trials, *Journal of Social Psychology*, 129, 491–7.

McCaffery, E. J. (1994) Cognitive theory and tax, *UCLA Law Review*, 41, 1861–947.

Monahan, J. & Slovic, P. (1995) Probability, danger, and coercion: A study of risk perception and decision making in mental health law, *Law & Human Behavior*, 19, 49–65.

Noll, R. G. & Krier, J. E. (1991) Some implications of cognitive psychology for risk regulation, *Journal of Legal Studies*, 19, 747–80.

Pennington, N. & Hastie, R. (1986) Evidence evaluation in complex decision making, *Journal of Personality and Social Psychology*, 51, 242–58.

Poser, S., Bornstein, B. H., & McGorty, E. K. (2003) Measuring damages for lost enjoyment of life: The view from the bench and the jury box, *Law and Human Behavior*, 27, 53–68.

Rachlinski, J. J. (1998) A positive psychological theory of judging in hindsight, *University of Chicago Law Review*, 65, 571–625.

Rachlinski, J. J. (2003) Misunderstanding ability, misallocating responsibility, *Brooklyn Law Review*, 68, 1055–91.

Rachlinski, J. J. & Farina, C. R. (2002) Cognitive psychology and optimal governmental design, *Cornell Law Review*, 87, 549–615.

Rachlinski, J. J. & Jourden, F. (2003) The cognitive components of punishment, *Cornell Law Review*, 88, 457–85.

Reckers, P., Jennings, M., & Lowe, D. J. (1997) The mitigation of the hindsight bias in judges' evaluations of auditor decisions, *Auditing: A Journal of Practice and Theory*, 16, 20–39.

Robbennolt, J. K. (2002) Punitive damage decision making: The decisions of citizens and trial court judges, *Law and Human Behavior*, 26, 315–42.

Robbennolt, J. K. & Studebaker, C. A. (1999) Anchoring in the courtroom: The effects of caps on punitive damages, *Law & Human Behavior*, 23, 353–73.

Ross, L. (1977) The intuitive psychologist and his shortcomings. In L. Berkowitz (ed.), *Advances in Experimental Social Psychology*, vol. 10 (pp. 174–214). New York: Academic Press.

Ross, L. & Shestowsky, D. (2003) Contemporary psychology's challenge to legal theory and practice, *Northwestern University Law Review*, 97, 1081–114.

Saks, M. J. & Kidd, R. F. (1986) Human information processing and adjudication: Trial by heuristic. In H. R. Arkes & K. R. Hammond (eds.), *Judgment and Decision Making: An Interdisciplinary Reader* (pp. 211–42). Cambridge: Cambridge University Press.

Salzman, J. & Thompson, B. H., Jr. (2003) *Enviro-mental Law and Policy*. New York: Foundation Press.

Seidenfeld, M. (2002) Cognitive loafing, social conformity, and judicial review of agency rulemaking, *Cornell Law Review*, 87, 486–548.

Slovic, P., Fischhoff, B., & Lichtenstein, S. (1982) Facts versus fears: Understanding perceived risks. In D. Kahneman, P. Slovic, & A. Tversky (eds.), *Judgment Under Uncertainty: Heuristics and Biases* (pp. 464–89). Cambridge: Cambridge University Press.

Sunstein, C. R. (2000) Cognition and cost–benefit analysis, *Journal of Legal Studies*, 29, 1059–96.

Sunstein, C. R. (2002) Probability neglect: Emotions, worst cases, and law, *Yale Law Journal*, 112, 61–107.

Sunstein, C. R., Kahneman, D., & Schkade, D. (1998) Assessing punitive damages (with notes on cognition and valuation in law), *Yale Law Journal*, 107, 2071–153.

Sunstein, C. R., Kahneman, D., Schkade, D., & Ritov, I. (2002) Predicatably incoherent judgments, *Stanford Law Review*, 54, 1153–214.

Thompson, W. (1989) Are juries competent to evaluate statistical evidence? *Law & Contemporary Problems*, 52(4), 9–42.

Thompson, W. C. & Schumann, E. L. (1987) Interpretation of statistical evidence in criminal trials: The prosecutor's fallacy and the defense attorney's fallacy, *Law and Human Behavior*, 11, 167–87.

Viscusi, W. K. (1999) How do judges think about risk? *American Law & Economic Review*, 1, 26–62.

Cases:
In re Estate of Chamberlain, 156 A. 42 (N.J. Perog. Ct. 1931).
First Alabama Bank v. Martin, 425 So. 2d 415 (Ala. 1982).

29

The Psychology of Medical Decision Making

Gretchen B. Chapman

Introduction

Good decision making is an essential part of good medicine. Patients have to decide what symptoms warrant seeking medical attention and whether to accept the medical advice received. Physicians have to decide what diagnosis is most likely and what treatment plan to recommend. Health policy makers have to decide what health behaviors to encourage and what medical interventions to pay for. The study of the psychology of decision making should therefore have much to offer to the field of medicine. Conversely, medicine should provide a useful test bed for the study of decisions made by experienced decision makers about high-stakes outcomes.

The current chapter reviews six intersections between the psychology of decision making and medicine:

1 One such intersection is the exploration of decision processes through the examination of decision biases in medical scenarios with physician or patient decision makers.
2 A second intersection is the exploration of whether decision phenomena demonstrated in hypothetical questionnaire scenarios are related to real-world health behavior.
3 A related area is the exploration of whether the decision domain (medical or nonmedical) affects the decision biases observed and implications of such domain effects for the decision processes underlying the biases.
4 Certain types of decisions may be especially likely to occur in medical settings. Consequently, these types of decisions comprise another intersection between decision research and medicine. One example is predicting one's preferences for future health states, such as occurs when making treatment decisions about a progressive disease.

5   Another example is decision making on behalf of another person, such as with advance directives.

6   A final area where decision process research intersects with medical applications is in the development and evaluation of decision analytic tools. A tool much utilized in medical decision-making research is utility assessment, used to quantify the quality of life afforded by various health states and medical treatments. Although utility assessment is intended to improve decision making, its validity may be limited by the decision biases displayed by the patients or lay people whose utility is assessed.

Heuristics and Biases

Many of the decision biases demonstrated in non-medical domains have also been demonstrated with clinicians, patients, or other participants reading medical scenarios or making real medical decisions. In general, these studies indicate that clinicians are not immune to decision biases and that decision biases show up in medical domains as they do in other domains. For example, physicians show framing effects (McNeil, Pauker, Sox, & Tversky, 1982), the hindsight bias (Arkes, Wortmann, Saville, & Harkness, 1981), unpacking (Redelmeier, Koehler, Liberman, & Tversky, 1995), and the certainty effect (Tversky & Kahneman, 1986). Preference reversals (Chapman & Johnson, 1995), the omission bias (Ritov & Baron, 1990), and biases in intertemporal choice (Chapman, 1996b) have all been demonstrated using medical scenarios. Decision biases demonstrated in medical domains will not be reviewed extensively here (for reviews see Chapman & Elstein, 2000; Dawson & Arkes, 1987). Some biases, however, are particularly noteworthy when demonstrated in a medical context because of their implications for health care reform and the effects of managed care on medical practice. Two such biases are summarized here and their implications discussed.

Added alternatives

Redelmeier and Shafir (1995) demonstrated that the addition of an option to a choice set alters preference for the original options in the choice set. They presented primary care physicians with a scenario describing a patient with osteoarthritis for whom many anti-inflammatory medications have been ineffective. In the two-option condition, physicians were given a choice between: (a) prescribing no new medications but referring the patient to an orthopedic specialist to discuss surgery; or (b) referring to the specialist and also prescribing an as-yet-untried anti-inflammatory medication. In the three-option condition, there were two as-yet-untried anti-inflammatory medications that could be tried; thus the choice options were referral only, referral plus one medication, and referral plus the other medication. Interestingly, physicians were more likely to select the referral-only option in the three-option condition than in the two-option condition. That is, the addition of the second medication option increased the preference for the referral-only option. This pattern violates the regularity principle, which states that adding more choice options to a consideration set should not increase preference for one of the existing options. If referral plus the first medication was better than referral only in the two-option condition, the same should hold true in the three-option condition.

Schwartz, Chapman, Brewer, and Bergus (2004) replicated the Redelmeier and Shafir (1995) result and found that the bias (the difference in percentage preference for the referral-only option in the two- vs. three-option condition) was accentuated when physicians were made to feel accountable for their choices. That is, physicians who were asked to write an explanation for their choices and to agree to be contacted later to discuss their choices showed a larger discrepancy in percentage preference between the two- and three-option conditions than did physicians who were simply asked to provide choices anonymously. This finding is important for two reasons – one theoretical and one practical. First, the finding illuminates the mechanism underlying the bias. Shafir, Simonson, and Tversky (1993) argue that decision makers make choices that can be easily justified by good reasons. In the three-option condition, there is no good reason to select one medication option over the other, so decision makers avoid that conflict by selecting the referral-only option. In the two-option condition, however, it is easy to construct good reasons for selecting the medication option, so the referral-only option is less popular. It can reasonably be assumed that an accountability manipulation would accentuate the tendency to make choices that can be justified by good reasons. Thus, the fact that the accountability manipulation increased the added alternative bias bolsters the reason-based choice account of the bias.

The second reason why the accountability results are important is because of their implications for medical practice. Accountability is usually considered a method for improving medical decisions. Indeed, physician performance is often evaluated by "report card" summaries, and physicians are called upon to explain adverse events. The Schwartz et al. (2004) findings demonstrate that, in contrast to much research showing that accountability improves decision making (e.g., Lerner & Tetlock, 1999), accountability can also have the undesirable effect of increasing decision biases and causing medical decisions to be driven by what is most defensible for the practitioner rather than what is best for the patient.

Single- vs. repeated-play gambles

A second bias with important implications for medical practice involves evaluating risky alternatives. Decision makers will sometimes make different decisions about a gamble to be played just once in comparison to a gamble to be played multiple times. For example, consider a gamble that offers a 50 percent chance to win $2,000 and a 50 percent chance to lose $500. Decision makers were more interested in playing this gamble five times than in playing it just once (Redelmeier & Tversky, 1992). That is, decision makers were more willing to accept a risky prospect if it was to be played many times. This result is in opposition to normative expected-utility theory.

Differences between risk preferences for single- and repeated-play gambles have important potential applications to medical decisions because some medical decisions are made about single instances, for example, a physician deciding on a single treatment for an individual patient. In contrast, other medical decisions are made about multiple instances, such as an insurance policy maker deciding whether to pay for a particular treatment for all patients with a given diagnosis. The practice decisions of individual physicians sometimes conflict with group-wide policies or practice guidelines. These disagreements might be explained in part by different preferences for single- and repeated-play gambles.

Redelmeier and Tversky (1990) demonstrated differences between individual and group medical decisions. For example, physicians were more likely to order an expensive blood test that might detect a rare, treatable condition if they were deciding on behalf of an individual patient than if they were deciding on behalf of a group of comparable patients. Some of Redelmeier and Tversky's results on medical decisions, however, appear opposite to those obtained with monetary decisions. For example, they presented college students and physicians with a scenario about a medical treatment that provided an 85 percent chance of adding two years to a patient's life and a 15 percent chance of shortening life by four years. Decision makers were more likely to advocate this treatment for an individual patient than for a group of patients. That is, they were more willing to accept a risky prospect if it was to be played only once (i.e., for a single patient). DeKay, Nickerson, Ubel, Hershey, Spranca, & Asch (2000) were unable to replicate this finding. Using the same scenario, they found either no effect of group vs. individual perspective or an effect in the opposite direction to that obtained by Redelemeier and Tversky (1990) (but consistent with the monetary results of Redelmeier and Tversky, 1992).

The effects of single- vs. repeated-play risky choices requires more research, and the implications of this research for understanding differences between medical decisions for individual patients vs. policy-level decisions is not yet clear. There are other plausible reasons for differences between individual-level and policy-level decisions in medicine besides the effects of repeated play. For example, when making decisions on behalf of a group, policy makers often have the goal of conserving resources or allocated resources so as to maximize medical benefits across the entire group. When making decisions on behalf of an individual patient, in contrast, a physician often has the goals of maximizing medical benefit for this patient (often while ignoring costs) and perhaps avoiding liability charges. It remains to be seen whether differences in risk preferences induced by single- vs. repeated-play perspectives plays a major role in explaining the tension between individual and group medical decisions.

Decision Making and Health Behavior

The usefulness of medical decision-making research on decision processes and biases would be bolstered if the research results improved prediction of actual health behavior. That is, one would hope that the constructs studied and measured in decision research were associated with real-world health behavior. We would expect, for example, that risk-seeking patients would choose risky treatments more often than risk-averse patients do, and that patients with low subjective time discount rates would engage in preventive health behaviors more than do patients with high discount rates. In addition, one might expect that people who demonstrate decision biases in hypothetical scenarios would make real-world decisions that could in some sense be characterized as worse than the real-world decisions made by people who do not demonstrate the biases. Such predictions rest on the assumption that decision theoretic constructs show stable individual differences, an assumption that has been the topic of recent research (e.g., Bromily & Curley, 1992; Stanovich & West, 2000).

Risk preferences

Decision makers who prefer a lottery to its expected value are called risk-seeking; those who prefer the expected value are risk-averse. If this distinction has implications for actual medical decisions, we would expect that risk-seeking patients would choose risky treatments more often than risk-averse patients do. Prosser, Kuntz, Bar-Or, & Weinstein (2002) found just that. Patients with relapsing-remitting multiple sclerosis answered a hypothetical lottery question as an assessment of risk preference. Those who were risk-seeking on the lottery question were more likely to have selected β-interferon treatment in real life than those who were risk-averse. β-interferon treatment is effective but can cause side-effect symptoms that may be experienced as worse than those of the disease. Thus, the treatment is a risky option that may result in a very good or very bad outcome, compared to no treatment, which yields the status quo.

Nightingale (1987a, 1987b, 1988; Nightingale & Grant, 1988) found that physicians who expressed risk-seeking preferences in a hypothetical scenario about lost life years were more likely to order laboratory tests and admit patients who presented to the emergency room in real life. They were also more likely to choose to intubate a lung disease patient in a hypothetical scenario. Each of these behaviors can be interpreted as selecting the riskier option. For example, admitting an ER patient to the hospital might result in a very good outcome (patient receives needed extensive care) or a bad outcome (patient receives unnecessary, expensive care), whereas the alternative of providing acute care and sending the patient home has a more certain outcome of medium value (patient receives limited care).

Time preferences

Preventive health behaviors instantiate a choice between a small immediate reward (e.g., eating a tasty dessert now) and a larger delayed reward (e.g., being thin and healthy later). Thus, a potential explanation for why many people fail to take preventive health measures is that they discount future outcomes very steeply. Decision makers who demand a large percentage increase in value in exchange for a delay in receiving the outcome are said to have high temporal discount rates. A strong relationship between discount rates and preventive health behaviors would suggest methods for encouraging these health behaviors. Specifically, manipulations that decrease discount rates should increase preventive health behaviors. Several studies have examined the correlation between discount rates as measured with hypothetical choices and a real-world health behavior. These studies assess whether individual differences in discount rates on the hypothetical choice task correspond to individual differences in the health behavior.

In one such study, Fuchs (1982) compared monetary discount rates to self-reports of several health behaviors: smoking, exercise, seat belt use, dental exams, and being overweight. Discount rates had a small relationship to smoking but not to the other behaviors. Chapman and Coups (1999) examined the relationship between responses to hypothetical intertemporal tradeoffs and acceptance of an influenza vaccine. They found a small but significant relationship between vaccine acceptance and a hypothetical monetary choice measure of time preferences. Chapman, Brewer, Coups, Brownlee, Leventhal, & Leventhal (2001) replicated the small but significant correlation between monetary (but not health) discount rates and flu shot acceptance. They also examined the relationship between discount rates and adherence with medication to control hypertension and high cholesterol but found no relationship.

In contrast to these studies, which found small and inconsistent relationships between time preference and health behavior, strong evidence for the relationship between time preference measures and health behavior comes from several studies of addictive behaviors (Bickel, Odum, & Madden, 1999; Kirby, Petry, & Bickel, 1999; Madden, Petry, & Badger, 1997; Vuchinich & Simpson, 1998). Addictive behavior can be understood as an instance of intertemporal choice in that the user makes a choice of whether to engage in an immediately pleasurable activity (using the substance) that carries a long-term cost (sustained addiction with negative consequences for health, job, etc.). In several studies, addicts and matched controls were presented with monetary choices between immediate and delayed sums of money. The resulting discount rates were higher for heroin addicts than for matched non-drug-using controls (Kirby et al., 1999; Madden et al., 1997), higher for heavy social drinkers and problem drinkers than for light social drinkers (Vuchinich & Simpson, 1998), and higher for current cigarette smokers than for ex-smokers and never-smokers (Bickel et al., 1999; see also Cairns, 1994). It is currently unclear why substance abuse shows a reliable relationship to hypothetical choice measures of time preference when other behaviors do not.

Decision biases

Decision research frequently demonstrates decision biases in hypothetical scenarios. Do such biases influence real-world health behavior? That is, are people who demonstrate decision biases in hypothetical scenarios more likely to exhibit poor real-world decision making? Is committing a decision fallacy on a questionnaire indicative of committing that same fallacy in real life?

The naturalism bias is a preference for natural over artificial products even when the two are indistinguishable. For example, Chapman (unpublished) presented university employees with a scenario (after Spranca, 1993) describing two medications – one derived from a natural herb, and the other synthesized in a laboratory. The two medications were described as chemically identical. A majority of subjects preferred the natural medication, comprising the naturalism bias. Furthermore, the subjects who preferred the natural option were more likely than those who did not to turn down a free flu shot offered to employees. This result indicates that to the extent that accepting a flu shot can be considered a better decision than declining the shot, demonstration of a bias in a hypothetical scenario is associated with quality of real-world health decisions. This association may exist because one reason people decline the flu shot is that they dislike unnatural medical interventions, even when naturalness is not associated with a better outcome.

In the same study, Chapman also gave subjects a scenario designed to assess the omission bias (Ritov & Baron, 1990; see also Chapter 5, this volume). The scenario asked subjects to imagine that they had a 10 percent risk of contracting a disease. A vaccine was available that would always prevent the disease but could also cause the disease itself. From a normative perspective, decision makers should accept the vaccine as long as it resulted in a risk of developing the disease that was less than 10 percent, because that is a better outcome than the outcome of non-vaccination. Many subjects, however, refused vaccines that posed risks of less than 9 percent. This pattern demonstrates the omission bias, or a preference for bad outcomes that result from omissions relative to identical outcomes that result from actions. Furthermore, subjects who demonstrated the omission bias were more likely to decline the flu shot. This result provides another demonstration that decision biases on a questionnaire are linked with poor real-world decision making. One reason people decline the flu shot may be that they prefer inaction over action.

Thus, there appears to be some evidence, though limited, that risk preferences, time preferences, and decision biases are associated with health behaviors in the predicted directions. These findings point to the real-world applicability of the study of decision processes. That is, decision phenomena studied in the lab or with hypothetical scenarios can have implications for understanding real health behavior.

Domain Differences

As demonstrated in the Redelmeier and Tversky (1990, 1992) studies reviewed above, decisions about health outcomes sometimes show different patterns from analogous decisions about other domains, such as money. These domain differences can provide clues about the underlying decision processes and also signal caution in generalizing findings from one domain to another. As an example of such domain differences, consider research on preferences for sequences of outcomes.

Decision makers often express a preference for improving sequences. For example, Loewenstein & Sicherman (1991) presented subjects with various ways in which a set amount of income money could be distributed across six years. Subjects preferred the distribution that provided less than one sixth of the money in the first year, with increasing amounts in each succeeding year. This response is surprising because subjects could have increased their consumption in every year (relative to the increasing sequence) by selecting the sequence that delivered more of the money in the early years, enabling them to invest part of the money in the early years and spend it in later years. A preference for improving sequences represents a negative time preference because decision makers prefer to put off good outcomes until later. Negative time preferences are commonly seen in the preferences for sequences, but are uncommon in preferences for individual outcomes. For example, if given a choice between $100 now or $100 in one year, most decision makers select the immediate money, showing a positive time preference (see Chapter 21, this volume).

Chapman (1996a) found that time preferences for sequences were influenced by the decision domain. Subjects rated their preferences for sequences that described how their health or monetary income could change over their entire lifetime. Whereas subjects preferred increasing monetary sequences, they preferred declining health sequences. This domain effect suggests one mechanism underlying sequence preferences – that preferences for sequences are influenced by expectations about how sequences are usually experienced. Specifically, subjects' preferences were in line with their stated expectations about how health and money would change over their lifespan. They expected monetary income to increase and health quality to decrease over the lifespan. In contrast, when evaluating short sequences (one year or 12 days), expectations about changes in health and money were similar to one another, and preferences were also similar in the two domains, with improving sequences preferred. Thus, domain (health vs. money) interacted with sequence length such that health and money preferences differed for long sequences but not for short sequences. Finally, ratings of expectations mediated this interaction.

The effect of expectations on preferences for sequences can produce different preferences for health and money outcomes. In addition, it can produce different preferences across health outcomes. Chapman (2000) found that college women were more likely to prefer an improving sequence of facial acne over a worsening sequence than to prefer an improving sequence of facial wrinkles over a worsening sequence. These preferences were in line with their expectations that acne improves but wrinkles worsen with age. It is not clear why preferences are aligned with expectations. One possible explanation is a reference point effect where decision makers compare each time period in the actual sequence with that same time period in the expected sequence and weigh negative differences (losses) more heavily than positive differences (gains). Other potential explanations include a type of naturalism bias or an attempt to match one's own sequence with the sequence that peers are likely to experience.

This research demonstrates a difference between health and money decisions. As a consequence, it also reveals a particular mechanism underlying preferences – namely that expectations are one factor driving preferences for sequences. Thus, medical decisions do not always mirror decisions in other domains. Although the majority of research on the psychology of decision making has employed monetary outcomes, the findings from such studies do not always generalize to other domains. Indeed, some psychological mechanisms are likely to be missed if cross-domain comparisons are not made.

Predicting Preferences

A current puzzle in medical decision-making research is that preferences expressed by different people for the same health state often differ systematically, as do preferences expressed by the same person at different points in time. For example, a common finding in the study of health state evaluation is that patients actually experiencing a health state assign higher utilities to it than do healthy adults who have not experienced that health state (e.g., Boyd, Sutherland, Heasman, Tritchler, & Cummings, 1990). These discrepancies raise questions about which utilities to use as the basis for a treatment or policy decision.

Utility assessment can be thought of as in some sense a prediction. Choosing among medical treatment options is difficult in part because, at the point of making the choice, the patient may not have experienced many of the possible consequences of each treatment. To make his decision, the patient must forecast her own preferences. That is, she must anticipate her future preferences for health states not yet experienced. Such anticipatory judgments are not always accurate because experience with a later adverse health state can impact health preferences in ways that may be difficult to predict.

Kahneman and Snell (1990; see also Kahneman, Wakker, & Sarin, 1997) introduced the distinction between predicted and experienced utility. Predicted utility is the forecast made at the time of the decision. That is, the decision maker predicts her utility or value for potential future outcomes and bases her decision on these forecasts. Experienced utility, in contrast, is the utility or value actually achieved from the outcome when it is experienced. Several studies have examined predictions of preferences for future health states.

Sieff, Dawes, and Loewenstein (1999) asked people getting tested for HIV to predict how they would feel five weeks after receiving either a positive or negative test result. About half the participants also later provided experienced-utility ratings following receipt of their actual test results. Most participants received a negative test result, and among this group, experienced distress levels were marginally higher than subjects had predicted, indicating that they were not as relieved as they had expected to be. Only a few of the participants received a positive result, so the predicted and experienced judgments could not be compared for this group. Instead, the judgments from the entire sample about predicted distress given a positive test result were compared to the experienced utilities provided by a separate sample of people who had recently received a positive HIV test result. The experienced distress judgments were significantly lower (less extreme) than the predicted judgments. Thus, people who had received a positive test result were less distressed than the predictions would indicate. Despite the discrepancy between mean predicted and experienced judgments, the correlation between these two judgments (for subjects who tested negative) was quite high ($r = 0.62$). The Sieff et al. study suggests that experience with a change in health status (diagnosis of HIV) can alter evaluations of health states.

In a longitudinal study of laryngeal cancer patients undergoing radiation therapy (Llewellyn-Thomas, Sutherland, & Thiel, 1993), patients gave utility judgments for three descriptions of common treatment-induced health outcomes before and after the treatment. Prior to therapy, none of the health states had yet been experienced. After treatment, each patient indicated which of the descriptions best matched his or her current health (the experienced health state). Pre- and post-treatment judgments of this health state were then compared. The means of these judgments were very close for the experienced health state – as close as were the mean pre- and post-treatment judgments of the alternative health states. This result suggests that pre-treatment predictions of preferences are quite accurate on average. Although mean predicted judgments were similar to mean experienced judgments, it is possible that individual subjects' judgments did not show close agreement. Llewellyn-Thomas et al. did not examine the correlation between predicted and experienced judgments as Sieff et al. (1999) had done.

Jansen and colleagues (2000) suggested several methodological accounts of why a predictive health state evaluation does not match a later experienced health state evaluation. In their study, breast cancer patients evaluated a hypothetical radiotherapy scenario before they started radiation treatment and then evaluated their actual experience during therapy. Utility judgments of actual experience were significantly higher than predicted judgments. The results indicated that this discrepancy was due to a mismatch between the hypothetical radiotherapy scenario used to elicit predicted judgments and the patients' actual health states during radiation treatment. That is, during radiation treatment, the patients evaluated the original radiotherapy scenario as worse than what they were actually experiencing. Evaluation of the original radiotherapy scenario, in contrast, was consistent before and during treatment.

Why else might predicted utility differ from experienced utility? Loewenstein and Schkade (1999) outlined several potential mechanisms of this effect. One possibility is that people have intuitive theories about health state utility, and these theories are sometimes inaccurate. For example, some patients may underestimate their ability to adapt psychologically to poor health (Gilbert, Pinel, Wilson, Blumberg, & Wheatley, 1998) and may instead theorize that the initial dysphoria felt at diagnosis is representative of the low quality of life that will be experienced throughout the illness. A second hypothesis is that a change in health states alters the salience of different aspects of health. When making a predicted judgment, people may focus too much importance on the salient aspects of the health state description, even if these aspects later turn out to be relatively unimportant contributors to experienced utility (Wilson, Wheatley, Meyers, Gilbert, & Axsom, 2000). These mechanisms are likely to operate in many domains in addition to health. Thus, although the discrepancy between predicted and experienced utility has important implications for medical decisions, its implications are much broader.

Surrogate Decision Making

Many decisions are made on behalf of others. Such surrogate decisions are especially common in medical settings, where clinicians make decisions on behalf of patients, and family members frequently decide on behalf of a sick or incapacitated loved one. Consequently, medical decision-making research has addressed the issue of how closely surrogate decisions match the preferences of the beneficiary. Often the beneficiary has the opportunity to express her preferences in advance, such as in an advance directive for health care. This raises the related question of how useful advance directives and similar communications are in improving the accuracy with which surrogates estimate the preferences of patients. Given that people often have difficulty predicting their own future preferences, it would not be surprising if they had equal or greater difficulty predicting the preferences of someone else.

Several studies have examined how well surrogate decision makers can predict patient preferences and the extent to which advance directives improve this predictive accuracy. Perhaps the largest study on the role of advance directives in end-of-life medical care is the Study to Understand Prognoses and Preferences for Outcomes and Risks of Treatments (SUPPORT) (Covinsky et al., 2000). The observational portion of this study found that both physicians and family surrogates were only moderately better than chance in predicting the preferences of seriously ill patients for resuscitation. An intervention to improve physician–family communication did not increase the physician knowledge of patient preferences for end-of-life care, nor did it increase the number of patients who had advance directives. The intervention did increase documentation of existing advance directives in medical charts, but this did not result in medical care that was more consistent with patient preferences (SUPPORT Principal Investigators, 1995). Thus, the SUPPORT study provides a pessimistic view both of surrogate decision making and of the prospects for tools such as advance directives to improve decision making.

Another notable study on surrogate decision making and advance directives is the Advance Directives Values Assessment and Communication Enhancement (ADVANCE) study by Peter Ditto and colleagues (Coppola, Ditto, Danks, & Smucker, 2001; Ditto et al., 2001; Fagerlin, Ditto, Danks, Houts, & Smucker, 2001). In this study, patients read illness scenarios and indicated which medical treatments they would choose while their surrogate decision makers (family members) predicted the treatments the patient would want. Several types of advance directives were examined, and none of them improved surrogates' accuracy in predicting patients' preferences (Ditto et al., 2001). The ADVANCE study included physicians as well as family member surrogates (Coppola et al., 2001). Primary care physicians who knew the patients were worse than family member surrogates in predicting patient preferences. Worse still were hospital-based physicians who did not know the patients. Advance directives helped only the hospital-based physicians, who knew nothing about the patients' preferences other than what was contained in the advance directive (Coppola et al., 2001). Thus, advance directives improve accuracy, but only when the surrogate has no other sources of information about the patients' preferences.

It is unclear whether the failure of advance directives to improve accuracy in ADVANCE was due to the patients' failure to express usable information in the advance directive or the surrogates' failure to use that information. The former could result if patients were not successful in expressing their preferences in the advance directive (e.g., the advance directive did not agree with the patient's own preferences as expressed in the scenarios) or if preferences expressed in the advance directives did not vary much across patients.

The ADVANCE study also pointed to a heuristic that surrogates use in predicting patients' preference. Family member surrogates' predictions about patient preferences were closer to the surrogates' own preferences for themselves than to the patients' actual preferences (Fagerlin et al., 2001). These results are similar to those from Schneiderman and colleagues (Schneiderman, Kaplan, Pearlman, & Teetzel, 1993; Schneiderman, Kaplan, Rosenberg, & Teetzel, 1997) who found that physicians' predictions of their patients' preferences for life-sustaining treatment corresponded more closely to the physicians' own preferences than to the patients' actual preferences. Fagerlin et al. (2001) noted that this correspondence between predictions and own preferences led to projection errors such that when surrogates mispredicted patient preferences, it was more likely to be in the direction of the surrogate's own preference than in the opposite direction. A projection heuristic (predicting patient preferences based on one's own preferences), however, also resulted in more accurate predictions than a counter-projection strategy. These results are consistent with the conclusion that surrogates used their own preferences as a guide when they were uncertain about patient preferences. Like many decision heuristics, this strategy produces more accurate responses than doing the opposite, but also results in a systematic error profile.

Some studies have explored how well physicians can represent the preferences of their patients without the benefit of advance directives. Elstein et al. (2004) asked both prostate cancer patients and their clinicians to judge the TTO utility of several health states, including the patient's own health state. In addition, both groups rank ordered the importance of six attributes that were used in the health state descriptions (e.g., fatigue, sexual function). Patients gave responses that reflected their own preferences, and clinicians gave responses that reflected what they thought the patient's preferences were. Each patient's responses were compared to those given by his clinician. The correlations between patient and clinician responses were low to moderate. Although one might predict that agreement would improve as patients progressed through treatment, as the patient became more familiar with the disease and treatment and the clinician became more familiar with the patient, this was not the case. Thus, this study indicates that physician judgments are often not a close approximation of patient preferences.

Studies of surrogate decision making paint a fairly pessimistic picture, with surrogates often not predicting patients' preferences very accurately and advance directives providing little benefit. Surrogate decision making occurs in many domains other than medicine, including business, real estate, and law. Consequently, an understanding of how to improve surrogate decisions would be of great value. Further research is needed on what types of advance directives or similar communications can improve surrogate decision making.

Health State Evaluation

Decision theory provides tools that can be used to improve decisions and circumvent decision biases. One tool that has been particularly influential in medical decision-making research is utility assessment. Researchers, policy makers, and individual clinicians frequently want to know how a particular patient, or a group of similar patients, evaluates a particular health state. Policy makers, for example, may want to evaluate how much increased quality of life is provided by a medical intervention so that they can decide whether to approve or pay for the intervention. They therefore need to know how patients evaluate the pre-treatment and post-treatment health states. A clinician may want to know how a particular patient evaluates a side effect of surgery, so as to help the patient decide between surgery and medication treatment. Patient educators who design decision aids for patients often advocate assessing individual patients' preferences for health states so that the decision aid can construct a customized treatment recommendation for the patient. Consequently, the ability to assess patients' health state utilities easily and accurately has many applications.

Utility judgments are often inputs into more complex decision analyses. Because intuitive decision making often exhibits decision biases, many decision analysts recommend that important personal and policy medical decisions be made explicitly using decision analysis. That is, a decision model is constructed that incorporates the probabilities and utilities of relevant outcomes. Such models depend on accurate assessment of utilities for relevant health states.

Utility assessment methods

The three most commonly used utility assessment techniques used in medical decision-making research are the visual analog scale (VAS), the standard gamble (SG) and the time tradeoff (TTO) (see Chapman & Elstein, 1998). With the VAS, the patient assigns the target health state a score on a scale from 0 to 100 where 0 corresponds to death and 100 to perfect health. A visual display (such as a "feeling thermometer") often accompanies the question. The VAS method is not derived from axioms of expected utility theory (EUT); thus, the values obtained from patients cannot be considered true utilities. Because the VAS is easy to administer and easy for patients to understand, however, some researchers have advocated using it as an approximation to utility or developing algorithms for converting VAS values to the utility values that would be obtained from other methods.

In the SG, the patient compares the prospect of experiencing the target health state for certain with a gamble with a p chance of experiencing perfect health and a $1 - p$ chance of dying. The patient specifies (often through a series of pairwise choices) what value of p would make her indifferent between the gamble and the certain health state. The utility of perfect health is set at 1.0 and that of death at 0. Thus, according to EUT, the utility of the target health state is p. Thus, if a patient said that she was indifferent between living with diabetes for sure and undergoing a treatment that offered an 85 percent chance of perfect health but a 15 percent chance of imminent death, we could conclude that the patient's utility for diabetes was 0.85 on a scale where 0 means death and 1.0 means perfect health.

In the TTO, the patient compares the prospect of living in the target health state for a set number of years (y) with living in perfect health for a shorter number of years (x). The patient sets the value of x (often through a series of pairwise choices) to make the two prospects equally appealing. The utility of the target state is thus inferred to be x/y. For example, if a patient said that living with diabetes for 10 years (followed by death) was equivalent to living in perfect health for 8.5 years (followed by death), we would conclude that the utility of diabetes was 0.85 on a scale where 0 means death and 1.0 means perfect health.

The TTO is noteworthy because it was developed specifically for assessment of the utility of chronic health states (Torrance, 1986). The VAS and SG can be used to assess utility for any outcome, health related or non-health related, assuming the top and bottom points of the scale are set appropriately for the outcomes. The TTO, in contrast, is based on the tradeoff between quality of life and length of life and therefore can only be used to evaluate chronic quality of life states (or other attributes that can be traded off multiplicatively with longevity). It represents an advancement in decision research methods that resulted from study in the medical domain. It has the advantage over SG that it represents a riskless measure of utility (which may be more appropriate for modeling riskless decisions) and one that does not require the respondent to use or understand probabilities. It has the disadvantage of being based on assumptions about the utility function for years of life (Miyamoto, 2000).

Quality-adjusted life years

The TTO is based on an underlying quality-adjusted life year (QALY) model. QALYs are the standardized measure of health benefit used in many decision analyses (Gold, Siegel, Russell, & Weinstein, 1996). For example, the expected benefit from heart by-pass surgery could be quantified as the additional life years it provides, corrected for the quality of life during those years. A treatment that actually shortened life but greatly improved quality of life during those years (relative to an alternative treatment or no treatment) might provide positive QALYs, as could a treatment that extended life but at the cost of decreased quality of life. QALYs are calculated simply as length of life where each time unit is multiplicatively weighted by quality of life. Quality of life is equivalent to the utility for the health state and is measured on a 0 to 1 scale where 0 corresponds to death or health states as bad as death, and 1 corresponds to perfect health. VAS, SG, and TTO are all measurement techniques that can be used to assess the utilities needed for QALY calculations. Because of the widespread use of QALY estimates for health treatment and policy decisions, it is important to know what psychological factors may stand in the way of obtaining accurate utility values from patients who are often ill and may lack education in quantitative methods.

Willingness to tradeoff

Both the SG and the TTO ask the respondent to make a tradeoff. In the SG, the respondent trades off health quality for risk of death. In the TTO the respondent trades off health quality for length of life. In order to express their true utilities, respondents must understand the tradeoffs and be willing to make them. For example, if a patient states that living 10 years with heart disease is equivalent to living 10 years with perfect health (that is, she will not give up any life expectancy to improve her health from having heart disease to having perfect health), a utility analyst would infer that the heart disease state has a utility of 1.0 for this patient – as good as perfect health. An alternative explanation, however, is that the patient doesn't understand the question or is following a general rule of never giving up years of life.

Chapman et al. (1998) found that a large number of patients with prostate cancer were unwilling to make tradeoffs when posed with TTO questions. Patients in that study were asked to give TTO responses to each of three health state descriptions composed of aspects of health that are influenced by prostate cancer and its treatments (e.g., fatigue, sexual function, incontinence). The descriptions were constructed such that state A dominated state B, which dominated state C. Thus, the correct ordering of the utilities of the three states was A > B > C. When asked how much life expectancy they would give up to improve each health state description to perfect health, 58 percent of patients (18 of 31) refused to tradeoff any life expectancy for health quality for one or more of three health states. Interestingly, a change in wording improved willingness to tradeoff. Another group of patients was asked to imagine two friends: Mr. Smith's health fits one of the health state descriptions, and he lives for 10 years. Mr. Jones has perfect health but lives for shorter (specified) amount of time. Patients were asked which friend they would rather be. Using this format, only 32 percent (9 of 28) refused to tradeoff any life expectancy for one or more of the three health states. In addition, this change in wording also increased the likelihood from 16 percent to 68 percent that patients would give TTO utilities that correctly ordered the three health states. Since correct ordering in this task is a measure of the validity of the utility responses, the study suggests that unwillingness to tradeoff hampers the validity of TTO utility responses.

Numerosity

VAS, SG, and TTO procedures all require respondents to use numbers. SG and TTO require the use of tradeoffs (e.g., a decrease in qualify of life is compensated by an increase in longevity), and the SG requires the use of probabilities. If respondents lack numerical skills, they may give noisy or biased responses to utility assessment methods. Woloshin, Schwartz, Moncur, Gabriel, and Tosteson (2001) assessed the relationship between utility measurement and numeracy or quantitative skills. Numeracy was measured by questions such as how to convert a proportion of 1 in 1,000 to a percentage. Patients with low numeracy gave SG and TTO utilities that lacked validity in that more desirable health states did not receive higher utilities. Patients high in numeracy, in contrast, gave SG and TTO utilities that tracked the desirability of the health states. Validity of VAS ratings was not associated with numeracy. These results indicate that although the TTO and SG methods have desirable axiomatic properties, their empirical validity depends on the quantitative skills of the respondent. In contrast, while the VAS lacks the formal properties of a utility scale, it can be used appropriately by even those with low numeracy.

Biases that affect utility assessment mean that the utilities incorporated in decision analyses do not reflect patients' true preferences. Consequently, the use of decision analysis may not succeed in reducing the incidence of decision biases. Methods for improving medical decisions and avoiding biases therefore continue to be a topic of current research.

Conclusion

The investigation of the psychology of decision making in medicine and health domains has resulted in a number of innovations, discoveries, and applications. Differences in how decision biases are manifest in health domains relative to other domains has shed light on the mechanisms underlying the biases. Even when biases occur in health domains just as they do in other domains they may have important implications for understanding or improving medical practice. It appears that the study of decision processes is not just an academic exercise – decision phenomena such as risk preferences, time preferences, and biases have been shown to be related to real-world medical decisions and health behaviors. The medical domain is often a useful testbed for the study of decision phenomena that are of broad interest and relevant to many domains. Examples include predicted utility and surrogate decision making. Certain decision theoretic tools have been used extensively in medical decisions, and the particularities of medical decision making have inspired new tools, such as the time tradeoff utility assessment. The goal of such decision analytic tools is to improve decision making in medicine and other domains.

References

Arkes, H. R., Wortmann, R. L., Saville, P. D., & Harkness, A. R. (1981) Hindsight bias among physicians weighting the likelihood of diagnoses, *Journal of Applied Psychology*, 66, 252–4.

Bickel, W. K., Odum, A. L., & Madden, G. J. (1999) Impulsivity and cigarette smoking: Delay discounting in current, never, and ex-smokers, *Psychopharmacology*, 146, 447–54.

Boyd, N. F., Sutherland, H. J., Heasman, K. Z., Tritchler, D. L., & Cummings, E. J. (1990) Whose utilities for decision analysis? *Medical Decision Making*, 10, 58–67.

Bromily, P. & Curley, S. P. (1992) Individual differences in risk taking. In J. F. Yates (ed.), *Risk-taking Behavior* (pp. 87–132). New York: John Wiley & Sons.

Cairns, J. A. (1994) Valuing future benefits, *Health Economics*, 3, 221–9.

Chapman, G. B. (1996a) Expectations and preferences for sequences of health and money, *Organizational Behavior and Human Decision Processes*, 67, 59–75.

Chapman, G. B. (1996b) Temporal discounting and utility for health and money, *Journal of Experimental Psychology: Learning, Memory, and Cognition*, 22, 771–91.

Chapman, G. B. (2000) Preferences for improving and declining sequences of health outcomes, *Journal of Behavioral Decision Making*, 13, 203–18.

Chapman, G. B., Brewer, N. T., Coups, E. J., Brownlee, S., Leventhal, H., & Leventhal, E. A. (2001) Value for the future and preventive health behavior, *Journal of Experimental Psychology: Applied*, 7, 235–50.

Chapman, G. B. & Coups, E. J. (1999) Time preferences and preventive health behavior: Acceptance of the influenza vaccine, *Medical Decision Making*, 19, 307–14.

Chapman, G. B. & Elstein, A. S. (1998) Utility assessment: Methods and research. In C. L. Bennett & T. J. Stinson (eds.), *Cancer Policy: Research and Methods* (pp. 13–24). Boston: Kluwer Academic Publishers.

Chapman, G. B. & Elstein, A. S. (2000) Cognitive processes and biases in medical decision making. In G. B. Chapman and F. A. Sonnenberg (eds.), *Decision Making in Health Care: Theory, Psychology, and Applications* (pp. 183–210). New York: Cambridge University Press.

Chapman, G. B., Elstein, A. S., Kuzel, T. M., Sharifi, R., Nadler, R. B., Andrews, A., & Bennett, C. L. (1998) Prostate cancer patient's utilities for health states: How it looks depends on where you stand, *Medical Decision Making*, 18, 278–86.

Chapman, G. B. & Johnson, E. J. (1995) Preference reversals in monetary and life expectancy evaluations, *Organizational Behavior and Human Decision Processes*, 62, 300–17.

Coppola, K. M., Ditto, P. H., Danks, J. H., & Smucker, W. D. (2001) Accuracy of primary care and hosptial-based physicians' predictions of elderly outpatients' treatment preferences with and without advance directives, *Archives of Internal Medicine*, 161, 431–40.

Covinsky, K. E., Fuller, J. D., Yaffe, K., Johnston, C. B., Hamel, M. B., Lynn, J., Teno, J. M., & Phillips, R. S. (2000) Communication and decision-making in seriously ill patients: Findings of the SUPPORT project, *Journal of the American Geriatrics Society*, 48, S187–S193.

Dawson, N. V. and Arkes, H. R. (1987) Systematic errors in medical decision making: Judgment limitations, *Journal of General Internal Medicine*, 2, 183–7.

DeKay, M. L., Nickerson, C. A., Ubel, P. A., Hershey, J. C., Spranca, M. D., & Asch D. A. (2000) Further explorations of medical decisions for individuals and for groups, *Medical Decision Making*, 20, 39–44.

Ditto, P. H., Danks, J. H., Smucker, W. D., Bookwala, J., Coppola, K. M., Dresser, R., Fagerlin, A., Gready, R. M., Houts, R. M., Lockhard, L. K., & Zyganski, S. (2001) Advance directives as acts of communication: A randomized controlled trial, *Archives of Internal Medicine*, 161, 421–30.

Elstein, A. S., Chapman, G. B., Chmiel, J., Knight, S. J., Chan, C., & Bennett, C. L. (2004) Agreement between prostate cancer patients and their clinicians about utilities and attribute importance, *Health Expectations*, 7, 115–25.

Fagerlin, A., Ditto, P. H., Danks, J. H., Houts, R. M., & Smucker, W. D. (2001) Projection in surrogate decisions about life-sustaining medical treatments, *Health Psychology*, 20, 166–75.

Fuchs, V. R. (1982) Time preference and health: An exploratory study. In V. R. Fuchs (ed.), *Economic Aspects of Health* (pp. 93–120). Chicago: University of Chicago Press.

Gilbert, D. T., Pinel, E. C., Wilson, T. D., Blumberg, S. J., & Wheatley, T. P. (1998) Immune neglect: A source of durability bias in affective forecasting, *Journal of Personality & Social Psychology*, 75, 617–38.

Gold, M. R., Siegel, J. E., Russell, L. B., & Weinstein, M. C. (1996) *Cost-effectiveness in Health and Medicine.* New York: Oxford University Press.

Jansen, S. J. T., Stigglebout, A. M., Wakker, P. P., Nooij, M. A., Noordijk, E. M., & Kievit, J. (2000) Unstable preferences: A shift in valuation or an effect of the elicitation procedure? *Medical Decision Making*, 20, 62–71.

Kahneman, D. & Snell, J. (1990) Predicting utility. In R. M. Hogarth (ed.), *Insights in Decision Making: A Tribute to Hillel J. Einhorn* (pp. 295–310). Chicago: University of Chicago Press.

Kahneman, D., Wakker, P. P., & Sarin, R. (1997) Back to Bentham? Explorations of experienced utility, *Quarterly Journal of Economics*, 112, 375–405.

Kirby, K. N., Petry, N. M., & Bickel, W. K. (1999) Heroin addicts have higher discount rates for delayed rewards than non-drug-using controls, *Journal of Experimental Psychology: General*, 128, 78–87.

Lerner, J. S. & Tetlock, P. E. (1999) Accounting for the effects of accountability, *Psychological Bulletin*, 125, 255–75.

Llewellyn-Thomas, H., Sutherland, H., & Theil, E. (1993) Do patients' evaluations of a future health state change when they actually enter that state? *Medical Care*, 31, 1002–12.

Loewenstein, G. & Schkade, D. (1999) Wouldn't it be nice? Predicting future feelings. In D. Kahneman, E. Diener, & N. Schwarz (eds.), *Well-being: The Foundations of Hedonic Psychology* (pp. 85–105). New York: Russell Sage.

Loewenstein, G. & Sicherman, N. (1991) Do workers prefer increasing wage profiles? *Journal of Labor Economics*, 9, 67–84.

Madden, G. J., Petry, N. M., Badger, G. J., & Bickel, W. K. (1997) Impulsive and self-control choices in opioid-dependent patients and non-drug-using control participants: Drug and money rewards, *Experimental and Clinical Psychopharmacology*, 5, 256–62.

McNeil, B. J., Pauker, S., Sox, H., Jr., & Tversky, A. (1982) On the elicitation of preferences for alternative therapies, *New England Journal of Medicine*, 306, 1259–62.

Miyamoto, J. M. (2000) Utility assessment under expected utility and rank-dependent utility assumptions. In G. B. Chapman and F. A. Sonnenberg (eds.), *Decision Making in Health Care: Theory, Psychology, and Applications* (pp. 65–109). New York: Cambridge University Press.

Nightingale, S. D. (1987a) Risk preference and laboratory test selection, *Journal of General Internal Medicine*, 2, 25–8.

Nightingale, S. D. (1987b) Risk preference and laboratory use, *Medical Decision Making*, 72, 168–72.

Nightingale, S. D. (1988) Risk preference and admitting rates of emergency room physicians, *Medical Care*, 26, 84–7.

Nightingale, S. D. & Grant, M. (1988) Risk preference and decision making in critical care situations, *Chest*, 93, 684–7.

Prosser, L. A., Kuntz, K. A., Bar-Or, A., & Weinstein, M. C. (2002) The relationship between risk attitude and treatment choice in patients with relapsing-remitting multiple sclerosis, *Medical Decision Making*, 22, 506–13.

Redelmeier, D. A., Koehler, D. J., Liberman, V., & Tversky, A. (1995) Probability judgement in medicine: Discounting unspecified possibilities, *Medical Decision Making*, 15, 227–30.

Redelmeier D. A. & Shafir E. (1995) Medical decision making in situations that offer multiple alternatives, *Journal of the American Medical Association (JAMA)*, 273, 302–5.

Redelmeier, D. A. & Tversky, A. (1990) Discrepancy between medical decisions for individual patients and for groups, *New England Journal of Medicine*, 322, 1162–4.

Redelmeier, D. A. & Tversky, A. (1992) On the framing of multiple prospects, *Psychological Science*, 3, 191–3.

Ritov, I. & Baron, J. (1990) Reluctance to vaccinate: Omission bias and ambiguity, *Journal of Behavioral Decision Making*, 3, 263–77.

Schwartz, J. A., Chapman, G. B., Brewer, N. T., and Bergus, G. B. (2004) The effects of accountability on bias in physician decision making: Going from bad to worse, *Psychonomic Bulletin & Review*, 11, 173–78.

Schneiderman, L. J., Kaplan, R. M., Pearlman, R. A., & Teetzel, H. (1993) Do physicians' own preferences for life-sustaining treatment influence their perceptions of patients' preferences? *The Journal of Clinical Ethics*, 4, 28–33.

Schneiderman, L. J., Kaplan, R. M., Rosenberg, E., & Teetzel, H. (1997) Do physicians' own preferences for life-sustaining treatment influence their perceptions of patients' preferences? A second look, *Cambridge Quarterly of Healthcare Ethics*, 6, 131–7.

Shafir, E., Simonson, I., and Tversky, A. (1993) Reason-based choice, *Cognition*, 49, 11–36.

Sieff, E. M., Dawes, R. M., & Loewenstein, G. (1999) Anticipated versus actual response to HIV test results, *American Journal of Psychology*, 112, 297–311.

Spranca, M. D. (1993) Some basic psychology behind the appeal of naturalness in the domain of foods, unpublished dissertation, University of California, Berkeley.

Stanovich, K. E. & West, R. F. (2000) Individual differences in reasoning: Implications for the rationality debate? *Behavioral and Brain Sciences*, 23, 645–726.

The SUPPORT Principal Investigators (1995) A controlled trial to improve care for seriously ill hospitalized patients: The Study to Understand Prognoses and Preferences for Outcomes and Risks of Treatments (SUPPORT), *Journal of the American Medical Association (JAMA)*, 274, 1591–8.

Torrance, G. W. (1986) Measurement of health state utilities for economic appraisal, *Journal of Health Economics*, 5, 1–30.

Tversky, A. & Kahneman, D. (1986) Rational choice and the framing of decisions, *Journal of Business*, 59, S251–S278.

Vuchinich, R. E. & Simpson, C. A. (1998) Hyperbolic temporal discounting in social drinkers and problem drinkers, *Experimental and Clinical Psychopharmacology*, 6, 292–305.

Wilson, T. D., Wheatley, T., Meyers, J. M., Gilbert, D. T., & Axsom, D. (2000) Focalism: A source of durability bias in affective forecasting, *Journal of Personality & Social Psychology*, 78, 821–36.

Woloshin, S., Schwartz, L. M., Moncur, M., Gabriel, S., & Tosteson, A. N. A. (2001) Assessing values for health: Numeracy matters, *Medical Decision Making*, 21, 382–90.

30

Judgment, Decision Making, and Public Policy

Nick Pidgeon and Robin Gregory

Introduction

Basic judgment and decision-making (JDM) research and methodology are being used in a wide range of contexts for arriving at better considered, and more equitable, public policy decisions. The emphasis in such research is, inevitably, towards investigations located in the "real" world, as when working with members of the general public to elicit their values, or when studying the nature of controversial public policy decisions in situ with directly affected stakeholders. Consideration of normative issues is never far from view in work in the public policy domain either. The coherence and accuracy of people's preferences and perceptions is a constant preoccupation of many of the sponsors and users of such research (if not always the researchers who conduct it), while the particular strengths and weaknesses of the judgments made by policy makers and experts have also proven fruitful areas of study. Equally, some of the political and economic stakes in public policy decisions are so high that the question of the "right" decision outcome or process may in itself become a core objective of a research study. Public policy issues also tend to merge disciplinary boundaries, albeit sometimes in unobtrusive ways, in the search for creative methodological and theoretical solutions to pressing resource allocation or other types of decision problem. A further key consideration is that of uncertainty. Almost all public policy decisions involve uncertainty, yet policy makers often prefer to avoid explicit consideration of such factors in their deliberations, which creates difficulties in communicating the outcomes of JDM research to sponsors and users.

In this chapter we highlight a number of central contributions that JDM research can deliver for public policy. In the first half we discuss the issue of *evidence* for informing public policy decisions. Here JDM research can contribute to the systematic collection, or sometimes critique, of basic data that feed into a wider public policy prioritization or decision process. In the second half of the chapter we turn to the provision of specific pre-scriptive tools for improving *decision quality*. By helping both lay and expert stakeholders to better organize and understand their own judgments and deliberations, we can strive for policies that better reflect their own views and opinions. The prescriptive paradigm of decision analysis provides the foundation for a number of such tools, and in a variety of ways. As Bell, Raiffa, and Tversky (1988, p. 9) point out, prescriptive approaches add something that is "far from the spirit of normative or descriptive analyses."

A third theme, running throughout the chapter, is the way in which the *basic theory* of JDM impacts upon public policy. The proper collection of evidence, and the development and use of tools, require advances in theory. However, quite subtle changes in theory can also have profound implications for the way in which public policy is framed and con-ducted. Encounters with the field usually, in turn, provide unique opportunities to reflect back upon some of the fundamental theoretical assumptions underpinning the subject as practiced in the psychology or economics laboratory. An example is achieving the proper balance between constructing theoretically "optimal" solutions and ones that are just robust enough to resolve the decision problem at hand.

The challenge that this diversity brings also raises a set of very real tensions and dilemmas that highlight some of the limitations on the direct transferability of findings from labor-atory science and normative theory to an inherently complex world. In this respect, the art of good applied research depends as much upon knowing the limits of what will work in any particular context, as it does on the use of particular well-established results, procedures or formal methods. Accordingly, throughout this chapter we illustrate specific public policy applications alongside some of the wider issues raised.

Evidence for Informing Public Policy

Insights provided by research in JDM are increasingly being used to generate, or alternat-ively critique, basic evidence informing public policy decisions. A common motivation, as Fischhoff (1990) points out, has been for decision makers to turn to such research only as a means of last resort, or when the behaviour of the public seems to threaten existing policy. Increasingly, policy makers are also seeking information about people's beliefs and preferences prospectively, and in a wide range of settings (e.g., health, envir-onment, safety, financial), particularly when they believe decisions need to be sensitive to basic social "values" or concerns.

Contingent valuation

The first example we discuss is Contingent Valuation (CV), a set of expressed preference methodologies now routinely used by economists to value a wide range of public goods not directly traded in any market. The basic approach posits a hypothetical market for an un-priced good and asks individuals to state the monetary value they place on proposed changes to its quantity, quality, or access. These might include individual health states (see Chapter 29, this volume), safety (Jones-Lee, 1989), or environmental resources such as air quality, natural habitats, and threatened species (Cummings, Brookshire, & Schulze, 1986). From a public policy perspective, valuation in a common scale is often necessary as part of a cost–benefit analysis comparing or prioritizing competing social or community concerns; for example, urban development versus wetlands pollution, more jobs from industry versus increased incidence of respiratory illnesses. Such issues have received particular attention because they typically involve controversial public policy tradeoffs. Where direct market values are not available, asking people what the good might be worth to them (that is, their "willingness to pay" for a gain or their "willingness to accept compensation" for a loss) might seem, on the face of it, a perfectly reasonable strategy.

JDM researchers have, in turn, become interested in CV, in part because the public policy stakes are often so high, but in part also because of the difficult intellectual challenges involved. Psychologists working from the behavioral decision theory perspective have always held, as one basic objective, an interest in the elicitation of preferences and values and the optimal conditions for doing this (see Fischhoff, Slovic, & Lichtenstein, 1980). Fischhoff and Furby (1988), for example, discuss a range of conditions that a CV survey ought to meet (to clarify the appropriate context of judgment for respondents) in order to optimize the chances of eliciting stable and meaningful values. These include providing information about what is being valued, why, how much of it, and the implied payment conditions for both respondents and others.

CV research is also instructive because it places a critical focus upon the methodological and normative aspects of JDM research itself. Differences in elicited preferences using rating versus choice response modes gain enormously in importance when the outputs of research matter (since policy conclusions may then be sensitive to choices over the methodology to be adopted). Here the basic laboratory science of heuristics, biases, and decision framing (e.g., Kahneman, Slovic, & Tversky, 1982) can provide a part of the theory needed to explain anomalies and inconsistencies of judgments apparent in CV elicitation. However, in interpreting the significance of particular biases in relation to real-world contexts, in CV or public policy more widely, it is always necessary to ask whether a particular judgmental phenomenon really matters, and with what consequences. On the one hand, a longstanding (if sometimes overlooked) observation is that while heuristics might indeed lead to persistent biases in laboratory conditions, they could still generally be useful in many of the decision environments ordinarily faced by people, particularly if judgment cues are inter-correlated (hence substitutable) and successful adaptation requires sufficient rather than strictly optimized solutions (Einhorn & Hogarth, 1981; see also Chapter 4, this volume). On the other hand, there is no necessary reason why particular heuristics should work well in the real world either, or that significant improvements to generally adaptive judgment strategies cannot be achieved. The question of judgmental competence, therefore, requires both careful empirical analysis of what strategies people do use alongside critical analytic work to uncover the implications of, and limits to, use in the context under consideration. Serving the interests of the ordinary citizen (and ultimately of policy makers) requires *appropriate* use of JDM models and findings in the public policy domain.

In our view CV does represent a task (admittedly one sometimes imposed by enthusiastic survey personnel on an unsuspecting public) where significant biases are evident *and* the outcomes of people's judgments genuinely matter. There exist two broad sources of inconsistency, as seen from the perspective of standard economic theory. A first concerns over-sensitivity to theoretically irrelevant aspects of the good and/or task, arising from a number of factors. For example, elicited values are highly sensitive to anchoring and range effects (Boyle, Bishop, & Walsh, 1985), while "willingness to pay" and "willingness to accept" judgments typically elicit different values for the same good (with a debate as to which is appropriate for policy; see Pearce, 1998). A second, more difficult challenge is insensitivity to theoretically relevant information. In standard economic terms people should, all other things being equal, be prepared to pay more for a good as the size or quantity of the benefit they receive increases. However, in the context of CV for environmental improvements a part-whole bias has been identified in which respondents state approximately the same willingness-to-pay for a "large" good as they do for a "small" one. Kahneman and Knetsch (1992) label this the "embedding effect" and argue it has origins in moral sentiments rather than economic values (see also Chapter 22, this volume).

In the safety domain it has been demonstrated that people's valuation of a small reduction of probability of harm in a road accident varies only partially in relation to the size of the risk reduction offered (Beattie, Covey, Dolan, et al., 1998). In part, this can be explained by respondents' inability to fully comprehend changes in the very small probabilities being valued (typically of the order of 10^{-4} or lower). For decision makers, however, such seemingly small anomalies in individual CV responses can have major implications. Beattie, Chilton, Cookson, et al. (1998) demonstrate through meta-analysis how the median "value of statistical life" (VoSL) implied by each of 28 separate CV safety studies varied between £80,000 and £25m. Systematic insensitivity was indicated by the fact that implied VoSL was inversely related to the order of magnitude of risk reduction (10^{-3}, 10^{-4} etc.) valued by participants (if people's underlying values for risk are stable, then the two should be strictly unrelated).

One interpretation of these anomalies is that the trouble lies in the various elicitation procedures themselves. That is, the conceptual basis for CV is sound, but care is needed in using the technique (Arrow, Solow, Portney, Leamer, Radner, & Schuman, 1993; Bateman, Carson, Day, et al., 2002). A second view is that people may not routinely hold well-formed or stable preferences for a good with which they are not directly familiar, or which is not routinely traded in a market. Complex environmental resources or public services often entail multiple attributes, involving difficult tradeoffs not readily reduced to any single dimension of "value" (Fischhoff, 1991). Gregory, Lichtenstein, and Slovic (1993) argue that expressed preferences for complex environmental goods are actively *constructed* (also Payne, Bettman, & Schkade, 1999; Chapter 6, this volume). That is, people deploy whatever heuristics, cues, and problem-solving strategies they have available to them to make sense of and structure a value elicitation task. This helps to reduce cognitive demands, while bringing to bear whatever general value or moral commitments people happen to hold about an issue. The importance of such factors has also been highlighted in recent qualitative approaches to elicitation of environmental values, including narrative (Satterfield, Slovic, & Gregory, 2000) and group-based (Henwood & Pidgeon, 2001) approaches.

At a conceptual level this work may ultimately challenge mainstream economic thinking about choice (which relies upon the assumption that an individual can articulate fully coherent preferences). In policy terms, the persistence and severity of anomalies suggests that, at minimum, the results of any single survey will always need to be treated with considerable caution by decision makers. It also implies, paradoxically, that conventional CV may be least useful for policy under precisely the circumstances where it is most often needed and used. Alternatively, approaches that *support* the constructive processes of elicitation, such as multiattribute and decision analytic methods (Gregory, 2000; Fischhoff, in press), may be needed where decision stakes are high.

Set against this is the issue of effort versus accuracy (Payne, Bettman, & Johnson, 1993; Chapter 6, this volume). We view this as a particularly important generic issue for all applications of JDM, but in particular for public policy. In many domains choices will indeed be highly sensitive to variations in input parameters, placing the precision of evidence under particular scrutiny. In others, however, a rough or "ballpark" estimate will fully meet the needs of a decision maker. In this latter case effort expended in eliciting increasing "accuracy," or in exploring the implications of different elicitation frames, must be set against a prior evaluation of the feasible options, as well as the requisite conditions (which may prove relatively modest) and the insight required for making a legitimate and defensible decision.

Risk perception research

A second example of the ways in which basic research can contribute to an important set of policy debates is provided by risk perception studies (see Pidgeon & Beattie, 1998; Slovic, 2000). From a psychological perspective there are three key research issues: the cognitive processes through which hazards are interpreted and mentally represented; the ways in which classes of hazards come to be viewed as risky; and the factors that influence the acceptability of hazards.

Research on risk perceptions arose during the 1970s and 1980s, initially in response to rising concerns about civilian nuclear power. For psychologists, risk perception research offered the possibility of an empirical understanding of some of the judgments and beliefs underlying this highly visible and complex social issue. Over time, of course, risk perception research has taken in a more diverse and evolving set of hazards (chemicals, electromagnetic fields, ecological hazards, genetically modified organisms, nanotechnology), although again more often than not in response to policy makers' worries about rising public concerns associated with particular technologies.

An initial hypothesis receiving some support was that lay perceptions of risks might be the result of limited knowledge, or the operation of simplifying cognitive heuristics, such as availability, in making judgments about the probability of future harm. Lichtenstein, Slovic, Fischhoff, Layman, and Combs (1978) indeed found that vivid imaginable causes of death (such as tornadoes) receive similar likelihood estimates to non-vivid ones (asthma) which occur with a much higher frequency (in this case, by a factor of 20). In addition, the findings also indicated systematic overestimation of absolute frequencies of rare causes of death and underestimation of common ones. However, a closer look at the findings revealed that respondents' *ordinal* judgments of the annual expected fatalities from a range of activities matched quite well with those of actuarial statistics (Daamen, Verplanken, & Midden, 1986). Commenting retrospectively upon the ways in which this research became used and quoted at the time, Fischhoff (1990, p. 648) illustrates some of the difficulties faced by researchers who care to enter a domain of hotly contested public policy issues:

> Typically, [the work] has been described as proving the public's ignorance (or even "irrationality") regarding risk issues with the attendant political ramifications. I have heard it described as proving the public's hopeless confusion about risks (e.g., nuclear power) that were not even in the study. Not only were these claims unwarranted by these results but they went far beyond what could be shown in any single series of studies.

The researchers' own interpretation was that further detailed empirical work was necessary, the findings suggesting the hypothesis (subsequently confirmed) that the concept of "risk" might mean far more to people than just expected fatalities (although, as Fischhoff also notes, an alternative response might be to ask how policymakers come to such misinterpretations in the first place). Accordingly, the now classic psychometric work conducted at Decision Research in Oregon (Slovic, Fischhoff, & Lichtenstein, 1980; Slovic, 2000) indicated that ratings of qualitative risk characteristics exhibit a systematic pattern, with three important factors emerging. First, "dread risk" relating to judgments such as uncontrollability, fear, catastrophic potential, involuntariness of exposure, and inequitable distribution of risk. Second, "unknown risk" relating to judgments of the observability of risk, effects delayed in time, familiarity, and level of scientific knowledge. Third, a factor related to the "number of people exposed," that is societal vulnerability to the effects of the hazard. The authors conclude that perceptions of risk are closely related to these factors, with the most important being "dread risk." According to Slovic (1987, p. 283) "the higher a hazard's score on this factor, the higher its perceived risk, the more people want to see its current risks reduced, and the more they want to see strict regulation employed to achieve the desired reduction in risk."

The early psychometric studies have provided a model for a growing body of research and literature (see Pidgeon, Hood, Jones, Turner, & Gibson, 1992; Slovic, 2000). Over time it has also become clear that while the basic approach adopted from judgment research has provided extensive empirical *descriptions* of the psychology of risk perceptions, it has not always yielded substantive *theoretical* progress towards explaining risk perceptions and behavioral responses in the face of risks. Accordingly, a range of further conceptual issues have subsequently gained attention from researchers, including: cultural factors (Dake, 1991); the social dynamics of risk amplification and attenuation through perception, media, and political processes (Kasperson, 1992); and the role of trust in institutions (Cvetkovich & Löfstedt, 1999). Such diversity of effort is healthy for promoting understanding and also cautions against any simple assumption that JDM research can, standing alone, provide definitive answers to many of the difficult risk policy questions society faces today.

The example of risk perception and policy is also particularly instructive, in contrast to that of CV discussed earlier, because it illustrates how research framed by a seemingly unproblematic question – why do people object, or not, to certain technologies? – has led to a transformation of *the question itself* over a period of time as more empirical evidence has accumulated. In particular, it appears that rather than being inevitably biased, or ill-informed, public risk perceptions exhibit a complexity and rationality that may be sensitive to factors sometimes ignored in expert analyses. In this respect, the focus shifts from where the "faulty" risk perceptions lie, and how to address (and mitigate) these, to understanding the contribution that perceptions research can offer for societal decision making and resolving societal conflicts. Accordingly, a significant policy debate now exists over whether people's perceptions and beliefs *should* form one input, directly or indirectly, to processes of public policy resource allocation (see contributions to Okrent & Pidgeon, 1998).[1] This debate touches upon a range of philosophical issues, in particular regarding the epistemological status of competing "expert" and "public" evaluations of risk as well as the appropriateness of making a distinction between "objective" and "subjective" depictions of risk (Pidgeon et al., 1992; Slovic, 1998).

The debate is unlikely to be resolved in the near future. On the one hand it can be argued that, most of the time, those who make policy decisions should base their choices on the preferences of those who will be affected. This is not only likely to lead to more legitimate outcomes, but also there are a range of situations where lay people know something that the experts do not (e.g., Wynne, 1992). Yet as Cross (1998) points out, if resource allocation is driven by the "worry of the week" (rather than by detailed expert analysis), perhaps fuelled by intense but temporary media interest, then in the long run lives may be lost, resources squandered, and opportunities for innovation spurned. However, public policy choices cannot be resolved solely by the science of risk assessment alone. They inevitably involve a judgment about facts *and* values, and as far as risk perception research taps legitimate value concerns then there may well be a case for reflecting some aspects of them in regulatory frameworks or policy decisions (Fischhoff, Watson, & Hope, 1984; Pidgeon, 1998).

Risk perceptions may also require attention by policy makers simply because they lead to real consequences (Sunstein, 2002), such as secondary social amplification impacts (see Pidgeon, Kasperson, & Slovic, 2003). For example, Frewer (2003) reports that the public announcement by the UK Health Minister in 1996 of a potential link between eating British beef, "mad cow" disease, and deaths from CJD (Creutzfeld-Jakob Disease) triggered major consumer avoidance of British sources of beef. In other cases, however, it can be argued that the decision maker should (with care) disregard the beliefs of the affected population (Lichtenstein, Gregory, Slovic, & Wagenaar, 1990). An obvious example is when people intentionally have been misinformed as to the consequences of actions; a less obvious example is when decision makers and citizens hold different priorities for saving known and unknown lives, or about incurring present as opposed to future costs.

Tools to Aid Decision Quality

Much JDM research has emphasized either normative issues or descriptive concerns. Less attention has been given to a third area, arguably the most critical for public policy applications, which emphasizes ways that people can be *helped to make better decisions* (Bell et al., 1988). In this section we focus on this topic of prescriptive decision aiding, exploring some of the insights, successes, and limitations of prescriptive approaches to public policy choices.

Implementation of a prescriptive approach typically requires guidance from a trained analyst and a willingness on the part of decision makers to work through the problem in a systematic, disaggregated fashion (von Winterfeldt & Edwards, 1986). It also requires the decision maker to at least be aware that a choice is to be made and that different decision-making responses are possible. Central to a prescriptive emphasis is the appropriate balancing of effort and accuracy discussed earlier in this chapter. In this and other respects, tools for aiding decision quality need to be linked appropriately to the judgment task. That is, they must be both understandable and accessible, and their use must be efficient in the sense that they readily provide help to people and take into account considerations of attention and possible outcomes and available resources. If the task is routine and the policy context relatively insignificant, such as a straightforward re-licensing of a facility, then requirements are fairly modest. If the task is novel or the context more significant, such as choosing among competing health standards or potential waste sites, then additional effort is warranted. This effort may take the form of thinking hard about what matters (to oneself and to others), confronting tradeoffs (to the extent that getting more of one thing requires giving up something else), or searching for additional (more comprehensive) and higher quality (more complete or precise) information. In this respect one goal of any prescriptive approach is to provide *adequate insight* to the decision maker, and through this a resolution of the problem that they face (Phillips, 1984).

The decision analysis model

Multiattribute utility theory (MAUT) provides a set of axiomatic theories of preference, which state that if people can make choices based on their preferences, and if these choices satisfy the axioms, then numbers can be assigned to values, utilities, and subjective probabilities (Raiffa, 1968; Chapter 17, this volume). Additionally, a rule can be specified for combining these numbers into a summary measure such that an option with a larger measure is preferred. This logic underlies MAUT's operational offspring, decision analysis. Keeney (1982) states that decision analysis offers "a formalization of common sense for decision problems that are too complex for informal use of common sense." It relies on human judgment to address, and to establish an explicit framework for integrating, values and facts, with people being asked to express judgments about facts in ways that reflect both the associated uncertainty and their own biases. Although the discussion in this section focuses on decision analysis techniques, a similar logic applies to a wide range of approaches that rely on the quantitative analysis of options using multiple objectives, including analytic hierarchy techniques (Saaty, 1980) and a variety of multicriteria methods (Hobbs, 1986).

The operationalization of a decision analysis approach is deceptively simple. It starts with structuring the problem at hand, which entails identifying the mandate of the decision makers, the principle participants, and the key constraints (see Chapter 14, this volume). The next step is to define relevant concerns in terms of what matters to the participants and, for each objective, to define measurable attributes such that they clarify how well the various actions and alternatives under consideration are able to satisfy these values (Keeney, 1992). For many public policy problems typical objectives will include a variety of economic, social, environmental, and cultural considerations. Often, multiple attributes for each objective are needed to track impacts over time. For example, jobs associated with a proposed factory might be measured by an overall number, the average salary, or their distribution; environmental concerns associated with a dam might reflect impacts on threatened fish species, water flows, or affected acres of agricultural land. Tools such as influence diagrams (Schacter, 1986) can be used to link hypotheses about management actions to these attributes and, in turn, to desired endpoints; for example, how might a change in water flows on a river affect fish populations and, in turn, angling opportunities and tourism revenues.

The choice of objectives and performance measures includes implicit value judgments that decision analysis techniques can help bring to the attention of decision makers. For example, many public policy choices that deal with health and safety decisions have as one objective to minimize mortality. Two possible attributes are the number of fatalities and the number of years of life lost. The former counts the death of any individual the same, whereas the latter counts the loss of a year of expected life of any individual the same. As a result, deaths of younger people count for more than the deaths of older people when years of life lost is used as an attribute. Which is the best measure? There is no right or wrong answer, except to say that a prescriptive approach requires that this type of value judgment be made *explicit* so that policy makers can recognize the implications of different measures.

Explicit attention to objectives can aid decision makers in several other ways. First, it helps to clarify what matters to the potentially affected population and thus provides a guide to communication, because people will especially want to hear about possible impacts on those concerns that matter most to them. Tools such as means–ends diagrams (Keeney, 1992) are helpful in distinguishing between values important in and of themselves (fundamental objectives) and those important because of their indirect contribution (means objectives). Second, giving explicit attention to objectives helps to enlarge the public debate and, to the extent that values are elicited from a broad population base, can help to bring back to policy deliberations groups who might have felt marginalized or disenfranchised. Third, it can help to establish common interests and thus aid negotiations among otherwise disparate or competing parties (Thompson, 1998). Even though environmental and commercial interests may seek different forest management policies, for example, both sides will care about many of the same economic, environmental, and social concerns (although presumably not to the same degree) and this reminder of commonalities can help to foster cooperation. Finally, decision analysis can help smooth the path for acceptance of new initiatives. For many elected officials, the bottom line is concerned with understanding the reasons why different individuals or different groups (e.g., communities, associations) either support or are opposed to an option; decision analysis explicitly links acceptance back to reasons, in the form of objectives and attributes.

Seen in relation to contemporary JDM theory, a decision analysis approach is fundamentally constructive, in that it provides a defensible basis for helping people to form and clarify their own preferences, and to understand the likely consequences of actions.

This structuring of both values and facts is, in turn, a means to creating and selecting improved policy alternatives. Decision analysts typically make use of tools such as consequence matrices, which show objectives (or attributes) down the side and different alternatives across the top (Clemen, 1996). This simple tool can be very effective at showing which alternatives are dominated (or nearly dominated, in that the differences in consequences are negligible), and therefore require no further attention. Tradeoffs are highlighted through the expression of one objective in terms of another. If both minimizing cost and maximizing safety are objectives of the problem, for example, the relevant policy question becomes how many additional dollars would be paid or exchanged to obtain a specified improvement in safety (Hammond, Keeney, & Raiffa, 1999). Consequence matrices therefore facilitate the creation of better options through encouraging thinking across objectives ("How much of this would I swap for that?") and, in some cases, by helping participants to combine the preferred portions of several different alternatives to create a new, preferred option.

Decision analysis offers, therefore, a different sort of prescriptive advice than would other tools, such as conventional probabilistic risk assessments. Despite its quantitative foundations, decision analysis fundamentally respects the subjectivity of both values and probabilities,[2] with the importance of impacts defined on a case-by-case basis. If, for example, a possible increase in crime is said to matter, then the next question is why? Does it matter because of possible injuries to property or to health? To what extent is fear important? What about implications for public sector spending in terms of additional policing or court costs? These various measures can use either natural scales (e.g., the increase in dollar costs) or constructed scales (e.g., an index of different physiological and psychological reactions to fear), depending on the subjective definition held by those concerned.

Explicit treatment of uncertainty in consequences is the other important element in the implementation of a decision analysis approach (Morgan & Henrion, 1990). Tools such as decision trees often are used to help keep track of these probabilistic relationships, distinguishing between choice points (squares) and uncertain events (circles) and allowing summary alternatives to be compared through the multiplication of values by probabilities. Reflecting its common axiomatic foundations with much of JDM research, prescriptive decision analysis places special emphasis upon eliciting subjective probabilities of events. Formal expert judgment elicitation procedures can help to refine probability estimates of the impacts of risk-inducing activities and to clarify the basis for technical judgments (e.g., Spetzler & Staël von Holstein, 1975; Keeney & von Winterfeldt, 1991). An important aspect of this procedure is to understand how different experts might think about the problem; complex problems typically are decomposed into more tractable parts, thereby focusing on areas of high uncertainty and clarifying why experts might perceive uncertainties in different ways.

An early application here for laboratory JDM findings and theory was for expert subjective probability elicitation to include training in heuristics and biases and to introduce specific techniques designed to "debias" judgments (Fischhoff, 1982; see also Chapter 16, this volume), while also recognizing the conditions (such as relevant and prompt feedback) that foster well-calibrated expert judgment. One example is that expressed confidence intervals typically are overly narrow; as a result, decision analysts help experts to think more carefully about extreme cases (i.e., the tails of the distribution) and to avoid anchoring on a mean estimate. Another example is the under-reliance on base rates; decision makers typically pay too much attention to highly salient or sensational examples (which may denote either failures or successes) and thereby fail to give sufficient weight to the full knowledge that is at hand. By introducing information covering a wide range of cases or geographic settings, prescriptive decision aids can often help decision makers to see the bigger picture and to pay more attention to the underlying factors and probabilities.

However, as noted in the introduction, the explicit incorporation of uncertainty in analysis (while a matter of strict intellectual hygiene for the JDM researcher and decision analysis practitioner alike) also raises particular dilemmas in the policy arena. Some policy makers find it exceptionally hard to accept that uncertainties attach to most policy problems, preferring to deal in all or nothing terms instead (Is climate change happening or not? Is British beef safe?). More often than not this is to make the analysis more tractable for themselves and in their communication to others,[3] while at other times it is driven by a desire for more clarity than actually exists. In some circumstances it may even serve explicit political ends; as in cases where acknowledgement of uncertainties might benefit the arguments of policy opponents or competing interest groups. Equally, and as noted by Fischhoff, Lichtenstein, Slovic, Derby, & Keeney (1981), uncertainties themselves may be directly exploited by policy makers, as one way of obfuscating or diffusing responsibility for the possible undesired outcomes of their decisions (it will always be unclear as to the *exact* extent of sea level rise possible during the twenty-first century, so why bother to spend resources to adapt now?). A further complexity arises because not all uncertainties in the policy arena, especially involving novel issues or technologies with long time-scales for potential impacts, can be meaningfully addressed in terms of relative frequency or subjective probability distributions. All of these situations raise rather difficult professional dilemmas for the decision analyst or researcher.

Uncertainty about consequences can be reduced directly through gathering more information, for example in the form of field studies or models that might be initiated as part of an assessment process. From a decision analysis perspective, information has value to the extent that it informs the decision at hand (or, in a sequenced decision process, to the extent that subsequent choices are informed) and influences the preferred choice. Thus money to be spent on collecting data can be subject to so-called "value of information" studies in which the benefits of new data are evaluated in terms of how they might affect the decision (Watson & Buede, 1987). A closely related concept is that of "value of learning," which has been applied by decision analysts to the analysis of a variety of health and environmental policy options – one example is the emerging field of adaptive management, which sets up experimental trials designed to reduce the uncertainty associated with management options (Walters & Green, 1997).

Some policy applications of decision aiding

Although decision analysis techniques originally were developed as aids to individual decision makers, they now have been used to elicit public value judgments in a wide variety of contexts, often involving the management of risks and the identification of preferred options. A well-known policy application has been to help develop estimates of the impacts of risk-reduction initiatives and proposed regulations on health and safety. Macartney, Douglas, and Spiegelhalter (1984), for example, used decision trees to examine alternative treatments for sick infants with coarctation of the aorta, a disease whose diagnosis may require an invasive procedure which itself increases the risk of death. Morgan, Morris, Henrion, Amaral, and Rish (1984) conducted careful expert judgments to explore the extent to which different options for controlling sulfur air pollution from coal-fired power plants would result in likely health effects. The results, expressed as subjective probability distributions, showed a general similarity among atmospheric scientists' estimates of sulfur emissions over time but, in contrast, a wide range of views concerning the likely health effects. Keeney and von Winterfeldt (1986) examined unintended side effects of health and safety regulations that could include accidents (e.g., through the operation of equipment) and stress (e.g., related to unemployment) as well as a range of adverse effects related to reduced household income. Strategies comparing the costs and effectiveness of different options for preventing mother-to-child HIV transmission are also being used to help control the spread of AIDs in Africa (Kahn & Marseille, 2002).

Environmental policies also have benefited from the application of decision analysis techniques. North and Merkhofer (1976) analyzed the effects of different controls on coal-fired power plants (e.g., taller stacks, low-sulfur coal use, treatment of flue gases) to reduce sulfur oxide emissions, a major contributor to air pollution. Other applications include evaluations of management options for endangered species (Maguire, 1986), the assessment of fisheries management options (McDaniels, 1995), and the development of water-use plans associated with relicensing of hydroelectric facilities (Gregory & Failing, 2002). Finally, environmental directorates in the US, the EC and elsewhere are using decision analysis and other multicriteria methods to suggest improved management options for the regulation of pesticides and chemicals (OECD, 2002).

Special policy considerations of prescription

In all these cases, the application of prescriptive methods has sought to identify key value-based components that could influence the decision and to isolate major contributors to the uncertainty of consequences. Often, decision makers simply need help in knowing how to think about a problem. One part of this concerns focusing on anticipated changes in key values relevant to the situation at hand. Environmental quality or economic and social development may matter to a decision maker in the abstract, but in the context of a particular action or initiative what matters is the likely range of possible effects and the decision makers' utility (including attitudes toward risk) over this range. A decision analysis approach emphasizes that if the impact of different alternatives on a specific concern is negligible, then that objective matters little or not at all in the context of the specific problem under consideration.

Of course, decision makers do not always want to be so explicit about what they are doing. One set of relevant cases, termed "taboo tradeoffs" (Fiske & Tetlock, 1997), involves situations where choices bring up emotional, moral, or ethical issues that are fundamentally hard for individuals to think about. Examples here include questions asking about a person's willingness to increase a present benefit in return for decreasing their own or another's future health; or their willingness to permit development that will provide jobs for a depressed community at the risk of degrading a sacred site. In some situations, such choices may simply be difficult because they are novel or because gaps exist in the information desired to make an informed choice. When this is the case, further structuring of the problem or further field studies and expert elicitations can help to make the problem easier. In other situations, however, individuals may be deeply offended by being asked to help make this type of policy choice, because they feel it is not their place to do so (instead, elected officials should take on this responsibility) or because a norm that is sacred or protected may be violated (e.g., the health of children or protection of a sacred site). In such situations, analysts and policy makers need to work in consort with stakeholders to determine whether the tools at their disposal will be helpful or, instead, if they run the risk of violating the rights of an individual or standards recognized by the society or community.

A generic policy issue for prescriptive JDM approaches is the question of how specific policy applications are framed and the effect that this might have on their acceptance or support. A well-known set of examples involve whether a proposed change is viewed as a loss or as a gain, a question of framing which in part depends also on the choice of a reference point (Kahneman & Tversky, 1979, 2000; Chapter 19, this volume). Asymmetrical evaluation of gains and losses has been demonstrated in diverse policy sectors. Gregory, Lichtenstein, and MacGregor (1993), for example, found that people believed restoring environmental quality to previous levels (i.e., restoring a loss) was significantly more valuable than making equivalent improvements (i.e., achieving gains) from the status quo. Johnson, Hershey, Meszaros, & Kunreuther (1993) examined actual choices made by residents of the US states of New Jersey and Pennsylvania between two automobile insurance policies, one which was cheaper but provided limited rights to further recovery of damages and another, more expensive one, that allowed this possibility. Although the limited rights policy was in place in New Jersey and the alternative, more expensive plan was in force in Pennsylvania, when presented with a choice large majorities of people in both states chose the default option rather than give it up for the alternative.

Almost *all* public policy choices, by definition, involve acceptance of losses (normally a finite risk) alongside economic or other gains. Such circumstances are always likely to yield potentially conflicting frames, depending upon whether an option is established in discourse primarily as a gain or primarily a loss, and where the dominant reference point lies. Under some circumstances "frames" might even be explicitly utilized by different stakeholders in a policy debate to advance their own particular cause (Fischhoff, Pidgeon, & Fiske, 1983). For prescriptive purposes, as the National Research Council (1996) report notes, there is no scientific way of identifying the "best" framing or reference point for an issue for a particular decision problem. The best one can do (if resources are available, and assuming the decision problem is sufficiently important and finely balanced) is to formulate competing frames with stakeholders or policymakers in order to explore potential impacts on final policy outcomes.

Most decision aids provide *cognitive assistance*, used to help disaggregate complex tasks into simpler problems or to clarify the relative importance of different elements in a particular decision context. As noted briefly above, recent research has shown the importance of affective considerations in judgments (Epstein, 1994; Slovic, Finucane, Peters, & MacGregor, 2002), with positive or negative reactions associated with a stimulus functioning as a cue for, and often a leading predictor of, subsequent cognitive evaluations. It is likely that future prescriptive approaches will need to give more attention to JDM research on such factors, and in turn JDM researchers should recognize the prescriptive implications of such work for developing advice and support to decision makers. In a recent study, for example, consumer choices about health care options were assisted by affectively enhancing information concerning the quality of different program alternatives (Hibbard & Peters, 2002).

A final key policy concern is that of evaluability (Hsee, 1996; Chapter 18, this volume). In contrast to many economic approaches used in assessing public policy options, a prescriptive decision analysis approach emphasizes the *context* within which alternatives are considered. Thus stated expenditures of $X to obtain more or less of Y can only be assessed as foolish or wise when compared to other possible options. The bottom line, for a prescriptive approach to policy, is not whether people are (on average) willing to pay $20 to obtain an improvement in health or visibility (in fact, the question, by itself, has no meaning) but, instead, whether this option is the best possible way to satisfy the underlying objectives or whether some other alternative is likely to be preferred.

Concluding Comments: Future Directions, Future Deliberations

We believe that the considerable scope for JDM research, methods and theory in the domain of public policy means that research has, to date, only touched the surface of the many potential applications and issues that this expanding field presents. A particular strength of more prescriptive JDM approaches is the respect paid to the subjectivity of problem structuring, values, and probabilities, something which is in keeping with the current move away from purely science-based public policy decision processes to ones that attempt to incorporate a wider range of values and concerns. Work in the public policy domain is also likely to extend theories well beyond the constraints of laboratory research, as when the operation of intuitive judgment strategies are explored in a range of richer, more naturalistic decision contexts (Klein, Orasanu, Calderwood, & Zsambok, 1993; Chapter 15, this volume). The issues of effort versus accuracy, evaluability, and the operation of intuitive affective processes all seem particularly important issues for defining future research priorities.

Applying JDM research (and researchers) to these topics will not always be straightforward. Many contemporary risk controversies are rooted in a combination of psychological, social and political factors, and as a result will require innovative and integrative research and policy solutions (Pidgeon et al., 2003). Also, as noted above, work in the policy domain brings challenges not ordinarily faced in the experimental laboratory.

Fischhoff (1990), for example, lists cautionary lessons from his own work on risk perception and communication issues in the public policy domain, including: (1) expect one's empirical results to be distorted, both deliberately and inadvertently; (2) expect "amateurs" to usurp the need for psychological expertise, replacing our research with their self-serving speculations; and (3) expect the temptation to overshoot one's competence.

A particularly exciting direction for future research and application in relation to JDM and public policy lies in the area of governance and the acceptability of decision-making processes. Changes in the basic understanding of the nature and efficacy of risk communication, from providing information about probabilities to promoting *dialogue* among parties (see Fischhoff, 1995), have had profound implications for the ways governments view the limits and possibilities of their own engagement with stakeholders and the wider public. This has resulted in moves toward use of so-called "analytic deliberative" decision processes (National Research Council, 1996), which seek to combine sound risk and systems analysis with an open and trusted consultative process that reflects both expert and lay views (also Renn, Webler, & Wiedemann, 1995; Beirle & Cayford, 2002).

A particular future challenge in the area of deliberative processes will be the *integration* of expert and (in many cases very culturally diverse) community perspectives on an issue. New approaches to risk communication, such as using mental models (Morgan, Fischhoff, Bostrom, & Atman, 2002) and risk rankings (Florig et al., 2001), have begun to explore this issue. Decision analysis seems well suited to help to formalize the aspirations of deliberative processes in that citizens' opinions should be both well informed and clearly expressed, in ways that are scientifically defensible and speak to the relevant decision makers. It can also support the difficult task of using stakeholder input to develop new creative decision alternatives (a development that would mark off true deliberation from more traditional forms of consultation). Experimental tests of decision aiding approaches have begun to identify some of the ways in which the quality of consultative processes could be evaluated and, in turn, improved through more closely linking decision analysis methods to specific deliberative and risk communication challenges (Arvai, Gregory, & McDaniels, 2001). Above all there is a challenge to link the operation of analytic-deliberative processes more closely to the needs of decision makers, since one of the expectations of deliberation (particularly among people who participate) is that it should lead to concrete policy outcomes. Again, further development of insights from JDM theory regarding effort and accuracy in choice are likely to be useful here. There may be no use at all, in terms of value of information (although there may be other more indirect benefits, such as enhancing trust in institutions), in undergoing extensive technical/deliberative analysis in cases where many potential decision options are dominated, or only an order of magnitude judgment is required for identifying the best decision for a community. An equal danger arises if deliberative processes settle for broadly acceptable but partial solutions, for example by failing to provide the precision necessary to decide between a set of competing alternatives or by failing to identify viable options. In all of the above, the "art" of prescriptive intervention needs to be further refined and developed through a wider consideration of basic JDM findings in the applied public policy context.

Notes

1   This same question, on the role of perceptions in evaluations of public policies, arises in other settings; an example is the current debate about the use of single vs. multiple discount rates when evaluating streams of project costs and benefits that occur over time (Frederick, Loewenstein, & O'Donoghue, 2002).
2   One can make the argument here that probabilistic risk assessment is itself a subjectivity-laden exercise, in relation to both definition of problems and terms as well as to judgments about the structuring of analytic models (see Fischhoff et al., 1981; Pidgeon et al., 1992). However, *as practiced* it typically fails to recognize that subjectivity.
3   Although there are recent signs that governments are recognizing the strategic need to explicitly address uncertainty in a wide range of policy processes (e.g., Cabinet Office Strategy Unit, 2002).

Acknowledgments

Work reported in this chapter was supported by the Leverhulme Trust under a programme award (RSK990021) to the University of East Anglia, the UK Economic and Social Research Council (Grant RES-336-25-0001), and by US National Science Foundation awards SES-0114924 to Decision Research and SBR95-21914 to Carnegie Mellon University. We wish to thank Baruch Fischhoff, Nigel Harvey, and Derek Koehler for insightful comments on earlier versions.

References

Arrow, K., Solow, R., Portney, P. R., Leamer, E., Radner, R., & Schuman, H. (1993) Report of the NOAA panel on contingent valuation, *Federal Register*, 58, 4602–14.
Arvai, J., Gregory, R., & McDaniels, T. (2001) Testing a structured decision-aiding approach: Value-focused thinking for deliberative risk communication, *Risk Analysis*, 21, 1065–76.
Bateman, I. J., Carson, R. T., Day, B., Hanemann, W. M., Hanley, N., Hett, T., Jones-Lee, M., Loomes, G., Mourato, S., Özdemiroglu, E., Pearce, D. W., Sugden, R., & Swanson, J. (2002) *Economic Valuation with Stated Preference Techniques: A Manual.* Cheltenham: Edward Elgar Publishing.
Beattie, J., Chilton, S., Cookson, R., Covey, J., Hopkins, L., Jones-Lee, M., Loomes, G., Pidgeon, N. F., Robinson, A., & Spencer, A. (1998) *Valuing Health and Safety Controls: A Literature Review.* Norwich: Health and Safety Executive Books.
Beattie, J., Covey, J., Dolan, P., Hopkins, L., Jones-Lee, M., Loomes, G., Pidgeon, N. F., Robinson, A., & Spencer, A. (1998) On the contingent valuation of safety and the safety of contingent valuation: Part 1 – Caveat investigator, *Journal of Risk and Uncertainty*, 17, 5–25.
Beierle, T. C. & Cayford, J. (2002) *Democracy in Practice: Public Participation in Environmental Decisions.* Washington, DC: Resources for the Future.
Bell, D., Raiffa, H., & Tversky, A. (1988) *Decision Making: Descriptive, Normative, and Prescriptive Interactions.* Cambridge: Cambridge University Press.
Boyle, K. J., Bishop, R. C., & Walsh, M. P. (1985) Starting point bias in contingent valuation, *Land Economics*, 61, 188–94.

Cabinet Office Strategy Unit (2002) *Risk: Improving Government's Ability to Handle Risk and Uncertainty*. London: UK Cabinet Office Strategy Unit.

Clemen, R. (1996) *Making Hard Decisions: An Introduction to Decision Analysis*. Belmont, CA: Duxbury Press.

Cross, F. B. (1998) Facts and values in risk assessment, *Reliability Engineering and System Safety*, 59, 27–40.

Cummings, R. G., Brookshire, D. S., & Schulze, W. D. (1986) *Valuing Environmental Resources: An Assessment of the Contingent Valuation Method*. Totowa, NJ: Rowman and Allanheld.

Cvetkovich, G. & Löfstedt, R. (1999) *Social Trust and the Management of Risk*. London: Earthscan.

Daamen, D., Verplanken, B., & Midden, C. (1986) Accuracy and consistency of lay estimates of annual fatality rates. In B. Brehmer et al. (eds.), *New Directions in Research on Decision Making*. Amsterdam: Elsevier.

Dake, K. (1991) Orienting dispositions in the perception of risk: An analysis of contemporary worldviews and cultural biases, *Journal of Cross-Cultural Psychology*, 22, 61–82.

Einhorn, H. & Hogarth, R. (1981) Behavioral decision theory: Processes of judgment and choice, *Annual Review of Psychology*, 32, 53–88.

Epstein, S. (1994) Integration of the cognitive and the psychodynamic unconscious, *American Psychologist*, 49, 709–24.

Fischhoff, B. (1982) Debiasing. In D. Kahneman, P. Slovic, & A. Tversky (eds.), *Judgement under Uncertainty: Heuristics and Biases* (pp. 422–44). Cambridge: Cambridge University Press.

Fischhoff, B. (1990) Psychology and public policy: Tool or toolmaker? *American Psychologist*, 45, 647–53.

Fischhoff, B. (1991) Value elicitation: Is there anything in there? *American Psychologist*, 46, 835–47.

Fischhoff, B. (1995) Risk perception and communication unplugged: Twenty years of process, *Risk Analysis*, 15, 137–45.

Fischhoff, B. (in press) Cognitive processes in stated preference methods. In K-G. Mäler & J. Vincent (eds.), *Handbook of Environmental Economics*. North Holland: Elsevier.

Fischhoff, B. & Furby, L. (1988) Measuring values: A conceptual framework for interpreting transactions with special reference to contingent valuation of visibility, *Journal of Risk and Uncertainty*, 1, 147–84.

Fischhoff, B., Lichtenstein, S., Slovic, P., Derby, S. L., & Keeney, R. L. (1981) *Acceptable Risk*. Cambridge: Cambridge University Press.

Fischhoff, B., Pidgeon, N. F., & Fiske, S. (1983) Social science and the politics of the arms race, *Journal of Social Issues*, 39, 161–80.

Fischhoff, B., Slovic, P., & Lichtenstein, S. (1980) Knowing what you want: Measuring labile values. In T. Wallsten (ed.), *Cognitive Processes in Choice and Decision Behaviour* (pp. 117–41). Hillsdale, NJ: Erlbaum.

Fischhoff, B., Watson, S., & Hope, C. (1984) Defining risk, *Policy Sciences*, 17, 123–39.

Fiske, A. & Tetlock, P. (1997) Taboo trade-offs: Reactions to transactions that transgress spheres of justice, *Political Psychology*, 18, 255–97.

Florig, H. K., Morgan, M. G., Morgan, K. M., Jenni, K. E., Fischhoff, B., Fischbeck, P., & DeKay, M. L. (2001) A deliberative method for ranking risks (I): Overview and test-bed development, *Risk Analysis*, 21, 913–22.

Frederick, S., Loewenstein, G., & O'Donoghue, T. (2002) Time discounting and time preference: A critical review, *Journal of Economic Literature*, 40, 351–401.

Frewer, L. J. (2003) Trust, transparency and social context: Implication for social amplification of risk. In N. F. Pidgeon, R. K. Kasperson, & P. Slovic (eds.), *The Social Amplification of Risk* (pp. 123–37). Cambridge: Cambridge University Press.

Gregory, R. (2000) Valuing environmental policy options: A case study comparison of multiattribute and contingent valuation survey methods, *Land Economics*, 76, 151–73.

Gregory, R. & Failing, L. (2002) Using decision analysis to encourage sound deliberation: Water use planning in British Columbia, Canada, *Journal of Policy Analysis and Management*, 21, 492–9.

Gregory, R., Lichtenstein, S., & MacGregor, D. (1993) The role of past states in determining reference points for policy decisions, *Organizational Behavior and Human Decision Processes*, 55, 195–206.

Gregory, R., Lichtenstein, S., & Slovic, P. (1993) Valuing environmental resources: A constructive approach, *Journal of Risk and Uncertainty*, 7, 77–97.

Hammond, K., Keeney, R., & Raiffa, H. (1999) *Smart Choices: A Practical Guide to Making Better Decisions*. Boston: Harvard Business School Press.

Henwood, K. L. & Pidgeon, N. F. (2001) Talk about woods and trees: Threat of urbanisation, stability and biodiversity, *Journal of Environmental Psychology*, 21, 125–47.

Hibbard, J. & Peters, E. (2002) Supporting informed consumer health care decisions, data presentation approaches that facilitate the use of information in choice, *Annual Review of Public Health*, 24, 413–33.

Hobbs, B. (1986) What can we learn from experiments in multiobjective decision analysis? *IEEE Transactions on Systems, Man, and Cybernetics*, 16, 384–92.

Hsee, C. K. (1996) The evaluability hypothesis: An explanation for preference reversals between joint and separate evaluations of alternatives, *Organizational Behavior and Human Decision Processes*, 67, 242–57.

Johnson, E., Hershey, E., Meszaros, J., & Kunreuther, H. (1993) Framing probability distortions and insurance decisions, *Journal of Risk and Uncertainty*, 7, 35–51.

Jones-Lee, M. (1989) *The Economics of Safety and Physical Risk*. Oxford: Basil Blackwell.

Kahn, J. & Marseille, E. (2002) A saga in international HIV modelling: Preventing mother-to-child HIV transmission, *Journal of Policy Analysis and Management*, 21, 499–505.

Kahneman, D. & Knetsch, J. L. (1992) Valuing public goods: The purchase of moral satisfaction, *Journal of Environmental Economics and Management*, 22, 57–70.

Kahneman, D., Slovic, P., & Tversky, A. (1982) *Judgement Under Uncertainty: Heuristics and Biases*. Cambridge: Cambridge University Press.

Kahneman, D. & Tversky, A. (1979) Prospect theory: An analysis of decision under risk, *Econometrica*, 47, 263–91.

Kahneman, D. & Tversky, A. (2000) *Choices, Values and Frames*. Cambridge: Cambridge University Press.

Kasperson, R. E. (1992) The social amplification of risk: Progress in developing an integrative framework of risk. In S. Krimsky & D. Golding (eds.), *Social Theories of Risk* (pp. 153–78). Westport, CT: Praeger.

Keeney, R. (1982) Decision analysis: An overview, *Operations Research*, 30, 803–38.

Keeney, R. (1992) *Value-focused Thinking: A Path to Creative Decision Making*. Cambridge, MA: Harvard University Press.

Keeney, R. & von Winterfeldt, D. (1986) Why indirect health risks of regulations should be examined, *Interfaces*, 16, 13–27.

Keeney, R. & von Winterfeldt, D. (1991) Eliciting probabilities from experts in complex technical problems, *IEEE Transactions on Engineering Management*, 33, 83–6.

Klein, G. A., Orasanu, J., Calderwood, R., & Zsambok, C. E. (1993) *Decision Making in Action: Models and Methods*. Norwood, NJ: Ablex.

Lichtenstein, S., Gregory, R., Slovic, P., & Wagenaar, W. (1990) When lives are in your hands: Dilemmas of the societal decision maker. In R. Hogarth (ed.), *Insights in Decision Making* (pp. 91–106). Chicago: University of Chicago Press.

Lichtenstein, S., Slovic, P., Fischhoff, B., Layman, M., & Combs, B. (1978) Judged frequency of lethal events. *Journal of Experimental Psychology: Human Learning and Memory*, 4, 551–78.

Macartney, F., Douglas, J., & Speigelhalter, D. (1984) To catheterise or not to catheterise? An approach based on decision theory, *British Heart Journal*, 51, 330–8.

Maguire, L. (1986) Using decision analysis to manage endangered species populations, *Journal of Environmental Management*, 22, 345–60.

McDaniels, T. (1995) Using judgement in resource management: A multiple objective analysis of a fisheries management decision, *Operations Research*, 43, 415–26.

Morgan, M. G., Fischhoff, B., Bostrom, A., & Atman, C. (2002) *Risk Communication: A Mental Models Approach*. Cambridge: Cambridge University Press.

Morgan, M. G. & Henrion, M. (1990) *Uncertainty: A Guide to Dealing with Uncertainty in Quantitative Risk and Policy Analysis*. Cambridge: Cambridge University Press.

Morgan, M. G., Morris, S., Henrion, M., Amaral, D., & Rish, W. (1984) Technical uncertainty in quantitative policy analysis: A sulphur air pollution example, *Risk Analysis*, 4, 201–16.

National Research Council (1996) *Understanding Risk: Informing Decisions in a Democratic Society*. Washington, DC: National Academy Press.

North, W. & Merkhofer, L. (1976) A methodology for analyzing emission control strategies, *Computers and Operations Research*, 3, 185–207.

OECD (2002) *Technical Guidance Document on the use of Socio-economic Analysis in Chemical Risk Management Decision Making*. Paris: Organization for Economic Co-operation and Development, Environment Directorate.

Okrent, D. & Pidgeon, N. F. (eds.) (1998) Special issue: Risk perception versus risk analysis, *Reliability Engineering and System Safety*, 59, 1–159.

Payne, J. W., Bettman, J. R., & Johnson, E. J. (1993) *The Adaptive Decision Maker*. Cambridge: Cambridge University Press.

Payne, J. W., Bettman, J. R., & Schkade, D. (1999) Measuring constructed preferences: Towards a building code, *Journal of Risk and Uncertainty*, 19, 243–70.

Pearce, D. (1998) Valuing risks. In P. Calow, (ed.), *Handbook of Environmental Risk Assessment and Management* (pp. 345–75). Oxford: Blackwell Science.

Phillips, L. D. (1984) A theory of requisite decision models, *Acta Psychologica*, 56, 29–48.

Pidgeon, N. F. (1998) Risk assessment, risk values and the social science programme: Why we do need risk perception research, *Reliability Engineering and System Safety*, 59, 5–16.

Pidgeon, N. F. & Beattie, J. (1998) The psychology of risk and uncertainty. In P. Calow, (ed.), *Handbook of Environmental Risk Assessment and Management* (pp. 289–318). Oxford: Blackwell Science.

Pidgeon, N. F., Hood, C., Jones, D., Turner, B., & Gibson, R. (1992) Risk perception. In *Risk: Analysis, Perception and Management* (pp. 89–134). London: The Royal Society.

Pidgeon, N. F., Kasperson, R. K., & Slovic, P. (eds.) (2003) *The Social Amplification of Risk*. Cambridge: Cambridge University Press.

Raiffa, H. (1968) *Decision Analysis: Introductory Lectures on Choices Under Uncertainty*. Reading, MA: Addison-Wesley.

Renn, O., Webler, T., & Wiedemann, P. (1995) *Fairness and Competence in Citizen Participation*. Dordrecht: Kluwer.

Saaty, T. (1980) *The Analytical Hierarchy Process*. New York: MacGraw-Hill.

Satterfield, T., Slovic, P., & Gregory, R. (2000) Narrative valuation in a policy judgment context, *Ecological Economics*, 34, 315–31.

Schacter, R. (1986) Evaluating influence diagrams, *Operations Research*, 34, 871–82.

Slovic, P. (1987) Perception of risk, *Science*, 236, 280–5.

Slovic, P. (1998) The risk game, *Reliability Engineering and System Safety*, 59, 73–7.

Slovic, P. (2000) *The Perception of Risk*. London: Earthscan.

Slovic, P., Finucane, M., Peters, E., & MacGregor, D. G. (2002) The affect heuristic. In T. Gilovich, D. Griffin, & D. Kahneman (eds.), *Heuristics and Biases: The Psychology of Intuitive Judgement* (pp. 397–420). Cambridge: Cambridge University Press.

Slovic, P., Fischhoff, B., & Lichtenstein, S. (1980) Facts and fears: Understanding perceived risk. In R. Schwing & W. Albers (eds.), *Societal Risk Assessment: How Safe is Safe Enough?* (pp. 181–214). New York: Plenum Press.

Spetzler, C. S. & Staël von Holstein, C.-A. (1975) Probability encoding in decision analysis, *Management Science*, 22, 340–58.

Sunstein, C. R. (2002) The laws of fear, *Harvard Law Review*, 115, 1119–68.

Thompson, L. (1998) *The Mind and Heart of the Negotiator*. New Jersey: Prentice-Hall.

von Winterfeldt, D. & Edwards, W. (1986) *Decision Analysis and Behavioral Research*. Cambridge: Cambridge University Press.

Walters, C. & Green, R. (1997) Valuation of experimental management options for ecological systems, *Journal of Wildlife Management*, 61, 987–1006.

Watson, S. & Buede, D. (1987) *Decision Synthesis*. Cambridge: Cambridge University Press.

Wynne, B. (1992) Risk and social learning: Reification to engagement. In S. Krimsky and D. Golding (eds.), *Social Theories of Risk* (pp. 275–300). Westport, CT: Praeger.

Author Index

Itzkowitz, J. 473, 477, 479
Iyengar, S. S. 80, 354, 458

Jacobs, E. A. 432
Jacobson, L. 186
Jacoby, J. 115
Jacoby, L. L. 169
Jacowitz, K. E. 244, 245
Jagacinski, C. M. 342
Janoff-Bulman, R. 366
Jansen, S. J. T. 594
Jarvis, W. B. G. 254
Jasper, J. D. 513
Jayasinghe, N. 267
Jeffrey, R. C. 14, 166
Jegadeesh, N. 528
Jenkins, H. M. 208, 213
Jennings, D. L. 234, 278
Jennings, M. 459
Jensen, K. L. 559
Jenson, M. E. 167
Jepson, D. 171–2, 317, 318, 324
Ji, L. 511, 512
Jia, J. 137
Jiranyakul, K. 411
Johns, M. 574
Johnson, E. J. 53, 67, 99, 111, 112, 114, 116, 117, 118, 119, 148, 203, 241, 242, 244, 246, 250, 297, 298, 299, 319, 362, 363, 366, 380, 385, 455, 495–6, 533, 557, 577, 578, 586, 616
Johnson, F. 449
Johnson, J. G. 80, 135, 265, 310
Johnson, M. K. 367
Johnson, P. E. 302
Johnson, S. 447
Johnson, T. R. 474
Johnson-Laird, P. N. 167, 168, 171, 278, 380, 381
Jones, D. 609
Jones, E. E. 252
Jones-Lee, M. 606
Jonides, J. 97
Joseph, J. S. 240
Josephs, R. 457
Joslyn, S. 261
Jourden, F. 573
Joyce, C. R. B. 38, 46
Joyce, E. 549

Jullien, B. 418n
Juslin, P. 38, 54, 66, 191, 194, 229, 261, 537
Juster, F. T. 435

Kachelmeier, S. J. 559
Kagel, J. 411
Kagel, J. H. 486
Kahn, B. E. 371
Kahneman, D. 7, 10, 12, 13, 14, 15, 16, 29, 30, 37, 51, 52, 53, 54, 65, 67, 69, 89, 90–1, 93, 94, 95, 96, 97, 98, 100, 101, 102, 103, 104, 112, 113, 114, 125, 128, 143, 144, 145, 147, 149, 158, 159, 160, 161, 163, 165, 168–9, 170, 172, 182, 187, 188, 241–2, 244, 245, 249, 258–9, 262, 264, 276, 280, 281, 284, 297–8, 301, 318, 319, 325, 333, 343, 345, 348, 349, 360, 365, 366, 367–8, 370, 371, 373, 379, 380, 381, 383, 386, 387, 388, 390, 391, 395, 404, 405, 406, 407, 408, 410, 411, 412, 413, 414, 415, 416, 418n, 419n, 444, 445, 446, 449–50, 451, 452, 454, 456, 493, 533, 536–7, 549, 557, 572, 573, 586, 593, 606, 609, 616
Kamin, K. A. 268, 269, 569
Kanouse, D. E. 91
Kao, S.-F. 213
Kaplan, R. M. 595
Kaplan, S. E. 331
Kaplow, L. 32, 33
Karney, B. R. 367
Karp, S. A. 519
Kasperson, R. E. 609
Kasperson, R. K. 610
Kassin, S. M. 568
Katsikopoulos, K. 71, 72
Kaye, D. 571
Kearns, D. T. 332
Kedmi, D. 267
Keeney, R. L. 34, 68, 290n, 306, 329, 341, 342, 346, 611, 612, 613, 614, 615
Kelley, C. M. 169
Kelly, J. R. 554
Kelman, M. 573–4
Keltner, D. 455
Kenny, D. A. 241
Kent, R. J. 241
Keppe, H.-J. 531

Subject Index

Lightning Source UK Ltd.
Milton Keynes UK
UKOW020717080313

207301UK00003B/7/P

9 781405 157599